Praise for PassPorter®

"A nifty travel guide that works overtime as a planner, organizer, and journal..."

– Jacky Runice
Daily Herald–Chicago

"[PassPorter] is a brilliant travel aid... the most practical, sanity-saving guide you could take along to Disney World."

– Stephanie Gold,
Amazon.com

"[PassPorter] has become the Bible for those of us who want to experience Walt Disney World to the max."

– Kim Cool,
Venice Gondolier Sun

"Vacationers who want to enjoy all that Disney World has to offer should make sure they take along this PassPorter guide."

– ForeWord Reviews

I love this book. It's my Disney Bible!!! Thank you to ALL for this incredible book! For first timers like ourselves this book is AMAZING!

— Ann Petersoli
in Massachusetts

PassPorter is wonderful. I call it the best and most complete Disney World guide. You are AWESOME! Thank you so much.

— Joey Morehead
in Tennessee

You guys are the best. You make an unorganized person feel like they have it all under control. This will be my first vacation that isn't utter chaos. Thank you.

— Sarah Rhue
in Pennsylvania

We love the full color, glossy pages and the number of pockets for holding receipts and other details. This is our only vacation guide that we buy -- others pale badly in comparison.

— Byron Etzel in N. Carolina

What's Unique in PassPorter

- **Coverage of the most recent changes** throughout Walt Disney World—thanks to our later production schedule, this is the most up-to-date 2016 guidebook available! We have coverage of MyMagic+, My Disney Experience, MagicBands, FastPass+, recent price changes, and new attractions and eateries.
- **Special glossy photo supplement** at the back of the book
- **Comprehensive yet concise information** is packed into our pages—PassPorter is information-rich and padding-free!
- **Full color** brings life and clarity to our maps and photos.
- **Blending of personal experience** and photographs from your authors and the collective wisdom of tens of thousands of readers means a guidebook that's full of heart and soul.
- **Well-organized chapters and pages** make it easy to find what you need. We edit our information carefully so that sections always begin at the top of a page.
- **Worksheets** to jot notes and make travel arrangements.
- **Our famous organizer PassPockets** (select editions) to plan your trip, store your maps and papers, and record your memories.
- **Floorplans of Disney resort hotel rooms** to give you a better sense of the layout.
- **Fold-out maps** of the four major Disney theme parks, printed in full color on heavy paper to stand up to rugged use.
- **Custom-designed attraction charts** provide all the information you need at a glance.
- **ToddlerTips, KidTips, TweenTips, and TeenTips** offer advice for kids by kids.
- **Color, self-stick tabs** to mark your chapters.
- **Original color photos** to see the *real* Walt Disney World!
- **Personalization labels and stickers** to customize your book.
- **Magical memories** from fellow travelers convey the spirit and wonder of Walt Disney World.
- **Disney changes highlighted** with a light green background to mark significant changes since our last edition.
- **Expert peer reviewers** to ensure accuracy and thoroughness.

...and much more! Visit us at http://www.passporter.com for a complete list of what's new and unique in PassPorter's Walt Disney World 2016!

PassPorter's® Walt Disney World® 2016

18th Edition

The unique travel guide, planner, organizer, journal, and keepsake

Jennifer Marx,
Dave Marx,
and Alexander Marx

PassPorter Travel Press

An imprint of MediaMarx, Inc.
P.O. Box 3880, Ann Arbor, Michigan 48106
877-WAYFARER

PassPorter's® Walt Disney World®–2016 Edition
by Jennifer Marx, Dave Marx, and Alexander Marx

P.O. Box 3880, Ann Arbor, Michigan 48106
E-Mail: support@passporter.com
Visit us online at http://www.passporter.com

Special Sales: PassPorter Travel Press publications are available at special discounts for bulk purchases for sales premiums or promotions. Special editions, including personalized covers and excerpts of existing guides, can be created in large quantities. For information, write to Special Sales, P.O. Box 3880, Ann Arbor, Michigan, 48106.

Distributed by Publishers Group West

ISBN-13: 978-1-58771-154-1
ISBN-10: 1-58771-154-0

10 9 8 7 6 5 4 3 2 1

Printed in China

About the Authors

Name: Jennifer Marx
Date of birth: 10/09/68
Residence: Ann Arbor, MI
Signature: ....

Jennifer Marx fell in love with Walt Disney World on her first visit as a teenager in 1983. She has since returned more times than she can count on her fingers and toes many times over, visiting every park, attraction, resort, and restaurant at least once. As author of more than a dozen popular books, she yearned to write one about Walt Disney World but felt no interest in churning out yet another travel guide when there were so many excellent books already available. When she hit upon the idea of the PassPorter, she knew she could offer her fellow vacationers something unique and valuable. With the help of the PassPorter, Jennifer has organized gatherings at Walt Disney World for individuals, groups, and families of all ages and stages. Jennifer lives in Ann Arbor, Michigan and is a loving mother to her amazing son Alexander.

Dave Marx may be considered a Renaissance Man, a jack-of-all-trades, or a dilettante, depending on how you look at things. He took a 20-year hiatus between his early journalism training and the commencement of his full-time writing career. Beyond co-authoring numerous books with Jennifer, he's been a radio writer/producer; recording engineer; motion picture music editor; broadcast engineering supervisor; tax preparer; cab driver; whitewater safety and rescue instructor; developer and instructor of online publishing courses; and board member for the Independent Book Publishers Association. He has also co-authored and contributed to numerous books about America Online and the Internet. He discovered the "World" (Walt Disney World, that is) in 1997 and spent more than six months there over the following five years. Dave is from New Jersey and now makes his home in Ann Arbor, Michigan.

Name: Dave Marx
Date of birth: 04/07/55
Residence: Ann Arbor, MI
Signature: ....

Alexander Marx is our 11-year-old son who has been to Walt Disney World over a dozen times. He loves technology (Sorcerers of the Magic Kingdom is one of his favorites) and dislikes roller coasters and big thrill rides. He shares his "A-OK!" ratings and his oldie-but-goodie **ToddlerTips** and KidTips on the attractions in the Touring the 'World' chapter. Alexander also offers his thoughts on various aspects of traveling and touring on the PassPorter Facebook page at http://www.facebook.com/passporter. Beyond Alexander's contributions to this book, he's created and designed a see-through backpack with a pocket sized for PassPorter. Get the details at our web site.

PassPorter Team

Our eight Expert Peer Reviewers painstakingly checked our text, photos, and maps, and helped us ensure PassPorter's accuracy, readability, and thoroughness. Thank you for helping to make PassPorter the best it can be!

Sandy Bostwick is an occupational therapist, educator, and writer. She is a PassPorter Guide for the Special Needs Forum and has visited Disney Parks in Florida, California, and Hong Kong, China. She enjoys traveling, riding roller coasters, learning new things, and having fun with special people.

Bernie Edwards served on the Disney Parks Moms Panel and the original Walt Disney World Moms Panel from 2010 through 2014. He, his wife Laura, and their two sons, Christopher and Thomas, all love visiting Walt Disney World and Disneyland as often as possible. Bernie travels worldwide for work, and his favorite hotel on the planet is the Wilderness Lodge—he loves taking the boat from the Lodge to the Magic Kingdom at night.

Debbie Hendrickson Debbie Hendrickson has been a PassPorter Guide for 12 years. She and her husband Lee love visiting Walt Disney World and Disneyland and have been to both locations many times. Debbie enjoys the magical atmosphere of the Disney Parks and loves that her inner kid comes out whenever she walks onto Disney Property.

Ginger Jabour is a PassPorter Guide, retired Air Force colonel, Assistant Scoutmaster, volunteer tutor, and former tv reporter. She's visited Walt Disney World and Disneyland 25+ times, usually with husband, Jay, and sons, Matt and Mark. She enjoys wrangling more Disney visits, scrapbooking, teaching, photography, beaches, and working with Scouts (camping she just tolerates). Anna is her hero.

Cam Matthews has been a Disney Vacation Club member since 2004 and has made 20 trips home. Knowing how much their daughter Stefanie loved trips to Disney World, Cam and husband Luke planned carefully to make every trip magical for her because, if anyone understood magic, it was Stefanie. Cam is also a PassPorter Message Board Guide.

PassPorter Team

Cheryl Pendry and her husband Mark usually visit Walt Disney World every year, despite the fact they live in England. They became Disney Vacation Club members in 2002 and Cheryl is the author of *PassPorter's Disney Vacation Club Guide*. She is also the author of *PassPorter's Walt Disney World for British Holidaymakers* and is a PassPorter Message Board Guide.

Ann Smith, a PassPorter Message Board Guide, has been to Disney World over 20 times. She's experienced many magical memories with her family—her husband, Jim, and children, Jamie, Brendan, and Shelby. One of her fondest Disney World memories was watching both of her sons perform on Main Street with their High School marching band several times over the past six years.

Mindy Stanton is a stay-at-home mom. She enjoys vacationing in Walt Disney World yearly with her husband Keith, two boys Nicholas and Aiden, and her parents Fran and Louann. Mindy also enjoys scrapbooking, trips to the beach, planning Walt Disney World vacations for others and being a PassPorter message board Guide in the Family Room forum.

A special thank you to the Guides (moderators) of our own message boards: Kathy Batzinger, Tiffany Bendes, Tanya Blissman, Sandra Bostwick, Dyan Chaplin, Dianne Cook, Michele Dakho, Kelly Davis, Pam Dorr, Lesley Duncan, Lisa Fredsbo, Marisa Garber-Brown, Will Garmer, Debbie Hendrickson, Linda Holland, Kelly Hughes, Ginger Jabour, Claudine Jamba, Ann Johnson, Deb Kendall, Robin Krening-Capra, Susan Kulick, Marcie LaCava, Eileen Lloyd, Keri Madeira, Heather Macdonald, Cam Matthews, Sarah Mudd, Bill Myers, Joby Normandeau, Rebecca Oberg, Allison Palmer-Gleicher, Cheryl Pendry, Danielle Primavera, Susan Rannestad, Sabine Rautenberg, Terri Sellers, Ann Smith, Marie St. Martin, Mindy Stanton, Marnie Urmaza, Sara Varney, Suzi Waters, Don Willis, and the 70,000+ readers in our amazing community at http://www.passporterboards.com/forums.

Special recognition goes to **Cheryl Pendry**, who not only peer reviewed this edition, but also contributed many of the photos that appear here.

Credit goes out to **Allison Cerel Marx** who contributed many of the KidTips when she was much younger!

Our gratitude to these very important folks "behind the scenes" at PassPorter:
Printer: Oceanic Graphic Printing (Thanks, Dean and Daisy!)
Online Coordinator and Newsletter Editor: Sara Varney

Acknowledgments

© Terri Sellers

This edition is dedicated to **Bill Myers**, a longtime PassPorter Guide and passionate Disney fan who fell in the line of duty. Bill was an avid photographer and you can see his photos throughout this edition, with a particularly magical photo on page 319. You are missed by us all, Bill!

A "world" of thanks to our readers, who've contributed loads of tips, stories, and photos since PassPorter's debut. A special thanks to those who generously allowed us to include their **contributions and photographs** in this edition:

Angela Amick, Julie Amling, Tiffany Andrisani, Jennifer Arnold, Tom Arreola, Matt Asplen, Heather Baker, Abbey Barnes, Diana Barthelemy-Rodriguez, Jennifer Berry, Alisa Boquet, Charity Boughner, Beth Borja, Tracy Bratlie, Lissette Brito, Carolyn Brooke-Millward, Jean Bussell, Megan Caceres, Michelle Clark, Nicole Clayton, Vicki Lynn Collins, Dawn Chugg, Genevieve Daniel, Katie Dattalo, Tricia Davids, Laura Dawson, Jyl Deshler, Heather DiFulvio, Lois Ann Dolley, Brigett Duncan, Sean Dunham, Dawn Elliot, Debbie Ernest, Byron Etzel, Susan Fadel, Eileen Farnsworth, Pamela Feavel, LilyAnn Fisherman, Elizabeth Ferris, Stephanie Fieldstad, April Fletcher-Yout, Nathan Franco, Sam Fuller, Brenda G., Cyndi Gai, Shirley Garcowski, Monica Gauvin, Victoria Goeler, Ben Gross, Susan Gross, Misty Hailey, Denise Hand, Gayle Hartleroad, Melissa Hasbrouck, Catie Hiltz, Alison Hinsley, Lura Honeycutt, Amanda Hulse, Teresa Humphries, Andrea Johnson, Lindsay Jones, Brad K., Patti Kalal, Brent Key, Elizabeth Key, Jill Koenigs, Angie Lambert, Jennifer Lambert, Denise Lang, David Latoundji, Jodi Leeper, Michelle Lisanti, Melissa Loflin, Julie Long, Priscilla Lopez, Suzie Lyle, Carlos Medina, Karen Majeau, Christine Mak, Joseph Marchewka, Stephanie Mason, Cam Matthews, Bonnie McCarty, Leanna Metteer, Lisa Miller, Rae Mills, Lynn Mirante, Joey Morehead, Darren Mosher, Sarah Mudd, Bill Myers, Amanda Nash, Kelly Michelle Narvaez, Beth N., Erin Newman, Alisa Niethammer, Amy Novak, Lisa O'Meara, Liliane Opsomer, Debra Ortiz, Carrie Owens, Melissa Lynn Page, Tom Panzella, Cheryl Pendry, Chris Perry, Gina Pesca, Ann Petersoli, Penny J. Pettigrew, Jean Philo, Andrea Popovits, Melissa Potter, Michelle Price, Denise Preskitt, Stacey Rahe, Shendl Rewitzky, Sarah Rhue, Barry Ristow, Rachel Robinson, Kim Roe, Sherry Rohlfing, Jana Ruf, Ben Rupp, Hope Rupp, Jamie S., Danielle Sabato, Amy Sellars, Heather Shevland, Janet Simonsen, Lisa Siverns-LeClair, Rebecca Smith, Keith Stanton, Mindy Stanton, Hiromi Stone, Wendy Suchomel, Marianne Swan, Francis T. Tewey, Regina Thomas, Tina Thornton, Kurt Ulrich, Marnie Urmaza, Kelly Van Eerden, Joy Vodnik, Rick Wagner, Teresa Weddelman Susan Weid, Shannon Wellnitz, Donald Willis, Teresa Wilson, Gina Winnette, Tammy Wright, Jeanne Young, Mark Zielberg, Ann, Disney Event Group, imadisneygirl, JustLorri, Nalagh, and SuperNemo. May each of you receive a new magical memory for every reader your words touch.

PassPorter would not be where it is today without the support of the **Internet Disney fan community**. Our thanks to the friendly folks below and to all whom we didn't have room to include!

- AllEars.net (http://www.allears.net). Thanks, Deb W., Deb K., and Mike S.!
- Disney Food Blog (http://www.disneyfoodblog.com). Thanks, AJ!
- MouseEarVacations.com (http//www.mouseearvacations.com). Thanks, Jami!
- Mouse Fan Travel (http://www.mousefantravel.com). Thanks, Beci, Annette, and Sara!
- MousePlanet.com (http://www.mouseplanet.com). Thanks Mike D., Mark, Adrienne, & Tony!
- MouseSavers.com (http://www.mousesavers.com). Thanks, Mary!
- Planning Strategy Calculator (http://pscalculator.net). Thanks, Scott!
- Sorcerer Radio (http://www.srsounds.com). Thanks, Wayne and Kirsten!
- Tikiman Pages (http://www.tikimanpages.com/poly). Thanks for checking our Poly pages, Steve!

A heartfelt thank you to our **family and friends** for their patience while we were away on trips or cloistered at our computers, and for their support of our dream: Allison Cerel Marx; Carolyn Tody; Fred Marx; Kim, Chad, Megan, and Natalie Larner; Dan, Jeannie, Kayleigh, Melanie, and Nina Marx; Jeanne and David Beroza; Greg Reese; Tracy DeGarmo, Ben Foxworth; and Bruce and Marta Metcalf.

About Our Cover Photo

This scenic photo of Cinderella Castle in the Magic Kingdom was taken by PassPorter author Jennifer Marx. The image was captured with a Panasonic Lumix DMC-FZ1000 on a brilliantly sunny day in February 2015 (can you spot the crane?). 50,000 more photos are online at the PassPorter Photo Archive at http://www.passporter.com/photos, where you can search and browse images.

Contents

List of Maps, Worksheets, and Charts

Contents
(continued)

Contents

(continued)

The PassPorter Way

PassPorter guidebooks are **independently published** by a family-owned and family-run small business. As journalists, we strive to present accurate information with a fair and balanced viewpoint. Our books are "unofficial," meaning we can call it as we see it.

We travel as our readers do. Although we enlist the help of local experts who live and breathe our destinations, we fly or drive long distances from our home base in Michigan, and stay in the hotels, giving us a perspective that no "local" can possess. We make all our own reservations and arrangements, sometimes with the help of a travel agent, but mostly we "shop direct." We pay our own way, so we're always looking for the best deal. We buy our own admission, pay for all our excursions, tours, and add-ons. We make our reservations through normal channels—no VIP treatment, no media discounts or freebies. We need to know that our experience will be like yours and hasn't been enhanced for the sake of a better review. While we may be invited to visit a hotel, restaurant, or attraction as members of the media, we do not use those visits to evaluate matters like quality of service or level of amenities offered, as regular guests may not receive quite the same treatment.

PassPorter guidebooks are truly a community effort. Through our PassPorter.com web site, message board community, PassPorter News weekly e-newsletter, and many face-to-face encounters, we interact with you, our readers, year-round. Whether or not we join a particular discussion, we're always watching the message boards to see what's important to you, and we're thinking of how we can better address those issues in our books. You contribute in so many ways! These pages are filled with your tips and photos, and your suggestions and questions over the years have led to improvements large and small. Your reports on our message board make you our field researchers, witnessing and experiencing far more than we could ever manage on our own. Dozens of you, as Peer Reviewers over the years, pore over each manuscript, and each manages to uncover items to be updated, clarified, or fixed that nobody else has managed to find. Few publishers, in any field, subject their manuscripts to this level of scrutiny. Unlike many travel books, which, once printed, are set aside until it's time to produce the next edition, we're immersed in our topic 365 days a year, following the news and rumors, and keeping in constant touch with you.

All of this makes PassPorter a uniquely interactive guidebook. Together, we've created what we like to think of as "book 2.0" and we're proud to be innovators of a new generation of guidebooks that encourage collaboration. Here are some of the special interactive features in this edition:

PassPorter Photos: We truly believe that a picture tells a thousand words, so this edition is enhanced with more than 500 full-color photos! The majority of these photos were contributed by our amazing readers, as we feel a wider range of perspective makes a better guidebook. The photos that appear at the top of pages are "Photo Slices," because they give you just a slice of Disney—they are intended to convey a general look, a feeling, or an idea. All of the photos were hand-picked from our vast personal collection and the online PassPorter Photo Archive. Want a closer look? If the ⓘ symbol and 4- to 5-digit code appears with the photo, go to http://www.passporter.com/i and look it up!

PassPorter Articles: You just can't fit everything in a guidebook, so when we have more to tell you, we lead you to one of our feature articles and/or photo collections on our web site. Just look in the lower right margin for the ⓘ icon accompanied by a keyword, visit http://www.passporter.com/i and enter the keyword (type it exactly as it appears). Note that multiple article keywords are separated by the | symbol. Here's an example ☛

More at ⓘ passporter-way | making-of-passporter

Congratulations!

First, congratulations are in order—you're going to Walt Disney World! You are about to embark on an experience that will amaze and, hopefully, delight you. This isn't an ordinary, run-of-the-mill trip—after all, you're going to spend your vacation in the heart of Mickey Mouse land!

The Walt Disney World Resort is a world unto itself, full of heralded amusements and hidden gems. Yet the very fact that it is so vast can make a visit to Walt Disney World seem more like a race in a maze than a relaxed vacation. And worse yet, pleasant memories of a great vacation may disappear beneath the stress and worries that accompanied it.

Happily, after fifty-plus trips to Walt Disney World, we've learned to dispel our stress with one simple and enjoyable task: **planning ahead**. In fact, it is no task at all—planning is as much fun as the vacation itself. Planning gave birth to the PassPorter concept. Originally, Jennifer made itineraries on her computer and placed them in a binder. During the trip she kept the binder handy, using it to store passes, brochures, and receipts. After the vacation, these organizers had turned into scrapbooks, full of pixie-dusted memories and goofy smiles. When Jennifer's writing career took off, she didn't have the time to create binders for every trip. She wished for a simpler version that she could use each trip without a lot of fuss. It was on a Disney bus that the idea came to her. She could make an easy-to-use, book-based version and offer it as a resource to fellow vacationers!

Now, after much work, you hold PassPorter in your hands. The first edition of PassPorter debuted in 1999, creating a sensation in the Disney fan community, winning 13 national awards, and helping hundreds of thousands plan great vacations. This edition is our eighteenth, which features large color photos on beautiful glossy paper for your viewing pleasure!

It is our greatest hope that PassPorter helps you "discover the magic" through your own eyes, as it did for us. To get you in the spirit, read "Disney Dreaming" on the next page and prepare for your adventure!

Smiles and laughter,

Jennifer, Dave, and Alexander

We'd love to hear from you! Visit us on the Internet (http://www.passporter.com) or drop us a postcard from Walt Disney World!

P.S. We finished this edition's updates in September 2015. For the latest changes, updates, and news, be sure to consult our page of free book updates at http://www.passporter.com/customs/bookupdates.htm.

Top Photo Slice: Wishes fireworks at the Magic Kingdom (11580) © Jamie S.

Disney Dreaming

A good part of the fun of going to the Walt Disney World Resort is the anticipation before your trip! To really get you into "Disney Dreaming," we present some of our favorite tips to feed your excitement and prepare you for the adventure that lies ahead. This is magical stuff—don't blame us if you get the urge to hop on the next plane to Orlando.

Watch a Movie

Disney movies—animations and live action alike—capture the Disney spirit wonderfully. Rent your favorite movie online and settle in for a cozy evening. You can also request a free vacation planning video of the Walt Disney World Resort at http://www.disneyvacations.com or call 407-934-7639. (To get a free Disney Cruise Line video, call 888-325-2500.)

Listen to Music

Load up your CD player with Disney music or listen to a Disney-themed Internet radio station. We recommend Sorcerer Radio, which features both Disney tunes and shows! Listen at http://www.srsounds.com.

Go Shopping

You may enjoy a visit to The Disney Store for its delightful theming and foot-tapping music. You can buy park admission at a discount, and special offers may be had with the Disney Rewards Visa (see page 10).

Reminisce

If you've visited the "World" before, think back to your vacation and the things you enjoyed most about it. Dig out your souvenirs, photos, and home movies and view them with fresh eyes. If you used a PassPorter last time, go through your PassPockets carefully to refresh your memory and find the notes you made "for next time." If you haven't gone to Walt Disney World before, talk to all the friends and family members who have gone and get their impressions, tips, and stories.

Network With Others

Disney fans tend to gravitate toward the Internet. You'll find many Disney sites—even one for PassPorter planners! (See page 7 for more information.) No access to the Internet? Try your library!

Plan, Plan, Plan

Few things are better than planning your own trip to the Walt Disney World Resort. Cuddle up with your PassPorter, read it through, and use it to the fullest—it makes planning fun and easy. PassPorter really is the ultimate in Disney Dreaming!

Top Photo Slice: A hammock at Disney's Caribbean Beach Resort © MediaMarx, Inc.

Planning Your Adventure

Planning is the secret to a successful vacation. The Walt Disney World Resort is vast and overwhelming without a game plan. Good planning is rewarded by a far more magical Disney experience. Planning is also wonderful fun. It increases the anticipation and starts the excitement months before your vacation begins.

PREPARE the best possible vacation

Planning begins with learning about the Walt Disney World Resort. Your PassPorter has all the information you need for a great vacation, and then some! Written to be complete yet compact, PassPorter can be your only guidebook or act as a companion to another. You can use it in a variety of ways: as a travel guide, a vacation planner, an organizer, a trip journal, and a keepsake. We designed it for heavy use—you can take it with you and revisit it after your trip is just a fond memory. You can personalize it with your plans, notes, souvenirs, and memories. We even crafted it with extra room in the binding to hold the things you'll squeeze and jam into the pockets along the way. PassPorter is the ultimate Walt Disney World Resort guide—before, during, and after your vacation.

MAKE the most of your PassPorter

This first chapter helps you with the initial planning stage: gathering information and budgeting. Your PassPorter then continues through the planning stages in order of priority. Sprinkled throughout are ways to personalize your trip, little-known tips, and magical Disney memories.

Above all else, have fun with your plans, both now and when you reach the Walt Disney World Resort. Leave room for flexibility, and include time to relax and refresh. You might be tempted to see and do it all, but an overly ambitious plan will be more exhausting (and frustrating) than fun. Don't get so bogged down with planning and recording that you miss the spontaneous magic of a Disney vacation. To paraphrase Robert Burns, "The best laid plans of mice and men go oft astray." Use your PassPorter to plan ahead and be aware of your options so you can relax and enjoy your vacation, no matter what it brings.

Top Photo Slice: It's never too early to plan your trip! (①14621) © Alisa Niethammer

Planning With Your PassPorter

Each important aspect of your vacation—budgeting, traveling, packing, lodging, touring, and eating—has a **special, dedicated worksheet** in your PassPorter. Don't be shy; we designed these worksheets to be scribbled upon at will. Not only do they take the place of easy-to-lose scraps of paper, they are structured specifically for your vacation.

We recommend you **use a standard ball point pen or soft-lead pencil** on the worksheets in your PassPorter, as it will work best on our glossy paper. You can **keep your pen handy, too**! Slip the pen inside the book's spiral binding and secure the pen's pocket clip to one of the spirals.

Additions and significant changes at Disney World since our last edition are highlighted in green, just like this paragraph. This is not to be confused with general changes and tweaks to PassPorter, which are plentiful.

Your PassPorter is most useful when you keep it handy before and during your vacation. It fits compactly into backpacks and shoulder bags. Or tuck your PassPorter into a **waist pack** (at least 6.5" x 9" or 17 x 23 cm).

Your PassPorter loves to go on rides with you, but try to **keep it dry** on Splash Mountain and Kali River Rapids. The heavy cover offers good protection, but a simple resealable plastic bag (gallon size) is a big help.

Personalize your PassPorter! **Write your name** under the front cover flap, along with other information you feel comfortable listing (we recommend that you do not list your room number for safety reasons). Your hotel name, trip dates, and cell phone number help if you misplace your PassPorter. Under the back cover flap are places for your important **phone numbers**, **reminders**, and **addresses**. Use the checkboxes to mark items when done. The **label page** at the end of the text is a fun feature—use the labels to personalize your PassPockets and attach the tabs to mark your chapters!

Two tools you may find helpful for planning are a **highlighter** (to mark "must-sees") and those sticky **page flags** (to mark favorite pages).

It's normal for the **handy spiral binding** in your PassPorter to rotate as you flip pages. If this causes your binding to creep up, you can easily rotate it back—just twist the binding while holding the pages securely.

Your PassPorter's **sturdy cover** wraps around your book for protection, and you can fold it back and leave the book open. The binding is a bit bigger than necessary to fit your stuff. We crafted a pocket for each day of your trip (up to 10 days), plus special ones for your journey, lodging, and memories. Read more about these "PassPockets" on the next page.

Note: Most of the tips on these two pages apply to the regular edition (spiral-bound); if you have a deluxe edition (ring-bound), visit http://www.passporter.com/wdw/deluxe.htm.

Top Photo Slice: PassPorter's map of Disney's Animal Kingdom park (see the full version in chapter 4) © MediaMarx, Inc.

Keep everything you need for your journey together here in one place, such as maps, tickets, coupons, reservation numbers... even passports!

Using Your PassPockets

In the back of your PassPorter are 14 unique "PassPockets" to help you plan before you go, keep items handy while you're there, and save memories for your return. Just pencil in your trip information and itinerary on the front; store brochures, maps, receipts, and such inside; and jot down impressions, memories, expenses, and notes on the back. Use the PassPockets in any way that suits you, filling in as much or as little as you like. You can even personalize your PassPockets with the included labels!

Read the advice or tip.

Use the pockets as printed, or personalize with a label.

Write your itinerary here, including times, names, and confirmation numbers. Or just record what you did.

Jot down things you want to remember, do, or visit.

Make notes before you go or add notes during your trip.

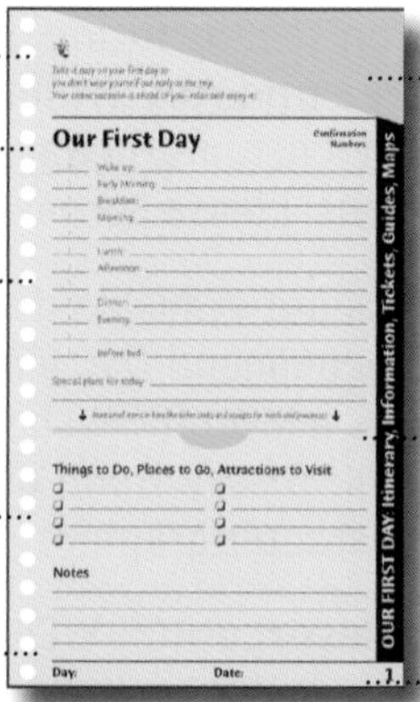

Store items you want to have on hand during your trip, or things you collect along the way, in this roomy pocket. Guidemaps, brochures, and envelopes all fit inside.

Slip small items in this smaller slot, such as receipts, claim tags, and ticket stubs.

Write the day of the week and the date for quick reference.

Record memories of your vacation to share with others or to keep to yourself. You can jot these down as you go or reminisce at the end of the day.

Keep track of photos taken so you can find them later!

Watch your expenses to stay within a budget or to track your resort charge account balance.

Remember all those great (or not-so-great) meals and snacks by noting them here. You can even include the price of the meal or snack, too!

What did you forget? What do you want to do again? What would you like to try next time? What wouldn't you touch again with a ten-foot pole? Make a note of it here!

Use the Vacation-at-a-Glance page just before the photos and PassPockets to record park hours, showtimes, meals, or anything that helps you plan your trip. If you prefer to travel light, don't be shy about removing a PassPocket and carrying it around for the day instead of toting your entire PassPorter. Just tuck it back in here at the end of the day! (If you have the spiral version and feel uncomfortable about tearing out a PassPocket, you may prefer our ring-bound Deluxe Edition with looseleaf pockets—see page 312.) You can also purchase extra PassPockets—visit http://www.passporterstore.com/store.

Top Photo Slice: The "Our Journey" PassPocket © MediaMarx, Inc.

Finding Disney Information

PassPorter can act as your **first source** of information for the Walt Disney World Resort. It can also be a companion to other Disney books you may already own or purchase later. Either way, we like to think it packs a lot of information into a small package. Everything you need to know to plan a wonderful Disney vacation can be found within its pages.

Do keep in mind that the Walt Disney World Resort is constantly changing. We've taken every step to ensure that your PassPorter is as up-to-date as possible, but we cannot foresee the future. So to help your PassPorter remain current, we **make free updates available** to you at our web site (http://www.passporter.com/customs/bookupdates.htm). If you have ideas, questions, or corrections, please contact us—see page 308.

Oodles of **travel guidebooks** are available if you have a hankering for second opinions. We highly recommend *The Unofficial Guide to Walt Disney World* by Bob Sehlinger for its irreverence, sheer quantity of detail, and touring plans. *Birnbaum's Walt Disney World* offers the official line and plenty of cheerful Disney character graphics.

Call the **Walt Disney World Resort** at 407-WDW-MAGIC (407-939-6244) or e-mail them through their web site (http://www.disneyworld.com) when you need answers to specific questions. In our experience, their representatives are very friendly, but they rarely volunteer information and won't offer opinions. Prepare questions in advance. If the person you reach doesn't have an answer, call back—several times if necessary. Don't hesitate to ask for a manager if you can't get the information you need.

Travel agents you know and trust can be a great source of information—many have web sites, too. Also check with **membership organizations** that arrange travel, such as AAA (see page 11).

Magazines and newsletters about Disney are also available. Our own free weekly PassPorter News has Disney and other travel features, book updates, news, reviews, reports, contests, tips, and deals—subscribe at http://www.passporter.com/news (subscribers are also entitled to a discount on PassPorter guidebooks). ALL EARS® Newsletter is a free unofficial weekly e-mail with Disney articles and news —subscribe at http://www.allears.net. Annual Passholders in the United States (see page 10) receive a quarterly newsletter from Disney. And, for the price of a gold membership fee ($79.99), D23 members receive the *Disney twenty-three* publication quarterly, which contains exclusive interviews with filmmakers and Imagineers, plus behind-the-scenes glimpses—all in glossy color (subscribe at http://www.d23.com).

Top Photo Slice: Authors' bookshelf with PassPorters and other travel guidebooks © MediaMarx, Inc.

More at ⓘ finding-answers | disney-podcasts (tip: enter this keyword at http://www.passporter.com/i for more information!)

Exploring a Whole New World Wide Web

The ultimate source of information, in our opinion, is the **Internet**. Of course, this requires access to a computer with access to the Internet, but with this you can connect to millions of vacationers happy to share their Disney knowledge.

The web offers hundreds of Disney-related sites. In fact, **PassPorter** has its own web site with updates, tips, ideas, articles, forums, and links. Visit us at http://www.passporter.com. We even have a special club—PassPorter's Club—just for vacation planners! More details are on page 316.

Disney's official web site at http://www.disneyworld.com is an excellent source for basic information, including park hours, rates, and maps. You can also call 407-824-4321 to get much of the same information. Also check out the Disney Moms Panel at http://disneyworldforum.disney.go.com and the Disney Parks Blog at http://disneyparks.disney.go.com/blog.

We also recommend several **unofficial web sites**, which we frequent ourselves when planning a trip. We introduce these web sites as appropriate throughout the book (check pages 304–305 in the index for a full list). Two special sites deserve mention now: AllEars.net is a comprehensive and up-to-date guide at http://www.allears.net, and MousePlanet.com has great articles and weekly updates at http://www.mouseplanet.com.

Another source of information (and camaraderie) is **discussion groups**. PassPorter has its own set of message boards with an active, supportive community of vacationers at http://www.passporterboards.com/forums—come chat with us, ask your questions, and share the fun! Fans also gather at the "**DIS**" (**Disney Information Station**) at http://www.disboards.com, as well as at **WDWMagic** at http://forums.wdwmagic.com and **Intercot** at http://www.intercot.com.

Podcasts are the latest way to learn about Disney online—they are similiar to talk radio shows and free to listen to on your computer or iPod. PassPorter has its own podcast with host "moms" Jennifer Marx and Sara Varney—listen to us weekly at http://www.passporter.com/podcast.

E-mail lists are yet another valuable Internet resource, allowing you to observe and participate in discussions from the safety of your e-mailbox. We have a newsletter list with regular feature articles—subscribe for free at our web site. Many other mailing lists are available, including **The Mouse For Less** for Disney fans on a budget—visit at http://www.themouseforless.com.

Top Photo Slice: Giant laptop at Pop Century Resort (ⓘ522) © MediaMarx, Inc.

Budgeting for Your Vacation

There's nothing magical about depleting your nest egg to finance a vacation. Too many Disney vacationers can tell you that money concerns overshadowed all the fun. Yet you can avoid both the realities and worries of overspending by planning within a budget. Budgeting ahead of time not only keeps you from spending too much, it encourages you to seek out ways to save money. With just a little bit of research, you can often get **more for less**, resulting in a richer, more relaxed vacation.

If you purchase a **vacation package**, you have the advantage of covering most of your major expenses up front. And while Disney's package prices haven't offered a real savings in the past, they've recently been offering decent deals. Consider adding the Dining Plan to your package (see pages 223–225). Can't find a package with a great deal? Planning each aspect of your vacation separately often saves you even more money, as we show throughout this book. You can learn about vacation packages on page 32 and inquire into prices with the Walt Disney Travel Co. at 407-828-8101 or online at http://www.disneytravel.com.

Your **vacation expenses** usually fall into six categories: planning, transportation, lodging, admission, food, and extras. How you budget for each depends upon the total amount you have available to spend and your priorities. Planning, transportation, lodging, and admission are the easiest to factor ahead of time, as costs are more or less fixed. The final two—food and extras—are harder to control, but can usually be estimated.

Begin your vacation budgeting with the **worksheet** on the following page. Enter the minimum you prefer to spend and the maximum you can afford in the topmost row. Establish as many of these ranges as possible before you delve into the other chapters. Your excitement may grow as you read more about Walt Disney World, but it is doubtful your bank account will.

As you uncover costs and ways to save money later, return to this worksheet and **update it**. Think of your budget as a work in progress. Flexibility within your minimum and maximum figures is important. As plans begin to crystallize, write the amount you expect to pay (and can afford) in the Estimated Costs column. Finally, when you are satisfied with your budget, **transfer the amounts** from the Estimated Costs column to the back of each PassPocket. Note that each PassPocket also provides space to record actual expenses, which helps you stay within your budget. Tip: This worksheet and many others are available in electronic, interactive versions, and some even do the calculations for you—see page 316 for details.

More at ⓘ saving-money-for-disney-world

Top Photo Slice: Piggy bank at The Great Piggy Bank Adventure in Epcot © MediaMarx, Inc.

Electronic, interactive worksheet available—see page 316

Budget Worksheet

Use this worksheet to identify your resources, record estimated costs, and create a budget for your vacation. When complete, transfer the figures from the Estimated Costs column to the back of each PassPocket.

	Minimum		Maximum		Est. Costs	
Total Projected Expenses	$		$		$	
Planning:						
Phone Calls/Faxes:						
Guides/Magazines:						
Transportation:	(transfer to your Journey PassPocket)					
Rental Car:						
Fuel/Maintenance/Tolls:						
Airfare/Travel Tickets:						
Luggage/Seat Fees:						
Shuttle/Town Car/Taxi:						
Stroller/Wheelchair/ECV:						
Parking:						
Lodging:	(transfer to your Rooms PassPocket)					
En Route Motel/Other:						
Resort/Hotel:						
Admission:	(transfer to appropriate PassPocket)					
Theme Park Passes:						
Water Park Passes:						
DisneyQuest Passes:						
Golf/Recreation:						
Guided Tours/Other:						
Food*:	Daily	Total	Daily	Total	Daily	Total
Breakfast:						
Lunch:						
Dinner:						
Snacks:						
Groceries/Other:						
	(transfer to each daily PassPocket)					
Extras:						
Souvenirs/Clothing:						
Gratuities:						
Vacation Wardrobe:						
Internet Access/Photos:						
Other:						
Total Budgeted Expenses	$		$		$	

* If you're on the Disney Dining Plan package (see pages 223-225), you may want to check off your included meals in the worksheet so you don't budget money for them.

Top Photo Slice: Filling out at PassPorter worksheet © MediaMarx, Inc.

Money-Saving Programs

You can save real money on a Walt Disney World Resort vacation by taking advantage of the following money-saving programs. Some require a membership fee, but they often pay for themselves quite quickly.

Disney Rewards Visa Card—This credit card from Chase gives cardholders special discounts on Disney resorts, packages, and tours, plus onboard credits on the Disney cruise. The card itself has no annual fee and earns "Disney Dream Reward Dollars" equal to 1% or more of your purchases. You can redeem your dollars relatively quickly for Disney travel, entertainment, and merchandise. Exclusive cardholder benefits are also typically offered, such as special character meet and greets. Another perk is the "pay no interest for 6 months" offer on Disney packages and cruises, but keep in mind initial deposits and all payments must be made with the card or you can lose the deal. Be sure to read the fine print carefully, too—if you carry a separate balance while floating a 0% vacation deal, your payments may apply to the higher interest balance first and you could end up paying some steep interest. Also, double-check exactly when you need to pay off the balance and be careful about confusing terminology. We have a Disney Visa ourselves and we think the "rewards" are just average, interest rates are high, and the available discounts are sparse (but attractive when offered). Disney Rewards Visa is available to U.S. residents only. If you have a Disney Rewards Visa, be sure to mention this when making reservations so they can offer any available incentives or deals. There's also a Chase Visa Rewards Disney debit card which offers some theme park benefits (but no longer earns Reward Dollars)—this card is available to those who bank with Chase. For details, visit http://www.disneyrewards.com or call 877-252-6576. Also see our in-depth article at http://www.passporter.com/credit.asp.

Annual Pass (AP)—An Annual Pass (regular or premium) saves big money on admission if you plan to visit for more than 10–14 days in a one-year period (depending on the pass)—this is the point at which it becomes less expensive than regular admission. It may also deliver discounts at selected resorts, meals, tours, and ticketed events, plus invitations to special events. And let's not forget Tables in Wonderland eligibility (see below). Florida residents can pay for their Annual Pass in monthly installments without extra fees. See pages 122–123 for details and call 407-WDW-MAGIC for prices.

Florida Residents—Those of you with proof of Florida residency (such as a valid Florida driver's license) can enjoy great savings on Disney tickets, resorts, cruises, and more. The deals are so good we're almost tempted to move to Florida. For more information, visit http://disneyworld.disney.go.com/florida-residents/.

Tables in Wonderland (formerly the Disney Dining Experience)—This program offers 20% discounts on food and alcohol (for up to 10 persons, paying with one credit card or with cash) at most Disney eateries, plus free theme park parking after 5:00 pm, and free resort valet parking when dining at the resort. Available to Annual and Seasonal Passholders, DVC members, and Florida residents ages 21 and up with a valid Florida driver's license or ID card. Membership is $150/year for Annual/Seasonal Passholders; $175/year for Florida residents without an Annual or Seasonal Pass (renewals are no longer offered). A second membership for your spouse or partner is $50/year. Call 407-566-5858 to order (allow 4–6 weeks, or request a confirmation letter if traveling within 6 weeks). The card is also available for purchase at Guest Services at each theme park. This discount program cannot be combined with any other discount or package, and there are some blackout dates (e.g., major holidays like Mother's Day, Easter, July 4th, Thanksgiving, Christmas Eve/Day, and New Year's Eve/Day). An 18% gratuity is added to all Tables in Wonderland transactions, regardless of party size. The person whose name is on the card must be present for the discount to be applied.

More at ⓘ credit-card-101

Top Photo Slice: A bowl of pennies ... save your spare change for your trip and watch it add up! © MediaMarx, Inc.

Disney Vacation Account–This program lets you set up automatic and recurring contributions to a savings account on the schedule that works best for you (weekly, bi-weekly, or monthly). It's like putting your vacation on layaway! There are no fees to setup or maintain the account, and you can withdraw your money at any time. You can also get a $20 Disney gift card for every $1000 you spend on Disney vacation purchases with the account. Jennifer loves it! Details at https://disneyvacationaccount.disney.go.com.

Disney Vacation Club (DVC)–This timeshare program may save money for families who plan ahead. DVC members also get discounts on select meals, admission, and backstage tours. See pages 108–109.

Disney "Postcard" Specials and Advertisements–Disney sometimes offers lodging discounts in direct mail and mass media advertisements. These offers may be sent to previous Disney guests and vacationers who've requested planning materials, or they may appear in newspaper or TV ads. These offers usually have eligibility requirements, such as residence in a particular state, or can only be used by the person who received the mailing. If you receive an offer, be sure to save it for your records. You'll need the "coupon code" and perhaps an ID number ("pin code") to make your reservation. Be sure you are eligible for the offer–if you show up at Disney and can't prove eligibility, you'll lose your "deal." Visit http://www.mousesavers.com for a listing of current offers. Tip: Be sure to check your "spam" e-mail folder for any wayward Disney offers that may wind up there.

Bounceback Offer–After you arrive at a Disney resort hotel, you may get an offer to return ("bounceback") to Walt Disney World at some point in the future at a great rate! Look for bounceback offers in your hotel room, or after you return home.

Orlando Magicard–This free card offers discounts on many non-Disney shows and park tickets, as well as rental cars and hotels. Call 888-416-4026 or visit them online at http://www.orlandoinfo.com/magicard.

Entertainment Book–This annual discount book offers coupons for rental cars, off-property hotels and restaurants, and non-Disney theme parks like Universal Orlando, SeaWorld, and Busch Gardens. Cost is about $35 for a new edition (older editions may be less). Call 888-231-SAVE (888-231-7283) or visit http://www.entertainment.com.

American Automobile Association (AAA)–Members enjoy discounts on tickets when purchased through AAA (resort discounts ended at the start of 2015).

Money-Saving Tips

- ✔ *MouseSavers.com is a web site dedicated to cataloging available Disney discounts and deals. Webmaster Mary Waring has built a huge following, both at http://www.mousesavers.com and through her free monthly newsletter.*
- ✔ *If you are flying, check newspapers and the Internet for fare sales–they occur more frequently than you might think and offer savings. Expedia.com (http://www.expedia.com) has great combo deals on fares and hotel rooms!*
- ✔ *If you are driving or arriving late in the evening, consider staying a night at a less expensive motel your first night.*
- ✔ *You can save money on meals by sharing entrees or by eating only two meals a day, as Disney portions tend to be quite large. Bring quick breakfast foods and snacks from home to quell the munchies and keep up your energy.*
- ✔ *Always ask about discounts when you make reservations, dine, or shop. You may discover little-known specials for Disney Visa Card, Florida residents, Annual Passholders, or simply vacationers in the right place at the right time.*
- ✔ *Join The Mouse For Less community for more money-saving tips–you can subscribe for free at http://www.themouseforless.com.*

More at ⓘ catching-deals

Plan It Up!

Use these tips and stories to make planning your vacation fun:

"If you have access to the **Internet**, make it a point to get online once a week for the latest news. We have many trip reports from fellow vacationers posted on our message boards at http://www.passporterboards.com/forums. MousePlanet also offers trip reports at http://www.mouseplanet.com/wdwtr."

"My kids love to measure their height in between our trips to Walt Disney World. It's always exciting when they reach a new height that includes new rides! We will pick up an 'I'm Celebrating' button that says 'I'm Celebrating 44 inches!' to celebrate the new milestone."

– Contributed by Tiffany Andrisani, a winner in our Reader Tip Contest

"Update your PassPorter! I came onto the site and I noticed that there was a link to update to my PassPorter that was so very important in my planning of my perfect trip. Now I have it written down in my calendar to check again about a week before I leave in order to make sure that I don't have any unpleasant surprises or that I don't miss out on something wonderful! Updates are at http://www.passporter.com/customs/bookupdates.htm"

– Contributed by Debbie Ernest, a winner in our Reader Tip Contest

"Before we go to Walt Disney World, I create a "playlist" on YouTube of rides/attractions that we plan to do/see. We sync our TV to our YouTube account, and the children spend tons of time watching videos. This is a great time to build anticipation and set expectations! (Tip: Preview the videos first, as some are far too extensive for young children, as they include long views of queues. I usually choose videos that are during the day and show rides only.)"

– Contributed by Angela Amick, a winner in our Reader Tip Contest

"I make spreadsheets prior to my trip to list out all my dining reservations, flight information, and things to do on the trip. That way when it comes to booking your reservations, you will have all your days and times planned out and you won't have to think too hard on that 180 day mark! I take all my information and write it in my PassPorter so that I always have the information at my fingertips while in the parks!"

– Contributed by Shendl Rewitzky, a winner in our Reader Tip

Magical Memory

"*My sister has had a very hard life and she doesn't often experience the fun things. So I saved up the money to take her to Walt Disney World, with some help from an understanding husband. I remember the moment when we stepped onto Main Street, U.S.A. for our first time ever and she stopped and just stood looking at Cinderella Castle. She turned to me with tears in her eyes and said, 'Thank you for giving me this moment.' It made all those weeks of saving every penny I could worth it all to see the look on her face. That was a magical moment for me.*"

...as told by PassPorter reader Teresa Humphries

More at ⓘ preparing-kids

Top Photo Slice: Authors' desktop while planning a trip © MediaMarx, Inc.

Getting There (and Back!)

So, you promised your family a trip to visit the Mouse, or for the tenth time today you've gleefully thought, "I'm going to Disney!" Eventually the moment of truth arrives: Just *how* are you going to get there?

Traveling in this age of tightened security requires more planning and patience, but you'll discover it is quite easy to get to the Walt Disney World Resort. The path to Orlando is well traveled by cars, planes, trains, buses, and tours. On the other hand, "easy" isn't always convenient or inexpensive. Choosing the best and most affordable way to get to Disney can take some doing. We can help!

In this chapter, we walk you through the process of making your travel arrangements. We brief you on weather, attendance levels, park hours, and seasonal rates so you can pick the best time to go or make the most of the dates you've already chosen. You'll find descriptions of each major path to the Walt Disney World Resort and a worksheet to help you pick a route and make your reservations. Then it's time to get packing, with the help of our special packing lists. Finally, we help you smile and enjoy your journey with tips for having fun along the way.

CHART your journey and make travel plans

What we won't do is take up space with the phone numbers of airlines and car rental companies or travel directions from every city. You can find that information on the Internet or in your phone book. Just jot down numbers and notes on the worksheet, and transfer the winners to the appropriate PassPocket in the back.

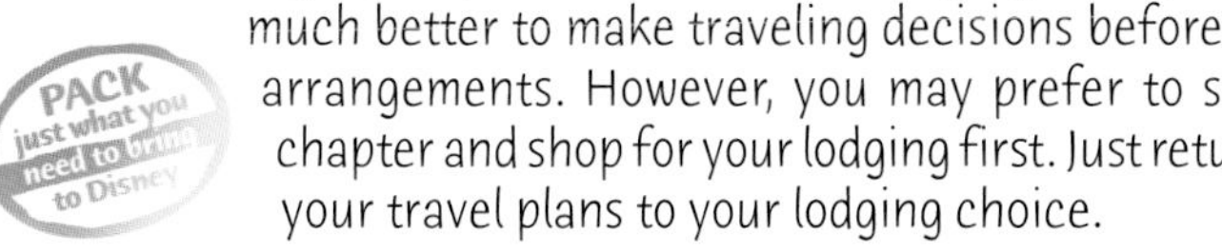

It's important to note that due to reservation change penalties, air and rail travel is generally less flexible than lodging. Thus, we find it works much better to make traveling decisions before finalizing hotel arrangements. However, you may prefer to skip to the next chapter and shop for your lodging first. Just return here to tailor your travel plans to your lodging choice.

The Best of Times

Most Disney veterans can tell you, in no uncertain terms, that some times are much better than others to visit the "World." We wholeheartedly agree, but there's more to it. While there are certainly times of the year that are less crowded or more temperate, only you can decide the best time to visit. To help you decide, we charted the **fluctuating factors** for each month below. If you ask us, the best time to visit is November–February, but avoid the holidays, when parks fill to capacity. Three-day weekends are also to be avoided whenever possible. The latter half of August and September are less crowded, though you'll battle the heat. For links to more temperature and rainfall data, visit http://www.passporter.com/wdw/bestoftimes.htm.

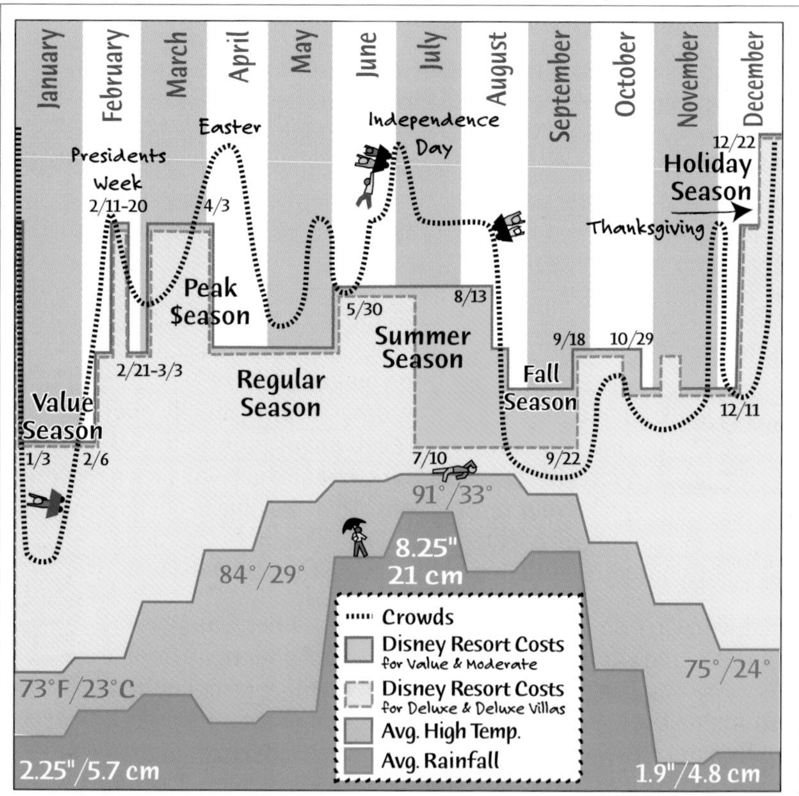

Disney resorts have six seasons—here they are from lowest price to highest price: **value, fall, regular, summer, peak, and holiday**. The exact dates of these seasons have become convoluted over the years, but the above chart shows you the relative timing of the six seasons. Also note that certain weekends, such as Easter, Memorial Day, and Independence Day, have higher rates (below holiday but usually about regular or peak). You can get the exact dates of each season online at http://www.disneyworld.com

Top Photo Slice: Walt Disney World Railroad station on a bright, sunny day © MediaMarx, Inc.

Getting There

One of the major hurdles to a Walt Disney World Resort vacation is figuring out how to get there in the first place. Many of us think along the traditional (and expensive) lines first and become discouraged. It doesn't have to be like that. There are **more ways** to get to Disney than you probably realize. Below we describe each, beginning with the most popular. At the end of the list, on page 23, a worksheet gives you space to make notes, jot down prices, and note reservation numbers. When your travel plans are finalized, record them on the first PassPocket.

By Car, Van, Truck, or Motorcycle

Many vacationers arrive at Disney in their own vehicle. It's hard to beat the **slowly rising sense of excitement** as you draw closer or the freedom of having your own wheels once you arrive. Driving may also eliminate the concerns you or family members may have with air travel. Additionally, driving might be less expensive than air travel for large families. Be sure to compare the costs of driving versus flying before you decide. On the down side, gas is very expensive these days and you may spend long days on the road, which cuts deeply into your time with Mickey.

If you opt to drive, carefully **map your course** ahead of time. You can do this with an AAA TripTik—a strip map that guides you to and from your destination. TripTiks can be created for free at the http://www.aaa.com web site, and AAA will print and mail them to members. If you're driving, we heartily recommend *Along Interstate-75* (http://www.i75online.com) and/or *Drive I-95* (http://www.drivei95.com). I-95 drivers should also visit http://www.i95exitguide.com. Or try a trip routing service, such as http://www.mapquest.com or http://maps.google.com. **Tip**: Have exact change ready for the unmanned toll booths along the Florida toll roads on your route. Check toll prices at http://www.floridasturnpike.com/TRI/index.htm and http://www.cfxway.com.

If you live more than 500 miles away, **spread out your drive** over more than one day, allotting one day for every 500 miles. Arriving at Walt Disney World overly road-weary is no way to begin a vacation. If your journey spans more than one day, decide in advance where to stop each night and make reservations accordingly. Check that your air-conditioning is in good working order and your cell phone is charged before heading out (bring a cell phone charger and headset, too). Secure rest areas are available once you hit the Florida border, making it a bit easier to drive at night. Also see our in-depth articles on driving at http://www.passporter.com/articles/driving.asp.

More at ⓘ driving | driving-with-kids | driving-at-night

Top Photo Slice: Tomorrowland Indy Speedway at the Magic Kingdom (ⓘ9514) © Cheryl Pendry

By Airplane

Air travel is the fastest way for most vacationers to get to Orlando. In fact, air travel may be less expensive than you think if you know the tricks to getting an **affordable flight**.

Be flexible on the day and time of departure and return. Fares can differ greatly depending on when you fly and how long you stay. Consider flying on Tuesdays, Wednesdays, and Saturdays, which are historically lower-fare days. Also include a Saturday night stay in your travel dates, when possible, as it may produce a lower fare. And try to avoid traveling during holidays, as this results in significantly higher fares (though flying on the actual day of a holiday can sometimes be a money-saver).

Take advantage of the many "**fare sales**." To learn about sales, visit airlines' web sites or travel sites such as Expedia (http://www.expedia.com), Orbitz (http://www.orbitz.com), Travelocity (http://www.travelocity.com), or Kayak (http://www.kayak.com). Note that not all airlines are represented on these travel sites. Subscribe to e-mail fare alerts from travel sites and from the airlines that serve your home airport(s). If Southwest Airlines is an option, be sure to check out their web site (see http://www.southwest.com). Tip: It pays to book at least 21 days in advance in most cases, but when you're not ready to book, check out Google Flights (http://www.google.com/flights/explore/) —it offers price predictions and shows you when fares are rising or dropping.

Be sure to include **luggage and/or seat assignment fees** when you compare fares. You'll find handy fee charts at http://www.kayak.com.

Try **alternate airports**, such as Orlando Sanford or Tampa, when researching fares. It may be less expensive to fly to another airport and rent a car to drive to Walt Disney World.

Be persistent. Ask for their lowest fare if you call the airline directly. When you find a good deal, put it on hold immediately (if possible), note your reservation number on page 23, and cancel later if necessary.

Consider **Priceline.com** (http://www.priceline.com), where you name your own price for a round-trip ticket (but once your price is met, you can't cancel).

Finally, **don't stop shopping**. If your airline offers a cheaper fare later, you may be able to rebook at the lower rate (watch out for penalties).

Once you reserve a flight, **make a note** of the reservation numbers, flight numbers, seat assignments, and layovers on your first PassPocket. To arrange **ground transportation** from the airport, see pages 21–22.

More at ⓘ flying-with-kids | waiting-to-take-off | surviving-long-flights | surviving-bumpy-flights

Top Photo Slice: Walt Disney's old survey plane seen on the Studio Backlot Tour (ⓘ3671) © Teresa Wilson

Our Top 10 Flying Tips & Reminders

It may be fastest to fly, but it's certainly not less complicated these days. Here are our top 10 flying tips, reminders, and warnings:

1. Visit http://www.tsa.gov for **travel security news and updates**. You can also use this web site to check security waitpoint times the day before you leave, and to check the status of your flight before departing for the airport. Speaking of web sites, we also suggest you use online check-in if it is offered by your airline, which most now do. Some airlines are also testing an "e-boarding pass" which is sent to your mobile device—you just bring it up on your cell phone and show it at the security checkpoint (but still print your pass as a backup).
2. Be aware that many airlines **charge extra fees** for baggage and certain seats, and that you may get a discount if you pre-pay these.
3. Pick up a **meal and drinks** for the flight after you pass through security, as most domestic flights have discontinued meal service.
4. Pack **sharp or potentially dangerous items** in checked luggage (or just leave them at home). This includes pocket knives and sport sticks. Cigarette lighters, scissors with blades under 4" and nail clippers without knives are allowed. For details, visit http://www.tsa.gov.
5. Remember the **3-1-1 rule** for liquids/gels in carry-ons: They must be in 3.4 oz. **or less** bottle(s), all in **1 quart-sized, clear, zip-top bag**, and **1 bag per person**, placed in a screening bin. Limit your carry-ons to one bag and one personal item (e.g., purse)., though note that medical devices (like a CPAP) are not counted in the limit for carry-on items.
6. Keep your **luggage unlocked** for inspections to avoid damage. Or buy TSA-approved luggage locks at any retail store—they are typically the same price as regular locks.
7. Plan to arrive at the airport at least **two hours prior to departure**. Add an extra 30–45 minutes if you are dropping off a rental car (and don't forget to fuel it up to avoid hefty charges).
8. **Curbside check-in** may be available (fees may apply), but you may need to obtain a boarding pass from your airline's desk anyway.
9. E-ticket holders should bring a **confirmation and/or boarding pass**. If you don't have one, print it from your airline's web site (your hotel's front desk should also be able to print boarding passes within 24 hours of departure).
10. Keep your **photo ID handy**. We use PassHolder Pouches (page 311)

➤

Top Photo Slice: Checking in at the Orlando International Airport (ⓘ15637) © Cheryl Pendry

More at ⓘ airline-security

Planning | Getting There | Staying in Style | Touring | Feasting | Making Magic | Index | Notes & More

Orlando International Airport

Orlando International Airport is a large, sprawling hub and one of the better (and cleaner) airports we've flown into. When you arrive, your plane docks at one of the **satellite terminals** (see map below). From there, follow the signs to the automated **shuttle** that takes you to the main terminal—there you'll find **baggage claim** and ground transportation. Once you reach the main terminal (Level 3), follow the signs down to baggage claim (Level 2). Shuttles, taxis, town cars, rental cars, and buses are found down on Level 1 (take the elevators opposite the baggage carousels). Disney's Magical Express (see page 21) check-in is located on Level 1, Side B. Each shuttle and bus company has its own ticket booth. If you get lost, look about for signs or an information desk that can get you back on track.

As your authors used to live in different cities, we became quite good at **meeting up at the airport**. It's best to meet your party at their baggage claim area as you won't be allowed past security without a valid boarding pass. The trick is knowing which airline and baggage claim area. Use the map and airline list below, or call the airport directly at 407-825-2001. Be careful when differentiating between Side A's and Side B's baggage claims. Gates 1–29 and 100–129 use Side A, while gates 30–99 use Side B. Check the arrival/departure boards in the terminal for flight status, too! Other terminal meeting spots are the Disney Stores (Disney's EarPort and the Magic of Disney—see stars on map below) or an eatery. Be sure to exchange cell phone numbers, too.

For **more details** on the Orlando International Airport, call 407-825-2001 or visit http://www.orlandoairports.net. Page travelers at 407-825-2000.

Aer Lingus, AeroMexico, Air Transat, Alaska Airlines, American Airlines, AviancaTaca, CanJet, Caribbean, Copa, Gol, JetBlue, MiamiAir, Norwegian, SunWing, TAM, Volaris, and WestJet use Gates 1–29; BahamasAir, Silver Airways, Spirit, United, and US Airways use Gates 30–59; AirCanada/rouge, British Airways, Delta, Frontier, Lufthansa, Sun Country, Thomas Cook, and Virgin Atlantic use Gates 60–99; AirTran Airways, Southwest, and Virgin America use Gates 100–129.

Top Photo Slice: Arrivals and departures board at Orlando International Airport © MediaMarx, Inc.

Orlando Sanford Airport

Travelers flying to Orlando **from Europe or via group charter** may arrive at the smaller Orlando Sanford International Airport (SFB), located about 18 miles northeast of Orlando and 67 miles from Port Canaveral. Airlines with scheduled service into Sanford include Allegiant Air, ArkeFly, BeauRivage, Icelandair, Jetairfly, SST Air, and Galaxy Vacations, as well as two international charter services with flights from the United Kingdom and Ireland (Monarch and Thomson Airways).

Alamo/National, Avis, Dollar, Enterprise, Hertz, and Thrifty all operate **in-terminal car rental desks**. Budget has an off-site rental office. Mears Transportation and several shuttle services provide bus/van service from Sanford to Orlando-area attractions and Port Canaveral.

International passengers arrive and depart from Terminal A, while domestic travelers use Terminal B. A Welcome Center is located across the street from Terminal A and is home to ground transportation services.

Dining options here include the Budweiser Tap Room (terminal A) and basic food courts (terminals A & B).

For more details on the Orlando Sanford International Airport, phone 407-585-4000 or visit http://www.orlandosanfordairport.com. If you plan to rent a car at the airport and drive to the Walt Disney World Resort, use a map routing service such as MapQuest.com before you leave home to get directions (the airport is located at 1200 Red Cleveland Blvd., Sanford, FL 32773).

More at sanford-airport

Top Photo Slice: Lobby at the Orlando Sanford Airport © Anonymous

By Train, Bus, Tour, and Boat

By Train

The train is a uniquely relaxing and fuel-saving way to travel to the Walt Disney World Resort. **Amtrak** serves the Orlando area daily with both **passenger trains** and an Auto Train, which carries your family and your car. The **Auto Train** runs between suburban Washington, DC (Lorton, VA) and suburban Orlando (Sanford, FL). Other trains go through to Kissimmee, which is a closer, less-crowded station. Prices vary depending upon the season, the direction, and how far in advance you make your reservation. The Auto Train is also available one-way, and in many seasons, one direction is less expensive than the other direction. You may need to take a taxi or town car (see page 22) from the train station to the Disney property. Hertz rental cars are available from the Sanford (Orlando) station, but not the Kissimmee station. For Amtrak reservations, call 800-USA-RAIL or visit them at http://www.amtrak.com. Also see the in-depth PassPorter article at http://www.passporter.com/autotrain.asp.

By Bus

Buses make good economic and environmental sense. **Greyhound** serves Orlando and Kissimmee. You can take the local LYNX buses from there, but it's not fast or easy (for more information on LYNX, see page 22 under "Riding a Bus"). Buses often take longer to reach a destination than cars or trains do driving the same route. Fares are lowest if you live within 10 hours of Walt Disney World. For fares, schedules, and tickets, call Greyhound at 800-231-2222 or visit them at http://www.greyhound.com.

By Tour

A number of **special tours** go to the Walt Disney World Resort, which you may want to consider if you prefer to go with a large group or with like-minded folks. Check with the associations, organizations, and societies you belong to, or contact a travel agent.

By Boat

If you book passage on the **Disney Cruise Line**, your package may include a stay at the Walt Disney World Resort. The boat doesn't pull up to the Magic Kingdom, but Disney offers optional, prearranged transfers to and/or from the Walt Disney World Resort—this transportation may be included in your cruise package, or you may add it for an additional fee. See pages 106–107 for details on the Disney Cruise, and see page 312 to learn about our award-winning, detailed guide to the Disney Cruise Line.

By Everything Else!

The list of ways to get to Disney is really endless. You could even combine business with pleasure, as many others do!

More at ⓘ auto-train

Top Photo Slice: An Amtak Auto Train en route to Sanford, Florida © MediaMarx, Inc.

Are We There Yet?

Once you reach Orlando Airport, you need to continue about 20 miles before you actually reach Disney property. Your options are to take advantage of Disney's Magical Express shuttle service, use a shuttle or town car, rent a car, ride a bus, or call a taxi. Here's the details of each:

Disney's Magical Express (DME)

Disney's Magical Express is a free perk for Disney's resort hotel guests, providing **free ground transportation** to and from Orlando International Airport. Included with this service is luggage "intercept" on arrival in Orlando—properly tagged luggage is pulled off the conveyor and is delivered directly to your Disney resort hotel room (if your flight arrives between 5:00 am and 10:00 pm). If you arrive between 10:00 pm and 5:00 am, get your own checked baggage off the luggage carousel. Now just head directly to Disney's Welcome Center (Level 1, Side B)—if you have the booklet or MagicBands mailed to you in advance by Disney, proceed directly to the bus lines. (No booklet or MagicBands? Go to the check-in desk here and they will print vouchers.) For your return to the airport, we recommend you reserve the return trip at the time you book, as it will save time later. You may be able to check in for your flight (and check your bags) before you leave your Disney resort. Disney's Magical Express is efficient, with guests being whisked to their resort with little wait and few (if any) stops at other hotels (though long waits and delays can still occur during peak arrival times). Nonetheless, Disney's Magical Express does take extra time. If you want another hour or two of park time on your first or last day, we suggest you pay for a town car service (see next page).

Arrival Tip: Travel with a **carry-on containing all your necessities**, including your park passes, a swimsuit, and a change of clothes. It may be many hours before your checked luggage arrives at your resort or before you're aware of any lost luggage.

Return Trip Note: You may **check your bags at the resort** on the day of your departure between 5:00 am and 1:00 pm (hours may vary). Check with your airline to learn if any baggage fees apply and, if so, pay them in advance. Guests on AirTran, Alaska, Delta, JetBlue, Southwest, United Airlines, and US Airways may only check one bag per passenger—if you have additional bags, you must check them at the airport or call BAGS at 407-284-1231 to pre-pay for excess luggage. Guests on American Airlines must pre-pay at the above number for all bags. All bags must be 50 pounds or less and must fit within the airline's dimension requirements. No oversize or overweight bags will be accepted.

You must **make reservations** for Disney's Magical Express at least one day prior to your arrival in Orlando, but do it at least ten days prior to allow time to receive your materials in the mail. (No time? Stop at the desk in the airport and show your Disney resort reservation.) To add this service, call Disney's regular reservations phone line or your travel agent, or visit http://www.disneyworld.com. Disney will need your airline flight numbers. Once reserved, Disney will send guests who reside in North America special luggage tags (one per person age 3 and above; more available by calling 866-599-0951) and an instruction booklet. If your flight is changed or delayed, notify Disney's Magical Express Guest Services at 866-599-0951.

Only **guests at Disney-owned resorts** can use Disney's Magical Express. Swan, Dolphin, Shades of Green, and all hotels on Hotel Plaza Boulevard (Regal Sun Resort, DoubleTree Suites, Hilton, etc.) are not included, and neither are travelers using Sanford Airport. Disney Vacation Club members wishing to use this service should contact DVC Member Services.

More at ⓘ magical-express

Top Photo Slice: A Disney's Magical Express bus © MediaMarx, Inc.

Are We There Yet?

(continued)

Taking a Shuttle or Town Car

A number of companies stay in business largely by transporting guests to and from Disney. Shuttle stands are located at the Orlando International Airport (Level 1), but all other pickup locations require advance notice. The major shuttle operator is Mears (800-759-5219). We prefer a **town car**, however. The town car driver greets us at baggage claim, carries our luggage, drives us to our hotel, and charges less than it costs a family of four to use a shuttle, taxi, or rental car. If you'd like to stop at a grocery store or if you need a car/booster seat, request this at reservation. We use Quicksilver Tours (888-468-6939, http://www.quicksilver-tours.com).

Driving a Car

If you're driving to Disney, you'll need specific directions. You can find detailed directions through a trip routing service (see page 15) or Disney (call 407-939-4636). Fliers planning to drive a car while in Orlando should rent at the airport. We don't feel a rental car is needed if you stay only on Disney property, as their internal transportation system works well (see pages 124–125) and even an occasional taxi fare can be cheaper than a rental car. Tip: Vacationers using I-75/Florida Turnpike can arrive via the Western Beltway (FL 429 Toll) and Disney's Western Way—see maps on cover flaps.

Renting a Car

If you plan to go off-property often, you may find a rental car helpful. Alamo and National (Disney's official rental car agencies), as well as Avis, Budget, Dollar, Enterprise, and Thrifty are located right at the airport on Level 1 (in-airport rentals incur a 10% fee). Hertz, Economy, and many others are off-site, and you'll need to take a shuttle on Level 1 to reach them (off-site rentals carry an 8.67% fee). The Dolphin Resort and several off-property hotels offer rental car desks, too. Inquire about all taxes and surcharges. See our rental car tips at http://www.passporter.com/rentalcars.asp.

Riding a Bus

The regional bus system, LYNX, has limited service to the Walt Disney World property. Call 407-841-LYNX or visit http://www.golynx.com. Please note that it takes about three hours to get from the Orlando Airport to Walt Disney World via LYNX. If you need to get from your hotel to many other theme parks in the Orlando area, Mears offers transportation ($16 and up for a round trip)—call a day in advance.

Using a Taxi

While taxis are available, we don't recommend them for airport travel due to the cost. Large parties may be able to ride in a taxi minivan economically, however, especially for occasional travel within Walt Disney World.

More at ⓘ town-cars | rental-cars

Top Photo Slice: Road signs on the way to Walt Disney World Resort (ⓘ4979) © Cheryl Pendry

Travel Worksheet

Use this worksheet to jot down preferences, scribble information during phone calls, and keep all your discoveries together. Don't worry about being neat—just be thorough! When everything is confirmed, transfer it to your first PassPocket in the back of the book. Circle the names and numbers once you decide to go with them to avoid confusion.

Arrival date: ________________ Alternate: ________________________
Return date: ________________ Alternate: ________________________

We plan to travel by: ❑ Car/Van ❑ Airplane ❑ Train ❑ Bus ❑ Tour
❑ Other: ____

For Drivers:
Miles to get to Orlando: ________ ÷ 500 = ______ days on the road
We need to stay at a motel on: ____________________________
Tune-up scheduled for: ________________________________
Rental car info: ____________________________________

For Fliers:
Airline phone numbers: _______________________________
Flight preferences: __________________________________
Flight availabilities: _________________________________
Reserved flight times and numbers: _____________________

For Ground Transportation:
Magical Express/town car/shuttle/rental car reservations: ________
____
Package ground transportation details: ___________________
____

Additional Notes:

Reminder: Don't forget to confirm holds or cancel reservations within the allotted time frame.

Electronic, interactive worksheet available– see page 316

Packing List

Packing for a vacation is fun when you feel confident you're packing the right things. Over the years, we've compiled this packing list for a great vacation. Just note the quantity you plan to bring and check off items as you pack. Consider carrying items in **magenta** on a daily basis as you tour.

The Essentials

- ❑ Casual clothing you can layer—the dress code nearly everywhere at Disney is casual, even at dinner. One "nice" outfit is usually enough.
  ___ *Shorts/skirts* ___ *Pants/jeans* ___ *Shirts* ___ *Sweaters*
  ___ *Underwear* ___ *Socks* ___ *Pajamas* ___ ________
- ❑ Jacket and/or sweatshirt (light ones for the warmer months)
  ___ ***Jackets*** ___ *Sweatshirts* ___ *Sweaters* ___ *Vests*
- ❑ Comfortable, well-broken-in shoes ... plus a second pair, just in case!
  ___ *Walking shoes* ___ *Sandals/Crocs* ___ *Sneakers* ___ ________
- ❑ Swim gear (bring one-piece suits for water slides)
  ___ *Suits/swim diapers* ___ *Cover-ups/towels* ___ *Water shoes* ___ *Goggles*
- ❑ Sun protection (the Florida sun can be brutal)
  ___ ***Sunblock*** ___ ***Lip balm*** ___ ***Sunburn relief*** ___ ***Sunglasses***
  ___ ***Sunhats*** ___ ***Caps*** ___ ***Visors*** ___ ________
- ❑ Rain gear (compact and light so you don't mind carrying it)
  ___ *Raincoat* ___ ***Poncho*** ___ ***Umbrella*** ___ ***Extra socks***
- ❑ Comfortable bags with padded straps to carry items during the day
  ___ ***Backpacks*** ___ ***Waist packs*** ___ *Shoulder bags* ___ ***Camera bag***
- ❑ Toiletries (in a bag or bathroom kit to keep them organized)
  ___ ***Brush/comb*** ___ *Toothbrush* ___ *Toothpaste* ___ *Dental floss*
  ___ *Favorite soap, shampoo, and conditioner* ___ *Deodorant* ___ ***Baby wipes***
  ___ ***Aspirin/acetaminophen/ibuprofen*** ___ ***Bandages*** ___ ***First aid kit***
  ___ ***Prescriptions*** *(in original containers)* ___ *Vitamins* ___ *Fem. hygiene*
  ___ *Hair dryer/iron* ___ ***Anti-blister tape*** ___ *Makeup* ___ *Hair spray*
  ___ *Razors and gel* ___ *Nail clippers* ___ *Cotton buds* ___ *Lotion*
  ___ *Mending kit* ___ *Spare eyeglasses* ___ *Lens solution* ___ ***Bug repellent***
  ___ *Medical/duck tape* ___ *Small scissors* ___ ***Safety pins*** ___ ***Insect sting kit***
- ❑ Camera/camcorder and more cards/film than you think you need
  ___ ***Camera*** ___ ***Camcorder*** ___ ***Memory cards*** ___ ***Film***
  ___ ***Batteries*** ___ *Chargers* ___ ***Case/tripod*** ___ ________
- ❑ Money in various forms and various places
  ___ ***Charge cards*** ___ ***Traveler's checks*** ___ ***Bank cards*** ___ ***Cash***
- ❑ Personal identification, passes, and membership cards
  ___ ***MagicBands*** ___ ***Driver's licenses*** ___ ***Passports/IDs*** ___ *Birth certificate*
  ___ ***AAA card*** ___ ***DVC member card*** ___ ***Discount cards*** ___ ***D23 card***
  ___ ***Tickets/passes*** ___ ***Insurance cards*** ___ ***Calling cards*** ___ *Air miles card*

Tip: Label everything with your name, phone, and hotel to help reunite you with your stuff if lost. Every bag should have this info on a luggage tag as well as on a slip of paper inside it. Use our Luggage Tag Maker at http://www.passporter.com/wdw/luggagelog.htm.

More at ⓘ luggage-tips | carry-ons

Top Photo Slice: The PassPorter luggage, ready to go! © MediaMarx, Inc.

For Your Carry-On

- ❑ Your **PassPorter**, **tickets**, **maps**, **guides**, and a **pen** or **pencil**! Remember to pack any sharp or potentially dangerous items in your checked luggage, not your carry-on.
- ❑ Your **MagicBands**, **personal identification**, **credit/debit cards**, and **money**.
- ❑ **Camera** and/or **camcorder**, along with **memory cards**, **film**, and **batteries**.
- ❑ Any **medications**, **written prescriptions**, important toiletries, **sunblock**, **sunglasses**, and **hats**—liquids/gels must each be 3.4 oz. or less and all fit in a single quart-size bag.
- ❑ **Snacks**, **gum**, favorite books, **toys**, **games**, blankets, change of clothes.

For Families

- ❑ Snacks, books, toys, and games
- ❑ Baby items (**diapers**, **food**, **bottles**, etc.)
- ❑ Stroller, carrier, and accessories
- ❑ **Autograph books** and **fat pens**
- ❑ EarPlanes (earplanes.com) or lollipops

For Couples

- ❑ Corkscrew and wine glasses
- ❑ Candles and matches
- ❑ Evening wear for nights out
- ❑ Jacket (if going to Victoria & Albert's)
- ❑ Portable CD player and CDs

For Connected Travelers

- ❑ Laptop and power supply
- ❑ Extension cord/surge suppressor
- ❑ Phone/network cables, coupler, splitter
- ❑ Security cable with lock
- ❑ **Cell phones/iPads** and chargers
- ❑ **Two-way radios**
- ❑ **iPod/MP3 players**
- ❑ Wi-fi router

For Heat-Sensitive Travelers

- ❑ **Personal fans/water misters**
- ❑ **Water bottles** (frozen, if possible)
- ❑ **Washcloth** to cool off face and neck
- ❑ Loose, breezy clothing
- ❑ **Hats** with wide brims
- ❑ **Sunshades** (for baby strollers)
- ❑ **Elastics** to keep long hair off neck
- ❑ **Sweatbands**

Everyone Should Consider

- ❑ Big beach towels (for pools and water parks)
- ❑ **Penlight** or flashlight (for reading/writing in dark places and to alleviate kids' fears)
- ❑ **Water bottles** and personal **fan/water misters**
- ❑ **Snacks** for any time of the day (plus gum, if you chew it, as it is not sold at Disney)
- ❑ Plastic cutlery for snacks or leftovers
- ❑ **Quarters** and **pennies** (and a way to hold them) for the coin presses and/or laundry
- ❑ Plastic storage bags that seal (large and small), plus trash bags
- ❑ Address book, stamps, and envelopes
- ❑ Laundry detergent/tablets, bleach, dryer sheets, stain stick, and a laundry tote
- ❑ Binoculars and magnifying glasses
- ❑ Collapsible bag or suitcase inside another suitcase to hold souvenirs on your return
- ❑ **Spare pair of prescription eyeglasses and a copy of your eyeglass prescription**

Your Personal Packing List

❑ ________	❑ ________
❑ ________	❑ ________
❑ ________	❑ ________
❑ ________	❑ ________
❑ ________	❑ ________
❑ ________	❑ ________
❑ ________	❑ ________
❑ ________	❑ ________

More at ⓘ must-pack-items | child-safety-seats | cares-harness

Adventuring!

Your journey is more pleasant when you consider it an adventure rather than a tiring trek. Here are our tried-and-true adventuring tips:

"Bring your own **snacks and beverages** aboard the plane. We also suggest you bring chewing gum (to offset air pressure), 3 oz. lotion (to offset dry air), and an iPod/MP3 player (to offset boredom)."

"Here are some things to remember to pack—I was so glad to have them during my Walt Disney World trip last week: Bring gallon-size, resealable bags to hold pennies and quarters for penny presses, sunscreen bottles, sticky cups or leftover snacks from meal or snack breaks, plus more. Pack liquid hand soap, toilet wet wipes/baby wipes, and air freshener for the hotel bathroom area. Bring ponchos to use for rain or to sit on wet seats for shows or on the ground to wait on parades. Pack a good hat and sunglasses for park touring. I would also suggest carrying a tube or bottle of easy-to-apply sunscreen for body, as well as a face sunscreen stick and lip sunscreen."

– Contributed by Abbey Barnes, a winner in our Reader Tip Contest

"If you plan to use a rental car while in Florida, consider flying into Tampa International Airport rather than Orlando. Airfare rates tend to be less expensive and the airport is less hectic."

– Contributed by April Fletcher-Yout, a winner in our Reader Tip Contest

"This is an old tip, but it never ceases to amaze me how many people don't think about it before they get to Walt Disney World. Always pack a throw blanket or beach towel and bring it into the park with you, especially if vacationing during the hot summer months. The sidewalks and curbs are very hot which makes sitting around waiting for a parade pretty miserable. Having a blanket/beach towel for your family to sit on will make things much more bearable and helps mark off the space you need if some of your group are still exploring the park."

– Contributed by Stefanie Mason, a winner in our Reader Tip Contest

Magical Memory

"*Here's our newest Disney tradition: After we've checked out of our resort and right before we drive all the way back to Ohio, we head to the Grand Floridian for breakfast and discuss the 'highs, lows, funnies and magical moments' of our trip together, summarizing things in our PassPorter. The notes are great to review when planning the next trip, but more importantly, it's a wonderful way to end the trip, with everyone reflecting on what they really enjoyed. This is MUCH better than rushing out of the resort, cramming everything in the car, and driving off!*"

...as told by vacationer Julie Amling

More at ⓘ 10-travel-tips

Top Photo Slice: Flying and driving into the sunset © MediaMarx, Inc.

Staying in Style

Nowhere in the "World" is Disney magic more evident than at the resort hotels on Walt Disney World property. In fact, the resorts are so impressive that we do not often consider staying "off-property" (as hotels outside of Walt Disney World are known), and we frequently plan our visits around our favorite resorts rather than our favorite parks. Staying in a Disney resort is unlike any other hotel experience we've had, and we've visited both the exotic and the expensive. It isn't just that staying at a Disney resort provides total immersion in the Walt Disney World experience. The resorts offer hidden surprises and a remarkable attention to detail.

With more than 30,000 guest rooms and campsites throughout the Walt Disney World Resort, it would take more than 82 years to stay once in each room. (Sign us up!) There's something for every taste and budget. Whether you want a romantic setting, space for a family reunion, disabled access, or bunk beds, you can find it somewhere in the "World." There are enough choices to preclude staying at a non-Disney hotel, but bargains off-property are also a factor. If you visit with friends or family, prefer to stay in another hotel, or even take a cruise, your PassPorter still serves you well—you can record your arrangements here with the same ease. We include basic information on the Disney Cruise Line, Disney Vacation Club, and off-site hotels at the end of this chapter, too.

EXPLORE your resort in detail with info and maps

If you've already decided to stay at a Disney resort, your PassPorter puts you a step ahead! Our Walt Disney World resort descriptions are the most comprehensive of any guidebook, and our resort maps, photos, floor plans, tips, notes, and recommendations can help the veteran vacationer, as well as the novice, get the most out of their resort.

To help you find your way through the staggering array of choices, we've prepared a detailed guide to choosing your resort. We heartily recommend you turn the page and take advantage of it.

Top Photo Slice: Our son Alexander asleep in a Mickey-themed bedroom at an ALL STAR Vacation Home © MediaMarx, Inc.

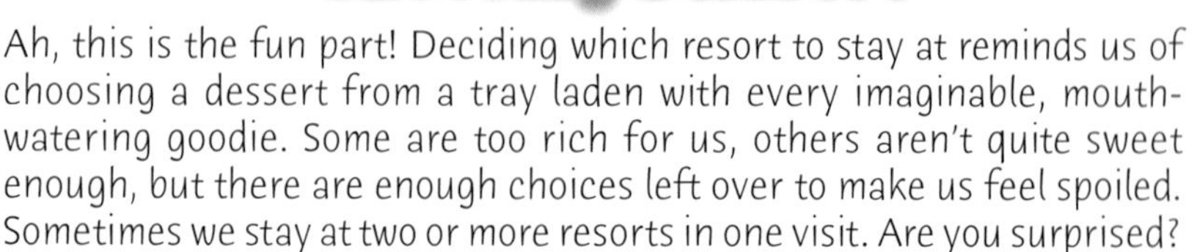

Choosing a Resort

Ah, this is the fun part! Deciding which resort to stay at reminds us of choosing a dessert from a tray laden with every imaginable, mouth-watering goodie. Some are too rich for us, others aren't quite sweet enough, but there are enough choices left over to make us feel spoiled. Sometimes we stay at two or more resorts in one visit. Are you surprised?

Start with the exhaustive **resort checklist** on the next page. Compare it with your preferences to uncover the resorts that meet your needs. Then carefully read the resort descriptions, beginning on page 37. Each description follows the same format, allowing you to find exactly what you seek as you **compare resorts**. The first and second pages of each description list resort essentials, along with floor plans and transportation times. The third page lists the best tips, notes, and ratings for each resort—this is the "good stuff" to help you make the most out of your experience. In the Ratings section, we and our readers grade each resort for value, magic, and satisfaction. An explanation of the ratings is at the bottom of this page. The fourth page features a detailed resort map and our ideas for the best rooms in the resort. Rates, addresses, and phone/fax numbers are listed at the end of each description. **Tip**: When researching resorts, use the darkest "stamp" (tab) at the top of the page to locate parks and eateries in the vicinity, which will have the same "stamp" at the top of their pages.

When you're ready, use the Lodging Worksheet on pages 116–117 to record your dates, preferences, and reservation options.

Resort Ratings Explained

We offer a variety of resort ratings in PassPorter to help you make the best decisions. Even so, we recommend you use these ratings as a guide, not gospel.

Value Ratings range from 1 (poor) to 10 (excellent) and are based on **quality** (cleanliness, maintenance, and freshness); **accessibility** (how fast and easy it is to get to attractions); and **affordability** (rates for the standard rooms)—**overall value** represents an average of the above three values. **Magic Ratings** are based on **theme** (execution and sense of immersion); **amenities** (guest perks and luxuries); and **fun factor** (number and quality of resort activities)—**overall magic** represents an average of the above three values. We use a point accumulation method to determine value and magic ratings.

Readers' Ratings are calculated from surveys submitted by experienced vacationers at our web site (http://www.passporter.com/wdw/rate.htm).

Guest satisfaction is based on our and our readers' experiences with how different types of guests enjoy the resort: ❤❤❤❤❤=love it ❤❤❤❤=enjoy it ❤❤❤=like it ❤❤=tolerate it ❤=don't like it

Top Photo Slice: Signpost to Disney resorts at Disney's Hilton Head Resort (ⓘ6149) © Cheryl Pendry

Resort Comparisons

* Kitchen facilities are present only in the villas or family suites of indicated resorts	All-Star Resorts	Animal King. Lodge/Villas	Art of Animation	Beach Club/Villas	BoardWalk Inn/Villas	Caribbean Beach	Contemporary/Villas	Coronado Springs	Fort Wilderness	Grand Floridian/Villas	Old Key West	Polynesian Village/Villas	Pop Century	Port Orleans	Saratoga Springs	Shades of Green	Swan/Dolphin	Wild. Lodge/Villas	Yacht Club
Deluxe		✓		✓	✓		✓			✓		✓				✓	✓	✓	✓
Disney's Deluxe Villas		✓		✓	✓		✓			✓	✓	✓			✓			✓	
Moderate						✓		✓	✓					✓					
Value	✓		✓										✓						
Rooms and Amenities																			
Total Rooms	5568	1293	1984	785	910	2112	963	1967	1195	1047	761	847	2880	3056	1260	586	2267	864	634
Occupancy	3-6	3-12	3-6	3-8	3-12	3-4	3-12	3-6	3-10	3-12	3-12	3-8	3-4	3-5	3-12	5-8	3-5	3-8	3-5
Fridges/coolers	✓	✓	✓	✓	✓	✓	✓	✓		✓	✓	✓	✓	✓	✓	✓		✓	✓
Coffeemakers		✓		✓	✓	✓	✓	✓	✓	✓	✓	✓		✓	✓	✓	✓	✓	✓
Hair Dryers	✓	✓	✓	✓	✓	✓	✓	✓	✓	✓	✓	✓	✓	✓	✓	✓	✓	✓	✓
In-Room Safes	✓	✓	✓	✓	✓	✓	✓	✓	✓	✓	✓	✓	✓	✓	✓	✓	✓	✓	✓
Kitchen Facilities*	✓	✓	✓	✓	✓		✓		✓	✓	✓	✓			✓			✓	
Turndown (on req.)		✓		✓	✓		✓			✓		✓					✓	✓	✓
Free wi-fi	✓	✓	✓	✓	✓	✓	✓	✓	✓	✓	✓	✓	✓	✓	✓	✓	✓	✓	✓
Eating and Drinking																			
Restaurants/Cafes	–	3	–	3	7	1	3	1	2	4	2	3	–	1	2	4	9	3	3
Character Meals				✓			✓		✓	✓		✓					✓		
Lounges	3	5	1	3	4	1	6	2	1	3	1	3	1	4	2	1	4	2	2
Food Courts	3	1	1	–	–	1	1	1	–	1	–	1	1	2	1	–	1	–	–
Room Service		✓		✓	✓	✓	✓	✓		✓		✓				✓	✓	✓	✓
Pizza Delivery	✓		✓			✓					✓		✓	✓		✓			✓
Recreational Activities																			
Beach (no swim)				✓	✓	✓	✓	✓	✓	✓		✓					✓	✓	✓
Pools	6	2	3	2	3	7	3	4	2	2	4	2	3	7	5	2	2	2	2
Kid Pool	3	2	1	1	1	1	2	1	1	1	1	1	1	2	1	1	1	1	1
Spa (Hot Tub)	–	4	–	5	3	1	3	1	1	1	2	1	–	2	6	1	1	3	5
Spa (Services)				✓	✓		✓	✓		✓	✓				✓		✓		✓
Health Club		✓		✓	✓		✓	✓		✓	✓				✓	✓	✓	✓	✓
Marina				✓	✓	✓	✓	✓	✓	✓	✓	✓		✓			✓	✓	✓
Tennis		✓		✓	✓		✓		✓	✓	✓				✓	✓	✓		✓
Jogging Path	✓		✓	✓	✓	✓	✓	✓	✓	✓	✓	✓	✓	✓	✓		✓	✓	✓
Kids' Program		✓		✓						✓		✓					✓	✓	✓
Access and Facilities																			
Monorail							✓			✓		✓							
Disabled Rooms	288	66	96	10	51	22	6	99	8	5	67	17	126	34	16	22	51	46	10
Conf. Center				✓	✓		✓	✓		✓							✓		
Your Favorites																			

Top Photo Slice: Panoramic of the Epcot area resorts (ⓘ3964) © Rick Wagner

Reserving a Room

Once you have an idea of where you want to stay at the Walt Disney World Resort, it's time to **make reservations**. A travel agent is not needed, but if you have a great travel agent, by all means consult him or her (they do not generally charge any fees for their services). Here's the lowdown on making Disney resort reservations:

Before you make your reservations, **use the worksheet** on pages 116–117 to jot down the dates you prefer to visit along with any alternates. Even a one-day change in your travel dates can open the door to availabilities. Be familiar with all resorts in your price range. We also suggest you finalize resort reservations after you make your flight reservations. Hotel room reservations may be changed or canceled without fees up to a certain date, but flight changes at any time almost always incur a fee.

You can make reservations for all Disney World resort hotels at http://www.disneyworld.com or at **407-WDW-MAGIC** (407-939-6244)—alas, all known toll-free numbers for Disney have been de-activated. Note that Walt Disney Travel Company agents answer the above number. Disney representatives can offer assistance in English, Spanish, Japanese, French, Portuguese, and German. Discounts are sometimes available on the Walt Disney World web site, but you must follow the specific links for the specials or you'll be charged regular rates. You may also want to try Travelocity or Expedia, both of which are popular Internet reservation systems—you can visit them at http://www.travelocity.com and http://www.expedia.com. Be sure to look for promotional rates while you're there, too! If you prefer, you can also make reservations through the mail by writing to Walt Disney World at Box 10100, Lake Buena Vista, Florida 32830.

Reservations can be made for just **lodging ("room only")** or for **vacation packages**, which include lodging, admission, and more (see page 32 for more details on the types of packages available). Prices and policies differ for each type of booking, which we describe on the next page.

Research **special deals or packages** by visiting MouseSavers.com (see page 11) or by calling Disney Reservations. If you have a Disney Visa card or Annual Pass, or if you are a Florida resident or military family, ask about those discounts, too. (The Swan and Dolphin offer discounts to nurses, teachers, and government employees.) If your dates aren't available, ask about alternates. Sometimes you can get a discount for part of your stay. Lock in whatever discount you can get, and book at the full price for the remainder. Keep calling back, as canceled reservations are released every morning. If a lower rate comes out later, you may be able to call back and get it applied.

Make any **special requests** at the time of reservation and again when you check in. If you need a barrier-free room, a refrigerator, or a crib, request this now. If you have a particular location or room in mind (we make many suggestions later), make sure to tell the reservations agent. It's best to make your request as general as possible. You'll have better luck requesting a "high floor with views of fireworks" than simply "room 5409." If Disney doesn't know why you want room 5409, they can't choose a suitable substitute. Disney will not guarantee a particular room or view, but if your request is "in the system," they will try their best to make your wish come true. Call your resort about three days before your arrival to confirm any requests you made.

More at ⓘ reserving-a-room

Top Photo Slice: Tools to reserve a room—your computer and phone! © MediaMarx, Inc.

In need of **ground transportation** between the Orlando International Airport and your Disney-owned resort? Disney's Magical Express provides free shuttle bus service from and to the airport, as well as luggage handling. If your reservation agent doesn't mention it, be sure to ask. If you forget, the service can be added to your reservation at least one day before your scheduled arrival, or you can even check in at the Disney's Magical Express desk at the Orland Airport with a copy of your Disney room reservation. See page 21 for the full details on Disney's Magical Express.

Miles of smiles on a Magical Express motorcoach

You may be able to hold more than one reservation for the same date, but eventually you have to put down a deposit or lose the reservation. Typically, Disney resort reservations are held three days without confirmation as a courtesy, but only if you have at least 45 days until your stay. **Deposit and cancellation policies do differ** between packages and room-only reservations. Room-only reservations have a more liberal deposit policy—the cost of one night's lodging is all that's required (due in 3 days), with a no-penalty cancellation possible up to six days prior. With less than six days' notice, you forfeit the full one-night deposit. Packages require a deposit of $200, also due in 3 days, and full payment for your vacation is due 30 days in advance. Package reservations made online can be canceled without a penalty at least 31 days before your arrival, or incur a $100 charge if made between 6 and 31 days prior, $200 for cancellations made less than 6 days prior, or full price for cancellations 1 day or less. There's a $50 charge for modifying package reservations within 46 days of your arrival, unless your change increases your package price.

Be sure to **pay your deposit** by 10:00 pm ET on your due date, or your reservation will be canceled. Your deposit can be made over the phone with American Express, MasterCard, Visa, Discover, JCB, Diner's Club, through mail or fax with the same credit cards or a personal check, or online in most cases. The Lodging Worksheet at the end of the chapter (pages 116–117) has spaces to check off confirmations and deposits made, too! **Tip**: You may be able to request an extension on your deposit if needed—inquire with Disney.

Once you've made your reservations, **record the details** on your Room(s) PassPocket, including the name of the resort, dates, type of room, price, reservation number, and any special information you want to note. This is also an ideal place to note any special requests you want to check on at check-in. Use a pencil if plans aren't final.

Higher Rates on Weekends, Holidays, and More

You should know that Disney charges higher room rates on weekends and some holidays. And if a stay straddles two lodging seasons, whenever the "season" changes, the rate changes, too. The weekend and holiday rates bump up by about $5–$30 per night at the value, moderate, and deluxe resorts. Affected holidays include Martin Luther King weekend, President's Day weekend, Easter week, Independence Day weekend, Columbus Day weekend, Thanksgiving weekend, and the week between Christmas and New Year's Day. It's possible that Disney may extend this practice to any period when demand for resort rooms is particularly high (or low), such as during a major convention or special event. You can learn the nightly rate for a given time period by calling Disney at 407-939-6244 or going online at http://www.disneyworld.com.

Choosing a Package

Disney's vacation packages offer the promise of peace of mind and luxury. Package rates may be lower than the list price for each component, but may include more components than you can possibly use. A good number of veteran vacationers tell us they love these packages! Note that everyone in your room must be on the same package and plan. For more information and reservations, ask your travel agent, call 407-939-6244, or visit http://www.disneyworld.com. Below are the 2016 packages:

Magic Your Way Basic Package—Get one or more nights at a Disney resort; an upgradeable Magic Your Way Base Ticket (see page 122); four vouchers (per package) for miniature golf; four vouchers (per package) for the ESPN Wide World of Sports complex; 10% off Sammy Duvall's water sports; 10% off Splitsville bowling and food; and a variety of other shopping and restaurant discounts from 10%–20%. Three-night package starting at $150/adult per night (based on double occupancy).

Magic Your Way Quick Service Dining Plan—Everything in the basic package plus two meals at participating quick-service eateries (see page 223) and one snack per day, and one Rapid Fill drink mug/person. About $42.84/adult, $17.47/child per night above basic package.

Magic Your Way Dining Plan—Everything in the basic package above plus one resort refillable Rapid Fill drink mug/person and dining at more than 100 participating Disney table-service restaurants* (see pages 223–225 for dining plan details). About $61.84/adult or $20.96/child per night above basic package cost.

Magic Your Way Deluxe Dining Plan—Everything in the above package, except you get three dining credits (good at table-service or counter-service) and two snack credits, plus one refillable mug/person. About $111.73/adult or $32.56/child per night above basic package cost.

Magic Your Way Premium Package—Everything in the basic package, plus breakfast, lunch, and dinner at more than 100 participating restaurants,* unlimited recreation, unlimited admission to Disney childcare clubs, in-room childcare, Cirque du Soleil tickets, and unlimited admission to selected theme park tours**. About $208.08/adult or $152.60/child per night above basic package cost. Requires a 3-night minimum stay.

Magic Your Way Platinum Package—Everything in the premium package listed above, but you can eat at any Disney eatery, including Victoria & Albert's (premium menu only), character meals, and dinner shows. You also receive two "magical evenings"—a ride on the Characters in Flight balloon and one fireworks cruise. Additional benefits include one selected spa treatment, a specially created keepsake, and itinerary planning services. About $260.10/adult or $201.65/child per night above basic package cost. Requires a 3-night minimum stay.

Annual Passholder Package with Dining—Annual passholders can purchase packages that include lodging (which may or may not be discounted) and the Quick Service Dining Plan, the standard Dining Plan, and/or the Deluxe Dining Plan.

Note: It is also now possible to book a package with a resort reservation and one of the Disney Dining Plans without the need to also include park admission.

* Participating Disney restaurants include all restaurants described in chapter 5 (see pages 221–270) **except the following eateries, which are excluded**: Victoria & Albert's (Grand Floridian) and Ghirardelli (Disney Springs). Note that this list is subject to change at any time—be sure to check with Disney before making plans. Kids ages 3–9 must order off the children's menu when available. Dining Plan credits may also be used for in-room private dining.

** Selected theme park tours include all tours described on pages 272–273 except Mickey's Magical Milestones, Backstage Magic, and VIP Tours.

Top Photo Slice: Cruising in a Sea Raycer, available at a discount on some packages (2462) © SuperNemo

Resort Key

Resort Locations—The Disney resorts described in your PassPorter are all located within minutes of the theme parks. We organize them into four areas: Magic Kingdom, Disney Springs, Epcot, and Disney's Animal Kingdom (use the map on the inside back cover for reference). Each resort's area is identified in its description. You can also use the blue "stamps" at the top of each page to locate all resorts in a neighborhood.

Room Locations—Room locations, such as a building or room number, can be requested, but are not guaranteed. However, if you note your preferences when you make your reservation, via phone about three days before arrival, and again when you check in, there is a chance you will get the room you want. Resort maps and suggestions are given for each resort in this chapter. If you don't like the particular room you've been assigned, do as you would with any hotel and politely ask for another.

Room Occupancy—All resorts have rooms that hold at least four guests, plus one child under 3 in a crib. Port Orleans Riverside (Alligator Bayou) rooms allow up to five guests with an optional trundle bed for a child. Many of the deluxe resorts have a day bed. Ft. Wilderness Cabins, All-Star Music family suites, and Art of Animation suites allow up to six. Treehouse Villas at Saratoga Springs and the two-bedroom villas in Disney's Deluxe Villa Resorts allow up to nine, and Grand Villas allow up to 12. There is an extra charge of $2–$25 per adult for more than two adults in a single room, except at Disney's Deluxe Villa Resorts.

Amenities—All rooms have the basics: television with remote control, phone, drawers, clothing rod with hangers, small table, and chairs, as well as simple toiletries. **Tip**: If your room doesn't have a coffeemaker or iron/ironing board, request it from housekeeping.

Check-In Time—Check-in time is 3:00 pm or 4:00 pm (varies by resort), although rooms may be available earlier (inquire upon your arrival). You can also check-in online at http://www.disneyworld.com within 60 days of your arrival! If you arrive early and your room is not ready, you can register, leave your luggage, and go play in the parks while your room is being prepared. Tip: You can request a voice or text message be sent to your cell phone—ask about this Mobile Room Ready Notification service when you check-in!

Check-Out Time—Check-out time is 11:00 am. If you need to check out an hour or two later (up to 1:00 pm), ask the Front Desk any time after check-in. If the resort isn't busy, they may grant your request at no extra cost. Extended check-out may also be available for an extra fee. You can also leave your bags with Bell Services and go play in the parks.

Childcare—Children's childcare "clubs" for ages 3–12 are available in many of the deluxe resorts (refer to the chart on page 29). In-room sitting is also available. Fees apply to all childcare. See pages 284–285 for details and opinions on childcare.

Concierge—Not to be confused with Lobby Concierge (see page 35), all of the deluxe resorts offer concierge services with extra perks like a continental breakfast, afternoon snacks, and planning services. Concierge services are associated with certain rooms (often on the higher floors) that come at a higher rate. Also known as Club Level service.

Convention Centers—Several resort hotels are popular among convention-goers due to their excellent facilities, including the BoardWalk, Contemporary, Coronado Springs, Grand Floridian, Swan, Dolphin, and Yacht Club. For more details on convention facilities, call 407-828-3200. Business Centers are available at each of the above resorts.

Data Services (Internet)—All Disney resorts have free wi-fi available in guest rooms and some public areas. Fort Wilderness has free wired Internet access. If you need technical support, call 407-827-2732 or 407-938-4357. The front desk will also receive and send your faxes for a fee.

Top Photo Slice: A Key to the World card and admission passes © MediaMarx, Inc.

Resort Key: Disabled Access to Information

Disabled Access—All resorts offer accommodations and access for differently abled guests. For details and reservations, call Disney's Special Requests Department at 407-939-7807 (voice) or 407-939-7670 (TTY). Be sure to ask that "Special Needs" be noted on your reservation. See page 29 for the number of barrier-free rooms at each resort.

Extra Magic Hours—Guests at Disney resorts and the Swan, Dolphin, and Shades of Green can enter the parks up to one hour earlier or stay two hours later. Resort-issued MagicBand or resort key card is required for entry, along with a valid admission. Only certain parks and attractions are open for Extra Magic Hours on any given day, however. The schedule changes from week to week (check http://www.disneyworld.com for the schedule during your visit), but here's a sample Extra Magic Hour schedule:

	Sunday	Monday	Tuesday	Wednesday	Thursday	Friday	Saturday
am	none	Animal Kingdom	none	none	Epcot	Magic Kingdom	Disney's Hollywood Studios
pm	none		Epcot	Magic Kingdom	none	Disney's Hollywood Studios	none

SAMPLE

Extra Magic Hour Attractions (underlined attractions are open only during evening Extra Magic Hours)—In the **Magic Kingdom**, this usually includes Space Mountain, Buzz Lightyear's Space Ranger Spin, Big Thunder Mountain, Stitch's Great Escape, Tomorrowland Indy Speedway, Haunted Mansion, Pirates of the Caribbean, Splash Mountain, Magic Carpets of Aladdin, and most of Fantasyland. **Epcot** opens Soarin', Mission: SPACE, Spaceship Earth, Test Track, The Seas With Nemo & Friends, Journey Into Imagination, "Captain Eo," Living with the Land, Gran Fiesta Tour Starring The Three Caballeros, and American Adventure. **Disney's Hollywood Studios** opens Rock 'n' Roller Coaster, Tower of Terror, Star Tours, Muppet*Vision 3-D, The Great Movie Ride, Voyage of the Little Mermaid, and Toy Story Midway Mania. **Disney's Animal Kingdom** opens Expedition Everest, It's Tough to be a Bug!, Kali River Rapids, Festival of the Lion King, Dinosaur, TriceraTop Spin, Primeval Whirl, The Boneyard, Pangani Forest Exploration Trail, and Kilimanjaro Safaris. Attractions are subject to change.

Food—Every resort has places to eat, such as food courts, cafes, fine dining, and room service. All resort eateries are noted in each resort's dining section later in this chapter. Details on the table-service restaurants start on page 230. If you are looking for snacks or groceries, each resort has a store with a small selection of food and drinks. No gum is sold on property. Special dietary requests can be made (see page 228).

Housekeeping Services—Every Disney resort has daily "mousekeeping" services and will happily provide you with extra towels, pillows, and blankets upon request, as well as a hair dryer, iron, and ironing board. If you require extra toiletries, just ask for them. For tipping suggestions, see page 36. Note: Disney's Deluxe Villa Resorts provide reduced services to DVC members using their points.

Ice and Soda—All resorts have ice machines within easy walking distance. Most, but not all, also have soda machines with Coke products. The more plush the resort, the harder it is to find a soda machine. If soda is important, pick up some before you arrive (it's cheaper anyway). Another option is to purchase a refillable souvenir mug (offered at most resorts) for free (or low-cost) refills of soda, coffee, tea, and cocoa at your resort—see page 36.

Information—Check the Walt Disney World information channels on your in-room TV. These channels are available at every resort and offer a nice introduction for newcomers, plus a peek at what's new. You can touch "0" on any resort phone for more information.

Top Photo Slice: Lobby Concierge at Disney's Pop Century Resort © MediaMarx, Inc.

Resort Key: Laundry to Recreation

Laundry—Every resort has either coin-operated/coinless machines in a laundry room near the pool (expect to pay at least $2/load) or a washer and dryer in your room. **Tip**: Most of Disney's Deluxe Villa resorts offer complimentary self-service laundry facilities (no coins needed). Laundry bags and forms are available in your resort room for same-day service.

Lobby Concierge—Each resort has a Lobby Concierge desk near the registration desk where you can buy park passes, make dining reservations, and find answers.

Mail and Packages—Purchase stamps in the resort shops; mail can be dropped off at Lobby Concierge or placed in mailboxes. Federal Express also picks up and drops off packages. The closest U.S. post office is at 601 Market St in Celebration.

MagicBand—A high-tech wristband issued to guests that unlocks your hotel room door, acts as your park admission, checks you in at FastPass+ entrances, and connects your PhotoPass images. MagicBands are in widespread use now. For details, see page 126.

Merchandise Delivery—Resort guests staying on Disney property can have park and Disney Springs purchases delivered free to their resort, usually by the next afternoon or the day after. Inquire before your purchase is rung up. Your package is delivered to your resort's gift shop or front desk, not your room (unless you're in concierge).

Money—Cash, Disney Dollars and Gift Cards, traveler's checks, MasterCard, Visa, American Express, Discover, Diner's Club, JCB, Apple Pay, and Google Wallet are accepted. Personal checks are accepted only at the resort where you are a guest. ATMs are near the front desk. Make your room deposit over the phone, Internet, or fax with the above credit cards or by mail with a credit card or check.

Parking—Secured, free, gated parking lots are available at all Disney resorts. The deluxe resorts also offer valet ($20/day, free to those with handicap parking permit/tags); Swan & Dolphin valet is $26/day. Show your MagicBand, resort ID, or confirmation at the security gate—parking is reserved for resort guests and those using a resort's restaurants or recreation.

Pets—Pets are not allowed in the parks or resorts (except for a few campsites at Fort Wilderness—see page 67) unless you travel with a companion (service) animal. You may board your pet for the day or overnight at the Best Friends Pet Care resort, located across from Port Orleans Resort. Daycare fees are $16–$69, while overnight boarding is $21–$69/night per animal for Disney resort hotel guests ($23–$76/night for non-Disney resort hotel guests). The pet resort can accommodate dogs, cats, and "pocket pets" (anything that's not a dog, a cat, a primate, or venomous). Special features and upgrades include bedtime stories, private dog park, grooming, and more. Get details and make reservations at 877-4-WDW-PETS (877-493-9738) or http://wdw.bestfriendspetcare.com.

Pools—Every Disney resort has at least one swimming pool. Hours vary, but usually the "themed" pools close in the evenings while the "leisure" pools may stay open all night. Only guests staying at a resort can use its pool (and your MagicBand/Key to the World card will often be checked), though some resorts share pools and Disney Vacation Club members using their points have access to all but Stormalong Bay, Bay Cove Pool, and the pools at Disney's Animal Kingdom Lodge and Art of Animation (unless they are staying there).

Preferred Rooms—Disney's value, moderate, and deluxe resorts offer preferred rooms with better locations and higher rates.

Recreation—Every resort has something to do, with many offering a wide variety of outdoor activities. You can visit another resort to use its recreational facilities (with the exception of swimming pools). Be sure to note the operating hours upon arrival or by phoning ahead.

Top Photo Slice: Sleepyheads after a magical day (22028) © Heather DiFulvio

Resort Key: Refillable Mugs to Voice Mail

Refillable Mugs—All Disney resorts sell mugs that can be refilled for multiple days, up to the length of your stay (which must be consecutive). The Rapid Fill mug contains an active RFID chip that allows refills at any Disney resort's soda station during the term of your stay (with a 2-minute mandatory wait time between refills). Cost is $8.99 for 1 day; $11.99 for 2 days; $14.99 for 3 days; and $17.99 for length of stay (4+ days). Guests on the Disney Dining Plan will receive the mug for the length of their stay. Neither milk nor juice is a refill option unless it appears on the soda fountain (but coffee and tea are available).

Refrigerators—In-room mini-refrigerators (without freezers) are provided free in Disney's resorts. One-bedroom and larger villas and Fort Wilderness cabins have full-size refrigerators.

Room Service—The deluxe resorts and some of the moderate resorts offer in-room dining. Most resorts offer a pizza delivery service in the afternoon and evenings.

Security—A gatehouse guards entry into every resort. If you arrive by car, plan to show your MagicBand, resort ID, or photo ID and explain that you are checking in, dining, or using the resort's recreational facilities. All resort rooms have electronic locks that open with your MagicBand or resort ID for added security. In addition, you can store small valuables in your in-room safe (most, though not all, rooms have them) or with the front desk.

Smoking—All Disney resort guest rooms (including patios/balconies) are nonsmoking. Designated outdoor smoking areas are indicated on resort maps.

Spa—Disney-speak for a hot tub. There's at least one spa at every Disney resort, with the exception of the value resorts (Polynesian Village finally got one in 2015). Traditional spa facilities (massages and manicures) are available in some resorts.

Tax—Sales tax is 6.5% in Orange County (most of Walt Disney World) and 7% in Osceola County (Pop Century, Art of Animation, and some parts of All-Star Resorts); sales tax is charged on all purchases and lodging. An additional lodging tax is 6% in both Orange and Osceola Counties.

Telephones—All rooms have a phone and information on how to use it. Local and toll-free calls are free; long-distance calls are the cost of the call plus a 50% surcharge. Use calling cards or cell phones instead. Incoming calls are free.

Turndown—Available at the deluxe resorts—request it from housekeeping.

Tipping—It's customary to tip valet parking attendants $1–$2 upon arrival and departure, bell services $1–$2/bag upon delivery and pick-up, and housekeeping $1/person/day. **Tip**: Leave your housekeeping tip daily with the housekeeper's name card so it's recognized.

Transportation—Every resort provides free transit to and from the parks via bus, boat, monorail, and/or pathway. We list each resort's options and in-transit times in this chapter.

Wheelchairs—You can borrow a wheelchair from any resort (inquire at Lobby Concierge or Bell Services). A deposit may be required; availability is limited. Motorized wheelchairs (ECVs) and a limited number of ESVs (electric standing vehicles) may be rented at the parks for in-park-only use. You can rent ECVs at the BoardWalk Resort for use anywhere from Buena Vista Scooters (866-484-4797, http://www.buenavistascooters.com). Note that only authorized vendors (Apple Mobility, Best Price, Buena Vista, C.A.R.E, Scooter Bug, Orlando Stroller Rentals, Kingdom Stroller, and Magic Strollers) can leave a rented ECV or stroller at a resort—unauthorized vendors must deliver and pick up from you in person.

Wi-Fi—See Data Services on page 33.

Voice Mail—Every resort offers free voice mail that can be retrieved from your room or any other phone in or outside of Disney property. You can personalize the message callers hear. If you are on the phone when a call comes in, the system still takes your caller's message.

Top Photo Slice: Turndown at an Animal Kingdom Lodge room (①3256) © Melissa Loflin

Disney's All-Star Resorts

Both economical and magical, the All-Star Resorts bring movies, music, and sports to life in three independent yet connected resort hotels. The All-Star Movies, All-Star Music, and All-Star Sports Resorts are located near Disney's Animal Kingdom theme park and the Blizzard Beach water park (use the blue tab at the top of the page for parks and eateries in the vicinity).

AMBIENCE

A star-studded production awaits you at the All-Star Resorts. From the painted stars everywhere you look to the autographed photos of famous celebrities lining the lobby walls, each resort greets you as a star in its **main hall**—Cinema Hall in All-Star Movies, Melody Hall in All-Star Music, and Stadium Hall in All-Star Sports. The halls house the registration desks, food courts, general stores, and arcades. Outside, the stars give way to larger-than-life movie, music, and sports icons, such as a towering Buzz Lightyear, a four-story-high conga drum, and a Coke cup that could hold 240 million ounces. Music plays in the background, providing you with an ever-changing soundtrack as you stroll through the grounds.

RESORT LAYOUT & ROOMS

The 5,568 guest rooms (1,728–1,920 in each resort) are situated in 15 differently themed areas encompassing a total of 30 buildings. **All-Star Movies Resort** showcases 101 Dalmatians, Fantasia and Fantasia 2000, The Love Bug, Toy Story, and Mighty Ducks; **All-Star Music Resort** features Calypso, Jazz Inn, Rock Inn, Country Fair, and Broadway; and **All-Star Sports Resort** sports Surf's Up!, Hoops Hotel, Center Court, Touchdown!, and Home Run Hotel. Each of the 15 areas features a themed courtyard flanked by two of the T-shaped buildings. The energetic and colorful themes are echoed in the guest rooms, with themed bedspreads, drapes, wallpaper, and a vanity area with one sink. Standard rooms have either two double beds or one king bed, a TV, a small table with two chairs, and drawers. Rooms with king-size beds are also the barrier-free rooms; thus, some of these rooms have only showers (no tubs). Rooms are small—260 sq. feet—but we find them adequate with the simple furnishings. 192 Family Suites are also available in All-Star Music—see page 39. No private balconies or patios, but each room has individual climate controls.

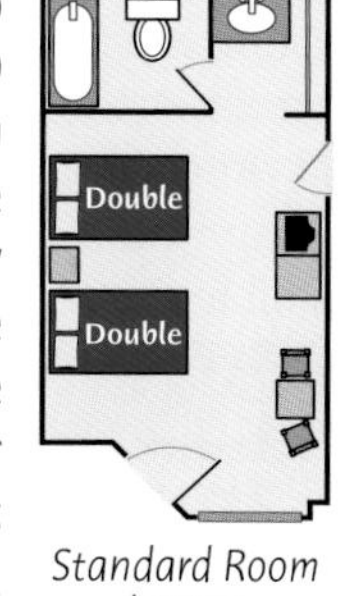

Standard Room Layout

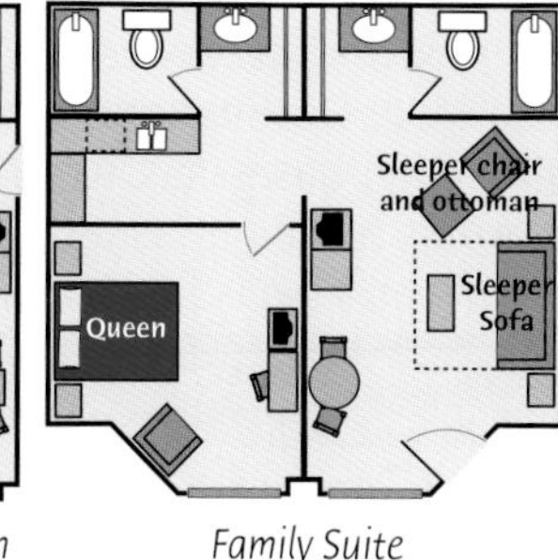

Family Suite Layout

Top Photo Slice: Cinema Hall at Disney's All-Star Movies Resort (ⓘ8867) © Cheryl Pendry

Using the Amenities at Disney's All-Star Resorts

EATING & DRINKING

Food courts: World Premiere (Movies), Intermission (Music), and End Zone (Sports), each with four food stations plus a snack shop. Breakfast (6:00 am to 11:00 am) menu items typically include a Breakfast Platter for $8.99, a Western omelet for $7.99, and Mickey waffles for $6.39. Lunch and dinner (11:00 am to midnight) items include a pepperoni pizza for $9.69, chicken nuggets for $8.99, a taco salad for $8.99, a bacon cheeseburger for $10.49, and child meals for $5.99+. Rapid Fill mugs ($8.99–$17.99) offer unlimited soft drink refills. **Pizza delivery** is from 4:00 pm to midnight. **Walk-up bars** are at each food court and main pool.

© MediaMarx, Inc.

Family Suite at All-Star Music

500+ more photos at http://www.passporter.com/photos

PLAYING & RELAXING

For Athletes: Well-marked paths are ideal for walks and jogs.
For Children: Quiet playgrounds are located within each resort (locations vary—see map on page 40 for playground locations).
For Gamers: Each resort's main hall has an arcade—note that games no longer reward players with tickets due to state law.
For Shoppers: Donald's Double Feature (Movies), Maestro Mickey's (Music), and Sport Goofy (Sports) offer gifts and sundries.
For Swimmers: Each resort offers a main pool and a smaller pool. Movies' main pool conjures up the fun of Fantasia, Music's main pool is in the shape of a guitar, and Sports' main pool is styled after a surfing lagoon. All main pools have children's wading pools nearby.

GETTING ABOUT

Buses (see chart below for in-transit times) are found outside the main halls in each resort. Stops are well-marked and offer benches. We find the bus service efficient, but some guests complain of waiting too long. Destinations other than those below can be reached by changing buses at Disney's Animal Kingdom (daytime) or Disney Springs (evening). Guests may find a car useful at this resort, and ample parking is freely available around the resort.

Magic Kingdom	Epcot	Disney's Hollywood Studios	Disney's Animal Kingdom	Downtown Disney
direct bus ~20 min.	direct bus ~10 min.	direct bus ~10 min.	direct bus ~10 min.	direct bus ~15 min.

Approximate time you will spend in transit from resort to destination during normal operation.

Top Photo Slice: The Calypso Pool at Disney's All-Star Music Resort © MediaMarx, Inc.

Making the Most of Disney's All-Star Resorts

TIPS

All-Star Music boasts **192 "Family Suites"** (see photo on previous page). These 520 sq. ft. rooms sport two full bathrooms, a kitchenette, a queen bed, a full sofa bed, and two convertible twin beds. Each suite sleeps up to 6 people, plus one child under 3 in a crib. We love them!

Walk around the resorts to catch all the neat props and details that make these resorts so fun. Even the walkways have fun designs.

If you need an escape from the activity of the All-Stars, look for the **quiet spots** around the resorts. Relax in a hammock behind a stand of palm trees in Fantasia at All-Star Movies, or try the picnic tables in Country Fair's courtyard in All-Star Music for a leisurely lunch.

Watch for **activities and movies** at the main pools in the evenings!

Mini-refrigerators without freezers are included in all rooms and suites at no extra charge.

NOTES

Plan to either carry your own luggage or wait a while (often 45–60 minutes) for their **luggage assistance service** to drop it off at your building. Unlike other Disney resorts, luggage is delivered at their convenience, not yours. Arrangements to pick up luggage on your departure day should be made the night before. You can borrow a luggage cart from the luggage assistance desk in the main hall, and you may need to leave your ID while you use the cart.

Toiletries are limited to a bar of facial soap at the sink and bath soap and shampoo in the shower/tub. You may want to bring your own.

Towels are not provided near the pools, so bring your own or use your room **towels**. Contact housekeeping for extra towels.

Check-in time is 4:00 pm. Check-out time is 11:00 am.

RATINGS

Ratings are explained on page 28.

Our Value Ratings:		Our Magic Ratings:		Readers' Ratings:
Quality:	6/10	Theme:	6/10	42% fell in love with it
Accessibility:	5/10	Amenities:	4/10	35% liked it well enough
Affordability:	9/10	Fun Factor:	2/10	12% had mixed feelings
Overall Value:	**7/10**	**Overall Magic:**	**4/10**	11% were disappointed

The All-Stars are enjoyed by...	(rated by both authors and readers)	
Younger Kids: ♥♥♥♥♥	Young Adults: ♥♥♥♥	Families: ♥♥♥♥
Older Kids: ♥♥♥♥♥	Mid Adults: ♥♥♥	Couples: ♥♥
Teenagers: ♥♥♥	Mature Adults: ♥♥	Singles: ♥♥♥

Top Photo Slice: The Touchdown section at Disney's All-Star Sports Resort (ⓘ17425) © Monica Gauvin

Finding Your Place at Disney's All-Star Resorts

ALL-STAR RESORT MAP

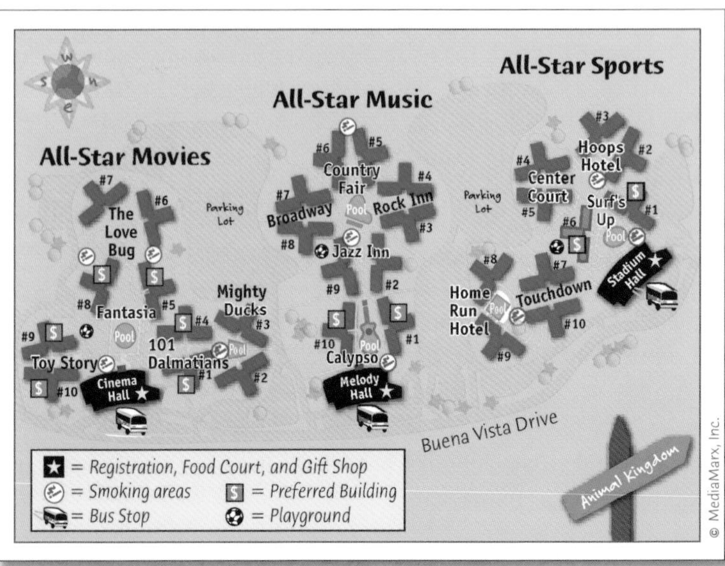

BEST LOCATIONS

Rooms at the All-Star Resorts vary mostly by location within the resorts and floor. For convenience, we recommend **101 Dalmatians**, **Fantasia**, or **Toy Story** (at All-Star Movies), **Calypso** (at All-Star Music), and **Surf's Up!** (at All-Star Sports)—they are closest to the main pools, food, and transportation. Our personal preferences are **Fantasia** (at All-Star Movies), **Country Fair** (at All-Star Music), and **Home Run Hotel** (at All-Star Sports) as they are relatively quiet and have good views from most windows—the latter two are a good distance from the main hall, however. Quieter rooms are those that face away from the pools and are on the **top floor**.

RATES

2016 Sample Room Rates

Seasons are noted on page 14.

Room Type	Value	Fall	Regular	Summer	Peak	Holiday
Standard	\$101–\$134	\$111–\$137	\$127–\$162	\$150–\$179	\$153–\$186	\$201
Preferred	\$120–\$141	\$129–\$151	\$153–\$181	\$168–\$197	\$171–\$205	\$219
Family Suites	\$244–\$273	\$253–\$304	\$313–\$350	\$345–\$401	\$354–\$411	\$447

13% tax is included in above rates. Preferred rooms are Fantasia, Toy Story, 101 Dalmatians, Calypso, and Surf's Up. Higher rate ranges are for weekend and holiday periods.

INFO

Disney's All-Star Movies/Music/Sports Resorts

1901/1801/1701 W. Buena Vista Dr., Lake Buena Vista, FL 32830

Phone: 407-939-7000/407-939-6000/407-939-5000

Fax: 407-939-7111/407-939-7222/407-939-7333

For reservations, call Central Reservations: 407-939-6244

Top Photo Slice: Sign at Disney's All-Star Music Resort © MediaMarx, Inc.

More at ⓘ all-star-movies | all-star-music | all-star-sports

Disney's Animal Kingdom Lodge & Villas Resort

Disney's Animal Kingdom Lodge and Villas share the ambience of its neighboring park, Disney's Animal Kingdom (use the blue tab at the top of the page for nearby parks/eateries). Guests at this deluxe resort can watch grazing wildlife on 44+ acres of African savanna from their balconies.

AMBIENCE

Your trek is rewarded as soon as you step into the lobbies of the two Lodge buildings, **Jambo House** and **Kidani Village**, which offer dramatic views to the animal reserves and "kopje" (rock outcrops) beyond. Sunlight pours in through high windows, painting the lobby's thatched ceiling and carved wooden decorations in a warm, intimate glow. African artwork greets you at every turn. Designed by the architect behind Disney's Wilderness Lodge, the hotel shares its sister resort's **rustic appeal**, but adds a welcome warmth and intimacy. Then, of course, there are the animals, which add a sense of delight unique to this resort.

LAYOUT & ROOMS

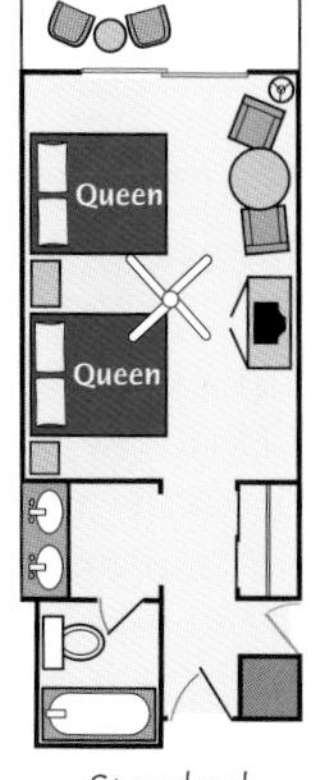

Standard Room Layout

Two **horseshoe-shaped buildings**, inspired by African Kraal (corral) villages, give most rooms a view of the private wildlife reserve. Rooms feature hand-carved furniture, gauze hangings at the head of the beds, and Kente-inspired fabrics. Standard rooms (344 sq. ft.) have two queen beds; one king bed and a daybed; or one queen bed and bunk beds. See page 43 for more details on the deluxe villas here. All rooms have a balcony, ceiling fan, table and chairs, refrigerator, coffeemaker, armoire with TV and drawers, double sinks, in-room safe, iron and ironing board, hair dryer, voice mail, and newspaper delivery.

DINING

A casual yet upscale restaurant, **Jiko**, is open for guests who want an elegantly inventive dinner. **Boma**, which means "place of refuge," offers an exciting, African-flavored dining adventure with all-you-care-to-eat buffets at breakfast and dinner. **The Mara** is a quick-service cafe open all day—typical menu items include a croissant sandwich ($6.49), a breakfast platter ($8.99), a kid's breakfast ($4.99), African stew ($8.49), chicken Caesar salad ($8.49), and pepperoni flatbread ($8.79). Rapid Fill mugs ($8.99–$17.99) can be purchased at The Mara. **Sanaa** is a full-service restaurant over at Kidani Village serving lunch and dinner. Room service is also available. The table-service restaurants are reviewed on page 253.

Using the Amenities at Disney's Animal Kingdom Lodge Resort

LOUNGING

Victoria Falls Lounge serves African- and Indian-inspired appetizers, coffees, wines, and beer. The **Cape Town Lounge and Wine Bar**, inside Jiko, serves great wines from South Africa. A small lounge is also inside **Sanaa**. **Uzima Springs** and **Maji** are poolside bars offering beer and mixed drinks. Snacks, beer, and wine are at the **Zawadi Marketplace**, **The Mara**, and **Johari Treasures**.

Sunrise on Animal Kingdom Lodge
More photos at http://www.passporter.com/photos

PLAYING & RELAXING

For Animal Watchers: Bring plenty of film/memory cards for your camera—you may also want a tripod. Binoculars are handy, too.
For Athletes: Keep in shape in the Zahanati and Survival of the Fittest Fitness Centers near the pools. Massage treatments are also offered. There is also a jogging path between the buildings.
For Children: Simba's Cubhouse is a supervised club (see page 284). There are also the Hakuna Matata and Uwanja Camp playgrounds, storytelling at the fire pit, and daily activities at Boma.
For Gamers: Pumbaa's Fun and Games and Safari So Good Arcade.
For Shoppers: The festive Zawadi Marketplace and Johari Treasures have sundries, foodstuffs, books, clothing, and African crafts.
For Swimmers: Soak in the Uzima and Samawati Springs pools, and enjoy water slides (close at 10:00 pm), kids' pools, and four spas (hot tubs). Both pools feature zero-entry sections where you can wade into the water. A pool wheelchair is available.
For Tours: Inquire in advance about the Sunset Safari (concierge guests only, $190.64) and Night Safari (resort guests only, $70) which tour the lodge's savannas. The Sunrise Safari ended Dec. 28, 2014.

GETTING ABOUT

Buses to theme parks and Disney Springs (see chart below for in-transit times) are a short walk out front of both buildings (see the map on page 44). Travel to other resorts via Disney's Animal Kingdom theme park (daytime) or Disney Springs (evening). Ample parking is available, as is valet parking ($20/day). This is the only deluxe resort to lack boat or monorail access to a nearby park.

Magic Kingdom	Epcot	Disney's Hollywood Studios	Disney's Animal Kingdom	Downtown Disney
direct bus ~20 min.	direct bus ~15 min.	direct bus ~10 min.	direct bus ~7 min.	direct bus ~15 min.

Approximate time you will spend in transit from resort to destination during normal operation.

Top Photo Slice: Pond near the Samawati Springs Pool at Disney's Animal Kingdom Lodge © MediaMarx, Inc.

Making the Most of Disney's Animal Kingdom Lodge Resort

TIPS

Disney Vacation Club has 134 studio and one-bedroom villas on the fifth and sixth floors of the original building ("Jambo House"), and Kidani Village has 324 studio, one-, two-, and three-bedroom villas, plus a full-service restaurant, savannas, pool, water play area, and a separate lobby area. Note that it is a 10-minute walk between the buildings, or you can take a bus (but it may take longer).

The Lodge has **44 acres of savanna**, which is distinct from the theme park, and is home to 36 species of mammals and 26 species of birds—more than 330 animals in all. Guests can see zebras, antelopes, giraffes, gazelle, wildebeests, ostriches, cranes, vultures, and storks. Animals may come within 15–30 feet from you, day or night. Each savanna has a few animal species that are unique to it. Each savanna closes daily for cleaning and animal care, but at least 2–3 savannas are always open. Best viewing times are typically early to mid-morning, and at dusk (ask about night-vision scopes).

African storytelling is held nightly around the firepit or in Sunset Overlook. "Safari guides" are also on hand to educate guests.

NOTES

Tour the resort's **African art collection** on a free self-guided tour or a daily guided tour in the afternoons. Inquire at the front desk.

Four separate savannas (each about 11 acres) can be viewed 24 hours a day. If your room doesn't have a view of the savanna, **watch the animals** from the kopje (the large observation area that extends into the savanna), the Sunset Overlook (a delightful room in the Jambo House lobby), the overlook near the Uzima pool, the alcoves along Zebra Trail and Kudu Trail (visit the second floor for outdoor platforms with rocking chairs and binoculars), and the viewing area near Sanaa.

Check-in is 3:00/4:00 pm. Check-out is 11:00 am. No late check-outs.

RATINGS

Ratings are explained on page 28.

Our Value Ratings:		Our Magic Ratings:		Readers' Ratings:
Quality:	9/10	Theme:	10/10	70% fell in love with it
Accessibility:	5/10	Amenities:	5/10	23% liked it well enough
Affordability:	6/10	Fun Factor:	8/10	7% had mixed feelings
Overall Value:	**6/10**	**Overall Magic:**	**8/10**	0% were disappointed

Disney's Animal Kingdom Lodge is enjoyed by... (rated by both authors and readers)		
Younger Kids: ♥♥♥♥♥	Young Adults: ♥♥♥♥	Families: ♥♥♥♥♥
Older Kids: ♥♥♥♥♥	Mid Adults: ♥♥♥♥♥	Couples: ♥♥♥
Teenagers: ♥♥♥	Mature Adults: ♥♥	Singles: ♥♥♥♥

Top Photo Slice: Giraffes on the savanna at Disney's Animal Kingdom Lodge (13190) © David Latoundji

Finding Your Place at Disney's Animal Kingdom Lodge Resort

ANIMAL KINGDOM LODGE MAP

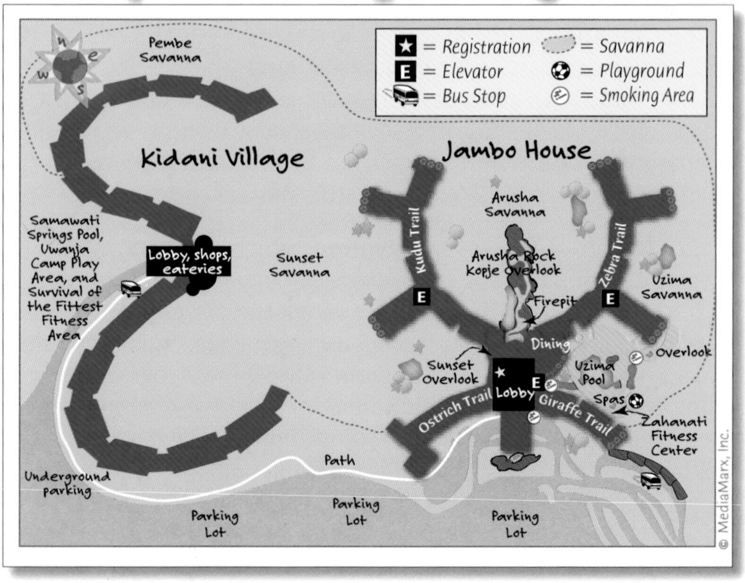

BEST LOCATIONS

At Jambo House, **standard rooms** are located on floors 1–4. Rooms come in three views: standard (Giraffe and Ostrich Trails), pool (Giraffe and Zebra Trails), and savanna (Zebra, Kudu, and Ostrich Trails). If animal-watching is your main draw, reserve a savanna-view room. Rooms on the far ends of the Zebra and Kudu Trails, and the far ends of Kidani Village, require a long walk. **Concierge rooms** (Jambo floor 5) are also available in pool and savanna views, as are several suites. **Villas** are located on floors 5 and 6 of Jambo House, also.

RATES

2016 Sample Room Rates

Seasons are noted on page 14.

Room Type	Value	Summer	Fall	Regular	Peak	Holiday
Standard View	$346-$376	$404-$410	$361-$417	$414-$464	$466-$506	$575
Pool View	$387-$422	$467-$492	$430-$506	$432-$478	$537-$600	$580
Savanna View	$495-$541	$577-$595	$526-$604	$597-$641	$650-$706	$735
Concierge (Club)	$514-$551	$573-$605	$561-$632	$592-$674	$673-$730	$760
Value Studio	$358-$366	$390	$374	$400	$489	$600
One-Bed. Savanna	$698-$739	$798	$758	$798	$939	$1028

12.5% tax is included in above prices. Suites start in the low $900s. Higher rates in price ranges are for weekends and holiday periods (see page 31).

INFO

Disney's Animal Kingdom Lodge & Villas Resort

2901 Osceola Parkway, Lake Buena Vista, FL 32830

Phone: 407-938-4799 Fax: 407-938-7102

For reservations, call Central Reservations: 407-939-6244

More at animal-kingdom-lodge | animal-kingdom-lodge-villas | kidani-village

Top Photo Slice: Signpost in Kidani Village at Disney's Animal Kingdom Lodge © MediaMarx, Inc.

Disney's Art of Animation Resort

The Art of Animation Resort focuses on value-priced accommodations for families of up to 6 in a suite. Disney's Art of Animation is right across from Disney's Pop Century Resort in the Epcot area (use the blue tab at the top of the page for parks and eateries in the vicinity) on the northeast corner of Osceola Parkway and Victory Way. This resort opened at Walt Disney World in May 2012.

AMBIENCE

Staying at Disney's Art of Animation Resort may be a bit like **stepping onto the screen** of your favorite Disney animated movies. Not unlike the All-Star and Pop Century resorts, the decor here is larger than life and vibrantly colored, reflecting the animated movies we all love. The resort features themed rooms and areas from four animated films: Finding Nemo, Cars, The Lion King, and The Little Mermaid. Look for Simba and friends on the African savannah, King Triton and Sebastian under the sea, Tow Mater and the Cozy Cone Motel, and Nemo and Marlin in their ocean home. The theme continues in the pools, play fountains, playgrounds, and food court!

RESORT LAYOUT & ROOMS

Disney's Art of Animation Resort features 1,984 guest rooms and family suites. All rooms at this resort are themed after one of **Disney's blockbuster animations**—family suites are decorated in the style of The Lion King, Finding Nemo, and Cars; standard guest rooms have a Little Mermaid theme. The family suites feature a master bedroom with a queen bed, a living room with a double-size sleeper sofa and a double-size Inova "TableBed" (a table that converts into a bed), two TVs, two full bathrooms (one with a shower, one with a tub), and a mini kitchen with small refrigerator, microwave, and coffeemaker. Standard guest rooms have either two double beds or one king bed, a TV, a small table with two chairs, and drawers. Rooms with king-size beds are also the barrier-free rooms; thus, some of these rooms have only showers (no tubs). Rooms are small—260 sq. feet for the standard guest rooms and about 525 sq. feet for family suites. There are no private balconies or patios, but each room has individual climate controls.

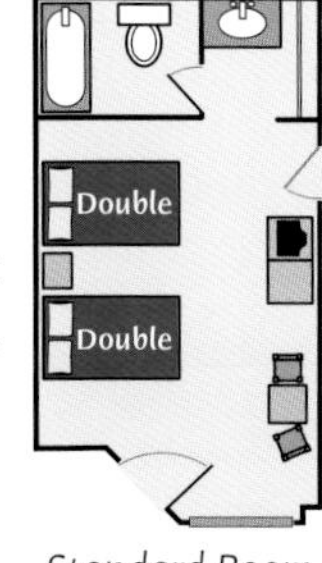

Standard Room Layout

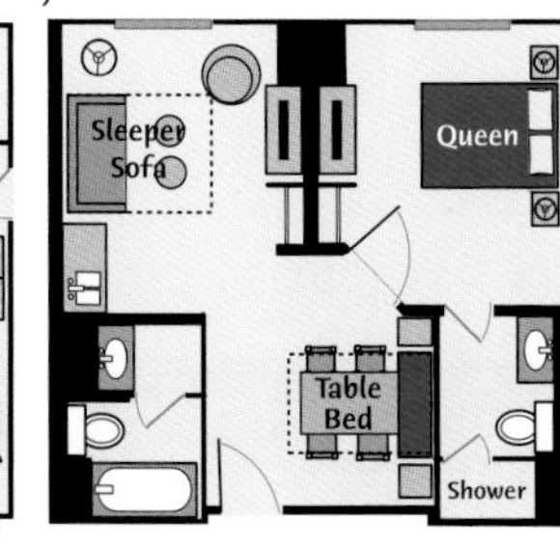

Family Suite Layout

Top Photo Slice: The colorful Art of Animation sign greets you upon arrival (ⓘ36732) © Barry Ristow

Using the Amenities at Disney's Art of Animation Resort

EATING & DRINKING

© Jennifer Marx
The innovative TableBed at Art of Animation
View more photos at http://www.passporter.com/photos

Art of Animation has a large food court called **Landscape of Flavors**, featuring a Mongolian grill and a design-your-own-burger station. It's open daily for breakfast, lunch, and dinner. Menu items include tandoori chicken ($9.99), pepperoni pizza ($9.69), and create your own smoothie ($5.79). Purchase a Rapid Fill mug for $8.99–$17.99 for refills. A pizza delivery service is available in the afternoons and evenings, along with seasonal snack carts near the pool and beverages at The Drop Off pool bar in the Finding Nemo courtyard.

PLAYING & RELAXING

For Athletes: The 12' wide lakeside path is ideal for walks and jogs. The lake does not offer a marina.
For Children: Two quiet playgrounds and an interactive play fountain are here (see map on page 48 for locations).
For Gamers: The Pixel Play arcade is located in Animation Hall.
For Shoppers: The large Ink and Paint shop offers Disney logo merchandise, clothing, sundries, and some snack foods.
For Swimmers: Cool off in the large The Big Blue pool in the Finding Nemo courtyard (which also features a wading pool), and two smaller themed pools called the Flippin' Fins Pool (The Little Mermaid courtyard) and Cozy Cone Pool (Cars courtyard).

GETTING ABOUT

Buses (see chart below for in-transit times) are outside the main building of the resort. Stops are well-marked and offer benches and shelter. Bus service is prompt and efficient. Destinations other than those below can be reached by changing buses at Disney's Hollywood Studios or Epcot (daytime) or Disney Springs (evening). Parking is freely available, though you should study the map to find the closest lot to your room.

Magic Kingdom	Epcot	Disney's Hollywood Studios	Disney's Animal Kingdom	Downtown Disney
direct bus ~25 min.	direct bus ~20 min.	direct bus ~15 min.	direct bus ~15 min.	direct bus ~20 min.

Approximate time you will spend in transit from resort to destination during normal operation.

Top Photo Slice: Larger-than-life characters on the main hall at Disney's Art of Animation (ⓘ37904) © Eddie Cabrera

Making the Most of Disney's Art of Animation Resort

Rooms at this resort were the first to have "**keyless" doors**. Guests need only to hold their MagicBand near the door handle to unlock it. By the end of 2013, Walt Disney World had retrofit all of its resorts with these locks.

Originally, this resort was to be an extension of Disney's Pop Century Resort (see pages 81–84) representing the first half of the 20th century, and would have been known as the **Legendary Years**!

The **33-acre lake** beside this resort is an added perk for a value resort—the other value resorts have no ponds, lakes, or rivers. Frequent park benches line the path, and you can see huge, colorful icons at the Pop Century across the lake reflected in the water.

Wondering how you would sleep on the unusual **Inova TableBed** in the family suites? It's really rather clever and space-saving! You can learn more about it at http://www.inovallc.com/cont_tablebed.html.

© Jennifer Marx

The opened TableBed at Art of Animation

Epcot's **IllumiNations** fireworks is visible from some locations at this resort. Best views are from the northeast end.

Self-service laundries are located near each pool. Wash loads and dry cycles are $2.00 each.

Check-in time is 4:00 pm. Check-out time is 11:00 am.

Ratings are explained on page 28.

Our Value Ratings:		Our Magic Ratings:		Readers' Ratings:
Quality:	7/10	Theme:	6/10	65% fell in love with it
Accessibility:	5/10	Amenities:	4/10	22% liked it well enough
Affordability:	8/10	Fun Factor:	4/10	7% had mixed feelings
Overall Value:	**7/10**	**Overall Magic:**	**5/10**	6% were disappointed

Art of Animation is enjoyed by...	(rated by both authors and readers)	
Younger Kids: ♥♥♥♥♥	Young Adults: ♥♥♥	Families: ♥♥♥♥♥
Older Kids: ♥♥♥♥♥	Mid Adults: ♥♥♥	Couples: ♥♥
Teenagers: ♥♥♥♥	Mature Adults: ♥♥	Singles: ♥♥

Top Photo Slice: The "Carwash" sign above the bathroom mirror in an Art of Animation Cars Family Suite © Jennifer Marx

Finding Your Place at Disney's Art of Animation Resort

ART OF ANIMATION RESORT MAP

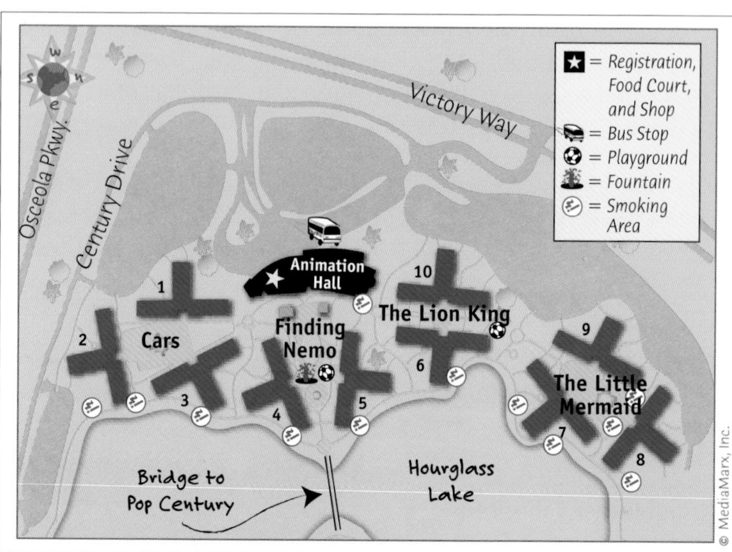

BEST LOCATIONS

Much like other **value resorts**, the guest rooms and suites at Art of Animation differ mostly by proximity to Animation Hall and floor level. As always, if you seek a quieter room, request a room/suite on the third or fourth floors of a building. There are no preferred-rate buildings at this resort. Cars, Finding Nemo, and The Lion King house the family suites, while standard rooms fill The Little Mermaid. Thanks to the layout, however, no rooms are really a great distance from Animation Hall—only The Little Mermaid section seems "out there" and it really isn't that far. The layout here is very similar to Pop Century (see page 84).

RATES

2016 Sample Room Rates

Seasons are noted on page 14.

Room Type	Value	Fall	Regular	Summer	Peak	Holiday
Standard	$123–$151	$142–$165	$158–$187	$183–$214	$184–$213	$224
Family Suite	$303–$336	$323–$366	$374–$426	$413–$472	$426–$494	$514

12.5% tax is included in above rates. There is a $10 per person charge for each additional adult in a room, but no extra charge for children under 18. Rooms may face parking lots, pools, the lake, or courtyards. Higher rates in price ranges are for weekends and holiday periods (see page 31).

INFO

Disney's Art of Animation Resort

1850 Century Drive, Lake Buena Vista, FL 32830

Phone: 407-938-7000 Fax: 407-938-4040

For reservations, call Central Reservations: 407-939-6244

Top Photo Slice: Seating in a Cozy Cone Cabana near the pool at Art of Animation (36916) © Jeffrey Kalasinski

Disney's BoardWalk Inn & Villas Resort

BoardWalk Inn & Villas Resort enjoys a favored location in the middle of the action, fronting Crescent Lake between Epcot and Disney's Hollywood Studios (use the blue tab at the top of the page for parks and eateries in the area). The Villas are affiliated with the Disney Vacation Club (see pages 108–109).

AMBIENCE

This "**seaside**" **resort** takes you back to the heyday of the Atlantic City Boardwalk in the 1920s and 1930s, where carefree days floated by on the summer breeze. Reminiscent of an elegant bed-and-breakfast inn, the BoardWalk continues this impression inside with its old-fashioned furnishings and soft, muted colors. Outside, a stroll along the vibrant promenade offers great views, family fun, and more eateries, clubs, and shops than you can visit.

LAYOUT & ROOMS

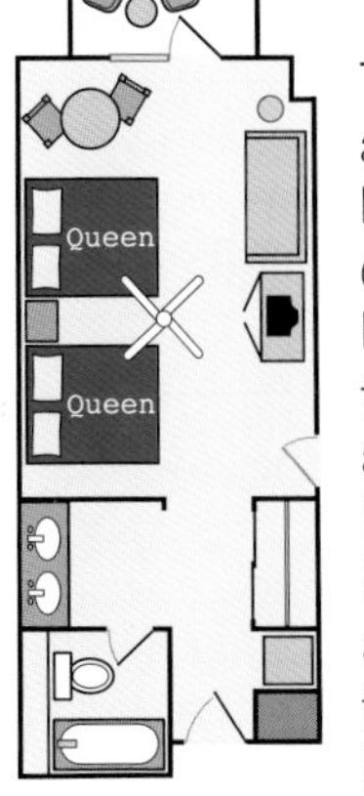

Standard Room Layout (Inn)

The two different sides of this resort offer varying accommodations, ranging from 359 to 2,142 sq. ft. **BoardWalk Inn** has 378 rooms with one king or two queens plus a daybed or queen sofa bed, and suites. **BoardWalk Villas** feature 532 studios and one-, two-, and three-bedroom villas (suites)—studios have a kitchenette, suites have a full kitchen, big-screen TV, DVD player, and washer/dryer. All rooms in the resort have a balcony or patio, double sinks, a marble vanity, a table and chairs, a sofa, an armoire, TV, ceiling fan, toiletries, and a hair dryer. Also available are housekeeping, turndown service (on request), voice mail, and, in most rooms, an in-room safe.

DINING

Unique to this resort is a lively entertainment complex along the waterfront promenade. This innovative mini-park offers a variety of dining options. BoardWalk table-service restaurants, detailed on page 254, include **Big River Grille & Brewing Works**, a modern brewpub; **ESPN Club**, an All-American sports cafe; **Flying Fish Cafe**, fine dining with an ever-changing menu; and **Trattoria al Forno** features Italian cuisine. The **Belle Vue Room** offers a quick bite in the mornings. Two quick-service cafes round out the menu. The **BoardWalk Bakery** tempts you with an expanded menu of sandwiches, baked goods, and coffee—try the Maine lobster sandwich ($18.29), an apple mixed greens salad ($11.29), egg bowl ($9.79), and chocolate peanut butter bar cake ($4.49). **Seashore Sweets** offers ice cream, cookies, fudge, saltwater taffy, and coffees.

Looking for the Beach Club and Villas? See pages 99–103.

Top Photo Slice: A view of the BoardWalk Inn from across Crescent Lake © MediaMarx, Inc.

Using the Amenities at Disney's BoardWalk Inn & Villas Resort

LOUNGING

The BoardWalk is rich with lounges and clubs. **Atlantic Dance Hall** and **Jellyrolls** (see page 214) serve up drinks and fun. In the resort itself is the **Belle Vue Room**, perfect for a quiet drink and a game of chess. **Leaping Horse Libations** is the pool bar near Luna Park. 24-hour room service.

ⓘ22892 © Matt Asplen

The BoardWalk is beautiful at night
350+ more photos at http://www.passporter.com/photos

PLAYING & RELAXING

For Athletes: Muscles and Bustles Fitness offers exercise equipment, steam room, sauna, and massage (for an extra fee). Rent bikes at Community Hall and surrey bikes on the BoardWalk. There are also two lighted tennis courts and a walking/jogging circuit around Crescent Lake and along the path to Disney's Hollywood Studios.
For Children: A playground and wading pool is at Luna Park. Harbor Club kids' care club is closed—see other options on page 284–285.
For Gamers: Side Show Games Arcade has video games. Rent DVDs at Community Hall (free to DVC members, $5 for guests).
For Shoppers: Dundy's Sundries and Screen Door General Store offer the basics, while Thimbles & Threads and Disney's Character Carnival stock apparel and gifts. Wyland Galleries has collectibles.
For Swimmers: Of the three pools, the largest is Luna Park with a 200-ft. "wooden coaster" slide. All pools have spas (hot tubs).
For the Curious: Take the free, 45-min. Ballyhoo Guided Tour every Wed. through Sat. at 9:00 am. Check in 15 min. prior at Belle Vue Lounge.

GETTING ABOUT

Buses are boarded in the front of the resort, while **boats** depart from the marina (see the chart below for in-transit times). Travel elsewhere via a park (daytime) or Disney Springs (evening). You can **walk** to Disney's Hollywood Studios, Epcot, Yacht & Beach Club, and Swan & Dolphin. If you miss the Disney's Hollywood Studios boat, just walk quickly to the Swan & Dolphin boat dock before your missed boat reaches it and hop on. Valet parking is a $20/day option.

Magic Kingdom	Epcot	Disney's Hollywood Studios	Disney's Animal Kingdom	Downtown Disney
direct bus ~20 min.	walk/boat ~10/~5 min.	walk/boat ~15/~20 min.	direct bus ~10 min.	direct bus ~15 min.

Approximate time you will spend in transit from resort to destination during normal operation.

Top Photo Slice: The coaster slide at BoardWalk Resort's Luna Park © MediaMarx, Inc.

Making the Most of Disney's BoardWalk Inn & Villas Resort

TIPS

The guest rooms at BoardWalk Inn were last **refurbished** in 2010.

The **Belle Vue Room** is a marvel of nostalgia. It's tucked away in a corner down the hall from the lobby on the Inn side of the resort. You'll find backgammon, chess, and checkers tables (ask a cast member for game pieces), as well as a single-malt scotch menu.

Take a stroll through the grounds, away from the busy Promenade. The **landscaping** is a delight. If you prefer the bustle of the BoardWalk, rent a **surrey bike** and tour around the promenade and lake.

The BoardWalk Inn's **Garden Suites** have to be the most romantic in the "World." Each of the 14 suites looks like a two-story cottage. All suites have private entrances and most have a unique garden surrounded by a white picket fence with a trellised arbor gate. Suites have a separate living room, sleeper sofa, and a wet bar on the first floor, while the open second floor has a king-size bed, a separate shower, and a large whirlpool tub.

Look for several quaint **sitting areas** scattered about the resort.

NOTES

Guests with rooms in the **small courtyard building** on the Inn side must use their room key to enter the building itself.

Noise and **light** levels are important considerations here due to the proximity of the BoardWalk Promenade. If these are concerns, request a room away from both the promenade and the pools.

Conference facilities are available at the BoardWalk.

Check-in time is 3:00 pm (BoardWalk Inn) or 4:00 pm (BoardWalk Villas). Check-out time is 11:00 am for both.

RATINGS

Ratings are explained on page 28.

Our Value Ratings:		Our Magic Ratings:		Readers' Ratings:
Quality:	9/10	Theme:	8/10	72% fell in love with it
Accessibility:	7/10	Amenities:	8/10	17% liked it well enough
Affordability:	3/10	Fun Factor:	6/10	8% had mixed feelings
Overall Value:	**6/10**	**Overall Magic:**	**7/10**	3% were disappointed

The BoardWalk is enjoyed by...	(rated by both authors and readers)	
Younger Kids: ♥♥♥♥	Young Adults: ♥♥♥♥	Families: ♥♥♥♥♥
Older Kids: ♥♥♥♥	Mid Adults: ♥♥♥♥♥	Couples: ♥♥♥♥♥
Teenagers: ♥♥♥	Mature Adults: ♥♥♥♥♥	Singles: ♥♥♥

Top Photo Slice: Rocking chairs on the porch at Disney's BoardWalk Resort © MediaMarx, Inc.

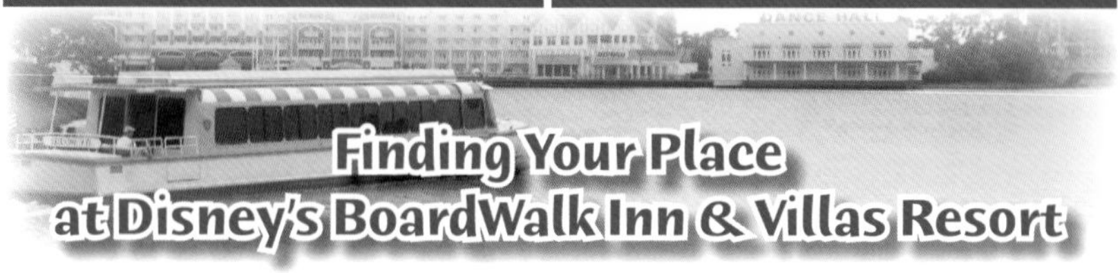

Finding Your Place at Disney's BoardWalk Inn & Villas Resort

BOARDWALK RESORT MAP

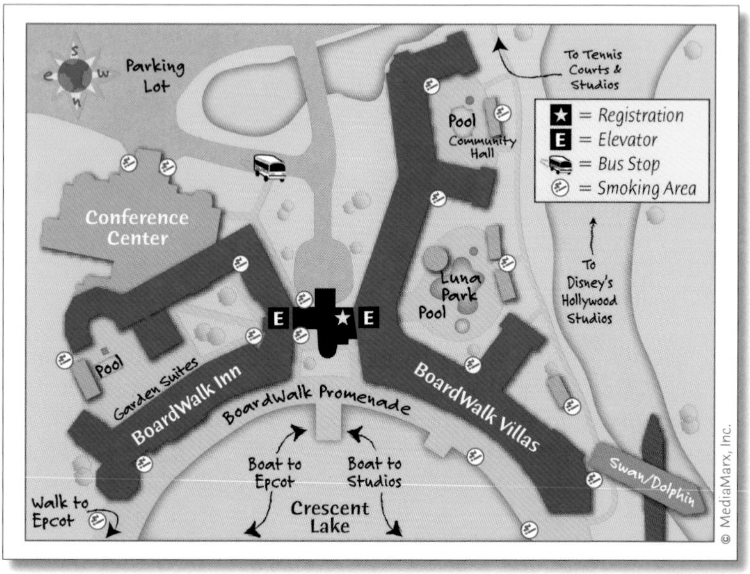

BEST LOCATIONS

It's hard to get a bad room here. Request a **water view** at the Inn if you want to watch the Promenade, but keep in mind it can be noisy. Water views in the Villas may overlook the canal leading to the Studios, but may also overlook the Promenade (you may request this). **Standard views** overlook attractive courtyards or the entrance driveway (not so bad as trees shield the parking areas). **Preferred views** in the Villas can overlook a pool, water, or garden view. Rooms around the leisure pools are more peaceful than those around Luna Park. Note that hallways on the Villas side can be very long.

RATES

2016 Sample Room Rates

Seasons are noted on page 14.

Room Type	Value	Fall	Regular	Peak	Holiday
Standard (Inn) or Studio (Villas)	$429-$448	$454-$490	$510-$529	$569-$612	$683
Water View (Inn)	$560-$598	$584-$630	$660-$691	$693-$776	$763
One-Bedroom (Villas)	$602-$616	$644	$686	$810	$860
Two-Bedroom (Villas)	$864-$878	$979	$1,119	$1,401	$1,529

12.5% tax is included in above prices. Concierge-level rooms begin in the mid-$600s and suites begin in the low-$800s. Two-bedroom concierge suites begin in the $1,600s. Higher rates in price ranges are for weekends and holiday periods at the Inn (see page 31).

INFO

Disney's BoardWalk Inn & Villas Resort

2101 N. Epcot Resort Blvd., Lake Buena Vista, FL 32830

Phone: 407-939-5100 Fax: 407-939-5150

For reservations, call Central Reservations: 407-939-6244

More at ⓘ boardwalk

Top Photo Slice: A Friendship boat cruises past the BoardWalk © MediaMarx, Inc.

Planning | Getting There | Staying in Style | Touring | Feasting | Making Magic | Index | Notes & More

Disney's Caribbean Beach Resort

The free spirit of the tropics greets you at the Caribbean Beach Resort, Disney's original moderately priced resort. Within easy distance of both Epcot and Disney's Hollywood Studios (use the blue tab at the top of the page for parks and eateries in the area), this large and sprawling resort is popular with families.

AMBIENCE

The bright, sunny colors of the buildings and rooftops are your first sign of the **laid-back lifestyle** you'll find at the Caribbean. After you check in at the Customs House, you make your way to one of the six "islands" that encircle 45-acre Barefoot Bay. Lush tropical foliage, hidden courtyards, and white sand beaches are the setting for your lively Caribbean adventure.

RESORT LAYOUT & ROOMS

The 2,112 rooms are well spread out among the six exotic "**islands**" of the Caribe—Aruba, Barbados, Martinique, Jamaica, Trinidad North, and Trinidad South. Each island has a cluster of stucco, pitched-roof buildings without elevators that make up the "village centers," all painted in their own distinctive colors. The rooms in the two-storied buildings have bright colors and oak furnishings. The beds (one king or two doubles) have posts carved into pineapples, the symbol of hospitality. Guest rooms have double sinks in the separate vanity area with under-sink shelves and a privacy curtain, a table and chairs, an armoire with TV, a set of drawers, and a ceiling fan. There are no balconies or patios. Guest rooms here are the largest of all the moderate resorts at 340 sq. ft. Amenities include a coffeemaker, refrigerator, toiletries, housekeeping, limited room service, and voice mail.

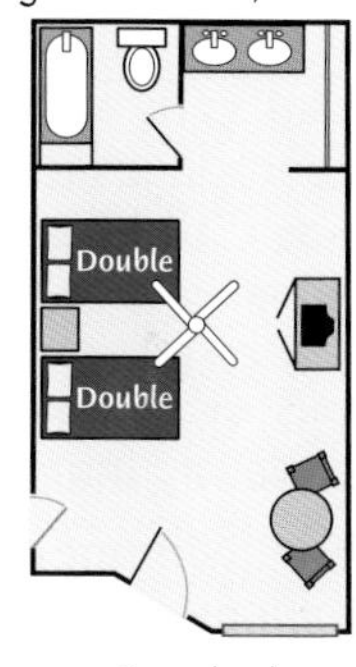

Standard Room Layout

DINING

The Caribbean Beach offers a table-service restaurant, as well as a breezy food court and the ubiquitous pool bar. All are available in **Old Port Royale**, also called "Center Towne," housing the eateries, shops, main pool, and marina. The food court's hours are 6:00 am–11:30 pm. **Banana Cabana**, a pool bar located at Old Port Royale, offers a variety of specialty drinks ($7.50+) and beer ($4.00–$5.00) during pool hours. **Bluerunner** is a limited room delivery service—typical menu items include domestic beer ($5.25), wine ($10.95+ for 1/2 bottles), 16" pizza ($13.99–$17.99), and cheesecake ($3.59). **Shutters**, the table-service restaurant, serves Caribbean-flavored fare for dinner only—see the restaurant's description on page 255.

Top Photo Slice: Top of the Aruba guest house at Disney's Caribbean Beach Resort (①12215) © Kurt Ulrich

Using the Amenities at Disney's Caribbean Beach Resort

MORE DINING

A bustling village atmosphere sets the stage for **Market Street**, the resort's food court. The various food stations offer chicken, pasta, sandwiches, burgers, pizza, and baked goods. Menu items include French toast with bacon ($6.39), Caribbean chicken salad ($9.69), bacon cheeseburger ($11.19), turkey BLT ($10.49), kids' cheese pizza ($5.99), and smoothie ($4.99). Get refills at the beverage island with a mug ($8.99–$17.99).

© MediaMarx, Inc.

A Caribbean Beach pirate-themed room

150+ more photos at http://www.passporter.com/photos

PLAYING & RELAXING

For Athletes: The Barefoot Bay Boat Yard rents boats and "toobies" (motorized inner tubes). Rent a bicycle or surrey bike for a ride around the bay. Walkers and joggers enjoy the many beautiful paths and will really enjoy the circuit around Barefoot Bay and the footbridges to Caribbean Cay island.

For Children: There are playgrounds on the beaches in Barbados, Jamaica, and Trinidad South.

For Gamers: Goombay Games in Old Port Royale has video games.

For Shoppers: The Calypso Trading Post & Straw Market offers themed gifts, sundries, clothing, and Caribbean items.

For Swimmers: The themed pool near Old Port Royale features cannons and waterfalls, as well as a wading pool for kids, a spa (hot tub), and a water slide. Six leisure pools are among the resort's "islands." Note that there is no swimming in the bay.

For Sunbathers: Each "island" has a beautiful, white sand beach.

GETTING ABOUT

Transportation to the theme parks and water parks (see chart below for in-transit times) is via frequent **buses**. Other resorts are accessible by changing buses at a nearby theme park (daytime) or Disney Springs (evening). You can also take an internal resort bus if you need to reach other areas within the resort. To go to the Customs House (lobby concierge/luggage services), get off at Barbados.

Magic Kingdom	Epcot	Disney's Hollywood Studios	Disney's Animal Kingdom	Downtown Disney
direct bus ~20 min.	direct bus ~15 min.	direct bus ~12 min.	direct bus ~20 min.	direct bus ~25 min.

Approximate time you will spend in transit from resort to destination during normal operation.

Top Photo Slice: Inside Old Port Royale at Disney's Caribbean Beach (10988) © Marianne Swan

Making the Most of Disney's Caribbean Beach Resort

TIPS

While you can't swim in the bay, the **white sand beaches** are great spots to relax. We found several hammocks set up along the beach—take some time to just kick back and watch the palm trees flutter.

You can catch a glimpse of the **Epcot globe** between Old Port Royale and Martinique—look in the evenings for a glimpse of IllumiNations.

There are "hidden" **courtyards** sporting tables with umbrellas in every "island" of the resort—these are now the designated smoking areas, but can still be very rewarding places to relax. Be sure to take a trip across the bridge to **Caribbean Cay** (formerly Parrot Cay) in the middle of Barefoot Bay. Beyond the lush foliage and dense bamboo stands, you'll find gazebos, picnic areas, and hammocks.

© MediaMarx, Inc.
Caribbean Cay

NOTES

All rooms have **refrigerators**.

There are **no elevators**.

This is a sprawling resort, making it difficult to get to Old Port Royale to eat or shop. Consider **stocking up** on snacks and quick breakfast foods. Board the "Internal" bus to move around the resort.

All rooms in Martinique and Trinidad North are **preferred rooms**. Pirate-themed rooms are found in Trinidad South (see photo on previous page and prices on the next page), while the remaining rooms have a very subtle Finding Nemo theme.

Check-in time is 3:00 pm. Check-out time is 11:00 am.

Ratings are explained on page 28.

RATINGS

Our Value Ratings:		Our Magic Ratings:		Readers' Ratings:
Quality:	6/10	Theme:	6/10	47% fell in love with it
Accessibility:	5/10	Amenities:	6/10	43% liked it well enough
Affordability:	8/10	Fun Factor:	6/10	8% had mixed feelings
Overall Value:	**6/10**	**Overall Magic:**	**6/10**	2% were disappointed

Caribbean Beach is enjoyed by...	(rated by both authors and readers)	
Younger Kids: ♥♥♥♥♥	Young Adults: ♥♥♥♥	Families: ♥♥♥♥
Older Kids: ♥♥♥♥♥	Mid Adults: ♥♥♥♥	Couples: ♥♥♥♥♥
Teenagers: ♥♥♥♥	Mature Adults: ♥♥♥♥	Singles: ♥♥♥

Top Photo Slice: Sailboat on Barefoot Bay at Disney's Caribbean Beach Resort © MediaMarx, Inc.

Finding Your Place at Disney's Caribbean Beach Resort

CARIBBEAN BEACH RESORT MAP

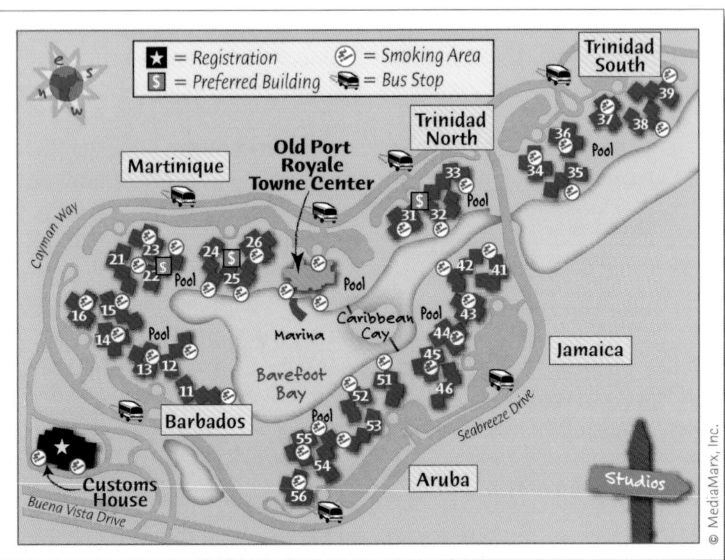

BEST LOCATIONS

Your "island" can make or break your experience. Though more expensive, we suggest **Martinique** or **Trinidad North**, which are close to Old Port Royale. **Aruba** and **Jamaica**, across the Barefoot Bay bridge, are good choices for a bit of seclusion. You don't need a **water view** to enjoy your room here, but if you prefer one, we found the following rooms to have outstanding water views: 2524, 2525, 2556, and 2557 in Martinique; and 3117, 3149, 3225–3228, and 3257–3261 in Trinidad North. Corner rooms (available with either double- or king-size beds) seem larger as they often have an extra window.

RATES

2016 Sample Room Rates

Seasons are noted on page 14.

Room Type	Value	Fall	Regular	Summer	Peak	Holiday
Standard Room	$182–$201	$204–$226	$212–$245	$220	$237–$260	$285
Preferred, Water, or King	$210–$227	$226–$243	$242–$270	$251	$268–$290	$318
Pirate Themed Standard	$259–$278	$277–$284	$296–$328	$306	$306–$327	$335
Pirate Themed Water	$276–$304	$282–$289	$302–$334	$312	$317–$341	$368

12.5% tax is included in above rates. King-bed rooms come in both standard or water view, and both are the same rate as a water-view room. Preferred rooms (any view, any bed size) are located in Martinique and Trinidad North. Higher rates in price ranges are for weekends and holiday periods (see page 31).

INFO

Disney's Caribbean Beach Resort

900 Cayman Way, Lake Buena Vista, FL 32830

Phone: 407-934-3400 Fax: 407-934-3288

For reservations, call Central Reservations: 407-939-6244

More at ⓘ caribbean-beach

Top Photo Slice: Reflections of Caribbean Beach Resort across Barefoot Bay (ⓘ22198) © Christine Mak

Disney's Contemporary Resort & Villas

The Contemporary Resort is one of the original and quintessential Walt Disney World hotels, built at the same time as nearby Magic Kingdom (use the blue tab at the top of the page for parks and eateries in the area). Bay Lake and the Seven Seas Lagoon surround the resort on three sides.

AMBIENCE

Every time we enter the Contemporary, we get the sense we've entered the **center of the "World."** It isn't just the soaring architecture, the massive steel and glass tower, or the monorail running right through it, though those are all a part of it. Rather, it is akin to the feeling city dwellers boast about: Everything you need, everyone you like, and every place that matters is right there. And that seems to be exactly the way Disney intended it, with the Grand Concourse housing many of the resort's services, restaurants, and shops.

RESORT LAYOUT & ROOMS

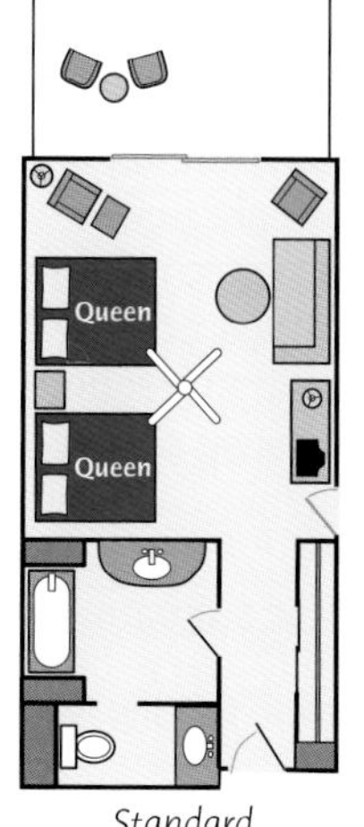

Standard Room Layout

The original 668 guest rooms are housed in the 15-story, A-frame **Tower** or within the three-story **Garden Wing**. These 436 sq. ft., modern rooms have Feng Shui-influences with flat-screen TVs, double closets, and dark cherry wood details with two queens or one king bed, and a daybed. Some rooms have large patios or balconies. Next door in the **Bay Lake Tower**, 295 Disney Vacation Club villas offer an "urban boutique" experience, with studios, one- and two-bedroom, and Grand Villas. Amenities include toiletries, safe, newspaper delivery, coffeemaker, refrigerator, hair dryer, turndown service (on request), voice mail, and valet parking ($20/day).

DINING

The Contemporary has a wide variety of dining options. The two most popular table-service restaurants—**Chef Mickey's** (a character dining experience) and the trendy **California Grill** (the Contemporary's centerpiece)—are detailed on page 255. **The Wave** offers American cuisine with an international flair at breakfast, lunch, and dinner. The **Contempo Cafe** is a quick-service eatery open all day—typical menu items include a cheeseburger ($9.39), smoked turkey sandwich ($9.49), pasta marinara ($7.29), and kid's meals ($5.99). Refillable mugs are available at the resort for $8.99–$17.99. The **Sand Bar** and **Cove Bar** by the pool also offers drinks ($2.99 & up), sandwiches ($9.49), and ice cream ($3.79).

Top Photo Slice: Bay Lake Tower and the original Contemporary Tower (21972) © Laura Dawson

Using the Amenities at Disney's Contemporary Resort

LOUNGING

The Wave offers a large lounge. **Outer Rim Lounge** on the 4th floor of the main tower has huge glass windows, though it is often congested with strollers. **California Grill Lounge** offers California wines and appetizers along with a magnificent view. **Contemporary Grounds** is a coffee bar near the front desk. The **Top of the World** lounge at Bay Lake Tower is open for DVC resort guests only. There are also two pool bars. **Room service** is open 24 hours a day.

Bay Lake Tower at the Contemporary
300+ more photos at http://www.passporter.com/photos

PLAYING & RELAXING

For Athletes: The Olympiad fitness center has exercise equipment, sauna, and massage therapies. Boat rentals add to the fun. Sammy Duvall's Watersports Centre at the resort offers waterskiing and parasailing. Tennis courts are also available near Bay Lake Tower.
For Gamers: A large resort arcade offers pinball and video games.
For Shoppers: The fourth-floor Concourse shops sell gifts and clothing. The marina pavilion offers swimwear and sun protection.
For Swimmers: The Bay Cove Pool (for Bay Lake Tower guests only) has a zero-entry, water slide, whirlpool spa, and an interactive children's water feature. There are also two more heated pools, two hot tubs, and another water slide, as well as a sand beach for sunbathers.

GETTING ABOUT

The Contemporary Resort offers myriad transportation options (see the chart below for in-transit times). For the Magic Kingdom, board the **monorail** on the fourth floor or walk the **path** on the north side (see map on page 60). For Epcot, monorail to the Transportation and Ticket Center (TTC) and transfer to the Epcot monorail. For other parks, take the **direct bus** just outside the lobby. For the Polynesian Village or Grand Floridian, take the monorail. For Fort Wilderness or the Wilderness Lodge, take the **boat**. For other destinations, go to the Magic Kingdom (daytime) or Disney Springs (evening) and transfer to the appropriate resort bus. Valet parking is a $20/day option.

Magic Kingdom	Epcot	Disney's Hollywood Studios	Disney's Animal Kingdom	Downtown Disney
monorail/walk ~20/~10 min.	monorail x 2 ~5+10 min.	direct bus ~20 min.	direct bus ~20 min.	direct bus ~35 min.

Approximate time you will spend in transit from resort to destination during normal operation.

Top Photo Slice: Entrance to The Wave restaurant at the Contemporary Resort © MediaMarx, Inc.

Making the Most of Disney's Contemporary Resort

TIPS

The Contemporary's **Bay Lake Tower** is a Disney Vacation Club property, but you don't have to be a member to reserve a room. Bay Lake Tower offers dramatic views of the Magic Kingdom next door and Bay Lake. The Skyway Bridge connects the Bay Lake Tower to the original tower for access to the monorail and other resort services.

The Magic Kingdom fireworks can be watched from a **viewing patio** on the Bay Lake Tower rooftop (alas, it's only accessible to Disney Vacation Club members), but there is a viewing patio on the 4th floor of the main tower—look for the door tucked in behind Fantasia Market. California Grill diners can also use their deck (see page 255).

The **Electrical Water Pageant**, a whimsical parade of lighted barges and music, can be seen from the shore of Bay Lake at 10:10 pm (or a bit later if the Magic Kingdom fireworks are at 10:00 pm).

The Contemporary Tower also offers one- and two-bedroom suites and two concierge levels, all with special amenities. Among the many amenities in the **suites** (bathrobes, triple sheeting, turndown service, etc.), the two-line speakerphones are great.

NOTES

The obvious method of transportation to Magic Kingdom is via the monorail, but consider **walking** instead on busy mornings or when the park lets out—it's much faster! The monorail goes around the lagoon clockwise, so it can take a while to reach the Magic Kingdom.

Guest rooms in the **Garden Wing** can be a hike from the Tower's restaurants and services. If this is a concern, reserve a Tower room.

The Contemporary Resort has a **large convention center** also.

Check-in time is 3:00 pm/4:00 pm. Check-out time is 11:00 am.

RATINGS

Ratings are explained on page 28.

Our Value Ratings:		Our Magic Ratings:		Readers' Ratings:
Quality:	8/10	Theme:	4/10	50% fell in love with it
Accessibility:	9/10	Amenities:	9/10	24% liked it well enough
Affordability:	5/10	Fun Factor:	5/10	10% had mixed feelings
Overall Value:	**7/10**	**Overall Magic:**	**6/10**	16% were disappointed

Contemporary is enjoyed by...	(rated by both authors and readers)	
Younger Kids: ♥♥♥	Young Adults: ♥♥♥♥♥	Families: ♥♥♥♥♥
Older Kids: ♥♥♥♥♥	Mid Adults: ♥♥♥♥	Couples: ♥♥♥♥
Teenagers: ♥♥♥♥♥	Mature Adults: ♥♥♥	Singles: ♥♥♥♥

Top Photo Slice: The striking windows in the Contemporary's original tower © MediaMarx, Inc.

Finding Your Place at Disney's Contemporary Resort

CONTEMPORARY RESORT MAP

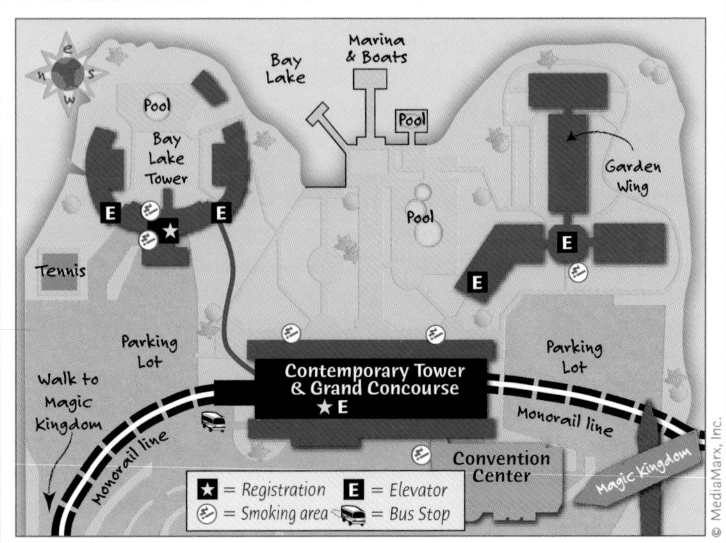

LOCATIONS

If you are drawn to the Contemporary by its proximity to the Magic Kingdom and you want to **see the castle** from your room, be sure to reserve this specifically—only certain **Tower** rooms get this breathtaking view. The **Garden Wing** may lack the Tower's excitement, but we found the rooms delightful and serene, especially those facing the water. Very few of the Garden Wing rooms have **balconies**, but first-floor rooms have **patios**.

RATES

2016 Sample Room Rates

Seasons are noted on page 14.

Room Type	Value	Fall	Regular	Peak	Holiday
Standard View (Wing)	$330-$355	$362-$411	$367-$406	$407-$452	$551
Garden/Water View (Wing)	$378-$407	$417-$474	$426-$472	$483-$537	$595
Tower Room (Bay View)	$447-$492	$490-$557	$502-$556	$586-$651	$650
Tower (Magic Kingdom view)	$507-$545	$535-$607	$557-$616	$646-$718	$715
Bay Lake Tower Studio	$431-$441	$462	$492-$493	$571	$609
Bay Lake Tower One-Bedroom	$535-$545	$584	$597-$599	$695	$776
Bay Lake Tower Two-Bedroom	$726-$737	$832	$939-$945	$1,188	$1,299

12.5% tax is included in above rates. Concierge-level rooms (floors 12 and 14) start in the $600s. Suites come in a variety of views and start in the $1000s. Higher rates in price ranges are for weekends and holiday periods (see page 31).

INFO

Disney's Contemporary Resort

4600 North World Drive, Lake Buena Vista, FL 32830

Phone: 407-824-1000 Fax: 407-824-3539

More at ⓘ contemporary

Top Photo Slice: Sunset over the Seven Seas Lagoon as seen from atop the Contemporary Resort (ⓘ12427) © Cheryl Pendry

Disney's Coronado Springs Resort

Coronado Springs is located near Disney's Animal Kingdom and Disney's Hollywood Studios (use the blue tab at the top of the page for parks and eateries in the area). The resort offers moderately priced rooms and convention facilities. The resort surrounds a 15-acre lake known as Lago (Lake) Dorado.

AMBIENCE

The architecture and decor trace the travels of explorer Francisco de Coronado in colonial Mexico and the **American Southwest**. Adventure awaits around every corner, from the colorful, bustling market to the Mayan pyramid overlooking the main swimming pool. Your visit begins in a sunny plaza, which leads to the large, open lobby graced by beamed ceilings, elegant columns, and intricately inlaid floors. Around the corner, a festive market offers native foods, just the thing to eat on the lakeside terrace. The resort's buildings are clustered around sparkling Lago Dorado, including the stately main building, El Centro.

RESORT LAYOUT & ROOMS

The renovated guest rooms in this 1,967-room resort are divided into three districts. Closest to El Centro are the **Casitas**, a bustling village of three- and four-story stucco buildings painted in soft pastels. Next around the lagoon are the rustic adobe-and-wood **Ranchos**. You could imagine Zorro dashing under the porch roofs and amid the cactus, while bubbling springs cascade into rock-strewn stream beds, ultimately to disappear into the parched desert earth. Finally, you reach the tropical **Cabanas**, vibrantly colored two-story buildings with the corrugated tin roofs of a rustic beach resort. Rooms are about 314 sq. ft. and offer two queen beds or one king bed, a separate vanity area with just one sink, table and chairs, armoire, and a TV. Amenities include toiletries, housekeeping, limited room service, hair dryer, iron and ironing board, coffeemaker, refrigerator, in-room safe, and voice mail. Newspaper delivery is available for $1.50/day. Concierge rooms and junior, one-bedroom, and executive suites are also available.

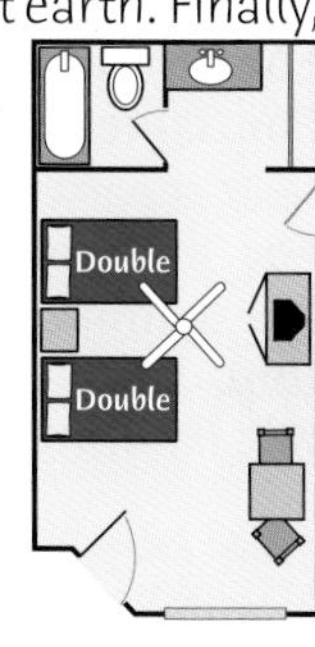

Standard Room Layout

The large 190,000 sq. ft. **Conference Center** is quite modern and generally lacks the regional character of the resort. It boasts the largest ballroom in the Southeast (60,214 sq. ft.). An 85,000 sq. ft. exhibit hall, meeting rooms, another 20,000 sq. ft. ballroom, and patios round out the facilities. A full-service business center is also available.

Top Photo Slice: Sunrise at Disney's Coronado Springs Resort (①2444) © Darren Mosher

Using the Amenities at Disney's Coronado Springs Resort

DINING

Coronado Springs' dining options are the real enchilada. **Maya Grill** (see page 256) is an upscale restaurant open for breakfast and dinner. **Las Ventanas** is a casual table-service eatery open all day. **Pepper Market** is an a la carte food court dressed up like a festive, outdoor market. Typical menu items include veggie frittata platter ($9.99), cheese omelet ($9.99), cheeseburger($9.99), chef's salad ($10.95), chicken quesadillas ($9.99), and kids' chicken nuggets ($6.50). An automatic 10% gratuity is added. **Siesta's** is the poolside bar serving sandwiches, nachos, fries, and various drinks. The **Rix Lounge** is a 300-seat lounge with music, appetizers, and specialty drinks. **Limited room service** is offered in the mornings and evenings. Refillable mugs ($8.99–$17.99) are available at the Pepper Market.

①2445 © Darren Mosher

Coronado Springs at dusk

75+ more photos at http://www.passporter.com/photos

PLAYING & RELAXING

For Athletes: La Vida Health Club has exercise equipment, whirlpool, and massage treatments. Boats, bikes, surreys, and fishing poles can be rented at La Marina, and there is a volleyball court. Enjoy a nature trail and a walk/jog around the lagoon.
For Charmers: Casa de Belleza offers beauty and hair treatments.
For Children: The Explorer's Playground is near the main pool.
For Gamers: Video games of all sorts are found at the Iguana Arcade near the main pool (note that the Jumping Bean Arcade closed).
For Shoppers: Panchito's has sundries, character items, and gifts.
For Swimmers: A leisure pool in each of the three districts, plus the Dig Site main pool, which is built around an ancient pyramid and features a water slide, spa (hot tub), and kids' pool.

GETTING ABOUT

Transportation to the theme parks is by frequent, direct **buses** (see chart below for in-transit times). There are four bus stops (see map on page 64). For other destinations, transfer at a nearby theme park (daytime) or at Disney Springs (evening). A sidewalk connects the resort to Blizzard Beach, and it's a quick drive to both Disney's Hollywood Studios and Disney's Animal Kingdom.

Magic Kingdom	Epcot	Disney's Hollywood Studios	Disney's Animal Kingdom	Downtown Disney
direct bus ~15 min.	direct bus ~15 min.	direct bus ~15 min.	direct bus ~10 min.	direct bus ~25 min.

Approximate time you will spend in transit from resort to destination during normal operation.

Making the Most of Disney's Coronado Springs Resort

TIPS

The **Dig Site** is really a miniature water park with delightful scenery and fun water attractions. The pool itself is huge (10,800 sq. ft.), and there's a large sandbox that masquerades as the "dig site" of the Mayan pyramid. The 123-foot-long water slide has a jaguar atop it that spits water. Oh, and they have the largest outdoor spa (hot tub) of any Disney resort—it fits 22 people!

Roll-away beds are available for $15/day (but rooms are still limited to four guests). Request a roll-away bed with your reservation and again at check-in.

NOTES

The **Pepper Market** food court works a bit differently. Upon arrival, you are seated by a cast member and given a ticket. You then visit the various food stations, and when you find an item you want, your ticket is stamped. Drinks are refilled for you. You pay after your meal. A 10% gratuity is added (unless you get your food to go).

This resort goes for the sun-drenched effect and, in the process, seems to **lack enough shade** to protect you from the scorching Florida sun. Use caution if you are fair-skinned (as Jennifer is) or if you are going during the summer months.

Coronado Springs strikes us as a bit more **buttoned-down** than the other moderate resorts, no doubt due to the conference center and business facilities. While we have no major complaints, it also didn't delight us in the same way that other moderate Disney resorts have. On the other hand, some of our fellow vacationers are very impressed with the resort, especially its quality service. We definitely feel this is a great resort for business travelers.

Check-in time is 3:00 pm. Check-out time is 11:00 am.

RATINGS

Ratings are explained on page 28.

Our Value Ratings:		Our Magic Ratings:		Readers' Ratings:
Quality:	7/10	Theme:	8/10	35% fell in love with it
Accessibility:	6/10	Amenities:	5/10	47% liked it well enough
Affordability:	8/10	Fun Factor:	4/10	15% had mixed feelings
Overall Value:	**7/10**	**Overall Magic:**	**6/10**	3% were disappointed

Coronado Springs is enjoyed by...	(rated by both authors and readers)	
Younger Kids: ♥♥♥♥	Young Adults: ♥♥♥♥♥	Families: ♥♥♥♥
Older Kids: ♥♥♥♥	Mid Adults: ♥♥♥♥	Couples: ♥♥♥♥♥
Teenagers: ♥♥♥♥	Mature Adults: ♥♥♥	Singles: ♥♥♥

Top Photo Slice: Cactus at in the Ranchos at Disney's Coronado Springs Resort (①1317) © Denise Preskitt

Planning | Getting There | Staying in Style | Touring | Feasting | Making Magic | Index | Notes & More

Finding Your Place at Disney's Coronado Springs Resort

CORONADO SPRINGS RESORT MAP

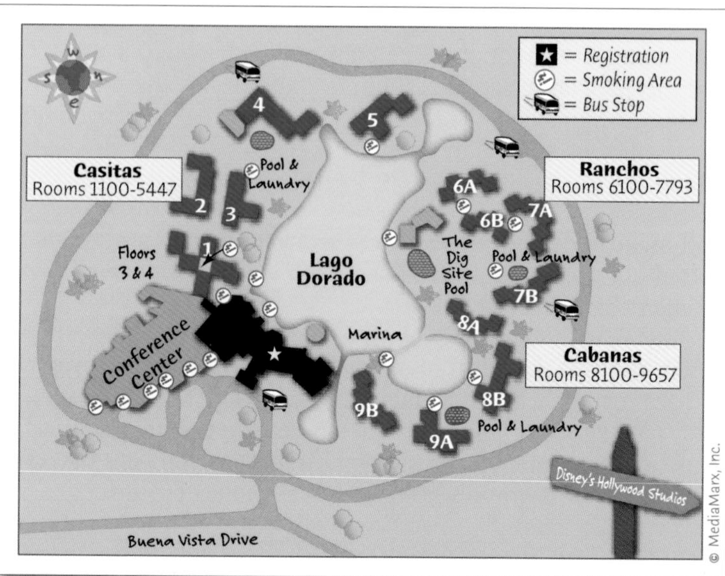

BEST LOCATIONS

The **Casitas** are the least interesting visually, but they are convenient to the Convention Center—in fact, they house the only rooms that you can reach from El Centro without leaving the protection of a roof or overhang. Building 1 is the closest to the Conference Center. The charming **Ranchos** are closest to the main pool and farthest from El Centro. We recommend building 6B for its view and proximity to the leisure pool. The **Cabanas** are convenient to El Centro. We loved our room in building 8B (close to pools and the bus); building 8A has good views, and 9B is next door to El Centro.

RATES

2016 Sample Room Rates

Seasons are noted on page 14.

Room Type	Value	Fall	Regular	Summer	Peak	Holiday
Standard Room	$188–$205	$204–$226	$217–$245	$226	$243–$266	$290
Preferred, Water, or King	$197–$219	$232–$249	$276–$313	$281	$298–$322	$326
Junior Suite (double beds)	$449–$504	$480–$515	$505–$579	$477	$515–$555	$704
One-Bedroom Suite	$809–$864	$840–$876	$865–$939	$800	$846–$901	$1078

12.5% tax is included in above rates. Higher rates in price ranges are for weekends and holiday periods (see page 31).

INFO

Disney's Coronado Springs Resort

1000 W. Buena Vista Drive, Lake Buena Vista, FL 32830

Phone: 407-939-1000 Fax: 407-939-1001

For reservations, call Central Reservations: 407-939-6244

More at coronado-springs

Looking for the Dolphin Resort? See page 105.

Disney's Fort Wilderness Resort & Campground

Much more than tents and hookups, Fort Wilderness is a resort in every sense of the word. It is pleasantly situated in a shady forest on Bay Lake, connected by a scenic waterway to the nearby Magic Kingdom theme park (use the blue tab at the top of the page for parks and eateries in the vicinity).

AMBIENCE

Enveloped by pine, cypress, and oak, this 700-acre campground is a **relaxing haven** after the noise and excitement of a long day at the parks. Rough-hewn log common buildings are nestled among towering pine trees and flowering meadows. Wilderness this is not, however. There are enough daily conveniences and services that the tents may be the only reminder that you are camping.

RESORT LAYOUT & ROOMS

All types of camping are available—tent, pop-up, trailer, and motor home (RV)—throughout the 788 **campsites**. Located on small loop roads connecting to larger thoroughfares, each site is relatively secluded by trees and shrubs and offers its own paved driveway, Coquina rock bed, charcoal grill, picnic table, and 110V/220V electrical service. Of the three types of campsites, non-preferred, partial-hookup sites supply water, but are farthest from services, preferred sites are closer and have water, sewer, and free Internet access, and some provide cable TV as well, and premium sites offer larger pads for big RVs along with all other amenities. Each site fits up to ten people and one car; pets are welcome at certain sites. All sites are close to clean, air-conditioned Comfort Stations with restrooms, private showers, phones, ice machines (extra fee), and laundry facilities. For guests without a tent or trailer, you can rent an RV from http://www.floridacamperrental.com (as we did) or book one of the 407 **Wilderness Cabins** are roomy, air-conditioned "log cabins" (504 sq. ft.) that hold up to six guests plus a child under 3 in a crib. Each cabin has a living room, bedroom, a full kitchen, and bathroom. Charmingly rustic yet comfortable, each cabin comes with pots and utensils, plus a coffeemaker, stove, microwave, refrigerator, dishwasher, cable TV, DVD player, free high-speed Internet, phone, hair dryer, and safe. The living room has a pull-down double bed. The bedroom has a separate vanity, TV, a double bed, and bunk beds. Outside is a charcoal grill, picnic table, and deck. All guests at cabins must be accommodated within them; no tents are permitted outside the cabin.

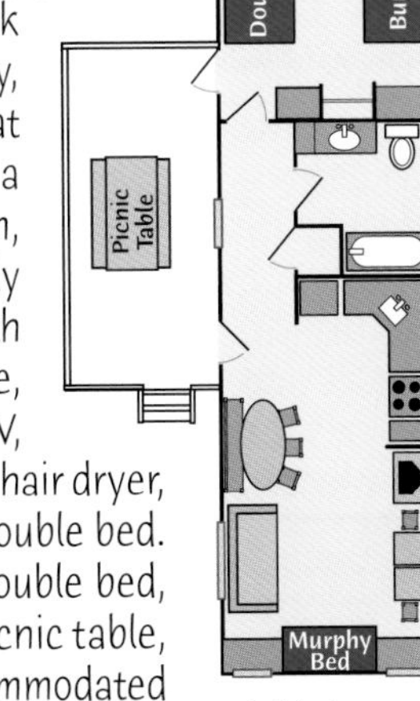

Cabin Layout

Top Photo Slice: Spanish moss and a covered wagon at Fort Wilderness Resort & Campground (14549) © Cheryl Pendry

Using the Amenities at Disney's Fort Wilderness Resort

DINING

Many guests cook at their sites or cabins. **The Chuck Wagon** is open during the nightly campfire and serves snacks, such as a hot dog ($4.79) and a s'more kit ($8.99). **Hoop-Dee-Doo Musical Revue** and **Mickey's Backyard BBQ** are dinner shows (see page 264). **Trail's End Restaurant** serves breakfast, lunch, and dinner (page 256). **Crockett's Tavern** serves drinks and snacks.

© MediaMarx, Inc.

A Fort Wilderness Cabin

PLAYING & RELAXING

For Athletes: You'll find two lighted tennis courts, plus volleyball, tetherball, basketball, and horseshoes. Rent a boat at the marina or a canoe or bike at the Bike Barn. Horseback rides ($42) at the livery (must be 9+ years, 48"+). Nature walks, too!
For Children: Pony rides ($5) and a nearby playground delight kids. Free nightly campfires with Chip and Dale and Disney movies, or go on a "hay ride" ($8/adult and $5/kids 3–9).
For Dogs: Enjoy the fenced, leash-free dog park near loop 300.
For Fishers: Try a bass fishing excursion in Bay Lake for $200–$230.
For Gamers: Two video arcades are within the resort.
For Romantics: Enjoy a relaxing, private carriage ride for $45.
For Shoppers: Gifts, sundries, and groceries at two trading posts.
For Show-Goers: Two dinner shows! See page 264 for details.
For Swimmers: The main Meadows pool has a slide, spa (hot tub), and children's play areas. The Wilderness Cabins have another pool. Beach is for sunbathing only. Child-size life vests are at the pools.
For Tours: A back trail Segway tour is offered here—see page 273.

GETTING ABOUT

Boats (see chart below) go to Magic Kingdom, Wilderness Lodge, and Contemporary. **Buses** to Disney's Hollywood Studios and Wilderness Lodge pick up/drop off at Settlement Depot. Buses for Epcot, Animal Kingdom/Blizzard Beach, and Disney Springs/Typhoon Lagoon pick up/drop off at Outpost Depot. Three bus routes—Yellow, Orange, and Purple—serve locations within the resort and all stop at Settlement Depot and Outpost Depot. For resorts, transfer at Magic Kingdom or Disney Springs. You can rent an **electric golf cart** to move about the resort easier.

Magic Kingdom	Epcot	Disney's Hollywood Studios	Disney's Animal Kingdom	Downtown Disney
boat ~15 min.	direct bus ~25 min.	direct bus ~30 min.	direct bus ~30 min.	direct bus ~35 min.

Approximate time you will spend in transit from resort to destination during normal operation.

More at ⓘ horseback-rides

Top Photo Slice: Marina and beach at Disney's Fort Wilderness Resort (ⓘ4631) © Amy Sellars

Making the Most of Disney's Fort Wilderness Resort

TIPS

Electric golf carts are very popular for moving about the resort but are hard to get. To reserve one up to a year in advance, call the Bike Barn at 407-824-2742. Rates are $59 + tax per 24-hour period.

The **Electrical Water Pageant**, a light and music barge parade on Bay Lake, can be seen from the beach at around 9:45 pm.

Fort Wilderness offers **many special features** not found at other resorts, including the nightly campfire and movie (see previous page), trail rides, and more. See page 215 for details.

Seasonal, weekly, and monthly **discounts** may exist for campsites.

NOTES

A **car** may come in handy at this resort, and there is 15-minute parking available at the Meadows Trading Post. Disney transportation to and from Fort Wilderness requires a transfer from internal to external transport, making it more time-consuming than most resorts. To reduce transit time, request a site in loops 100–800, as these are within walking distance of Settlement Depot and the marina.

Bring your **groceries**, or buy them at Winn-Dixie about a mile north of Disney Springs. You can pick up some items from the trading posts.

Pets are allowed for $5/day in loops 300–900, and 1600–1900 (request at booking). No pets in pop-ups or tents. Dogs may also visit the fenced-in Waggin' Trails Dog Park near loop 300.

Creekside Meadow offers rustic **group camping** with a Comfort Station, grills, and fire pits. Six-person tents and cots can be rented.

Campfires are not allowed at individual campsites.

Check-in time is 1:00 pm (campsites) or 3:00 pm (cabins). Check-out time for all is 11:00 am.

RATINGS

Note: The two Affordability Ratings below correspond to lodging and camping.

Ratings are explained on page 28.

Our Value Ratings:		Our Magic Ratings:		Readers' Ratings:
Quality:	7/10	Theme:	6/10	80% fell in love with it
Accessibility:	4/10	Amenities:	5/10	7% liked it well enough
Affordability:	6 & 10/10	Fun Factor:	8/10	10% had mixed feelings
Overall Value:	**6 & 7/10**	**Overall Magic:**	**6/10**	3% were disappointed

Fort Wilderness is enjoyed by...	(rated by both authors and readers)	
Younger Kids: ♥♥♥♥♥	Young Adults: ♥♥♥♥	Families: ♥♥♥♥♥
Older Kids: ♥♥♥♥	Mid Adults: ♥♥♥♥	Couples: ♥♥♥
Teenagers: ♥♥♥♥	Mature Adults: ♥♥♥♥	Singles: ♥♥

Top Photo Slice: Checkboard in the Reception Outpost at Disney's Fort Wilderness Resort © MediaMarx, Inc.

Finding Your Place at Disney's Fort Wilderness Resort

FORT WILDERNESS RESORT MAP

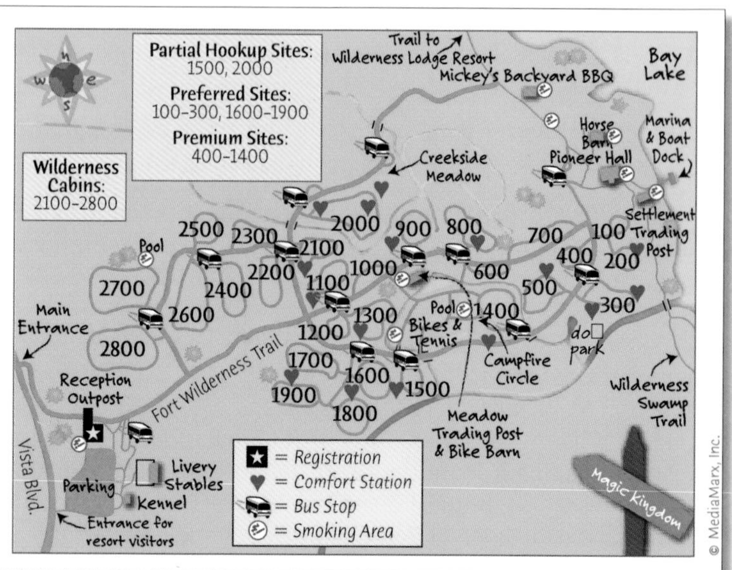

BEST SPOTS

Campsites and cabins are located on loops, circular drives with about 40 sites or cabins each. The most popular **cabins** are on loops 2500–2700 near the west pool, though we loved our cabin on loop 2100 near a bus stop. The most popular **campsites** are on loops 100 and 200. Most preferred and all premium sites are **close to Pioneer Hall** in the 100–800 and 1400 loops. **Full hookup campsites** are in loops 900–1300 and 1600–1900—we highly recommend loop 1400 (we stayed here in 2014). **Partial hookups** are located in the 1500 and 2000 loops.

RATES

2016 Sample Campsite/Cabin Rates *Seasons are noted on page 14.*

Room Type	Value	Fall/Pre-Holiday	Regular	Peak	Holiday
Partial Hookup Campsite	$56-$68	$60-$72	$84-$96	$93-$110	$120
Full Hookup Campsite	$78-$88	$84-$91	$102-$119	$133-$141	$145
Preferred Campsite	$89-$97	$90-$95	$123-$133	$145-$151	$158
Wilderness Cabin	$336-$363	$368-$394	$404-$421	$457-$482	$562

12.5% tax is included in above rates. There is an additional charge of $5/night for more than two adults in a cabin, or $2/night for more than two adults at a campsite. Higher rates in price ranges are for weekends and holiday periods (see page 31).

INFO

Disney's Fort Wilderness Resort & Campground

4510 N. Fort Wilderness Trail, Lake Buena Vista, FL 32830
Phone: 407-824-2900 Fax: 407-824-3508
For reservations, call Central Reservations: 407-939-6244

More at ⓘ camping

Top Photo Slice: A boat makes its way home across Bay Lake to the Fort Wilderness Resort © MediaMarx, Inc.

Disney's Grand Floridian Resort & Spa and Villas

The most luxurious of Disney's resorts, the Grand Floridian Resort & Spa is a breathtaking Victorian hotel with turrets and gabled roofs. It extends into the Seven Seas Lagoon between the Polynesian Village and the Magic Kingdom (use the blue tab at the top of the page for parks and eateries in the area).

AMBIENCE

From the moment you step into the **Grand Lobby**, you will feel as though you've been transported back to the 1890s and the days when the well-to-do wintered in style at grand seaside resorts. As in that unhurried time, the warm whites and marble floors draw you in, just as the towering lobby and stained glass skylights draw your eyes upward. It is the picture of charm, romance, and luxury.

RESORT LAYOUT & ROOMS

900 guest rooms are generously spread out among five **lodge** buildings and the Grand Lobby, along with 147 Disney Vacation Club villas (opened in 2013). The luxurious rooms are decorated in four different whimsical-yet-subtle themes: floral, cameo (fairies), swans (Wind in the Willows), and Alice in Wonderland. Rooms are about 400 sq. ft. and are resplendent with marble-topped double sinks and balconies or patios. Most guest rooms offer two queen-size beds and a daybed, accommodating five people. The lodge buildings also house the slightly smaller "dormer" rooms, plus suites. Amenities include signature toiletries, turndown service, mini-bar, large in-room safe, hair dryer, newspaper delivery, valet parking, 24-hour room service, free high-speed Internet—and best of all—comfy robes.

Standard Room Layout

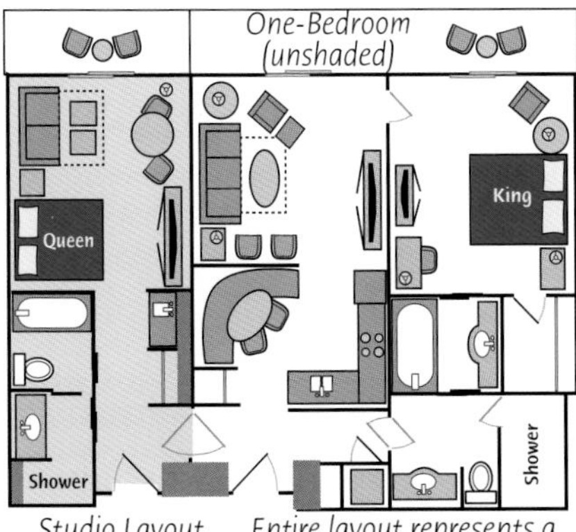

Studio Layout (shaded) *Entire layout represents a Two-Bedroom Villa*

The **Villas** are available in studio, one-bedroom, two-bedroom, and three-bedroom grand villas. All have queen or king beds, queen-size sleeper sofas, pull-down bunk-size beds, and private porches or balconies. All villas (except the studios) have Victorian-style tubs with bubble jets!

Top Photo Slice: The Grand Floridian as seen from the Magic Kingdom (ⓘ8216) © Brigett Duncan

Using the Amenities at Disney's Grand Floridian Resort & Spa

DINING & LOUNGING

Culinary delights await you in any of the restaurants and lounges, largely located on the first two floors of the Grand Lobby. Table-service restaurants, which are described on pages 256–257, include: **1900 Park Fare**, a festive character dining experience; **Cítricos**, sophisticated Floridian and Mediterranean cuisine; **Grand Floridian Cafe**, a sun-splashed cafe with traditional fare; **Garden View Lounge**, high tea in the afternoon; **Narcoossee's**, seafood with a view of Seven Seas Lagoon; and **Victoria & Albert's**, Disney's finest restaurant. Quick-service options include the **Grand Floridian Pool Bar** for snacks and **Gasparilla's Grill and Games** for light fare 24 hours a day. Typical menu items at Gasparilla's Grill include an egg croissant ($6.49), a cheeseburger ($10.99), pepperoni flatbread($9.99), and a veggie stromboli ($7.99).

PLAYING & RELAXING

For Athletes: Two clay tennis courts are available for a fee. Rent a variety of boats at the marina. You'll also find walking/jogging paths.
For Charmers: The Ivy Trellis Salon pampers you with hair and nail treatments. The Grand Floridian Senses Spa is a full-treatment spa and health club in a Victorian-themed setting.
For Children: There is no traditional playground here, but kids love the Alice in Wonderland splash playground near the Villas.
For Gamers: Gasparilla's Grill and Games has a video arcade.
For Shoppers: On the first floor, Sandy Cove stocks sundries and Summer Lace offers upscale women's clothing. On the second floor, M. Mouse Mercantile has gifts; Basin White offers upscale bath products; and Commander Porter's has men's and women's apparel.
For Swimmers: A moderately-sized leisure pool and hot tub are available, as is a themed, zero-entry pool near the beach with a slide and play fountain. Sunbathers enjoy the beach (no swimming).

GETTING ABOUT

A **monorail** goes to Magic Kingdom as well as the Contemporary, the Polynesian Village, and the Transportation and Ticket Center (TTC), where you can transfer to the Epcot monorail. **Boats** also take you to the Magic Kingdom and the Polynesian Village. For other parks (see chart below for in-transit times), use the **direct buses** in front of the resort. For other resorts, monorail to the Magic Kingdom (daytime) or bus to Disney Springs (evening) and transfer to a resort bus.

Magic Kingdom	Epcot	Disney's Hollywood Studios	Disney's Animal Kingdom	Downtown Disney
monorail/boat ~3/~10 min.	monorail x 2 ~12+10 min.	direct bus ~10 min.	direct bus ~15 min.	direct bus ~20 min.

Approximate time you will spend in transit from resort to destination during normal operation.

Top Photo Slice: Monorail entering the Grand Floridian Resort station © MediaMarx, Inc.

Making the Most of Disney's Grand Floridian Resort & Spa

TIPS

The Grand Lobby is often filled with the sound of **live music**, ranging from solo pianists to full dance bands.

New **Disney Vacation Club villas** (147 to be exact) opened in late 2013. They are located on the beach between the resort and the Wedding Pavilion. To read about our experiences in a studio villa, visit http://www.passporter.com/grand-floridian-villas.asp.

Many **children's activities** are offered, including scavenger hunts, arts and crafts, and story time (complimentary). Additional-fee activities like fishing trips, the Wonderland Tea Party, and the Pirate Cruise (see page 274) are also available.

Private dining is available for a quiet or romantic evening. You can have a meal on your balcony, on the beach, or even on a boat in the lagoon. Make arrangements in advance with room service.

NOTES

For a touch of magic, end your day with a romantic, nighttime **stroll along the beach**. You may even catch the Electrical Water Pageant on the Seven Seas Lagoon around 9:15 pm.

Four extra-special types of rooms are available. The **lodge tower** rooms have a separate sitting area, an extra TV and phone, and five windows. **Concierge** rooms offer personalized services, continental breakfast, evening refreshments, and a private elevator. Of the concierge rooms, special **turret rooms** have wet bars and windows all around, while **honeymoon suites** pamper with whirlpool tubs!

The Grand Floridian Resort & Spa also has a **conference center**.

Check-in time is 3:00 pm. Check-out time is 11:00 am.

RATINGS

Ratings are explained on page 28.

Our Value Ratings:		Our Magic Ratings:		Readers' Ratings:
Quality:	10/10	Theme:	8/10	80% fell in love with it
Accessibility:	8/10	Amenities:	9/10	4% liked it well enough
Affordability:	2/10	Fun Factor:	6/10	11% had mixed feelings
Overall Value:	**7/10**	**Overall Magic:**	**8/10**	5% were disappointed

Grand Floridian is enjoyed by...	(rated by both authors and readers)	
Younger Kids: ♥♥♥♥	Young Adults: ♥♥♥♥	Families: ♥♥♥
Older Kids: ♥♥♥♥	Mid Adults: ♥♥♥♥♥	Couples: ♥♥♥♥♥
Teenagers: ♥♥♥	Mature Adults: ♥♥♥♥♥	Singles: ♥♥♥

Top Photo Slice: Inlaid marble floor at the Grand Floridian Resort (ⓘ24373) © oldmom

Finding Your Place at Disney's Grand Floridian Resort & Spa

GRAND FLORIDIAN RESORT MAP

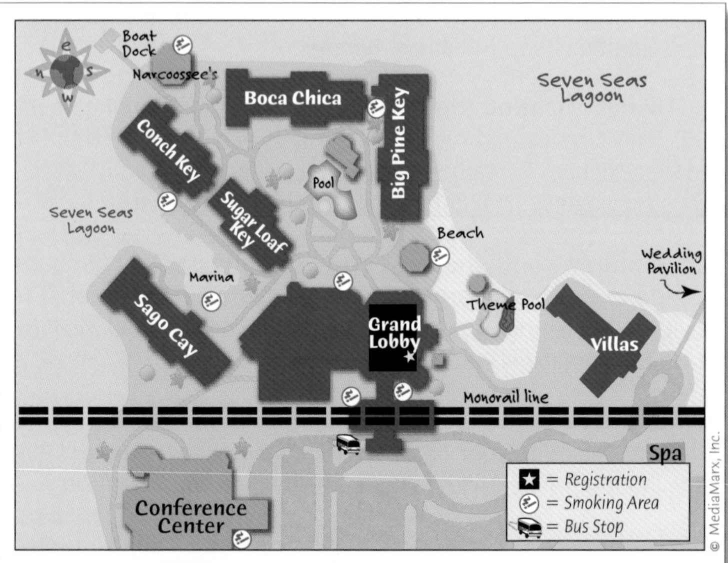

BEST SPOTS

The **dormer rooms** on the top floors of the lodge buildings may be a bit smaller (they only fit 4 rather than 5), but they feature vaulted ceilings, a secluded balcony, and a charming window above the French doors. The **best views of Cinderella Castle** come in the theme park-view rooms in Sago Cay and Conch Key lodges. Sugar Loaf Key is the closest lodge house to the Grand Lobby, but it also sees the most traffic and hears the most noise. Big Pine Key is near the beach, and its lagoon-view rooms offer picturesque vistas.

RATES

2016 Sample Room Rates

Seasons are noted on page 14.

Room Type	Value	Fall	Regular	Peak	Holiday
Garden View	$582-$624	$602-$675	$642-$675	$714-$783	$856
Lagoon View	$618-$663	$657-$737	$685-$741	$830-$911	$969
Magic Kingdom View	$716-$767	$758-$848	$794-$858	$961-$1,054	$1,107
Main Building Concierge	$970-$1,041	$1,033-$1,158	$1,087-$1,190	$1,295-$1,386	$1,451
Deluxe Studio (Standard View)	$570	$591	$610	$741	$890

12.5% tax is included in above room rates. Honeymoon concierge rooms start in the $1400s. Suites, which are available in one- and two-bedrooms, are upwards of $1,500. Higher rates in price ranges are for weekends and holiday periods (see page 31).

INFO

Disney's Grand Floridian Resort & Spa

4401 Floridian Way, Lake Buena Vista, FL 32830

Phone: 407-824-3000 Fax: 407-824-3186

For reservations, call Central Reservations: 407-939-6244

More at ⓘ grand-floridian | grand-floridian-villas

Disney's Old Key West Resort

Old Key West Resort caters primarily (but not exclusively) to Disney Vacation Club members. Old Key West is located roughly between Disney Springs (formerly known as Downtown Disney) and Epcot (use the blue tab at the top of the page for parks and eateries in the area).

AMBIENCE

If Disney's Grand Floridian and BoardWalk set the pace for elegant turn-of-the-century seaside resorts, this is the dressed-down, laid-back antidote. Lush vegetation and low, white **clapboard buildings** with sky-blue eaves evoke authentic Key West style, and the public areas of the resort exude small-town intimacy. The quaint waterside shop, restaurant, and bar are connected by wooden walkways, and the Conch Flats Community Hall offers homey choices like table tennis and board games. The atmosphere is lively, friendly, and not at all hectic. Accommodations are spacious, comfy, and attractive.

RESORT LAYOUT & ROOMS

Intimate is not necessarily small. Old Key West is big enough to get lost in. (We speak from experience!) The resort's 761 guest "homes" range from **studios** (390 sq. ft.) with kitchenettes that sleep 4 adults, to spacious **one-bedrooms** (942 sq. ft.) with full kitchens that sleep 5 adults, **two-bedrooms** (1,395 sq. ft.) also with full kitchens that sleep 8 adults, and the incredible three-bedroom/four-bath **Grand Villas** (2,375 sq. ft.) that sleep up to 12. All have a private patio or balcony perfect for breakfast, and all but the studios include a master suite with a large two-person whirlpool tub; a sprawling great room with full kitchen, dining area, and queen-size sleeper sofa; and washer and dryer. Villas sport views of the golf course, waterways, or woods. Amenities in all rooms include a TV, refrigerator, microwave, coffeemaker, free high-speed Internet, and voice mail. One-bedroom and larger villas boast a fully equipped kitchen, big-screen TV, DVD player, and in-room safe. These "homes" are excellent for groups who wish to stay together.

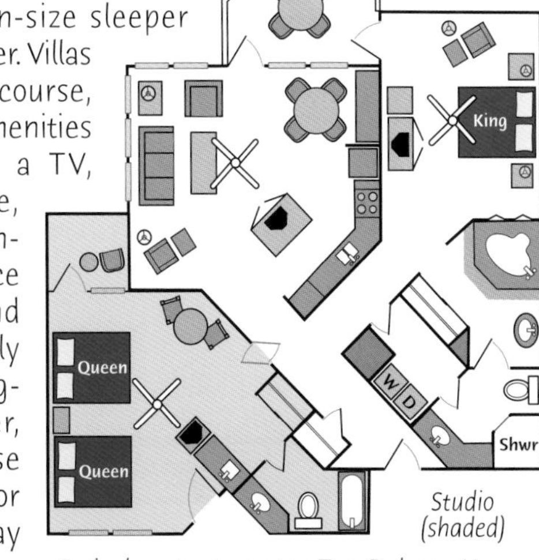

Entire layout represents a Two-Bedroom Home

Using the Amenities at Disney's Old Key West Resort

DINING & LOUNGING

Olivia's Cafe (see page 258) is a kind of casual, small-town place loved by locals. **Good's Food to Go** over by the main pool serves up breakfasts, burgers, and snacks—typical menu items include a tuna sandwich ($7.49) and a child's meal ($5.99). Refillable mugs are available for $8.99–$17.99. Also by the main pool, the **Gurgling Suitcase** has drinks and appetizers like shrimp fritters ($5.99) and crab cake ($7.59). **Turtle Shack** by the Turtle Pond Road pool offers snacks seasonally. **Pizza delivery** is also available.

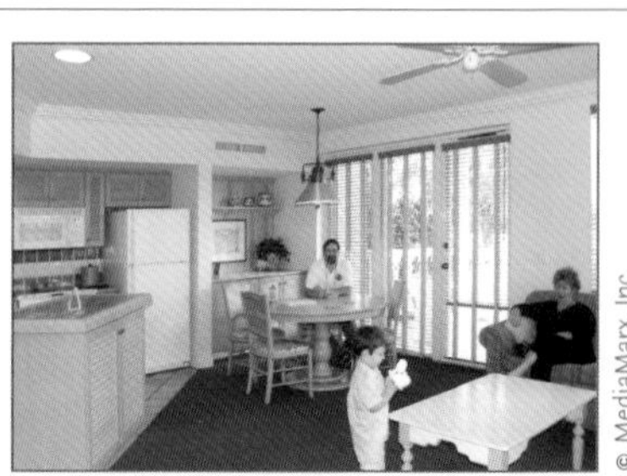
© MediaMarx, Inc.

Father, son, and grandma enjoy a one-bedroom villa at Old Key West

PLAYING & RELAXING

For Athletes: Tennis, basketball, shuffleboard, and volleyball courts are available. Rent boats and bikes at Hank's Rent 'N Return. Golf at the nearby course, or try the walking/jogging path. A health club has Nautilus equipment, plus a sauna and massages (extra fee).
For Children: The Conch Flats Community Hall offers games and organized events for kids. Playgrounds are near some of the pools.
For Gamers: The two arcades—Electric Eel Arcade and The Flying Fisherman—have plenty of video games to keep the kids happy.
For Shoppers: The Conch Flats General Store offers general and Disney merchandise, plus groceries and sundries.
For Swimmers: Three leisure pools and a large themed pool with a water slide, hot tub, sauna, and sandy play area round out the "R.E.S.T. Beach Recreation Department." A children's wading pool is near the main pool.

GETTING ABOUT

Direct **buses** to the four major parks and Disney Springs (see chart below for in-transit times) stop at the resort's five bus stops. A **boat** from the marina also travels to Saratoga Springs and the Marketplace at Disney Springs between 11:00 am and 11:00 pm—check the schedule. To get around the resort, hop on a bus, as they always stop at the Hospitality House before heading out. You can also take a (long) **walk** to Disney Springs via a footpath.

Magic Kingdom	Epcot	Disney's Hollywood Studios	Disney's Animal Kingdom	Downtown Disney
direct bus ~25 min.	direct bus ~10 min.	direct bus ~10 min.	direct bus ~15 min.	bus/boat ~5/~15 min.

Approximate time you will spend in transit from resort to destination during normal operation.

Top Photo Slice: Sandcastle water slide at Disney's Old Key West Resort © MediaMarx, Inc.

Making the Most of Disney's Old Key West Resort

TIPS

Some one-bedroom homes have a slight variation that can make a big difference if your party is large: There is a **second door to the bathroom** through the laundry room (see layout on page 73) that avoids the master bedroom. If this is important, request buildings 30 or higher at reservation and again at check-in.

Buildings 62–64 are the newest—they opened in early 2000. These are also the only buildings that have elevators.

Renovations to this resort brought a **sleeper chair** to all one-bedroom villas, bumping capacity up to five guests in those villas.

The **three-bedroom Grand Villas** are luxurious (and expensive). They are two-storied with private baths for each bedroom plus an extra bath for guests using the sleeper sofa. They have all the amenities of the other vacation homes, plus a 32" television and a stereo. They're very popular with families, so reserve as early as possible.

NOTES

Hank's Rent 'N Return offers more than just bikes and boats. You can rent videos, board games, balls, and more. There are often daily activities and games—inquire when checking in.

If you stay in a studio, you won't have a washer and dryer in your room, but there are air-conditioned **laundry rooms** available near the pools at no extra charge. You can buy soap and bleach, too.

①10601 © Casi Neveleff

Wildlife at Old Key West

Check-in time is 4:00 pm. Check-out time is 11:00 am.

RATINGS

Ratings are explained on page 28.

Our Value Ratings:		Our Magic Ratings:		Readers' Ratings:
Quality:	7/10	Theme:	7/10	85% fell in love with it
Accessibility:	5/10	Amenities:	6/10	15% liked it well enough
Affordability:	4/10	Fun Factor:	5/10	0% had mixed feelings
Overall Value:	**5/10**	**Overall Magic:**	**6/10**	0% were disappointed

Old Key West is enjoyed by...		(rated by both authors and readers)
Younger Kids: ♥♥♥	Young Adults: ♥♥♥♥	Families: ♥♥♥♥♥
Older Kids: ♥♥♥♥	Mid Adults: ♥♥♥♥♥	Couples: ♥♥♥♥♥
Teenagers: ♥♥♥♥	Mature Adults: ♥♥♥♥♥	Singles: ♥♥♥

Finding Your Place at Disney's Old Key West Resort

OLD KEY WEST RESORT MAP

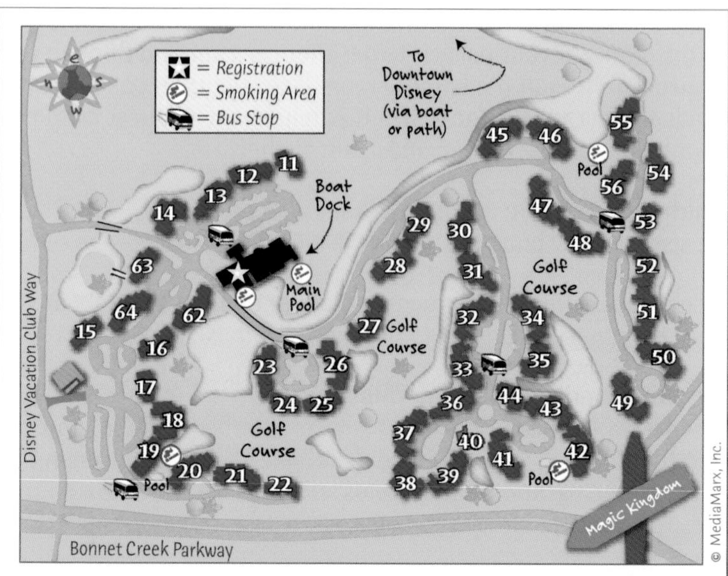

BEST LOCATIONS

Location is important in this sprawling resort. Though there are bus stops throughout the resort, we found staying near the **Hospitality House** to be a huge benefit. Buildings 11–14 and 62–64 are the closest (we loved our one-bedroom home in building 11), with buildings 15–16 and 23–26 also within reasonable walking distance. Most locations enjoy relative **peace and quiet**, but if you really want seclusion, 47–48 and 52–54 are nice as they are away from pools and roads, yet are near a bus stop. We suggest you avoid 30–44 as they feel remote, have traffic noise, and bus stops are often inconvenient.

RATES

2016 Sample Villa Rates

Seasons are noted on page 14.

Room Type	Value	Fall	Regular	Peak	Holiday
Studio Villa	$368–$386	$399	$414–$418	$485	$531
One-Bedroom Villa	$508–$520	$537	$572	$659	$748
Two-Bedroom Villa	$695–$721	$767	$835	$1,016	$1,142
Grand Villa	$1,481–$1,591	$1,641	$1,717	$1,939	$2,022

12.5% tax is not included in the above rates. Three views are available—water, golf course, and woods—but with no difference in price.

INFO

Disney's Old Key West Resort

1510 North Cove Road, Lake Buena Vista, FL 32830

Phone: 407-827-7700 Fax: 407-827-7710

For reservations, call Central Reservations: 407-939-6244

More at ⓘ old-key-west

Disney's Polynesian Village Resort

The Polynesian Village is a lush, tropical paradise that brings the romance of the South Pacific to life. It rests tranquilly on the Seven Seas Lagoon between the Transportation and Ticket Center and the Grand Floridian Resort (use the blue tab at the top of the page for parks and eateries in the area).

AMBIENCE

The blooming gardens are your first hint of the beauty and color of the **tropics**, which are captured so splendidly here at this Adventureland-themed resort. You may not even notice that you've entered the main building, the Great Ceremonial House, with its atrium filled with tropical plants. "Aloha!" is more than a word here—it is a way of life—and you will be reminded of this again and again during your visit.

RESORT LAYOUT & ROOMS

Guest rooms are arranged throughout **longhouses and bungalows** on 12 "islands" of Polynesia. The longhouses are two or three stories; the first-floor rooms have patios, third-floor rooms have balconies, but most second-floor rooms have sliding glass doors to a railing with no external balcony. The lush, laid-back feeling of the resort is carried into the recently renovated rooms with tropical blues and greens, dark, hand-carved wood furniture, and flat-screen TVs. Spacious rooms (415 sq. ft.) offer two queen beds and a daybed, accommodating five people (king beds in some rooms in Samoa, Fiji and Rarotonga). The roomy bathroom has a large mirror and toilet behind a partition. Suites and concierge-level rooms housed in the Tonga and Hawaii longhouses offer personal service and great views. New deluxe studio villas (465 sq. ft.) and two-bedroom bungalows were built in Tokelau, Moorea, Pago Pago, and Bora Bora (see page 79).

Standard Room Layout

DINING & LOUNGING

Paradise offers bounty in food, too. Two table-service restaurants (see page 258) are **Kona Cafe**, offering a filling breakfast and inventive lunch and dinner, and '**Ohana**, serving up food and fun with skewered meats. 24-hour **Captain Cook's Snack Company** is good for a quick breakfast and light meals. Typical items are waffles ($4.99) and a pork sandwich ($9.49). Refillable mugs are $8.99–$17.99. The **Pineapple Lanai** has Dole Whips ($3.99). A family-style **character breakfast** is served at 'Ohana. And let's not forget the Spirit of Aloha dinner show (page 265). **Tambu**, the lounge by 'Ohana, serves snacks and drinks, **Kona Island** serves morning coffee and evening sushi, and the poolside **Barefoot Bar** has drinks. **Trader Sam's Grog Grotto** (opened March 2015) pours Tiki Room whimsy with its drinks.

Top Photo Slice: Samoa Longhouse and the Great Ceremonial House at Disney's Polynesian Village Resort © MediaMarx, Inc.

Using the Amenities at Disney's Polynesian Village Resort

PLAYING & RELAXING

For Athletes: Boaters rent Sea Raycers and sailboats at the marina. Joggers enjoy the Walk Around the World that partially encircles the Seven Seas Lagoon, and a 1.5-mile path winds through the resort.
For Charmers: The Senses Spa is nearby (see page 215).
For Children: Lilo's Clubhouse is a childcare club (see page 285). A playground is near the main pool.
For Gamers: The arcade closed in 2014 (no word on what replaces it).
For Shoppers: On the first floor, BouTiki has Polynesian-themed gifts and clothing. The second floor houses Moana Mercantile (souvenirs and sundries) and Samoa Snacks.
For Show-Goers: Tucked in the back of the resort is Luau Cove, home to Polynesian-style dinner shows. More details on page 265.
For Swimmers: The renovated Lava Pool features a large pool, a water slide, and a zero-entry section (pool wheelchair available). There is also a new kids' water play area, a sunbathing beach, and a new hot tub.

Jennifer enjoys a spacious standard room at the Polynesian Village

GETTING ABOUT

A **monorail** shuttles you to the Magic Kingdom (see chart below for in-transit times), the Grand Floridian, and the Contemporary, as well as the Transportation and Ticket Center (TTC). A **boat** also goes to the Magic Kingdom. To reach Epcot, walk to TTC and board the monorail. To reach other parks and Disney Springs, take **direct buses** (see map on page 80 for the bus stop). To reach most resorts, take a monorail to the Magic Kingdom and transfer to a resort bus (daytime), or bus to Disney Springs and transfer to a resort bus (evening).

Magic Kingdom	Epcot	Disney's Hollywood Studios	Disney's Animal Kingdom	Downtown Disney
monorail/boat ~10/~5 min.	walk + monorail ~10+10 min.	direct bus ~15 min.	direct bus ~15 min.	direct bus ~25 min.

Approximate time you will spend in transit from resort to destination during normal operation.

Top Photo Slice: Relaxing in a hammock on the beach at Disney's Polynesian Village Resort © MediaMarx, Inc.

Making the Most of Disney's Polynesian Village Resort

TIPS

The Polynesian Village **underwent massive renovations** to its facilities, as well as adding Disney Vacation Club bungalows. The pool received a major upgrade (new hot tub!), as did the Great Ceremonial House—both completed in 2015.

The resort now has **20 unique bungalows** in Bora Bora around the shores of the resort—these are two-bedroom villas and sleep 8 guests. Each bungalow has a large deck with a plunge pool and views of the Magic Kingdom. The bungalows come at a hefty price tag, however—rates start at $2,137 per night. In addition to these bungalows, connecting studios (465 sq. ft.) were built in the Moorea, Pago Pago, and Tokelau longhouses. Note that there are no "regular" one-bedroom or two-bedroom villas at this Disney Vacation Club property.

The **Electrical Water Pageant** passes right by the Polynesian Village around 9:00 pm. If you don't have a water-view room, take a stroll down to the beach or to the end of the dock near the marina.

NOTES

Families love the Polynesian Village and it may get a bit **noisy** in the pool areas (near Samoa, Niue, Hawaii, Rarotonga, and Tokelau).

Walk to the Transportation and Ticket Center for the **Epcot monorail**. The monorail around the lagoon adds 20 minutes otherwise.

The Polynesian Village sometimes shares **bus routes** with the Contemporary and Grand Floridian resorts, picking up/dropping off guests at the Contemporary first and Grand Floridian last.

Daily activities are available for kids of all ages, such as coconut races, torch lightings, and hula lessons. Inquire at Lobby Concierge.

Check-in time is 3:00 pm. Check-out time is 11:00 am.

RATINGS

Ratings are explained on page 28.

Our Value Ratings:		Our Magic Ratings:		Readers' Ratings:
Quality:	8/10	Theme:	9/10	62% fell in love with it
Accessibility:	9/10	Amenities:	7/10	29% liked it well enough
Affordability:	3/10	Fun Factor:	8/10	7% had mixed feelings
Overall Value:	**7/10**	**Overall Magic:**	**8/10**	2% were disappointed

The Polynesian Village is enjoyed by... (rated by both authors and readers)		
Younger Kids: ♥♥♥♥	Young Adults: ♥♥♥♥♥	Families: ♥♥♥♥♥
Older Kids: ♥♥♥♥♥	Mid Adults: ♥♥♥♥♥	Couples: ♥♥♥♥♥
Teenagers: ♥♥♥♥	Mature Adults: ♥♥♥♥♥	Singles: ♥♥♥

Top Photo Slice: Drums at Disney's Polynesian Village Resort © MediaMarx, Inc.

Finding Your Place at Disney's Polynesian Village Resort

POLYNESIAN VILLAGE RESORT MAP

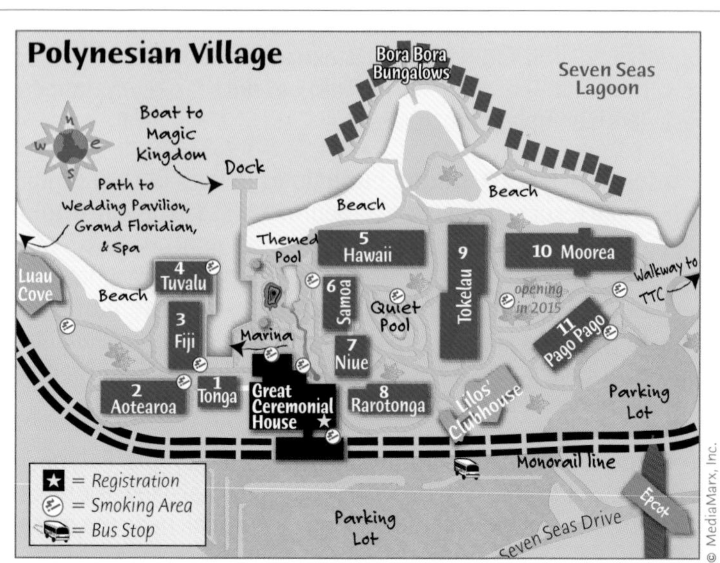

BEST LOCATIONS

All **first-floor rooms** have patios, and all **third-floor rooms** have balconies. Most **second-floor rooms** have no balconies, with the exception of Tonga, which does. Particularly nice water views can be found in Tuvalu, Hawaii, and Fiji. The first-floor rooms in Roratonga facing away from the water have pleasant, secluded patios. If you opt for a garden view, we recommend Aotearoa with beautiful landscaping and an up-close view of the monorail. For added **privacy**, request a room on the top floor. Of the new DVC areas, Bora Bora and Moorea have the best views.

RATES

2016 Sample Room Rates

Seasons are noted on page 14.

Room Type	Value	Fall	Regular	Peak	Holiday
Garden View	$508-$533	$528-$592	$600-$658	$649-$706	$793
Lagoon View	$654-$714	$693-$792	$768-$806	$870-$938	$1016
Lagoon View/Suite Concierge	$864-$925	$914-$1,027	$963-$1,042	$1,118-$1,217	$1,224
One-Bedroom Suite Concierge	$1,245-$1,334	$1,307-$1,496	$1424-$1,617	$1,601-$1,801	$1,783
Deluxe Studio (Lake View)	$529	$558	$628	$677	$804

12.5% tax is included in the above. Two-bedroom suites start in the $1800s. Higher rates in price ranges are for weekends and holiday periods (see page 31).

INFO

Disney's Polynesian Village Resort

1600 Seven Seas Drive, Lake Buena Vista, FL 32830

Phone: 407-824-2000 Fax: 407-824-3174

For reservations, call Central Reservations: 407-939-6244

More at ⓘ polynesian

Top Photo Slice: Resort entrance sign at Disney's Polynesian Village Resort © MediaMarx, Inc.

Disney's Pop Century Resort

Auld acquaintance shall be remembered at Pop Century, one of the Walt Disney World Resort's value-priced resorts. At this innovative resort, you'll find the last half of the 20th century immortalized for its contribution to popular culture—icons and references to the 1950s–1990s are everywhere. Pop Century Resort is located in the Epcot area (use the blue tab at the top of the page for parks and eateries in the vicinity) on the northeast corner of Osceola Parkway and Victory Way.

AMBIENCE

Whether you're 8 or 80, a **blast from your past** awaits at Pop Century. Pop Century sits beside a 33-acre lake with a scenic bridge that leads to Disney's Art of Animation Resort, which opened in 2012. Go from the rockin' days of sock hops "to infinity and beyond" in eye-popping style with a uniquely themed check-in lobby, food court/shop/lounge, and pool bar. Outside, giant cultural icons fill the senses, including a monumental Rubik's Cube®, a huge foosball field, and a billboard-sized laptop computer. The themes continue with three imaginative themed pools. Each guest lodge building is festooned with cultural icons and "groovy" catch phrases. This resort's plans originally called for an expansion across the lake (representing the decades of the first half of the 20th century), but that fell by the wayside when the Art of Animation Resort was announced in its place.

RESORT LAYOUT & ROOMS

The 2,880 guest rooms in Pop Century are situated in five differently themed areas encompassing a total of 10 guest lodges. **Pop Century** celebrates the decades of the 1950s, '60s, '70s, '80s, and '90s. Themed courtyards are formed between two or more of the ten T-shaped guest lodges. Each decade's theme is reflected in the guest room decor, but rich, wood-grain furniture adds elegance to the fun. Rooms have either two double beds or one king bed, a large TV with remote, a small table with two chairs, and a roomy chest of drawers. Rooms hold up to four guests plus one child under three in a crib (a folding crib is available on request). Rooms are small—about 260 sq. ft.—but as with the All-Star Resorts, furnishings allow adequate floor space. Rooms have no private balconies or patios, but each offers climate controls. Amenities include soap, housekeeping, large in-room safe, mini-refrigerator, free wireless Internet, table-side modem jack, iron and ironing board, and voice mail.

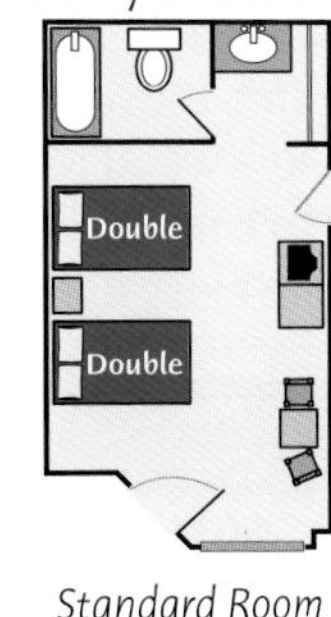

Standard Room Layout

Top Photo Slice: The '60s at Pop Century Resort (ⓘ3240) © Cheryl Pendry

Using the Amenities at Disney's Pop Century Resort

EATING & DRINKING

A standard guest room at Pop Century
400+ more photos at http://www.passporter.com/photos

Pop Century has a large **food court** with a variety of food stations. It's open daily for breakfast, lunch, and dinner. Menu items include a breakfast platter ($8.99), a create-your-own burger ($11.49), and a create-your-own salad ($11.49). Purchase a mug for $8.99–$17.99 and get refills from the beverage bar. A pizza delivery service is available in the afternoons and evenings, along with seasonal snack carts near the pool.

PLAYING & RELAXING

For Athletes: The 12' wide lakeside path is ideal for walks and jogs. The lake does not offer a marina.
For Children: A quiet playground and play fountain is located within the resort (see map on page 84 for locations).
For Gamers: An arcade is located in the resort's main building.
For Shoppers: The resort offers a large shop with Disney logo merchandise, clothing, sundries, and some snack foods.
For Swimmers: Cool off in the main pool (which also features a wading pool), and two smaller themed pools. The fun pools are shaped like a bowling pin, a flower, and a computer. There are no spas (hot tubs) at this resort.

GETTING ABOUT

Buses (see chart below for in-transit times) are outside the main building of the resort. Stops are well-marked and offer benches and shelter. Bus service is prompt and efficient. Destinations other than those below can be reached by changing buses at Disney's Hollywood Studios or Epcot (daytime) or Disney Springs (evening). Parking is freely available, though you should study the map to find the closest lot to your room.

Magic Kingdom	Epcot	Disney's Hollywood Studios	Disney's Animal Kingdom	Downtown Disney
direct bus ~25 min.	direct bus ~20 min.	direct bus ~15 min.	direct bus ~15 min.	direct bus ~20 min.

Approximate time you will spend in transit from resort to destination during normal operation.

Top Photo Slice: Kids water play fountain at Disney's Pop Century Resort © MediaMarx, Inc.

Making the Most of Disney's Pop Century Resort

TIPS

The **33-acre lake** beside this resort is an added perk for a value resort—the equivalent All-Star Resorts have no ponds, lakes, or rivers. Frequent park benches line the path, and "roadside" signs note landmark cultural events of each era.

The other side of the lake is Disney's Art of Animation Resort, which features 2000 new rooms, more than half of which are **family suites** with living rooms and bedrooms. Themes include The Lion King, Cars, Finding Nemo, and Little Mermaid. This resort opened May 2012. To learn more, see photos, read tips, and get rates, see our description on pages 45–48 and visit http://disneyworld.disney.go.com/resorts/art-of-animation-resort

Epcot's **IllumiNations** fireworks are visible across the lake. Best views are from the '50s buildings—try the fourth floor!

Food court patrons are treated to a **dance routine** performed by the resort's cast members at breakfast and dinner! They do the Twist at 8:00 am and the Hustle at 6:00 pm. Be there or be square!

A **children's pop-jet fountain** is tucked away in a corner between the '60s and '70s—look for a statue of Goofy and a red Corvette.

Plan to either **carry your own luggage** or wait a while (perhaps 45–60 minutes) for the resort's luggage service to drop it off at your building. Arrangements to pick up luggage on your departure day should be made the night before.

Coin-operated laundries are located near each pool. Bring lots of quarters—wash loads and dry cycles are $2.00 each.

Check-in time is 4:00 pm. Check-out time is 11:00 am.

NOTES

RATINGS

Ratings are explained on page 28.

Our Value Ratings:		Our Magic Ratings:		Readers' Ratings:
Quality:	6/10	Theme:	6/10	63% fell in love with it
Accessibility:	5/10	Amenities:	4/10	18% liked it well enough
Affordability:	9/10	Fun Factor:	4/10	11% had mixed feelings
Overall Value:	**7/10**	**Overall Magic:**	**5/10**	8% were disappointed

Pop Century is enjoyed by... (rated by both authors and readers)

Younger Kids: ♥♥♥♥♥	Young Adults: ♥♥♥♥	Families: ♥♥♥♥
Older Kids: ♥♥♥♥♥	Mid Adults: ♥♥♥	Couples: ♥♥
Teenagers: ♥♥♥	Mature Adults: ♥♥	Singles: ♥♥♥

Top Photo Slice: The Pop Century laundry room looks like a huge bowling shoe shelf! © MediaMarx, Inc.

Finding Your Place at Disney's Pop Century Resort

POP CENTURY RESORT MAP

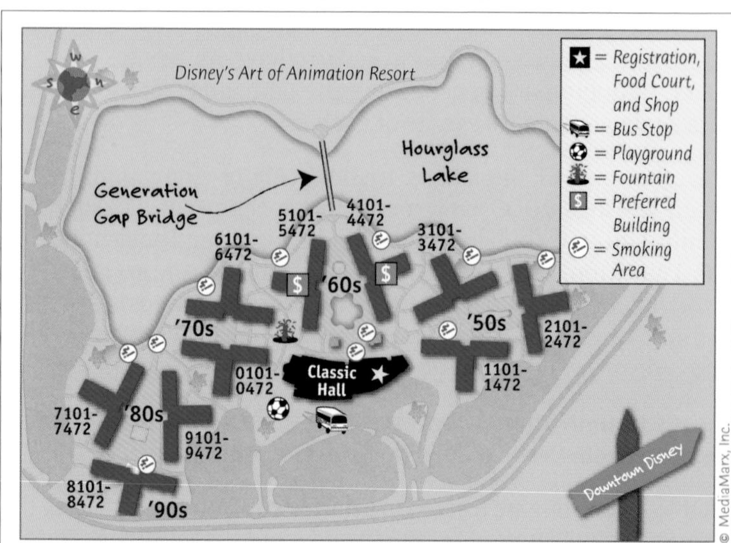

BEST LOCATIONS

Rooms at Pop Century **vary only by location** within the resorts and floor level. For convenience, we recommend the '50s, '60s, or '70s as they are closest to pools, food, and transportation. Our personal pick is the '70s as it is relatively quiet and has good views from most windows. Note that several buildings offer excellent views of Hourglass Lake, notably '50s, '60s, and '70s. If you seek quiet, request a room on the third or fourth floors. Note that rooms in the '60s are extra because they are the closest to Classic Hall, but we don't feel this resort is so spread out that you need to stay there.

RATES

2016 Sample Room Rates

Seasons are noted on page 14.

Room Type	Value	Fall	Regular	Summer	Peak	Holiday
Standard	$96–$129	$111–$134	$123–$156	$150–$179	$153–$186	$199
Preferred	$118–$145	$129–$151	$149–$177	$168–$197	$171–$205	$217

12.5% tax is included in above rates. Preferred rooms are in the guest lodges closest to the main building. There is a $10 per person charge for the third and fourth adult in a room, but no extra charge for children under 18. Rooms may face parking lots, pools, the lake, or courtyards. Higher rates in price ranges are for weekends and holiday periods (see page 31).

INFO

Disney's Pop Century Resort

1050 Century Drive, Lake Buena Vista, FL 32830

Phone: 407-938-4000 Fax: 407-938-4040

For reservations, call Central Reservations: 407-939-6244

More at ⓘ pop-century

Top Photo Slice: The '80s section at Disney's Pop Century Resort © MediaMarx, Inc.

Disney's Port Orleans Resort

In 2001, sister resorts Port Orleans and Dixie Landings merged into one resort known as Port Orleans. The large, moderately priced resort is located along the banks of the Sassagoula River, north of Disney Springs—use the blue tab at the top of the page for other places in the same vicinity. Port Orleans is popular with young couples, families, and children, both for its value and for its fun atmosphere.

AMBIENCE

The romance of the Old South awaits you at Port Orleans. The resort is divided into two separate districts: the French Quarter (the smaller district and the original Port Orleans) and Riverside (the former Dixie Landings). The **French Quarter** recaptures the feeling and flavors of historic New Orleans as it prepares for Mardi Gras. The Mint is your first stop in the French Quarter, a large building with wrought ironwork details and a soaring glass atrium that safeguards the district's front desk, Lobby Concierge, and shop. A step outside reveals narrow cobblestone lanes, complete with "gas" lamps, wrought iron benches, and grand magnolia trees. A leisurely 10-minute walk along the Sassagoula River takes you over to **Riverside**. Banjo music and southern hospitality greet you as you enter Riverside's Sassagoula Steamboat Company, a replica of an old riverboat depot. The depot is the crossroads of this quaint settlement, housing the district's front desk and services. Venture out along meandering paths and wooden bridges to antebellum mansions in one direction or the quaint bayou dwellings in the other.

RESORT LAYOUT

The resort's 3,056 guest rooms are scattered among the two districts, with 1,008 in the French Quarter and 2,048 in Riverside. Rooms in the French Quarter are housed in seven large buildings (see map on page 89), each designed to resemble **rows of townhouses** with differing architectural styles, varying rooflines, and facades bricked or painted in shades of blue, cream, or peach. Most buildings have their own yards and gardens in front, which are charmingly fenced with wrought iron. Up the Sassagoula in Riverside you'll find 1,024 rooms gracing "Gone With the Wind," plantation-style mansions in an area called **Magnolia Bend**. These three-storied, elegant buildings are situated majestically along the Sassagoula River. An equal number of rooms are housed within crackerbox-style dwellings in the **Alligator Bayou** section. These two-storied, rough-hewn, elevator-less dwellings peek through the trees, with quaint paths winding through the "bayous." Alligator Bayou has a more intimate feel to it than its neighbor, Magnolia Bend.

Top Photo Slice: Riverside Mill at Disney's Port Orleans Riverside Resort (①4166) © Michelle Clark

Lodging and Dining at Disney's Port Orleans Resort

RESORT ROOMS

Rooms are 314 sq. ft. in size and **decorated in three styles**. In the French Quarter, you find faux French Provincial furniture, gilt-framed mirrors, and Venetian blinds. Over in Riverside's Magnolia Bend, antebellum rooms delight with cherry furniture and brocade settees. Riverside's Alligator Bayou rooms sport beds made of hewn "logs" and patchwork quilts. All rooms accommodate up to four and come with either two queen beds or one king bed (king bed rooms are located on building corners); 963 Alligator Bayou rooms house up to five guests by offering a complimentary trundle bed in rooms with queen beds (trundle beds slide out from under the queen bed and fit a child or small adult). Rooms include a TV, armoire, table and chairs, ceiling fan, and a separate vanity area with double pedestal sinks and privacy curtain. Every room has a window (corner rooms have two), but none have private balconies. Amenities include toiletries (soap and shampoo only), hair dryers, coffeemakers, housekeeping, limited room service, in-room safe (most rooms), refrigerator, and voice mail.

ⓘ21728 © Charity Boughner
A standard guest room at Port Orleans Riverside
300+ more photos at http://www.passporter.com/photos

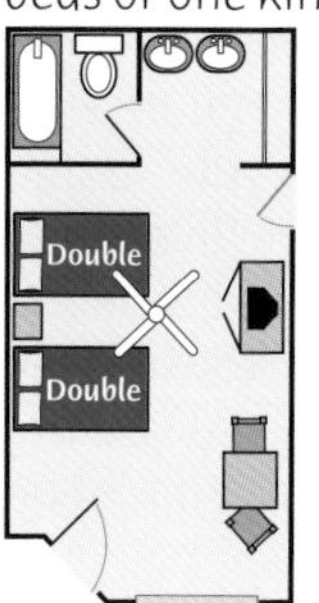

Standard Room Layout

DINING & LOUNGING

Port Orleans plays host to one of the more popular resort eateries: **Boatwright's Dining Hall**. This table-service restaurant in the Riverside district offers dinner only—see page 258. Two large food courts—**Sassagoula Floatworks and Food Factory** in the French Quarter and the **Riverside Mill** at Riverside—offer breakfast, lunch, and dinner. Typical menu items are beignets ($2.99), French toast with eggs ($5.19), cheesecake ($3.89), grilled chicken sandwich ($8.59), pasta with meatballs ($8.09), and kids' chicken nuggets ($4.99). Purchase a mug for $8.99–$17.99 and get refills. The French Quarter's **Scat Cat's Club** is a full-service bar with live music on the weekends, while **Mardi Grogs** pool bar has drinks and snacks. In Riverside, the **River Roost** offers specialty drinks, appetizers, and music in the evenings, and **Muddy Rivers Pool Bar** has drinks and snacks. Limited room service.

Top Photo Slice: Sassagoula Floatworks and Food Factory sign at Port Orleans French Quarter (ⓘ3324) © Lynn Mirante

Using the Amenities at Disney's Port Orleans Resort

PLAYING & RELAXING

For Athletes: The Dixie Levee marina in Riverside rents pedal boats, rowboats, canopy boats, and bikes (including surrey bikes). Be sure to check the rental hours early on to avoid disappointment later. Both districts offer plenty of paths for walkers and joggers, too.
For Fishers: An old-fashioned fishin' hole on Ol' Man Island in Riverside lets you hang a cane pole over a pond stocked with catfish, perch, bass, and bluegill (catch and release only). For more adventure, you can book a fishing excursion down the Sassagoula.
For Children: Two playgrounds are near the two themed pools.
For Gamers: South Quarter Games (French Quarter) has plenty of video games, as does the Medicine Show Arcade (Riverside).
For Romantics: Enjoy a relaxing, private carriage ride for $35.
For Shoppers: Jackson Square Gifts & Desires (French Quarter) and Fulton's (Riverside) stock sundries, souvenirs, and snacks.
For Swimmers: The French Quarter's Doubloon Lagoon is a moderately sized themed pool with a huge dragon housing the water slide (you slide right down its tongue). A Mardi Gras band of crocodiles shoots water at unsuspecting swimmers. The French Quarter also has a wading pool for the young ones and a hot tub (spa) nearby. In Riverside, Ol' Man Island offers a particularly nice "swimmin' hole" with a large free-form pool, complete with a water slide, a waterfall cascading from a broken sluice, and a fun geyser. A hot tub and kids' wading area are also here. Riverside also has five quieter pools spread throughout the resort.

GETTING ABOUT

Direct **buses** to the major theme parks and Disney Springs stop regularly (see chart below for in-transit times). Buses usually pick up guests at French Quarter's single bus stop first, then go on to the four stops in Riverside. To get to other resorts and destinations, take a bus to Epcot (daytime) or to Disney Springs (evening), and transfer to the appropriate bus. A **boat** also picks up guests from Riverside and the French Quarter and goes to and from Disney Springs Marketplace until 11:00 pm (weather permitting). Boats run about once an hour until 4:00 pm and every 15 minutes thereafter. A **shuttle boat** also operates between the French Quarter and Riverside on a frequent basis, especially at meal times. Parking throughout the resorts.

Magic Kingdom	Epcot	Disney's Hollywood Studios	Disney's Animal Kingdom	Downtown Disney
direct bus ~10 min.	direct bus ~10 min.	direct bus ~15 min.	direct bus ~15 min.	direct bus/boat ~15/~20 min.

Approximate time you will spend in transit from resort to destination during normal operation.

Top Photo Slice: Rose-covered archways leading to Magnolia Bend at Port Orleans Riverside (①4163) © Michelle Clark

Making the Most of Disney's Port Orleans Resort

TIPS

The two **spas** (hot tubs) near the themed pools are heavenly after a long day at the parks. The spa in the French Quarter is a bit of a walk from the pool and quite secluded (look near the laundry), but large enough for several people to soak comfortably (and sociably).

Explore the **resort's grounds** for the quaint parks and gardens scattered throughout. The French Quarter's street and park names are a treat unto themselves, with names like Mud du Lac Lane and Beaux Regards Square. An evening stroll in the French Quarter when the "gas" lamps are lit is particularly magical.

Enjoy an **evening carriage ride** through the two sister resorts. Carriages depart from in front of Boatwright's in Riverside between 6:00 pm and 9:00 pm. Cost is $35 for a 25-minute ride for up to four adults or two adults and two to three children.

Small **refrigerators** are included in your room. Roll-away/trundle beds are also free of charge—request these at reservation time.

NOTES

The **beds** are pretty high off the floor. Watch young ones so they don't fall out, or request complimentary bed rails from housekeeping. If you are concerned, note that some rooms in Alligator Bayou at Riverside come with a pullout trundle bed, which you can request upon reservation and check-in. In fact, this trundle bed allows for a fifth person, making Port Orleans Riverside the only moderately priced resort to accommodate five people. Do note that the trundle is small and is really intended for a child or very short person.

Due to the resort merger, Port Orleans has **two front desks**, one in each district. Refer to your reservation to know whether to check-in at French Quarter or Riverside.

Check-in time is 3:00 pm. Check-out time is 11:00 am.

RATINGS

Ratings are explained on page 28.

Our Value Ratings:		Our Magic Ratings:		Readers' Ratings:
Quality:	7/10	Theme:	8/10	65% fell in love with it
Accessibility:	7/10	Amenities:	6/10	22% liked it well enough
Affordability:	8/10	Fun Factor:	6/10	4% had mixed feelings
Overall Value:	**7/10**	**Overall Magic:**	**7/10**	9% were disappointed

Port Orleans is enjoyed by...	(rated by both authors and readers)	
Younger Kids: ♥♥♥	Young Adults: ♥♥♥♥♥	Families: ♥♥♥♥
Older Kids: ♥♥♥♥♥	Mid Adults: ♥♥♥♥	Couples: ♥♥♥♥♥
Teenagers: ♥♥♥	Mature Adults: ♥♥♥	Singles: ♥♥♥

Top Photo Slice: A horse and carriage passes a fountain at Disney's Port Orleans French Quarter Resort © MediaMarx, Inc.

Finding Your Place at Disney's Port Orleans Resort

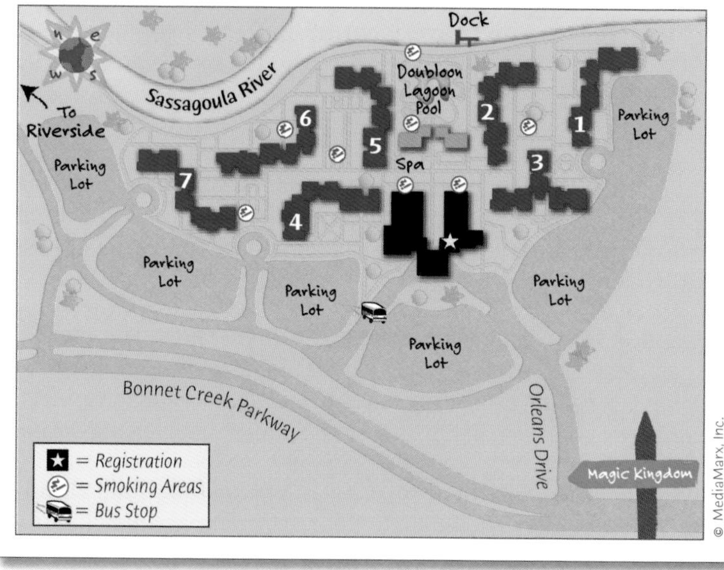

FRENCH QUARTER MAP

The French Quarter has a more compact, orderly layout.

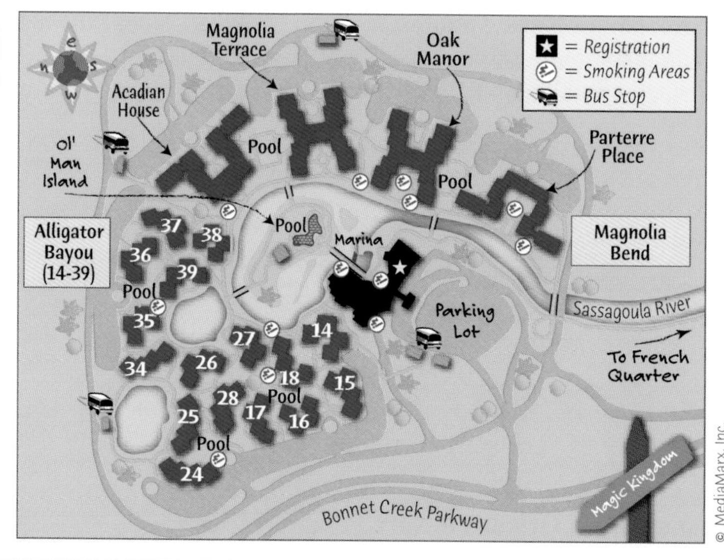

RIVERSIDE MAP

Riverside is large and meandering, with an island in the middle.

Top Photo Slice: A "gas lamp" in the evening at Disney's Port Orleans French Quarter Resort © MediaMarx, Inc.

Choosing Your Room at Disney's Port Orleans Resort

BEST LOCATIONS

Thanks to the merger of the two resorts, Port Orleans is exceptionally large and sprawling and **room location** can really make a difference in your resort experience. Each of Port Orleans' three distinctive sections is beloved by its fans. There's no right or wrong section. Request the style that suits you best.

Most rooms in the **French Quarter** are within easy distance of Lobby Concierge, the gift shop, and the food court. Buildings 2–5 are the nearest. The best views are of the Sassagoula River, as the opposite river bank is pristine—consider upgrading to a river view.

Riverside's Magnolia Bend features 512 **Royal Guest rooms** which let you "stay where royalty has stayed" featuring rooms with regal touches left behind by beloved Disney characters. Highlights include ornate beds with special optic effects, banners, and custom drapes.

The grand "mansions" and formal gardens of **Magnolia Bend** in Riverside add a luxurious air to your stay. The Magnolia Terrace building is a good pick for proximity to recreation and dining.

Our personal favorite is **Alligator Bayou** in Riverside. The buildings in Alligator Bayou are smaller (only two stories) and have lush landscaping. We often request building 14, which is near the main building, Ol' Man Island, a leisure pool, and a bus stop—it has no bad views. Buildings 15 and 18 are also good choices.

For a **quieter** room, request a room not on the ground floor. Corner rooms are particularly nice as they provide two windows.

RATES

2016 Sample Room Rates

Seasons are noted on page 14.

Room Type	Value	Fall	Regular	Summer	Peak	Holiday
Standard Room	$182–$201	$204–$226	$212–$245	$220	$237–$260	$285
Preferred, Water, or King	$210–$227	$226–$243	$242–$270	$251	$268–$290	$318
Royal Guest Room	$244–$252	$254–$279	$278–$309	$298	$292–$305	$336

12.5% tax is included in above rates. River-view rooms are more than a water-/pool-view room and are about the same price as a Royal Guest Room. Higher rates in price ranges are for weekends and holiday periods (see page 31).

INFO

Disney's Port Orleans Resort

2201 Orleans Dr. and 1251 Dixie Dr., Lake Buena Vista, FL 32830
Phone: 407-934-5000 (French Quarter) or 934-6000 (Riverside)
Fax: 407-934-5353 (French Quarter) or 934-5777 (Riverside)

More at ⓘ port-orleans

Top Photo Slice: Bedspread in Magnolia Bend at Disney's Port Orleans Riverside Resort (ⓘ10778) © Leanna Metteer

Disney's Saratoga Springs Resort & Spa

The largest of Disney's Deluxe Villa Resorts is just across the lake from Disney Springs. Opened in May 2004 and completed in 2009, Disney's Saratoga Springs Resort and Spa offers deluxe villas for Disney Vacation Club members and nightly rentals for everyone.

AMBIENCE

Saratoga Springs stretches out over 65 acres adjacent to the Lake Buena Vista Golf Course and across Village Lake from Disney Springs. This **Victorian-styled resort** is modeled on the historic vacation escape in Upstate New York. The fashionable elite of New York City journeyed up the Hudson on Commodore Vanderbilt's railroad to sip the health spa's waters, stroll its shady byways, and cheer their race horses to victory. Disney's architects soaked up the town's Arts and Crafts atmosphere to bring its essence to Walt Disney World. Saratoga Spring's 18 lodges cluster around the resort's lakes in six districts. Of those, Congress Park, The Springs, The Paddock, The Carousel, and The Grandstand represent the resort's theme of history, health, and horses. The new Treehouse Villas weigh in as the sixth district. The Carriage House check-in and hospitality building also offers dining and shopping.

RESORT LAYOUT & ROOMS

Studio villas (355 sq. ft.) accommodate up to four guests with one queen bed, a sofa bed, sink, microwave, and a small refrigerator. The one-bedroom (714 sq. ft.) and two-bedroom (1,075 sq. ft.) villas hold up to 4 or 8 guests respectively and offer master suites with king beds and whirlpool tubs, DVD players, sofa beds, full kitchens, and washers/dryers. The Grand Villas (2,113 sq. ft.) sleep up to 12 on two levels and feature three bedrooms—the living room, dining room, and master suite (with its whirlpool tub) are on the first level, and on the second level are two more bedrooms with queen beds and private baths. The Treehouse Villas (1,074 sq. ft.) sleep up to 9 people in three bedrooms. All villas have a laptop-sized safe, and high-speed Internet access is available at no charge.

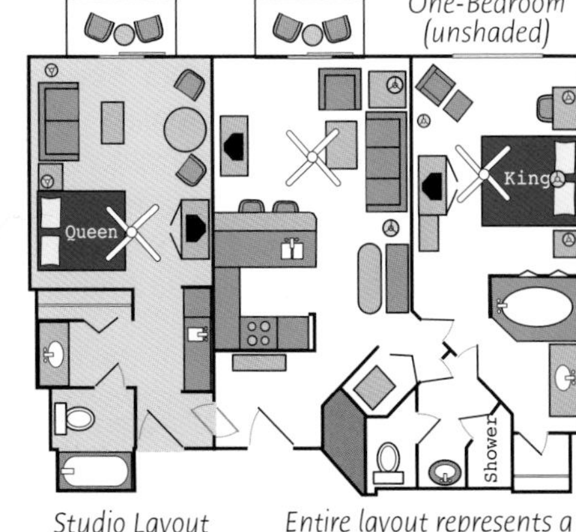

Studio Layout (shaded)

Entire layout represents a Two-Bedroom Villa

Using the Amenities at Disney's Saratoga Springs Resort

DINING & LOUNGING

Hungry? The **Turf Club Bar & Grill** is a full-service restaurant (see details on page 259). **The Artists' Palette** is an eatery and market resembling an artist's loft. Open all day, it has pizzas, salads, sandwiches, bakery items, meals, groceries, gifts, and sundries. **The Rocks** and **Backstretch** pool bars are open daily.

Allie and Jennifer relax in their one-bedroom villa at Saratoga Springs

PLAYING & RELAXING

For Athletes: Rent surrey bikes at Horsing Around Rentals. There are also two clay tennis courts, basketball, shuffleboard, jogging path, and golf at the Lake Buena Vista Golf Course.
For Charmers: Senses Spa (formerly Saratoga Springs Spa) has a fitness center and a full range of spa treatments.
For Children: Organized activities are offered at Community Hall. Children's playground. "Pop-jet" play fountains are by the main pool and The Grandstand pool. Board games are in The Turf Club.
For Gamers: Win, Place, or Show Arcade games in Community Hall.
For Romantics: Enjoy a relaxing, 25-minute carriage ride for $35.
For Shoppers: Visit The Artists' Palette for groceries and sundries.
For Swimmers: The High Rock Spring pool features a zero-entry/children's wading area, a 125-foot-long water slide, two free-form hot-tub spas, and an adjoining kids' play area. The Paddock is a 3,200 sq. ft. pool with zero entry, water slide, and play area. There are three other leisure pools with spas (hot tubs).

GETTING ABOUT

Direct buses to the four major parks, water parks, and Disney Springs (see chart below for transit times) stop at the resort's five bus stops. These buses also provide internal transportation within the resort. A **boat** from the dock near the Carriage House goes to the Marketplace at Disney Springs and Old Key West. **Walking paths** connect the resort with Disney Springs West Side (the pathway crosses the footbridge near the boat dock). Park next to each lodge building.

Magic Kingdom	Epcot	Disney's Hollywood Studios	Disney's Animal Kingdom	Downtown Disney
direct bus ~25 min.	direct bus ~10 min.	direct bus ~15 min.	direct bus ~20 min.	walk/bus/boat ~15/10/7 min.

Approximate time you will spend in transit from resort to destination during normal operation.

Making the Most of Disney's Saratoga Springs Resort

TIPS

The **Main Street Railroad Station** at Magic Kingdom was modeled on the former station in Saratoga Springs, New York. The Carriage House, theater, and other nearby buildings were originally modeled on the architecture of Upstate New York resort, Chautauqua.

Want to **relax**? Barbecue pavilions, lakeside pavilions, formal gardens, and gazebos/fountains for "taking the waters" all add to the relaxed resort atmosphere.

A **refillable mug** ($8.99–$17.99) is available for purchase at The Artists' Palette—you can refill it here and also at the pool bars.

The **Turf Club** is a full-service "bar and grill" serving creatively-prepared American favorites such as crab cakes ($13.49), a signature grilled romaine salad ($5.99), root beer brined pork chop ($22.99), prime rib ($31.49). Kids meals are $8.59. Open 5:00 to 10:00 pm.

NOTES

The **Treehouse Villas** are back! These old favorites were completely rebuilt and now feature three bedrooms (one bedroom with a queen-size bed and a whirlpool tub, another bedroom with a queen-size bed, a third bedroom with bunk beds), and a queen-size sleeper sofa and sleep chair in the living room. The Treehouse Villas also have two bathrooms, a fully-equipped kitchen, laundry, and a deck. The fun thing about the treehouses is that they are perched on pedestals, so you're sleeping on the second floor amidst all the trees! Note that these villas no longer have a downstairs bedroom as they did in their previous incarnation.

The classroom and meeting areas of the old Disney Institute are now the **main sales offices** and show-villas for Disney Vacation Club.

Check-in time is 4:00 pm. Check-out time is 11:00 am.

RATINGS

Ratings are explained on page 28.

Our Value Ratings:		Our Magic Ratings:		Readers' Ratings:
Quality:	6/10	Theme:	6/10	67% fell in love with it
Accessibility:	6/10	Amenities:	6/10	18% liked it well enough
Affordability:	6/10	Fun Factor:	5/10	10% had mixed feelings
Overall Value:	**6/10**	**Overall Magic:**	**6/10**	5% were disappointed

Saratoga Springs is enjoyed by...		(estimated by the authors)
Younger Kids: ♥♥♥♥	Young Adults: ♥♥♥♥	Families: ♥♥♥♥♥
Older Kids: ♥♥♥♥	Mid Adults: ♥♥♥♥♥	Couples: ♥♥♥
Teenagers: ♥♥♥	Mature Adults: ♥♥♥♥♥	Singles: ♥♥

Top Photo Slice: A Treehouse Villa at Disney's Saratoga Springs Resort © MediaMarx, Inc.

Choosing Your Room at Disney's Saratoga Springs Resort

SARATOGA SPRINGS RESORT MAP

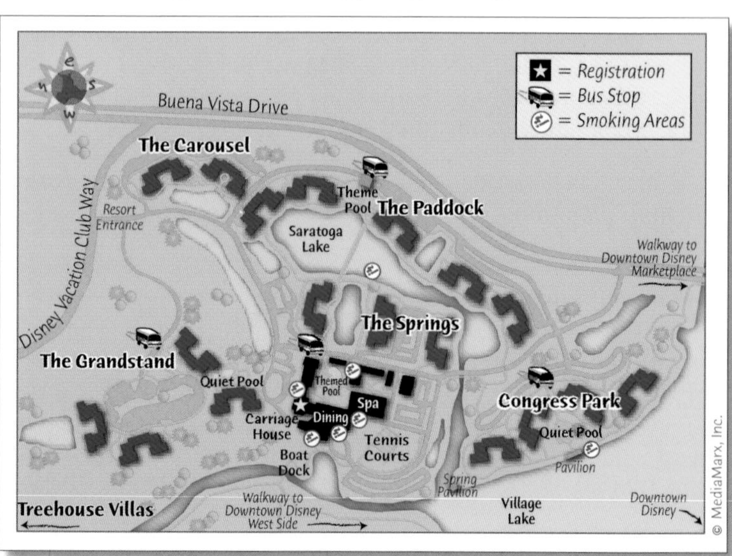

BEST LOCATIONS

Rooms in **Congress Park** have views of Disney Springs and/or gardens and offer a short walk to the Disney Springs Marketplace and a moderate walk to The Carriage House. Some garden views include parking lots. **The Springs** offers closest proximity to The Carriage House and themed pool, with views of Saratoga Lake or gardens/parking. **The Paddock** and **The Carousel** are the most spread out and distant from other facilities. Request to be close to the pool and/or footbridge if that's important. **The Grandstand** is close to the main facilities and has a superior pool area. The **Treehouse Villas** are secluded and a fair distance away from services. Requests for particular locations are honored when possible.

RATES

2016 Sample Villa Rates

Seasons are noted on page 14.

Room Type	Value	Fall	Regular	Peak	Holiday
Studio Villa	$368–$386	$399	$414	$485	$531
One-Bedroom Villa	$508–$520	$537	$572	$659	$748
Treehouse Villa	$818–$866	$920	$971	$1,210	$1,377
Three-Bedroom Grand Villa	$1,481–$1,491	$1,541	$1,636	$1,839	$1,922

12.5% tax is included in the above rates.

INFO

Disney's Saratoga Springs Resort & Spa
1960 Broadway, Lake Buena Vista, FL 32830
Phone: 407-827-1100 Fax: 407-827-1151
For reservations, call Central Reservations: 407-934-7639

More at saratoga-springs

Top Photo Slice: A gazebo at Disney's Saratoga Springs Resort © MediaMarx, Inc.

Looking for Shades of Green? Page 104. Swan Resort? Page 105.

Disney's Wilderness Lodge & Villas Resort

The Wilderness Lodge and Villas are nestled in a dense forest of pines on Bay Lake, accessible by waterway from the Magic Kingdom (use the blue tab at the top of the page for parks and eateries in the area). The Lodge and Villas were inspired by the U.S. National Park lodges built in the 1900s.

AMBIENCE

Ah, wilderness! Rustic log buildings, swaying pines, babbling brooks, and the faintest whiff of wood smoke from the crackling fireplace. The Wilderness Lodge pays homage to the **grand log lodges** of the Pacific Northwest, with its towering lobby, 55-foot totem poles, and deluxe rooms. The Villas at Wilderness Lodge offer Disney's Deluxe Villa accommodations for Disney Vacation Club members (see pages 108–109) and all other guests. Architecturally, the Villas represent an earlier era than the main Lodge building and draw influences from the lodges created by America's railroad workers.

RESORT LAYOUT & ROOMS

The Wilderness Lodge and the Villas offer varying accommodations, ranging from 340 to 1,071 sq. feet. The **Lodge** houses 728 guest rooms and suites, with some encircling the cavernous lobby but most in the two wings. The cozy Lodge rooms are outfitted with new furniture and bed spreads with Hidden Mickeys. Most Lodge rooms have two queen beds, but some offer a bunk bed in place of the second bed. The **Villas** feature 136 studios and one- and two-bedroom suites, each with a kitchenette or full kitchen, DVD player, and washer and dryer. All rooms have a balcony or patio, a small table and chairs, TV, double sinks, toiletries, in-room safe, refrigerator, turndown service (on request), newspaper delivery, voice mail, and valet parking.

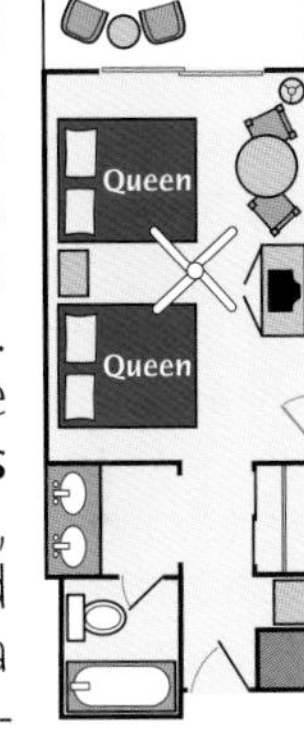

Standard Lodge Room Layout

DINING

As you would expect from a Lodge, the food here is served in hearty, healthy portions. The two table-service restaurants (see page 260) are **Artist Point** for fine dining in the evening and **Whispering Canyon Cafe** for a fun, western-style adventure serving all-you-can-eat meals throughout the day. **Roaring Fork Snack Shop** is a self-service cafe serving breakfast foods, burgers, sandwiches, and snacks—purchase a refillable mug here for $8.99–$17.99 and includes self-serve refills. Typical menu items include breakfast platter ($9.99), roast beef sandwich ($11.29), grilled chicken sandwich ($10.19), and wilderness salad ($10.79). **Miss Jenny's In-Room Dining** is available for limited room service at breakfast and dinner.

Top Photo Slice: One of the wings of the main lodge at Disney's Wilderness Lodge Resort (ⓘ4389) © Amy Sellars

Using the Amenities at Disney's Wilderness Lodge & Villas Resort

LOUNGING

Territory Lounge, a saloon adjacent to Artist Point, serves up beers, wines, spirits, and snacks. The **Trout Pass Pool Bar** offers cocktails and light snacks you can enjoy at tables overlooking the main pool and Bay Lake. Beer and wine are also available from the resort shop.

ⓘ7031 © Gina Pesca

Having fun at the Wilderness Lodge

PLAYING & RELAXING

For Athletes: Rent watercraft and bicycles at Teton Boat & Bike Rentals. A bike and jogging path extends about a mile to Fort Wilderness. A health club, Sturdy Branches, is available.
For Children: The Cub's Den is a supervised program for kids ages 4–12 (see page 285). A playground is located near the beach.
For Gamers: Buttons and Bells arcade, across from Cub's Den.
For Shoppers: The large Wilderness Lodge Mercantile in the Lodge carries clothing, sundries, foodstuffs, newspapers, and gifts.
For Swimmers: Cleverly designed to seem like part of Silver Creek, a free-form swimming pool is nestled among craggy rocks and waterfalls. A water slide and wading pool, as well as two hot tubs, are also available nearby. A leisure pool and another hot tub are located near the Villas. The white sand beach here on Bay Lake is ideal for relaxing upon, but swimming is not permitted.

GETTING ABOUT

You can take a direct **boat or bus** to the Magic Kingdom (see chart below for in-transit times). Boats also ferry you to Fort Wilderness and the Contemporary. **Buses** take you directly to Magic Kingdom, Epcot, Disney's Hollywood Studios, Disney's Animal Kingdom, Disney Springs, and the water parks. To reach other resorts, go to the Magic Kingdom (daytime) or Disney Springs (evening), and then transfer to a resort bus. Fort Wilderness and Wilderness Lodge share many of their bus routes, so travel to and from Fort Wilderness for the Hoop-Dee-Doo show (see page 264), horseback riding, etc., is quite convenient.

Magic Kingdom	Epcot	Disney's Hollywood Studios	Disney's Animal Kingdom	Downtown Disney
boat or bus ~8 or ~10 min.	direct bus ~10 min.	direct bus ~15 min.	direct bus ~15 min.	direct bus ~25 min.

Approximate time you will spend in transit from resort to destination during normal operation.

Top Photo Slice: Elevated wooden walkway at Disney's Wilderness Lodge Resort (ⓘ4394) © Amy Sellars

Making the Most of Disney's Wilderness Lodge & Villas Resort

TIPS

Disney's Wilderness Lodge will undergo multiple **renovations** through 2017. Work will begin as early as Oct. 26, 2015 on the pools, as well as the resort beach, playground, boardwalk, and recreation fire pit. Additionally, more Disney Vacation Club villas are being built, including 26 waterfront cabins.

For good rainy day activities, ask for a **kids' activity/coloring book** at the bell station or a list of **Hidden Mickeys** at Lobby Concierge. You can also get a list of the resort's music at the Mercantile shop.

Explore the resort. Indian artifacts, historic paintings, and survey maps are displayed. Follow Silver Creek from its indoor origin as a hot spring and onward outside as a bubbling brook and waterfall.

Ask about becoming a **Flag Family**. Each morning, a family is selected to go on the Lodge roof to help raise or lower the flag! This is popular, so inquire at check-in for a better chance.

Inquire about the "**Wonders of the Lodge" tour** at Lobby Concierge. The walking tour explores the architecture, landscaping, totem poles, and paintings. Offered Wednesdays–Saturdays at 9:00 am.

Watch **Fire Rock Geyser**, modeled after Old Faithful, erupt like clockwork every hour on the hour from 7:00 am to 10:00 pm. The **Electrical Water Pageant** is visible from the beach at 9:35 pm.

NOTES

Courtyard-view rooms can be **noisy** with the sounds of children and rushing water. Opt for a Lodge view if you prefer serenity.

About 37 Lodge rooms with **king beds** double as the barrier-free (handicap-accessible) rooms and have a large shower with no tub.

Check-in time is 3:00/4:00 pm. Check-out time is 11:00 am.

RATINGS

Ratings are explained on page 28.

Our Value Ratings:		Our Magic Ratings:		Readers' Ratings:
Quality:	9/10	Theme:	10/10	79% fell in love with it
Accessibility:	6/10	Amenities:	6/10	17% liked it well enough
Affordability:	6/10	Fun Factor:	8/10	3% had mixed feelings
Overall Value:	**7/10**	**Overall Magic:**	**8/10**	1% were disappointed

Wilderness Lodge is enjoyed by...	(rated by both authors and readers)	
Younger Kids: ♥♥♥♥	Young Adults: ♥♥♥♥♥	Families: ♥♥♥♥
Older Kids: ♥♥♥♥	Mid Adults: ♥♥♥♥♥	Couples: ♥♥♥♥♥
Teenagers: ♥♥♥♥	Mature Adults: ♥♥♥♥	Singles: ♥♥♥

Top Photo Slice: Overhead lamps in the lobby at Disney's Wilderness Lodge (ⓘ3271) © Melissa Loflin

Choosing Your Room at Disney's Wilderness Lodge & Villas Resort

LODGE AND VILLAS RESORT MAP

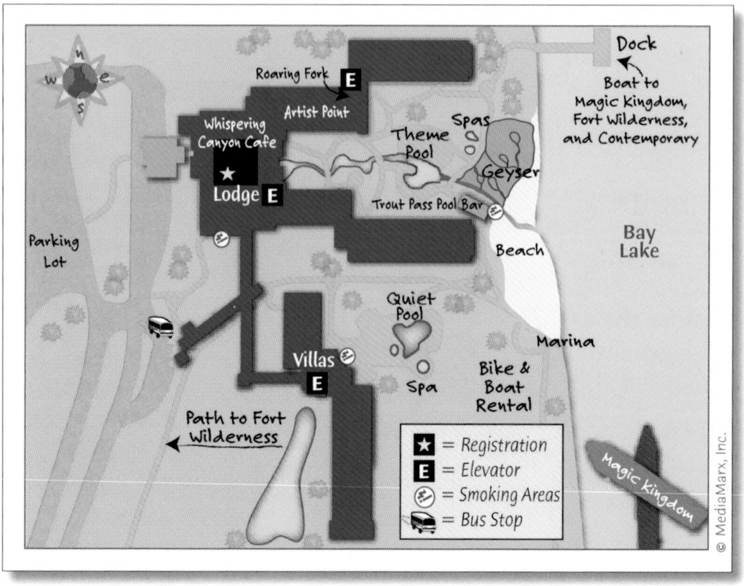

BEST LOCATIONS

Standard rooms overlook the parking areas yet are close to the Lobby. **Lodge views** overlook woods (north side) or the Villas (south side). **Top-floor rooms** facing the woods on the Magic Kingdom (north) side may catch a glimpse of fireworks. Rooms facing the **courtyard or lake** offer panoramic views and cheerful resort sounds. If you seek privacy, consider a **honeymoon suite** at the top of the Lobby or a top-floor room with solid balcony railings. Concierge service is offered for suites and rooms on the seventh floor. **Villas** in the northeast corner offer views of the pool.

RATES

2016 Sample Room and Villa Rates

Seasons are noted on page 14.

Room Type	Value	Fall	Regular	Peak	Holiday
Standard View	\$325–\$336	\$367–\$407	\$389–\$429	\$471–\$512	\$561
Woods View	\$377–\$406	\$395–\$439	\$422–\$450	\$438–\$476	\$584
Courtyard View	\$382–\$412	\$405–\$451	\$439–\$484	\$529–\$575	\$610
Studio Villa	\$421–\$432	\$451	\$488	\$582	\$621
One-Bedroom Villa	\$576–\$587	\$610	\$665	\$808	\$839

12.5% tax is included in the above. Suites and concierge start in the \$600s. Higher rates in price ranges are for weekends and holiday periods (see page 31).

INFO

Disney's Wilderness Lodge and Villas Resort
901 Timberline Drive, Lake Buena Vista, FL 32830
Phone: 407-824-3200 Fax: 407-824-3232
For reservations, call Central Reservations: 407-939-6244

More at ⓘ wilderness-lodge

Top Photo Slice: Bed headboard in guest room at Disney's Wilderness Lodge Resort (ⓘ4241) © Michelle Clark

Disney's Yacht and Beach Club & Villas Resorts

Offering luxury, convenience, and added amenities, the Yacht Club and Beach Club are sister resorts. Both resorts feature a relaxing atmosphere on Crescent Lake within walking distance of Epcot and Disney's Hollywood Studios (use the blue tab at the top for parks and eateries in the area).

AMBIENCE

These resorts evoke the charm of **bygone seaside resorts**. The Yacht Club is housed in a dove-gray clapboard building, exuding elegance and grace. The Beach Club atmosphere is casual, bringing to mind sun-filled days you might have found along the eastern seaboard generations ago. Windows in the sky-blue building may gaze out upon the "beach houses" nestled alongside the beach. The Beach Club Villas are housed in a separate building evoking the charm of Cape May, New Jersey. The Villas' clapboard walls are painted in seafoam green with white railings and columns, and gingerbread trim. Colorful pennants flap in the breeze from atop the roofs and turrets, and strings of light bulbs dangle gracefully between old-fashioned street lamps.

RESORT LAYOUT & ROOMS

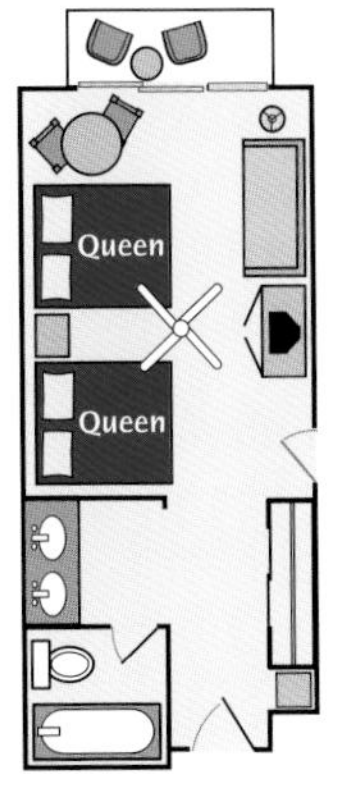

Standard Room Layout

Each of the standard rooms at the Yacht and Beach Club is housed within five floors of one deceptively large yet creatively shaped building, while the villas are located within a free-standing addition. Covered walkways connect the Villas to the Beach Club lobby. Well-appointed and understated, the standard rooms are large (380 sq. ft.) and sunny. The 634 **Yacht Club** rooms are outfitted in ocean blues, floral patterns, and antiqued wood. The 580 **Beach Club** rooms are recently renovated and playfully decorated. Guest rooms have one king or two queen beds, a daybed, ottoman, double sinks, a make-up mirror, a small table and chairs, an armoire with a TV, and a small refrigerator. Some smaller rooms have a king-size Murphy bed and an extra sink and counter. Many rooms—but not all—have balconies or patios (all Yacht Club guest rooms have balconies). Amenities include room service, hair dryers (most rooms), iron, newspaper delivery, turndown service (on request—not available in the Villas), in-room safe, toiletries, and voice mail. Both the Yacht Club and the Beach Club offer concierge service with slightly larger rooms on the fifth floor. In addition, 40 special suites (20 in each resort) range in size from a junior suite to a two-bedroom suite to the ultimate Presidential Suite.

Top Photo Slice: The morning sun on Disney's Yacht Club Resort (ⓘ6716) © Cheryl Pendry

Lodging and Dining at Disney's Yacht and Beach Club Resorts

VILLAS

Added in mid-2002 are the 205 Beach Club Villas with studio, one-, and two-bedroom **villas** for Disney Vacation Club members (see pages 108–109) and the public at large. Studios accommodate up to four guests with one queen-size bed, a double-size sofa bed, and a kitchenette (with a sink, microwave, and a small refrigerator). The one- and two-bedroom villas accommodate up to four or eight guests respectively and offer full kitchens, DVD players, king-size beds, delightful whirlpool tubs in the master bathroom, double-size sleeper sofas in the living room, and washers/dryers. All villas are quite homey and feel like a cottage you might have on the beach. Amenities for all villas include room service, iron and ironing board, hair dryer, newspaper delivery, in-room safe, toiletries (shampoo and soap), and voice mail.

Exploring the Beach Club

One-Bedroom (unshaded)

Queen

King

Shower

Studio Layout (shaded)

Entire layout represents a Two-Bedroom Villa

DINING

With the Yacht and Beach Club sharing restaurants, there are more dining options here than at almost any other resort. Table-service options (see page 261) include **Beaches and Cream**, a popular soda fountain; **Cape May Cafe**, a character breakfast and all-you-can-eat clambake; **Yachtsman Steakhouse** for dinner; and the **Captain's Grille** for breakfast, lunch, and dinner. The **Crew's Cup** offers a good snack menu. For a quick meal, try **Hurricane Hanna's**, a poolside grill, or the **Beach Club Marketplace**, offering breakfast items, baked goods, sandwiches, salads, gelato, coffee, and beverages (refillable mugs—$8.99–$17.99) for eat-in or take-out.

Using the Amenities at Disney's Yacht & Beach Club Resorts

LOUNGING

Several lounges will help you relax after a long day of playing. **Ale & Compass** and **Crew's Cup** in the Yacht Club serve drinks and munchies. At Beach Club, **Martha's Vineyard** features an award-winning wine list and appetizers. **Hurricane Hanna's** is a pool bar and grill—menu items include a pulled pork sandwich ($9.49), cheeseburger ($10.19), and veggie wrap ($10.29). Room service is always available.

PLAYING & RELAXING

For Athletes: The Ship Shape Health Club is a complete fitness club offering a spa, sauna, and massage therapies. The resorts also sport two lighted tennis courts and a sand volleyball court. The Bayside Marina rents watercraft for cruises and surrey bikes to ride around.
For Charmers: Periwig's Beauty and Barber Shop is a full-service salon for hair, skin, and nail care.
For Children: A playground is near Stormalong Bay. Sandcastle Club offers supervised activities for children ages 4–12 (see page 284).
For Gamers: Lafferty Place Arcade has video games.
For Shoppers: The Beach Club Marketplace (Beach) and Fittings and Fairings (Yacht) offer sundries and resort wear.
For Swimmers: The three-acre Stormalong Bay water park is resort swimming at its best. Three free-form, sandy-bottomed pools create deceptively complex waterways with whirlpools, bubbling jets, "rising sands," a water slide in a shipwreck, and two hot tubs. Stormalong Bay is for Yacht and Beach Club and Villas resort guests only (bring your resort ID). Leisure pools are located at the far ends of the resorts. The Villas has its own leisure pool, called "Dunes Cove," and a hot tub.

GETTING ABOUT

Boats (see chart below for in-transit times) depart from the marina for Epcot and Disney's Hollywood Studios. **Buses** outside the lobby go to the Magic Kingdom, Disney's Animal Kingdom, and Disney Springs. Reach other destinations by transferring at Disney's Hollywood Studios (day) or Disney Springs (evening). Parking is available, as well as valet parking ($20/day). The BoardWalk, Dolphin, and Swan are all within **walking distance**, as is the International Gateway to Epcot. You can walk to Disney's Hollywood Studios along the path beside the BoardWalk Villas (see map on page 52).

Magic Kingdom	Epcot	Disney's Hollywood Studios	Disney's Animal Kingdom	Downtown Disney
direct bus ~20 min.	walk/boat ~10/~10 min.	walk/boat ~20/~15 min.	direct bus ~20 min.	direct bus ~15 min.

Approximate time you will spend in transit from resort to destination during normal operation.

More at ⓘ surrey-bikes

Top Photo Slice: Lounge chairs on the beach at Disney's Yacht and Beach Club Resort (ⓘ14386) © Cheryl Pendry

Making the Most of Disney's Yacht and Beach Club Resorts

TIPS

Enjoy a **waterfront stroll** around Crescent Lake using the boardwalks and bridges encircling it. This is a very lively place!

Request **turndown service** from housekeeping before you go out for the evening, and return to find your bedcovers turned down with a chocolate. This service is not available in the Beach Club Villas.

A **bank of elevators** near each resort's lobby serves most rooms. If your room is at one of the far ends, look for a **single elevator or stairway** rather than trek down the hallways. If you're going to Epcot, the exit near Beach Club's leisure pool is convenient.

Yacht and Beach Club have **separate entrances** and **front desks**. Beach Club Villas guests check in at the Beach Club's front desk.

Explore the charming **public areas**, such as The Solarium (just off the Beach Club lobby), The Drawing Room (near the Villas' entrance), and The Breezeway (near the Dunes Cove pool).

NOTES

Bring your **MagicBand** with you to Stormalong Bay—it will be checked. It can be noisy with the sounds of happy children late into the night, so avoid it and places nearby if you seek peace.

All rooms on the first floor have pleasant patios. Most rooms on the top floor have full **balconies**, as do some on the intervening floors. Be aware that some balconies are standing room only, however. If a full-size balcony is important, request it.

A **conference center**, reminiscent of a town hall, is available.

Check-in time is 3:00/4:00 pm. Check-out time is 11:00 am.

RATINGS

Ratings are explained on page 28.

Our Value Ratings:		Our Magic Ratings:		Readers' Ratings:
Quality:	8/10	Theme:	8/10	55% fell in love with it
Accessibility:	8/10	Amenities:	9/10	34% liked it well enough
Affordability:	3/10	Fun Factor:	6/10	7% had mixed feelings
Overall Value:	**6/10**	**Overall Magic:**	**8/10**	4% were disappointed

Yacht and Beach Clubs are enjoyed by... (rated by both authors and readers)

Younger Kids: ♥♥♥♥	Young Adults: ♥♥♥♥	Families: ♥♥♥♥
Older Kids: ♥♥♥♥♥	Mid Adults: ♥♥♥♥♥	Couples: ♥♥♥♥♥
Teenagers: ♥♥♥♥	Mature Adults: ♥♥♥♥♥	Singles: ♥♥♥

Top Photo Slice: Disney's Yacht & Beach Club Resort at night, as seen from the BoardWalk Resort (ⓘ12191) © Cheryl Pendry

Finding Your Place at Disney's Yacht and Beach Club Resorts

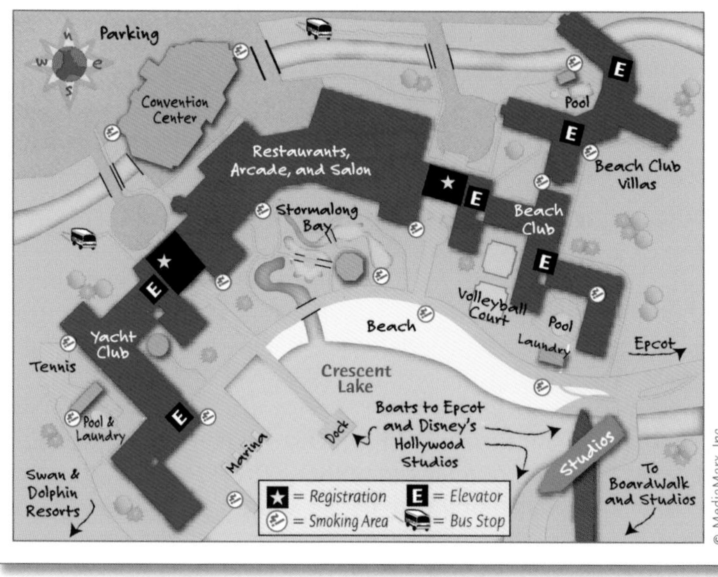

RESORT MAP

BEST LOCATIONS

Your room location can make or break your experience. We strongly recommend you indulge in a room with a **water view** at either the Yacht or Beach Club. Specifically, try to avoid the standard-view, even-numbered Beach Club rooms between 3662–3726, 4662–4726, and 5662–5726, which overlook an ugly rooftop. You may also want to request a room **closer to the lobby** for easier access. Rooms with a king-size Murphy bed are slightly smaller than other rooms. The slightly larger rooms on the Beach Club's fifth floor are concierge. Rooms at the **Beach Club Villas** have views of Epcot, gardens, or the pool, but rates are the same for all.

RATES

2016 Sample Room and Villa Rates

Seasons are noted on page 14.

Room Type	Value	Fall	Regular	Peak	Holiday
Standard View or Studio Villa	$400–$432	$436–$492	$470–$512	$554–$600	$672
Water/Pool View	$498–$534	$546–$602	$569–$626	$637–$690	$744
One-Bedroom Villa	$576	$610	$659	$808	$839
Two-Bedroom Villa	$904	$1,035	$1,171	$1,408	$1,563

12.5% tax is included in the above. Concierge rooms start in the high-$600's. Higher rates in price ranges are for weekends and holiday periods in non-Villa rooms (see page 31).

INFO

Disney's Yacht and Beach Club and Villas Resorts

1700/1800 Epcot Resort Blvd., Lake Buena Vista, FL 32830
Phone: 407-934-7000/8000 Fax: 407-934-3450/3850

More at ⓘ yacht-club

Shades of Green Resort

Shades of Green is a U.S. Armed Forces Recreational Center on Walt Disney World property, located near the Magic Kingdom theme park. Formerly The Disney Inn, this self-supporting resort is exclusively for active and retired military personnel in the Army, Navy, Air Force, Marines, and Coast Guard, as well as those in the Reserves and National Guard. Department of Defense civilians and U.S. Public Health Officers are also eligible.

ROOMS

Nestled in the woods **between two golf courses**, Shades of Green offers 586 rooms with deluxe accommodations. Guest rooms remain among the largest on property at 450 sq. feet, accommodating up to five guests. Features include two queen-size beds, plus a sitting area with a daybed or sleeper sofa. Rooms have a refrigerator, coffeemaker, iron and ironing board, hair dryer, and an in-room safe. While the rooms are large and very pleasant, with a balcony or patio in every room, some feel the lack of Disney theming is a drawback (and they don't give MagicBands either). The resort (and all rooms) are smoke-free (smoking may be allowed on the balcony/patio). Eleven 1–3 bedroom suites are available, sleeping 6–8 guests each.

AMENITIES

Dining choices include the Garden Gallery family restaurant, Evergreens sports bar, a specialty Italian restaurant (Mangino's), the Express Cafe for quick meals, a coffee counter, and room service. There's also a lounge (Eagles). Resort amenities include two lighted tennis courts, two heated pools, wading pool, playground, exercise room, arcade, and laundry facilities. Military-discount tickets are available for Disney and other area attractions at the hotel's ticket office. **Buses** run on regular schedules to Animal Kingdom, Hollywood Studios, Epcot, the Transportation and Ticket center, and Disney Springs (and the Polynesian Village is a 10-minute walk away). You must show your Shades of Green resort ID or military ID to board their buses. A multi-level parking structure is available ($5/day).

RATES

Rates are based on rank or pay grade and begin at **$98** (**$108** for pool views). Reserve up 53 weeks in advance (limit three rooms). **Tip**: Shades of Green is offering discounts on early bookings—visit http://www.militarydisneytips.com for news and announcements.

INFO

Shades of Green Resort

P.O. Box 22789, Lake Buena Vista, FL 32830

Phone: 407-824-3400 Fax: 407-824-3460

For more information, call 888-593-2242 or 407-824-3665

Web site: http://www.shadesofgreen.org

More at ⓘ shades-of-green

Top Photo Slice: Shades of Green © MediaMarx, Inc.

Walt Disney World Swan and Dolphin Resorts

Crowned by five-story-high sculptures of swans and heraldic dolphins, the Walt Disney World Swan and Dolphin resorts tower above the nearby Epcot area resorts. Westin and Sheraton, both of which are divisions of Starwood Hotels, jointly manage this pair of luxury hotels popular with business and international visitors. Renovations are in progress here.

ROOMS

Guest rooms feature either one king-size bed or two double-size beds, separate vanity and bath areas, two 2-line phones, mini-bar, hair dryer, iron, coffeemaker, weekday newspaper delivery, and in-room safe. The mandatory $23/night resort services fee gives you use of the health club, Internet access, 60 minutes of local calls, unlimited local and domestic long-distance calls, and two bottles of water daily. Some rooms have balconies, and 195 suites offer a bit more room. Guest rooms at both resorts sport a modern design by Michael Graves and "Heavenly Beds" with pillow-top mattresses and down comforters. The sister resorts offer conference facilities, too.

AMENITIES

Between the resorts, there are **17 eateries**, including Il Mulino, Garden Grove, Kimonos, Shula's Steakhouse, bluezoo (an upscale seafood restaurant by chef Todd English), and Fresh (an innovative market-style buffet)—see pages 259–260 for details. Picabu is a 24-hour quick-service buffet/cafeteria with a whimsical atmosphere. The BoardWalk entertainment district is just a stroll away, as is Fantasia Gardens miniature golf. Free **buses** serve Disney's parks and Disney Springs, and boats run to Disney's Hollywood Studios and Epcot. Guests receive many of the benefits enjoyed at the Disney-owned resorts, including package delivery, Extra Magic Hours, MyDisneyExperience, and the option to purchase park tickets. Guests cannot charge Disney purchases to their room, nor do they get complimentary MagicBands (you can buy them for $12.95).

RATES

Rooms begin in the **low $300s**, but discounts and special rates are available—ask about discounts for AAA, Annual Passholders, teachers, nurses, and military. Great rates have been found on Sheraton.com, Westin.com, Hotwire.com, and Priceline.com (see page 16). Starwood members earn points (see http://www.spg.com).

INFO

Walt Disney World Swan and Dolphin Resorts

1200/1500 Epcot Resort Blvd., Lake Buena Vista, FL 32830
Phone: 407-934-4000 Fax: 407-934-4884
For reservations, call 888-828-8850 or 407-934-4000
For more information, visit http://www.swandolphin.com

Top Photo Slice: The Walt Disney World Swan and Dolphin Resorts at sunset © Cheryl Pendry

Disney Cruise Line

The Disney Cruise Line set sail in 1998 with the same enthusiasm and energy you find at the Walt Disney World Resort. Each of the four ships (the Disney Magic, Disney Wonder, Disney Dream, and Disney Fantasy) have 5+ themed restaurants, including one or more for adults only. Experience Broadway-quality productions, first-run and classic Disney movies, and nightclubs. Separate areas of the ship were designed exclusively for adults and children.

ITINERARY

Cruises convenient for Walt Disney World guests depart Disney's own terminal in Port Canaveral at 4:00 pm. Four-night **cruises** spend the next day in Nassau, followed by a day at Castaway Cay, Disney's private island, then a full day at sea. Guests debark at Port Canaveral at 9:00 am the following morning. Three-night cruises follow the same plan, but skip the day at sea. Seven-night cruises offer different itineraries—one to the Eastern Caribbean (with stops at St. Maarten, St. Thomas/St. John, and Castaway Cay), one to the Western Caribbean (with stops at ports like Grand Cayman, Cozumel, and Castaway Cay), and some special cruises. In 2016, ships will sail to the Bahamas, Caribbean, Europe, Atlantic Canada, and Alaska in itineraries from 3- to 12-nights long.

STATEROOMS

Staterooms range from downright comfortable to out-and-out luxurious. Even the least expensive staterooms are decorated in glowing, warm woods and include a television, phone, cooler, and in-room safe. The bright and cheery bathrooms include a hair dryer and tub. Deluxe staterooms include a split bathroom, which makes family travel especially comfortable, and up to 44% of all staterooms offer a verandah. Staterooms that sleep four usually have one queen bed, a single daybed, and a single berth—great for families but not so great for two couples. At the high end, the two-bedroom Walter E. and Roy O. Disney suites are a feast for the eyes, decorated with exotic wood paneling and cut crystal—they include a whirlpool tub!

RATES

Many vacationers book add-on **packages** that combine a three- or four-night cruise and three or four nights at the Walt Disney World Resort. During the 2016 value season, three-night cruises start at $654/person (for double occupancy) for a standard inside stateroom to more than $4,539/person for a Royal Suite. Third, fourth, and fifth occupants pay much less. Airfare and ground transfers are extra. Add-on packages now allow you to stay at any of Disney's resort hotels, for any length of time.

More at ⓘ preparing-to-cruise | cruising-for-adults

Top Photo Slice: The Disney Magic in St. Thomas, U.S. Virgin Islands © Janet Simonsen

Making the Most of the Disney Cruise Line

DINING

Your cruise includes all food onboard (including room service) and lunch at Castaway Cay. Soft drinks are free at meals and at the beverage station. Alcoholic beverages are extra. Each night you'll be assigned to a different dining room. **Royal Palace** (Dream), **Royal Court** (Fantasy), **Lumiere's** (Magic), or **Triton's** (Wonder) is the most formal dining room, which is also open daily to all for full-service breakfast and lunch. **Enchanted Garden** (Dream/Fantasy) and **Carioca's**/**Parrot Cay** (Magic/Wonder) are more casual, and also host the breakfast buffets. **Animator's Palate** is an extraordinary room that transforms before your eyes. **Palo** is the ships' intimate, adults-only restaurant with an elegant Italian menu and marvelous service. You may reserve a table at Palo ($25/person surcharge) in advance online or in person on the afternoon that you board, and seats can go quickly. The Dream and Fantasy add adults-only **Remy**, a fine French restaurant, for $75. Breakfast and lunch buffets and snacks are served on Deck 9/11. Fountain drinks are complimentary from the beverage station on Deck 9/11.

NOTES

State any preferences at reservation time and again a month before you sail. Your **cruise documentation** with your room assignment arrives a few weeks before you sail, and you can check-in online.

Passports are not required for regular itineraries, but we still suggest them. Get your required **papers** in order long before you depart.

All shore-side food, transportation, and entertainment in every port of call except Castaway Cay is **at your own expense**. Unless you are especially adventuresome, we suggest you either book a shore excursion (listed in your cruise documentation) or stay onboard.

Dress is casual, but wear a dress/ jacket at the Captain's reception, dinner at Royal Palace/Court/Lumiere's/Triton's, and Palo and Remy.

TIPS

To **save money**, book a cruise-only passage as early as possible. You can still book ground transfers through Disney.

Your day at **Castaway Cay** is short. Be sure to wake up early!

Need more details? We have a **550+ page guidebook** all about the Disney Cruise! See page 312 and visit http://www.passporter.com/dcl/guidebook.asp.

For more information, visit http://www.disneycruise.com or call 888-DCL-2500.

More at ⓘ cruise-security | cruising-special-diets | disney-dream

Top Photo Slice: The AquaDuck water coaster on the Disney Dream (ⓘ24887) © MediaMarx, Inc.

Disney Vacation Club

Can you ever get enough of Walt Disney World? Disney Vacation Club (DVC) members are betting that they can't. DVC is Disney's kinder, gentler version of a vacation timeshare, and offers several enticing twists on the timeshare experience. The DVC offers the promise of frequent, reduced-cost Disney vacations in exchange for a significant up-front investment.

RESORTS

Disney operates **13 Disney's Deluxe Villa Resorts**: Old Key West (page 73), Boardwalk Villas (page 49), Villas at Wilderness Lodge (page 95), Beach Club Villas (page 99), Saratoga Springs (page 91), Animal Kingdom Villas (page 41), the Bay Lake Tower villas at the Contemporary (page 57), Grand Floridian Villas (page 69), Vero Beach (Florida coast), Hilton Head Island (South Carolina), Grand Californian Villas (Disneyland), and the Aulani Resort (Hawaii). The newest addition are the bungalows and villas at the Polynesian Village, which opened in 2015 (see page 77). Studios, one-, two-, and three-bedroom villas with kitchen and laundry facilities are offered (studios have kitchenettes and access to laundry rooms). Housekeeping is limited, with full services every eight days.

THE PROGRAM

With a typical vacation timeshare, you buy an annual one-week (or multiple-week) stay during a particular time period in a specific size of accommodation. DVC uses a novel **point system** that adds far greater flexibility and complexity to the process. You can use your points however you wish to create several short getaways or a single, grand vacation—at any time of the year and at any DVC or other Disney resort. Here's how it works: You buy a certain number of points at the going rate (from $165 per point as of press time). 100 points is the minimum—so every year you'd have at least 100 points to apply toward accommodations. You might need 20 points/night for a one-bedroom at Old Key West weeknights during the off-season. 90 points/night may be needed for a two-bedroom at BoardWalk weekends in peak season. Just as with a regular resort room, rates are affected by size, view, location, season, and day. You also pay annual dues based on the number of points purchased. Rates vary, depending on your "home" resort—from about $5.05 to $8.06 per point—so dues on a 160-point purchase would be about $808–$1,290. If you compare the combined cost of points and fees to renting comparable, non-discounted resort rooms, it takes about seven years to recover the value of the points purchased. After that, vacations might cost half the prevailing rental rates. Membership contracts expire in 2042, with the exception of Saratoga Springs (2054), Animal Kingdom Villas (2057), Bay Lake Tower and Grand Californian (2060), Aulani (2062), Grand Floridian (2064), and Polynesian Village(2066).

More at ⓘ dvc-secret | hilton-head

Top Photo Slice: Shuttered windows in a villa at Old Key West Resort © MediaMarx, Inc.

Making the Most of the Disney Vacation Club

TIPS

While you can reserve up to eleven months in advance at your **home resort**, you can only book seven months in advance at others.

You can **borrow points** from the next year or save unused points until next year. You can buy more points from Disney at the going rate, or buy/sell points on the open market—we heartily recommend DVC By Resale (http://www.dvcbyresale.com, 800-844-4099).

Don't let unused points expire! If you can't use all your points this year or prefer to use them later, you must contact DVC Member Services. Otherwise, those **points expire** at the end of your use year. If you can't use points, bank them or try "renting out" your points (and non-DVC members may consider "renting" points to try out DVC).

Use points to book **at most Disney resorts in the world**, Disney Cruise Line, Adventures by Disney, luxury hotels, and adventure travel vacations, or barter points for "swaps" at non-Disney resorts.

DVC members receive many **discounts** on items including annual passes, resort rooms, dining, guided tours, etc. They also qualify for the Tables in Wonderland dining discount program (see page 10).

DVC members staying at a DVC resort on points may purchase the **Disney Dining Plan** for the length of stay (see pages 223–225).

Anyone may **rent Disney Vacation Club points** from a DVC member, and this can be a great money-saver. For details and folks willing to rent points, visit http://www.mouseowners.com.

NOTES

Vacancies at DVC resorts, called Disney's Deluxe Villa Resorts, are made available to **nonmembers**—they are booked just like regular Disney resort reservations, and daily housekeeping is included. Thus, it may be very difficult to use your DVC points at a resort if you are booking near to your intended arrival date.

Want to learn more? Get our 200+-page DVC guide at http://www.passporter.com/disney-vacation-club.asp (paperback or e-book) and visit our DVC forums online at http://www.passporterboards.com/forums/owning-magic-disney-vacation-club/

PassPorter's Disney Vacation Club Guide
For Members and Members-to-Be

INFO

200 Celebration Place, Celebration, FL 34747-9903
Phone: 800-500-3990 Fax: 407-566-3393
DVC information kiosks are at most Disney parks and resorts.
Sales offices and models are at Disney's Saratoga Springs.

More at ⓘ dvc-cruise

Top Photo Slice: Disney's Vero Beach Resort on the Florida coast (ⓘ11055) © Alison Hinsley

Hotel Plaza Resorts

Each of these hotels is located on Disney property across from Disney Springs, but are independently owned and operated. A variety of discounts may be available. Some of the Disney resort hotel benefits mentioned earlier in this chapter do not apply (such as Extra Magic Hour and package delivery, even at the Hilton). All the Hotel Plaza Resorts offer scheduled buses to the parks (see next page) and are within walking distance of Disney Springs. Visit http://www.downtowndisneyhotels.com.

Hotel Name	*Starting Rates*	*Year Built*	*Year Renovated*
Buena Vista Palace Hotel & Spa	**$299+**	**1983**	**2007**

A high-rise hotel with 1,014 luxury guest rooms and suites. This is the largest of the hotels on Hotel Plaza Boulevard. It's also the closest hotel to Disney Springs Marketplace. All rooms feature balconies or patios, two double beds or one king bed, flat screen TV, Herman Miller chair, cordless phone, coffeemaker, in-room safe, hair dryer, iron and ironing board, newspaper delivery, and toiletries. Wireless Internet access, WebTV, Sony PlayStation games, and premium movies are available for an additional fee. Resort amenities include three heated pools, whirlpool spa, tennis and sand volleyball courts, full-service European-style spa with fitness center and beauty salon, arcade, three restaurants (one with character breakfasts every Sunday), a cafe, two lounges, a pool bar, and room service. Formerly known as Wyndham Palace Resort & Spa. Web: http://www.buenavistapalace.com. Call 407-827-2727.

DoubleTree Suites Resort	**$129+**	**1988**	**2008**

This all-suite hotel offers 229 one- and two-bedroom suites. All rooms come with dining areas, kitchenettes (refrigerator, microwave, and coffeemaker), separate living rooms with sofa beds, double-size or king-size Sweet Dream beds, three TVs, two phones, in-room safe, hair dryer, iron and ironing board, and toiletries (no balconies). Suites accommodate up to six people (up to four adults). Amenities include a heated pool, wading pool, fitness center, arcade, one restaurant, one lounge, one pool bar, and room service. Look for the freshly baked chocolate chip cookies upon your arrival. Web: http://www.doubletreeguestsuites.com. Call 800-222-8733 or 407-934-1000.

Hilton Orlando Lake Buena Vista	**$99+**	**1984**	**2008**

This first-class business hotel is located right across the street from the Downtown Springs Marketplace. The 814 rooms are luxurious, each offering "Serenity" beds (two doubles or one king), overstuffed chair, flat screen TV, MP3 clock radios, two phones, hair dryer, iron and ironing board, coffeemaker, mini-bar, newspapers, Internet access ($9.95/day), and toiletries (no balconies or in-room safes). Amenities include two heated pools, kids water play area, two whirlpool spas, fitness center, arcade, shopping area, three eateries (one with character meals every Sunday), two cafes, and one lounge, one pool bar, and room service. The Hilton no longer offers the Extra Magic Hour perk (see page 34). Web: http://www.hiltonlakebuenavista.com. Call 800-445-8667 or 407-827-4000.

Holiday Inn	**$109+**	**1978**	**2010**

With 323 standard rooms and one suite, this renovated 14-story hotel offers clean, basic accommodations. Standard rooms come with two double beds or one king bed, balconies, satellite TV, hair dryer, iron and ironing board, coffeemaker, in-room safe, newspaper delivery, toiletries, and high-speed Internet. Additional amenities include Nintendo games (extra fee), two heated pools, wading pool, whirlpool spa, fitness center, arcade, one restaurant, one cafe, and room service. Web: http://www.downtowndisneyhotels.com/hotels/holiday-inn. Call 800-223-9930 or 407-828-8888.

Top Photo Slice: The Hilton © MediaMarx, Inc.

Hotel Name	Starting Rates	Year Built	Year Renovated
Lake Buena Vista Best Western Resort	**$99+**	**1973**	**2010**

This 18-story, Caribbean-themed hotel is on the shores of Lake Buena Vista. The renovated resort offers 321 standard rooms (345 sq. ft.) and four suites, all of which have balconies. Rooms come with two queen beds or one king bed, satellite TV, hair dryer, iron and ironing board, coffeemaker (with coffee and tea), in-room safe, newspaper delivery, free wireless Internet, and toiletries. Other amenities include Nintendo games and premium movies for an extra fee, one heated pool, a wading pool, privileges to the DoubleTree fitness center, two eateries, two lounges, and room service. Web: http://www.lakebuenavistaresorthotel.com. Call 800-348-3765 or 407-828-2424.

B Resort & Spa	**$140+**	**1975**	**2013**

This hotel offers 394 standard rooms that each accommodate up to five guests and have a sitting area, balcony or patio, coffeemaker, and phone, in addition to the new "Blissful Beds" (two queen beds or one king bed), sofa bed, 47" LCD TV, desk, mini beverage cooler, in-room safe, hair dryer, iron and ironing board, newspaper delivery, wifi Internet access, and Aveda toiletries. "Stunning" rooms in the tower are slightly larger and offer upgraded bathrooms. Hotel amenities include a heated zero-entry pool, four tennis courts, arcade, 24-hour fitness center, the American Q restaurant, a pool bar and grill, and in-room dining. Mandatory $20/night service fee. Self-parking is $16; valet parking is $21. Note: This hotel was formerly The Royal Plaza and changed in late 2013. Web: http://www.bhotelsandresorts.com/b-walt-disney-world. Call 888-66B-HOTE or 407-828-2828.

Wyndham Lake Buena Vista Resort	**$109+**	**1972**	**2007**

Formerly the Grosvenor Resort and then the Regal Sun Resort, this hotel offers 626 rooms in a 19-story high-rise nestled beside Lake Buena Vista. All rooms come with standard two double-size beds or one king-size bed, 37" HD TV, MP3 clock radio, coffeemaker, refrigerator, in-room safe, wireless Internet access, hairdryer, iron and ironing board, and toiletries (no balconies). Resort amenities include two heated pools, whirlpool spa, a new kids' water playground, two tennis courts (as well as basketball, volleyball, and shuffleboard courts), scheduled kids activities, business center, fitness center, thermal spa, arcade, one restaurant (with character breakfasts thrice weekly), one casual dining cafe, one pool bar, one lounge, and room service. Web: http://www.wyndhamlakebuenavista.com. Call 800-624-4109 or 407-828-4444

Hotel Plaza Resort Transportation to the Parks

Guests staying at these Hotel Plaza Resorts get free bus transportation to the four major Disney parks, Downtown Disney, and the water parks. Hotel Plaza buses—which differ from the standard Disney buses—run every 30 minutes and typically start one hour before park opening and continue up to two hours after park closing. Note that buses to the Magic Kingdom drop you off at the Transportation and Ticket Center (TTC), where you can take a monorail or boat to the park entrance or transfer to another bus to another Disney destination. Disney's Animal Kingdom buses may operate only once an hour during the slower times of the day. Within walking distance is Downtown Disney, where you can also board Disney buses to other resorts. Those bound for the water parks should check with their hotel for bus schedules. Guests who want to venture off to Universal Studios/Islands of Adventure, SeaWorld, Wet 'n' Wild, or the Belz Outlet Mall can take a shuttle for $12/person round-trip—check with your hotel on pick-up times. Many guests who stay at these hotels recommend you get a rental car—all hotels but the Lake Buena Vista Best Western and Hotel Royal Plaza have a rental car desk.

Top Photo Slice: Bus transportation for guests staying at the Hotel Plaza Resorts © MediaMarx, Inc.

Hotels Near Disney World

Below are several hotels and motels near Walt Disney World (but not on Disney property) that either we've stayed in and recommend or at which our readers report good experiences. More hotels are listed on following pages.

Hotel Name (in alphabetical order)	*Starting Rates*	*Year Built*	*Year Renovated*
Nickelodeon Family Suites	**$119+**	**1999**	**2005**

Besides the resort's close proximity to Walt Disney World (just 3 miles/5 km), the hotel offers unique and very convenient "KidSuites" with a living room, kitchenette, master bedroom, and kids' room. The kids get a bunk bed, TV, game system (fee applies), and a small table and chairs—decorated with SpongeBob SquarePants, Rugrats, The Fairly OddParents, Jimmy Neutron, or Danny Phantom. A three-bedroom KidSuite with an extra adult bedroom is also available. If you don't have kids, you can get a room with a different configuration, such as the Nick@Nite Suite (whirlpool tub and 50" TV) and the Kitchen Suite (full kitchen). A breakfast buffet and Nickelodeon character breakfast are available. The resort also has a huge pool complex with seven water slides, four-story water tower, zero-entry pool, water playground, two hot tubs, and a small miniature golf course. There is a free scheduled shuttle bus to Walt Disney World, but we found it more convenient to drive. Visit http://www.nickhotel.com or call 407-387-5437 or 866-462-6425. Hotel address: 14500 Continental Gateway, Orlando, FL 32821

Radisson Resort Orlando Celebration	**$118+**	**1987**	**2012**

We enjoyed our stay at this 718-room, 6-story deluxe hotel just 1.5 miles (2.5 km) from the gates of Walt Disney World. Guest rooms accommodate up to four guests with either one king-size bed or two double-size beds. Recently refurbished rooms come in either pool or courtyard views and feature modern Italian furniture and marble bathrooms. Amenities include a 25" TV, mini refrigerator, in-room safe, coffeemaker, iron and ironing board, hair dryer, make-up mirror, voice mail, and data ports. For a $11.30 daily service fee, you get scheduled shuttles to attractions, 24-hour access to the fitness center, high-speed Internet access (most rooms), use of lighted tennis courts, free local and toll calls, and free newspaper delivery. The resort has two pools, a water slide, a wading pool, and two hot tubs, as well as playground, and arcade. Food service includes a full-service restaurant (open for breakfast and dinner), a deli with Pizza Hut items, a sports bar, a pool bar, and room service. Note that kids under 10 eat free when accompanied by a paying adult. For the best rates, visit http://www.radissonorlandoresort.com or call 866-358-5609 or 407-396-7000. 2900 Parkway Boulevard, Kissimmee, FL 34747

Sheraton Lake Buena Vista Resort	**$161+**	**1994**	**2013**

This recently-renovated resort (formerly Sheraton Safari) now has contemporary/casual Floridian decor, and a line-up of kids' activities led by "Pool Captains." The 490-room, 6-story hotel is located just 1/4 mile (1/2 km) from Disney property (you can't walk to it, but it is a short drive or ride on the scheduled shuttle). Guest rooms come in standard (one king-size or two double-sized beds), Junior and Family Suites (with kitchenette and separate parlor), and deluxe suites (with full kitchens and large parlors). Standard rooms accommodate up to four guests, or five guests with the rental of a roll-away bed. All rooms have a balcony or patio, TV with PlayStation, two phones with voice mail, dataports, and high-speed Internet access, hair dryer, make-up mirror, coffeemaker, iron and ironing board, and in-room safe. The resort features a large pool with a 79-ft. water slide, wading pool, hot tub, fitness center, and arcade. One full-service restaurant (Zest) offers lunch and dinner, and the 27 Palms pool bar and grill offers lighter fare. Visit http://www.sheratonlakebuenavistaresort.com or call 407-239-0444 or 800-423-3297. Hotel address: 12205 Apopka-Vineland Road, Orlando, FL 32836

Top Photo Slice: Radisson Resort © MediaMarx, Inc.

Hotels Near Universal Studios

Below are the four on-site hotels at Universal Studios Florida (about 7 miles/11 kilometers from Walt Disney World property). Guests staying here get special privileges at Universal Studios and Islands of Adventure, such as the "Universal Express" ride access system to bypass attraction lines (all but Cabana Bay), early admission to Wizarding World, priority seating at some restaurants, complimentary package delivery, on-site transportation, and more. Each of these hotels accepts pets and offers pet-related services. All of these resorts are operated by Loews Hotels (http://www.loewshotels.com).

Hotel Name (in alphabetical order)	*Starting Rates*	*Year Built*
Hard Rock Hotel	**$244+**	**2001**

If you think Hard Rock Cafe is great, this 650-room hotel really rocks. Step inside a rock star's mansion filled to the rafters with a million-dollar rock memorabilia collection. Standard guest rooms (365 sq. ft.) feature two queen beds or one king bed, flat-panel TV, MP3 station, stereos, two-line cordless phones, mini-bar, coffeemaker, in-room safe, hair dryer, bathroom scale, iron and ironing board, and toiletries. There are 14 Kids Suites with a separate sleeping area for the kids. Heated pool with a water slide and underwater audio system, wading pool, two whirlpool spas, sand beach, fitness center, two restaurants (including a Hard Rock Cafe), a cafe, a lounge, a pool bar, and room service. Web: http://www.hardrockhotelorlando.com. Call 800-BE-A-STAR or 407-445-ROCK. Hotel address: 5800 Universal Blvd., Orlando, FL 32819

Portofino Bay Hotel	**$279+**	**1999**

Stay in this remarkably themed resort and get a big taste of the Italian Riviera. The hotel is a deluxe recreation of the seaside village of Portofino, Italy, developed with the help of Steven Spielberg. There may be cobblestone streets outside, but luxury abounds inside. 750 rooms and suites are available, including several Kids Suites. Standard rooms come with either two queen beds or one king bed and double sofa bed, cable TV, two phones, mini-bar, coffeemaker, in-room safe, hair dryer, iron and ironing board, and toiletries. Resort amenities include three heated pools, a water slide, whirlpool spas, a full-service spa, fitness center, a Bocce ball court, four restaurants, three cafes, a lounge, and room service. Web: http://www.portofinobay.com. Call 407-503-1000 or 800-232-7827. Hotel address: 5601 Universal Blvd., Orlando, FL 32819

Royal Pacific Resort	**$224+**	**2002**

This hotel boasts 1,000 guest rooms with a South Seas theme and lush landscaping. Standard rooms (355 sq. ft.) hold up to five guests (four adults) and feature two queen beds or one king bed, cable TV, mini-bar, coffeemaker, in-room safe, hair dryer, iron and ironing board, and toiletries. The Club Rooms add robes, turndown service, newspaper delivery, continental breakfast, and afternoon beer/wine/snacks. Resort amenities include a huge pool, kids' water play area, wading pool, two whirlpool spas, sand beach, volleyball court, putting green, fitness center, arcade, a supervised children's program, two restaurants, a cafe, a lounge, a pool bar, and room service. Web: http://www.universalorlando.com/Hotels/Loews-Royal-Pacific-Resort.aspx. Call 888-322-5541 or 407-503-3000. Hotel address: 6300 Hollywood Way, Orlando, FL 32819

Cabana Bay Beach Resort	**$179+**	**2014**

This new retro-themed hotel features 1,800 moderate and value priced guest rooms and family suites. Cool features include a 10,000 sq. ft. zero-entry pool, lazy river, and bowling alley! Web: http://www.universalorlando.com/Hotels/Cabana-Bay-Beach-Resort.aspx. Call 407-503-4000. Hotel address: 6550 Adventure Way, Orlando, FL 32819. We stayed here in 2015 and loved it!

Top Photo Slice: Hard Rock Hotel as seen from CityWalk at Universal Studios (3087) © Cheryl Pendry

More Hotels Outside Disney

You may prefer to stay "off-property" to attend a conference, visit other parks, or pay a bargain rate. Below are several popular hotels, motels, and inns off property. We've included starting rates for standard rooms (off-season), driving distance to Disney Springs, available transportation to Disney, the year it was built (plus the year it was renovated, if available), if it is a Disney "Good Neighbor Hotel" (able to sell multi-day passes), a short description, web site (if available), and a phone number.

Hotel/Motel Name (in alphabetical order)	Starting Rates	Distance to WDW	Trans. Avail.	Year Built	Good Neighbor
Calypso Cay Resort	$90+	3mi/5km	Bus	'00 ('12)	
151-suite resort with free breakfast. http://www.calypsocay.com. 407-997-1300					
Caribe Royale Resort	$150+	4mi/6km	Bus($)	'97 ('14)	✔
Ten-story suite hotel with living rooms and wet bars. AAA discount. 407-238-8000					
The Celebration Hotel	$260+	8mi/12km	Bus	'99	
Upscale business hotel within Disney's town of Celebration. 407-566-6000					
Embassy Suites LBV	$140+	3mi/5km	Bus	'85 ('07)	✔
All-suite hotel with a Caribbean theme in Lake Buena Vista. 407-239-1144					
Gaylord Palms	$200+	1mi/1.5km	Bus	'02	
1,406-room luxury resort near Disney. http://www.gaylordpalms.com. 407-586-0000					
Hawthorne Suites LBV	$100+	1mi/1.5km	Bus	'00	✔
Rooms and suites, free breakfast. http://www.hawthornlakebuenavista.com. 407-597-5000					
Holiday Inn Maingate East	$69+	6mi/10km	Bus($)	'73('02)	✔
Standard rooms and Kidsuites. Located in Kissimmee. 407-396-4222					
Hyatt Regency Grand Cypress	$260+	3mi/5km	Bus	'84('13)	
750-room hotel with balconies, private lake, nature trails, and golf. 407-239-1234					
Marriott Orlando World Center	$275+	4mi/6km	Bus($)	'86('04)	
28-floor, 2,000-room resort with four restaurants and a convention center. 407-239-4200					
Orlando Vista Hotel	$112+	1.5mi/2km	Bus	'86('04)	
246 rooms and kid suites. http://orlandovistahotel.com . AAA discount. 407-239-4646					
Quality Suites Maingate	$80+	6mi/10km	Bus	'90('10)	
One- and two-bedroom suites with living rooms and kitchenettes. 407-396-8040					
Red Roof Inn	$49+	5mi/8km	–	'89('12)	
Basic budget lodging with a good reputation. Located in Kissimmee. 407-396-0065					
Sheraton's Vistana Resort	$150+	3mi/5km	Bus	'80('12)	
One- and two-bedroom villas. Details at http://www.sheraton.com. 407-239-3100					
Staybridge Suites	$155+	2mi/3km	Bus	'93('12)	✔
All-suite hotel with one- and two-bedroom suites and free breakfast. 407-238-0777					
The Palms Hotel & Villas	$90+	6mi/10km	Bus	'91('01)	
Two-room suites with kitchen, living area, and bedroom. AAA discounts. 407-396-2229					

Tip: You really need a car when staying at off-property hotels. Even when shuttles to the parks are provided, the schedules and drop-off/pick-up points aren't accommodating. If you are flying to Orlando and staying off-site, be sure to factor in the cost of renting a car.

Top Photo Slice: The Celebration Hotel © MediaMarx, Inc.

Vacation Homes

Another off-property lodging option that can provide excellent value is a vacation home rental. Vacation homes are typically free-standing **houses or condos with several bedrooms, kitchens, and pool access** ... some vacation homes even have their own private pools and hot tubs. Vacation homes are ideal for large families and groups. Many vacation home rental companies operate near Walt Disney World, and choosing from among them can get confusing. Important points to look for in a vacation home rental company include proximity of homes to Walt Disney World, quality of customer service, prices, and extra fees. We've only tried one rental company—ALL STAR Vacation Homes—but we've been so impressed that we've been back several times. Below is their information, followed by general contact information for some other vacation home companies for which we've received positive reviews from our readers.

ALL STAR Vacation Homes really shines in our book. ALL STAR Vacation Homes has a full guest service center near their properties; more than 150 homes within four miles of Walt Disney World (we can see Expedition Everest from the patio of our favorite home at 8009 Acadia Estates); excellent amenities in clean, luxurious homes; and great deals on a wide variety of home sizes. Most homes have computers with Internet, and all guests have free access to their Internet Cafe. Their customer service has always been helpful and friendly, and their vacation homes have secured and gated entrances. Vacation home rentals start as low as $119/night. We could go on and on ... actually, we have in the form of several feature articles (see http://www.passporter.com/asvh.asp). For more information and to make a reservation, phone 888-825-6405 or visit http://www.allstarvacationhomes.com and ask for the PassPorter rate deal (free standard rental car or $125 off a 7-night home rental).

Relaxing in our ALL STAR Vacation Home

Florida Spirit Vacation Homes—More than 100 vacation homes within six to ten miles of Walt Disney World, which you can pre-select online. http://www.floridaspiritvacationhome.com, 866-357-7474.

FlipKey by TripAdvisor—Comprehensive vacation home rental search site, with over 5,000 listings in Orlando alone. http://www.flipkey.com.

More at ⓘ all-star-vacation-homes

Top Photo Slice: Playing in the private pool at an ALL Star Vacation Home in Windsor Hills © MediaMarx, Inc.

Electronic, interactive worksheet available–see page 316

Lodging Worksheet

Use this worksheet to jot down preferences, scribble information during phone calls, and keep all your discoveries together. Don't worry about being neat–just be thorough! Circle your final choices once you decide to go with them (to avoid any confusion) and be sure to transfer them to your Room(s) PassPocket.

Arrival date: ________________ Alternates: ________________

Departure date: ________________ Alternates: ________________

Total number of nights: ______ Alternates: ________________

We prefer to stay at: ______________________________

Alternates: ______________________________

____

Using your preferences above, call Disney's Reservations phone line at 407-939-6244 or visit http://www.disneyworld.com and jot down resort availabilities in the table on the next page. It works best for us when we write the available days in the far left column, followed by the resort, view/type, special requests, rate, and total cost in the columns to the right. Draw lines between different availabilities. Circle those you decide to use, and then record the reservation numbers, as you'll need them to confirm, cancel, or make changes later. The two columns at the far right let you note confirmations and room deposits so you don't forget and consequently lose your reservation.

Additional Notes:

Top Photo Slice: Filling out a PassPorter worksheet © MediaMarx, Inc.

Collect information on lodging in the table below. We've included some sample notes to show you how we do it, but you're welcome to use this space in any way you please.

Dates	Resort	View/Type/Requests	Rate	Total	Reservation #	Confirm by	Dep.
7/10 - 7/16	Port Orleans	Water View (Riverside)	$233	$1,398	2635 1419 8419	2/14/16 ✓	✓
7/11 - 7/16	All-Star Movies	Standard (Fantasia)	$150	$1,250		2/15/16	

The Last Resort

Your resort or hotel is your home-away-from-home, and deserves special consideration. Here are our some of our best lodging tips:

"There is **so much to do at your Walt Disney World Resort**! Be sure to pick up an activities list, every resort has them and plan some time (an hour, an afternoon or a whole day) at your resort! The activities range from trivia games, pool parties to crafts, and evening movies and campfires!! Most of the activities are free; ask guest services to be sure. And if you are staying over a special event or holiday; there may be something extra special! (we participated in a mardi gras parade through Port Orleans and received beads and candy during one visit)!"

– Contributed by Jennifer Lambert, a winner in our Reader Tip Contest

"Most Disney Resorts offer **online check-in** before your arrival to speed up the registration process in the lobby. On our last stay at Pop Century, we were also given the opportunity to provide our email or cell phone number and receive a text with the number of our room. We were traveling by car to the Disney area that morning, not sure whether we should head to the parks or take a chance and stop at the resort to see if our room was ready (check in was at 3:00 pm). Then we received a text stating our room was ready and the room number. We opened our PassPorter to the Pop Century map and parked near the building we were in! No need to stop at the lobby and check in—just use your Magic Band as your room key! We unloaded our luggage in our room and headed to the parks! Big time-saver!"

– Contributed by Lisa O'Meara, a winner in our Reader Tip Contest

"My family loves the refillable mugs but doesn't like carrying them into the parks. When we use them for breakfast, instead of carrying them to parks or bringing back to room, **store your mugs at bell services**. I bring an extra bag and get bell services to hold them. Then after our day at the parks we retrieve them and get a refill on the way back to room. Just keep track of the claim ticket bell services gives you!"

– Contributed by Alisa Boquet, a winner in our Reader Tip Contest

Magical Memory

"Don't be afraid to stay at the value resorts! For years we only stayed at the Moderates but we recently tried All Star Sports and really liked it. While we missed a few of the amenities of the moderates, the price couldn't be beat. We got two rooms at All Star Sports for less money than one room at Port Orleans. Our two 20+ children shared a room and my husband and I had our own room. And we had excellent bus service!"

...as told by vacationer Kim Roe

24626 © Sarah Mudd

A "Win!" at All-Star Sports!

Top Photo Slice: Epcot area resorts at sunset © Amy Sellars

Touring the "World"

The Walt Disney World Resort has been called many things—a world-class resort, an endless playground for young and old alike, and even a mecca for capitalism—but we have never heard it called boring.

The "World" (as it is known to insiders) began in 1971. Opening on October 1st of that year, it offered a small fraction of what we enjoy today: the Magic Kingdom park and the Contemporary and Polynesian Village resort hotels. It was the dream of an all-American leader, Walt Disney, who didn't live to see opening day. Yet his legacy flourished, becoming the 43-square-mile wonderland we know and love today.

DECIDE what parks to visit and which attractions to see

One of the things that makes the Walt Disney World Resort so special is the attention to detail and service. It takes tens of thousands of people, known as "cast members," working together to stage the "show" we see as "guests." You'll notice that Disney often uses special words to describe their unique services and attractions. There's nothing mundane here.

LEARN the basics of having fun in the parks

To help you recognize these terms, we begin with Park Passwords, defining the "Disneyese" you'll hear and read, such as the much-touted FastPass+ ride reservation system. We then move on to practical matters, such as transportation and admission to the parks. Next come our expanded and detailed attraction descriptions for the four major theme parks, along with plenty of color photos and the largest theme park maps you'll find in any Disney guidebook. (They fold out!) Descriptions and maps of the smaller parks follow, along with hints, tips, and a Touring Worksheet to help you decide what to do. Don't overlook our at-a-glance attraction lists and theme park touring plans.

DISCOVER the parks and attractions of Disney

GET where you want to go with ease

So let's go around the "World" in 102 pages!

Top Photo Slice: A smiley face appears in the sky over Dumbo The Flying Elephant at the Magic Kingdom (①4010) © Tina Thornton

Park Passwords

Admission—Park passes (tickets and MagicBands). See pages 122–123 for pass details.

Attraction—An individual ride, show, or exhibit.

Baby Care Centers—Special centers are found in each of the major parks. All restrooms (men's included) support diaper changing.

Cast Member—Disney employees are "cast members"—they wear white or blue name tags with their names.

Disney Dollars and Gift Cards—Disney's own currency, good throughout the Walt Disney World Resort.

ECV—Electric Convenience Vehicle. You can rent these four-wheeled scooters at the parks and elsewhere. See page 36.

Extra Magic Hour—Resort guests can enjoy certain parks earlier or later on certain days. See page 34 for details.

FastPass+—Disney's ride "reservation" system (see below).

ⓘ48341 © Jennifer Marx

MagicBands

FastPass+

Tired of waiting in long lines? Disney's high-tech FastPass+ ride reservation system reduces the time you spend in line and is free to all park guests! To begin making FastPass+ reservations, first go to the MyDisneyExperience app (online at disneyworld.com or on your smart device) and link your park pass by ID number. Once you have a valid park pass in the system, you can make up to three FastPass+ reservations per day of your visit up to 60 days in advance (Disney resort guests) or up to 30 days in advance (everyone else). Currently, your three FastPass+ reservation selections must be in the same park, even if you have a park-hopping ticket. Additionally, there is a "tiered" approach to reservations, meaning you can only select one headliner and two minor attractions at Epcot and Disney's Hollywood Studios. After you use all three initial FastPass+ reservations on the day of your visit (or your arrival windows have passed), you can select one more FastPass+ to use that same day at one of the FastPass+ kiosks in the parks (and you can select an attraction in a different park). The extra FastPass+ reservation is a rolling FastPass+ experience—each time you use it, you can select a new one.

So how do you actually use FastPass+? Just swipe your park pass or MagicBand on the Mickey head RFID reader at the entrance to an attraction and, if you're within your one-hour reservation window, Mickey lights up green and you're good to go. Too early? You'll need to wait. Too late? You won't get in, but you can go online or to a kiosk to make a new FastPass+ reservation. Once you're in the FastPass+ queue, there's usually still a short wait, and you'll experience most or all "pre-show" activities. Most FastPass+ attractions still have a "Standby" line for those without FastPass+, though at press time Disney was experimenting with making some venues FastPass+ only. Our attraction descriptions in this chapter indicate if an attraction has FastPass+ (look for the icons: FP for headliner FastPass+, FP for all other FastPass+), and our touring plans give recommendations on which reservations to get. Read more about MyDisneyExperience and MagicBand wristbands on page 126.

More at ⓘ fastpass (tip: enter this keyword at http://www.passporter.com/i for more information!)

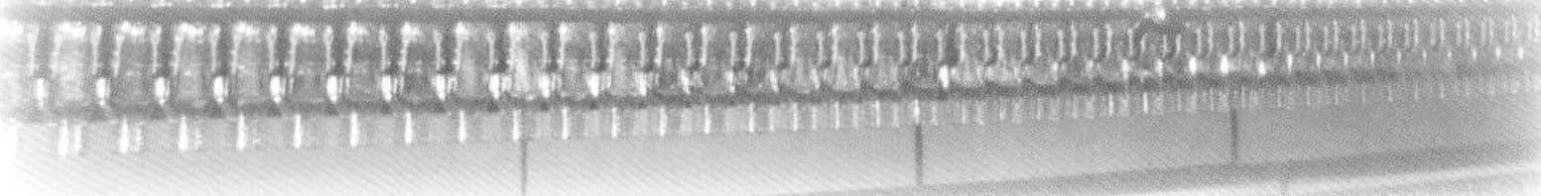

First Aid—First aid stations are at the four theme parks and two water parks (see maps).

Guest Relations—An information desk, located inside and outside the front gates of all four parks and Disney Springs. Lobby Concierge at resorts provides a similar range of services.

Guidemaps—Free maps available at the parks. See also "Times Guide."

Lockers—Available for a fee ($8–$10 + $5 deposit) in each park and at the Transportation and Ticket Center. Save your receipt for a new locker at another park on the same day.

Lost & Found—Lost items or children can be claimed at a central location in each park. Consult a guidemap or a cast member. Also see page 281.

Money—Pay with Disney Dollars, Disney Gift Cards, cash, traveler's checks, American Express, MasterCard, Visa, Discover, JCB, Diner's Club, Disney Visa Reward Vouchers, Apple Pay, and Google Wallet. Disney Gift Cards are sold at parks, resorts, and most U.S. Disney Stores. ATMs are in the parks, resorts, and Disney Springs. Disney resort guests can charge to their room.

Packages—Park purchases can be delivered and held for pick-up near the park exit at all major parks, and Disney resort guests can have packages delivered to their resort the next afternoon free of charge. Inquire about package delivery before purchasing.

Park—Disney's recreational complexes requiring admission, which include the four major parks (Magic Kingdom, Epcot, Disney's Hollywood Studios, and Disney's Animal Kingdom) and four minor parks (Blizzard Beach, Typhoon Lagoon, ESPN Wide World of Sports, and DisneyQuest). Descriptions begin on page 129. You must be 14 or older to enter a park alone.

Parking—Fee is $17 a day for cars, $18 for camper/trailers, and $21 for bus/tractor trailers. Parking is free to Disney resort guests; Swan/Dolphin, Shades of Green, and Disney Springs Hilton guests; and Annual Passholders. Tables in Wonderland members park free after 5:00 pm. Tip: Save your receipt to park free at another park on the same day.

PhotoPass—This service lets you view all photos taken by Disney's photographers at http://www.disneyphotopass.com. No more waiting in long queues to view/buy photos.

Queue—Waiting area/line for an attraction or character meet.

Re-Entry—Guests may exit and re-enter the same park on the same day. Be sure to hold on to your pass and bring photo ID. Disney uses a safe finger scan (biometrics) when you enter and re-enter a park (see photo).

© MediaMarx, Inc.
Finger scan upon park entry

Security—All bags are searched before entering parks.

Shopping—Shops sell Disney and themed items. We list the best shops in this chapter.

Smoking—Prohibited in resorts, buildings, queues, and parks, except in designated smoking areas (see park maps).

Strollers & Wheelchairs—Strollers ($15/single stroller, $31/double, $13–$27/day for length-of-stay rental), wheelchairs ($12/day—no deposit, $10/day for length-of-stay rental), and ECVs ($50/day + $20 deposit) can be rented at the parks. Limited availability—arrive early, bring your own, or rent elsewhere (see page 36). Save your receipt for a free rental at another park on the same day, but there's no guarantee a rental will be available. Tip: Save money and get better strollers by renting from Orlando Stroller Rentals (http://www.orlandostrollerrentals.com).

Tax—Florida and county sales tax totals 6.5%.

Times Guide—Free listing of attraction hours and showtimes—pick up as you enter the parks.

Top Photo Slice: A wall of candy at the Mouse Gear shop at Epcot (ⓘ5359) © Eileen Farnsworth

More at ⓘ first-aid-on-vacation | single-rider-lines

Park Admission

Budget **$104**/day for ages 10+ (**$97**/kids ages 3-9), the single-day/single-park base price with tax for the major parks ($8 extra for Magic Kingdom), based on the last price increase in February 2015. The "Magic Your Way" multi-day admission delivers flexibility and savings (especially for stays of five days and longer), so you can do more at a lower price. The prices here include tax. Estimate a 4%-12% increase when rates go up again (sometime in early 2016).

Magic Your Way Admission — *Actual 2015-2016 Rates*

Magic Your Way tickets are available for 2-10 days. Guests can stick to basic admission or add one or more options at the time of purchase (see explanations below). Magic Your Way includes single-day passes and all varieties of Park Hopper passes. A Magic Your Way ***Base Ticket*** *($204-$388) is good for entry to a single major park (Magic Kingdom, Epcot, Disney's Hollywood Studios, or Disney's Animal Kingdom) for each day of the ticket. Multiday Base Tickets bring substantial discounts (see chart on the next page), so it pays to buy your admission all at once. Multiday Base Tickets expire 14 days after the first use, but they do not have to be used on consecutive days. More days—and options—can be added to a Base Ticket within 14 days of first use, provided that at least one day's admission remains. The* ***Park Hopping*** *option (add $48-$68) lets you visit more than one major park on the same day, for the length of your ticket. If you intend to visit more than one park a day, the Park Hopping option is necessary because you cannot simply buy extra days of admission on a Base Ticket and then use more than one admission in a single day. The Magic Your Way* ***Water Parks Fun and More*** *option (add $64) adds a limited number of single-park admissions for the minor parks (Blizzard Beach, Typhoon Lagoon, DisneyQuest (closing in 2016), Wide World of Sports, and Disney's Oak Trail golf course) to any Base Ticket. Each Water Parks Fun and More option is worth $13-$55. Purchase this feature with 1-day Base Tickets and you receive two Water Parks Fun and More options, while 2- to 10-day Base Tickets receive the same number of options as there are days on the pass. Regardless of how many options you receive, the cost to add this feature is always the same. As long as you make a minimum of two visits to the more costly minor parks, you'll get your money's worth. Combining park-hopping and water park fun and more options adds $95 to the price of an adult base ticket. The* ***No Expiration*** *option is no longer offered. Prices for the various tickets are listed in the comparison chart on the next page.*

Premium Annual Pass — *Actual 2015-2016 Rates*

Unlimited admission to the four major parks for 356 days, plus special privileges. A Premium Annual Pass ($749, or $649 for Florida residents/DVC members) costs less than two 4-day Magic Your Way Base Tickets with Park Hopping. Premium Annual Passes also kick in theme park parking, a complimentary MagicBand, park hopping privileges, and unlimited downloads from Disney's PhotoPass. You cannot share an Annual Pass (or any other multiday pass).

Platinum Annual Pass Plus — *Actual 2015-2016 Rates*

A Platinum Annual Pass ($829/$729 for Florida residents/DVC members) offers the same privileges as the Premium Annual Pass plus unlimited admission to both water parks, Disney's Oak Trail, and Wide World of Sports for $80 more. A Platinum Annual Pass costs less than two 4-day Magic Your Way tickets with park-hopping, water parks, and no-expiration options.

Premier Annual Pass — *Actual 2015-2016 Rates*

The Disney Premier Passport ($1439) offers premium annual pass benefits at both Walt Disney World and Disneyland Resort in California. Available only at park ticket booths.

More at ⓘ park-passes-on-a-budget

Top Photo Slice: A park pass/room key in the hot little hands of Alexander, who is ready to go already! © MediaMarx, Inc.

Old Ticket Media: If you have an old Park Hopper with unused days on it, you may use those days, but you can no longer upgrade old ticket media if it has been used. With the removal of old-style turnstiles, most older ticket media will have to be exchanged for the new RFID-enabled media before park entry. This can only be done at Guest Relations at the Parks and Disney Springs, or at the TTC. There is no charge.

Upgrades and Exchanges: Within 14 days of your admission's first use or before the admissions on the original tickets are used up (whichever comes first), upgrade or apply the unused value to better admission. Visit Guest Relations/Concierge before you go home.

Disney Vacation Club Discounts: Discounts of about $100 are available on Annual Passes for members of the immediate family residing in the same household.

AAA: Members (see page 11) can still expect some sort of discount (historically 5%) on some passes. You must purchase tickets directly from AAA to get the discount.

Florida Resident Discounts: Florida Resident Seasonal Passes work like Annual Passes, but with blackout dates in busy seasons. Other deals for Florida residents include Gold Passes (no blackouts), weekday passes, and Epcot after 4 passes. Parking is now included in all resident passes. A multi-day ticket is available with a small, advance purchase discount.

Military Discounts: Discounts of roughly 7%–8% may be available on admission—check with your Exchange shop or MWR office. Disney's Military Promotional Tickets in the past have offered significant discounts for active, reserve, and retired military members and their spouses on four-day passes, often up to 50% or more below regular prices. Blackout dates usually apply. Some MWR offices may need to pre-order your tickets, so check with them well in advance. Keep an ear out for special programs for active military personnel. Visit http://www.disneyworld.com/special-offers, phone 407-939-4636, or visit Shades of Green online at http://www.shadesofgreen.org (see page 104) or upon arrival.

Online Ticket Brokers—These folks sell legitimate, unused passes at excellent rates: http://www.mapleleaftickets.com (800-841-2837), http://www.ticketmania.com (877-811-9233), http://www.floridaorlandotickets.net (407-344-0030). Be wary of others hawking tickets, including eBay, craigslist, and timeshares.

Kids Play Free (Well, Some Do): Kids under 3 are admitted into the parks for free (and get a free ride if the ride allows someone that small). Anyone 10 and over is considered an adult in the eyes of the ticket booth. Admission for kids ages 3–9 cost about 20% less than adult passes. Also, the option-filled pass you buy for yourself is usually more than your child needs, especially if you use childcare programs (detailed on pages 284–285).

Admission Comparison Chart: Options and prices for your number of days in the parks. *(2015/2016 prices for adult, nondiscounted passes purchased at the gate, including 6.5% tax.)*

Admission Type Days:	1	2	3	4	5	6	7	8	9	10	11	12	13
Base (single day/park)	$103 ($112)	$204	$293	$325	$335	$346	$357	$367	$378	$389			
Base + Park Hopping (PH)	$143	$257	$346	$393	$404	$414	$425	$436	$446	$457			
Base + Water Parks & More	$167	$268	$357	$389	$399	$410	$421	$431	$442	$453			
Base + Water Parks + PH	$192	$300	$389	$421	$431	$442	$453	$463	$474	$485			
Premium Annual Pass											$749 →		
Platinum Annual Pass											$829 →		

More at ⓘ replacing-lost-passes

Tip: Copy down or take a photo of the numbers on the back of your admission, as you will need these to replace lost tickets. Record the numbers on the worksheet on page 317.

Top Photo Slice: Ticket windows at Disney's Animal Kingdom © MediaMarx, Inc.

Getting Around the Parks and Resort

The internal **transportation system** at the Walt Disney World Resort is quite extensive, with buses, boats, and the famed monorail all doing their part to shuttle guests around the property. Transportation hubs exist at each major theme park and Downtown Disney, where you can reach nearly any other place in the "World" by bus, monorail, or boat. The Transportation and Ticket Center (TTC) near the Magic Kingdom forms another hub, where you can get the monorail, ferryboat, and various buses. For current route information, see our property transportation chart on the right, check with a transportation cast member, or call 407-WDW-RIDE (407-939-7433).

Bus service is the cornerstone of the Walt Disney World transportation system. It is efficient, if occasionally confusing. With a few exceptions, bus routes run every 15 to 20 minutes, from about one hour prior to park opening until about one hour after closing. Bus stops are clearly marked. Travel times vary by route. Be sure to build in extra time for travel. Tip: Special early-morning buses pick up guests who have early character breakfasts—ask about it at your resort. All buses are equipped to board guests in wheelchairs or ECVs. If a lift is out of service, another will be dispatched.

ⓘ18975 © Cheryl Pendry

A Disney bus passes under a monorail

Monorail trains run along two circular routes for the Magic Kingdom. The express route visits the park and the Transportation and Ticket Center (TTC), while the resort route also stops at the Contemporary, Polynesian Village, and Grand Floridian resorts. A separate line connects the TTC to Epcot. Monorails run from 7:00 am until one hour after park closing (they do not always continue to operate for Extra Magic Hours).

If you **drive**, you'll find ample parking at the parks. Use the map on the back flap of your PassPorter to get around the "World." **Tip**: Jot down your vehicle location in your PassPorter, or take a digital photo, so you don't forget where you parked. Also, if you intend to take advantage of Extra Magic Hour (EMH) mornings (see page 34), we recommend you avoid driving to the Magic Kingdom—it may be difficult to get into the park early enough. If you do drive, the gates at the TTC generally open 30–45 minutes before EMH time on EMH mornings.

From several locales, **boats** (also known as launches, ferries, cruisers, and Friendships) usher guests to the Magic Kingdom, Epcot, Disney's Hollywood Studios, Downtown Disney, and between some resorts. Boats generally depart every 15–30 minutes. At the Magic Kingdom, large ferries transport guests from the TTC to the gates, and a **railroad** encircles the park. Small boats run between the Magic Kingdom and the nearby resorts. At Epcot, "**Friendship**" boats shuttle you between points in the World Showcase.

By far the most reliable and common method of transportation within the "World" is **walking**. You can't walk between most parks and resorts—it's too far and there are few sidewalks, making it unsafe. You will, however, walk a lot around the parks, the resorts, and even between some parks and resorts. Bring comfortable, broken-in, walking shoes!

More at ⓘ monorails

Top Photo Slice: Monorail Lime glides over Epcot (ⓘ13293) © Wendy Suchomel

Disney Property Transportation Chart

Note: TTC = Transportation and Ticket Center (see previous page)

To get to the Magic Kingdom from...	Take the...
Polynesian Village or Grand Floridian	Monorail or boat
Contemporary	Monorail or walk
Wilderness Lodge or Fort Wilderness	Boat (or bus from Wilderness Lodge)
All other resorts	Bus
Disney's Hollywood Studios or Animal Kingdom	Bus to TTC, then monorail or boat
Epcot	Monorail to TTC, then monorail or boat
To get to Epcot from...	**Take the...**
Polynesian Village	Monorail (or walk) to TTC, then monorail
Contemporary or Grand Floridian	Monorail to TTC, then monorail
BoardWalk, Yacht/Beach Club, Swan/Dolphin	Boat or walk (to World Showcase)
All other resorts	Bus (to Future World)
Disney's Hollywood Studios or Animal Kingdom	Bus (or boat/walk from Studios)
Magic Kingdom	Monorail or boat to TTC, then monorail
To get to Disney's Hollywood Studios from...	**Take the...**
BoardWalk, Yacht/Beach Club, Swan/Dolphin	Boat or walk
All other resorts	Bus
Epcot or Disney's Animal Kingdom	Bus (or boat/walk from Epcot)
Magic Kingdom	Monorail or boat to TTC, then bus
To get to Disney's Animal Kingdom from...	**Take the...**
All resorts	Bus
Disney's Hollywood Studios or Epcot	Bus
Magic Kingdom	Monorail or boat to TTC, then bus
To get to Disney Springs/Typhoon Lagoon from...	**Take the...**
Port Orleans	Boat *(DS Marketplace only)* or bus
Old Key West or Saratoga Springs	Boat *(DS Marketplace only)*, bus, or walk
All other resorts	Bus
All parks (except Magic Kingdom)	Bus, boat, monorail to a resort, then bus
Magic Kingdom	Walk/monorail to Contemporary, then bus
To get to Blizzard Beach/Winter Summerland from...	**Take the...**
Disney's Animal Kingdom	Any resort bus going to Blizzard Beach
All resorts (or other theme parks)	Bus (or take resort bus and transfer)
To get to Fantasia Gardens from...	**Take the...**
All resorts *(guests at Swan, Dolphin, BoardWalk, and Yacht & Beach Club can walk)*	Travel to Disney's Hollywood Studios, boat to Swan, then walk
To get to Wide World of Sports from...	**Take the...**
All resorts	Go to Disney's Hollywood Studios, then bus
To get to Hoop-Dee-Doo Revue from...	**Take the...**
Magic Kingdom, Wilderness Lodge, or Contemporary	Boat to Fort Wilderness
Any other park	Bus to Fort Wilderness
Any other resort	Bus to Magic Kingdom, then boat
To get to a Disney Resort Hotel from...	**Take the...**
Any resort *(Swan, Dolphin, BoardWalk, Yacht & Beach Club are in walking distance of each other)*	Bus to a nearby theme park or Disney Springs, then bus, boat, or monorail

Top Photo Slice: A Friendship boat cruises through the International Gateway at sunset (5395) © Amy Sellars

MyMagic+

My Disney Experience, MagicBands, and FastPass+

MyMagic+ is Disney's suite of **new high-tech tools designed to enhance your planning** and touring experiences. These new technologies, including My Disney Experience, MagicBands, and FastPass+, work together and are changing how we vacation at Disney. Some elements of MyMagic+, such as FastPass+, are continuing to evolve as we write this. You should expect changes as tweaks are made in the coming years.

My Disney Experience—This is a web- and mobile-based app that acts as a centralized point for your Disney plans and reservations. Use My Disney Experience to customize your MagicBands (see below), complete online check-in, make resort room requests, make advanced dining reservations, link admission, create day-by-day plans, and make FastPass+ selections. You can also link family and friends in your travel group, so they can make and share the plans. Access it online at http://mydisneyexperience.com or download it free to your mobile device via the Apple App Store, Google Play, or Amazon Apps. The mobile app has GPS-enabled maps, displays wait times, show times, and character greeting times, and gives you access to create and modify dining and FastPass+ selections.

MagicBands— The MagicBand is a wristband for Disney resort guests that uses radio (RFID) technology to identify you at park and attraction entrances, shops, restaurants, your resort... everything you could use your Key to the World card for, "plus." Your information is securely stored on Disney's computers. To use it, you just touch the band to a special sensor, and in some cases enter a PIN number afterwards. You can use the MagicBand to check in for Disney's Magical Express at the airport, register at your Disney resort, unlock your resort room door, get free parking at the parks, enter the Disney parks (provided you've purchased admission, of course), reserve and check-in for dining and FastPass+ (attractions, character greetings, entertainment, parades, and fireworks), link your PhotoPass images, and play interactive games and attractions (such as Sorcerers of the Magic Kingdom). The waterproof wristband uses a non-latex, hypoallergenic material that is soft and flexible—one size fits all (those with small wrists can peel away part of the band to make it smaller). Disney resort guests can customize the color (red, blue, green, pink, yellow, orange, or gray) and the name that appears under the wristband at My Disney Experience (if entered at least 10 days prior to your vacation). If you'd rather not use a MagicBand you can request an RFID card when you arrive at your Disney resort. Note also that you will create a PIN number at check-in, to be used when charging to your account with a MagicBand (for added security). Tip: You can further personalize your MagicBand by purchasing buttons (Bandits, $6.95-$12.95), frames (Sliders, $12.95-$14.95), and bands (CoverBands, $6.95-$15.95). Only Disney resort guests get complimentary MagicBands, but everyone can buy one for about $13.

FastPass+—This is an enhanced version of the popular FASTPASS program (see page 120) that utilizes your MagicBand, Key to the World card, or park pass, and does away with paper. You can also book FastPass+ selections (up to three per day) up to 30-60 days in advance at My Disney Experience or at a kiosk when you arrive at the parks—you get to pick from several different available times offered when you make the selection. You can change your FastPass selections at any time up to your return time at My Disney Experience or at a kiosk, and if you miss a return time, you can reschedule it for a different time or attraction. Each person in your group can choose their own FastPass+ selections, or you can do them all together. The new FastPass+ system currently has more than 60 attractions, shows, and parades (the legacy FASTPASS system only had 28), so there are things you can reserve with FastPass+ that you can't reserve otherwise. You can use your MagicBand at all attractions marked in this book with either the FP headliner symbol or the FP regular symbol (see next page).

More at disney-tech

Top Photo Slice: Customized MagicBand screen at My Disney Experience © MediaMarx, Inc.

Understanding and Using the Attraction Descriptions and Ratings

PassPorter's custom-designed attraction charts include background, trivia, tips, restrictions, queues, accessibility details, enhanced ratings, and much more! We've organized this wide array of information into a consistent format so you can find what you need at a glance. Below is a key to our charts, along with notes and details. Enjoy!

Description Key

Icons[4] Ratings[5]

1 **Attraction Name** [D-3[2]] (Bar Color[3]) FP 🚹 A-OK! # # #	
An overview of the attraction, what to expect (without giving too much away), historical background, trivia and "secrets," our suggestions for the best seating/viewing/riding, tips and tricks, waiting/queue conditions (e.g., covered, outdoor, etc.), wheelchair and stroller access, height/age restrictions, and **Alex's ToddlerTips** *(ages 1-4),* KidTips *(ages 5-11),* **Allie's TweenTips** *(ages 11-12), and* **Allie's TeenTips** *(ages 13-16)—hints and tips by kids for kids!*	**Type**[6] Scope[6] Ages[7] Thrill Factor[8] Avg. Wait[8] Duration[8]

[1] Each chart has an empty **checkbox** in the upper left corner—use it to check off the attractions you want to visit (before you go) or those you visited during your trip.

[2] **Map coordinates** are presented as a letter and a number (i.e., A-5). Match up the coordinates on the park's map for the attraction's location within the park.

[3] The **bar color** indicates the attraction's target audience, as follows:

Thrill Seekers	Family Friendly	Loved by Little Kids	Everything Else

[4] Icons indicate when an attraction accepts a FastPass+ reservation (FP for a headliner attraction, FP for all other attractions), or a height/age restriction (🚹).

[5] Our **ratings** are shown on the far right end. An **A-OK!** indicates that an attraction is approved as little kid-friendly by our kids Allie and Alex. The three boxes on the right side show ratings on a scale of 1 (poor) to 10 (don't miss!). The first is **Jennifer's** rating, the second is Dave's, and the third is our Readers' ratings. We offer our personal ratings to show how opinions vary. You can also use our ratings as a point of reference—Jennifer appreciates good theming and dislikes sudden spins or drops, while Dave enjoys live performances and thrills. We both appreciate detail-rich attractions.

[6] The boxes on the right below the numeric ratings give basic information. The first box is **attraction type**. The second box is always **attraction scope**, which we rate as follows:

E-Ticket	Headliner attraction; the ultimate; expect long lines
D-Ticket	Excellent fun, not-to-be-missed
C-Ticket	Solid attraction that pleases most guests
B-Ticket	Good fun, but easily skipped in a pinch
A-Ticket	A simple diversion; often overlooked

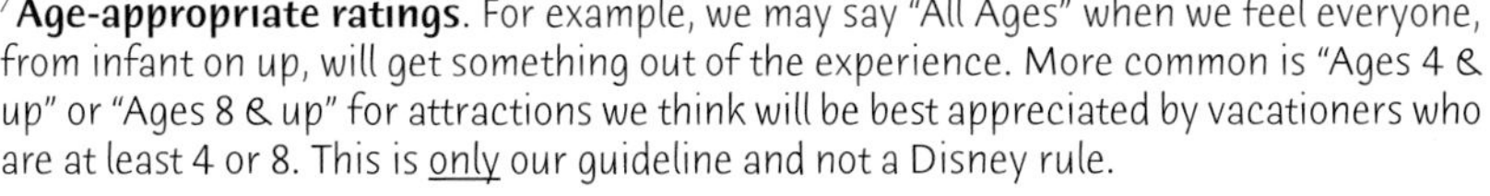

[7] **Age-appropriate ratings**. For example, we may say "All Ages" when we feel everyone, from infant on up, will get something out of the experience. More common is "Ages 4 & up" or "Ages 8 & up" for attractions we think will be best appreciated by vacationers who are at least 4 or 8. This is only our guideline and not a Disney rule.

[8] **Thrill/scare factor, average wait**, and **duration** follow the age ratings, though we eliminate these if they don't apply or expand them if deserving. We did our best to format this information so you can understand it without having to check this key, too!

Top Photo Slice: Thumbs up for the Magic Kingdom © MediaMarx, Inc.

The Parks

Disney's parks are quite spread out. To gain a better overall mental image, take a look the park map below. Note how the four major Disney parks form the **anchor of the resort**. Each park in the map below has its own map (go to the page number in parentheses). A similar "property map" marked with all roads and hotels is on the back flap of your book.

Check **theme park hours** by calling 407-WDW-INFO (407-939-4636) or by visiting the web site at http://www.disneyworld.com. Resort guests may also consult the resort's update sheet/board, park maps, and Times Guides on arrival. Park hours are typically published six months in advance. Once you know the park hours for your trip, write them on the appropriate PassPocket. Don't be surprised if the park hours change.

Study the descriptions and maps to **familiarize yourself** with the names and themes of the lands before you arrive. We provide handy, fold-out, full-color maps for each major park in this chapter—on the inside of each map are our favorite touring plans and a list of attractions. Feel free to pull them out and take them along with you for quick reference.

Plan your visit around the things that are **most important** to you or require advance planning (like restaurant seatings or show times). If you're just not sure, you can use our favorite touring plans included in each major park description as a starting point.

Note: The old **Tip Boards** at the parks are being phased out or are gone entirely now. To get wait times now, you need to check the MyDisneyExperience app (see page 126) on your smart device or visit the attraction itself.

Park Ratings

We rate each park to help you make the best decisions. Even so, our ratings may differ from your opinions—use the ratings as a guide only. **Value Ratings** range from 1 (poor) to 10 (excellent) and are based on **quality** (cleanliness, maintenance, and newness); **variety** (different types of things to do); and **scope** (quantity and size of things to do)—**overall value** represents an average of the above three values. **Magic Ratings** are based on **theme** (execution and sense of immersion); **excitement** (thrills, laughs, and sense of wonder); and **fun factor** (number and quality of entertaining activities)—**overall magic** represents an average of the above three values. We use a point accumulation method to determine value and magic ratings. **Readers' Ratings** are calculated from surveys submitted by vacationers at our web site (http://www.passporter.com/wdw/rate.htm).

♥♥♥♥♥=love it ♥♥♥♥=enjoy it ♥♥♥=like it
♥♥=tolerate it ♥=don't like it

More at ⓘ overcoming-kids-fears

Top Photo Slice: Aerial view of Epcot as seen from the Characters in Flight by Aerophile balloon © MediaMarx, Inc.

Magic Kingdom

The Magic Kingdom is a true fantasyland, playfully painted in bold strokes upon the canvas of the imagination. This is quintessential Disney and often the first park guests visit. It is located the farthest north of all parks, on the shore of the Seven Seas Lagoon.

The Magic Kingdom conjures up fantasy, nostalgia, youth, and most of all, **magic**. One thing it does especially well is blend the ordinary with the unusual, enhancing both to make it all seem better than reality. This giant, 107-acre playground attracts people of all ages to its bygone boulevards, tropical gardens, western landscapes, living cartoons, and yesterday's vision of tomorrow. All roads lead to Cinderella Castle in the park's hub, the crown of the Kingdom.

39668 © Danielle Sabato

A young princess stopped in the middle of Main Street to stare at Cinderella Castle

11389 © Katey Touchette

Sign above head as you enter the park

15052 © Lois Ann Dolley

Tomorrowland Indy Speedway

Top Photo Slice: Enchanting evening view of the Cinderella Castle looking down Main Street, U.S.A. (14671) © Andrea Johnson

Orienting Yourself at the Magic Kingdom

Fold out the next page for touring plans and a handy attraction chart

Six "lands" **radiate like spokes from the hub** of Cinderella Castle, located in the center of the park, with one more land added on for good measure (see the fold-out map on the facing page). Below are the lands in clockwise order, along with descriptions and headline attractions. Look behind the map to see our favorite itineraries and an at-a-glance list of attractions, and then turn to pages 137–148 for attraction details.

Main Street, U.S.A.

Walt Disney World Railroad Station ☛

ⓘ13308 © Jodi Leeper

An early 1900s Main Street bustles with shops, eateries, a barbershop quartet, and City Hall.
Headline Attraction: Walt Disney World Railroad

Adventureland

Enchanted Tiki Room ☛

ⓘ1872 © Brad K.

Walk to the beat of jungle drums in a paradise filled with pirates, parrots, crocs, and camels.
Headline Attractions: Pirates of the Caribbean, Enchanted Tiki Room, Jungle Cruise, The Magic Carpets of Aladdin

Frontierland

Harper's Mill on Tom Sawyer Island ☛

ⓘ13375 © Janet Simonsen

Journey back to the American Frontier, complete with a fort, mill, shootin' gallery, and "mountain range."
Headline Attractions: Splash Mountain, Big Thunder Mountain

Liberty Square

Liberty Belle Riverboat ☛

ⓘ11223 © Dana Berlestein-Rodriguez

Step back in time to Colonial America with her presidents, riverboats, and a haunted house.
Headline Attractions: The Haunted Mansion, The Hall of Presidents

Fantasyland

Teacups at the Mad Tea Party ☛

ⓘ5234 © Amy Sellars

An enchanted, brightly colored "small world" where elephants fly, teacups spin, dwarves mine, and princesses hold court.
Headline attractions: Under the Sea ~ Journey of the Little Mermaid, Winnie the Pooh, Dumbo, Mickey's PhilharMagic, Seven Dwarfs Mine Train, Peter Pan's Flight

Tomorrowland

Entrance to Tomorrowland ☛

ⓘ3285 © Cheryl Pendry

The future as imagined in the 1930s, complete with space flights, aliens, and time travel.
Headline Attractions: Space Mountain, Buzz Lightyear's Space Ranger Spin, Monsters Inc. Laugh Floor

Top Photo Slice: The Partners Statue in the hub at the Magic Kingdom (ⓘ13554) © Janet Simonsen

Our Favorite Touring Plans for the Magic Kingdom

NOTES

While we don't believe in the "commando" approach to fun, relaxing vacations, we realize that you may want guidance. Use these touring plans, which focus on the highest-rated attractions, as a starting point. You can do these plans in one day if you start by 9:00 am. If you can start earlier or stay later, add in additional attractions. The plans work best if you go in the same order, but feel free to re-order based on showtimes and wait times. Vacationers with infants and toddlers, or thrill-shy adults, may prefer to skip all attractions in blue.

ITINERARIES

Touring With Adults

Get FastPass+ (can be reserved 30-60 days in advance on My Disney Experience—see page 126) for Seven Dwarfs Mine Train, Space Mountain, Jungle Cruise for as early as possible.

Enter Tomorrowland
Visit Buzz Lightyear
Visit Stitch's Great Escape!
Visit Space Mountain
Enter Adventureland
Visit Enchanted Tiki Room
Visit Pirates of the Caribbean
Visit Jungle Cruise
Enter Frontierland (and have a snack)
Visit Big Thunder Mountain
Visit Splash Mountain
Eat lunch at Liberty Tree Tavern* or Columbia Harbour House (*about 4 hours after entering park*)
Enter Fantasyland
Visit Seven Dwarfs Mine Train
Get another FastPass+ of your choice
Visit Under the Sea
Visit Mickey's PhilharMagic
Visit Peter Pan's Flight
Enter Liberty Square (and have a snack)
Watch parade from Sleepy Hollow
Visit Haunted Mansion
Visit Hall of Presidents
Visit whatever FastPass+ attraction you managed to get, or ride the Walt Disney World Railroad
If the park is still open, do the following:
Eat dinner at Skipper Canteen*, Be Our Guest*, Crystal Palace*, or Tony's Town Square* (*about 8 1/2 hours into your day*)
Watch nighttime parade from Main Street, Cinderella Castle, or Liberty Square
Watch fireworks from same spot
(Tour duration: About 10 1/2 hours)

Touring With Kids

Get FastPass+ (can be reserved 30-60 days in advance on My Disney Experience—see page 126) for Princess Fairy Tale Hall, Peter Pan's Flight, and Jungle Cruise for as early as possible.

Enter Fantasyland
Visit Seven Dwarfs Mine Train
Visit Under the Sea ~ Journey of The Little Mermaid
Visit Dumbo the Flying Elephant
Visit The Barnstormer (Great Goofini)
Visit Enchanted Tales with Belle
Visit Peter Pan's Flight
Visit Winnie the Pooh
Visit Mickey's PhilharMagic
Watch castle show (if showing)
Eat lunch at Be Our Guest* or Pinocchio Village Haus
Enter Adventureland
Visit Pirates of the Caribbean
Enter Frontierland
Visit Splash Mountain or Big Thunder Mtn.
Enter Adventureland (and have a snack)
Visit Magic Carpets of Aladdin
Visit Jungle Cruise
Get another FastPass+ of your choice
Enter Liberty Square
Watch parade from Sleepy Hollow
Visit Haunted Mansion
Enter Tomorrowland
Visit Stitch's Great Escape!
Visit Monsters, Inc. Laugh Floor
Visit Space Mountain
Visit Buzz Lightyear
Eat dinner at Skipper Canteen*, Tony's Town Square*, Crystal Palace*, or Cosmic Ray's (*about 8 hours after entering park*)
Watch nighttime parade from Main Street
Watch fireworks from hub or Liberty Square
(Tour duration: About 9 1/2 hours)

** These restaurants may be difficult to impossible to get in as a walk-up. Advance dining reservations can be made up to 180 days in advance (see page 226).*

Top Photo: Detail of Cinderella Castle, complete with gargoyle (①7808) © Wendyismyname

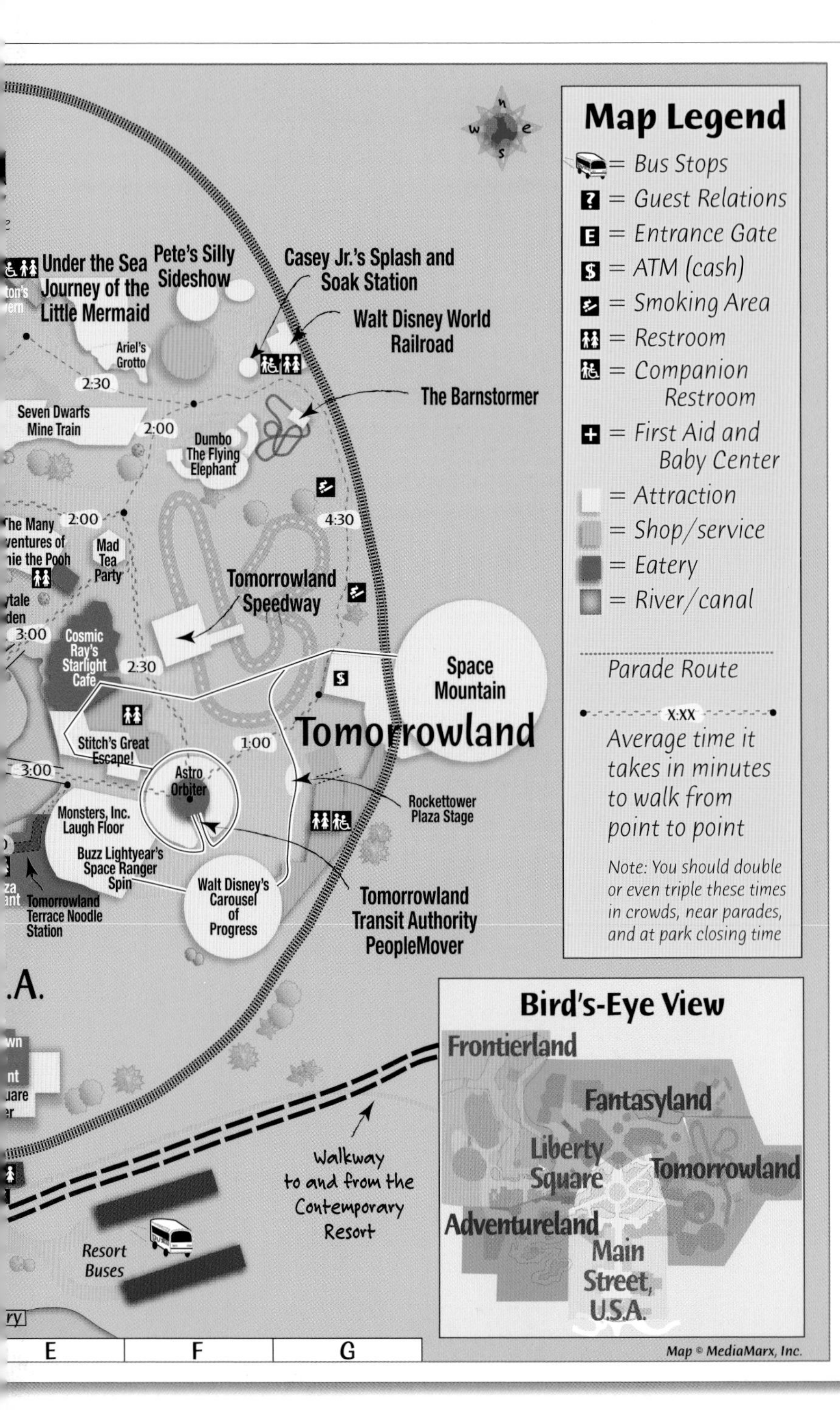
Map Legend
= Bus Stops
= Guest Relations
= Entrance Gate
= ATM (cash)
= Smoking Area
= Restroom
= Companion Restroom
= First Aid and Baby Center
= Attraction
= Shop/service
= Eatery
= River/canal
Parade Route
X:XX
Average time it takes in minutes to walk from point to point
Note: You should double or even triple these times in crowds, near parades, and at park closing time
Under the Sea Journey of the Little Mermaid
Pete's Silly Sideshow
Casey Jr.'s Splash and Soak Station
Walt Disney World Railroad
Ariel's Grotto
The Barnstormer
Seven Dwarfs Mine Train
Dumbo The Flying Elephant
Mad Tea Party
Tomorrowland Speedway
Cosmic Ray's Starlight Cafe
Space Mountain
Tomorrowland
Stitch's Great Escape!
Astro Orbiter
Rockettower Plaza Stage
Monsters, Inc. Laugh Floor
Buzz Lightyear's Space Ranger Spin
Walt Disney's Carousel of Progress
Tomorrowland Transit Authority PeopleMover
Tomorrowland Terrace Noodle Station
2:30
2:00
2:00
4:30
3:00
2:30
1:00
3:00
Walkway to and from the Contemporary Resort
Resort Buses
Bird's-Eye View
Frontierland
Fantasyland
Liberty Square
Tomorrowland
Adventureland
Main Street, U.S.A.
E
F
G
Map © MediaMarx, Inc.

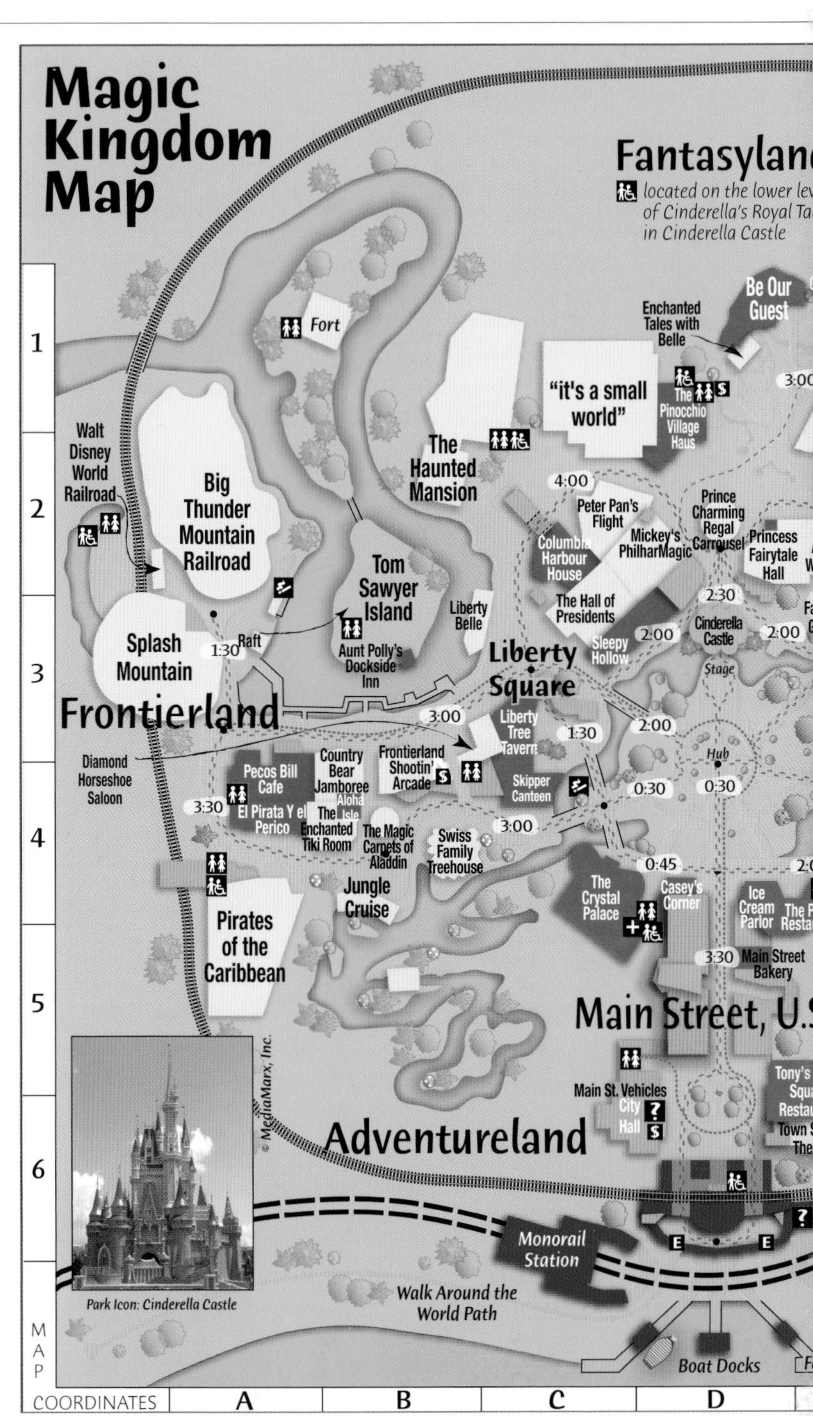

Park Icon: Cinderella Castle

Magic Kingdom Attractions At-A-Glance

(alphabetical order)

Attraction	Type	Allow	Page
☐ Astro Orbiter [F-4]	Ride	20+	146-T
☐ Barnstormer, The (Great Goofini) [F-2]	Coaster	30+	143-Fa
☐ Big Thunder Mountain Railroad [A-2]	Coaster	50+	140-Fr
☐ Buzz Lightyear [F-4]	Track Ride	30+	146-T
☐ Carousel of Progress [F-4]	Show	30+	146-T
☐ Casey Jr. Playground [G-1]	Playground	20+	145-Fa
☐ Country Bear Jamboree [B-4]	Show	30+	140-Fr
☐ Diamond Horseshoe Saloon [B-3]	Pavilion	20+	141-LS
☐ Dumbo The Flying Elephant [F-2]	Ride	30+	142-Fa
☐ Enchanted Tales with Belle [D-1]	Show	40+	142-Fa
☐ Fairytale Garden [E-3]	Live Show	30+	143-Fa
☐ Frontierland Shootin' Arcade [B-4]	Arcade	15+	140-Fr
☐ Hall of Presidents, The [C-3]	Show	30+	141-LS
☐ Haunted Mansion, The [C-2]	Track Ride	30+	141-LS
☐ "it's a small world" [C-2]	Boat Ride	25+	143-Fa
☐ Jungle Cruise [B-4]	Boat Ride	40+	138-A
☐ Liberty Belle Riverboat [C-3]	Boat Ride	30+	141-LS
☐ Mad Tea Party [E-2]	Ride	20+	143-Fa
☐ Magic Carpets of Aladdin [B-4]	Ride	30+	138-A
☐ Main Street Vehicles [D-5]	Vehicles	30+	137-MS
☐ Mickey's PhilharMagic [D-2]	3-D Show	40+	144-Fa
☐ Monsters, Inc. Laugh Floor [E-4]	Show	45+	147-T
☐ Peter Pan's Flight [C-2]	Track Ride	40+	144-Fa
☐ Pirates of the Caribbean [A-4]	Boat Ride	30+	139-A
☐ Prince Charming Regal Carrousel [D-2]	Ride	15+	144-Fa
☐ Princess Fairytale Hall [D-2]	Character	30+	145-Fa
☐ Seven Dwarfs Mine Train [E-2]	Coaster	60–90+	145-Fa
☐ Space Mountain [G-3]	Coaster	60+	147-T
☐ Splash Mountain [A-3]	Coaster	60–90+	140-Fr
☐ Stitch's Great Escape! [E-4]	Show	50+	148-T
☐ Swiss Family Treehouse [B-4]	Walk-thru	30+	139-A
☐ Tiki Room, The Enchanted [B-4]	Show	20+	138-A
☐ Tom Sawyer Island [A-3]	Playground	60+	140-Fr
☐ Tomorrowland Arcade (closed) [G-3]	Arcade	20–40+	148-T
☐ Tomorrowland Speedway [F-3]	Ride	50+	148-T
☐ Tomorrowland Transit Authority [F-4]	Track Ride	10+	148-T
☐ Town Square Theater [E-6]	Pavilion	30+	137-MS
☐ Under the Sea (Ariel's) [E-1]	Ride	60–90+	142-Fa
☐ Walt Disney World Railroad [D-6, A-2, G-1]	Train Ride	30+	137-MS
☐ Winnie the Pooh, Many Adv. [E-2]	Track Ride	30+	144-Fa

See page 151b for an explanation of this chart.

Catching the Shows at the Magic Kingdom

Fun and excitement surround you in the Magic Kingdom. Live entertainment fills the streets with parades, performers, bands, and fireworks. Every afternoon, the 20-minute-long parade highlights favorite Disney moments (see the parade route on the foldout map). The current parade, **Disney Festival of Fantasy** FP, debuted in February 2014 with innovative new floats. We like to watch the parade from Frontierland or Liberty Square.

The dazzling **Wishes fireworks show** FP is generally held whenever the park is open after dark. Stand in front of Cinderella Castle to see Tinker Bell as she flies toward Tomorrowland during the 12-minute show. The fireworks are preceded by "**Celebrate the Magic**," a show in which character images are projected on the castle. If you don't mind missing the castle show, Tomorrowland (near the Speedway) and Liberty Square are good viewing locations, too. Fantasyland is also possible, but it is very loud. Tip: The "Made with Magic" Ear Hats and accessories will light up and interact with Wishes!

Cinderella Castle is the backdrop for live musical stage shows such as Dream Along With Mickey stage show. In the evening, **Disney's Electrical Parade** (if showing) adds lights and music to the fun and follows the same route as the day parade. Disney characters make appearances throughout the park, especially at park opening and after some shows.

ⓘ15071 © Nicole Clayton

The glorious Wishes fireworks show over Cinderella Castle, as seen from the hub

More at ⓘ magic-kingdom-parades

Top Photo Slice: Fireworks over Cinderella Castle during the Dream Along with Mickey show (ⓘ24239) © Bill Myers

Making the Most of the Magic Kingdom

TIPS

Take a **spin around the park** when you first arrive by boarding the train at the Walt Disney World Railroad station in Main Street, U.S.A. The 20-minute journey is a great introduction to the park.

Get a **haircut** at the Harmony Barber shop in Main Street. Try some colored hair gel at no extra charge, but watch out for the pixie dust! Young 'uns can get their very first haircut, too! Walk up or reserve at 407-WDW-STYLE.

© MediaMarx, Inc.

Alexander got his first haircut at the Harmony Barber Shop

Want a hairdo? The **Bibbidi Bobbidi Boutique** inside Cinderella Castle offers fancy do's for girls and boys ages 3 and up. Open from 8:00 am–7:00 pm—reserve up to 180 days at 407-WDW-STYLE.

Is your little prince or princess more of a pirate? Journey to the **Pirates League** in Adventureland for pirate "makeovers" for girls, boys, and even adults! Girls may also choose the "Mermaid Transformation" package! The "First Mate" package includes a bandanna, choice of facial effect (scar, tattoo, fake tooth, earring, or eye patch), sword and sheath, and personalized pirate oath for $29.95 plus tax. Reserve at 407-WDW-CREW.

Make time for the **Flag Retreat** in the Main Street town square, usually held at 5:00 or 5:30 pm daily. A color guard takes down the flag, and most days a marching band plays as well. Are you a veteran? Inquire at City Hall about assisting in the flag lowering, too.

Looking for interactive fun? "**Sorcerers of the Magic Kingdom**" is a role-playing game using playing cards and electronic game kiosks, where guests battle the Disney Villains who are trying to take over the Magic Kingdom. Look for the "Sorcerer Recruitment Center" at the Firehouse on Main Street to pick up your quest, an activated Portal Key card, a pack of five random cards, and a map. Challenges are found everywhere but Tomorrowland. You can play (and trade with others for needed cards) as you and/or your group tour the park. See page 283 for more details on the different kinds of cards you can collect. On a smaller scale, "**A Pirate's Adventure - Treasures of the Seven Seas**" is a hunt for five treasures around Adventureland. Pick up your map to the right of Pirates of the Caribbean.

Top Photo Slice: An engineer waves from the Roger E. Broggie along the Walt Disney World Railroad (ⓘ2305) © Janet Simonsen

Getting the Best at the Magic Kingdom

SHOPPING

Sure stops for general Disney merchandise include much of Main Street, U.S.A.—shops here are open for 30–60 minutes after park closing. Here are some of our favorite **themed shops**:

Shop	Land	What makes it special
The Chapeau	Main Street, U.S.A.	Hats with embroidered names
Disney Clothiers	Main Street, U.S.A.	Upscale yet casual Disney clothes
Memento Mori	Liberty Square	Haunted Mansion-themed items
Agrabah Bazaar	Adventureland	Themed, open-air marketplace
Plaza del Sol Caribe Bazaar	Adventureland	Pirate clothing and decor
Briar Patch	Frontierland	Great theme, Pooh and friends
Castle Couture	Fantasyland	Disney princess costumes
Mickey's Star Traders	Tomorrowland	Sci-fi toys and gadgets

NOTES

Free wireless Internet is available throughout the park! Look for the "Disney-Guest" network on your wireless device. Charge your device in Fantasyland (Rapunzel area) or buy a charger at a gift shop.

Alcohol is served in just one location at the Magic Kingdom: Be Our Guest restaurant (see page 231). If you're not dining here but want a drink, try one of the nearby resort hotels.

Need a **good place to meet**? The Liberty Bell in Liberty Square and the waterside seating across from the Plaza Restaurant are good choices. We recommend you avoid Cinderella Castle.

Main Street, U.S.A. closes a half hour later than the rest of the park. So while other folks fight the crowds in the parking lot, feel free to linger. Note that the stores are extremely busy at the end of the day.

Dining options abound, although table-service isn't as prevalent as at Epcot. There are seven table-service restaurants and many counter-service cafes and carts. See pages 231–233 for details.

RATINGS

Ratings are explained on page 128.

Our Value Ratings:		Our Magic Ratings:		Readers' Ratings:
Quality:	7/10	Theme:	7/10	82% fell in love with it
Variety:	9/10	Excitement:	10/10	15% liked it well enough
Scope:	7/10	Fun Factor:	7/10	2% had mixed feelings
Overall Value:	**8/10**	**Overall Magic:**	**8/10**	1% were disappointed

Magic Kingdom is enjoyed by...	(rated by both authors and readers)	
Younger Kids: ♥♥♥♥♥	Young Adults: ♥♥♥♥	Families: ♥♥♥♥♥
Older Kids: ♥♥♥♥♥	Mid Adults: ♥♥♥	Couples: ♥♥♥♥
Teenagers: ♥♥♥♥	Mature Adults: ♥♥♥	Singles: ♥♥♥

Top Photo Slice: Windows above the Disney Clothiers shop in Main Street, U.S.A. (ⓘ9685) © Karen Majeau

Finding Your Way to the Magic Kingdom

BEST TIMES TO GO

The park tends to be the **busiest on Saturdays and Sundays**, and any day there are Extra Magic Hours scheduled (see page 34). We recommend you check the Extra Magic Hour schedule on Disney's web site and avoid those days if you prefer fewer crowds. The park is drawing larger crowds in general due to the recent expansion. Popular attractions such as Seven Dwarfs Mine Train and Splash Mountain are best done first thing in the morning to avoid long lines. Visit lands on the west (left) side of the park **earlier in the day**. Parents of young children are best off doing Fantasyland (particularly Peter Pan's Flight) first as it gets busier later in the day. If you go to Splash Mountain and/or Big Thunder Mountain **during parade times**, note that the area can be very congested—use the riverside boardwalk or railroad instead. **Shop in the afternoon** to avoid crowds.

GETTING THERE

By Monorail—From the Contemporary, Polynesian Village, or Grand Floridian resorts, take the monorail directly to the park. From Epcot, take the monorail to the Transportation and Ticket Center (TTC) and transfer to a Magic Kingdom express monorail or boat.

By Boat—From the TTC, ferry boats take guests to and from the Magic Kingdom. Guests at Polynesian Village, Grand Floridian, Wilderness Lodge and Villas, and Fort Wilderness also have a boat service.

By Bus—From all other resorts, buses take you directly to the Magic Kingdom. From Disney's Hollywood Studios or Disney's Animal Kingdom, bus to the TTC and transfer to monorail or boat. From Downtown Disney, bus to the Contemporary and walk.

By Car—Take I-4 to exit 67 (westbound) or exit 62 (eastbound) and continue about four miles to the toll plaza. All-day parking is $17 (free to resort guests and annual passholders) and the pass is valid at other parks' lots on the same day. Park, take a tram to the Transportation and Ticket Center, and monorail or boat to the park.

By Foot—You can walk from the Contemporary Resort.

ⓘ22826 © Cam Matthews

A ferry boat transports guests across the Seven Seas Lagoon

More at ⓘ most-magical-attractions

Top Photo Slice: An early morning view of the Magic Kingdom from the Contemporary Resort (ⓘ3113) © Jennifer Berry

Charting the Attractions at Main Street, U.S.A.

Jennifer | Dave | Readers

Main Street Vehicles [D-5] — A-OK! — 3 | 2 | 5

Catch a one-way ride to or from the hub in vehicles fashioned after those popular at the turn of the century. We've seen horseless carriages, trolleys pulled by draft horses, and even a fire engine. These vehicles are fun to ride in if you're willing to wait in the slow, long lines. No time? Just walk instead. Vehicles tend to stop operating later in the day and during parades. Must transfer from wheelchair. **Alex's ToddlerTip:** *"Look at the horses! ☺"* **Allie's TeenTip:** *"It's a bit boring."*

Vehicles | A-Ticket | All ages | Gentle ride | Long waits

Town Square Theater (Meet Mickey) [D-6] — FP — A-OK! — 3 | 5 | 5

Mouse fans gather in the theater's ornate lobby before being ushered into a backstage world of steamer trunks and whimsical theatrical props, where Mickey graciously greets (and sometimes talks) to guests. Wonderful details make this an above-average meet-n-greet. This is also the park's PhotoPass Center.

Exhibit | A-Ticket | Ages 3 & up | Simple fun

Walt Disney World Railroad [D-6] — A-OK! — 5 | 5 | 7

Circle the Magic Kingdom on a popular steam train, with stops at Main Street, U.S.A., Frontierland, and Fantasyland. You'll catch glimpses of all but Liberty Square along the 1.5-mile journey. Ride the full route for fun, or disembark at any stop to travel through the park. Personal strollers must be folded before entering station. Replacement rental strollers may be available at other stops (hold on to your name tag!), but are not guaranteed. Attraction is closed during fireworks. Wheelchair and ECV friendly. **Alex's ToddlerTip:** *"Choo choo! ☺"* **Allie's KidTip:** *"Kids like this train! It doesn't go too fast."*

Train Ride | B-Ticket | All ages | A bit loud | Gentle ride | Short waits | 20 min. ride (roundtrip)

Attraction descriptions and ratings are explained on page 127.

What Is and Isn't an Attraction?

We defined an "attraction" on page 120 as an individual ride, show, or exhibit. These are the destinations at the park and almost invariably come with a queue. We cover virtually all the attractions that Disney lists in their own guidemaps, plus a few that aren't listed but we still think are deserving of the "attraction" title (such as Main Street Vehicles). Like Disney, we don't consider things like street entertainers to be attractions as they rarely need a queue. We also don't consider outdoor stage shows, parades, or fireworks to be attractions, either—we cover these in the Entertainment sections in the park introduction pages of your PassPorter. Character greeting areas are less straightforward—if Disney considers one to be an attraction or we feel it offers more than simple character greetings, we include a description of it. For a list of character greeting locations, refer to the guidemap and Times Guide available upon your arrival. We also list popular spots to find favorite characters at Disney's Hollywood Studios on page 171b. For more specific information or hard-to-find characters, ask at Guest Relations in any of Disney's parks. Also check out our *Disney Character Yearbook*—details on page 314.

© MediaMarx, Inc.
Alexander finds attractions everywhere

Top Photo Slice: A panoramic view of Main Street, U.S.A.(ⓘ14640) © Nicole Clayton

Charting the Attractions at Adventureland

Jennifer Dave Readers

Walt Disney's Enchanted Tiki Room [B-4] A-OK! 8 7 8

A perfectly cool place to sit and rest while more than 225 Audio-Animatronics creatures sing and cavort above you. This classic attraction is similar to the original, which debuted at Disneyland in 1963. This fun musical revue grew from Walt Disney's notion for an unusually entertaining Chinese restaurant. Don't miss the pre-show in the outdoor, covered queue area. Best views are on the left side. Wheelchair friendly. Assistive listening devices. **Alex's ToddlerTip**: ☺ **Alex's KidTip**: "It's dark and loud, but the birds tell funny jokes." **Allie's KidTip**: "Look for the Tiki gods." **TeenTip**: "It may seem lame, but it's not!"

ⓘ6889 © Joy Vodnik

Singing Tiki Gods

Show
D-Ticket
All ages
Dark, loud, angry gods
Short waits
3 min. intro
11 min. show

Jungle Cruise [B-4] FP+ A-OK! 6 6 7

See the sights along the "rivers of the world" in the company of a silly skipper. You and your fellow explorers will go chug-chugging up river in an open-air, awning-covered river boat inspired by the "African Queen." Every skipper tells a slightly different tale. Audio-Animatronics animals and "natives" liven things up. You may get damp. Watch for the Jingle Cruise during the holidays. Outdoor, covered queue. Transfer from ECV to wheelchair. **Alex's ToddlerTip**: ☺ **Allie's KidTip**: "Lions, and tigers, and King Cobra!" **TweenTip**: "One of my favorites!"

ⓘ13623 © Janet Simonsen

Scenes along the Jungle Cruise

Boat Ride
D-Ticket
Ages 3 & up
Corny jokes
FASTPASS or long waits
10 min. ride

The Magic Carpets of Aladdin [B-4] FP+ A-OK! 5 6 5

Take a spin through a whole new world. Colorful, rider-controlled carpets go around, up, and down—sit in the front to control the height, or sit in the back to tilt forward and back. Similar to Dumbo (see page 142). Water-spitting camels add to the fun. Transfer from ECV to wheelchair. **Alex's ToddlerTip**: "Wow! ☺" **Allie's KidTip**: "Sit in the front so you can zoom up and get sprayed by camels."

ⓘ13724 © Patti Kalal

Margaret anticipates her carpet ride

Ride
D-Ticket
Ages 3 & up
Med. waits
$1\frac{1}{2}$ min. ride

Top Photo Slice: A goddess statue seen while riding the Jungle Cruise (ⓘ13628) © Janet Simonsen

Charting the Attractions at Adventureland

Pirates of the Caribbean [A-4]

FP+ A-OK! — Jennifer 8, Dave 7, Readers 9

Boat Ride | E-Ticket | Ages 6 & up | Gentle drop, dark, scary to young kids | 9 min. ride

"Yo ho, yo ho!" The ride that inspired the movies is a slow, dark cruise through a subterranean world of Audio-Animatronics pirates (including Captain Jack Sparrow and Barbossa) and the townsfolk they plunder. Enjoy scene after riotous scene and fun special effects while riding in new boats. Captain Blackbeard and the Mermaids are the latest additions. Lines can be long, especially on hot days because you get to wait in a cool cellar. Take the left line—it's shorter. You aren't likely to get wet, but seats can be damp. Transfer from ECV to wheelchair and transfer from wheelchair. **Alex's ToddlerTip:** *"Scary! ☹"* **Alex's KidTip:** *"It's dark and there is a drop ... and you can sometimes get wet."* **Allie's TeenTip:** *"Very cool! I love Jack!"*

①39484 © Liliane Opsomer

"A pirate's life for me!"

Swiss Family Treehouse [B-4]

Jennifer 5, Dave 5, Readers 4

Walk-thru | B-Ticket | Ages 4 & up | Lots of stairs | Allow 15–30 min. to tour

Walk through the home of the shipwrecked family from the Disney classic "Swiss Family Robinson." The branches of the huge (and very fake) banyan tree, known as "Disneyodendron eximus," cradle the family's heirlooms and contraptions. The treehouse has multiple levels that you need to climb. Thus, this attraction is not wheelchair or stroller accessible, and it can be tiring for some. The line of guests winds through slowly. **Alex's KidTip:** *"You'll love the inventions in the treehouse!"*

Strollers: To Bring or Rent

See page 121 for more on rentals.

If you bring your own stroller (a boon for the airport and travel to and from the buses/parking lot), we recommend a compact, umbrella stroller, as it's easy to tote about. If you prefer to bring a larger, folding stroller (the kind with cup holders and serious cargo capacity), try to travel the buses at off-hours, when the stroller won't prevent you from getting onboard due to crowded conditions. Rentals in the parks are good for kids who only need an occasional ride and weigh less than the 70-lb. weight limit. All rental strollers in the parks are now either "jogging style" or molded plastic (see photo). Need an alternative? Rent a nicer stroller for a better price from a place like Orlando Stroller Rentals (http://www.orlandostrollerrentals.com), which we've used and recommend.

© MediaMarx, Inc.

Rental at Magic Kingdom

Charting the Attractions at Frontierland

Jennifer | Dave | Readers

Big Thunder Mountain Railroad [A-2] FP+ A-OK! 7 8 9

Be prepared to grin as you ride this not-so-scary roller coaster through a wild western landscape. There is plenty of speed and lots of curves, but no fearsome drops on this 4-min. mine train ride. You'll shake and rattle, though! Look around and enjoy Disney's lovingly built scenes. Night rides are extra fun! Lines can be long, but there is a new, interactive queue in which you get to help the miners. 40"/102 cm height restriction, adult supervision required. Transfer from wheelchair. Health warning. **Allie's KidTip:** "Listen for the howls of the wolves. I loved this ride! Can we go again?"	**Coaster** E-Ticket Ages 6 & up Fast turns, dark caves FASTPASS or long waits

Country Bear Jamboree [B-4] A-OK! 5 4 5

A troupe of Audio-Animatronics bears sings, dances, and jokes in this loving country music sendup. Grown-up city slickers might find the jokes and songs a bit corny, but the young 'uns just might take a hankerin' to 'em. This is another cool, dim place to duck out of the hot Florida sun. Wheelchair accessible. Reflective captioning. Assistive listening devices. **Alex's ToddlerTip:** ☺ **Allie's KidTip:** "Listen carefully for the words to the songs. They're funny!" **TeenTip:** "Boring."	**Show** C-Ticket Ages 2 & up Loud Med. waits 15 min. show

Frontierland Shootin' Arcade [B-4] 4 6 3

Have fun shootin' targets with electronic rifles. Aim at cactus, tombstones, and bits of the landscape. Pay 1 dollar (four quarters) for about 35 shots. **Allie's KidTip:** "Shoot the red dots. But beware: The guns are heavy." **TweenTip:** "Awesome! Rest your elbow on the pad to get the best shot."

© MediaMarx, Inc.

Arcade | A-Ticket | Ages 9 & up

Splash Mountain [A-3] FP+ 4 6 9

Even bystanders can get soaked when riders slide down this five-story log flume into the Briar Patch. The first ten minutes of this attraction are a gentle ride through an Audio-Animatronics wonderland with all the "brer" creatures from "The Song of the South." Then, kersplash! 40"/102 cm height restriction, adult supervision required. Little ones can play in the charming Laughin' Place playground near the attraction's exit while big kids ride. Health warning. Transfer from wheelchair to ride. **Alex's ToddlerTip:** ☺ (for the playground) **Allie's KidTip:** "I love Splash Mountain. On the last big drop, you might want to lean back."	**Coaster** E-Ticket Ages 9 & up Very steep drop at end! FASTPASS or long waits 11 min. ride

Tom Sawyer Island [A-3] A-OK! 6 6 5

Young 'uns can explore caves, tunnels, and Fort Langhorn as they scamper over Tom and Huck's legendary hangout. Kids love the bridges; oldtimers wander the winding paths and play checkers. Caves are fun, but can be very dark and confining. Board a raft near Big Thunder Mountain to reach the island. This is a great place for a break—try Aunt Polly's Dockside Inn for a snack (seasonal). Must be able to walk. Closes at dusk. Tip: Look for the hidden whitewash brushes—if you find one, tell a cast member for a surprise! **Alex's ToddlerTip:** "Caves! ☺" **Alex's KidTip:** "The caves are cool but a little dark and scary!"	**Playground** C-Ticket All ages Dark, scary caves Short waits Allow 1 hr.

Tips: You can board the Walt Disney World Railroad (see page 137 for details) at the Frontierland Station [A-2]. Need a break? Look for the rocking chairs scattered about Frontierland and Liberty Square.

Top Photo Slice: Riding Big Thunder Mountain in Frontierland (ⓘ13645) © Misty Hailey

Charting the Attractions at Liberty Square

Jennifer | Dave | Readers

Diamond Horseshoe Saloon [B-3] 5 – 4

The Diamond Horseshoe Saloon is serving light refreshments most of the time; buffet meals in peak seasons. This attraction has had difficulty finding its place in recent years, and we wouldn't be surprised if it changes in the near future. Let's hope they bring back a live show. If it's open, it should remain wheelchair accessible.

Pavilion
A-Ticket

The Hall of Presidents: A Celebration of Liberty's Leaders [C-3] 5 4 6

Ladies and gentlemen, the Presidents of the United States! The show begins with a 180° film presenting a patriotic, stirring view of our past. Every U.S. President is represented in full Audio-Animatronics glory—look for President Obama (see photo), who debuted here in July 2009. The revamped show focuses on the bond between a president and his people, and is now narrated by Morgan Freeman. A red brick colonial hall houses the large, 700-seat theater, a cool, quiet hideaway. Wheelchair accessible. Reflective captioning. Assistive listening devices. Shows are every half hour. **Allie's KidTip:** "You might like the movie—it talks about freedom." **TeenTip:** "I'd rather do something else."

© MediaMarx, Inc.
President Obama joins the line-up

Show
C-Ticket
Ages 10 & up
Dark theater
Short waits
23 min. show

The Haunted Mansion [B-2] FP A-OK! 9 8 9

Go for a gore-free ride through a world of 999 grinning ghosts in this popular attraction. The spooky visual effects are astounding, but the scares are served up with a wink and lots of chuckles. There's a fun storyline, nifty special effects, and enough delicious detail here that you'll ride again and again. Just be sure to leave room in your two- to three-person "doom buggy" for hitchhiking ghosts! A new interactive queue is great fun, but you can bypass it for a quicker wait. May be too intense for young kids (though Allie liked it, she was a bit scared even at 12). Transfer from wheelchair to ride. Visit http://www.doombuggies.com for more details. **Allie's KidTip:** "Can you find the dog skeleton? Hint: It's on a cliff in the graveyard."

© MediaMarx, Inc.
Spooky fun!

Track Ride
E-Ticket
Ages 6 & up
Mild scares, very dark
Medium waits
3 min. intro
7 min. ride

Liberty Square Riverboat [B-3] 5 6 5

Take a cruise on a steam-driven sternwheeler. Mark Twain narrates your spin around Tom Sawyer Island, but the real joy is the attention to detail. The boat and its steam power plant are more interesting than the scenery—be sure to tour the decks. Dodge the sun in the middle deck salon. The "Liberty Belle" replaced the "Richard F. Irvine" in 1996. Wheelchair accessible. Adult supervision. Departs on the hour and half-hour. **Alex's KidTip:** "Ask if you can help steer the boat!"

Boat Ride
C-Ticket
All ages
Gentle rides
Med. waits
20 min. ride

Attraction descriptions and ratings are explained on page 127.

Top Photo Slice: The Liberty Bell in front of the Hall of Presidents (ⓘ9449) © Cheryl Pendry

Charting the Attractions at Fantasyland

Jennifer Dave Readers

Under the Sea ~ Journey of the Little Mermaid [E-1] FP+ 7 7 8

Track Ride
E-Ticket
All ages
Expect long waits
7 min. ride

Enter Prince Eric's Castle and go under the sea to see Ariel and her friends. Board your two- to three-person Omnimover clamshell to be immersed in favorite scenes and music from the beloved film. Ariel, Eric, Sebastian, Scuttle, and evil Ursula are brought to Audio-Animatronic "life" using classic techniques and innovative lighting. The ride is identical to The Little Mermaid—Ariel's Undersea Adventure at Disney California Adventure, though the interactive queue is unique. Some dark and scary moments. Wheelchair and ECV accessible, transfer from ECV to wheelchair. Hearing disability services. Alex's KidTip: *"Good ride for those who love Ariel (not me)."*

ⓘ42608 © Carlos Medina

"We got no troubles, life is the bubbles"

Dumbo The Flying Elephant [F-2] FP+ A-OK! 6 6 7

Ride
D-Ticket
All ages
Spins high in the air
Long waits
2 min. flight

Every child wants to ride around, up, and down on Dumbo. Two-seater flying elephants take you for a short, fast spin. Show your child how to lift the control lever to rise higher. Grown-ups will enjoy the pachyderm's-eye view. Dumbo has flown to a new location where a second ride system and innovative queue ease the long waits. Kids cavort in an indoor playground, parents sit in comfort, and the family is paged when it's time to ride. Adults must ride with small children. Must transfer from wheelchair. Alex's KidTip: *"Use a fun flying style, like up and down! This is still one of my favorite rides!"*

ⓘ42545 © Amanda Hulse

Dumbo is better than ever!

Enchanted Tales with Belle [D-1] FP+ 8 7 7

Show
C-Ticket
All ages
Happy ending
15 min. story

Explore Maurice's cottage and whimsical workshop, then step through a magic mirror into Beast's Castle. Madame Wardrobe is on hand to greet you, and to cast her guests for roles in a telling of the "tale as old as time." Then, an animatronic Lumière invites all into the Library, to await Belle's arrival and to watch or play their parts as she presents her famous story. The staging is similar to Storytime with Belle, which was formerly held in Fairytale Garden. Alex's KidTip: *"You can volunteer for parts!"*

© Jennifer Marx

Welcome to Beast's Castle!

Top Photo Slice: The top of the Dumbo ride (ⓘ42545) © Amanda Hulse

Charting the Attractions at Fantasyland

Jennifer Dave Readers

Fairytale Garden [E-3] — A-OK! — 6 6 5

Merida from "Brave" started to "play and greet" guests here in 2013 (and Storytime with Belle now has its own home at Enchanted Tales). Sit on stools and benches among the rose bushes and watch characters at various times throughout the day. Characters may take volunteers from the audience. Arrive about ten minutes early to get a seat. No shade. Wheelchair friendly. **Allie's Kid Tip:** "You might want to be in the show because it could be fun!!!"

Live Show | B-Ticket | All ages | Happy ending | 15 min. story

The Barnstormer (Great Goofini) [F-2] — FP — A-OK! — 7 7 6

Even grown-up coaster fans love this fast, swooping "flight" featuring The Great Goofini, a barnstorming pilot who came to town with Dumbo's Circus. This attraction was re-themed during the Fantasyland expansion. Long lines move quickly through an uncovered queue, but take time to enjoy the Goofy artifacts. Cars may be small for big/tall adults. May close during wet weather. Transfer from wheelchair. **Alex's Toddler Tip:** "I like Goofy's plane! ☺"

ⓘ39669 © Danielle Sabato
The Great Goofini's latest "trick"

Coaster | D-Ticket | Ages 2 & up (35" and up) | Fast turns | Med. waits | 1 min. flight

"it's a small world" [C-2] — FP — A-OK! — 5 6 6

"It's a world of laughter, a world of tears..." Yes, these are Disney's famous singing and dancing dolls, who first debuted their act at the 1964–65 New York World's Fair. Their catchy song adapts to the local surroundings as your boat floats sedately past scenes depicting the world's continents and cultures. Must transfer from ECV to wheelchair to ride. **Alex's Toddler Tip:** ☺ **Allie's Kid Tip:** "Ask your grown-ups for a seat at the end of a row so you can see more."

Boat Ride | C-Ticket | All ages | Short to med. waits | 11 min. cruise

Mad Tea Party [E-2] — FP — A-OK! — 2 3 6

Spin and spin and spin some more inside a giant teacup. Young kids love to get dizzy, so this ride draws them like a magnet. Turn the metal wheel at the center of your teacup to make it spin even faster. You'll be as dizzy as the Mad Hatter. This is one ride that lasts a bit longer than you'd like. Sit this one out if you're prone to dizziness. Adult supervision of children under 7. Must transfer from wheelchair to ride. **Alex's Toddler Tip:** "I want to ride the 'teacups' again! ☺" **Alex's Kid Tip:** "Spin as fast as you can! If you get dizzy, look down at your seat."

© MediaMarx, Inc.
Alexander and Dave twirl about in the teacups

Ride | C-Ticket | Ages 4 & up | Scares adults | Short waits | 2 min. spin

Attraction descriptions and ratings are explained on page 127.

Top Photo Slice: Beast's Castle (ⓘ42613) © Carlos Medina

Charting the Attractions at Fantasyland

Jennifer | Dave | Readers

The Many Adventures of Winnie the Pooh [E-2] FP+ A-OK! 6 5 7

Track Ride
D-Ticket
All ages
Kid-friendly; dark could be slightly scary
FASTPASS or long waits
3 min. ride

Take a gentle ride through the world of that fabulously popular bear. Blow through the Blustery Day, bounce along with Tigger, dream of Heffalumps and Woozles, and float away in a mighty spring flood, all in a four-seat "honey pot" that moves along an indoor track. Pooh fans will exit feeling warm and fuzzy—the better you know Pooh's tales, the more you'll get from your tour through the cartoon cutout scenery. The interactive, covered queue winds through pages blown away from a huge storybook—look for signs and fun things to do while you wait, including walls covered in "honey." Transfer from ECV to wheelchair. **Alex's ToddlerTip:** *"Tigger and Pooh! ☺"* **Allie's KidTip:** *"Sit in the front."*

Mickey's PhilharMagic [D-2] FP+ A-OK! 8 9 9

3-D Show
E-Ticket
All ages
Intense effects may be scary
FASTPASS or med. waits
10 min. show

Trouble's brewing in Fantasyland in this 3-D movie experience, when Donald "borrows" (and loses) Mickey's sorcerer hat. The audience, assembled in front of a giant, 150-foot-wide screen in PhilharMagic Concert Hall, awaits a concert conducted by Mickey. Donald, naturally, gets into deep trouble. Soon he's scurrying through scenes from Disney classic films, trying to regain the lost hat. Along the way he meets Simba, Peter Pan, Lumiere, Aladdin, Ariel, and other favorite Disney characters. Look for Donald at the "end." The 3-D movie effects and sensations are kid-friendly. Best seats in middle or back of theater. Covered queue. Wheelchair accessible. Assistive listening devices. Reflective captioning. **Alex's ToddlerTip:** ☺ **Allie's TeenTip:** *"Wow! Good for all ages."*

Peter Pan's Flight [C-2] FP+ A-OK! 6 6 8

Track Ride
D-Ticket
Ages 3 & up
Dark, heights
FASTPASS or long waits

Climb aboard a flying, three-seat pirate ship that twists and turns sedately through the clouds. Follow Peter Pan and the Darling children from London to Neverland. Scenes featuring the Lost Boys, mermaids, Captain Hook's ship, and the crocodile unfold below, then you're safely home. Very dark, 4-minute ride. Covered, interactive queue area. Transfer from wheelchair to ride. **Alex's ToddlerTip:** ☺ **Allie's KidTip:** *"Can you find the mermaids? One of them looks like Ariel!"*

Prince Charming Regal Carrousel [D-2] A-OK! 5 5 6

Ride
B-Ticket
Ages 2 & up
High horses can be scary
Short waits
2 min. ride

ⓘ16956 © Brenda G.

A princess and her horse

This colorful, lovingly maintained carrousel painted with scenes from Cinderella sits at the center of Fantasyland. Many of the 84 horses were rescued from a historic New Jersey carousel, but you'd have a hard time telling which ones. The horses closer to the perimeter tend to rise higher. One chariot (an original) holds six. Look for Cinderella's horse with a golden ribbon on its tail. Disney tunes make it a joy for the ears! The carousel is particularly enchanting in the evening. Note that the name changed from Cinderella's Golden Carrousel in 2010 in anticipation of the recent Fantasyland expansion. Guests must transfer from wheelchair to board. Adult supervision of children required. **Alex's ToddlerTip:** ☺ **Allie's KidTip:** *"Sit carefully on the horse."*

More at ⓘ fantasyland-for-adults

Top Photo Slice: The entrance to Storybook Circus in Fantasyland (ⓘ43040) © Barry Ristow

Charting the Attractions at Fantasyland

Jennifer | Dave | Readers

Princess Fairytale Hall [D-2]

FP+ A-OK! 7 – 8

Pavilion
A-Ticket
All ages
Expect long waits

With the Seven Dwarfs Mine Train Ride open across the way, the classic Snow White's Scary Adventure closed in early 2012 to make way for a new Princess meet-and-greet. Anna, Elsa, Aurora, Cinderella, and other, less-traditional princesses like Tiana and Rapunzel are on hand for autographs and photos. FastPass+ for Anna and Elsa goes very fast, and the standby wait can exceed 60–90 minutes, depending on the season.

Seven Dwarfs Mine Train [E-2]

FP+ 8 8 8

Coaster
E-Ticket
Ages 4 & up
Fast turns, modest drops
FastPass+ or long waits
3 min. ride

This moderate roller coaster boasts an innovative ride vehicle that pendulum-swings from side to side as you ride the banked curves of the Seven Dwarfs' fabled mine. It's something of a cross between Big Thunder Mountain Railroad and Splash Mountain. The journey begins like any tubular-track coaster, up and into the mine. Inside, the track levels out and you pass Audio-Animatronics depicting scenes from Snow White. Then, emerge from the mine to finish up with short drops and fast turns. 38" (97 cm.) height restriction. If you do not have a FastPass+ reservation, make a beeline for this first thing in the morning.
Alex's KidTip: *"I think it's too scary and fast for kids who don't like coasters."*

© Amanda Nash

Riding the Seven Dwarfs Mine Train

Meet Your Favorite Characters FP+

The new Fantasyland has more "character" than ever. The Princess Fairytale Hall brings your favorite princesses, including the extremely popular Anna and Elsa from Disney's "Frozen." Beyond that is Enchanted Tales With Belle (see page 142). Ariel's Grotto has returned, in a new spot near the exit of the mermaid's ride—once more, her fans have a chance to chat and smile for some Ariel photos. Just around the corner in Storybook Circus is Pete's Silly Sideshow, where you can meet The Astounding Donaldo, The Great Goofini, Madame Daisy Fortuna, and Minnie Magnifique!

More at ⓘ new-fantasyland

Top Photo Slice: Mosaic of Cinderella and her prince in Cinderella Castle (ⓘ13571) © Janet Simonsen

Charting the Attractions at Tomorrowland

Jennifer Dave Readers

Astro Orbiter [F-4] — A-OK! — 1 | 3 | 3

Ride
C-Ticket
Ages 5 & up
Heights
Long waits
1 1/2 min. flight

Go for a short, fast spin in a two-seat rocket high above Tomorrowland. Often mistaken for a futuristic sculpture, the fanciful planets of Astro Orbiter go into motion with each launch. Think "Dumbo" with small, silvery space ships. Pull back on the stick to "soar" high. Get a dizzying view as your ship whirls. Must ride an elevator to board. Motion sickness warning. Outdoor, covered queue. Adults must accompany kids under 7. Transfer from wheelchair to ride. **Allie's KidTip:** *"You can get a great view of the park."* **TweenTip:** *"Faster than Dumbo and Aladdin."*

①2151 © Laura Dawson

Michael, Victoria, Rick, and Miranda soar above Tomorrowland on the Astro Orbiter

Buzz Lightyear's Space Ranger Spin [F-4] — FP — A-OK! — 8 | 8 | 8

Track Ride
D-Ticket
Ages 2 & up
Mild "space flight" effects
FASTPASS or med. waits
4 min. flight

All right, Space Rangers, it's time to help Toy Story's Buzz Lightyear defeat the evil Emperor Zurg! Buzz himself briefs new cadets before you're sent into battle in a Day-Glo, comic book world of planets and space creatures. Your two-seat space vehicle (an "XP-37 Space Cruiser") is equipped with a pair of "ion cannons" (laser pointers) mounted on the dashboard. Aim and shoot the electronic targets to accumulate points (aim for the higher targets for more points). Move the joystick to make your vehicle spin and home in on your targets. Compare your score at the end. Covered queue area is mostly indoors. Wheelchair accessible. **Alex's ToddlerTip:** ☺ **Allie's KidTip:** *"Check your score. I made Space Cadet!"*

Walt Disney's Carousel of Progress [F-4] — A-OK! — 9 | 6 | 6

Show
C-Ticket
Ages 6 & up
No scares
Short waits
22 min. show

See the march of modern technology through the eyes of an American family. Each of the four scenes in this Audio-Animatronics show highlights another 20 years (or so) of progress in the 20th century. When the scene changes, the entire theater moves around to the next stage. One of Walt Disney's favorite attractions. (Jennifer loves it, too!) Limited hours. Outdoor, covered queue. Wheelchair accessible. Assistive listening devices. Closed captioning (pre-show only). **Allie's KidTip:** *"Rover is cute."*

①7174 © Dawn Erickson

The 1940s scene at Carousel of Progress

①6932 © Priscilla Lopez

Progress is all around us!

Top Photo Slice: Astro Orbiter in Tomorrowland (①13392) © Janet Simonsen

Charting the Attractions at Tomorrowland

Monsters, Inc. Laugh Floor [E-4]

FP A-Ok! Jennifer 6 Dave 7 Readers 7

Show
D-Ticket
All ages
Dark, playful monsters
12 minute show

This fun attraction picks up where the movie left off, inviting guests into a monster comedy club to collect their laughter and power Monstropolis. The fun show uses the same cool technology from "Turtle Talk with Crush" (see page 159), meaning the monsters onscreen like Mike Wazowski can interact with audience members. Expect some good natured ribbing, and some audience members even appear on screen. Indoor queue. Guests sit on hard plastic benches in the 458-seat theater. Wheelchair/ECV accessible. Assistive listening. Handheld and video captioning for portions of show.

Monster vending machine ... how yummy!

Space Mountain [G-3]

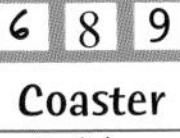

6 8 9

Coaster
E-Ticket
Ages 8 & up
Dark, rough, jerky, fast
FASTPASS or long waits
$2\frac{1}{2}$ min. flight

Blast off into the blackness of space on the Magic Kingdom's most exciting roller coaster. You'll depart from 'Space Station Seventy-Five,' your gateway to the galaxies! This fast, indoor ride has sudden turns and short drops, but no big, stomach-in-your-throat drops. The darkness makes it scarier than it really is. The indoor queue and ride loading areas are rich with visual detail and interactive video games you can play while you wait (in the standby queue only). There are two slightly different coasters—go left for one, right for the other when you reach the loading area. Renovations in 2010 brought a smoother ride, more comfortable 'ships,' a darker 'flight' (with brighter 'stars'), better effects, new soundtrack, in-vehicle sound system, and a general sprucing up! Transfer from ECV to wheelchair, then transfer from wheelchair to ride. 44"/112 cm height restriction. Adult supervision. Health warning. **Allie's Kid Tip:** *"I loved it! But it is bumpy. Try to sit in the middle. Ride it again if you can!"*

Taking off into the star tunnel at Space Mountain

Attraction descriptions and ratings are explained on page 127.

More at ⓘ laugh-floor

Top Photo Slice: Space Mountain as seen from the monorail (ⓘ7928) © Janice Kovacs

Charting the Attractions at Tomorrowland

Attraction	Jennifer	Dave	Readers
Stitch's Great Escape! [E-4]	6	5	6

Stitch's Great Escape! [E-4]

Guests are recruited by the Grand Councilwoman, Captain Gantu, and Pleakley to guard "Experiment 626" (Stitch), and mischief ensues when that wily captive escapes into the theater. Even Skippy, from this attraction's previous incarnation, has a part. Animation, Audio-Animatronics, surround sound, lighting, and tactile effects combine to make an immersive experience. Alas, restrictive shoulder restraints, periods of total darkness, and a barrage of fire from "laser cannon" leave Stitch with too many scare factors and too little charm. Outdoor, covered queue. 40"/102 cm minimum height. Handheld captioning. Assistive listening. Wheelchair and ECV accessible. **Allie's TweenTip:** *"I love it when the power goes out!"*

Ratings: 6 | 5 | 6 — Show; D-Ticket; Ages 7 & up; May be scary for the young, yucky smells!; Short to medium waits; 12 min. show

Tomorrowland Arcade (closed) [G-3] A-OK!

Closed permanently in February 2015 due to a new state law that forbids video game arcades that dispense prizes. Some video and pinball machines have been moved to other resort arcades. No word yet on what is replacing it.

Ratings: 3 | 2 | 3 — Arcade; A-Ticket; Ages 6 & up

Tomorrowland Speedway [F-3] FP+ A-OK!

Every kid wants a chance to drive, and when they're tall enough they can at this popular attraction. Experienced drivers won't be as thrilled. Guide rails, shock-absorbing bumpers, and a low top speed (7 mph maximum) make these gas powered "race cars" safe. Family members can cheer from an enclosed grandstand (the entrance is to the right). Shortest waits are early in the morning. Covered outdoor queue. Transfer from wheelchair to ride. 52"/132 cm height restriction to drive solo. Health warning. Adult supervision required. **Allie's KidTip:** *"Even if you're tall enough, make sure your feet can touch the pedals before you drive."*

Ratings: 4 | 3 | 4 — Ride; C-Ticket; Ages 4 & up; Cars may bump yours from behind; Long waits; 4 min. drive

Tomorrowland Transit Authority Peoplemover [F-4] A-OK!

Take a grand tour of Tomorrowland on an elevated, automated people mover. The four-seat vehicles move sedately along a route that takes you through Space Mountain and past nearly every other attraction in Tomorrowland. Along the way you can look down upon Tomorrowland's crowds and view a scale model of Progress City (formerly of Disneyland's Carousel of Progress). It makes a great introduction to Tomorrowland. Outdoor, mostly covered queue. Must be ambulatory to ride. Name changed to add Peoplemover in summer 2010. **Allie's KidTip:** *"Look for the stars when you go through Space Mountain."*

Ratings: 6 | 6 | 6 — Track Ride; B-Ticket; All ages; Dark; Short waits; 12 min. grand tour

Tomorrowland is a bright sight at night

Top Photo Slice: Tomorrowland sign (9529) © Cheryl Pendry

Epcot

Triple the size of the Magic Kingdom, Epcot opened its doors (and many minds) in 1982. Epcot is the ultimate world's fair, showcasing a future where technology improves our lives, the countries of the world live in peace, and dreams really can come true.

Striving to educate and inspire as well as entertain, Epcot introduces millions to new **technological and international frontiers**. Epcot began as Walt Disney's dream of an "Experimental Prototype Community of Tomorrow;" it's a far cry from the ordinary communities where most of us live. The first of two "worlds," Future World greets you with its awe-inspiring, 180-foot-tall, geodesic sphere (Spaceship Earth). Streamlined structures and broad vistas transport you into the future of today's hopes and dreams. Beyond Future World is World Showcase, offering an inspiring glimpse into faraway lands, different customs, and exotic peoples.

ⓘ37948 © Eddie Cabrera

Holding onto his Viking roots in Norway

ⓘ141349 © Sam Fuller

Fish may not be food, but it looks like tourists are on the menu

ⓘ16921 © MediaMarx, Inc.

PassPorter fans in front of Spaceship Earth during PassPorter's 10th anniversary

Top Photo Slice: Spaceship Earth at sunset (ⓘ2624) © Beth Borja

Orienting Yourself at Epcot

Fold out the next page for a touring plan and a handy attraction chart

The **two worlds of Epcot** offer a variety of attractions, all housed in "pavilions"—nine in Future World and eleven in the World Showcase (see the fold-out map on the next page). Below are the headline attractions in the west and east sides of Future World and World Showcase. See the other side of the map for our favorite itinerary and an at-a-glance list of attractions, and pages 157–166 for attraction details.

Future World East

Science and technology take center stage with an up-close look at space travel, vehicle testing, communications, and energy.

Headline Attractions: Mission: SPACE, Test Track, Spaceship Earth, Universe of Energy

Mission: SPACE ☛

ⓘ12729 © Cheryl Pendry

Future World West

Explore the nature of the world on land and in the sea, and the nature of imagination and perception in the recesses of our minds.

Headline Attractions: Soarin', The Seas with Nemo & Friends

The Seas with Nemo and Friends ☛

ⓘ11570 © Kelly Michelle Narvaez

World Showcase East

Cruise a river in Mexico, get "Frozen" in Norway, see the wonders of China, celebrate in Germany and Italy, and explore the American adventure.

Headline Attractions: Gran Fiesta Tour, Reflections of China

Mexico pavilion ☛

ⓘ11410 © Diana Barthelemy-Rodriguez

World Showcase West

Hear drummers in Japan, view treasures in Morocco, see the sights in France, tour gardens in the United Kingdom, and explore the wonders of Canada.

Headline Attractions: Impressions de France, O Canada!

Japan pavilion ☛

ⓘ2165 © Janet Simonsen

Top Photo Slice: The World Showcase Lagoon at Epcot (ⓘ3963) © Rick Wagner

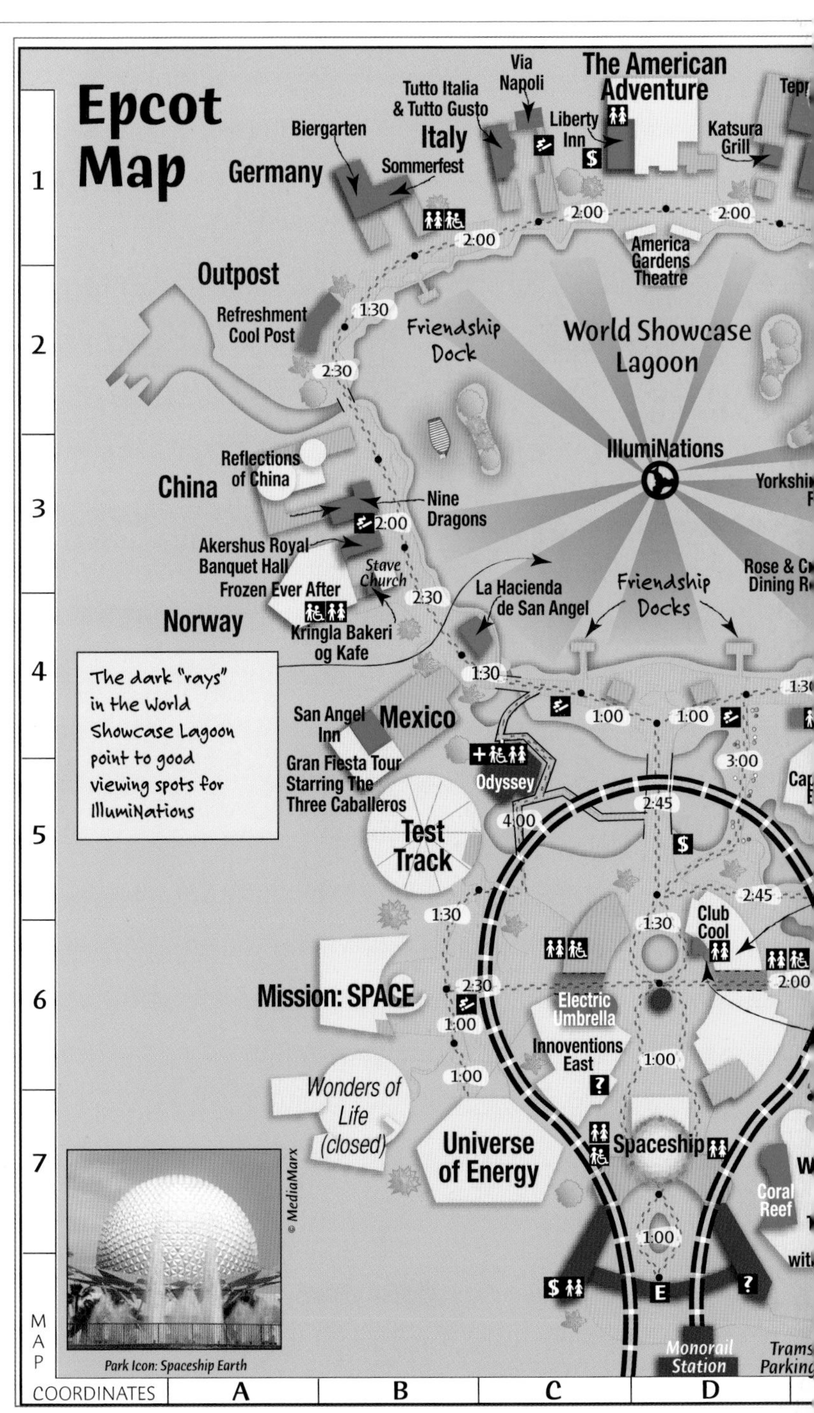
Epcot Map
1
2
3
4
5
6
7
MAP COORDINATES
A
B
C
D
Germany
Biergarten
Sommerfest
Tutto Italia & Tutto Gusto
Via Napoli
Italy
The American Adventure
Liberty Inn
Katsura Grill
America Gardens Theatre
Outpost
Refreshment Cool Post
Friendship Dock
World Showcase Lagoon
IllumiNations
China
Reflections of China
Nine Dragons
Akershus Royal Banquet Hall
Frozen Ever After
Stave Church
Norway
Kringla Bakeri og Kafe
La Hacienda de San Angel
Friendship Docks
The dark "rays" in the World Showcase Lagoon point to good viewing spots for IllumiNations
San Angel Inn
Mexico
Gran Fiesta Tour Starring The Three Caballeros
Odyssey
Test Track
Club Cool
Mission: SPACE
Electric Umbrella
Innoventions East
Wonders of Life (closed)
Universe of Energy
Spaceship
Coral Reef
Monorail Station
Trams Parking
© MediaMarx
Park Icon: Spaceship Earth

Epcot Attractions At-A-Glance

(alphabetical order)

Attraction	Type	Allow	Page
☐ America Gardens Theatre [D-1]	Show	30–40+	164-WS
☐ The American Adventure [D-1]	Pavilion	(80+)	164-WS
☐ The American Adventure Show [D-1]	Show	(50+)	164-WS
☐ Canada [E-4]	Pavilion	30–40+	166-WS
☐ Captain EO [E-5]	3-D Film	25–45+	161-FW
☐ China [B-3]	Pavilion	(35+)	163-WS
☐ Club Cool [D-6]	Walk-thru	15-20+	159-FW
☐ The Circle of Life [F-6]	Film	15-20+	160-FW
☐ France [F-2]	Pavilion	30–40+	165-WS
☐ Frozen Ever After [B-3]	Boat Ride	?	162-WS
☐ Germany [B-1]	Pavilion	(15–30+)	163-WS
☐ Gran Fiesta Tour [B-4]	Boat Ride	20+	162-WS
☐ ImageWorks [E-5]	Playground	20–30+	161-FW
☐ Impressions de France [F-2]	Film	20–25+	165-WS
☐ Innoventions East [C-6]	Playground	40–60+	157-FW
☐ Innoventions West [D-6] ***closed***	Playground	40–60+	159-FW
☐ Italy [C-1]	Pavilion	(15–30+)	164-WS
☐ Japan [D-1]	Pavilion	15–30+	165-WS
☐ Journey Into Imagination [E-5]	Track Ride	15–20+	161-FW
☐ The Land [E-6]	Pavilion	(90+)	160-FW
☐ Living With the Land [F-6]	Boat Ride	30–40+	160-FW
☐ Mexico [B-4]	Pavilion	(25+)	162-WS
☐ Mission: SPACE [B-6]	Thrill Ride	40–90+	158-FW
☐ Morocco [E-1]	Pavilion	20–30+	165-WS
☐ Norway [B-3]	Pavilion	(45+)	162-WS
☐ O Canada! [E-4]	Film	(20–25+)	166-WS
☐ Reflections of China [A-3]	Film	25–30+	163-WS
☐ The Seas with Nemo & Friends [E-7]	Pavilion/Ride	40–60+	159-FW
☐ Soarin' [F-5]	Simulator	60–75+	160-FW
☐ Spaceship Earth [D-7]	Track Ride	30–40+	157-FW
☐ Test Track [B-5]	Thrill Ride	40–90+	158-FW
☐ Turtle Talk with Crush [E-7]	Show	30–40+	159-FW
☐ United Kingdom [F-3]	Pavilion	15–30+	166-WS
☐ Universe of Energy [B-7]	Film/Ride	40–60+	157-FW

The Allow column gives the amount of time (in minutes) you should allow for an attraction, assuming you do not have a FASTPASS and there are no ride breakdowns. Times in parentheses are approximate totals for all attractions in that pavilion—component times for that pavilion's attractions are also in the attraction list.

The letters after the page numbers stand for the first two letters of the land in which that attraction is located: FW for Future World and WS for World Showcase.

Our Favorite Touring Plan for Epcot

NOTES

Epcot is so large it's really difficult to do in one day, and we don't recommend it if at all possible. We recognize that many families may only have one day for Epcot, however, so we're sharing our best, one-day touring plan (which assumes entry by 9:00 am). If you can enter earlier, spend that extra time in Future World. Those lucky enough to have more time to spend at Epcot probably don't need a touring plan at all. But if you'd like to use ours anyway, you can easily split Future World and World Showcase into two days—just add in all the optional attractions and plan to sleep in on the day you do World Showcase (as it opens later than Future World). As with our other touring plans, you can skip items in blue if you're with young kids or sedate adults.

ITINERARY

Touring With Adults and/or Kids

Get FastPass+ (can be reserved 30-60 days in advance on My Disney Experience—see page 126) as early as possible.
Enter Future World East
Visit Mission: SPACE
Visit Test Track
Visit Spaceship Earth
Visit Club Cool
Enter The Seas with Nemo & Friends
Visit The Seas with Nemo & Friends
See Turtle Talk with Crush
Enter The Land
Visit Living With the Land
(Optional: Visit The Circle of Life)
Eat lunch at Electric Umbrella or Sunshine Seasons (*estimate lunch time at about two hours after you enter the park*)
Visit Soarin'
Enter Imagination!
Visit Captain EO
Visit Journey Into Imagination with Figment
Enter Canada
Browse Canadian pavilion
Enter United Kingdom
Browse United Kingdom pavilion
Enter France
Browse French pavilion
Visit Impressions de France
Enter Morocco
Browse Moroccan pavilion
Have a snack in World Showcase East (try a baklava in Morocco or Kaki Gori in Japan)
Enter Japan
Browse Japanese pavilion
Enter American Adventure
Visit The American Adventure
Eat dinner in World Showcase East. Try La Hacienda de San Angel* in Mexico, or Akershus Royal Banquet Hall* in Norway (*estimate time at 7 1/2 hours after you enter the park*)
Enter Norway
Visit Frozen Ever After
Enter Mexico
Visit Gran Fiesta Tour Starring The Three Caballeros
Enjoy any extra "free time" at the World Showcase
Find an IllumiNations viewing spot (see pages 168 and 266 for tips)
Watch IllumiNations

(Tour duration: About 11 hours)

Touring With Kids

Start at The Land or The Seas with Nemo & Friends rather than Mission: SPACE (be sure to see Turtle Talk with Crush). Proceed with the plan, omitting those items in blue that won't appeal to your kids. The extra time you gain can be used at the Epcot Character Spot or Kidcot stations/Agent P. World Showcase Adventure (see page 163) around the World Showcase.

** These restaurants may be difficult to impossible to get in as a walk-up. Advance dining reservations can be made up to 180 days in advance (see page 226).*

Top Photo: U.S. flag in front of Spaceship Earth (488) © MediaMarx, Inc.

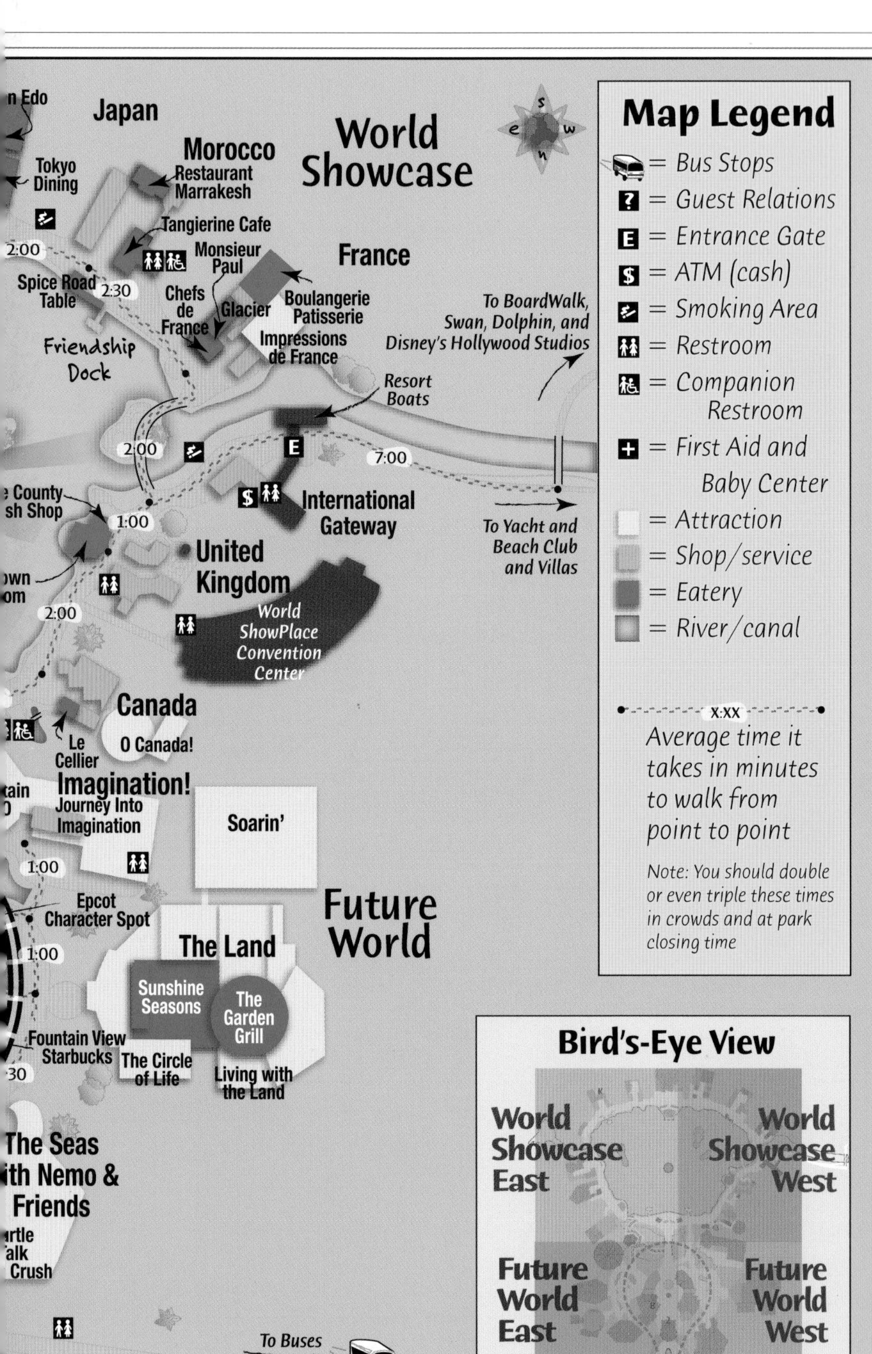
World Showcase
Japan
Morocco
Restaurant Marrakesh
Tokyo Dining
Tangierine Cafe
Monsieur Paul
France
Spice Road Table
Chefs de France
Glacier
Boulangerie Patisserie
Impressions de France
Friendship Dock
To BoardWalk, Swan, Dolphin, and Disney's Hollywood Studios
Resort Boats
2:00
2:30
7:00
1:00
International Gateway
United Kingdom
To Yacht and Beach Club and Villas
World ShowPlace Convention Center
Canada
Le Cellier
O Canada!
Imagination!
Journey Into Imagination
Soarin'
Epcot Character Spot
Future World
The Land
Sunshine Seasons
The Garden Grill
Fountain View Starbucks
The Circle of Life
Living with the Land
To Buses
E
F
G
Map Legend
= Bus Stops
= Guest Relations
= Entrance Gate
= ATM (cash)
= Smoking Area
= Restroom
= Companion Restroom
= First Aid and Baby Center
= Attraction
= Shop/service
= Eatery
= River/canal
X:XX
Average time it takes in minutes to walk from point to point
Note: You should double or even triple these times in crowds and at park closing time
Bird's-Eye View
World Showcase East
World Showcase West
Future World East
Future World West
Map © MediaMarx, Inc.

Catching the Shows at Epcot

Epcot presents a rich medley of sounds and sights for the strolling visitor. Guests may encounter acrobats, dancers, actors, and musicians—more than **two dozen groups** in all. Most shows last about 10-20 minutes. Axe-throwing lumberjacks in Canada and flag-wavers in Italy join old favorites like the Voices of Liberty at The American Adventure, British rockers in the United Kingdom, and the Mariachi Cobre band in Mexico. You'll flip for China's acrobats, and Japanese and African drummers set your pulse pounding. The spectacular **Fountain of Nations** dances in time to the music (see page 167).

6466 © Janet Simonsen

Fountain of Nations

Beyond casual entertainment, check your Times Guide for the open-air **America Gardens Theatre**, which offers half-hour performances, plus the Flower Power concerts in the spring, Eat to the Beat concerts in autumn, and Candlelight Processional in December (see page 289).

Crowds throng the World Showcase every evening at park closing for the popular **IllumiNations** fireworks and light show (see page 168 for all the details).

16831 © Elizabeth Ferris

Serveur Amusant entertains in France

Top Photo Slice: IllumiNations (12693) © Cheryl Pendry

Making the Most of Epcot

TIPS

If you arrive at Epcot via the **monorail**, you get a wonderful aerial view of Future World and a glimpse of World Showcase.

Little ones adore the **Kidcot Fun Stops** at each World Showcase pavilion around the lagoon. Cast members offer kids various craft projects to color and decorate. Activities vary, sometimes giving kids something different to add to their creation at each country. Alexander loves it!

ⓘ22960 © Andrea Popovitis

Showing off a mask made at the Kidcot Fun Stops

Kids also love the **play fountains** on the promenade between Future World and the World Showcase, and behind Innoventions East. Come prepared with suits under clothing and/or dry clothes and shoes.

Looking for **characters** at Epcot? Check out the Epcot Character Spot in Future World West, near Innoventions West.

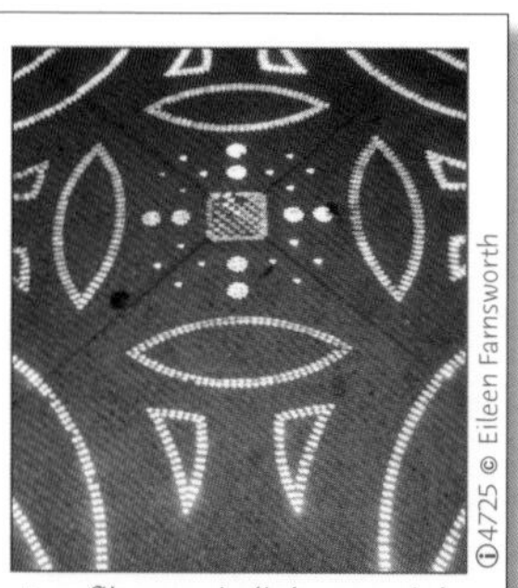

ⓘ4725 © Eileen Farnsworth

Fun fiber optic lights at night

Consider an Epcot **guided tour**, such as the Undiscovered Future World. See pages 272–273.

On your way out of the park in the evening, glance down at the path as you pass Innoventions—you'll discover **fiber-optic lights** embedded in the pavement that make beautiful patterns.

Epcot is the dining capital of the "World." Nearly all the good stuff encircles the lagoon in an **international dining extravaganza**, offering everything from the upscale Monsieur Paul to tacos at Cantina de San Angel. Future World offers less table-service dining, but it has some counter-service opportunities. See pages 234–241.

Epcot's main gate is at the **north end** of the park (the opposite of all the other parks), so east is to the right and west is to the left.

Top Photo Slice: Fiber optic lights outside Innoventions (ⓘ4724) © Eileen Farnsworth

Getting the Best at Epcot

① 15300 © Lindsay Jones
Sombrero Love

SHOPPING

The World Showcase makes Epcot the center for unusual shopping, too. A wide array of **international gifts and crafts** graces every pavilion, from British woolens and Japanese silks to German cut crystal and Moroccan leather. Here are our favorite shops:

Shop	Location	What makes it special
Art of Disney	Near Innoventions	Collectibles and animation cels
Disney Traders	World Showcase	Disney-themed merchandise
Mouse Gear	Future World	Huge store with clothes and gifts
ImageWorks	Imagination!	Unique photos and photo gifts
Plaza de Los Amigos	Mexico	Sombreros and tequila!
Yong Feng Shangdian	China	Huge store with a wide variety
Mitsukoshi Dept. Store	Japan	Authentic Japanese gifts, snacks
Tangier Traders	Morocco	Open-air, exotic shopping
La Maison du Vin	France	Two words: wine tastings!
The Crown and Crest	United Kingdom	Family name histories

NOTES

"**Friendships**" (boats) convey you to different points within World Showcase. You can usually get there faster if you walk, however.

Good viewing locations for **IllumiNations** FP+ go quickly. See page 168 for hints on getting the best possible view of the action.

After IllumiNations ends, step aside and wait for the crowds to thin. Take a **leisurely stroll** around the lagoon. Enjoy the music and the lights—you'll have a nice, quiet walk with very few people around. About 30 minutes after the show, you might even get to witness a huge fireball as cast members burn off excess fuel from the fire barges. As a bonus, you'll miss the traffic in the parking lot and bus queues.

RATINGS

Ratings are explained on page 128.

Our Value Ratings:		Our Magic Ratings:		Readers' Ratings:
Quality:	8/10	Theme:	8/10	58% fell in love with it
Variety:	8/10	Excitement:	8/10	34% liked it well enough
Scope:	10/10	Fun Factor:	6/10	7% had mixed feelings
Overall Value:	**9/10**	**Overall Magic:**	**7/10**	1% were disappointed

Epcot is enjoyed by...		(rated by both authors and readers)
Younger Kids: ♥♥♥	Young Adults: ♥♥♥♥	Families: ♥♥♥♥
Older Kids: ♥♥♥	Mid Adults: ♥♥♥♥♥	Couples: ♥♥♥♥♥
Teenagers: ♥♥♥	Mature Adults: ♥♥♥♥♥	Singles: ♥♥♥♥♥

Top Photo Slice: Hand-crafted wall tile in Morocco (①10669) © Melissa Potter

Finding Your Way to Epcot

BEST TIMES TO GO

The **best time to visit World Showcase** is when it first opens at 11:00 am, as most guests are still in Future World. It follows then that the **best time to tour Future World** is in the late afternoon and during dinner time (most attractions in Future World now stay open until 9:00 pm). World Showcase becomes congested in the evenings due to the many restaurants and IllumiNations show. Because of the focus on dining at Epcot, traditional lunch and dinner times are better spent at the attractions while others are eating. Along the same vein, you will find restaurants less busy and noisy if you dine before or after the normal lunch and dinner hour. **IllumiNations** is held nightly at park closing (usually 9:00 pm)—for a good view, start looking about one hour prior (see page 168). If you've already seen IllumiNations, consider **dining during it** for a quieter experience.

GETTING THERE

By Monorail—From the Magic Kingdom, Contemporary, Polynesian Village, or Grand Floridian, take the monorail to the Transportation and Ticket Center (TTC) and transfer to the Epcot monorail.
By Boat—From Disney's Hollywood Studios, Swan/Dolphin, BoardWalk, and Yacht & Beach Club, boats go to Epcot's International Gateway.
By Bus—From other resorts, Disney's Hollywood Studios, or Disney's Animal Kingdom, buses take you directly to Epcot. From Disney Springs, take a bus to a nearby resort and transfer to an Epcot bus, boat, or walk. (Tip: Bus to BoardWalk and walk/boat to Epcot.)
By Car—Take I-4 to exit 67 (westbound) or exit 62 (eastbound) and continue on to the Epcot toll plaza. All-day parking is available for $17 (free to resort guests and annual passholders).
By Foot—From the BoardWalk Inn & Villas, Yacht & Beach Club and Villas, Swan & Dolphin, and Disney's Hollywood Studios, Epcot is within walking distance. Follow the paths toward International Gateway—it emerges between United Kingdom and France. Walk through United Kingdom and Canada to reach Future World.

ⓘ2411 © Janet Simonsen

A monorail glides over the water during the International Flower and Garden Festival

Charting the Attractions at Future World (East)

Jennifer | Dave | Readers

Spaceship Earth [D-7]

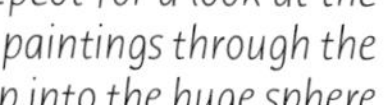

A-OK! 9 7 8

Track Ride
E-Ticket
Ages 3 & up
Dark, steep incline
Short waits
15 min. ride

Go inside the huge geodesic sphere that towers above Epcot for a look at the development of communication technologies from cave paintings through the space age. Four-seat "time machine" vehicles take you up into the huge sphere past dozens of Audio-Animatronics reenacting milestones in communication. A renovation in 2007 added new ride scenes, changes to existing scenes, an interactive touchscreen in the "time machine" vehicle, and narration by actress Dame Judi Dench. At the end of the ride, you'll exit into a post-show exhibit, Project Tomorrow, sponsored by Siemens, where you can do things such as "build a body" in 3-D, experience a driving simulation game, and check out an illuminated globe with a collage of futuristic images. Adults should accompany and sit beside children. We suggest you visit at park opening or in the evening for shorter waits. Outdoor queue is mostly covered. Guests must transfer from wheelchair. **Alex's ToddlerTip:** ☺ **Allie's KidTip:** *"You'll love all the lights. And it's good for learning."* **Allie's TeenTip:** *"Really boring."*

ⓘ4788 © Keith Stanton

An Audio-Animatronics Steve works on a computer prototype on Spaceship Earth

Innoventions East [C-6]

A-OK! 7 5 6

Playground
B-Ticket
All ages
Noisy
Short waits
Allow about 1 hour to explore

If gee-whiz technology pushes your buttons, pay a visit to Innoventions—Epcot's high-tech, hands-on trade exhibit. Innoventions East exhibits include the new Colotopia (paint exhibit), The Sum of All Thrills (custom design your own 4-min. thrill ride, then ride it in a simulator), Internet activities (send electronic and video e-mail back home), the "Habit Heroes" exhibit (learn the advantages to following a healthy lifestyle), the StormStruck exhibit (experience a hurricane simulation), and the Agent P. signup area (see page 163 for information about Agent P.). Short queues in some exhibits. Wheelchair accessible. **Allie's TeenTip:** *"Video e-mail is fun."*

Universe of Energy (Ellen's Energy Adventure) [B-7]

A-OK! 5 6 7

Film/Ride
E-Ticket
Ages 4 & up
Dark, loud, dinosaurs
Med. waits
8 min. intro 37 min. ride

Join Ellen DeGeneres for a humorous crash course in energy, the stuff that powers our world. Widescreen films, thunderous sound effects, and gigantic Audio-Animatronics dinosaurs help tell the tale. Ellen's cast includes Bill Nye the Science Guy, Jamie Lee Curtis, and Alex Trebek. Shows start every 17 minutes. Indoor queue with uncovered, outdoor, overflow queue. The queue moves quickly once the show begins. Effects may be too intense for small kids and some adults. ECV must transfer to wheelchair. Wheelchair accessible. Assistive listening. No flash photo or video lights. **Alex's ToddlerTip:** *"Dinosaurs roar! ☺"* **Allie's KidTip:** *"Dinosaurs!!! Oh, and it has a movie about energy, too. May be loud."* **Allie's TeenTip:** *"It's still cool to me, and a fun way to learn."*

© MediaMarx, Inc.

Dinosaur topiaries

Attraction descriptions and ratings are explained on page 127.

Top Photo Slice: Looking up at Spaceship Earth (ⓘ12676) © Cheryl Pendry

Charting the Attractions at Future World (East)

Jennifer Dave Readers

Mission: SPACE [B-6]

FP+ | 9 | 9 | 8

Prepare for space flight at the International Space Training Center. As a civilian "astronaut," you board a four-person training centrifuge to experience the sensations of liftoff and zero gravity. Guests can choose between the original, high-intensity version (Orange Team) or a low-intensity experience (Green Team). In the high-intensity version, sensations are intense—the simulator spins rapidly and you may get queasy. If you go for the full-octane experience, heed the warnings and don't close your eyes or look to the side during the ride. If you'd rather not take the chance of getting sick, try the milder version—it's the same ride but without the spinning. Save time to enjoy the post-show exhibits. Young kids enjoy the Space Base playground. Indoor, themed queue. 44"/112 cm height restriction. Young kids must be with an adult.

Thrill Ride
E-Ticket
Ages 8 & up
Disorienting
FastPass+ or long waits
7 1/2 min. pre-show
5 min. ride

© Jennifer Marx
Strapped in for take off!

ⓘ12729 © Cheryl Pendry
The entrance to Mission: SPACE in the early evening

Test Track [B-5]

FP+ A-OK! | 8 | 8 | 9

Do you feel the need for speed? How does 65 miles per hour in a rapidly accelerating six-seat, open-air test vehicle on a tightly banked track sound? This popular attraction was recently renovated and now has a new, interactive queue experience where you design a virtual car. You then board a "sim car" to try out your ideas on the track. The ride track remains the same as before, but now you test out your new car design in four scenes: capability (rough road and weather conditions), efficiency (your carbon footprint), responsiveness (maneuvering), and power (speed!). The attraction has even got a fresh new look with bright colors, reminding us of the movie "Tron." Reserve a FastPass+ if possible, or use the "single-rider queue" on the left for the shortest wait. Front seat offers more leg room. Indoor/outdoor queue. 40"/102 cm height restriction. Young children must be accompanied by adult. Health warning. Must transfer from wheelchair to ride. Assistive listening. Closed captioning. Alex's KidTip: "The test car only seems faster than your own car on the highway because the car is open (no roof). It's fun, but maybe still a little scary for me." Allie's KidTip: "Sit in the middle of the car so you don't get sprayed!" TeenTip: "I love the end of the ride when you go SUPER fast!"

Thrill Ride
E-Ticket
Ages 7 & up
Fast, jerky
FastPass+ or very long waits or singles line
3 min. intro
5 min. ride

More at ⓘ mission-space

Top Photo Slice: Spacesuits in the queue at Mission: SPACE (ⓘ13697) © Janet Simonsen

Charting the Attractions at Future World (West)

Jennifer Dave Readers

Club Cool [D-6] 7 6 8

Walk-thru
A-Ticket
Ages 2 & up
Noisy, sticky floor

Sample free Coke beverages from other countries at this "clubby" diversion. This is a fun place to cool off and enjoy a soft drink, including an unusual aperitif called Beverly. You can purchase Coke merchandise here, including t-shirts, vintage-shaped bottles, and other "pop" art. Wheelchair accessible. **Alex's KidTip:** *"Be sure to try all the drinks! You never know what you might like."* **Allie's TeenTip:** *"The drink from Japan is the best!"*

© Jennifer Marx
Alexander loves Beverly!

The Seas with Nemo & Friends [E-7] FP+ A-OK! 6 7 6

Pavilion/ Ride
D-Ticket
All ages
Sharks!
Med. waits
Allow about one hour

Board "Clamobiles" and explore the world's largest saltwater aquarium tank and artificial coral reef. New technology allows your favorite characters from "Finding Nemo" to swim among the real marine life in the aquarium. View dolphins, sharks, manatees, and thousands of sea creatures. Check with a cast member for a demo schedule. For programs that explore the aquarium in more depth, see page 275. After the tame ride, don't miss Turtle Talk with Crush (see below). Indoor queue. Wheelchair accessible. Assistive listening. Reflective captioning. Closed captioning. **Alex's ToddlerTip:** *"I found Nemo! ☺"* **Allie's KidTip:** *"I love the dolphins."*

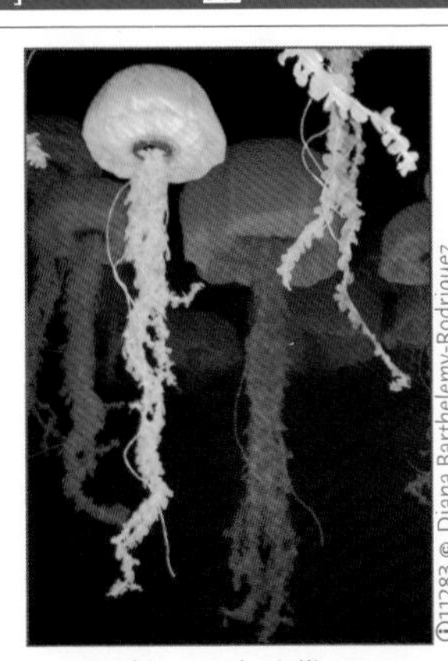
ⓘ11283 © Diana Barthelemy-Rodriguez
Takin' on the jellies!

Turtle Talk with Crush [E-7] FP+ A-OK! 9 9 9

Show
D-Ticket
Ages 3 & up
Long waits
12 min. film

State-of-the-art technology allows guests to interact with Crush (the sea turtle from "Finding Nemo")—he can see and hear you, and talk back! This animated, interactive experience engages kids and impresses adults. Encourage young kids (ages 3–8) to sit up front for the best experience. Inside The Seas pavilion. Wheelchair accessible. **Alex's ToddlerTip:** *☹ (bored)* **Allie's TeenTip:** *"Totally awesome, dude! It's so cute to hear the little kids' questions and answers."*

Note: Innoventions West closed in 2015, but we're not sure whether it will simply re-open with new exhibits or become something entirely new. Watch PassPorter.com for news and announcements. Innoventions East remains open.

Attraction descriptions and ratings are explained on page 127.

More at ⓘ the-seas

Top Photo Slice: Hidden Mickey in the floor of an aquarium at The Seas with Nemo & Friends (ⓘ11285) © Diana Barthelemy-Rodriguez

Planning | Getting There | Staying in Style | Touring | Feasting | Making Magic | Index | Notes & More

Charting the Attractions at Future World (West)

Jennifer Dave Readers

The Land [E-6] A-OK!	7	6	7
Agriculture and the environment take center stage, hosted by Nestlé. Rides, film, food court, and restaurant. "Behind the Seeds" guided greenhouse tour.	**Pavilion** D-Ticket		

The Circle of Life [F-6] A-OK!	6	5	6
Timon and Pumbaa from The Lion King set out to build the Hakuna Matata Village Resort—without regard to their ecosystem. Simba reminds them (and us) how important it is to protect the environment. Great photography. Indoor queue with benches. Inside The Land pavilion. Wheelchair accessible. Assistive listening. Reflective captioning. **Alex's ToddlerTip:** *"Simba! ☺"* **Allie's KidTip:** *"Simba tells us about the earth and how to take care of it."* **TeenTip:** *"Great for everyone!"*	**Film** C-Ticket Ages 3 & up Short waits 12 min. film		

Soarin' Around the World (2016) [F-6] FP+	10	9	9
With a new movie and score set to begin in 2016, you can soar over some of the world's most unique natural landscapes and man-made wonders, complete with all-new digital screens. Currently guests are strapped into oversized porch swings and rise from the floor for a simulated hang glider tour. An eye-filling, IMAX-quality movie screen, gentle motion, stirring music, and scented breezes combine for an exhilarating journey. Queue is indoors and offers fun games to play while waiting. Inside The Land pavilion. 40"/102 cm height restriction. Transfer from wheelchair to ride. Closed captioning. **Alex's KidTip:** *"It's like gliding! ☺"* **Allie's TeenTip:** *"Wow!"*	**Simulator** E-Ticket Ages 7 & up Heights, brief darkness FastPass+ or very long waits 5 min. ride		

© MediaMarx, Inc.
Soarin' over Big Sur

ⓘ13362 © Wendy Suchomel
Readers did Soarin' eight times over eight days!

Living With the Land [F-6] FP+ A-OK!	7	6	7
Learn how modern agriculture serves the needs of a hungry world and protects the environment. Your boat cruises through a multimedia exhibit and Disney's amazing experimental hydroponic greenhouses. See veggies that may be served for dinner upstairs (more than 30 tons are produced annually). Flash photos only allowed in the greenhouses. Indoor queues. Inside The Land pavilion. Must transfer from ECV to wheelchair. Wheelchair accessible. **Alex's ToddlerTip:** ☺ **KidTip:** *"More fun than school. Look for Hidden Mickeys!"* **TeenTip:** *"Boring but educational."*	**Boat Ride** D-Ticket Ages 4 & up Dark FastPass+ or med. waits 13 min. ride		

Top Photo Slice: A Mickey-shaped pumpkin grows in the hydroponic gardens in The Land © MediaMarx, Inc.

Charting the Attractions at Future World (West)

Jennifer | Dave | Readers

Captain EO [E-5] FP — 7 | 6 | 7

In June 2010, Honey I Shrunk the Audience closed to make way for the return of Captain EO, the "4D" film starring Michael Jackson and produced by filmmakers Francis Ford Coppola and George Lucas. The film graced Epcot from 1986–1994, the era of Michael Jackson's "Thriller," and Captain EO is more of the same. Michael captains a spaceship with a cute, cuddly, and klutzy crew of aliens with a mission to deliver a gift to the Supreme Leader, a truly scary-looking female alien portrayed by Anjelica Huston. Music, of course, conquers all, and the Universe lives happily ever after. The "4D" in-theater effects are mostly limited to seats that shake to the music, and everything may seem a bit quaint and dated, but the pre-show "Making of..." film alone makes it worthwhile. Eo is in for an "indefinite" run, and there's no hint that Honey, I Shrunk the Audience will return (we think a new show is in development). Wheelchair accessible. Assistive listening.	**3-D Film** E-Ticket Ages 5 & up Loud, intense Medium waits 5 min. intro 17 min. film

Journey Into Imagination with Figment [E-5] FP A-OK! — 5 | 5 | 3

Figment, the cute purple dragon, comes roaring back to Epcot in a reenergized version of Journey Into Your Imagination. Figment and Dr. Nigel Channing (Eric Idle) team up to stimulate our imaginations with sight, sound, smell, a bit of whimsy, and music from Disney legends Richard and Robert Sherman. Highlights include Figment's House and the final rendition of the theme song, One Little Spark. The ride still doesn't rate an "A," but you'll be charmed and tickled. Riders exit into the ImageWorks interactive playground. Indoor queue with outdoor overflow queue. Effects too intense for some children. Wheelchair accessible. **Alex's ToddlerTip:** *"Ride again, please! ☺"*	**Track Ride** C-Ticket Ages 5 & up Portions are very dark, loud, with bright flashes Med. waits 6 min. ride

ImageWorks: Kodak "What If" Labs [E-5] A-OK! — 6 | 6 | 7

Hands-on sound and image exhibits and a gift shop, at the exit to Journey Into Imagination with Figment. Digital portraits (which can be sent via e-mail), inventive photo gifts, and a unique Kodak photo lab. "Backdoor" entrance through shop. **Allie's KidTip:** *"It's cool! Check out the floor piano!"*	**Playground** B-Ticket All ages Allow 30 min.

ⓘ5398 © Amy Sellars

The Imagination pavilion in the evening

Top Photo Slice: The glass pyramid atop the Imagination pavilion (ⓘ10666) © Victoria Goeler

Charting the Attractions at World Showcase

(clockwise order)

Jennifer Dave Readers

Mexico [B-4] A-OK! 7 6 8

Enter Mexico's Mayan pyramid to find yourself in a magical, twilit village plaza with a volcano smoking ominously in the distance. Enjoy a fine exhibit of art and artifacts, eateries, a ride (see below), shops, and musicians. Allie's KidTip: "Don't worry, that's not a real volcano. Looks like it, though!"

Pavilion | D-Ticket | All ages | Low light

Gran Fiesta Tour Starring The Three Cabelleros [B-4] A-OK! 6 6 5

Tour Mexico in this revamped boat ride (formerly El Rio del Tiempo) featuring Audio-Animatronics, music, and short film/animation clips with the Three Caballeros (Donald Duck, Jose Carioca, and Panchito Pistoles). Jose and Panchito fly through Mexico in search of Donald for the big show. Don't miss the cool fiber-optic fireworks display. Your boat floats past diners at the San Angel Inn restaurant. Indoor queue inside the Mexico pavilion. Transfer from ECV to wheelchair to ride. Wheelchair accessible. **Alex's KidTip:** "This is one of my favorite rides! ☺" Allie's KidTip: "Be sure to look up and see the fireworks on the ceiling!"

Skeleton fiesta seen on the Gran Fiesta Tour
ⓘ8451 © Cheryl Pendry

Boat Ride | C-Ticket | All ages | Dark, but very tame | Short waits | 7 minute cruise

Norway [B-3] A-OK! 6 6 7

This taste of Norway features shops, a future Frozen-themed ride (see below), eateries, and a wooden Stave church. Peek inside the church for a history of the Vikings. Allie's KidTip: "If you see a troll, rub its nose for luck."

Pavilion | C-Ticket | All ages | Allow 30 min.

Castle in Norway
ⓘ11398 © Kate Touchette

Spelmanns Gledje perform in Norway
ⓘ1348 © Brad K.

Frozen Ever After (2016) [B-3] – – –

Celebrate "Winter in Summer" in this new Frozen-themed flume ride that takes you to Arendelle. Along the way you'll see Sven, Olaf, trolls, Elsa's ice castle, and even some fireworks. Cutting-edge Audio-Animatronics make the world of Frozen come alive! You can also meet Elsa and Anna in the "Royal Summerhus." Watch for more details after it opens at the PassPorter.com web site and newsletter.

Boat Ride

Top Photo Slice: Mural in Mexico (ⓘ11414) © Diana Barthelemy-Rodriguez

Charting the Attractions at World Showcase

(clockwise order)

	Jennifer	Dave	Readers
China [B-3] A-OK!	4	5	6

Explore China through a film (see below), museum exhibits, gardens, eateries, and the Yong Feng Shangdian department store. Visit a half-scale model of Beijing's Temple of Heaven. Acrobats and gymnasts perform. Allie's Kid Tip: *"When you walk into the temple to see the movie, look up."*

Pavilion | C-Ticket | All ages | Allow 20 min.

	Jennifer	Dave	Readers
Reflections of China [A-3]	7	6	7

Experience marvels of China in a sweeping, Circle-Vision 360° motion picture. Grand scenes of the Great Wall, the Yangtze Gorge, and Beijing's Forbidden City alternate with views of bustling cities. The film—previously called "Wonders of China"—was improved in 2003 with vibrant new footage of modern China including Macau and Hong Kong. You must stand to view. Indoor waiting area with wooden benches. Wheelchair accessible. Assistive listening devices. Reflective captioning. Allie's Kid Tip: *"Don't sit down or you'll miss part of the movie."*

5131 © Amy Sellars

Temple of Heaven ceiling in China

Film | C-Ticket | Ages 6 & up | Could cause dizziness | Short waits | 13 min. show

	Jennifer	Dave	Readers
Germany [B-1]	3	4	7

Steep-roofed stone buildings, oompah bands, eateries, and shops evoke a quaint German square. Look for the model railroad, and listen for the glockenspiel that chimes on the hour. Allie's Kid Tip: *"Find the train set in the toy shop."*

Pavilion | C-Ticket | All ages

Agent P's World Showcase Adventure

Go on an interactive scavenger hunt with a little help from Agent P (from "Disney's Phineas and Ferb" show) and his "F.O.N.E." This high-tech and entirely free activity leads you through many of the countries of the World Showcase—when you find the answer to a clue, your F.O.N.E. will often trigger a special event, such as the ringing of the glockenspiel in Germany. You should try this out, even if you're not a Phineas and Ferb fan! To sign up, visit one of the three kiosks early in the day (located at the International Gateway, Italy, and Norway) and you'll receive a mission time and starting location. Agent P's adventure replaced Kim Possible's mission in summer 2012.

© MediaMarx, Inc.

Agent P's F.O.N.E. can trigger the glockenspiel in Germany

Top Photo Slice: Rooftop creatures on the China pavilion (①7940) © Elizabeth Ferris

Charting the Attractions at World Showcase

(clockwise order)

Jennifer Dave Readers

Italy [C-1] 5 4 6

Disney faithfully captures the spirit and architecture of Venice in this Italian piazza. Eateries, shops, jugglers, music, and entertainers in a Mediterranean garden set the scene at this pavilion. Look closely at the angel atop the 83-foot-tall bell tower—it is covered in real gold leaf. The tower itself is a replica of the Campanile in St. Mark's Square, Venice. While there are no rides or movies at this pavilion, it's still worth a visit. Allie's Kid Tip: "Make a good wish at King Neptune's fountain."

①13290 © Wendy Suchomel

Maggie & Julianne

Pavilion | C-Ticket | All ages | Allow 15-20 minutes

The American Adventure [D-1] 6 5 7

This all-American pavilion is halfway around the lagoon from Future World. Home to the American Adventure show, theater, art gallery, a hamburger joint, wonderful singers, and a shop. Allie's Kid Tip: "See the fife and drum corps."

Pavilion | D-Ticket | All ages

The American Adventure Show [D-1] 7 7 7

Ben Franklin and Mark Twain take you on a patriotic tour of U.S. history. A large cast of Audio-Animatronics characters, including Thomas Jefferson and Susan B. Anthony. Martin Luther King Jr. takes center stage in updated filmed segments. Famous events are recreated and famous Americans share their ideas. Don't expect a critical view of history, however. The wide stage is easier to see if you don't sit in the front. See Epcot Times Guide for shows. Indoor queue. "Voices of Liberty" may sing. Wheelchair accessible. Assistive listening. Reflective captioning. Allie's Kid Tip: "Look on the walls for the statues."

Show | D-Ticket | Ages 5 & up | Dark at times | Med. waits | 15 min. intro with singers 30 min. show

America Gardens Theatre (seasonal) [D-1] 6 7 6

Live, musical entertainment is the hallmark of this outdoor theater on the edge of the lagoon. Check the Times Guide for show times—usually three half-hour shows daily. Seating is free, but the front rows may be reserved for "package" guests. Shows are visible from the promenade. Seating is on benches with sycamore trees providing some shade. Wheelchair accessible. Allie's Kid Tip: "Sit in the front because it's covered and the back is just trees."

Show | C-Ticket | Ages 2 & up | Short waits | Most shows 30 min.

①5436 © Cyndi Gai

Rainbow over The American Adventure on July 4th (really!)

Top Photo Slice: A golden eagle in front of the American Adventure pavilion (①2286) © Janet Simonsen

Charting the Attractions at World Showcase

(clockwise order)

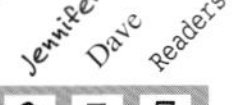

Japan [D-1]

A-OK! 8 7 7

The sound of Taiko drummers may draw you to this pavilion, featuring traditional Japanese architecture and gardens, entertaining exhibits, updated eateries, and the Mitsukoshi department store. A beautiful and peaceful retreat. Allie's KidTip: "Go through the Japanese garden. The goldfish are neat."

Pavilion | C-Ticket | All ages | Allow 20 min.

Morocco [E-1]

A-OK! 7 6 7

Morocco's Moorish architecture, art exhibits, exotic cuisine, live entertainers, and crafts beckon to the adventuresome traveler. Much is hidden from the casual visitor—take the time to explore the museum and other areas. You'll find a character meet-and-greet area virtually hidden across from Restaurant Marrakesh, plus artisans and cultural representatives scattered throughout. Excellent shopping opportunities. Allie's KidTip: "You'll feel like you want to go to Africa. I like the entertainers here, too."

Pavilion | C-Ticket | All ages | No scares | Allow about 20–30 min. to explore

ⓘ8522 © Cheryl Pendry

Twilight in Morocco

ⓘ2168 © Janet Simonsen

Garden maze in front of the France pavilion

France [F-2]

A-OK! 7 7 7

The Eiffel Tower, cobblestone streets, renovated eateries, shops (including a Guerlain boutique), street performers, and a film (see below) evoke the essence of France. **Allie's TeenTip:** "I want to go to Paris, and this is almost as good."

Pavilion | D-Ticket | All ages

Impressions de France [F-2]

A-OK! 9 9 7

The beauty and romance of France's villages, cities, and countryside come to life in a breathtaking film. Fabulous scenery, wonderful 200° widescreen photography, and the best musical soundtrack at Walt Disney World (great French classical tunes) make this one of our favorites. Cool, dark theater offers seating and welcome relief. Shows on the hour and half-hour. Wrought-iron benches and small exhibits make even the indoor, air-conditioned queue enjoyable. Wheelchair accessible. Assistive listening. Reflective captioning. **Alex's ToddlerTip:** ☹ (bored) Allie's KidTip: "You get to see Notre Dame, like in 'Hunchback of Notre Dame.'"

Film | D-Ticket | Ages 5 & up | Dark theater, loud music | Short waits | 18 min. film

More at ⓘ japan-epcot

Attraction descriptions and ratings are explained on page 127.

Top Photo Slice: Torii gate in front of the Japan pavilion (ⓘ11572) © Kelly Michelle Narvaez

Charting the Attractions at World Showcase

(clockwise order)

Jennifer Dave Readers

United Kingdom [E-3]

A-OK! 7 6 7

Pavilion
C-Ticket
All ages will enjoy

This is Florida's British Colony, full of quaint shops, gardens, a park with live entertainment (check the Epcot Times Guide for the British Revolution band—they're excellent!), a busy pub, and deliciously British eateries. Well-themed. **Allie's Kid Tip:** "You gotta play in the hedge maze! And there's really cool music."

© MediaMarx, Inc.

Allie and Melanie in the classic British phone box

ⓘ 2982 © Cheryl Pendry

The large park nearly hidden in the back of the pavilion

Canada [E-4]

5 5 7

Pavilion
C-Ticket

The architecture and natural beauty of Canada are captured in a 360° movie (see below), nifty waterfall, gardens, shops, eateries, and live entertainment.

O Canada! [E-4]

A-OK! 7 6 6

Film
C-Ticket
Ages 5 & up
Dark, a little dizzying
14 min. film

Experience the natural and manmade wonders of Canada in an updated Circle-Vision 360° film. Swooping aerials and dramatic scenery highlight this tour encompassing the Rockies and old-world Montreal. The updated film includes about 50% new footage and features Martin Short and Eva Avila. Shows start every 20 minutes. Stand to view. Indoor queue. Wheelchair accessible. Assistive listening. Reflective captioning. **Alex's Toddler Tip:** ☹ (bored) **Allie's Kid Tip:** "I got tired of standing for so long."

© MediaMarx, Inc.

Looking out at Canada

ⓘ 3942 © Mark Zielberg

Canada at sunset

More at ⓘ world-showcase

Top Photo Slice: The crenelated roofline of the United Kingdom pavilion (ⓘ 8351) © Cheryl Pendry

Cooling Off at Epcot's Fountains

Water is everywhere at Epcot, but nowhere does it draw our attention more than the beautiful fountains throughout the park.

You can't help but notice Epcot's spectacular **Fountain of Nations** at the heart of Future World (see photo on page 153). You may even have been cooled (or chilled) by its drifting mists. But have you really taken the time to savor this carefully choreographed water ballet? Every 15 minutes, the fountain dances to another musical number, with special seasonal music during the Christmas holidays. Thousands of water jets and lights are computer-synchronized to the rhythms and melodies. 30,000 gallons of water course through the fountain, and 2,000 gallons can be airborne at one time, shooting up to 150 feet high. While the mists are more chilling at night, the fountain's lights make the display that much more magical. Enjoy a meal at the Electric Umbrella (see page 235) and catch the show!

Beyond this, nearly **every pavilion has its own water feature**, from the tidal splashes in front of The Seas with Nemo & Friends to the upside-down waterfall at the Imagination pavilion. Even the countries in World Showcase get into the watery act, with delightfully-detailed fountains that evoke each country's charms.

© MediaMarx, Inc.

This water is flowing up, not down!

ⓘ3942 © Denise Lang

Cooling off on a warm day

And let's not forget Epcot's **play fountains**, which are beloved by kids and kids-at-heart. You'll find two in Future World, one near the plaza as you pass into Future World and the other on the way to Test Track. If you intend to play in them, be sure to bring a change of dry clothing!

Top Photo Slice: The Fountain of Nations at Epcot (ⓘ10638) © Brigett Duncan

Making the Most of IllumiNations

FP

IllumiNations finale

IllumiNations: Reflections of Earth brings every night to a spectacular close. Brilliant fireworks and a rousing, original musical score fill Epcot's World Showcase Lagoon every evening at park closing, heralding the creation of Earth. A shower of sparkling comets paves the way, a huge globe glides across the lagoon to take center stage, and a pageant of breathtaking scenery, wildlife, and the peoples of the earth plays across a giant video display covering the continents of the globe. Lasers, blazing torches, and more fireworks tumble forth as the music builds to a rousing climax.

Although the show is visible anywhere around the lagoon, there are definitely **better viewing sites**. You can judge a viewing site well in advance of the show as you stroll around the lagoon, or check our map on page 152. A clear view of the water at the center of the lagoon is critical, as is a clear view of the sky (watch those tree limbs). It also helps if the wind is to your back or side (to avoid fireworks smoke). The bridge between France and the United Kingdom is a prime (and popular) location. Italy and Norway are other good viewing spots. Or try for a 7:30 pm advance reservation at the Rose & Crown. Check in at the podium early and request a patio table. You may get lucky with a great view. If not, enjoy your meal anyway—diners are invited outside to stand and enjoy the show. Another place to stay seated is at La Hacienda de San Angel in Mexico. Arrive at least 90 min. early for a lagoon-side table. We also highly recommend the excellent views from the lagoon-side patios in the United Kingdom and France, if they aren't already occupied by private parties. If you opt to use your Headliner (Tier 1) FastPass+ for IllumiNations, which is rarely necessary in our opinion, the viewing area for FastPass+ holders is at the intersection of the World Showcase Lagoon and Future World, between the two Tower gift shops.

IllumiNations lights up the sky

Top Photo Slice: Fireball seen during the nightly IllumiNations show (ⓘ12700) © Cheryl Pendry

Disney's Hollywood Studios

This park's 154 acres spotlight the golden era of Hollywood and the glamorous silver screen. It's located southwest of Epcot and is connected to Epcot by Friendship boats and walkways. Disney's Hollywood Studios was renamed from Disney-MGM Studios in January 2008 (and may get yet another name change again soon). Big changes are in store for this park as it adds two new areas: Star Wars Land and Toy Story Land.

Tinseltown never looked so good. All the glamour, glitz, and pageantry of Hollywood come out to greet you at Disney's Hollywood Studios. Disney's rendition of Hollywood Boulevard is done up in 1930s art deco architecture, and an old-fashioned water tower (complete with Mickey ears) sets the stage. Disney's Hollywood Studios gives you a behind-the-scenes glimpse at movie-making as well as an opportunity to get involved in shows and tours. Celebrities may put in live appearances at Disney's Hollywood Studios as well, complete with a procession down Hollywood Boulevard and a handprint ceremony. The whole effect is of being a special guest at a major movie studio in the heart of Hollywood.

© Melissa Loflin

The Great Movie Ride

ⓘ14256 © Heather Baker

Getting an autograph

ⓘ36350 © Christopher Perry

Speeder-ing Outside Star Tours

Top Photo Slice: Marquee inside The Great Movie Ride) © Jennifer Marx

Orienting Yourself at Disney's Hollywood Studios

Fold out the next page for touring plans and a handy attraction chart

Unlike other parks, Disney's Hollywood Studios' layout is free-form, much like Hollywood's artistic personalities (see the park map on the next page). See the inside of the fold-out map for daily touring itineraries and an attractions-at-a-glance list, and pages 177–182 for attraction details.

Hollywood Boulevard Area

Stroll among the stars—this is the "main street" of Tinseltown in its heyday.

Headline Attraction: The Great Movie Ride

The Great Movie Ride ☛

①2323 © Janet Simonsen

Sunset Boulevard Area

Step back in time to the Hollywood that never was on this famous, palm-lined boulevard.

Headline Attractions: Rock 'n' Roller Coaster, Tower of Terror, Beauty and the Beast

Tower of Terror on Sunset Boulevard ☛

①14821 © Janet Simonsen

Echo Lake Area

Go for a journey into a galaxy far, far away with tours of the stars and a training academy. Expect this area to morph into Star Wars Land in the upcoming years.

Headline Attraction: Star Tours

Star Tours ☛

①48010 © Carlos Medina

Streets of America Area

Visit a movie set evoking famous urban skylines. It even has "towering" skyscrapers!

*Headline Attractions: Muppet*Vision 3-D; Lights, Motors, Action! Extreme Stunt Show*

Streets of America ☛

①4858 © Amy Sellars

Pixar Place Area

Play with "the Toys" and mermaids. Expect this area to become Toy Story Land in the future.

Headline Attractions: Toy Story Midway Mania!, Voyage of the Little Mermaid

Green Army Men in Pixar Place ☛

①13633 © Lura Honeycutt

Top Photo Slice: Entrance to Disney's Hollywood Studios (①12607) © Cheryl Pendry

Our Favorite Touring Plan for Disney's Hollywood Studios

NOTES

While Disney's Hollywood Studios has fewer attractions than the Magic Kingdom and Epcot, it's harder to see everything you want to visit due to show times and lengths. It is important to check your Times Guide and note showtimes. We recommend you jot down these showtimes on this page once you know them—you'll find a fill-in-the-blank line for those attractions/events with specific showtimes. The plans work best if you go in the same order, but you should feel free to skip an attraction or two (and return to it later) if it makes sense for you. You should be able to accomplish either of these plans in one day if you start by 9:00 am. Those with infants and toddlers, or thrill-shy adults, may prefer to skip all attractions in blue.

ITINERARIES

Touring With Adults

Get FastPass+ (can be reserved 30-60 days in advance on My Disney Experience—see page 126) as early as possible.

Enter Sunset Boulevard
Visit Rock 'n' Roller Coaster
Visit Tower of Terror
Enter Streets of America Area
Visit Lights, Motors, Action! @ _____
Visit Muppet*Vision 3-D
Enter Echo Lake Area
Visit Star Tours
Eat lunch at Studio Catering, Sci-Fi Dine-In*, Backlot Express, '50s Prime Time*, or Hollywood & Vine* *(about 3 hours after you enter the park)*
Enter Streets of America Area
Visit Streets of America Set
Enter Pixar Place Area
Visit One Man's Dream @ _____
Visit Voyage of the Little Mermaid or watch the afternoon parade @ _____
Visit Toy Story Midway Mania!
Eat dinner at Hollywood Brown Derby*, Hollywood & Vine*, '50s Prime Time*, or Catalina Eddie's *(about 7 1/2 hours after you enter the park)*
Watch Fantasmic! @ _____
(Tour duration: About 10 hours)

Touring With Kids

Get FastPass+ (can be reserved 30-60 days in advance on My Disney Experience—see page 126) as early as possible.

Enter Echo Lake Area
Visit Star Tours
Enter Pixar Place Area
Visit Toy Story Midway Mania!
Visit Disney Junior @ _____
Enter Streets of America Area
Visit Lights, Motors, Action! @ _____
Visit Muppet*Vision 3-D
Eat lunch at Hollywood & Vine*, '50s Prime Time*, ABC Commissary, or Backlot Exp. *(about 3 1/2 hours after you enter the park)*
Enter Streets of America Area
Visit Honey, I Shrunk the Kids Movie Set
Visit Team McQueen Headquarters Character Greeting
Enter Echo Lake Area
Watch the afternoon parade @ _____
Enter Hollywood Boulevard Area
Visit Great Movie Ride
Enter Pixar Place Area
Visit Voyage of the Little Mermaid @ _____
Eat dinner at Hollywood & Vine*, '50s Prime Time*, or Catalina Eddie's *(about 7 1/2 hours after you enter the park)*
Watch Fantasmic! @ _____
(Tour duration: About 10 hours)

** These restaurants may be difficult to impossible to get in as a walk-up. Advance dining reservations can be made up to 180 days in advance (see page 226).*

Top Photo: Giant guitar in front of Rock 'N' Roller Coaster (ⓘ1300) © BradK

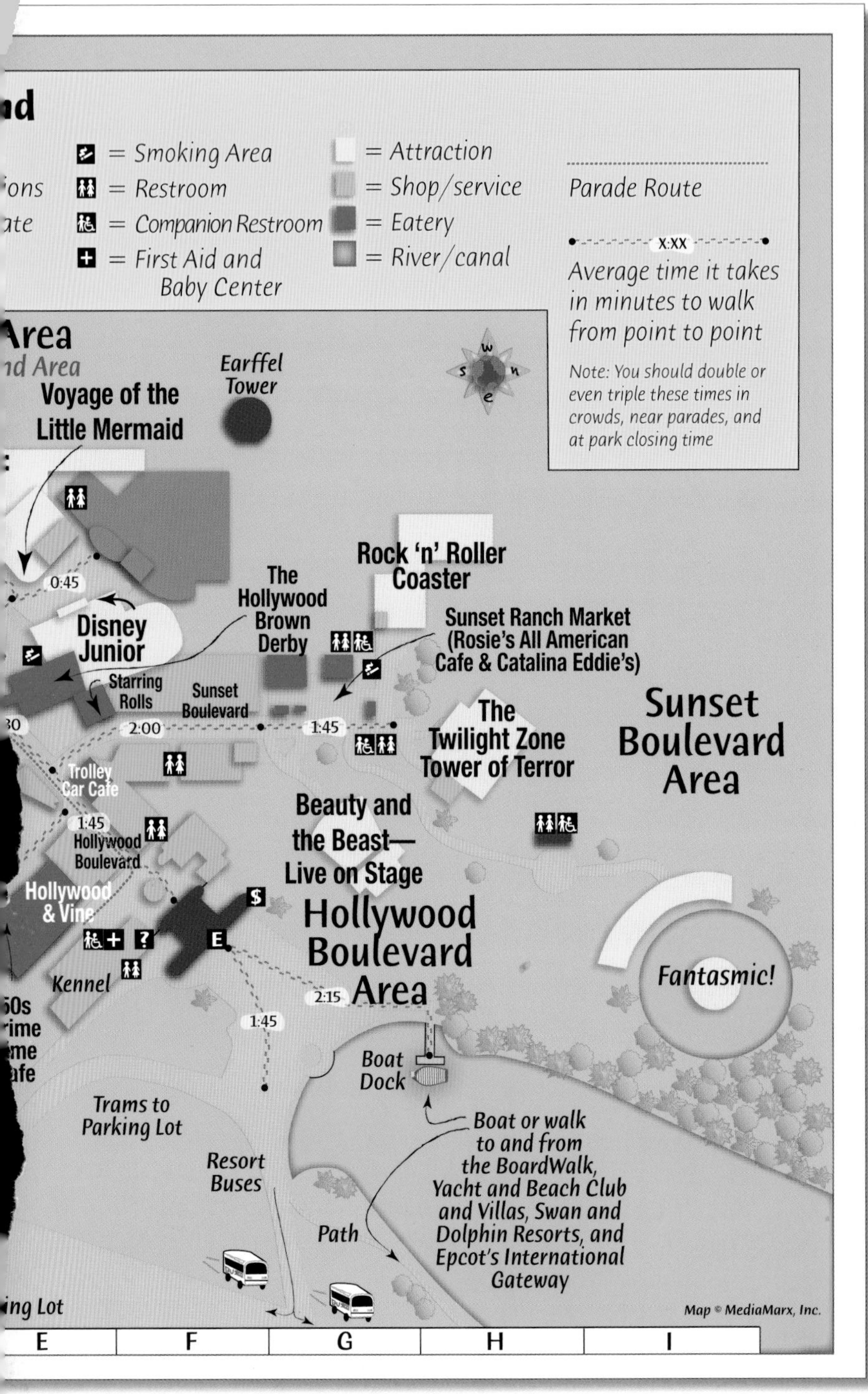

nd
ons
ate
= Smoking Area
= Restroom
= Companion Restroom
= First Aid and Baby Center
= Attraction
= Shop/service
= Eatery
= River/canal
Parade Route
X:XX
Average time it takes in minutes to walk from point to point
Note: You should double or even triple these times in crowds, near parades, and at park closing time
Area
nd Area
Voyage of the Little Mermaid
Earffel Tower
w
s
n
e
0:45
Disney Junior
The Hollywood Brown Derby
Rock 'n' Roller Coaster
Sunset Ranch Market (Rosie's All American Cafe & Catalina Eddie's)
Starring Rolls
Sunset Boulevard
2:00
1:45
30
The Twilight Zone Tower of Terror
Sunset Boulevard Area
Trolley Car Cafe
1:45
Hollywood Boulevard
Beauty and the Beast—Live on Stage
Hollywood & Vine
$
E
Hollywood Boulevard Area
Kennel
50s rime me afe
2:15
1:45
Fantasmic!
Boat Dock
Trams to Parking Lot
Resort Buses
Boat or walk to and from the BoardWalk, Yacht and Beach Club and Villas, Swan and Dolphin Resorts, and Epcot's International Gateway
Path
ing Lot
Map © MediaMarx, Inc.
E
F
G
H
I

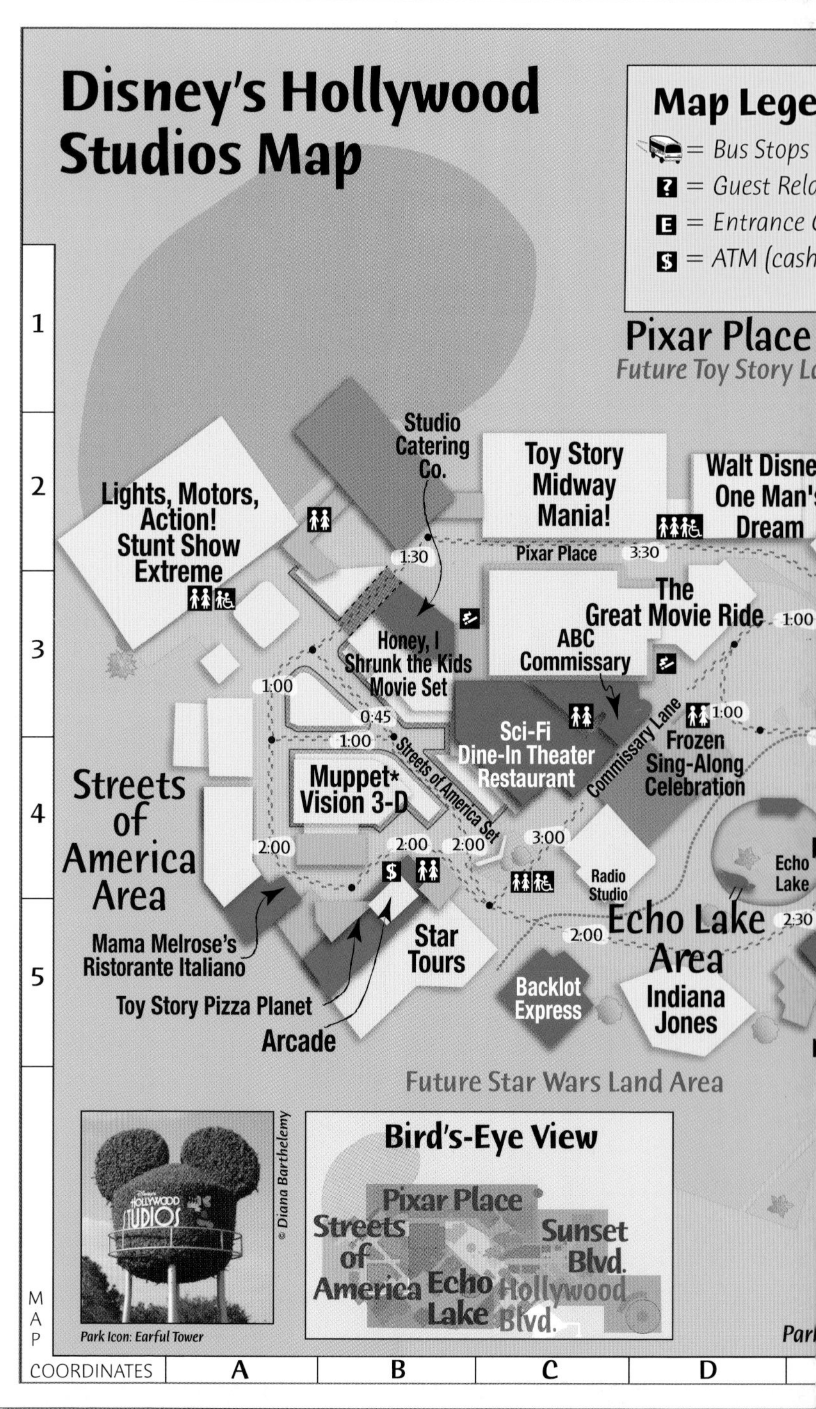
Disney's Hollywood Studios Map
Map Lege
= Bus Stops
= Guest Rela
= Entrance G
= ATM (cash
Pixar Place
Future Toy Story La
Studio Catering Co.
Toy Story Midway Mania!
Walt Disne One Man's Dream
Lights, Motors, Action! Stunt Show Extreme
1:30
Pixar Place
3:30
The Great Movie Ride
1:00
Honey, I Shrunk the Kids Movie Set
ABC Commissary
1:00
0:45
1:00
Sci-Fi Dine-In Theater Restaurant
Commissary Lane
1:00
Frozen Sing-Along Celebration
Streets of America Set
Muppet* Vision 3-D
Streets of America Area
2:00
2:00
2:00
3:00
Radio Studio
Echo Lake
2:30
Echo Lake Area
2:00
Mama Melrose's Ristorante Italiano
Star Tours
Backlot Express
Indiana Jones
Toy Story Pizza Planet
Arcade
Future Star Wars Land Area
© Diana Barthelemy
Park Icon: Earful Tower
Bird's-Eye View
Pixar Place
Streets of America
Sunset Blvd.
Echo Lake
Hollywood Blvd.
Par
MAP COORDINATES
A
B
C
D
1
2
3
4
5

Disney's Hollywood Studios Attractions At-A-Glance

(alphabetical order)

Attraction	Type	Allow	Page
☐ Beauty and the Beast [G-4]	Live Show	40–55+	182-HS
☐ Disney Junior–Live on Stage! [E-3]	Live Show	20–30+	180-MA
☐ For the First Time in Forever–A Frozen Sing-Along Celebration	Live Show	30–40+	177-EL
☐ The Great Movie Ride [D-3]	Film/Ride	25–45+	182-HS
☐ Honey, I Shrunk the Kids [B-3] Movie Set Adventure	Playground	20–30+	178-SA
☐ Indiana Jones Epic Stunt [D-5]	Live Show	40–50+	177-EL
☐ Lights, Motors, Action! Extreme Stunt Show [A-2]	Live Show	45–60+	178-SA
☐ Muppet*Vision 3-D [B-4]	3-D Film	30–40+	180-SA
☐ One Man's Dream [D-2]	Walk-thru	30–40+	180-MA
☐ Rock 'n' Roller Coaster [G-3]	Coaster	20–45+	182-HS
☐ Star Tours [B-5]	Thrill Ride	20–40+	177-EL
☐ Streets of America Set [B-4]	Walk-thru	20–30+	179-SA
☐ Toy Story Midway Mania [D-2]	Ride	45–60+	181-MA
☐ Toy Story Pizza Planet [B-5]	Arcade	15–20+	179-SA
☐ Twilight Zone Tower of Terror [H-4]	Thrill Ride	25–60+	182-HS
☐ Voyage of the Little Mermaid [E-2]	Live Show	25–40+	181-MA

The Allow column gives the amount of time (in minutes) you should allow for an attraction, assuming you do not have a FastPass+ and there are no ride breakdowns. The letters after the page numbers stand for the first one or two letters of the land in which that attraction is located: EL=Echo Lake, SA=Streets of America, MA=Mickey Avenue, and HS=Hollywood/Sunset Blvds.

Finding the Stars at Disney's Hollywood Studios

Disney's Hollywood Studios is the perfect star-gazing spot. The chart below shows typical locations of popular Disney characters.

Star(s)	Location(s)
☐ Various characters	Near Great Movie Ride
☐ Toy Story friends	Pixar Place
☐ Mickey Mouse	Near Studio Catering Co.
☐ Mike & Sulley	Near Studio Catering Co.
☐ Phineas and Ferb	Near Mama Melrose's Ristorante Italiano
☐ Cars vehicles	Team McQueen HQ near Streets of America

Note: Greeting locations and characters vary (check your guidemap), but Pixar Place, Hollywood Boulevard near the Chinese Theater, and Studio Catering Co. are the likely locations.

Catching the Shows at Disney's Hollywood Studios

© Jennifer Marx
Alexander gets "swindled" in the street

Entertainment is simply a matter of course at Disney's Hollywood Studios. The unique "**streetmosphere**" performers make their home along famous boulevards of Hollywood and Sunset, as well as Echo Lake. Dressed in 1940s-style garb, they're responsible for all sorts of on-the-street shenanigans.

Frozen fans enjoy **For the First Time in Forever: A Frozen Sing-Along Celebration** FP+ held in the Hyperion Theater area several times during the day at press time. This 25-minute retelling of the story is a big hit with Anna and Elsa fans. The show grew out from the Frozen Summer Fun event, so there's no telling how long it will last.

3835 © Stephanie Fieldstad
Fantasmic!

Come evening, it's Mickey versus villains in **Fantasmic!** FP+ at the expanded Hollywood Hills Amphitheater. Fantasmic! is a spectacular 25-minute mix of live action, music, and fireworks. Schedule changes seasonally, so check the Times Guide. The "Made with Magic" Ear Hats and accessories light up and interact with Fantasmic!

Fantasmic Tip: Later shows have shorter waits and better seating. Fantasmic! is popular, though we can take it or leave it. A Fantasmic! Meal Package may be available with special seating—see page 243.

Big Changes at the Studios: Disney announced in August 2015 that two new lands are coming to the park: Toy Story Land and Star Wars Land! The 11-acre Toy Story Land will shrink guests to the size of a toy to go on a family-friendly Slinky Dog roller coaster and spin about in an Alien saucers attraction. Star Wars Land will feature two new attractions (including a chance to pilot the Millenium Falcon), new restaurants, shopping, and interactive experiences in its 14 acres. No official opening dates have been announced for either, but our best guess is 2018–2019 for Toy Story Land and 2019–2020 for Star Wars Land. Bob Iger also mentioned earlier in 2015 that the park would be renamed, but we do not yet know to what. Subscribe to the free, weekly PassPorter News at http://www.passporter.com/news to learn more.

Top Photo Slice: Fire dances on the water during Fantasmic! (2977) © imadisneygirl

Making the Most of Disney's Hollywood Studios

TIPS

If you're interested in the **live shows**, check the Times Guide for showtimes and plan accordingly to avoid long waits or mad dashes.

Autograph seekers, be prepared! Characters come out in force for meet-and-greets in the park, especially in front of Great Movie Ride. See page 171b for a "star" chart, and see page 276 for tips.

ⓘ14254 © Heather Baker

Waiting to meet Buzz Lightyear and Woody

Some of the shows involve **audience participation**. If you like this sort of thing, volunteer enthusiastically for the fun by immediately standing up, waving, and calling out when the call for volunteers goes out! And remember to smile!

Seniors won't want to rush through Disney's Hollywood Studios—make enough time to slow down and enjoy the ambience of the park.

ⓘ28361 © Jamie Blaylock

New padawans take on Darth Vader at the Jedi Training Academy

Top Photo Slice: Tower of Terror © MediaMarx, Inc.

Getting the Best at Disney's Hollywood Studios

SHOPPING

General merchandise shopping is on Hollywood and Sunset Boulevards. Many major attractions have a **themed shop**, too. All shops can be entered without going on a ride. Here are our favorites:

Shop	Location	What makes it special
Crossroads of the World	Hollywood Blvd.	Guidemaps, Times Guides, ponchos
Sid Cahuenga's	Hollywood Blvd.	One-of-a-kind movie memorabilia
Head to Toe	Hollywood Blvd.	Custom embroidery and engraving
Keystone Clothiers	Hollywood Blvd.	Quality Disney clothes
Villains in Vogue	Sunset Blvd.	Disney Villain clothing and gifts
Stage One Company Store	Streets of America	Quirky shop with Muppets!
Writer's Stop	Streets of America	Books! (We can't resist 'em!)
Tatooine Traders	Echo Lake	Star Wars items, fun theme
Hollywood Tower Hotel	Sunset Blvd.	Scary stuff and Tower of Terror gifts

NOTES

Disney's Hollywood Studios has several **unique restaurants** and cafes, and many participate in a Fantasmic! Meal Package. See pages 242–244 for dining and package details.

The focus at this park is on **independent shows and rides** rather than on a never-ending stream of entertainment. Be prepared for walking and waiting. Your reward is longer, lovingly produced shows, more intense rides, and fascinating backstage glimpses.

The pavement in front of Grauman's Chinese Theater (The Great Movie Ride) is full of **celebrity footprints** and handprints.

ⓘ13284 © Wendy Suchomel

Kermit was here!

RATINGS

Ratings are explained on page 128.

Our Value Ratings:		Our Magic Ratings:		Readers' Ratings:
Quality:	8/10	Theme:	8/10	64% fell in love with it
Variety:	7/10	Excitement:	9/10	33% liked it well enough
Scope:	6/10	Fun Factor:	7/10	2% had mixed feelings
Overall Value:	**7/10**	**Overall Magic:**	**8/10**	1% were disappointed

Disney's Hollywood Studios is enjoyed by... (rated by both authors and readers)

Younger Kids: ♥♥♥♥	Young Adults: ♥♥♥♥♥	Families: ♥♥♥♥♥
Older Kids: ♥♥♥♥	Mid Adults: ♥♥♥♥♥	Couples: ♥♥♥♥♥
Teenagers: ♥♥♥♥♥	Mature Adults: ♥♥♥♥♥	Singles: ♥♥♥♥

Top Photo Slice: Streetmosphere characters outside shops on Hollywood Boulevard (ⓘ4412) © Melissa Potter

Finding Your Way to Disney's Hollywood Studios

BEST TIMES TO GO

Disney's Hollywood Studios can be enjoyed in one day, although it is best to **visit the most popular attractions earlier** to avoid long lines. Arrive before the scheduled opening time for the best advantage. The most popular attractions—Toy Story Midway Mania!, Rock 'n' Roller Coaster, and The Twilight Zone Tower of Terror—generate very long lines. Make a beeline for these rides first thing, unless you've just eaten breakfast. Several of the shows have **limited seating capacity** (such as Voyage of the Little Mermaid) and can require a lengthy wait if busy. Your FastPass+ priority is Toy Story Midway Mania! Check the entertainment schedule in the park Times Guide for show times. Take the length of show times into account when planning your route and keep in mind that several shows take a considerable amount of time. Many attractions and restaurants empty immediately before and during the parade, affording shorter lines or the chance to get a table without advance dining arrangements.

GETTING THERE

By Boat—From Epcot's International Gateway, BoardWalk Inn & Villas, Yacht & Beach Club & Villas, and Swan & Dolphin, take the Friendship boat.

By Bus—Take a direct bus from all other resorts, Epcot's main entrance, and Disney's Animal Kingdom. From the Magic Kingdom, catch a bus at the Transportation and Ticket Center (TTC). From Disney Springs, Typhoon Lagoon, or Blizzard Beach, take a bus or boat to a resort and transfer to a Disney's Hollywood Studios bus.

By Car—Take I-4 to exit 67 (westbound) or exit 62 (eastbound) and continue on to Disney's Hollywood Studios parking. All-day parking is available for $17 (free to resort guests and annual passholders).

By Foot—You can walk from the BoardWalk, Swan & Dolphin, and Yacht & Beach Club, and even Epcot's International Gateway. Follow the marked pathways along the canal beside the BoardWalk Villas (see resort map on page 52 for path location).

ⓘ2611 © Gayle Hartleroad

Friendship boat dock at Disney's Hollywood Studios

More at ⓘ disneys-hollywood-studios

Top Photo Slice: A stunt car drives on two wheels in Lights, Motors, Action! Stunt Spectacular (ⓘ4850) © Amy Sellars

Charting the Attractions at the Echo Lake Area

(in clockwise order starting from the left side of the park)

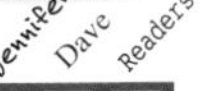

Indiana Jones Epic Stunt Spectacular (closing) [D-5] FP+ A-OK! 7 6 8

①2561 © Jyl Deshler

Saving the day!

The Indiana Jones films set the stage for an action show of epic proportions. Disney has built a huge indoor/outdoor set to demonstrate the stuntperson's craft, including the famous rolling boulder, an Egyptian marketplace, and a flaming German airplane. Adults may be picked to join the show—arrive early and show enthusiasm if this interests you. Theater opens 25 minutes before the show and guests sit in a covered, outdoor theater. Loud explosions and hot flames may scare young children. Wheelchair accessible. Assistive listening. Rumored to be closing (see page 173).

Live Show | E-Ticket | Ages 4 & up | Loud, fire, violence | FastPass+ or med. waits | 30 min. show

A Frozen Sing-Along Celebration [C-4] FP+ A-OK! 8 – 8

Fans of Disney's Frozen enjoy this heartwarming show narrated by the funny Arendelle historians. Anna, Elsa, Kristoff appear onstage during this retelling of the popular tale. Audience is encouraged to sing along to every song from the movie (lyrics are shown on big screens above). Jennifer really enjoyed the show even though when it comes to Frozen she's ready to let it go already. Snow and lighting effects. Wheelchair and ECV accessible. Now in the Hyperion Theater.

Live Show | C-Ticket | All Ages | FastPass+ or med. waits | 30 min. show

Star Tours: The Adventures Continue [B-5] FP+  8 8 8

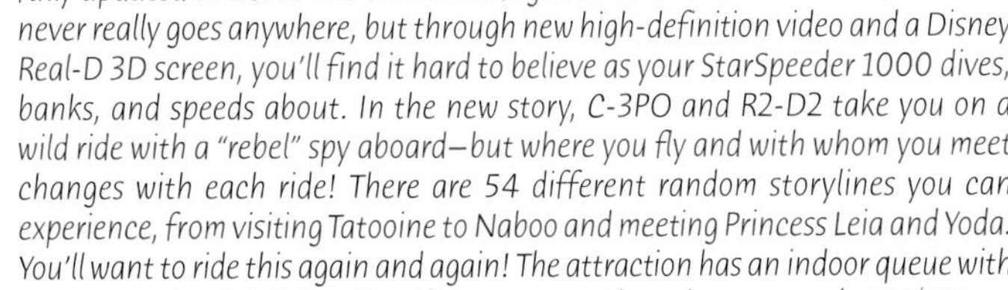

Take a flight to a galaxy far, far away in this "must ride" for all Star Wars fans, fully updated in 2011! The enhanced flight simulator at the heart of this ride never really goes anywhere, but through new high-definition video and a Disney Real-D 3D screen, you'll find it hard to believe as your StarSpeeder 1000 dives, banks, and speeds about. In the new story, C-3PO and R2-D2 take you on a wild ride with a "rebel" spy aboard—but where you fly and with whom you meet changes with each ride! There are 54 different random storylines you can experience, from visiting Tatooine to Naboo and meeting Princess Leia and Yoda. You'll want to ride this again and again! The attraction has an indoor queue with many new visual delights. Overflow queue outdoors is uncovered. 40"/102 cm height restriction. Young kids should be with an adult. Health warning. Guests must transfer from ECV to wheelchair, and from wheelchair to ride. Closed captioning. Non-moving rides may be available for ECV-bound and motion-sensitive—ask a cast member. **Allie's Kid Tip:** "This is good, but hold on tight!" **TeenTip:** "The back seats really are the best."

①48013 © Carlos Medina

A StarSpeeder

Thrill Ride | E-Ticket | Far-out fun | May be rough, rocky, may cause motion sickness | FastPass+ or expect long waits | 3 min. intro 4.5 min. flight

Attraction descriptions and ratings are explained on page 127.

Expect this area to be in flux as Star Wars Land takes shape. Rumor has it we may see a new Star Wars Launch Bay preview attraction appear or even a new adventure added to Star Tours with scenes from "Star Wars: The Force Awakens." See page 173 for more information.

Top Photo Slice: Droid spotted in the queue for Star Tours (①3834) © Stephanie Fieldstad

Charting the Attractions in the Streets of America Area

Jennifer | Dave | Readers

Honey, I Shrunk the Kids Movie Set Adventure [B-3] A-OK! 6 5 6

Kids climb, cavort, and caper amidst huge plants, insects, and spider webs in this playground based on the popular movies and TV show. Keep cool with various water sprays (it gets very hot here) and slide down giant rolls of film and leaves. Officially kids must be at least 4 years old to play, and adults must be with a child to enter. Wheelchair accessible.

Playground | B-Ticket | Ages 4 & up | Giant bugs | Short waits

ⓘ8724 © Elizabeth Key

Readers cavort in the playground

© MediaMarx, Inc.

Alexander plays on fungi

Lights, Motors, Action! Extreme Stunt Show [A-2] FP+ 7 8 8

You'll be wowed by an epic display of the stuntperson's art in this updated show originally from Disneyland Paris. Villains in cars and motorcycles roar across the set in pursuit of the hero, as filmmakers shoot scenes for a spy movie. Giant video screens show how special effects action is turned into movie magic. Lightning McQueen and Mater, stars of Cars and Cars 2, have also joined the cast! A 5,000-seat partially shaded grandstand offers metal bench seats. With only 2–3 shows daily, plan to arrive early. Brief, hot flames can make the front rows uncomfortable. Assistive listening. Wheelchair accessible. Unshaded queue. Lightning and Mater meet and greet available after the show.

Live Show | E-Ticket | Ages 3 & up | Loud! | Long waits or FastPass+ | 25 minutes

Muppet*Vision 3-D [B-4] FP+ A-OK! 7 7 9

Your 3-D glasses get a real workout as Kermit and his pals show you around the Muppet Labs. The Muppets are at their zany, pun-filled best in a frenetic good time that was Jim Henson's last production. The multiscreen videos and hilarious props shown in the pre-show area deserve your full attention. The digital projection theater is large and air-conditioned, with comfy seats. There's no need to sit in front to get a good view. Some effects may be scary for young kids. Indoor queue is fun. Wheelchair accessible. Assistive listening. Closed captioning. Reflective captioning. **Alex's Toddler Tip:** *"I like Kermit! ☺"* Allie's Kid Tip: *"Keep your 3-D glasses on."*

3-D Film | E-Ticket | Ages 4 & up | Intense, loud, some violence | Med. waits | 15 min. intro 17 min. film

ⓘ6905 © Keith Stanton

Balloon atop the Muppet Labs

Top Photo Slice: A stuntman on fire at Lights, Motors, Action! (ⓘ4204) © Lynn Mirante

Charting the Attractions in the Streets of America Area

Streets of America Movie Set [B-4]

Jennifer	Dave	Readers
6	6	6

© MediaMarx, Inc.

If you go to San Francisco, wear a flower in your hair

Whether or not you've been to the big city, you'll enjoy the movie set-style renditions of New York and San Francisco. The buildings are all facades, of course, but the detail is rich and pretty accurate. You'll find familiar bits of Chinatown and a London street in here, too. Disney entertainers may appear on the Plaza Hotel-like steps or roll down the streets in parade fashion. Look for the "Singin' in the Rain" umbrella (see photo), but don't be surprised if it gets a little damp! Wheelchair accessible.

Walk-thru
A-Ticket
All ages
Few waits
Unlimited

ⓘ8834 © Dawn Chugg

Singin' in the rain

Toy Story Pizza Planet Arcade [B-5]

A-OK!

Jennifer	Dave	Readers
2	3	6

This is a spacious, pleasantly themed arcade adjacent to the Pizza Planet cafe with a typical selection of video games. There's a depressing lack of Toy Story-themed arcade games, however. Tokens are needed to play. Most games require 2 to 4 tokens, and the tokens are 25 cents each. Not very magical. Wheelchair accessible. Allie's KidTip: *"Fun games."*

Arcade
A-Ticket
Ages 5 & up
Loud!
Few waits

Osborne Family Spectacle of Dancing Lights *(closing in 2016)*

The late Jennings Osborne's Christmas lights were too much for his Arkansas neighbors, so Disney invited him to the studio backlot, where his lights became a Thanksgiving through New Year's tradition. The more than five million lights grace the Streets of America Set. Look for them November 6, 2015 through January 3, 2016, but say goodbye after that—they close for good on January 4, 2016 after 20 years in order to make way for the new lands (see page 173).

ⓘ11667 © Donald Willis

The Osborne Family Spectacle of Dancing Lights light up the holiday nights

More at ⓘ osborne-lights

Top Photo Slice: Close-up of the Osborne Family Spectacle of Lights in Streets of America (ⓘ4643) © Dawn Elliott

Charting the Attractions in the Pixar Place Area

Jennifer Dave Readers

The Magic of Disney Animation [F-2] (closed)

This attraction closed on July 12, 2015. The Mickey Mouse and Minnie Mouse character meets were moved near Studio Catering Co. There's no word on what will be replacing The Magic of Disney Animation, but it's likely it closed to make way for the new Toy Story Land (see page 173).

Walt Disney: One Man's Dream presented by D23 [D-2]

8 | 8 | 8

This attraction illustrates Walt's impact on his company and the world. Follow Walt's imaginings as they grow and learn how his boyhood experiences affected his lifelong accomplishments. Hundreds of priceless and never-before-seen artifacts are on display, as well as a showing of the moving "One Man's Dream" presentation at the end. Wheelchair accessible.

Walk-thru
D-Ticket
Ages 10 & up
Allow 30 min.

Walt's Desk at One Man's Dream

ⓘ32411 © Harold and Dawn D.

Disney Junior–Live on Stage! [E-3]

FP+ A-OK! 7 | 6 | 8

Puppets give a live version of Disney Channel favorites, including characters from "Mickey Mouse Clubhouse," "Little Einsteins," "Handy Manny," and the newest show, "Jake and the Never Land Pirates." Seating is on a carpeted floor. This attraction becomes a kid-friendly dance party on Extra Magic Hour evenings. Outdoor, covered queue. Wheelchair access. **Alex's ToddlerTip:** ☺ *"Bubbles fall from the ceiling!"*

Live Show
C-Ticket
All ages
22 min. show

Toy Story Land is coming to this area and construction is likely to bring changes to the attractions in this area (see page 173).

Top Photo Slice: Toodles from Mickey Mouse Clubhouse at Playhouse Disney (ⓘ14275) © Heather Baker

Charting the Attractions in the Pixar Place Area

Jennifer | Dave | Readers

Studio Backlot Tour [B-2] (closed)

The park's backstage movie magic blockbuster and the American Film Institute exhibit and shop at the attraction's exit closed in September 2014.

Toy Story Midway Mania! [D-2]

FP+ | A-OK! | 10 | 10 | 10

This dark ride is based on Pixar's Toy Story and is Disney's first interactive 3-D ride. It makes use of digital sets, effects like wind and water spray, and spring-action pointers to shoot virtual projectiles like eggs, darts, balls, and rings. Look for hidden targets to get extra points and enjoy different levels of play. The "Toy Story Trams" seat four guests each (two groups of two). A third track system is being added to increase the capacity of this very popular attraction, but it may not be done until late 2016. Toy Story Midway Mania will become part of the new Toy Story Land (see page 173). This ride has fast spins and may cause motion sickness. Indoor queue with interactive Mr. Potato Head (in standby queue only). Wheelchair accessible.

3-D Ride
E-Ticket
Ages 3 & up
Some fast spins
Very long waits
5 1/2 min. ride

ⓘ9992 © Alisa Niethammer

Pixar Studios ... a sign of more attractions to come?

© MediaMarx, Inc.

Toy Story Trams on the way to play!

ⓘ22348 © Jessibean1

Mr. Potato Head in the queue

Voyage of the Little Mermaid [E-2]

FP+ | A-OK! | 8 | 7 | 8

Enjoy your favorite tunes while live action, puppets, falling water, and laser effects bring Ariel and her friends to life onstage, making you feel as if you're truly under the sea! Cool theater offers comfy seats. Middle rows are best for view of stage and effects. Stand to right during 5-min. pre-show for up-front seating. No flash photos or video lights. Covered outdoor queue. Wheelchair accessible. Assistive listening. Reflective captioning. **Alex's ToddlerTip:** *"Ariel is here! ☺"* **Allie's KidTip:** *"I love this! Look up!"* **Allie's TeenTip:** *"Boring!"*

Live Show
E-Ticket
Ages 3 & up
Dark, strobe
FastPass+ or long waits
17 min. show

Top Photo Slice: The Earful Tower topiary, seen on the Studio Backlot Tour (ⓘ11185) © Diana Barthelemy-Rodriguez

Charting the Attractions on the Hollywood & Sunset Boulevards

Jennifer | Dave | Readers

Beauty and the Beast–Live On Stage [G-4] FP+ A-OK! 6 7 8

Be Disney's guest! See Belle, Beast, Lumiere, Mrs. Potts, Chip, and that other beast, Gaston, live and on stage. An enthusiastic cast sings and dances its way through musical numbers from the animated film. The original story line all but disappears, but you'll hardly mind, thanks to the good performances, eye-filling costumes, and fine staging. Lines are long, but the theater opens 25 minutes prior to show. Live, pre-show entertainment on some days. Outdoor queue is uncovered. Wheelchair accessible. Assistive listening.

Live Show | E-Ticket | Ages 5 & up | Loud effects | Med. waits | 10 min. intro | 25 min. show

The Great Movie Ride [D-3] FP+ A-OK! 6 6 8

Hollywood's famed Grauman's Chinese Theater sets the stage for a sedate ride through famous scenes from classic movies enacted by Audio-Animatronics characters. Some live-action excitement and two short films add a bit of Hollywood pizzazz. Turner Classics Movies is the new sponsor, providing new narration and an updated finale with footage from Star Wars: The Force Awakens and Guardians of the Galaxy. Long lines snake through a props and costumes exhibit. Following the pre-show film, the queue separates—each line sees a scene that the other does not. Indoor queue with overflow queue outdoors. Effects may be too intense for small children. Transfer from ECV to wheelchair. Wheelchair accessible.

Film/Ride | D-Ticket | Ages 4 & up | Loud noises, scary scenes | Long waits | 3 min. intro | 18 min. ride

Rock 'n' Roller Coaster Starring Aerosmith [G-3] FP+ 8 10 9

Experience Disney's first high-speed coaster launch. Hurtle through twists, 4–5G turns, and three inversions (yes, upside down)—in the dark! Rock band Aerosmith invites you to take a limo crosstown and join them backstage. Aerosmith also provides the soundtrack for your ride—five different tunes are possible depending upon which "limo" you get. Upon boarding, we recommend you press your head against the headrest to prepare for the very fast start (0–58 in 2.8 seconds). Beyond that, this may be the smoothest coaster you ever ride—even the coaster-shy have enjoyed it. Interactive indoor queue area takes you through a recording studio's display of historic memorabilia. Take the single rider line for a shorter wait, or the "chicken exit" if you just want to enjoy the queue. 48"/122 cm height restriction. Transfer from ECV to wheelchair, and then transfer from wheelchair to ride. **Alex's KidTip:** *"Just no."* **Allie's KidTip:** *"You won't believe how fast it goes! Make sure your stuff is safe."* **TweenTip:** *"The loops are my favorite!"* **TeenTip** *"This ride rocks!"*

Coaster | E-Ticket | Ages 8 & up | Very fast, very dark, can cause motion sickness, headaches | FastPass+ or long waits | 2 min. intro | 3 min. ride

The Twilight Zone Tower of Terror [H-4] FP+ 3 9 9

Delight in the delicious spookiness of this haunted hotel, long before you ride its legendary "down and up and down and up again" elevator. The gut-wrenching drops are matched by wonderful visual effects. The queue splits in the basement—go left, it's typically shorter. To enjoy just the fabulous queue and pre-show, take the "chicken exit" before you board the elevator (ask a cast member). Outdoor queue is mostly shaded. 40"/102 cm height restriction. Health warning. Young children should be accompanied by an adult. Transfer from wheelchair to ride. Closed captioning. **Allie's KidTip:** *"I like the up and down part, but the rest is scary."* **TweenTip:** *"There are handles to hold beside the seats if you're scared. (But I'm not scared!)"* **TeenTip** *"This is the best ride at Disney World! And I got Jennifer to go on it with me finally!"*

Thrill Ride | E-Ticket | Ages 8 & up | Dark, scary, sudden drops | FastPass+ or long waits | 10 min. intro | 4 min. ride

More at ⓘ rock-n-roller-coaster

Attraction descriptions and ratings are explained on page 127.

Top Photo Slice: The Hollywood Tower Hotel, also known as The Twilight Zone Tower of Terror © MediaMarx, Inc.

Disney's Animal Kingdom

Disney's Animal Kingdom is the youngest and largest park (580 acres) at the Walt Disney World Resort. Part zoological park and part theme park, Disney's Animal Kingdom charms, delights, and thrills guests with a uniquely Disney look at the wild world. Disney's Animal Kingdom is located the farthest west of all the parks on the Walt Disney World property.

The Tree of Life towers above Disney's Animal Kingdom, reminding us of the wonder, glory, and fragility of nature's creations. This is the quietest of the parks out of respect to the animals who make their home here, but "quiet" doesn't mean "boring." Adventure awaits, as discoveries lurk around every bend. Like Epcot, Disney's Animal Kingdom is a place to explore with open eyes and eager minds. Lace up your boots, grab your safari hat, and load your camera—the adventure is about to begin!

14336 © Denise Lang

Honorary "bug eyes" at It's Tough to Be a Bug!

22855 © Amanda Hulse

Elephants spotted on a "two-week" safari

8462 © Janice Kovacs

Broken tracks at the top of Expedition Everest ... evidence of the Yeti?

Orienting Yourself at Disney's Animal Kingdom

Fold out the next page for touring plans and a handy attraction chart

To set the tone for the day, all guests pass through **The Oasis**, a lush jungle teeming with exotic wildlife, sparkling waters, and rocky crags. Then, standing on Discovery Island at the center, the **Tree of Life** binds the four lands of Disney's Animal Kingdom in a circle of life (see map). A new land, based on James Cameron's Avatar films, is currently in development (see page 191). See the inside of the map for our favorite touring plans and a list of attractions, and pages 191–196 for attraction details.

Discovery Island

Journey to the center where the waters meet, the Tree of Life looms large, and the little creatures scurry.

Headline Attraction: It's Tough to be a Bug!

Tree of Life ☛

© MediaMarx, Inc.

PANDORA: The World of Avatar

Coming in 2017, you can explore the exoplanetary moon of Pandora, with its floating mountains and bioluminescent plants (see page 191).

PANDORA Boat Ride Rendering ☛

© Disney

Africa and Rafiki's Planet Watch

Come together in the port town of Harambe, complete with thatched huts and baobab trees, and set off on safaris, treks, and adventures.

Headline Attractions: Kilimanjaro Safaris, Pangani Forest Exploration Trail, Festival of the Lion King

Sign at the entrance to Africa ☛

ⓘ15067 © Nicole Clayton

Asia

Step into the mythical kingdom of Anandapur (meaning "place of all delights") to experience the beauty, wonder, and peace of Asia.

Headline Attractions: Kali River Rapids, Maharajah Jungle Trek, Expedition Everest

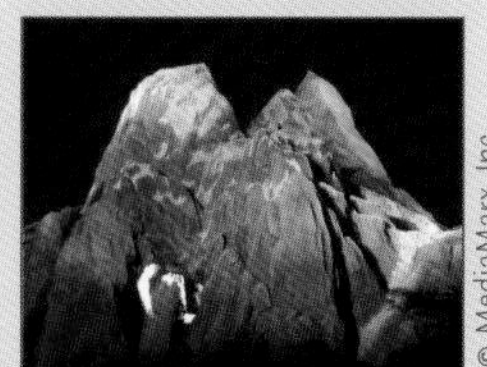

Expedition Everest ☛

© MediaMarx, Inc.

DinoLand, U.S.A.

Get tourist-trapped in the wacky world of an old dinosaur dig site, scattered with dino bones, then meet the "real" dinosaurs on a thrilling ride.

Headline Attractions: Dinosaur, Primeval Whirl, "Finding Nemo–The Musical"

Dino statue at Chester & Hester's! ☛

ⓘ11355 © Diana Barthelemy-Rodriguez

Top Photo Slice: A welcoming pterodactyl atop a building in DinoLand U.S.A (ⓘ3615) © Melissa Hasbrouck

Our Favorite Touring Plan for Disney's Animal Kingdom

NOTES

Like Disney's Hollywood Studios, Disney's Animal Kingdom has several attractions with specific showtimes, making it harder to fit the best attractions into one day. And because Disney's Animal Kingdom has about the same number of attractions as Disney's Hollywood Studios, its shorter hours make it harder to see and do everything you want. We've come up with touring plans—one for adults and one for kids—that take the typical showtimes into account to minimize waiting and backtracking. If you plan to use these plans, or modify them, be sure to check your Times Guide for showtimes. Use the fill-in-the-blank lines below to record showtimes on the day you visit to help you stay on track. As always, the touring plans work best if you go in the same order that we've listed, but you should feel free to skip an attraction or two (and return to it later) if that works best. You should be able to accomplish either of these plans in one day if you start by 9:00 am. Those with infants and toddlers, or less-adventuresome adults, may prefer to skip all attractions in blue.

ITINERARIES

Touring With Adults

Get FastPass+ (can be reserved 30-60 days in advance on My Disney Experience—see page 126) as early as possible.

Stroll through The Oasis

Enter Africa

Visit Kilimanjaro Safaris

Visit Pangani Forest Exploration Trail

Have a snack at Kusafiri Coffee Shop

Visit Festival of the Lion King @ _____

Enter Asia

Visit Expedition Everest

Visit Maharajah Jungle Trek

Visit Kali River Rapids

Eat lunch at Harambe Marketplace, Tusker House*, Pizzafari, or Flame Tree BBQ (*plan lunchtime for about 3 ½ hours after you arrive*)

Enter DinoLand U.S.A.

Visit "Finding Nemo—The Musical" @ _____

Visit Dinosaur

Visit Primeval Whirl

Enter Discovery Island

Visit It's Tough to be a Bug!

(Tour duration: About 8 hours)

Touring With Kids

Get FastPass+ (can be reserved 30-60 days in advance on My Disney Experience—see page 126) as early as possible.

Stroll through The Oasis

Enter Africa

Visit Festival of the Lion King @ _____

Visit Kilimanjaro Safaris

Visit Pangani Forest Exploration Trail

Take Wildlife Express Train to Rafiki's Planet Watch

Visit Rafiki's Planet Watch

Take Wildlife Express Train back to Africa

Eat lunch at Pizzafari, Harambe Marketplace, Tusker House*, or Flame Tree BBQ (*plan lunchtime for about 3 hours after you arrive*)

Enter DinoLand U.S.A.

Visit The Boneyard

Visit TriceraTop Spin

Visit "Finding Nemo—The Musical" @ _____

Enter Discovery Island

Visit It's Tough to be a Bug! or Maharajah Jungle Trek

(Tour duration: About 8 hours)

** These restaurants may be difficult to impossible to get in as a walk-up. Advance dining reservations can be made up to 180 days in advance (see page 226).*

Top Photo: A slice of Asia (①6539) © Dopey007

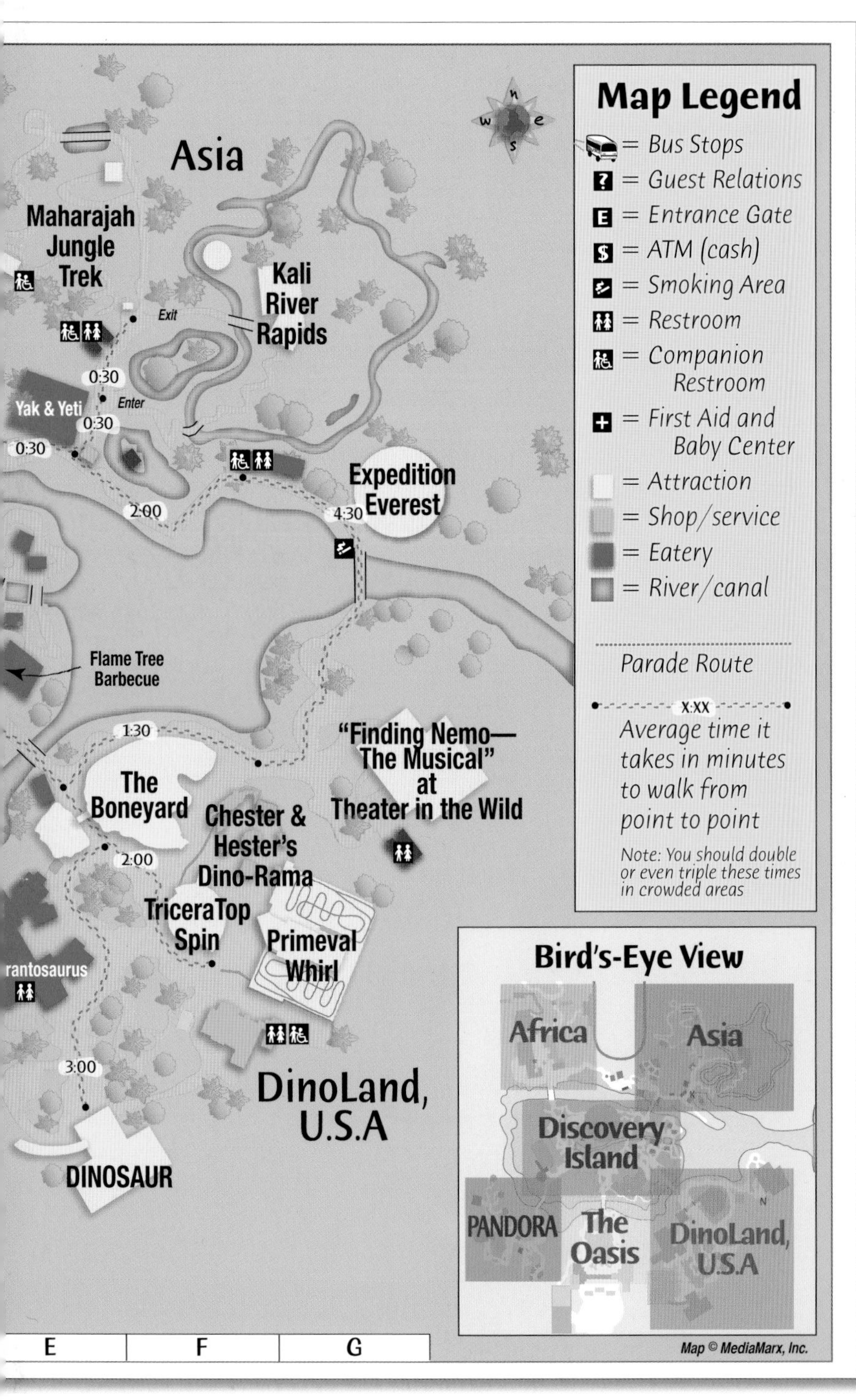
Asia
Maharajah Jungle Trek
Exit
Enter
Kali River Rapids
Yak & Yeti
0:30
0:30
0:30
2:00
4:30
Expedition Everest
Flame Tree Barbecue
1:30
"Finding Nemo—The Musical" at Theater in the Wild
The Boneyard
Chester & Hester's Dino-Rama
2:00
TriceraTop Spin
Primeval Whirl
rantosaurus
3:00
DinoLand, U.S.A
DINOSAUR
E
F
G
Map Legend
= Bus Stops
= Guest Relations
= Entrance Gate
= ATM (cash)
= Smoking Area
= Restroom
= Companion Restroom
= First Aid and Baby Center
= Attraction
= Shop/service
= Eatery
= River/canal
Parade Route
X:XX
Average time it takes in minutes to walk from point to point
Note: You should double or even triple these times in crowded areas
Bird's-Eye View
Africa
Asia
Discovery Island
PANDORA
The Oasis
DinoLand, U.S.A
Map © MediaMarx, Inc.

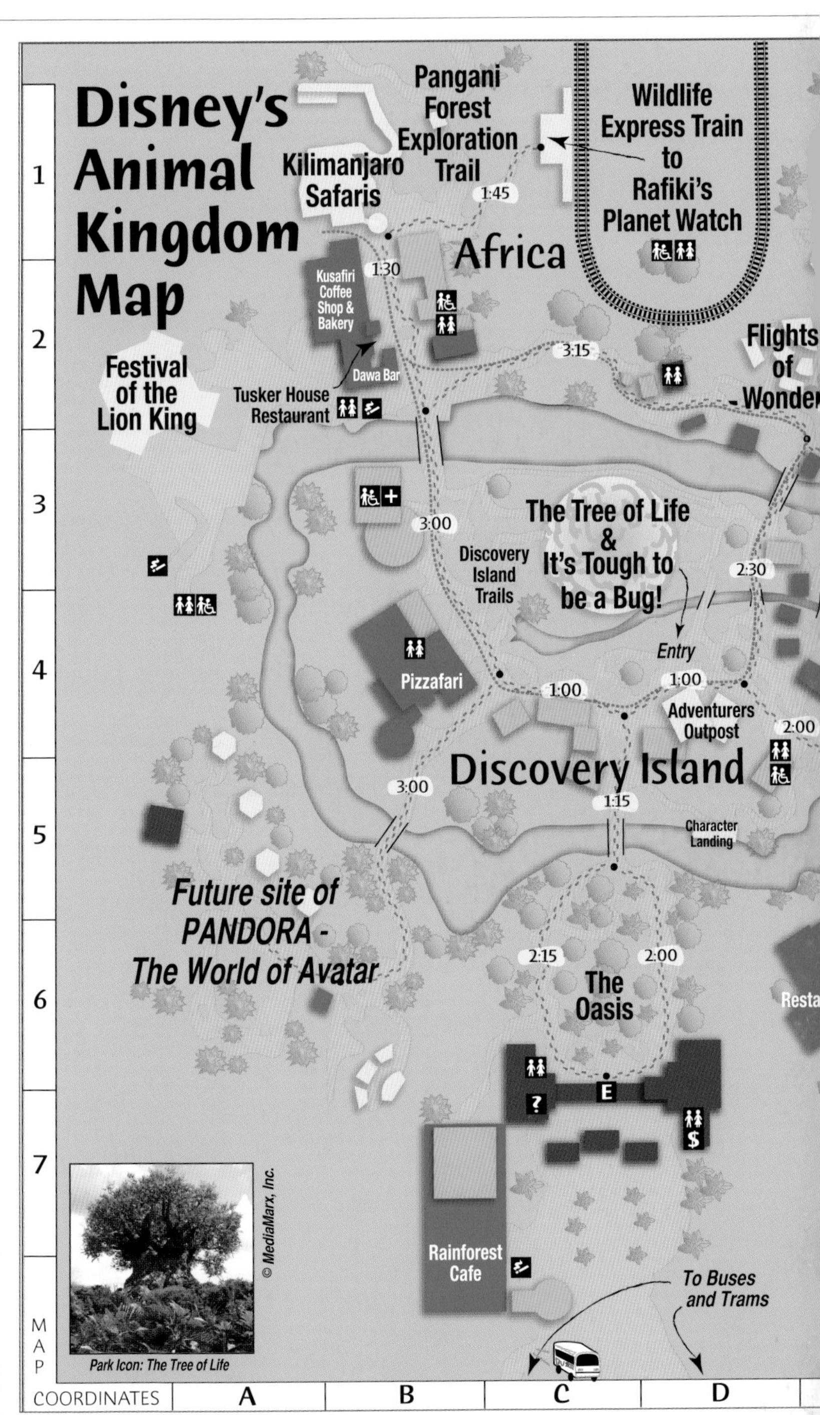

Park Icon: The Tree of Life

Disney's Animal Kingdom Attractions At-A-Glance

(alphabetical order)

Attraction	Type	Allow	Page
☐ Adventurers Outpost [D-4]	Character	30+	
☐ The Boneyard [F-5]	Playground	30–40+	196-DL
☐ DINOSAUR [E-7]	Thrill Ride	20–40+	196-DL
☐ Expedition Everest [G-3]	Coaster	60–120+	194-Asia
☐ Festival of the Lion King [A-2]	Live Show	40–55+	193-Afr
☐ "Finding Nemo—The Musical" [G-5]	Live Show	45–50+	196-DL
☐ Flights of Wonder [D-2]	Live Show	30–40+	194-Asia
☐ It's Tough to be a Bug! [D-4]	3-D Show	15–25+	191-DI
☐ Kali River Rapids [F-2]	Raft Ride	25–40+	195-Asia
☐ Kilimanjaro Safaris [B-1]	Ride	30–50+	192-Afr
☐ Maharajah Jungle Trek [E-1]	Walk-thru	30–45+	195-Asia
☐ The Oasis [C-6]	Walk-thru	5–20+	191
☐ Pangani Forest Exp. Trail [B-1]	Walk-thru	30–45+	192-Afr
☐ Primeval Whirl [F-6]	Coaster	30–60+	196-DL
☐ Rafiki's Planet Watch [off map]	Exhibit	60–90+	193-RP
☐ The Tree of Life and Trails [C-3]	Walk-thru	20–30+	191-DI
☐ TriceraTop Spin [F-6]	Ride	30–40+	196-DL
☐ Wildlife Express Train to Rafiki's Planet Watch [C-1]	Train Ride	20–25+	193-RP

The Allow column gives the amount of time (in minutes) you should allow for an attraction, assuming you do not have a FastPass+ and there are no ride breakdowns. The letters after the page numbers stand for the first two, three, or four letters of the land in which that attraction is located: DI=Discovery Island, Afr=Africa, RP=Rafiki's Planet Watch, Asia=Asia, and DL=DinoLand U.S.A.

Finding the Animals at Disney's Animal Kingdom

Everyone has their favorite furry and feathered friends. The chart below shows typical locations of popular animals.

Animal(s)	Location(s)
☐ Parrots, macaws, turtles	The Oasis
☐ Gorillas, meerkats, hippos	Pangani Forest Trail
☐ Lions, elephants, rhinos	Kilimanjaro Safaris
☐ Tigers, giant bats	Maharajah Jungle Trek
☐ Otters, giant tortoise	Discovery Island Trails
☐ Goats, sheep, llamas	Rafiki's Planet Watch
☐ Gibbons	Asia temple ruins

Tip: Keep your eyes open for live animal encounters with Disney naturalists. You're most likely to stumble across these on Discovery Island and Rafiki's Planet Watch.

Catching the Shows at Disney's Animal Kingdom

The best entertainment at Disney's Animal Kingdom is its themed live **theater shows**, described in detail on pages 191–196. Roving entertainers take a back seat to the wildlife, of course. Fireworks shows don't fit in here, either—they would just scare the animals.

Finale of Festival of the Lion King

A new nighttime spectacular, **Rivers of Light**, will debut along the natural stage of the River of Discovery. Guests will sit in two amphitheater-style viewing areas to enjoy the water show that will feature live music, floating lanterns, a water screen with projected imagery. We're expecting it to open in March 2016—watch our newsletter for details!

Other entertainment includes **The Adventure Begins** show, which starts 15 minutes before park opening every day—Minnie, Pluto, and Goofy arrive in a safari truck to start your adventure!

In Africa's Harambe Village, **live bands** and acrobats keep the Dawa Bar and Tusker House's outdoor tables hopping.

Visitors to Rafiki's Planet Watch may get lucky and catch **live animal acts** on the outdoor stage! Also be on the lookout for **DiVine**, a ten-foot-tall, towering and wandering "vine."

If you stay until park closing, you may get a little "**kiss goodnight**" from Donald, Goofy, Mickey and Minnie as they wave good-bye to all the guests leaving the park. Look for them in The Oasis just as you exit.

Simply DiVine

Top Photo Slice: Friendly birds wait for their cue at Flights of Wonder in Asia (ⓘ14325) © Janet Simonsen

Making the Most of Disney's Animal Kingdom

TIPS

Disney's Animal Kingdom is a paradise, where delightful and often subtle details can work their magic if you **take the time** to notice. This is not a do-it-all-in-a-day-or-die park. Slow down, revel in the beauty, wonder at the animals, and enjoy yourselves!

Trails lead off in all directions—don't be afraid to explore them. A bridge and path connects DinoLand and Asia (see map on page 186).

This park is one big photo op! Bring plenty of **memory cards/film** and **batteries**, and even **binoculars** for viewing animals.

Dining options here include the expanded Harambe Marketplace in Africa, full-service and counter-service restaurant (Yak & Yeti) in Asia, and Tusker House buffet with a character breakfast and lunch. See the listings on pages 245–247.

The outdoor, sheltered **seating** by Flame Tree Barbecue is a wonderful spot, whether you want to dine or simply rest. Tables and dining pavilions are set amidst lush tropical gardens.

"Caw caw, roar roar!" **Wilderness Explorers** encourages guests to discover the natural surroundings and earn more than 30 sticker badges! With the help of the free Wilderness Explorers Handbook, you'll encounter various challenges and activities stationed around the park. Learn how to track animals, how animals communicate, and the benefits of recyling. The free, self-guided program is inspired by the Disney-Pixar movie "UP" and while it's aimed at kids ages 7–10, anyone can play!

Reflecting pool at Flame Tree Barbecue

Getting the Best at Disney's Animal Kingdom

SHOPPING

The best shopping at Disney's Animal Kingdom can be found in two places: Discovery Island around the Tree of Life and Africa's Village of Harambe. Of the two, Harambe offers more in the way of handcrafted and **imported goods**, while Discovery Island offers themed **Disney merchandise**. Here are our favorite shops:

Shop	Location	What makes it special
Outpost	Outside park entrance	Guidemaps, hats, sunglasses
Garden Gate Gifts	Inside park entrance	Film, stroller/wheelchair rentals
Adventurers Outpost	Discovery Island	Safari hats, logowear
Island Mercantile	Discovery Island	Disney-themed gifts
Disney Outfitters	Discovery Island	Upscale clothing, decorative items
Mombasa Marketplace	Africa	Crafts demonstrations
Out of the Wild	Rafiki's Planet Watch	Conservation-themed items
Chester & Hester's	DinoLand U.S.A.	Kitschy, quirky gifts (and junk!)

NOTES

Not all **animals** can be seen all the time. On the plus side, you'll often see new ones each time, making subsequent visits unique.

Beverages sold in Disney's Animal Kingdom generally do not come with lids, for the animals' safety.

It always seems **hotter** at Disney's Animal Kingdom than at any other park. Be prepared with hats, sunglasses, sunscreen, and ways to keep yourself cool, like plenty of cold water and/or a personal misting fan ($16). Take advantage of the mist-spraying fans throughout the park when you need relief. Take frequent breaks in air-conditioned spots—try the eateries, shops, or attractions.

Disney announced in 2011 that they would bring the **fantasy world of AVATAR** to Disney's Animal Kingdom. Construction began in 2014. For more details, see page 191 and watch our web site and newsletter!

RATINGS

Ratings are explained on page 128.

Our Value Ratings:		Our Magic Ratings:		Readers' Ratings:
Quality:	8/10	Theme:	9/10	44% fell in love with it
Variety:	7/10	Excitement:	7/10	33% liked it well enough
Scope:	6/10	Fun Factor:	6/10	15% had mixed feelings
Overall Value:	**7/10**	**Overall Magic:**	**7/10**	8% were disappointed

Animal Kingdom is enjoyed by... (rated by both authors and readers)		
Younger Kids: ♥♥♥♥♥	Young Adults: ♥♥♥♥	Families: ♥♥♥♥♥
Older Kids: ♥♥♥♥	Mid Adults: ♥♥♥♥	Couples: ♥♥♥♥
Teenagers: ♥♥♥♥	Mature Adults: ♥♥♥♥	Singles: ♥♥♥♥

Top Photo Slice: Flamingos seen on the Kilimanjaro Safari (ⓘ13965) © Heather Baker

Finding Your Way at Disney's Animal Kingdom

BEST TIMES TO GO

Most guests arrive in the morning and leave in the afternoon, making **late afternoon** the best time to visit. Not only are the crowds thinner, but the park's animals prefer the cooler temperatures found in the earlier and later parts of the day, so you're more likely to see them. If possible, take advantage of Extra Magic Hours, especially in the cool of the evening. You may have more luck spotting animals during and after a rainstorm, too. When you **first arrive**, head for Expedition Everest or Kilimanjaro Safaris to pick up a FastPass+ (or just go ahead and ride if the wait is short enough). Another strategy is to get FastPass+ for three of the attractions early in the day and then immediately get a FastPass+ for another attraction. Check the Animal Kingdom **Times Guide** for show times and durations, and plan your day accordingly—these shows can chew up more time than you'd expect. You can use our touring plans on page 185a to give you an idea of what you can expect to do in one day. Finally, if your park pass allows it, consider spreading out your visit over a **couple of days** rather than packing it all into one. Midday is best avoided due to the big crowds, the intense heat/sun, and sleeping animals.

GETTING THERE

By Bus—All resorts, Epcot, and Disney's Hollywood Studios have buses that take you directly to Disney's Animal Kingdom. From the Magic Kingdom, walk or monorail to the Contemporary and catch a bus. From Disney Springs, take a bus to an Epcot-area resort and catch a Disney's Animal Kingdom bus.

By Car—From I-4, take exit 65 (eastbound or westbound) and follow signs to Disney's Animal Kingdom parking. All-day parking is available for $17 (free to resort guests with resort ID and annual passholders). The parking lot is some distance from the entrance. You'll appreciate the free trams to the front gate.

Note: There is no boat, path, or monorail access to this theme park.

ⓘ4978 © Cheryl Pendry

Parking lot tram at Disney's Animal Kingdom

More at ⓘ animal-trekking

Top Photo Slice: Directional signpost at Disney's Animal Kingdom (ⓘ10892) © Gina Pesca

Charting the Attractions in The Oasis and Discovery Island

Jennifer | Dave | Readers

The Oasis [C-6]

A-OK! 7 | 6 | 7

Chatty Flamingos

All guests pass through this lush jungle habitat of gurgling waters and exotic plants on their way in and out of the park. Many of the paths lead to small animal exhibits. Look for shady seats in a rocky grotto. Wheelchair accessible. KidTip: *"Can you spot the camouflaging lizards anywhere here?"*

Walk-thru | A-Ticket | All ages | Allow 20 min.

Adventurers Outpost [D-4]

A-OK! 4 | – | 5

Located in the former Beastly Bazaar, this new character meet and greet is just the place to find Mickey and Minnie. A sign outside indicates wait times, and the travel-themed interior is nicely air-conditioned.

Pavilion | A-Ticket | All ages

It's Tough to be a Bug! [D-4]

FP+ A-OK! 8 | 8 | 9

Delve into the insect world beneath the Tree of Life on Discovery Island for a humorous show hosted by Flik from "A Bug's Life" and featuring a pint-sized cast of animated and Audio-Animatronics characters. 3-D effects, creepy sensations, and yucky smells can terrify the bug-wary. Queue offers close-up views of the tree's animal sculptures. Look for hilarious movie posters in the "lobby." Air-conditioned, 430-seat theater. Outdoor queue is uncovered. Special effects may be too intense for some. Wheelchair accessible. Assistive listening. Reflective captioning. The entrance is marked on the map on page 186. KidTip: *"Sit between two grown-ups in case you get scared."*

3-D Show | E-Ticket | Ages 6 & up | Dark, smells, bug noises, "stings" | FastPass+ or med. waits | 8 min. show

The Tree of Life and Discovery Island Trails [C-3]

6 | 5 | 8

Tropical gardens and exotic animals surround the Tree of Life at the center of the park. Walk the winding paths, and get a close-up view of the tree, too. How many animals can you see in the trunk and roots? (Hint: 366, including a "hidden Mickey.") Wheelchair accessible. KidTip: *"The animals are cool."*

Walk-thru | A-Ticket | All ages | Allow 30 min.

Attraction descriptions and ratings are explained on page 127.

PANDORA: The World of Avatar

Disney broke ground on a new land early in 2014 based on the popular movie franchise "Avatar" by James Cameron. The new land will occupy the former Camp Minnie-Mickey area, and Festival of the Lion King and the character meet and greets have been moved out elsewhere. The next Avatar movie is set to debut in December 2017, and Avatar Land is likely to open in 2017 or 2018. You can expect to ride AVATAR Flight of Passage, where you get to experience what it is like to fly with the Banshees of Pandora in a flight simulator ride that incorporates some 3-D technology. We also anticipate a slow boat ride through the bioluminescent forest of Pandora. Expect elements from the original Avatar film as well as its three, yet-to-be-released sequels. Keep an eye on PassPorter.com for news!

Top Photo Slice: Detail of the trunk of the Tree of Life on Discovery Island (ⓘ8309) © Cheryl Pendry

Charting the Attractions at Africa

Jennifer | Dave | Readers

Kilimanjaro Safaris [B-1]

FP A-OK! 8 | 8 | 9

Board a safari truck to explore 100 acres of African habitat with lions, giraffes, crocodiles, ostriches, gazelle, and many other live animals. Wildlife may be plentiful or scarce, since it's free to roam. Disney also includes a vague story line in case the animals are feeling shy. The ride gets very bumpy, so hang on tight. We recommend you ride first thing in the morning, late afternoon, or after it rains, when the animals are more active. Sit in outside seats for best views and photos. Disney announced a new after-dark experience called Sunset Kilimanjaro Safaris that will allow guests to experience two new species: African wild dogs and hyenas (no word yet on when that will begin). Outdoor queue is covered and has overhead monitors. Height restriction for children riding in front two seats. Young children should be accompanied by an adult. Health warning. Transfer from ECV to wheelchair to ride. Wheelchair accessible. Assistive listening. Closed captioning. **Alex's ToddlerTip:** ☺ **Alex'sKidTip:** *"It's more bumpy and more fun in back."* **TweenTip:** *"Look at the signs in the truck to identify the animals."*

Ride
E-Ticket
Ages 4 & up
Bumpy, live birds and animals, "close escapes"
FastPass+ or long waits
19 min. vehicle ride

ⓘ8284 © Cheryl Pendry

Wildebeest graze on the savanna as a safari truck passes by

Pangani Forest Exploration Trail [B-1]

A-OK! 6 | 8 | 7

ⓘ1834 © imadisneygirl

This gorilla loves his blankie

Animal lovers will stroll enthralled through this exhibit of African wildlife in an artfully built natural habitat. African birds, hippos, meerkats, and a troop of gorillas make their home here. Hands-on exhibits in the naturalist's hut add interest. A habitat—the Endangered Animal Rehabilitation Centre—calls attention to the African bushmeat crisis. The meerkat viewing area is especially popular, and plan to spend extra time in the aviary. Walk slowly or sit, and the wonders will unfold. Allow several hours if you love to watch animals. Early morning or late afternoon is the best time to visit. Wheelchair accessible. Closed captioning. **Alex'sKidTip:** *"The animals can't get close to you. It's ok!"*

Walk-thru
D-Ticket
All ages
Live animals, birds flying overhead
Short waits
Allow at least 30 minutes

Top Photo Slice: Savanna visited during the Kilimanjaro Safaris (ⓘ11336) © Diana Barthelemy-Rodriguez

Charting the Attractions at Africa

Jennifer | Dave | Readers

Festival of the Lion King [A-2]  A-OK! 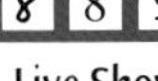 8 | 8 | 9

①23090 © Francis T. Tewey

Broadway-caliber performance

Live Show
E-Ticket
Ages 2 & up
Long waits (check showtimes in Times Guide)
30 min. show

This colorful, dynamic pageant set to music from "The Lion King" features singers, dancers, acrobats, and floats, and really sets your hands to clapping! The 1,000-seat theater-in-the-round affords many great vantage points, but arrive early to sit down front. Try the first or last shows for shortest waits. Lots of audience participation and lots of fun! This theatre is fully air-conditioned. This show moved in 2014 from Camp Minnie-Mickey to Africa (see map on page 186). Outdoor queue is uncovered. No external video lights. Wheelchair accessible. Assistive listening. **Alex's ToddlerTip:** ☺ **Allie's KidTip:** *"If you sit in the front you might get asked to play music!"* **TweenTip:** *"Try to make the animal sounds."*

Wildlife Express Train to Rafiki's Planet Watch [C-1] A-OK! 5 | 4 | 5

Train Ride
B-Ticket
All ages
Glimpses of backstage
Short waits
15 min. ride (each way)

All aboard! This train at Harambe station is the only route into or out of Rafiki's Planet Watch (formerly called Conservation Station). Enjoy a ringside glimpse of the park's backstage animal care areas. A guide describes the sights as the train chugs slowly along the track. Note: Everyone must disembark at Rafiki's Planet Watch. As always, Disney's eye for detail shines forth around Harambe Station and onboard the train. The best seats are in the front row. Themed, outdoor queue is mostly covered. Wheelchair accessible. Assistive listening. **Alex's ToddlerTip:** ☺ **Allie's KidTip:** *"Sit in the front row of the train to see better."*

Rafiki's Planet Watch [off map] A-OK! 5 | 6 | 5

Exhibit
C-Ticket
All ages
Backstage, educational fun
Live animals
Short waits
Allow at least 90 minutes for a good exploration

This is the park's most remote and most under-appreciated attraction, a must-visit for animal lovers of all ages. Formerly called Conservation Station, it was renamed and jazzed up with live animal encounter shows, more hands-on activities, and visits from Rafiki. The 5-min. walk from the train station to Rafiki's Planet Watch is interspersed with fun, conservation-themed exhibits and activities. See short films, use interactive video displays, and relax in darkened rain forest "soundscape" booths. View the park's nursery and veterinary hospital. Enjoy the cleanest, most animal-friendly petting zoo anywhere (it even has a hand-washing fountain at the exit). The Wildlife Express Train from Harambe is the only way into or out of Rafiki's Planet Watch. Wheelchair accessible. Assistive listening. **Alex's ToddlerTip:** ☺ **Allie's KidTip:** *"Look for the fishes, lizards, and frogs. And go to the petting farm!"*

①7295 © Melissa Potter

Petting a goat at Rafiki's

Top Photo Slice: Animal sign above entrance to Rafiki's Planet Watch (①1720) © Brad K.

Charting the Attractions at Asia

Jennifer / Dave / Readers

Expedition Everest [G-3]

FP+ | 9 | 10 | 9

This popular thrill ride takes guests on a rickety tea plantation train up and into 199-foot-tall Forbidden Mountain on the way to Mount Everest. Once inside the chilly mountain interior, you'll have a startling encounter with the fearsome Yeti—part god, part beast—and the largest and most complex Audio-Animatronics figure ever built. Banished, you'll hurtle through darkness and even ride backward. The coaster has several steep drops and sharp turns, and some parts are very intense. The incredibly detailed queue snakes through a Himalayan village filled with artifacts, a museum, and a Yeti shrine. Single rider line available. 44"/112 cm. height restriction. Health warning. Must transfer from wheelchair to ride. Visit http://www.disneyeverest.com.

Coaster
E-Ticket
Ages 8 & up
Dark, drops, heights
FastPass+ or very long waits
3 min. ride

ⓘ10336 © Melissa Loflin

Yeti poster near Expedition Everest

Flights of Wonder [D-2]

A-OK! | 7 | 7 | 7

Duck! Owls or hawks may fly right above your head during a show starring more than 20 species of free-flying exotic birds and their talented animal handlers. Guano Joe (or Jane), a tour guide from Anandapur Tours, adds some comic relief to this conservation-themed show. Guests are selected from the audience to join in the action. Afterward, everyone has a chance to come down to ask questions, view the "stars" up close, and take photos. Sit near the aisles for the closest animal encounters. Outdoor, shaded theater. Outdoor queue is uncovered. Theater opens 15 minutes beforehand. No food or drink allowed. Leave strollers at the door. Wheelchair accessible. Assistive listening. **Allie's Kid Tip:** *"Volunteer to go on the stage! I'm too shy to do it, but it looks like fun."*

Live Show
D-Ticket
Ages 3 & up
Live birds overhead
Med. waits (showtimes listed in Times Guide)
25 min. show

ⓘ12598 © Cheryl Pendry

Birds at Flights of Wonder

ⓘ10869 © Gina Pesca

This bird flew right overhead!

More at ⓘ expedition-everest

Top Photo Slice: Hidden Mickeys in the brick wall at Flights of Wonder (ⓘ6192) © Alisa Niethammer

Charting the Attractions at Asia

Jennifer | Dave | Readers

Kali River Rapids [F-2]

FP+ A-OK! 8 8 8

Drift through jungle mists, unexpected geysers, and smoking devastation on a somewhat daring ride in a 12-person raft. The roaring rapids boast one thrilling (albeit tame) drop. Just when you think it's all over, Disney tosses in one last little surprise. You will get wet—possibly damp, more likely soaked—and there's no way to predict (or control) how much. A small storage area is available on board, but it won't keep things very dry. Some guests wisely bring a poncho and a dry change of clothing—plastic ponchos are available for sale nearby. Shoes/sandals must be worn at all times. Long lines are common, but they snake through fascinating Asian architecture rich with fine detail. 38"/97 cm height restriction. Special effects may be too intense for some children and adults. Health warning. Must transfer from wheelchair to ride. Allie's KidTip: *"If you go backward on the drop, be prepared to get soaked."* **TweenTip:** *"It's good when it's really hot out!"*

Raft Ride
E-Ticket
Ages 7 & up
Med. drop, flames, geysers, and you will get wet!
FastPass+ or long waits
5 min. cruise

ⓘ4184 © Melissa Hasbrouck

Rafters getting squirted on Kali River Rapids

Maharajah Jungle Trek [E-1]

A-OK! 6 8 7

Walk a winding path through ancient ruins in a lush Asian setting. Tigers, tapir, fruit bats, deer, antelope, a Komodo dragon, and a walk-through aviary filled with tropical birds highlight this beautifully designed zoo. Artfully hidden barriers make you feel like you can reach out and touch the animals, but fortunately for them (and us) you can't. Cast members are on hand to enrich your animal-viewing adventure. We think the tigers, aviary, and bats are the highlights, but you'll find your own favorites. Be sure to pick up a guidemap on your way in. Animal lovers may be tempted to spend hours here—bring your camera! Wheelchair accessible. Allie's KidTip: *"Tigers! How many can you find?"*

Walk-thru
D-Ticket
All ages
Live animals, birds overhead
Short waits
Allow at least 30 minutes

ⓘ2925 © Cheryl Pendry

Tiger seen on the jungle trek

ⓘ14600 © Janet Simonsen

Birdhouse

Charting the Attractions at DinoLand U.S.A.

Ratings: Jennifer / Dave / Readers

The Boneyard [F-5] A-OK! — 7 5 6

Kids can climb, slide, crawl, scamper, excavate, and explore to their hearts' content in a funky dinosaur dig. Parents are welcome, too. One of the places at Disney's Animal Kingdom with a water spray for hot days. Keep an eye on your young ones! Bring a towel and dry clothes. Wheelchair accessible. **Alex's ToddlerTip:** ☺ **Allie's KidTip:** "You can get wet here if you are hot. I love this place!"

- **Playground**
- B-Ticket
- Ages 1 & up
- Allow 30 min.

DINOSAUR [E-7] FP+ A-OK! — 7 7 8

Intrepid riders are sent back through time to fetch a dinosaur before the dinos (and the riders) become extinct. Be prepared to be bounced, jostled, and scared as your Time Rover vehicle hurtles into the past and races through a dark forest. The "pre-show" and science exhibits in the indoor queue areas make the wait interesting. Front row "outside" seats for maximum thrills, inside seats for the less bold. No flash photography. 40"/102 cm height restriction. Young children should be accompanied by an adult. Effects may be too intense for some. Health warning. Must transfer from wheelchair to ride. Closed captioning (pre-show). **Allie's KidTip:** "Cover your eyes in the dark parts if you're scared. Ask your grown-ups to tell you when a dinosaur shows up so you can look."

- **Thrill Ride**
- E-Ticket
- Ages 7 & up
- Dark, loud, very scary, rough and bumpy ride
- FastPass+ or long waits
- 3.5 min. ride

"Finding Nemo–The Musical" [G-5] FP+ A-OK! — 7 8 8

The "Finding Nemo" themed stage show features original songs by a Tony Award-winning composer and the theatrical puppetry of the same artist who did the puppets for the Broadway version of "The Lion King." Joining the show are acrobats, dancers, and animated backgrounds. The covered, air-conditioned theater opens 20 minutes before show time. No external video lights. Uncovered outdoor queue. Wheelchair accessible. Assistive listening. **Alex's ToddlerTip:** ☺ **Allie's KidTip:** "Cool puppets!"

- **Live Show**
- E-Ticket
- Ages 4 & up
- FastPass+ or med. waits
- 30 min. show

Primeval Whirl [F-6] FP+ A-OK! — 7 7 8

Chester and Hester cooked up a dizzy bit of fun for Primeval Whirl, a totally whacky wild mouse coaster (with style). Your round "time machine" car spins as it goes around tight curves, over mild drops, and even through the jaws of a dinosaur. (What else?) Two identical coasters each boast 13 spinning, four-person ride vehicles. 48"/122 cm height restriction. Health warning. Must transfer from wheelchair to ride. **Alex's KidTip:** "This is a crazy ride! It goes so fast!"

- **Coaster**
- D-Ticket
- Ages 7 & up
- Fast, drops
- FastPass+
- 2.5 min. ride

TriceraTop Spin [F-6] A-OK! — 5 5 7

Dumbo morphs into a Dino! Sixteen dinosaur-shaped, four-rider cars swoop around a huge, spinning toy top. Part of Chester & Hester's Dino-Rama! (see below). Must transfer from ECV to wheelchair to ride. **Alex's ToddlerTip:** ☺ **Allie's KidTip:** "Sit in the front and make the dinosaur tilt forward or backward."

- **Ride**
- C-Ticket
- Ages 2 & up
- 1.5 min. ride

Chester & Hester's Dino-Rama!

Chester & Hester, the operators of DinoLand's crazy roadside-style gift shop, have created a roadside "carnival" with two attractions and about a half-dozen games of skill or chance. Play midway games for $2 a pop and maybe win a prize. Games include Mammoth Marathon, Bronto-Score, and Fossil Fueler.

Top Photo Slice: Comet atop the TriceraTop Spin ride in DinoLand U.S.A. (5532) © Amy Sellars

Typhoon Lagoon Water Park

Typhoon Lagoon is a 56-acre water park with lush foliage, lazy rivers, roaring waterfalls, and a huge surfing "lagoon." The water park is located near Disney Springs West Side.

AMBIENCE

Legend has it that this was once the Placid Palms Resort in Safen Sound, Florida, a **tropical hideaway** nestled on a sparkling lagoon. Disaster struck when a typhoon raged through the sleepy resort, flooding the lagoon and tossing ships about. In its wake, they discovered sharks in the harbor, a surfboard through a tree, and ships scattered everywhere. Most amazing was the Miss Tilly shrimp boat, impaled on a craggy mountain (Mt. Mayday) that kept trying to dislodge the boat with a huge plume of water. Water was everywhere, forming waterfalls, rapids, pools, and surf. In true Disney form, misfortune was turned into luck and the Typhoon Lagoon water park was born. Or so the story goes.

PARK LAYOUT

The park's attractions are arrayed around its focal point, the gigantic, 2½-acre **wave pool** at the foot of Mt. Mayday. The "mountain" offers the advantage of height to several tube and body slides that slither down it. Around the perimeter of the park is a "lazy river" called Castaway Creek, offering a relaxing retreat to swimmers drifting lazily along in inner tubes. Finding your way around the park can be confusing at first—the dense foliage and meandering paths recreate the tropical look quite convincingly. Just keep in mind that one path encircles the park, and you can see Miss Tilly perched atop Mt. Mayday from almost everywhere. This park is worth exploring, too—the lush Mountain Trail on Mt. Mayday presents photo opportunities, and many hidden groves and glens offer quiet getaways.

EATING

Leaning Palms is the largest of the cafes, offering combo meals with a hot dog ($7.99), shrimp basket ($10.49), fish basket ($9.49), barbecued pork sandwich ($9.49), chicken wrap ($9.49), turkey pesto sandwich ($9.49), and Caesar salad ($8.99). A kids' meal is $7.49 and includes your choice of corn dog nuggets, turkey sandwich, or PB&J, plus chips, drink, and a sand pail. **Happy Landings** has ice cream and a fun water play area where you can take aim at the guests drifting by on Castaway Creek. **Typhoon Tilly's Galley & Grog** has fish & chips, snacks, ice cream, and beverages. **Let's Go Slurpin'** offers alcoholic drinks and snacks. **Low Tide Lou's** (seasonal) has sandwiches. **Surf Doggies** offers hot dogs and turkey legs. Look for a cart selling yummy donut holes, too! Three **picnic areas** have shade and tables.

Top Photo Slice: The Miss Tilly shrimp boat atop Mt. Mayday at Typhoon Lagoon (①7055) © Elizabeth Key

Charting the Attractions at Typhoon Lagoon

Attraction	Description	Jennifer / Dave / Readers	Info
Typhoon Lagoon Surf Pool [C-4] — A-OK!	*Waves in the world's largest inland wave pool at the base of Mt. Mayday change every half-hour, alternating between gentle bobs and 6-foot waves. Kids enjoy the two Bay Slides to the far left and the small tidal pools near the front. Observe the waves before entering.* **Allie's KidTip:** *"Don't scrape yourself on the bottom."*	8 / 8 / 9	Pool; E-Ticket; Surfing waves scary to kids
Crush 'N' Gusher [E-5]	*This "water roller coaster" has jets of water pushing you uphill, followed by short drops. Three slides: Pineapple Plunger and Coconut Crusher (1–3 riders), Banana Blaster (1–2 riders). 48"/122 cm restriction. Transfer from wheelchair/ECV.*	6 / 7 / 8	Tube Slide; E-Ticket; Ages 7 & up
Castaway Creek [Entry points: A-3, A-4, D-2, D-3, D-5] — A-OK!	*Relax on a half-mile, 20-minute circuit around the park on inner tubes. Catch a free tube at one of five entrances. Note where you entered, too!* **Allie's KidTip:** *"This is nice and relaxing. Little kids will like the yellow inner tubes the best."*	9 / 8 / 8	Pool; D-Ticket; Ages 3 & up
Ketchakiddee Creek [A-2]	*Several fountains, two body slides, and a 30-sec. tube ride—just for little squirts (48"/122 cm or under). Shady, thatched-roof shelters.* **Alex's ToddlerTip:** ☺	6 / 6 / 7	Playground; B-Ticket
Keelhaul Falls [B-1] — A-OK!	*A slow, solo tube ride with a surprise! (Warning—ride spoilers ahead.) Rafters plunge unexpectedly into a pitch-black tunnel about half the way down.* **Allie's KidTip:** *"The waterfall is fun! You don't get as wet as you think you will."*	6 / 7 / 7	Tube Slide; C-Ticket; Ages 7 & up
Mayday Falls [B-1] — A-OK!	*Like Keelhaul Falls, this tube ride is solo. Unlike it, Mayday Falls is fast, twisting and turning through caves and waterfalls.* **Allie's KidTip:** *"This is very bumpy!"*	5 / 6 / 7	Tube Slide; C-Ticket
Gang Plank Falls [B-1] — A-OK!	*Bring the family on this three- to five-person raft ride down the mountain. Watch out for waterfalls and those twisty-turny rafts!* **Allie's KidTip:** *"This is fun! Hold on tight because you go a little fast, but that's no problem."*	8 / 6 / 6	Raft Slide; C-Ticket; Ages 4 & up
Humunga Kowabunga [C-1]	*This is the ultimate thrill slide, shooting sliders down one of two slides in less than 10 seconds. Viewing bleachers at the bottom. 48"/122 cm height requirement. Health requirement. Ages 9 & up.* **Allie's KidTip:** *"It gave me a wedgie."*	1 / 5 / 7	Body Slide; E-Ticket; Fast, steep
Storm Slides [D-1]	*Three body slides (Stern Burner, Jib Jammer, and Rudder Buster) corkscrew through waterfalls and caves. Viewing bleachers at the bottom. Ages 8 & up.*	5 / 6 / 7	Body Slides; E-Ticket
Shark Reef [E-1] — A-OK!	*Line up at Hammerhead Fred's Dive Shop for your snorkel (no charge), shower, 5-minute lesson, then snorkel across the small, chilly, saltwater lagoon. You may see a variety of fish, including three kinds of passive sharks. Bring an underwater camera. Scuba-assisted snorkel (extra fee).* **Allie's KidTip:** *"I love the sharks!"*	9 / 8 / 8	Pool; E-Ticket; Ages 6 & up; Cold, salty

Top Photo Slice: Shark Reef at Typhoon Lagoon (ⓘ12225) © Cheryl Pendry

Making the Most of Typhoon Lagoon

TIPS

A **refillable mug** ($9.99) uses barcode scanners so you can refill without cast supervision. Buy a new barcode ($5) on future visits.

Avoid **two-piece suits** on slides—they may come down the slide at a different speed than you. Also, swimsuits with rivets, buckles, or exposed metal are not permitted. Wear water shoes—the sand and pavement can get quite hot.

A reader has fun at Castaway Creek

Want to go premium? Rent one of the **premium spaces**. The four spaces at Typhoon Lagoon are known as the "Beachcomber Shacks." Cost is $250 plus tax per day for up to six guests. Services include a personal attendant, private lockers, drink mugs, bottled water, lounge furniture, and towels. Available on a first come, first serve basis. Want something less pricey? You can rent "premium chairs" for $40 plus tax—this gets you two beach chairs, an umbrella, small table, and two towels.

Get your first taste of **scuba** in a special section of the Shark Reef. Cost is $20 for the first 30 min. and $15 for the rest of your party or for repeat dives. Pay at the booth near the dive shop.

NOTES

You can rent lockers ($13–$15, with a $5 deposit) and towels ($2 each). Bring hotel towels rather than rent them—they're close to the same size. Changing rooms are also available. Life vests are free (refundable deposit). Some personal flotation devices may be permitted.

Park hours: Usually 10:00 am–5:00 pm or later. A one-day pass is $61.77/adults and $53.25/kids 3–9 with tax, but you can get seasonal tickets (not valid May 28–Aug. 8) for $56.45/adults and $47.23/kids.

RATINGS

Ratings are explained on page 128.

Our Value Ratings:		Our Magic Ratings:		Readers' Ratings:
Quality:	7/10	Theme:	8/10	76% fell in love with it
Variety:	8/10	Excitement:	7/10	21% liked it well enough
Scope:	3/10	Fun Factor:	7/10	3% had mixed feelings
Overall Value:	**6/10**	**Overall Magic:**	**7/10**	0% were disappointed

Typhoon Lagoon is enjoyed by... (rated by both authors and readers)		
Younger Kids: ♥♥♥♥	Young Adults: ♥♥♥♥♥	Families: ♥♥♥♥
Older Kids: ♥♥♥♥♥	Mid Adults: ♥♥♥	Couples: ♥♥♥
Teenagers: ♥♥♥♥♥	Mature Adults: ♥♥♥	Singles: ♥♥♥

Top Photo Slice: A surfboard stuck in a tree, presumably from the fictional typhoon that passed through (12209) © Cheryl Pendry

Finding Your Way at Typhoon Lagoon

TYPHOON LAGOON PARK MAP

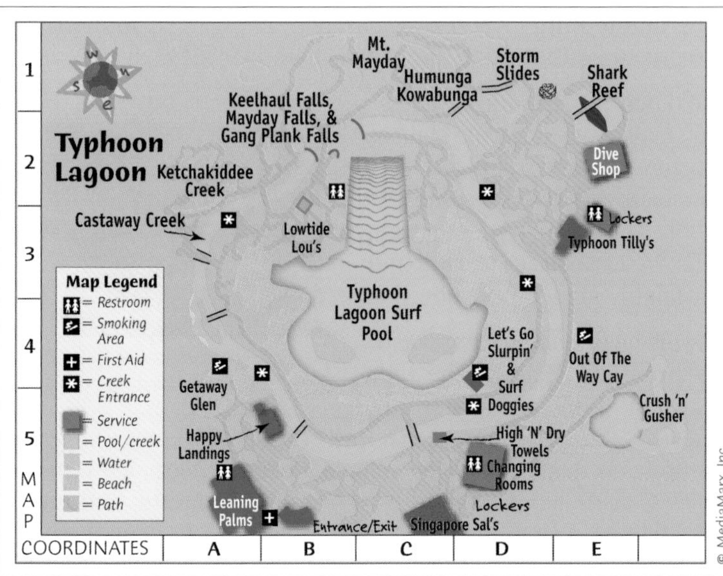

BEST TIMES

Typhoon Lagoon is very popular during the **hot months** and gets crowded fast—arrive early, as gates close when the park reaches capacity. It's also wise to stake out your beach chairs early as the good ones are grabbed quickly. We prefer to visit when it's a bit **cooler** as crowds are lighter and the water is heated. The park closes annually for refurbishment (this year it is Jan. 3–Mar 12, 2016)—call 407-560-4141 to confirm. If this park's closed, Blizzard Beach will be open. Beyond that, **weekdays** are better than weekends (locals love to visit the park). Visit in the **late afternoon** when the park empties a bit and the sun is less intense. The park may **close during storms**—when it reopens, it may be nearly empty. If you arrive when there are long lines, bypass them by getting your tickets at the Automated Ticket Vending Machines available here.

GETTING THERE

By Bus—All Disney resorts have direct buses to Typhoon Lagoon. From Magic Kingdom, Epcot, Disney's Hollywood Studios, and Disney's Animal Kingdom, take a bus or monorail to a nearby resort and transfer to a Typhoon Lagoon bus (which may also be the Disney Springs bus). Allow about 30–60 minutes if you travel by bus. **By Car**—Take exit 67 off I-4, take the first exit and turn right on Buena Vista Dr.—the park is on the right. From Disney Springs, turn right to Buena Vista Dr. and the park is on the left. Free parking.

Top Photo Slice: Swimmers enjoy the huge surf pool at Typhoon Lagoon (12219) © Cheryl Pendry

Blizzard Beach Water Park

Is it a water park, or a ski resort? The Blizzard Beach water park brings the chills and thrills of a Colorado winter to the warm Florida sun. Ski jumps, toboggan rides, and slalom runs zip you past snow that never melts in Disney's most action-oriented water park.

AMBIENCE

Disney's Imagineers scattered magic white stuff over the rocks and pines of towering Mount Gushmore to create a water park that'll make you shiver on the hottest August day. Oh, don't worry, the water is always a warm 80 degrees, but just a look at some of those water slides can freeze your insides. Luckily, Disney never abandons the idea of family fun—even the meekest snow bunny will have a ball!

ATTRACTIONS

Before you "hit the slopes" you'll discover the park's "**base lodge**" facilities—the major food, merchandise, and locker room areas. Then, as you face the mountain, the Tike's Peak children's area will be to your right. Straight ahead are two bridges over Cross Country Creek, the drift-along tube ride that encircles the mountain and most of the fun. Additional lockers can be found close to the action, near Downhill Double Dipper on the left and Ski Patrol on the right. Of course, Mount Gushmore dominates the park in every way. Its slopes are home to nearly two dozen lanes of slides and flumes. Most slides can be seen from the Lodge area, but Runoff Rapids is tucked away on the back slope of the mountain. You can also watch your daredevils in comfort, from shaded grandstands at the bottom of many slides. Three footpaths and a chairlift scale the 90-foot (9-story) mountain. After your first ascent on foot in the hot, Florida sunshine, you'll know why folks wait patiently for the chairlift, which takes you to the top in the comfort of a three-person, umbrella-shaded chair (32"/81 cm height restriction; under 48"/122 cm must be with an adult).

EATING

Water park meals are never fancy, which is fine when you're only wearing a swimsuit. **Lottawatta Lodge** serves up a Black Diamond Burger ($10.49), harvest salad with chicken ($9.99), Korean barbecue chicken flatbread ($9.99), chicken nuggets ($9.29), chicken wraps ($9.49), and kosher selections. A kid's meal is $7.99 with a choice of PB&J, chicken nuggets, or turkey sandwich, plus chips, drink, and a sandpail. **Avalunch** and **The Warming Hut** offer hot dogs, sandwiches, ice cream, and usually close before dinnertime. The thirsty line up at **Frostbite Freddie's Frozen Freshments**, **Polar Pub**, and **The Cooling Hut**. There are also **picnic areas**.

Top Photo Slice: The "ski jump" atop Mount Gushmore at Blizzard Beach (ⓘ6244) © Cheryl Pendry

Charting the Attractions at Blizzard Beach

Attraction	Jennifer	Dave	Readers	Type
Summit Plummet [D-2]	2	5	9	Body Slide
Only the boldest ride the world's highest body slide, which drops 120 feet. Go feet first, cross your arms, and it's over in eight seconds. Be prepared for a steep drop and a wedgie! 48"/122 cm height requirement. Health requirement.				E-Ticket; Ages 9 & up
Slush Gusher [D-2]	3	6	8	Body Slide
Ninety-foot-high double-bump slide is the second-tallest body slide in the park. One-piece suits recommended! 48"/122 cm height requirement. Ages 8 & up.				D-Ticket
Downhill Double Dipper [C-2]	5	7	8	Tube Slide
Race head-to-head on a half-enclosed innertube slide. Your race results are flashed on a scoreboard. 48"/122 cm height requirement. Ages 8 & up.				D-Ticket
Snow Stormers [C-2] A-OK!	7	5	8	Mat Slide
Zig and zag your way down this three-flume, family-friendly slalom mat slide. 12-second ride. **Allie's Kid Tip:** *"Fun, but it's a little bumpy." Ages 6 & up.*				C-Ticket
Toboggan Racers [D-3] A-OK!	6	5	7	Mat Slide
On your mark, get set, go! Race headfirst down an eight-lane mat slide. 10-second ride. **Allie's Kid Tip:** *"Push yourself off to go down." Ages 6 & up.*				D-Ticket
Teamboat Springs [E-3] A-OK!	9	8	9	Raft Slide
Whitewater-loving families can pack up to six in a large, round, river raft for a long, twisting ride—at 1,400 feet it is the longest ride of its kind anywhere. **Allie's Kid Tip:** *"Hold on to the bottom of the raft when you go down."*				D-Ticket; Ages 4 up
Runoff Rapids [D-2]	8	7	7	Tube Slide
Ride a tube down this twisty, turny, family-friendly course. Three different open and enclosed slides. Up to two can share a tube on the open slides. **Allie's Kid Tip:** *"Pick up your behind over the bumps, or it won't feel good."*				C-Ticket; Ages 6 & up
Cross Country Creek [Entry points: B-4, A-4, B-2, C-1, E-3, D-4] A-OK!	8	7	7	Pool
Float around the park on a moderately flowing creek. Enter and exit at any of six spots around the park. Return to your starting point in 20 minutes. **Allie's Kid Tip:** *"Don't get wet under the freezing waterfalls."*				D-Ticket; Ages 2 & up
Melt Away Bay [B-3] A-OK!	7	6	7	Pool
Bob in the sedate waves of a one-acre wave pool. Kids under 10 must be with an adult. **Allie's Kid Tip:** *"The tide pools are cool to play in!" All ages.*				C-Ticket
Ski Patrol Training Camp [D-3] A-OK!	8	7	7	Playground
Scaled-down area for kids 12 and under. Try Snow Falls slide, Cool Runners tube slalom, and Thin Ice Training Course—a walk across a field of "ice floes." **Allie's Kid Tip:** *"If an iceberg is far away, lean back to move toward it."*				D-Ticket; Ages 6-12
Tike's Peak [D-5]	6	5	7	Playground
Even the littlest ones have a mini version of the park, with slides, wading pools, and fountains. Must be 48"/122 cm or shorter. Ages 0-6. **Alex's Toddler Tip:** ☺				C-Ticket

Top Photo Slice: Ski Patrol Training Camp at Blizzard Beach (①6269) © Cheryl Pendry

Making the Most of Blizzard Beach

TIPS

Save time—buy park passes at Guest Relations or Lobby Concierge.

There's **little shade** here—use waterproof sunscreen and cover-ups! Wear water shoes to ward off the heat of the sand and sidewalks.

Play **miniature golf** at Winter Summerland, adjacent to the water park. See page 214 for more on this imaginative mini golf course.

Pick up a **map** on your way in to locate the lockers ($13–$15) and towels ($2). Life jackets are free if you leave an ID and/or deposit.

You'll find **chaise lounges** wherever you go, but on busy days, follow the path around the back end of the mountain where you'll find secluded lounging areas and the main entrance to Runoff Rapids. Or rent a "**Polar Patios**" premium space here—see page 199.

This is the "**big thrill**" water park, so it draws a young crowd. Typhoon Lagoon is a better choice for families.

NOTES

If you ride the big slides, bikinis are a very risky fashion statement. You'll have better luck with a **one-piece suit**. Also, swimsuits with rivets, buckles, or exposed metal are not permitted.

The **Beach Haus** near the entrance sells just about anything you may have forgotten or lost, from sunscreen to swimsuits.

When the **summer weather** is at its hottest, the parking lots fill up early. Use Disney buses instead, which can always drive in.

Park hours: Usually 10:00 am–5:00 pm or later. A one-day pass is $61.77/adults and $53.25/kids 3–9 with tax, but you can get seasonal tickets (not valid May 28–Aug. 8) for $56.45/adults and $47.23/kids.

RATINGS

Ratings are explained on page 128.

Our Value Ratings:		Our Magic Ratings:		Readers' Ratings:
Quality:	7/10	Theme:	8/10	94% fell in love with it
Variety:	8/10	Excitement:	8/10	2% liked it well enough
Scope:	4/10	Fun Factor:	7/10	2% had mixed feelings
Overall Value:	**6/10**	**Overall Magic:**	**8/10**	2% were disappointed

Blizzard Beach is enjoyed by... (rated by both authors and readers)

Younger Kids: ♥♥♥♥	Young Adults: ♥♥♥♥♥	Families: ♥♥♥♥♥
Older Kids: ♥♥♥♥♥	Mid Adults: ♥♥♥	Couples: ♥♥♥
Teenagers: ♥♥♥♥♥	Mature Adults: ♥	Singles: ♥♥♥♥

Top Photo Slice: The Snow Fall Slides at Blizzard Beach (ⓘ1980) © Hiromi Stone

Finding Your Way at Blizzard Beach

BLIZZARD BEACH PARK MAP

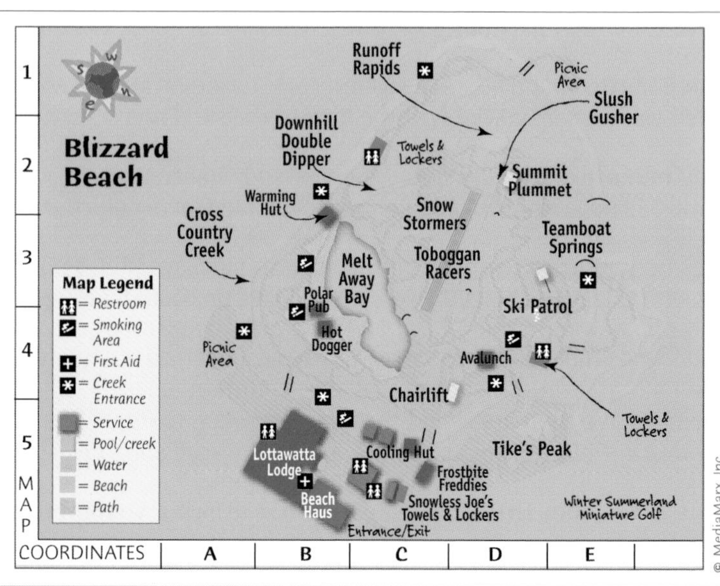

BEST TIMES

Thanks to the heated waters, you'll be comfortable throughout the **cooler months**, and the sun is kinder. The crowds are thinner, but the days are shorter, and an overcast, rainy winter day can make life miserable. Note that the park may be closed on Fridays and Saturdays in the cooler months. Summer at Blizzard Beach brings **huge crowds** that arrive early in the day. If the park reaches capacity, the gates close to all. By **mid-afternoon**, the crowds have thinned, as those who are worst-wilted have packed it in. That's a good time to arrive, refreshing yourself after a long morning at nearby Disney's Animal Kingdom. Operating hours vary with the season, so check before you trek. Closed Oct. 4, 2015–Jan. 3, 2016 for its annual rehab (Typhoon Lagoon will be open during that time).

GETTING THERE

By Bus—All resorts and Disney's Animal Kingdom have direct buses to Blizzard Beach. From Disney's Hollywood Studios, take the Coronado Springs bus. From Epcot, take the Disney's Animal Kingdom Lodge bus. From the Magic Kingdom and Downtown Disney, take a bus or monorail to a Disney resort and board a bus to Blizzard Beach. We recommend you take Disney transportation when you can, because the parking lot can fill up on busy days.
By Car—From westbound or eastbound I-4, take exit 65 (west on Osceola Parkway), exiting at Buena Vista Drive. Free parking.

Top Photo Slice: Melt Away Bay at Blizzard Beach (①6261) © Cheryl Pendry

Disney Springs
(formerly Downtown Disney)

If "heading downtown" is your idea of rest and recreation, the Walt Disney World Resort's Disney Springs district is a major treat. From the world's largest Disney Store to mind-boggling Lego sculptures, super dining, and thrilling entertainment, you'll have a ball Downtown.

AMBIENCE

The district is getting a major makeover along with its new name. Disney Springs has three unique **districts**. The **Marketplace** is a charming village of shops, **The Landing** features shopping and dining, and the **West Side** is the urban-style shopping, dining, and fun capital of the "World." Disney Spring's pedestrian-only streets and sprawling layout avoid the "mall" feeling completely.

SHOPPING

Disney Springs satisfies the urge to "shop 'til you drop." There's no admission charge here, and you'll find much more than Disney merchandise. The **Marketplace** shops are The Art of Disney, Basin (bath products), Disney's Days of Christmas, Eurospain/Arribas Brothers (crystal shop), Goofy's Candy Co., Once Upon a Toy, Design-A-Tee (make your own t-shirts), Tren-D (latest fashions), Disney's Pin Traders, Lego Imagination Center, LittleMissMatched, Team Mickey's Athletic Club/Rawlins Making the Game, RideMakerz, the World of Disney (and its Bibbidi Bobbidi Boutique for little kids), Mickey's Mart (everything under $10), and Mickey's Pantry. **West Side, The Landing** (formerly Pleasure Island), and **Town Center** (opening in 2016) concentrate on shopping. Look for Splitsville (bowling), Sunglass Icon, Disney's Candy Cauldron, DisneyQuest Emporium, Pop Gallery, Hoypoloi, Magnetron, Mickey's Groove (funky Disney gifts), Harley Davidson, Curl by Sammy Duvall, Planet Hollywood, Sosa Family Cigars, Starabilias (collectibles), Wetzel's Pretzels, and shops at House of Blues, Cirque du Soleil, and DisneyQuest. Magic Masters offers top-flight magic gear, demos, and even a hidden room. Packages can be delivered to your Disney resort!

PLAYING

Downtown Disney builds fun into nearly every shop and restaurant, but five spots put entertainment first. The **Characters in Flight by Aerophile** attraction is a tethered observation balloon that lifts riders up to 400 feet in the air—cost is $18/adult and $12/child age 3–9. Movie fans flock to the **AMC 24 Theatres Complex**, the Southeast's largest—their theaters sport stadium seating and new dining options. **Splitsville Luxury Lanes** features 30 bowling alleys, billiards, dining, and entertainment—see page 251. The innovative **Cirque du Soleil** also makes its home Downtown—see page 208. **DisneyQuest** (closing in 2016) is detailed on pages 209–212.

Top Photo Slice: Aerophile observation balloon at Disney Springs West Side © MediaMarx, Inc.

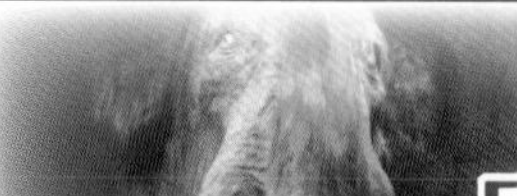

Finding Your Way at Disney Springs

DISNEY SPRINGS MAP

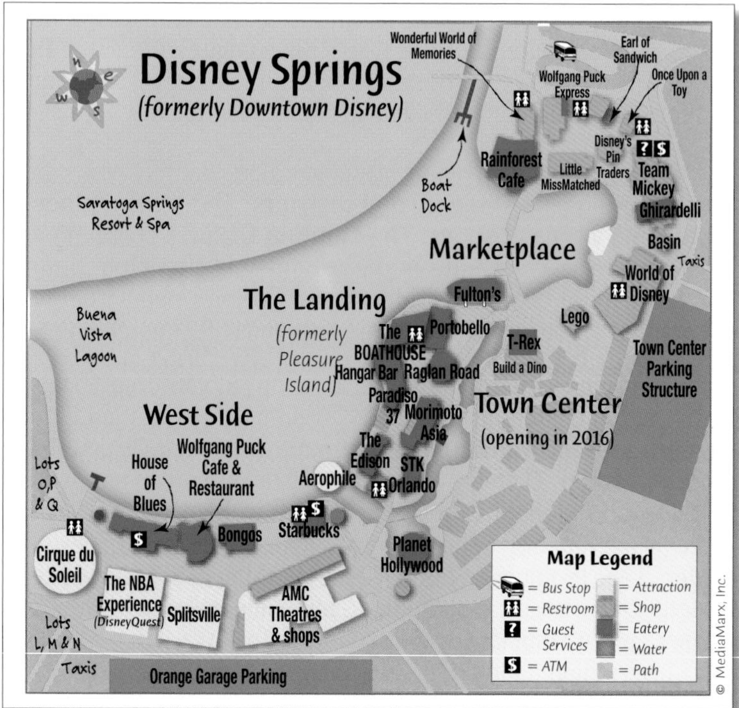

DINING

With the exception of Epcot, you won't find a more **diverse array** of dining in the "World" than at Disney Springs. For a heaping serving of showbiz, head to the West Side. The House of Blues serves up fabulous live music, Wolfgang Puck Grand Cafe offers famously innovative California fare, and Bongos Cuban Cafe has sizzling Latin rhythm and foods. Disney Spring's showplace is the famous Planet Hollywood, which drips with movie memorabilia. Fulton's Crab House serves upscale seafood on a riverboat, the Rainforest Cafe cooks up imaginative fare, and T-Rex offers big portions alongside big dinos. On The Landing, Portobello offers Northern Italian food, Raglan Road and Cookes of Dublin offer authentic Emerald Isle fare, and Paradiso 37 features Mexican and South American cuisine. The BOATHOUSE and Morimoto are new here. Busy shoppers like the lighter fare at The Earl of Sandwich, Starbucks, Wetzel's Pretzels, Wolfgang Puck Express, Ghirardelli Soda Fountain & Chocolate Shop, and the awesome Food Truck Park in the West Side. Complete descriptions begin on page 248.

Top Photo Slice: Wooly Mammoth near the Ice Cave at T-Rex in Disney Springs (①13809) © Janet Simonsen

Making the Most of Disney Springs

TIPS

Disney's **multi-year remodel** is still well underway at press time. The updated area features more shopping, dining and entertainment options, growing to more than 150 establishments. The Marketplace and the West Side keep their names and many of their current businesses, with the Marketplace adding a walking bridge to Saratoga Springs and an expanded World of Disney! The former Pleasure Island has become The Landing with restaurants and shops. The Town Center will be all new shopping area near The Landing, but details on the shops that will be there are not known at press time. Construction began in 2013 and should be done in 2016.

The World of Disney Store houses the popular **Bibbidi Bobbidi Boutique salon**, which offers hair styling and makeover services for both young girls ($55–$190) and boys ($16), ages 3–12. Appointments recommended (407-WDW-STYLE). Tip: Another location is inside Cinderella Castle—see page 134.

Kids can **play for free** at the Lego Imagination Center and in the water play fountain near the Marketplace bus stop entrance.

Little-known **discounts and specials** may be available. Be sure to ask! For example, movies at the AMC Pleasure Island 24 are just $6.00 before noon on weekdays.

Christmas brings fun activities. There's also a year-round toy train ride (for a fee). Don't forget Disney's Days of Christmas shop, too.

NOTES

Follow the signs to the new **Parking Structures, which are free!**

Most **shops** in the Marketplace open at 9:30 am, while West Side shops open at 10:30 am. Closing is at 11:00 pm, with seasonal variations. For **more details**, call Disney Springs at 407-828-3058.

GETTING THERE

By Bus—Buses are available from every Disney resort. From the parks, bus or monorail to a nearby resort and transfer.
By Car—From I-4, take exit 67, then take the first exit and turn right on Buena Vista Drive. Self-parking is free in the parking garages and lots; valet parking is $20.
By Boat—Boats may shuttle between the Marketplace and West Side seasonally. Resort guests at Port Orleans, Old Key West, and Saratoga Springs can take a boat to the Marketplace, too.

Top Photo Slice: World of Disney store at Disney Springs Marketplace (①1558) © Sharon Ellis

Cirque du Soleil

A circus has come to Walt Disney World, the likes of which you've probably never seen—magical, musical, a little mystical, and poetically graceful. Cirque du Soleil ("Circus of the Sun") from Montreal, Canada, has redefined the concept of "circus" for millions around the world and has a company-in-residence at Disney Springs West Side.

SHOWS

Cirque du Soleil weaves its magic with acrobats, clowns, jugglers, dancers, aerialists, lights, original music, and fabulous costumes (and not one animal). The long-running show, **La Nouba** (from the French "to live it up"), weaves a continuous, dream-like thread. There's a story here, but many guests hardly notice or care. This isn't Big Top-style circus, either. It has as much in common with modern dance as it does with circus. It's not for everyone (Dave likes it, Jennifer doesn't), but it adds yet another dimension to the magic. Note that this 90-minute show has no intermission.

INFO

Housed in its own **1,671-seat theater** at the west end of the West Side, Cirque du Soleil offers its shows at 6:00 and 9:00 pm, Tues.–Sat. Tickets are $59–$139/adults and $48–$115/kids ages 3–9 depending on category and date—see chart below. If you are a DVC member or a Florida resident, inquire about possible discounts. Call 407-939-7600 or visit http://www.lanouba.com to reserve up to six months in advance or visit the box office. Seats within categories are assigned based on availability, but you might get your pick at the box office.

SEATING PLAN

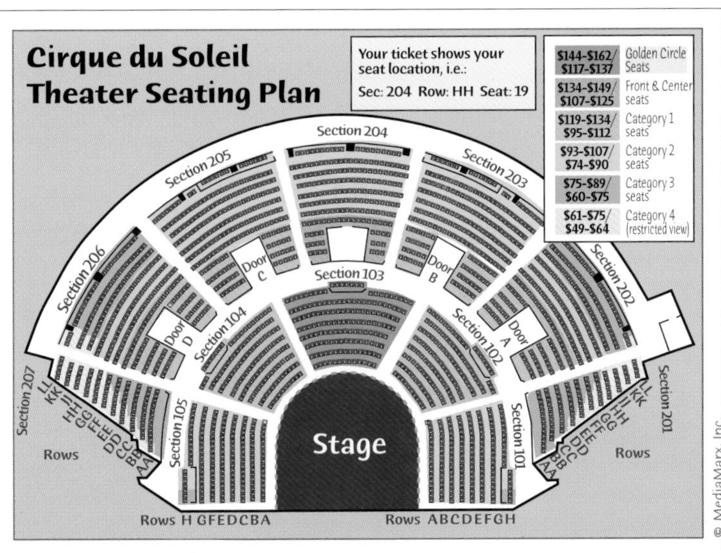

More at ⓘ cirque-du-soleil

Top Photo Slice: Cirque du Soleil building in Disney Springs © MediaMarx, Inc.

DisneyQuest

DisneyQuest on the West Side features ride simulators, high-tech games, and hands-on activities, but it's closing sometime in 2016 (we think the first half of the year) to make way for the NBA Experience.

LAYOUT

Attractions run the gamut from simple video arcade games to a you-design-it, you-ride-it roller coaster simulator. Take the "Cyberlator" elevator to the Ventureport, where you can enter four zones: **Explore Zone**, **Score Zone**, **Create Zone**, and **Replay Zone**. Each zone organizes the attractions (described below) by theme. Each zone spans at least two floors, with various stairs and walkways linking them. This makes for a bewildering maze—study our map on page 212 to orient yourself before you go.

☐ **Aladdin's Magic Carpet Ride** [Floor 2] A-OK!	6 4 6
Don virtual reality goggles for a wild, 4-min. ride on Aladdin's magic carpet. Swoop through Agrabah and the Cave of Wonder to search for jewels and free the Genie. Motion sickness warning. Explore Zone. Allie'sKidTip: *"Make sure your helmet is on tight so it doesn't fall off when you play."*	**Virtual** D-Ticket Ages 6 & up Dizziness

☐ **Animation Academy** [Floor 2] A-OK!	7 7 6
Take your seat at a computer workstation as an instructor draws out your artistry. Hands-on lessons in drawing and/or animating characters. Several 20-minute lessons are offered. After the class, you can buy your creation. Create Zone. Allie'sKidTip: *"Check the schedule for a class that draws a character you like."*	**Hands-on** D-Ticket Ages 6 & up Skill helps

☐ **Buzz Lightyear's Astroblasters** [Floor 3]	7 5 7
Ride fully enclosed two-person bumper cars mounted with "cannons" that shoot large rubber balls. The driver pilots to scoop up ammo, and the gunner fires on other cars to make them spin out of control. 3-min. game. 51"/130 cm height restriction. Replay Zone. Allie'sKidTip: *"Try to hit a lot of cars so they spin around."*	**Vehicles** D-Ticket Ages 9 & up Bumpy

☐ **CyberSpace Mountain** [Floor 2]	9 8 9
Design and ride your own coaster! Start by choosing a theme and designing the coaster tracks on a computer screen. Then get strapped into a two-person flight simulator to experience your coaster, or choose from a ready-made coaster. Be prepared to be shaken, rattled, and rolled on a ride more dizzying than the real thing. Simulator seats are small. 51"/130 cm height restriction. Create Zone. Allie'sKidTip: *"If you feel sick, just hit the red stop button."*	**Simulator** E-Ticket Ages 9 & up Upside-down during inversions

☐ **Invasion! An ExtraTERRORestrial Alien Encounter** [Floor 5] A-OK!	6 7 5
Dash across the galaxy to rescue Earth colonists from an invading horde in this simulator ride that borrows characters and fun from the former Magic Kingdom attraction. One teammate pilots the rescue vehicle, while three other teammates keep the bad guys at bay. Great pre-show film. Score Zone. Allie'sKidTip: *"I think kids will have more fun being a gunner than a pilot."*	**Simulator** E-Ticket Ages 7 & up Mildly violent theme

Attraction descriptions and ratings are explained on page 127.

Top Photo Slice: DisneyQuest building at Disney Springs West Side (2255) © Laura Dawson

Charting the Attractions at DisneyQuest

Living Easels [Floor 2] A-OK! 5 4 4

Draw animated landscapes on a touch-sensitive screen. You can buy print-outs if you like. Create Zone. **Allie's Kid Tip:** *"Use your imagination!" Ages 3 & up.*

Hands-on | B-Ticket

Midway on the Moon [Floors 4 and 5] A-OK! 6 8 5

Disney-themed versions of arcade games like Ursula's Whirlpool and traditional games like Skeeball. All games are free play, but prize redemption is no longer offered. Adults will love the classic games like Pac-Man, Frogger,and Donkey Kong. Replay Zone. **Allie's Kid Tip:** *"Look at all the games before you play."*

Arcade | A-Ticket | Ages 5 & up

Mighty Ducks Pinball Slam [Floor 3] 5 4 7

Use body motion/weight to move a "puck" around a huge screen and "body check" opponents on this simulator. 3-min. game. 48"/122 cm height restriction. Score Zone. **Allie's Kid Tip:** *"If you're tall enough but skinny, it might not work."*

Simulator | D-Ticket | Ages 9 & up

Pirates of the Caribbean: Battle for Buccaneer Gold [Floor 1] A-OK! 8 8 9

Yo ho, yo ho! DisneyQuest's newest attraction pits you and up to four shipmates in a 3-D simulated sea battle in quest of pirate gold. Fire virtual cannonballs against your foes, and feel the deck shudder when you take a hit. 35"/89 cm height restriction. Explore Zone. **Allie's Kid Tip:** *"Shoot the ships that you pass!"*

Simulator | E-Ticket | Ages 7 & up | Violent theme

Radio Disney SongMaker [Floor 2] A-OK! 6 6 4

Create your own hit song in a soundbooth. Combine styles and lyrics for laughs. You can buy a CD of it. Create Zone. **Allie's Kid Tip:** *"Don't be shy." Ages 4 & up.*

Hands-on | D-Ticket

Ride the Comix [Floors 4 and 5] (closed) 2 3 5

This 3-D virtual reality game closed in September 2014. With the announcement of DisneyQuest closing in 2016, we feel confident to state that there will not be a replacement.

Virtual | D-Ticket | May feel dizzy

Sid's Create-A-Toy [Floor 2] 3 4 5

Create a demented toy from spare toy parts—on a computer screen. You can buy a real version of your creation. Create Zone. **Allie's Kid Tip:** *"Boring." Ages 4 & up.*

Hands-on | B-Ticket

Virtual Jungle Cruise [Floor 1] A-OK! 9 6 6

Board a raft, grab a paddle, and take a 4-min. whitewater river cruise back in time on this motion simulator ride. Dr. Wayne Szalinski guides you and your teammates on this riotous journey over waterfalls and into the age of the dinosaurs. This is the only Jungle Cruise where you can see Walt Disney World's Cinderella Castle and Disneyland's Matterhorn at the same time! You may get a little damp. Explore Zone. **Allie's Kid Tip:** *"Paddle hard."*

Simulator | E-Ticket | Ages 6 & up | You must paddle on this ride

Top Photo Slice: Ride the Comix at DisneyQuest (6457) © Janet Simonsen

Making the Most of DisneyQuest

DINING

You won't go hungry at DisneyQuest. Disney operates a satisfying **counter-service eatery** called FoodQuest spread over two levels (see page 251). FoodQuest offers an appetizing variety of pizzas, salads, burgers, sandwiches, and wraps, plus tempting desserts. All sorts of luxurious coffee concoctions are available as well. And while you sip your latté, you can browse the Internet on limited-use computer terminals. Note that the Cheesecake Factory no longer operates this eatery.

TIPS

First-time visitors should spend time exploring the entire place before splitting up. While you're at it, choose a **meeting place** and time. FoodQuest is a good choice with places to sit, and the Ventureport on the third floor is highly visible.

Allow about **three to four hours** to tour, more if you love arcades.

Be sure to wear a **wristwatch**—it's easy to lose track of time! Also, it's faster to use the stairs to go up or down one level. On the other hand, the elevators are less disorienting than the curving staircases.

The Wonderland Cafe sports tables with **free Internet access**, but the custom browser makes it tough to surf at will.

NOTES

Best times to visit are during the mornings and afternoons and on the weekends. It gets pretty busy in the evenings, after other parks are closed. Crowds are huge on foul-weather days.

Stop by the **tip board** on floor 3 for wait times and notes.

Discounted admissions may be available in the evening.

RATINGS

Ratings are explained on page 128.

Our Value Ratings:		Our Magic Ratings:		Readers' Ratings:
Quality:	6/10	Theme:	5/10	78% fell in love with it
Variety:	4/10	Excitement:	5/10	22% liked it well enough
Scope:	3/10	Fun Factor:	6/10	0% had mixed feelings
Overall Value:	**4/10**	**Overall Magic:**	**5/10**	0% were disappointed

DisneyQuest is enjoyed by...	(rated by both authors and readers)	
Younger Kids: ♥♥♥♥	Young Adults: ♥♥♥♥♥	Families: ♥♥♥♥
Older Kids: ♥♥♥♥♥	Mid Adults: ♥♥♥	Couples: ♥♥♥
Teenagers: ♥♥♥♥♥	Mature Adults: ♥	Singles: ♥♥♥♥♥

Top Photo Slice: Sign above the door to DisneyQuest (ⓘ6461) © Janet Simonsen

Treasure Map of The Caribbean

Finding Your Way at DisneyQuest

DISNEYQUEST MAP

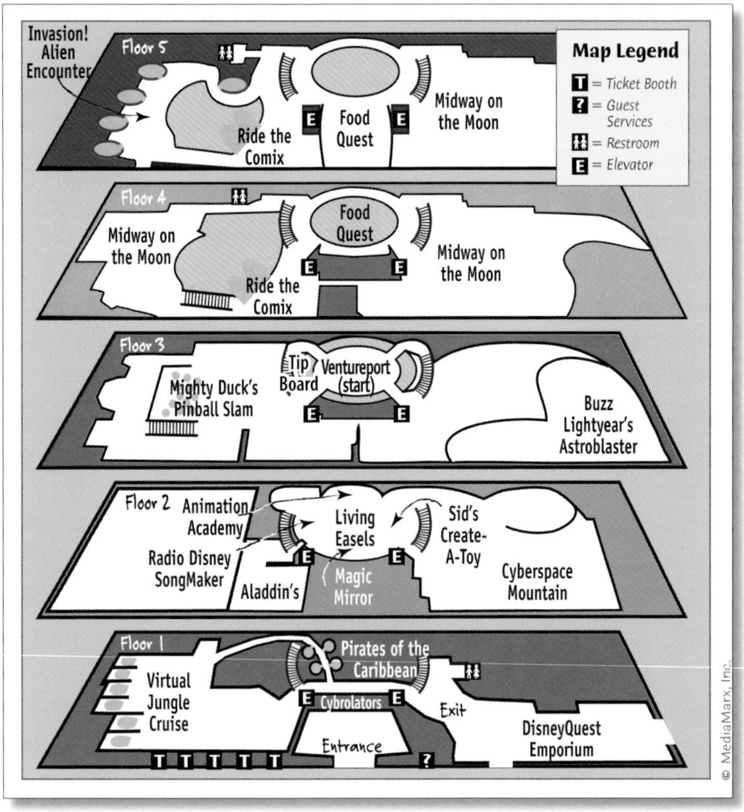

Invasion! Alien Encounter
Floor 5
Ride the Comix
Food Quest
Midway on the Moon

Map Legend
T = Ticket Booth
? = Guest Services
= Restroom
E = Elevator

Floor 4
Midway on the Moon
Food Quest
Midway on the Moon
Ride the Comix

Floor 3
Mighty Duck's Pinball Slam
Tip Board
Ventureport (start)
Buzz Lightyear's Astroblaster

Floor 2
Animation Academy
Radio Disney SongMaker
Aladdin's
Living Easels
Magic Mirror
Sid's Create-A-Toy
Cyberspace Mountain

Floor 1
Virtual Jungle Cruise
Pirates of the Caribbean
Cybrolators
Exit
Entrance
DisneyQuest Emporium

© MediaMarx, Inc.

ADMISSION

In keeping with Disney's approach to park admission, you pay a **single all-day price** and enjoy unlimited use of all rides, games, and activities. Adults pay $47.93 for a full-day admission, and kids ages 3–9 pay $41.54 (prices include tax). Children under 10 must be accompanied by an adult, but feel free to leave the older kids here while you shop elsewhere. Annual passes are available—see page 122. DisneyQuest **admission is included** in Magic Your Way tickets that have Plus options and Premium Annual Passes. DisneyQuest hours are 11:30 am–10:00 pm on Sundays–Thursdays, and 11:30 am–11:30 pm on Fridays and Saturdays (operating hours are subject to change).

INFO

For more DisneyQuest **information**, call 407-828-4600 or visit http://www.disneyquest.com. There is also a DisneyQuest kiosk in Disney Springs Marketplace that offers information.

More at ⓘ disneyquest

Top Photo Slice: Treasure map in the queue for Pirates of the Caribbean: Battle for Buccaneer Gold © Michelle Clark

Disney Celebrations in 2016

Nothing adds to a vacation like a **reason to celebrate**, and Disney knows this better than most. If you don't have a celebration of your own, Disney has one you can borrow. The 25th anniversary of Walt Disney World in 1996, the Millennium Celebration in 1999/2000, the 100th anniversary of Walt Disney's birth in 2001, and Disneyland's 50th birthday in 2005 all marked company or worldwide milestones. Sometimes, the celebratory focus has shifted to the guests themselves. "The Year of a Million Dreams" (well two years–2007 and 2008) started the trend. Then, "What Will You Celebrate?" promoted the "celebration vacation"–families that celebrate milestones like birthdays and anniversaries at Disney. In other words, your celebration became Disney's celebration. Regardless of focus, celebrations give Disney a chance to dress up its parks and introduce new rides and attractions, and give guests even more reasons to come visit.

In 2013, Disney Parks presented "**Limited Time Magic**" at both Walt Disney World and Disneyland. Some of the announced festivities were obvious, such as Valentine's Week and Independence Week. Of course, it's harder to find a theme for other weeks. "Long Lost Friends Week" (rarely-seen characters were out to meet and greet, and guests had a vote in who appears), and "Pirates Week" are among the gap-fillers. They dedicated a Friday the 13th to the Villains–Disney Hollywood Studios were open September 13th 'til the 13th hour (1:00 am) for a special dance party. Overall, we liked the idea; no matter when you visited Walt Disney World (or Disneyland) during 2013, something special and unique was happening. Of course, it's just a new wrapper for an old practice. The Disney Parks schedule is already crammed with special, short-term events. Why not weave them together into an all-encompassing theme? Curious what special thing Disney did in 2014? Alas, not much, unless you count introducing a "Frozen" theme to several things around the parks. Walt Disney World's 50th birthday is coming up in 2021, and we expect they'll put on a grand celebration of some sort!

Special celebrations come and go, but other events are **annual fixtures**, each spreading over many weeks. These include Epcot's Flower and Garden Festival, Epcot's Food and Wine Festival, Star Wars Weekends at Disney's Hollywood Studios, and the Thanksgiving/Christmas holiday season, which now begins about a week after Halloween. Then there are seasonal, after-hours parties–Mickey's Very Merry Christmas Party and Mickey's Not-So-Scary Halloween Party. Want to keep track of Disney's ever-changing lineup of celebrations? Subscribe to PassPorter News at http://www.passporter.com/news.htm.

Top Photo Slice: Balloons on Main Street, U.S.A. in the Magic Kingdom (ⓘ5851) © Amy Sellars

More Places to Play

BoardWalk—The BoardWalk resort has its own entertainment complex with clubs, restaurants, and entertainment. Jellyrolls is a dueling piano bar that serves drinks and free popcorn ($10 cover, 21 and up, no smoking allowed). Atlantic Dance Hall serves specialty drinks while open-request DJ music lures you onto the floor (no cover, 21 and up, open Tuesday–Saturday from 9:00 pm to 2:00 am). ESPN Club (page 254) is a popular sports bar. Midway games and street performers add to the fun. For details and directions to the BoardWalk resort, see pages 49–52.

Celebration, Florida—Imagine what would happen if Disney created a real town and you've got the community of Celebration, located just a few miles from the parks. Disney has divested most of its control over the years, but it remains a quaint neighborhood. Visitors may stroll or shop, have a bite in a restaurant, take in a movie at the theater, or stay in the luxury hotel. Others dream of moving to this carefully planned development. For details, call 407-566-2200 or visit http://www.celebrationfl.com.

Golf—The Walt Disney World Resort boasts four championship courses and one nine-hole course, operated by Arnold Palmer Golf Management, which redesigned the Palm course (now an Arnold Palmer Signature Course). The recently-added Tranquillo Golf Club (replacing the Osprey Ridge course) opened in late 2014. All courses are open to the public and feature full-service facilities, including driving ranges, pro shops, cafes, and lessons. Walt Disney World resort hotel guests receive a free golf club rental when they purchase another club rental and a round of golf, as well as free transportation for their scheduled tee times, at Magnolia, Lake Buena Vista, Palm, and Oak Trail. Call 407-WDW-GOLF or visit http://www.golfwdw.com.

Miniature Golf Courses—Disney has miniature golf, too! **Fantasia Gardens**, near the Swan Resort, has two 18-hole courses. One course is based on Disney's classic animated film, "Fantasia." The other is a "grass" course (Fantasia Fairways) with wildly undulating par-three and par-four holes from 40 to 75 feet long. Waits for tee times for this challenging course can be double the wait for the Fantasia course. **Winter Summerland** is a miniature golf park at Blizzard Beach with two 18-hole courses—one is blanketed in "snow," and the other celebrates the holidays in the tropics. Both are fun, and neither is very difficult. Tip: Ask about the "secret hole of the day" after you play at either course—if you get a hole-in-one in the secret hole, you may get a surprise. Cost with tax is $14.91 for adults and $12.78 for kids ages 3–9 (second round is half price), with discounts for Annual Passholders. Guests get one Disney logo golf ball for each round played! Hours: 10:00 am to 11:00 pm.

Top Photo Slice: Mickey sand trap at Disney's Magnolia Golf Course © MediaMarx, Inc.

More Places to Play

Fort Wilderness Resort—Fort Wilderness is a respite from the bustle of the parks, offering canoeing, boating, fishing excursions, biking, tennis, horseback trail rides, horse-drawn carriage rides, wagon rides, and a back trail adventure on Segways (see tours on pages 272–273). You can also visit the horse barn (pony rides cost $4, and are for guests ages 2+, 45 inches or less, 80 lbs. or less), blacksmith shop, and a nightly campfire program (with character visits and free movies). The 45-minute guided trail ride is another hidden gem—we really enjoyed our horseback ride! Cost is $46 for ages 9+ (guests must be at least 48" tall and under 250 lb.). Phone 407-824-2832 for trail ride reservations (recommended). For more information on Fort Wilderness, see pages 65–68.

© Jennifer Marx
Paul the Percheron

Health Clubs & Spas—Many of the deluxe resorts have Disney-owned health clubs with exercise equipment—some even offer massage treatments, steam rooms, and saunas. Use of a fitness center (excluding treatments) is complimentary to resort guests or $12/day/person for non-resort guests. If you've got relaxation in mind, we recommend the remodeled and re-branded **Senses spas at the Saratoga Springs and Grand Floridian resorts**. These world-class, full-service centers offer many beauty and wellness treatments, nutrition and fitness counseling, and lots of pampering. Call 407-WDW-SPAS (407-939-7727), or visit their web site at https://disneyworld.disney.go.com/spas/senses.

Tennis—Tennis enthusiasts will find tennis courts at most of Disney's deluxe resorts, Fort Wilderness, Swan and Dolphin, and Shades of Green. For more information, call 407-939-7529.

Walt Disney World Speedway—Disney has its own speedway, a one-mile, tri-oval track for **auto racing**. However, the Richard Petty Driving Experience that made its home there closed in August 2015. As to why they closed, we hear it was to make way for transportation improvement at Walt Disney World (which may mean nothing more than enlarging the Magic Kingdom parking lot).

More at ⓘ richard-petty-experience

Disney Nature Reserve—The Nature Conservancy runs this 12,000-acre hiking haven at the headwaters of the Everglades. For information, visit http://www.nature.org and search on "disney."

Top Photo Slice: Horses at the Tri-Circle D Ranch at Fort Wilderness Resort (ⓘ14565) © Cheryl Pendry

More Places to Play

Waterways (Boating, Fishing, etc.)—Water, water everywhere—and lots of things to do! You can rent boats at nearly every deluxe and moderate resort and Downtown Disney. Probably the most popular rental craft are little, two-person speed boats called Sea Raycers—the old Water Mice have been replaced by these more up-to-date craft. They're available at most marinas around Disney for $32 per half-hour, $40 for 45 minutes; $45 for 60 minutes (driver must be 12+ and at least 60" tall to pilot with an adult, or 16+ with a driver's license to pilot alone; 320 lb. max, two persons per boat, weight limit per boat). Fishing excursions and cane pole rentals are also available in most of those same places. A bass fishing program allows guests to reserve two-hour, guided, catch-and-release bass expeditions at many Disney marinas. All equipment is provided (even a digital camera to document your catch), fishing licenses are not needed thanks to the state-licensed guide on board, and participants even get a free subscription to Bassmaster Magazine. Excursions accommodate up to five guests and cost $200–$230. Phone 407-WDW-BASS for info.

ESPN Wide World of Sports Complex—Disney's state-of-the-art **athletic center** features a 9,500-seat baseball stadium, 70,000- and 80,000-square-foot fieldhouses, a track & field complex, volleyball, tennis, baseball, softball, football, and more. In 2005, Disney added another 20 acres of baseball, softball, and multi-sport fields under the sponsorship of Hess. The complex hosts 180 youth, amateur, and professional sporting events annually. General admission is $16/adults or $11/kids 3–9, but tickets for professional sporting events are typically more money. Note that the Multi-Sport Experience exhibit here has been closed. The 220-acre center is also the home of the Atlanta Braves Spring Training. The new PlayStation Pavilion offers high-end gaming, outside the admission gates. For more information, call 407-828-FANS (recorded information), or 407-939-1500 (to speak with a person), or visit http://www.disneyworldsports.com.

runDisney (Walt Disney World Running Events)—Disney's Wide World of Sports isn't just for spectators. Runners can register for the Walt Disney World Marathon, Half-Marathon, Family Fun Run 5K, and Goofy's Race and a Half Challenge (January 6–10, 2016). Disney's Princess Half-Marathon Weekend will return again February 18–21, 2016 (Jennifer and Alexander are doing the 5k in 2016!). Jeff Galloway, a leading marathon trainer, is runDisney's official training consultant. Visit http://www.rundisney.com to learn more and to register.

Top Photo Slice: A Sea Raycer zips about the Seven Seas Lagoon (ⓘ14550) © Cheryl Pendry

Deciding What To Do

Whew! We bet you're now wondering how in the world (no pun intended) you'll find the time to **fit everything** at Walt Disney World into your vacation. It's simple: You can't do it. Even a month-long stay wouldn't be enough to do and see everything. Rather than try to fit everything into your vacation, make a practical plan.

Naturally, you can't plan everything in advance, nor should you try—spontaneity and discovery are two elements of a great vacation. Yet it is a good idea to get a feeling for the parks, attractions, and activities before you go and to make a note of the ones you simply "must" do. This helps you **create an itinerary** and keeps you from missing the things you've got your heart set on.

First, read the preceding pages carefully to gain a solid idea of what the Walt Disney World Resort is all about. Next, **make a list** of all the things you'd like to see and do. This can be a great family activity. Make it a free-for-all, no-holds-barred event—what we call a "blue-sky session." List everything, no matter how impractical, silly, or expensive. Once you've got a good list, pare it down to the things that are most important and copy them to the worksheet on the next two pages. List the activity, where in the "World" it is located (i.e., which park or resort), its approximate cost, and any notes (including why it's on the list).

When you're done with the list, take a good look at the locations. Are several located in the same park? If so, can you do them all on the same day? Go through the list and note other patterns. With luck, you'll have a better sense of where you're headed. Next, **assign the activities** to specific days of your vacation, using the Day/Date column on the far right. For example, on a recent trip, we wanted to visit Spaceship Earth, race around Test Track, and watch IllumiNations. All those activities are at Epcot, so we grouped them together on our third day. We wrote a "3" next to each of those items, but you could write "Wed" or the date instead. If you've planned too much for one day or place, your Cost and Notes columns may help you decide which activities to keep and which to throw out or schedule for another day.

Not all activities can be decided this way, nor should they. Some choices should be **spur of the moment**. Be sure to "schedule" some free time in your trip—preferably a whole day or two. Use these techniques as a general game plan to a great vacation!

More at ⓘ planning-park-days | four-parks-in-one-day

Top Photo Slice: A bulletin board full of things to do in the now-closed Minnie's Country House (ⓘ6771) © Joy Vodnik

Electronic, interactive worksheet available—see page 316

Touring Worksheet

Use this worksheet to figure out the things you want to do most on your trip. Match up attractions to determine the parks you want to visit, noting the day/date (you may wish to refer to the Extra Magic Hour schedule on page 34). Fill in the park schedule grid at the bottom of the next page once you've picked days—the park schedule can help you complete your itinerary and choose eateries (in the next chapter).

Activity	Park	Land	Cost	Notes	Day/Date

Useful Abbreviations:
MK (Magic Kingdom)
EP (Epcot)
DHS (Disney's Hollywood Studios)
DAK (Disney's Animal Kingdom)
BB (Blizzard Beach)
TL (Typhoon Lagoon)
BW (BoardWalk)
DS (Disney Springs)
DQ (DisneyQuest)
WWOS (ESPN Wide World of Sports)
FG (Fantasia Gardens)
WS (Winter Summerland)
DCL (Disney Cruise Line)
VB (Disney's Vero Beach)
OFF (Off-site)
USF (Universal Studios)
IOA (Islands of Adventure)
SW (SeaWorld)
COVE (Discovery Cove)
BG (Busch Gardens)
KSC (Kennedy Space Center)
CB (Cocoa Beach)
LF (LEGOLAND Florida)
FH (Friend/Family's House)

Activity	Park	Land	Cost	Notes	Day/Date

Write your park schedule in this calendar grid—note the date in the corners. You can get Disney park schedules online at http://www.disneyworld.com.

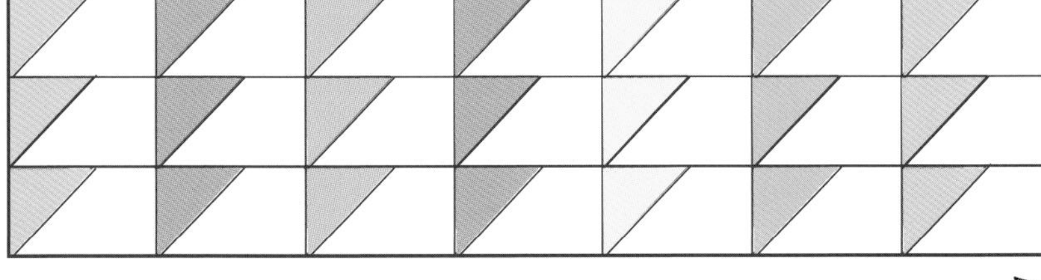

It's Not Such a Small World After All

If you've read this chapter, you know that touring Walt Disney World is no simple walk in the park. Here are some tips and tricks to help you:

"It's easy to add additional FastPasses after you've used your first three. Just stop by one of the kiosks in a park and select from one of the attractions available—even if the time shown isn't optimal. Once you've made the reservation on the kiosk, you can easily change the time on the MyDisneyExperience app on your smartphone. One final tip: The kiosk screens work better if you use your fingernail rather than your finger tip."

– Contributed by Sherry Rohlfing, a winner in our Reader Tip Contest

"If you're staying on-site (and why wouldn't you?), and a park is open quite late, be sure to stay as late as possible (take a rest during the day if needed). The park thins out considerably, first with those staying off-site and then even with those staying on-site. You can get on everything with no wait time. Plus the parks look particularly beautiful at night. There's something about walking around when it's pitch black with all of the lights and no crowds. You can really immerse yourself into the experience. Oh, and keep in mind that some parks may stay open later than publicized times—check with a cast member while you're at the park. For instance, during Christmas season Disney may publicize an 11:00 pm closing for the Magic Kingdom but it won't close until 1:00 am!"

– Contributed by Shirley Garcowski, a winner in our Reader Tip Contest

"*It can be hard to slow down when you're at the parks because it feels like 'time is money' (wanting to make the most of your day by getting a lot in). However, some of the sweetest moments can happen when you find a quiet spot to sit and enjoy an ice cream with your family. Plan on some rest even while at the park. It may just be one of your favorite memories.*"

– Contributed by Genevieve Daniel, a winner in our Reader Tip Contest

Magical Memories

"*We were standing at a tall table in Epcot, near the Port of Entry, on a beautiful, sunny day. The sky was clear and deep blue, there was a gentle breeze, and we were happy! We were sipping on glasses of sparkling, rosé champagne to celebrate our surprise engagement the week before. That's when a lovely couple approached us and said that they had to leave now, and would we like their FastPass tickets for Soarin' - oh my! (This was before FastPass+.) Our favourite ride in our favourite Disney park - yes, please! It was a brief yet perfect moment, and has stayed with us as one of our favourite Magical Moments from Walt Disney World.*"

...as told by Disney vacationer Carolyn Brooke-Millward

"*One of my most precious Disney memories happened on my kids' first trip. On our first morning there, my husband hustled out of the hotel room with our three-year-old to make rope-drop. I was feeling left out as I finished getting our nine-month-old son ready for the day. What was I going to do with a baby at the Magic Kingdom? My mother and I arrived at the gates, and the park was still almost empty. The Main Street Trolley was loading, with the Dapper Dans standing at the back. I usually skip the Trolley, but I thought, why not? I rode up Main Street with my mom next to me and my baby in my arms, while being serenaded by the Dapper Dans, and I realized this was going to be a magical trip!*"

...as told by Disney vacationer Tracy Bratlie

More at ⓘ what-a-wonderful-world

Top Photo Slice: Farewell signs in different languages at the end of "it's a small world" (ⓘ2240) © Laura Dawson

Feasting and Snacking

You can't have a good vacation without a good meal (or two), and your Disney vacation is no exception. Disney knows how to make your mealtimes as entertaining, adventuresome, and satisfying as the rest of your vacation experience. Disney eateries go out of their way to give everyone a unique and delicious dining experience, so you'll find that even the most exotic restaurant can please any taste, including the finicky eaters in your family. From the atmosphere to the service to the food itself, it has all been created to fill your imagination as well as your belly.

DISCOVER the fine points of dining at Disney

The choices can be awesome, ranging from basic hot dogs and burgers to once-in-a-lifetime elegance, from ultra-romantic dinners for two to foot-stompin' family hoedowns, and from exotic samplings of far-off places to the magic of a breakfast hug from Winnie the Pooh himself.

PLAN meals and reserve tables

For us, meal planning is more important than choosing which attractions to visit. It's easier to jump in an unexpectedly short line for a show than it is to get a table at the better eateries.

The six basic types of Walt Disney World Resort meals are table-service restaurants, counter-service cafes, quick-service snack shops, "special experiences" (such as dinner shows and character meals), room service, and meals you fix yourself. We devote most of the space here to table-service and special dining experiences, which are more costly and require the most planning. We also include details on the counter service and snacks in the parks. Resort counter service and room service is discussed in the "Staying in Style" chapter. We can't say much about your home cooking until we're invited to your villa or campsite, though.

The chapter begins with a meal planning guide, then moves to mealtime tips, park-by-park and resort-by-resort eatery reviews, and the low-down on the big shindigs, and ends with worksheets to plan your meals.

Top Photo Slice: Alexander enjoys a Mickey ice cream bar at the Magic Kingdom © MediaMarx, Inc.

Deciding On Dining

If you thought selecting a restaurant in your hometown was tough, you haven't seen anything. The Walt Disney World Resort has more than **300 places to eat**. But before you go running for the exit, take heart. We've been to virtually every restaurant on property at least twice (often much more) and we offer easily digestible descriptions and yummy ratings for you in this chapter. Better yet, we have a tried-and-true system for deciding where and when to eat.

First, decide **how often** you want to eat out. Many folks (including ourselves) bring or buy some food for in-room snacks or meals, with light breakfasts being the most practical choice. All Disney resorts now supply a refrigerator at no charge, some include a coffeemaker, and Disney's Deluxe Villas resorts have kitchen facilities, too. You can, of course, eat out every meal. We like to eat a light breakfast in our room with food we've packed or purchased, such as peanut butter and jelly on English muffins. We then do one or two special breakfasts "out" (such as a character breakfast—see pages 262–263). We often eat lunch and dinner at the parks, resorts, or Disney Springs. If you're doing the Disney Dining Basic or Quick-Service Plan (see the next three pages), you'll probably do about two meals a day. Some vacationers prefer to eat a big meal mid-morning and another mid-afternoon to save time and money (it's easy to fill up at many restaurants). More money-saving ideas are on page 229.

Once you have an idea of how often you want (and can afford) to eat out, your next task is to decide **when and where**. Revisit your Touring Worksheet (pages 218–219) and check the parks you want to visit—it is much easier to choose a restaurant in or near your day's destination. Every park offers table-service restaurants, counter-service eateries, and snack shops and carts. To help you choose from the overwhelming number of dining choices at Walt Disney World, this chapter offers descriptions of nearly all eateries. Descriptions are organized alphabetically within each park and resort to help you focus on your choices. Pick the eateries that fall within your budget, tastes, and needs—you may find it helpful to highlight or circle those eatery descriptions that interest you.

As you make decisions about your meals and the eateries you want to visit, jot them down on your **Meal Worksheet** at the end of the chapter on the next page. Make note of those table-service eateries for which advance reservations may be made. Continue on to page 226 to learn the what, when, and how of advance reservations at the Walt Disney World Resort.

Top Photo Slice: The tempting pastry case in Boulangerie Patisserie at Epcot (ⓘ15312) © Monica Gauvin

Disney Dining Plan

There's a never-ending buzz about the Disney Dining Plan packages. Available as an add-on to a Magic Your Way package (see page 32), and sometimes free as a promotional item, the Disney Dining Plan has **revolutionized the way many vacationers dine at Disney**. While a hands-down winner in the past, saving money and maximizing value is a challenge today.

Disney offers several Dining Plan packages in 2016. The **Basic Dining Plan** is most popular, and can be added to any Magic Your Way package that includes at least one day of park admission. The add-on price is $61.84/adult (includes tax) and $20.96/ages 3–9 per night of your stay, regardless of season. Those under age 3 may share their parent's meal. The Basic plan provides **one table-service credit, one counter-service credit, and one snack credit for each night of your stay**, plus a resort refillable mug. Compared to the average cost of meals, **you lose 7%**. To win, focus on higher-cost eateries and avoid all two-credit dining except for dinner shows and pizza delivery.

The **Deluxe Dining Plan** costs $111.73 (includes tax)/guests ages 10 and up and $32.56/guests ages 3–9 per night of your stay. The Deluxe Dining Plan includes **three meal credits (use for either table or counter service) and two snack credits per night**, plus one refillable mug. Savings and value can be very good on this plan if you avoid counter service meals, but it's easy to exceed your normal calorie count. (After paying tips, it can cost $120–$130/day per adult). For the **best value**, only dine at one-credit table-service restaurants. Three meals per day too much? A few two-credit meals won't destroy your savings. Pay out-of-pocket for all or most of your counter-service meals, and apply the extra credits to Signature Dining.

Disney also has a **Quick-Service Dining Plan**. For $42.84/adult and $17.47/ ages 3–9 per night of your stay, you get two counter-service meal credits (each credit is good for one entree or one combo meal, juice at breakfast, dessert at lunch/dinner, and one non-alcoholic beverage) and one snack per person per night, plus one refillable drink mug per person. **This is 2% less than break-even**.

How do credits work? Table-service credits on the Basic Dining Plan include an entrée, dessert, regular soft drink, and sales tax. Dessert can be swapped for a side salad or cup of soup. Meal credits on the Deluxe Plan add an appetizer. Most gratuities are not included. Counter-service meals on all plans provide an entrée, dessert, regular soft drink, and sales tax. Snack credits provide a single item, such as a soft drink, baked item, ice cream, or a Dole Whip, and can be applied to breakfast items like cereal, French toast sticks, oatmeal, grits, hard-boiled eggs, a side of bacon, sausage, potatoes or eggs. Disney affixes DDP icons to its menus to identify snack-credit items.

More at ⓘ dining-plans | dining-plan-tips | deluxe-dining-plan

Top Photo Slice: Menu showing "DDP" icons beside prices to identify snack credit items © MediaMarx, Inc.

Disney Dining Plan

(continued)

You can **use Disney Dining Plan credits at any time**, in any combination, for the duration of your stay (beginning at check-in), and they can be used to pay for your friends' meals (ask your server). Table-service credits are good at more than 100 participating eateries (noted in this chapter), as well as in-room private dining, pizza delivery, and dinner shows (gratuities are included on these last three). All unused credits expire without refund at 11:59 pm on your check-out day; use 'em or lose 'em!

The **Premium and Platinum Packages** (see page 32) combine dining and recreation. Premium meal benefits are comparable to the Deluxe Dining Plan. Platinum vacationers use just a single meal credit for Signature dining, including Victoria and Albert's (which can't be had at all on the other plans).

How do you get a Dining Plan? Add the plan to your reservation at least five days prior to your arrival. Disney Vacation Club members can purchase the Basic, Quick-Service, and Deluxe dining plans when staying on points—contact DVC for the details. Annual Passholders can buy a lodging package that includes dining, but no admission—see details on page 32.

Dining Plan Tips:

Use your PassPorter! **It's packed with features** to help you maximize your dining plan. Our eatery descriptions include average meal prices to help you judge relative values. We also note Disney Dining Plan participation and Signature dining restaurants (which require two table-service credits per meal). Our Meal Worksheet on page 268 includes columns for budgeting your dining credits, and to record actual usage. You can also use the Meals and Snacks section of each PassPocket to track these items.

Consider **sharing meals** to stretch your Dining Plan credits.

The **computed cost** of Basic Dining Plan credits is $35.59 (table service), $16.94 (counter service), and $4.59 (snack)—7% more than the price you'd pay off the plan. On the Basic and Deluxe Plans, you get decent bang from dinner shows and pizza delivery, as gratuities are also included. The two-credit Cinderella's breakfast is a money-waster under either plan.

According to our calculations, **the counter-service and basic dining plans are money-losers**. Yet on the **deluxe dining plan, average savings are around 20%**, and it's even more if you use every meal credit for table service. You'd have to use one out of four deluxe plan credits for counter-service meals to lose money.

➢

Top Photo Slice: A receipt on the table at 50s Prime Time Cafe at Disney's Hollywood Studios (①4464) © Eileen Farnsworth

Disney Dining Plan

(continued)

If you're eating counter service at your resort hotel and have the resort's **Rapid Refill mugs** (see page 36), use the soft drink portion of your counter-service credit on a bottled beverage from the Grab-n-Go, and save it for later.

On the Basic Dining Plan, it matters little if you dine at a la carte or **buffet/ character table-service restaurants**—the value of each meal is similar.

At counter-service spots you can **convert your dessert** or non-alcoholic drink into a snack item or a snack credit to be used later—ask at check-out. You can also substitute a single Quick Service meal for up to three snack items.

Disney tracks your dining credit balance by computer, but watch your meal credits carefully. Each meal receipt lists the number of credits you have remaining, **but there can be errors**. Your resort's Lobby Concierge can print out a detailed accounting. Note the credits you've used (and plan to use) on our Dining Worksheet on page 268.

Your entire travel party's **credits are grouped together by type (adult and child)** so you can use your credits as you wish. You can also pay for someone else's meal with your credits, and, if you're on the Deluxe, Premium, or Platinum dining plans, you can use any child meal entitlements for adult entrees.

You may **exchange two table-service credits** for selected dinner shows, Signature Dining, in-room dining, and pizza delivery—one pizza serves two adults. The average values (and quality) of many one-credit table-service restaurants are nearly as high as Signature Dining experiences, which can mean you'll get far **more bang for your buck** by avoiding the Signature establishments altogether.

Eateries participating in the Dining Plan can **change at any time**. You can download the most recent list of eateries at Disney's web site and/or request one at 407-WDW-DINE.

Leftover snack credits? Use them to buy snacks for the trip home.

Here are some "**secret numbers**"—these are the average values of adult meals based on our calculations (includes tax and 18% gratuity):

Meal Type	breakfast	lunch	dinner
Counter-service	$13.29	$17.69	$17.69
Table-service - B(asic) Plan	$28.82	$46.35	$50.17
Table-service - D(eluxe) Plan	$28.82	$54.57	$58.50
Table-service Signature (B/D)	$57.71	$56.66/$65.18	$77.57/$85.90

Top Photo Slice: Referigerated cases with beverages and snacks at Captain Cook's in the Polynesian Village (854)

Advance Reservations

With the popularity of the Disney Dining Plan (see pages 223–225), reservations have become essential at many restaurants. Virtually every table-service restaurant within Disney World allows anyone (whether or not you're on the Dining Plan) to make "Advance Reservations." Unlike traditional reservations, in which a table is held for your party at a designated time, Disney's advance reservations give you the **first table that becomes available**. Wait times for the first-available table vary, but we typically wait 10–30 minutes once we check-in at the eatery.

Most Disney table-service restaurants **accept advance reservations**, and we note this fact with each eatery description in this chapter. The only restaurants that don't accept advance reservations are some Disney Springs restaurants, Big River Grille (24-hour reservations only), and ESPN Club (see detailed listings in this chapter). Some restaurants do take traditional reservations, such as Victoria & Albert's, the Swan & Dolphin restaurants (see pages 259–260), and the character meals at Cinderella's Royal Table and Akershus Royal Banquet Hall (see pages 262–263).

Advance reservations can be made **before your arrival** by calling 407-WDW-DINE (407-939-3463) from 7:00 am to 10:00 pm Eastern Time seven days a week. You can also make advance reservations online at http://disneyworld.disney.go.com/dining or in the My Disney Experience app (see page 126). You can make them up to **180 days ahead of your visit** for reservations at most restaurants. Tip: Disney resort guests have the advantage of being able to book reservations for the first ten days of their trip at 180 days from their check-in date.

Already at Disney? Search for table-service availability using your iPhone or Android device—just download Disney's free **My Disney Experience** app (see page 126). Book in advance or search what's "Here & Now."

When you make an advance reservation, you will be asked to supply the name of your hotel, your phone number, your reservation number, and your date of arrival—you can record this information in your **Advance Reservations Worksheet** on page 269. If you aren't staying at a Disney resort, no problem—simply provide a daytime phone number. All advance reservations now require a credit card guarantee at the time of booking, and a few require full pre-payment. No-show penalties ($10/person or more) may be charged if you don't cancel a day prior. Emergencies are often excused, but be sure to call! You will get a **confirmation number** for each reservation. Link this to My Disney Experience (see page 126) and record this in your worksheet, and later transfer it to your daily PassPockets. You may wish to call and confirm your reservations a few days before you arrive, too.

More at ⓘ advance-reservations

Top Photo Slice: The beautiful stained glass windows of Cinderealla's Royal Table at the Magic Kingdom (ⓘ14781) © Amy Novak

If you don't get the advance reservation time and/or restaurant you want, **don't give up**—keep trying! Vacationers cancel their plans and spots open up all the time. We've gotten reservations for hot restaurants even on the day itself just by continuing to call and ask for any openings or by returning to My Disney Experience and checking on our preferred dates.

Want that **popular Be Our Guest, Cinderella's, or Chef Mickey's reservation**? These are hot tickets and can be very difficult to get. Your best bet is to call exactly 180 days before the date you want to eat here. Get online by 5:55 am (online bookings begin at 6:00 am), or pick up the phone and start dialing 407-WDW-DINE at 6:55 am Eastern Time (phone lines open at 7:00 am). If you get a recording, listen carefully—if the recording indicates the office is closed, hang up and redial right away. Otherwise wait on the line and do not hang up—you're in a queue for the next available representative. When you get an actual representative on the line, tell them immediately (even if you have to interrupt them) that you need a reservation for the restaurant of your choosing—be sure to include the exact date and number of people. It is important to convey this information as quickly as possible, because hundreds of other people are doing the same thing right now and every second counts. We suggest you write down the line you will speak on your worksheet and simply rattle it off to avoid any delays. Do not specify a time—let the representative search for any available time.

You will need a **credit or debit card when you make your reservation**—payment in full is required at time of booking for character meals and dinner shows (even if you're using Disney Dining Plan credits), and a credit/debit card guarantee is required for other meals. If you do not have a credit/debit card, the reservation cannot be made.

If you decide not to eat at a particular restaurant, just **cancel your reservation** online or via phone before 11:59 pm Eastern Time on the day before your reservation to avoid cancellation fees. If you are unable to get a reservation, check the day before the desired date and again on the morning you want to dine.

Check in at the restaurant's podium 15 minutes before your seating time. You may also need to wait anywhere from 5 to 30 minutes for a table to become available, depending upon how busy it is. Some restaurants issue a pager, and most have a comfortable waiting area or bar. If your restaurant opens before the park opens, simply tell the cast member at the park entrance turnstiles about your advance reservation—you may need to show your confirmation number. Daily bus transportation is available for these early advance reservations beginning at 6:30 am (Magic Kingdom area) and 7:00–7:15 am (all other parks). Be sure to tell the bus driver when you board where you need to go, and allow ample time to transfer if your reservation is at a resort.

Top Photo Slice: Cast members at the Sanaa podium at Disney's Animal Kingdom Lodge resort © MediaMarx, Inc.

Restaurant Menu

Alcoholic Beverages—Most eateries serve alcoholic drinks, though the only eatery in the Magic Kingdom that serves alcohol is Be Our Guest. Bars and lounges are located around the "World." Legal drinking age is 21 and they do check your identification.

Character Dining—Dine with Disney characters! See pages 262–263.

Children's Meals—Nearly every eatery has a special menu for kids age 3–9. Kid staples like macaroni & cheese and chicken tenders can usually be had at the most exotic of restaurants even when they're not on the menu—ask your server. Mickey Check meals ensure healthy options, but you may be able to substitute fries for the healthy choices. Kids also get free refills on child-size beverages at table-service restaurants, including juice, milk, bottled water, and soda (but not including specialty drinks). All eateries also provide high chairs and booster seats, as needed. As you can imagine, Disney is one of the most kid-friendly places to eat in the world. (Special note to parents of infants and toddlers: Jars of baby food are not available in the eateries, but you can purchase them at the Baby Care Centers of each park if necessary—see page 120.)

Counter Service—Most food at Disney is sold fast-food style. The quality does vary—it's generally worse at the Magic Kingdom and best at Disney's Animal Kingdom. At Magic Kingdom, we like Pecos Bill Cafe in Frontierland and Columbia Harbour House in Liberty Square. Disney's Animal Kingdom only has three table-service restaurants, but the counter-service food is several cuts above the ordinary. We especially like Flame Tree Barbecue.

Coupons/Discounts—Don't plan on finding coupons for restaurants. We know only of AAA discounts at some Swan/Dolphin eateries. Discounts for annual passholders and Disney Vacation Club members (mostly at lunch) do exist—be sure to ask your server. You may qualify for the Tables in Wonderland program—see page 10 for details.

Dietary Requirements—Low-cholesterol, low-salt, low-fat, and/or vegetarian meals are a regular part of the menu in most restaurants. Special allergy-friendly menus are available at all counter- and table-service locations. With 72 hours of advance notice, gluten-free, kosher and other special dietary needs can be met. Cosmic Ray's at Magic Kingdom has a no-advance-notice kosher menu at the check-out (ask for this at other counter-service restaurants, too). You may contact Disney regarding your special dietary requirements by e-mail at specialdiets@disneyworld.com or phone 407-824-5967.

Dinner Shows—Disney offers several dinner shows, combining all-you-care-to-eat meals with live entertainment. See pages 264–266.

Dress—Casual clothing is appropriate for most eateries in the "World" except Victoria & Albert's (see page 257), which requires that men wear a jacket. Several spots also require "resort casual" dress (sometimes called "business casual"), which means that men should wear dress slacks, jeans, trousers, dress shorts, collared shirts, and/or t-shirts (jackets are optional) and women should wear skirts, jeans, dress shorts, dresses, blouses, sweaters, and/or t-shirts. Resort casual dress code prohibits hats, swimsuits, swim coveralls, tank tops, torn clothing, or flip flops. Resort casual restaurants include Artist Point, California Grill, Citricos, Flying Fish, Jiko, Narcoossee's, and Yachtsman Steakhouse.

Entertainment—Some restaurants supply entertainment, while others like the Whispering Canyon Cafe and 'Ohana provide activities for kids.

Menus—To see eatery offerings and prices before you arrive, go to My Disney Experience (see page 126) for up-to-date menus direct from Disney.

More at ⓘ eating-healthy | food-allergies

Top Photo Slice: Front of the Restaurant Marrakesh menu (ⓘ2314) © Janet Simonsen

Money—Pay with Cash, Disney Gift Cards, traveler's checks, Disney Visa Reward cards, MasterCard, Visa, American Express, JCB, Discover, Diner's Club, most debit cards, Apple Pay, and Google Wallet. Disney MagicBands with charging privileges are welcomed, even at some of the smallest snack carts. Note that Disney resort room charging is accepted at the Swan and Dolphin eateries. The Shopping & Dining Gift Card, which can be purchased in amounts between $5 and $1,500, is also accepted at select shops and eateries. Sales tax is 6.5%. Gratuities may be applied automatically to large parties (eight or more persons).

Peak Periods—Prices for character meals and some other popular eateries may increase by 10%–20% during peak periods and weekends.

Smoking—Florida law prohibits smoking in all enclosed restaurants and other indoor public spaces. Only outdoor establishments and freestanding bars (no restaurants or hotel lobbies allowed) can allow smoking, but Disney bans smoking at most of these, too.

Time- and Money-Saving Dining Tips

- ✔ *If you're staying at a Walt Disney World resort hotel, you can make all of your advance dining reservations for the length of your stay (up to 10 days in advance) at 180 days from your arrival date.*
- ✔ *Inquire with Disney about Dining Plan add-ons to resort reservations (see pages 223–225). At press time, Disney is offering a free Dining Plan for select packages and dates. If the Dining Plan is not free, the Basic and Quick-Service Dining Plans only offer marginal savings. The Deluxe Dining Plan is a better deal, but only for those who normally eat three table-service meals a day and typically spend at least $90/day per adult.*
- ✔ *At counter-service eateries, there are usually several lines. The line farthest from the entry is often shorter. Look before you leap. Also note that counter-service eateries have lines on both sides of the cash register. If you see a short or nonexistent line on one side of an open register, jump in!*
- ✔ *Consider eating earlier or later than traditional mealtime hours. You'll be more likely to get a seat (if you haven't made reservations) or simply find the restaurant less crowded and noisy.*
- ✔ *Every item at counter-service restaurants can be ordered a la carte. If you don't want fries with that burger "meal," just ask, and you'll pay a reduced price.*
- ✔ *Landry's Select Club offers discounts at Rainforest Cafe, T-Rex, Yak and Yeti's, and 400 other Landry's locations. Get details at http://www.landrysinc.com. Annual passholder discounts may also be offered at these spots.*
- ✔ *The Tables in Wonderland program is for Florida residents and annual passholders. It offers 20% discounts on select restaurants in the parks and resorts, and more. See page 10 for details.*
- ✔ *Resort eateries are frequently less crowded than those in the parks. Consider a visit to a nearby resort restaurant before, during, or after a park visit. The Contemporary, Polynesian Village, and Grand Floridian resorts are close to the Magic Kingdom, the Yacht & Beach Club, BoardWalk, and Swan & Dolphin restaurants are close to Epcot and Disney's Hollywood Studios, and Disney's Animal Kingdom Lodge is a short drive/bus ride from Disney's Animal Kingdom.*

More at ⓘ saving-money-on-dining

Top Photo Slice: Sushi at Teppan Edo in Epcot (ⓘ8030) © Cheryl Pendry

Understanding and Using the Eatery Descriptions and Ratings

PassPorter's popular capsule reviews cover all table-service restaurants, as well as counter-service eateries at the parks. Our reviews include all important details, plus ratings. Below is a key to our eatery charts. Dig in!

Description Key

Ratings[7] ↓

[1] **Eatery Name** [D-2[2]] (Bar Color[3]) **B $, L $, D $, S[4]** DDP[5] [6]	# # #
Description offering an overview of the eatery, including comments on the theming, quality, and menu range. We try to give you an idea of what sort of foods you'll find at a particular eatery, along with typical prices and our recommendations. We also include information on the availability of lighter fare, children's meals, and alcoholic beverages. Whenever possible, we describe the type of seating (tables, booths, etc.) and whether it is indoor or outdoor.	**Type[8]** Cuisine[8] Noise Factor[8] Reservations[8] Avg. Wait[8] Hours[8]

[1] Each chart has an empty checkbox in the upper left corner—use it to check off the eateries that interest you (before you go) or those at which you ate (after your return).

[2] Map coordinates—match them up to park maps in "Touring the 'World'" for locations.

[3] The **bar color** indicates the eatery's main draw, as follows:

Gourmet Tastes | **Eateries for Everyone** | **Fun Food** | **Character Meals**

[4] Meals are indicated by letters: B (breakfast), L (lunch), D (dinner), and S (snack). The dollar figures that follow each meal type represent the average cost of a full adult meal. Table-service meal costs include appetizer, entree, dessert, soft drink, tax, and 18% tip. Average counter-service meal costs include entree, dessert, soft drink, and tax.

[5] The "DDP" symbol indicates that an eatery participates in the Disney Dining Plan (see pages 223–225) at press time. Note that the eateries are subject to change at any time—check with Disney before making plans. The color and letter in the lower right corner shows the type of Dining Plan eatery: blue "S" DDP S is snack, red "Q" DDP Q is quick service (counter service), purple "T" DDP T is table service, and gold "2" DDP 2 is signature (because a Signature eatery requires two table-service credits). Verify participation at 407-WDW-DINE.

[6] Eateries with a reasonable selection of healthy items (low-fat/low-sodium/low-calorie) are indicated with a tape measure symbol. These are also friendly to weight watchers!

[7] The three white boxes on the right show ratings on a scale of 1 (poor) to 10 (loved it!). The first rating is Jennifer's, the second is Dave's, and the third is our Readers' rating. We offer our personal ratings to show how opinions vary, even between two like-minded people. You can also use our ratings as a point of reference—Jennifer likes eateries with extensive theming and well-prepared foods that aren't too exotic or spicy. Dave has more cultured tastes, enjoys unusual, spicy, and barbecue dishes, and loves seafood!

© MediaMarx, Inc.
Kona Cafe

[8] The boxes on the right beneath the numeric ratings give basic information: eatery type (Table, Counter, or Buffet), cuisine, noise factor (from quiet to very noisy), seating (if reservations are accepted, needed, suggested, recommended, or required, and how many days in advance you can call), average wait time, and the eatery's hours.

Top Photo Slice: Windows in the atrium at Crystal Palace in the Magic Kingdom (①14476) © Cheryl Pendry

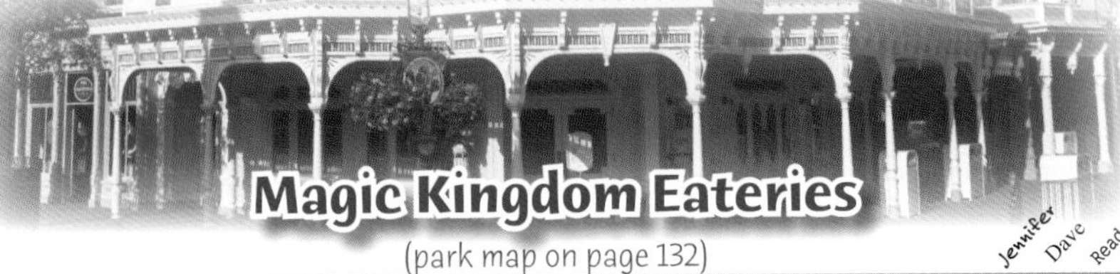

Magic Kingdom Eateries

(park map on page 132)

Jennifer | Dave | Readers

Be Our Guest [D-1] B $21, L $20 DDPO D $51 DDPT — 9 | 7 | 9

Step into the most delicious part of Belle and Beast's world. This restaurant has three themed wings: West Wing, Rose Gallery, and Ballroom. Breakfast and lunch are counter service—order, find a table, and your food arrives on a cart! Breakfast is prix fixe ($19.99) and offers entrées such as croissant doughnut, eggs florentine, and vegetable quiche. At lunch, sandwiches—carved turkey, steak, and grilled ham and cheese—are $11.49-$12.49, while Niçoise salad with tuna, vegetable quiche, and braised pork are $9.49-$14. Desserts are just $4.19. Dinner morphs to table service, and breaks Magic Kingdom tradition—beer and wine are served! Entrees are $18.49 to $33.49: pork chops, lamb, steak, and seafood are dressed-up French style and the veggie choice is ratatouille. Kids fare is unusual, but you can still get grilled cheese.

Counter and Table | French | Advance reservations | Call 180 days | 8-10 am, 10:30-2:30 pm, 4:00-8:30 pm

Casey's Corner [D-4] L $16, D $16, S $4 DDPO — 6 | 5 | 7

Casey's at the bat, and there's a hot dog at the plate. Old-time stadium foods—Chili cheese dogs ($10.29), fries ($2.99), Cracker Jack ($2.59), and drinks ($2.99 & $3.29). Seating is outdoors; some indoor grandstands and tables near a big-screen TV.

Counter | American | 11 am-closing

Cinderella's Royal Table [D-3] B $57, L $61, D $72 DDP2 — 6 | 6 | 7

For Disney magic, you can't beat dining inside Cinderella Castle! The character meals at "Cindy's" are hot tickets and very expensive as a result—the pre-plated breakfast is $55.29 or $34.64/kids 3-9. And lunch is $58.04 or $35.89/kids (see pages 262-263). Dinner is $67.96 or $41.84/kids with your choice of appetizer, entrée, dessert, and beverage. The price includes tax and gratuity, plus a gift for any children ages 3-9 in your party (a princess wand or a prince's sword). You will be able to meet and greet Cinderella, and have your photo taken with her, before you ascend to the dining room. If you'll be celebrating a special occasion, mention it at booking. Full payment is required at time of reservation (except for those on a dining plan). During holiday periods, meal prices are approximately an extra $6/adult and $4/kid.

Table | American | Med. noise | Advance reservations essential | Call 180 days | 8:05-10:40 am, 11:45-2:40 pm 3:50 pm-park closing

Columbia Harbour House [C-2] L $18, D $18, S $7 DDPO — 6 | 6 | 7

This cozy inn provides cool relief and attractive decor despite the inexpensive menu. Fried shrimp with fries ($9.99), fried fish with fries ($8.49), clam chowder ($4.99), garden harvest salad ($8.99), and sandwiches ($9.49) dominate the menu, but several veggie dishes—such as the vegetarian chili ($4.99)—create a rare port in the storm at Magic Kingdom. Kids meals ($5.99) include salad with chicken and mac & cheese. The quiet, upstairs dining room is usually open.

Counter | American | Med. noise | 10:30 am-1 hour before closing

Cosmic Ray's Starlight Cafe [E-3] L $18, D $18, S $9 DDPO — 6 | 5 | 6

Ray runs the biggest cafeteria at the Magic Kingdom. There's an excellent choice of chicken ($8.99-$10.99), sandwiches ($9.99-$10.79), burgers ($9.99-$10.69), and salads ($8.49), but not all food items are available from all stations. Kids can get peanut butter and jelly, turkey sandwich, and chicken nuggets ($5.99 each). Toppings bar. Sadly, the ½ chicken and BBQ rib combo is no longer offered. Kosher meals available upon request.

© MediaMarx, Inc.
Loving the big portions

Counter | American | Very noisy | Med. waits | 10:00 am-closing

Top Photo Slice: Casey's Corner at the Magic Kingdom (13588) © Janet Simonsen

Magic Kingdom Eateries

(continued)

Jennifer | Dave | Readers

The Crystal Palace [C-4] B $32 L $35, D $48 DDP T — 6 | 6 | 8

Little more than a stone's throw away from Cinderella Castle (but please, don't throw stones), this replica of a Victorian glass conservatory serves character meals all day long. Breakfast is $24.99 ($13.99/kids 3-9), lunch is $27.62 ($14.99/kids), and dinner is $37.99 ($17.99/kids), tax included ($4-$6 higher during holidays). Winnie the Pooh is your host at this popular buffet. The dinner menu changes weekly, but usually offers carved meats, roasted vegetables, shrimp, and salads. There's even a separate kids' buffet and an ice cream sundae "bar." Potted and hanging plants and wrought-iron tables and chairs add to the lovely garden setting. See pages 262-263 for details on the character meal.

Buffet | American | Very noisy | Reservations suggested | Call 180 days | ~8-10:45 am, 11:30-2:45 pm, 3:15 pm-closing

Gaston's Tavern [E-1] L $18, D $18, S $4 DDP O — 6 | 6 | 6

No one eats like Gaston, no one drinks like Gaston, and his decorating ... wow! Roasted pork shank ($9.79), veggies ($3.99) and hummus ($4.39) are the savories. Sweets include chocolate croissant, cinnamon roll, and fruit cup ($3.69-$4.19). LeFou's Brew is an apple juice slushie in a souvenir cup ($9.99) or paper cup ($4.49).

Counter | French | Long waits

Liberty Tree Tavern [C-3] L $42, D $35 DDP T — 6 | 6 | 7

One if by land, two if by monorail! Disney's elegant, Colonial-styled inn serves a la carte lunches and all-you-can-eat dinners (note that character dining is no longer offered here). At lunch, choose from an assortment of enticing soups and appetizers ($5.99-$14.99), sandwiches ($14.99), salads ($5.99-$14.99), veggie sandwich ($12.99), turkey ($17.99), and New England Pot Roast ($19.99). Kids' meals are $8.59 (turkey, meaty macaroni, chicken flatbread, mac and cheese). The fixed-price dinner offers turkey, carved beef, smoked pork loin, and all the trimmings for $31.99 ($15.99/kids). Seating is at tables and chairs, and the dining rooms are well-themed. Closed until Nov. 20, 2015.

Table | American | Noisy | Reservations suggested | Call 180 days | Short waits | 11 am-3:30 pm, 4pm-closing

Main Street Bakery Starbucks [D-5] B $11, L $11, S $5 DDP O — 5 | 6 | 6

The Bakery offers Starbucks coffees ($3.99-$5.79) alongside its smoothies ($4.99), pastries, and fruit. The popular ice cream cookie sandwiches are no longer served here; you will find them at the Plaza Ice Cream Parlor. Enjoy your treats in the cute dining area with granite-topped tables and counters, or take it outside to the tables near the Plaza Restaurant.

Counter | American | Med. noise | Med. waits | Open all day

Pecos Bill Tall Tale Inn & Cafe [A-4] L $18, D $18, S $7 DDP O — 7 | 6 | 6

Just the place to rustle up a bowl of chili ($3.99), BBQ pork sandwich ($10.29), or cheeseburger ($9.59-$10.79)—they even have a well-stocked fixin's bar. Veggie burger and chicken salads ($9.99-$10.99) please the health-conscious. Sit on the covered porch to watch the parade. Themed rooms provide delightful indoor seating. Self-service ordering kiosks are in operation here! Tortuga Tavern is next door.

Counter | American | Very noisy | 10:30 am-1 hour before closing

Pinocchio Village Haus [D-1] L $16, D $16, S $7 DDP O — 6 | 6 | 5

Pinocchio's has a popular Italian menu that is nothing to "lie" about. Individual flatbreads ($8.79-$9.99), chicken nuggets ($9.29), Caesar salad with chicken ($8.99) and a chicken parmesan sandwich ($9.49) are on the menu. The Swiss-styled stone building fits perfectly with its surroundings. Sit outside at a patio table for Fantasyland sights; some inside tables have a great view of "it's a small world."

Counter | Italian | Noisy | 11 am-1 hour before closing

Top Photo Slice: Charming window boxes above Pinocchio Village Haus at the Magic Kingdom (9396) © Cheryl Pendry

Magic Kingdom Eateries

(continued)

Jennifer Dave Readers

The Plaza Restaurant [D-4] L $33, D $33, S $11 | 7 7 7

This small Main Street standby has an old-fashioned ice cream parlor atmosphere, offering large hot and cold sandwiches, including a Reuben ($12.49), Angus chuck burgers ($15.99), proper malts and shakes ($4.99), banana split ($8.49), and sundaes ($4.99–$6.49). A veggie sandwich ($11.99) and the chicken and strawberry salad ($15.49) are offered as "lighter" fare. Kids' meals are $8.59 with drink. Walk-up guests can expect a short wait before being seated. Tables and half-booths.

Table | American | Reservations suggested | 11 am–1 hour before closing

Jungle Skipper Canteen (coming in late 2015) | ? ? ?

This new Jungle Cruise-themed restaurant has several unique dining rooms, including a "once-hidden secret meeting room of the Society of Explorers and Adventurers." Not open at press time—see PassPorter.com for more details.

Unknown

Tomorrowland Terrace [E-4] L $15, D $15, S $7 | 5 5 6

Open seasonally with American and Italian fare, including a chicken sandwich ($9.99), bacon cheeseburger ($9.99), lobster roll ($12.49), Caesar salad ($8.99), and triple chocolate cake ($4.29). Tables and chairs are in a shaded, open-air (not air-conditioned) terrace. Seasonal fireworks dessert parties—see page 282.

Counter | American | Med. noise | 5–9 pm

Tortuga Tavern [A-4] L $16, D $16, S $7 | 6 6 7

Open seasonally. Informal meals near Pirates of the Caribbean. The brief menu includes burritos ($9.49), rice bowls ($11.49), and southwest salad ($10.99). The kid's meal offers a quesadilla or PB&J, carrots, grapes, and a drink ($5.49–$5.99).

Counter | Mexican | 11 am–4 pm

Tony's Town Square Restaurant [D-6] L $41, D $47 | 8 8 8

Tony's serves Italian cuisine in the heart of Main Street, U.S.A. Familiar dinner entrees include Tony's "special" spaghetti and meatballs from Lady and the Tramp ($18.99) and shrimp scampi pasta ($20.99). Less familiar but perhaps more interesting is a strip steak with port wine sauce ($32.99) and cannelloni ($17.99). The lunch menu offers pizzas and sandwiches ($12.99–$16.99), plus more elaborate entrees ($13.49–$17.99) like baked ziti. Kids' meals are $8.59.

Table | Italian | Reservations suggested | 12–3:00 pm, 5 pm–closing

Selected Magic Kingdom Snack Shops and Carts

Shop	Location	Offerings
Plaza Ice Cream Parlor	Main Street, U.S.A.	Hand-dipped ice cream
Aloha Isle*	Adventureland	Pineapple Dole Whips (frozen dessert)
Sunshine Tree Terrace*	Adventureland	Citrus Swirl, frozen yogurt
Aunt Polly's Dockside Inn*	Frontierland	Ice cream, sundaes, pie (seasonal)
Golden Oak Outpost	Frontierland	Chicken sandwiches, carrot cake
Liberty Square Market*	Liberty Square	Fresh fruit, baked potatoes
Sleepy Hollow	Liberty Square	Funnel cakes, root beer floats, coffee drinks
Friar's Nook	Fantasyland	Hot dogs, fries, apples, carrot cake
Storybook Treats	Fantasyland	Soft-serve ice cream, shakes
Maurice's Cart	Fantasyland	Ice cream, frozen bananas, drinks
Auntie Gravity's	Tomorrowland	Ice cream, smoothies
The Lunching Pad	Tomorrowland	Coney island dogs, frozen drinks
Cool Ship	Tomorrowland	Corn dogs, Mickey pretzels, turkey legs

Note: Some shops and carts may be seasonal. Eateries marked with an asterisk (*) close as early as 3:00–5:00 pm.

Top Photo Slice: The indoor fountain at Tony's Town Square at the Magic Kingdom (3212) © Jean Philo

Epcot Eateries

(park map on page 152)

Ratings: Jennifer / Dave / Readers

Akershus Royal Banquet Hall [B-3] B $52, L $54, D $60 — 7 | 8 | 8

Enjoy authentic Nordic fare (lunch is $41.53/$28.75 kids ages 3-9, dinner is $46.85/$25.55–includes tax) in a replica of a rustic Norwegian castle, complete with Disney princesses all day long. Many diners have been happily surprised by food that's both remarkably familiar and somewhat unusual. Cold buffet. Hot specialties are brought to your table. Enjoy meats, cheeses, pasta, pan-seared salmon, Kjøttkake (Norwegian meatballs), and a variety of salads. Kids can get chicken breast, salmon, junior beef, meatballs, macaroni, or pizza. Soft drinks and dessert are included. Breakfast ($40.46-$46.85/$24.49-$27.68 kids ages 3-9) offers a Norwegian Smorgasbord plus eggs, sausage, bacon, and potato casserole. For character meal details, see pages 262-263. Photo package discontinued in 2014.

Table | Norwegian | Med. noise | Reservations recommended | Call 180 days | 8:00-10:10 am, 11:55 am-3:30 pm, 4:55-8:35 pm

Biergarten [B-1] L $30, D $44 — 5 | 8 | 8

Willkommen! A Bavarian town square in the midst of Oktoberfest is the setting for a hearty and satisfying German buffet (lunch is $23.42/$12.77 kids; dinner is $37.99/$17.99 kids–tax included). Wurst (sausages) with sauerkraut, pork schnitzel, Spätzle, red cabbage, and roast chicken reign supreme at lunch. A first-rate sauerbraten and beef rouladen are added at dinner. Every dish and side dish is several cuts above the typical German eatery. Musicians in lederhosen are on stage to entertain. Can you say "Gemütlichkeit"? (It roughly translates to "good feeling.") A large salad bar may even please some vegetarians, but this isn't the place for a light meal. Desserts and soft drinks are included; beverages are extra. There's Beck's beer on tap and a good German wine list.

© MediaMarx, Inc.

Dancing during a Biergarten show

Buffet | German | Very noisy | Reservations recommended | Call 180 days | Short waits | Noon-3:10 pm, 4:00-closing

Monsieur Paul *(was Bistro de Paris)* [F-2] D $93 — 8 | 9 | 7

This upscale restaurant offers a leisurely, quintessentially French meal in quiet, elegant surroundings. And, no, it's not as stuffy as you might think. The escargot ravioli with parsley cream was a refreshing take on a classic, the filet of beef forestier spot on, and our companions were equally pleased with their picks. We see no values on the optional prixe fixe menu. The wine list is excellent, but pricey. Ask for a window seat and linger until IllumiNations.

Table | French | Reservations recommended | Short waits | 5:30-8:35 pm

Boulangerie Patisserie les Halles [F-2] L $18, S $7 — 7 | 7 | 9

Along with the changes to the France pavilion comes a move to bigger digs for this popular bakery, which is now inside the Galerie les Halles shop. The expanded menu has offerings such as a turkey and bacon sandwich ($8.50) and Poulet au Pistou ($8.50). The ham and cheese croissants ($4.75), a cheese plate ($9.50) and French bread ($2.95) make a nice, light lunch, while croissants ($2.25-$4.75), eclairs ($4.25), chocolate mousse ($4.50), and fruit tarts ($3.85-$4.75) satisfy sweet tooths. The bakery's old space became the new Glacier ice cream parlor!

Counter | French | Long waits | 9 am-closing

Epcot Eateries

(continued)

Jennifer Dave Readers

Chefs de France [F-2] L $55, D $65 — 6 7 8

Traditional French favorites such as escargot ($12.99), onion soup ($8.99), seafood Bouillabaisse ($32.99), and grilled beef tenderloin with black pepper sauce ($35.99) carry the imprint of some of France's most famous chefs. The bright, bustling brasserie atmosphere, crowded seating, and overtaxed serving staff can be at odds with the desire for a slow, enjoyable meal. Lunchtime choices such as Crepe a la Tartiflette de Savoie ($15.99), croque monsieur with side salad ($14.99), and quiche Lorraine ($14.99) will keep things affordable—save the heavier entrees ($16–$23) until dinnertime. Prix fixe menus available. Kids' meals are $8.50–$10. Chairs and half-booths. Special dietary requests are hit or miss here. Remy the rat (from "Ratatouille") makes visits here.

Table | French | Very noisy | Reservations strongly recommended | Call 180 days | Med. waits | Noon–3 pm 4:30 pm–closing

Coral Reef [D-7] L $56, D $59 — 6 7 7

Few restaurants are as breathtakingly beautiful as the Coral Reef—brightly glazed blue mosaic tiles and brushed metal shimmer in the light cast by The Seas with Nemo & Friends aquarium, as fish of all sizes and colors swim by. The inventive seafood menu ($22–$30) covers a variety of international tastes and styles and is generally well-prepared. Meat and veggie lovers will also find foods to enjoy here ($18–$33). If only there was more elbow room, the noise more restrained, and the service more consistent. Tip: Request a tank-side table for the best views. Sweets here are special, especially The Chocolate Wave ($8.99). Kids' meals are $8.99. Enjoy the same view at lunch (entrees $19–$32).

Table | Seafood | Noisy | Reservations strongly recommended | Call 180 days | 11:30–3:30 pm, 4:00–9:00 pm

Electric Umbrella [C-6] L $18, D $18, S $7 — 5 4 6

If you're looking for basic burgers ($9.99) at Epcot, this is the place. It's also decent for healthier fare, like veggie flatbread ($9.99) and Veggie Naanwich ($9.49)—you can also swap your fries for an apple. The main seating area is noisy—look for quieter seating upstairs, or dine outside on the terrace. Kids meals are $5.99–6.49. Tip: This eatery has an unlimited drink station for refills!

Counter | American | Med. noise | Short waits | ~11 am–9 pm

Fountain View Starbucks [D-6] B $11, S $8 — 6 6 8

Re-opened in September 2013 as a Starbucks. You can get Starbucks drinks ranging in price from $3.59–$5.49 along with lighter fare, such as breakfast sandwiches and wraps ($4.99), smoothies ($4.49), pastries, and fruit.

Counter | Coffee | ~9 am–9 pm

The Garden Grill Restaurant [F-6] B ?? L ?? D $47 — 8 7 8

This popular character dining experience is tucked away in The Land pavilion. Farmer Mickey, Pluto, Chip, and Dale make the rounds of this rotating restaurant at breakfast, lunch, and dinner. Watch an ever-changing American landscape while you eat. Breakfast (which begins Nov. 2015) has biscuits and gravy, scrambled eggs, bacon, Mickey waffles and Chip's Sticky Bun Bake. Lunch and dinner are the same—breads with maple butter, salad, turkey breast, beef strip loin, fish of the day, smashed potatoes, and greenhouse vegetables. A "homegrown" salad features veggies from Disney's hydroponic gardens. Vegetarians can make special requests. Kids ages 3–9 get a chicken drumstick or turkey breast—dessert is a "Life's a Bug" cake. Soft drinks included. Dinner price is $37.97/$19.10 ages 3–9. Try for a booth on the lower tier, which is closer to the scenery. See pages 262–263 for character meal details.

Table | American | Med. noise | Reservations suggested | Call 180 days | Short waits | Hours not known at press time

Top Photo Slice: Chefs and servers at Les Chefs de France (8409) © Cheryl Pendry

Epcot Eateries

(continued)

Jennifer | Dave | Readers

Kringla Bakeri og Kafé [B-3] L $15, D $15, S $7 — 5 | 6 | 8

This is a must stop for veteran World Showcase visitors. Have a light meal with gourmet sandwiches and soups ($7.49–$8.49). Or treat yourself to a "kringle" (sweet pretzel–$4.69), schoolbread ($2.69), troll cloudberry horn (a cream-filled pastry–$3.39), or other desserts ($2.19–$4.69). Kids meals are $5.49. Beer and wine by the glass. Nice outdoor tables. Popular before IllumiNations.

Counter | Norwegian | Med. noise | Long waits | ~11 am-closing

La Cantina de San Angel [B-4] L $20, D $20, S $10 — 6 | 6 | 6

This recently expanded waterside eatery is now offering both indoor and outdoor seating, including viewing areas for IllumiNations. The taco plates are $11.95–$12.25, cheese empanadas are $10.95, nachos are $10.95, and guacamole with chips are $7.50. The ever-popular churritos for dessert are $3.99. Kids meals $7.95. Their popular margaritas are $9.95–$14.50. Full service offered at dinner (see below).

Counter | Mexican | Med. noise | Med. waits | ~11 am-closing

La Hacienda de San Angel [B-4] D $61 — 5 | 8 | 7

This lagoon-side table-service restaurant serves dinner only. A mix of the familar and unusual, the flavors are well above typical "Mex." The excellent taco trio starter ($11.25) feeds two, roasted and grilled meats and fish entrees are $25.50-$32. Large windows overlook the lagoon and IllumiNations. Kids meals $8.99–$9.50.

Table | Mexican | Call 180 days | 4 pm-closing

Le Cellier [E-4] L $83, D $83 — 7 | 8 | 7

Oh, Canada! This steakhouse-in-a-stone-cellar is one of World Showcase's most popular spots, and reservations may be hard to get. Warm lighting, brocade upholstery, and stained glass make this the coziest cellar around—an upscale steakhouse style with Canadian accents. Both lunch and dinner are Signature Dining, and now serve the same menu all day. Appetizers ($10-$17) include wagyu carpaccio and lobster salad. Entrees ($28–$49) include a bone-in ribeye, mushroom filet mignon, Kurobuta pork, lamb rack, grilled waygu short rib, roasted free-range chicken, and yellow tail snapper. Sides of poutine fries, marble potatoes, and lobster mac and cheese are also available. The luscious cheddar cheese soup ($10) is a big favorite at any time. Leave room for dessert—smoking chocolate moose ($10) anyone?

A PassPorter reader shows off the kids' chocolate "moose"

Table | Canadian | Medium noise | Reservations strongly recommended | Call 180 days | Long waits | 12:30 am–3:55 pm | 4:00 pm–closing

Liberty Inn [C-1] L $18, D $18, S $7 — 4 | 4 | 5

Hot dogs, hamburgers, and chicken nuggets ($7.99–$11.99) weren't as American as peach cobbler ($5.99) back in Colonial days, but they are now. A toppings bar adds relish to the basic fare, while a Southwest chicken Caesar salad ($8.99) provides an alternative. Kosher items available. Seating indoors and out.

Counter | American | Short waits | ~11 am-closing

Eatery descriptions and ratings are explained on page 230.

Top Photo Slice: The roof of Kringla Bakeri of Kafé in Norway has plants growing on it! (ⓘ4197) © Lynn Mirante

Epcot Eateries

(continued)

Jennifer Dave Readers

Lotus Blossom Café [B-3] L $18, D $18, S $10 — 4 4 5

Counter | Chinese | Med. noise | Med. waits | ~11 am-closing

Chinese food at Epcot leaves a bit to be desired, and what for a while was an interesting menu has been dumbed-down. Start with pot stickers ($5.25) or egg rolls ($3.99). Main course choices are orange chicken, beef noodle soup, beef rice bowl, Hong Kong-style curry, and shrimp fried rice (each $9.99), and sesame chicken salad ($7.95). Desserts are $3.50. Kids' meal (sweet and sour chicken) is $7.95. Indoor and covered outdoor seating.

© MediaMarx, Inc.

Enjoying a meal at Lotus Blossom Cafe

Restaurant Marrakesh [F-1] L $45, D $55 — 9 7 8

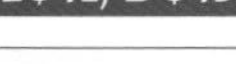

Table | Middle Eastern | Noisy | Reservations not always needed | Call 180 days | Short waits | 11:30 am–3:15 pm, 3:30 pm-closing

Enjoy exotic food in an authentic Moroccan setting as modest belly dancers and live musicians lend even more atmosphere. Lamb and chicken are the backbone of the cuisine, either roasted or stewed ($27.99). The flaky pastry-based appetizers ($5.95-$9.95) are a must, especially the chicken bastilla ($8.95)—this is one of Jennifer's all-time favorite foods in the World! If you've always wanted to try couscous, the Moroccan national dish of stewed meat and/or vegetables over steamed semolina, you'll find it is quite good here ($17.95-$19.95). Order a la carte, or choose from a variety of family-style feasts ($45 per person) at dinnertime. Plan to sample a variety of appetizers and desserts (desserts $5.95-$8.95). Check for bargain-priced specials at lunch. The kids' menu offers "Moroccan" pasta with meatballs, chicken tenders, and kefta (hamburger) with fries ($7.99).

Nine Dragons [B-3] L $41, D $43 — 7 8 6

Table | Chinese | Med. noise | Reservations suggested | Call 180 days | Medium waits | 12:00 pm–3:25 pm, 3:30 pm–park closing

Nine Dragons has improved the variety and adventure on its menu. Many regions of China are represented by familiar and unusual menu items. Appetizers ($4-$12) include pot stickers, hot and sour soup, and cold spicy beef. Main courses ($13-$26) include fried rice, sweet and sour pork, stir-fried veggies, kung pao chicken, fragrant five-spiced fish, and Chinese chicken salad. The Nine Dragons family dinner set includes soup, entree, and dessert ($23.98/person). Lunch choices and prices are similar, but you could create a dim sum-style meal from the cold and hot appetizers. A lunch set with a beef soup, choice of entree, and Chinese coleslaw is $18.98/person. Kids' entrees (sweet & sour shrimp, honey chicken, or shrimp and chicken) are $7.68-$10.98.

15864 © Cheryl Pendry

The renovated Nine Dragons

Top Photo Slice: Restaurant Marrakesh before diners arrive (1340) © Brad K.

Epcot Eateries

(continued)

Jennifer Dave Readers

Rose & Crown Pub and Dining Room [E-3] L $47, D $51 DDP T — 7 6 8

They say "heck" is a place where the cooks are English, but the food in this boisterous, crowded pub is quite nice. It's so cozy inside you'd swear you just walked in out of a London fog. Traditional specialties include fish & chips ($19.99), Shepherd's pie ($18.99), grilled steak with Yorkshire pudding ($28.99) and veggie cottage pie ($15.99). Start your meal (or simply snack) on a cheese plate ($12.49). Pub-style entertainers put in a regular appearance. A quieter meal with a view of IllumiNations may be had on the terrace—request a 7:30 pm (or earlier) reservation, check in early, request an outside table (no guarantee you'll get one, but ask anyway), and have a leisurely dinner. Don't forget a pint of ale, porter, or stout, a side of bubble and squeak ($4.99). And how about the sticky toffee pudding for dessert ($5.99)? Kids meals $8.59–$10.59.

Table | English | Very noisy | Reservations strongly recommended | Call 180 days | Long waits | ~12:00 pm–3:20 pm, 4:00–closing

San Angel Inn Restaurante [B-4] L $58, D $60 DDP T — 7 7 7

Where but Disney can you dine at noon in a romantic, twilit Mexican plaza, while a cool evening breeze caresses your skin, a volcano steams ominously on the horizon and boats float by on the Gran Fiesta Tour (see page 162)? Despite the fine, authentic Mexican food, it's the atmosphere that makes San Angel Inn (pronounced "San Anhel") a favorite. For appetizers, we suggest tostados ($10.50) or sopa Azteca (tortilla soup, $7.50). For your entree, try their wonderful Pollo a las Rajas (chicken with red peppers and onion cream sauce—$19.95) and Enchiladas Verdes con Pollo (pulled chicken tortillas—$18.95). Check the Chef's Selections for tempting items that go beyond simple "Mex." A separate vegetarian menu offers two choices ($13-$18). The kids can choose from quesadillas, tacos, or chicken tenders with Mexican rice ($8.50). La Cava del Tequila lounge is adjacent to this eatery, and offers more than 70 types of authentic tequilas ranging in price from $8 to upwards of $50. You can also get margaritas, tapas, and other appetizers in this 30-seat lounge.

Table | Mexican | Noisy | Reservations strongly recommended | Call 180 days | Med. waits | 11:30 am–4:00 pm 4:30–closing

Sommerfest [B-1] L $15, D $15, S $7 DDP O — 5 6 7

Hearty, German fare for light eaters. Sommerfest serves bratwurst ($9.49), frankfurters (with sauerkraut, of course—$9.29), Nudel Gratin ($3.79), Black Forest cake ($4.29), and apple strudel ($4.29). Wash it down with German wine ($7.50), schnapps ($7.50), or German beer ($8.25, or $13.25 in a souvenir mug). Covered seating is outdoors, within earshot of the oompah bands.

Counter | German | Noisy | Med. waits | ~11 am–closing

Spice Road Table [E-1] L $57, D $57, S $8 — 7 - 6

This waterfront eatery features tapas, small plates, olive oils, and wines from the Mediterranean. Menu items include (Alexander's favorite) fried calamari ($12), Harissa chicken roll ($8), and lamb sliders ($8), Mediterranean omelet ($7), Moroccan lamb sausage ($9), mussels tagine ($10), rice stuffed grape leaves ($8). Entrees include mix grill skewers ($38), yellowfin tuna ($27), Coriander-crusted lamb ($30), roasted chicken ($26), and Mediterranean vegetable platter ($24). Desserts include assorted baklava ($7), chocolate pyramid ($7), and lemon custard ($7). There's also an extensive drink menu—Jennifer enjoyed the red Spice Road Signature Sangria ($10.99), but didn't care for the white version. The restaurant has 120 outdoor terrace seats (some with a good view of IllumiNations) and 60 indoor seats.

Table | Moroccan, Mediterranean | Call 180 days | Med. waits, but long waits at end of day | 11:30 am–3:55 pm 4:00–9:00 pm

Top Photo Slice: Balloons above Sunshine Seasons in The Land (ⓘ4185) © Melissa Hasbrouck

Epcot Eateries

(continued)

Jennifer Dave Readers

Sunshine Seasons [F-6] B $12, L $18, D $18 — 7 7 8

Designed to look like an airport food court (to go along with Soarin' nearby), this eatery features an open kitchen and food stations themed to the seasons. The Soup and Salad station (spring) offers a tuna noodle salad ($11.49). The Asian station (summer) has a sweet and sour chicken ($11.39) and a vegan Tamarind beef with rice ($7.99). The Grill (fall) has a rotisserie chicken ($12.29) and grilled fish ($12.49). And the Sandwich station (winter) offers fish tacos ($11.79) and a turkey sandwich ($10.49). The Bakery offers various pastries, cakes, pies, espresso, and ice cream. Kids' meals ($5.99-$6.99) include a pizza panini, mac and cheese, mongolian beef, or a chicken leg. Seating is inside at tables and chairs.

Counter | Cuisine varies | Noisy | Long waits | ~9:00 am–closing

Tangierine Cafe [E-1] L $19, D $19, S $10 — 7 7 7

Tangierine Café offers traditional Middle Eastern sandwiches and combo platters served in a delightfully decorated, open-air café. Choose from shawarma (sliced chicken or lamb), roast chicken or vegetarian platters, and sandwiches and wraps ($8.99-$14.99). Desserts are a deal—for $2.50 you can add baklava to your meal. A coffee and pastry counter is tucked in the back, making this cafe an excellent choice for mid-afternoon espresso and honey-drenched desserts. Kids' meals are $7.99. Indoor and outdoor seating.

Counter | Middle Eastern | Med. noise | Med. waits | 11:00 am–closing

Teppan Edo [E-1] L $56, D $56 — 8 6 8

The Teppanyaki Dining Room got refreshed decor and a new name a few years ago, but the "teppan" dining concept survives. Guests sit around steel-topped griddle/tables, upon which meat and veggies are cooked by a flamboyant chef. Starters include tempura ($8.95), a bit of sushi ($9.95), or novel Yaki-Sushi—sushi rolls cooked at the table. Entree choices are steak ($30.95-$31.95), chicken ($24.95), or seafood ($25.95-$29.95), alone or in a variety of combos ($17.95-$29.95), all cooked the same way and served with the same veggies and rice. It's tasty, fun, and a good "adventure" for families and timid eaters. Tables seat eight and are often shared by several parties.

Your food is prepared in front of you on the grill ⓘ22851 © Cam Matthews

Table | Japanese | Noisy | Reservations recommended | Call 180 days | Long waits | 12–3:45 pm, 4:00–closing

Tutto Italia Ristorante [C-1] L $62, D $69 — 7 8 7

"Tutto Italia" means "all Italy," and this eatery's menu surveys the cuisine from south to north. Prices are high, but the quality is easily a match. The mixed antipasto for two ($29) is a delight. Pastas ($19.40-$29) include fettuccine with pancetta and parmesan cream, lasagna, and seafood risoto. Braised lamb shank, swordfish, rosemary chicken, and polenta with braised meats are hearty entrees ($26-$30). Lunch offers salads ($17-$20), entrees ($24-$28) and panini ($17-$19). Kids meals are $10 and offer pastas or mozzarella sticks. Desserts ($9-$13) include bugie/chiacchere (their signature anise and Sambuca-flavored crisp pastry) and cannolis. The casual Tutto Gusto wine bar offers wine flights, a mouth-watering array of antipasti, "small plates" ($8-$22), and the full Tutto Italia menu.

Table | Italian | Very noisy | Reservations strongly recommended | Call 180 days | 11:30–3:30 pm | 4:30–closing

Top Photo Slice: Chandelier at Tangierine Cafe (ⓘ12714) © Cheryl Pendry

Epcot Eateries

(continued)

Jennifer | Dave | Readers

Tokyo Dining [E-1] L $61, D $61 DDPT 10 | 8 | 9

Like Teppan Edo, this restaurant was renovated from a previous incarnation (the former Tempura Kiku and Matsu No Ma eateries) into a larger, more trendy eatery. Tokyo Dining showcases the traditional cuisine of Japan, with an emphasis on sushi. Appetizer choices include edamame ($5.95), miso soup ($3.95), and tempura ($9.95). Entrees range from tempura ($16.95-$25.95), deep-fried cutlets ($21.95-$28.95), grilled meats ($21.95-$29.95), to bento boxes with a sampling of traditional Japanese delicacies ($29.95). Kids meals come in a shinkansen (bullet train) shaped bowl and include your choice of tempura or teriyaki chicken ($10.50-$11.50). Desserts such as green tea cheesecake ($6.95) are excellent. The sushi bar has a large "mood screen" showing iconic Japanese images—very relaxing on a busy theme park day. The main dining room offers lovely views of the World Showcase Promenade. During IllumiNations, the lights are dimmed and the music is broadcast over the eatery's speakers.

Table | Japanese | Med. noisy | Medium waits | 12 pm-3:45 pm, 4:00-closing

Via Napoli Ristorante e Pizzeria [C-1] L $57, D $57 DDPT 7 | 7 | 7

In a pizza mood? This eatery in Italy offers wood-fired pizzas and other Southern Italian favorites. With a design inspired by Naples 45 Ristorante e Pizzeria in NYC, this casual restaurant seats 300 and features three wood-burning ovens named after active volcanos in Italy: Etna, Vesuvius, and Stromboli. Menu items include a variety of appetizers and salads, including Gamberetti Fagioli ($9) and calamari ($14). Pizzas are made with imported flour and tomatoes, and water closely resembling that found in Naples—they are available in three sizes (individuals for $16–$18, large 8-slices for $28–$30, and ½ meter 12 slices for $39–$41) and nine varieties. Lasagna ($20) and spaghetti ($21) are also offered, as well as Piatti alla Parmigiana with eggplant ($22), chicken ($26), and veal ($30). Desserts range from tiramisu ($9) to gelato ($9) to Zeppole di Ricotta ($10).

ⓘ23775 © Erin Newman

Via Napoli

Table | Italian | Reservations recommended | Call 180 days | Long waits | ~11:30 am-4:25 pm, 4:30 pm-closing

Katsura Grill [D-1] L $18, D $18, S $9 DDPO 7 | 5 | 8

Formerly Yakitori House. Of the Japan pavilion's three eateries, we visit here most often for tasty, filling, and economical fare. This classic Japanese quick-meal spot serves skewers of grilled teriyaki chicken, salmon, or beef as a platter or in a combo with shrimp tempura ($8.99-$12.99), satisfying beef curry over rice ($9.99), sushi ($7.99-$9.99) and big, filling bowls of Udon noodle soup ($10.99). Wash it down with hot sake or cold Kirin beer. Dine at tables indoors or out, and take a few minutes to stroll through the nearby bonsai display. Kids' meal is $7.50.

Counter | Japanese | Medium noise | ~11:30 am-closing

Yorkshire County Fish Shop [E-3] L $17, D $17, S $4 DDPO 7 | 8 | 7

Crowds have been queuing up and strolling away with Harry Ramsden's legendary Fish & Chips ($9.99), and for good reason—it's the real thing! (Dave can't resist it!) An extra side of chips is $2.69. Wash it down with a Bass ale or Harp lager draft ($8.25). Soft drinks also available. Seating at patio tables is often available to the right, or visit the United Kingdom gardens to eat.

Counter | English | Med. noise | ~11:30 am-closing

Eatery descriptions and ratings are explained on page 230.

Top Photo Slice: Patio seating for Yorkshire County Fish Shop on the World Showcase Lagoon (ⓘ5555) © Amy Sellars

Epcot Eateries

(continued)

Snacking at Epcot is every bit as diverse and rewarding as feasting in its fine restaurants. The snack carts and shops seem to appear and change regularly, however, so a definitive snack list isn't practical. Instead, we've listed our favorite treats at Epcot and where you can find them—this will give you an idea of the variety of snacks available. If you can't locate one of our favorite munchies, chances are very good you'll find a new tidbit that we haven't yet discovered!

Our Favorite Snacks at Epcot

Treat	Found At
Churros (fried dough rolled in cinnamon sugar) DD PS	Mexico (Cantina de San Angel)
Pretzels, Lefse, and School Bread DD PS	Norway (Kringla Bakeri og Kafé)
Italian pastries and cappuccino	Italy (along promenade)
Funnel cakes (deep-fried batter with powdered sugar)	The American Adventure
Kaki Gori (shaved ice with sweet flavoring)	Japan (along promenade)
Baklava (flaky pastry with honey, rosewater, and nuts)	Morocco (along promenade)
Wine by the glass	France (along promenade)

Note: Some shops and carts may be seasonal.

International Food and Wine Festival

Eager to sample more international cuisine and exotic tastes? Visit the "World" in autumn, when Epcot hosts the International Food and Wine Festival. Just stroll around the World Showcase Promenade and sample food and drink at more than 25 booths. The generously sized appetizer treats range in price from $2 to $7, while small plastic glasses of wine, beer, champagne, cognac, and port begin at $3 and go up from there. Guests on the Disney Dining Plan may be able to use their snack credits for many of the food items. You can easily make a meal out of the offerings, stopping at booths whenever you discover another appetizing snack. Eating while strolling around isn't always the most relaxing, but there are plenty of benches and quiet nooks at which to munch away. In addition to the treats, you can watch cooking demonstrations by top chefs, participate in beer and wine seminars and tastings, and attend the Eat to the Beat concert series at the America Gardens Theater (no extra charge). With advance reservations, you can join special wine tasting events ($95–$150), a Party for the Senses (a $145 wine-sipping and food-sampling extravaganza), wine schools (day-long education programs for $150), and one-hour Food and Wine Pairings ($65). Sweets lovers will enjoy the 3D Disney's Dessert Discovery event, which includes desserts, cordial samplings, and a VIP viewing of IllumiNations ($55). The 17th annual festival is likely to run from September 23 to November 14, 2016. For more information, call 407-WDW-INFO.

ⓘ12664 © Cheryl Pendry

Food booth at the Food and Wine Festival

Top Photo Slice: The frozen sweetness of a Kaki Gori from Japan © MediaMarx, Inc.

Disney's Hollywood Studios Eateries

(park map on page 172)

Ratings: Jennifer / Dave / Readers

ABC Commissary [C-3] — L $18, D $18, S $7 — DDP QS — 5 | 6 | 5

Carpeted floors, potted palms, and sleek decorating make you feel like a special employee. The International menu features a seafood platter ($9.99), New York Strip Steak ($11.99), Asian salad ($7.69), chicken club ($9.59), and burgers ($9.99–$11.49). Kids can get chicken nuggets, a cheeseburger, or a ham and cheese wrap ($5.99). Kosher items available. Shady outdoor seating, too.

Counter | American | Med. noise | Med. waits | Open all day

Backlot Express [C-5] — L $18, D $18, S $7 — DDP QS — 5 | 5 | 7

Rarely crowded and often overlooked, this backstage-themed cafeteria serves up burgers, hot dogs, chicken nuggets, pressed turkey club, and a Southwest chicken salad ($6.79–$8.99). Kids meals are $5.49–$6.49 (includes drink). Pleasant indoor and outdoor seating. Perfect spot for watching the parade—stake out a table about a half-hour beforehand. Not always open.

Counter | American | Noisy | Short waits | 11 am–closing

Cantina (coming with Star Wars Land) — – | – | –

Disney just announced that a new Star Wars-themed cantina will open in the new Star Wars Land (see page 173). Details are sketchy still, but based on the concept art it will bear a strong resemblance to the Mos Eisley cantina seen in Episode 4. We even hear they will serve blue milk! Watch passporter.com for more details as we draw closer to the new Star Wars Land.

Unknown

Catalina Eddie's [G-3] — L $14, D $14, S $5 — DDP QS — 4 | 5 | 6

Part of the outdoor Sunset Ranch Market mini food court. Cheese and pepperoni pizzas ($9.49–$9.99), chicken Caesar salad ($8.99), hot Italian deli sandwich ($9.49), and vanilla cake with chocolate custard ($4.29) make up the menu. Outdoor, shaded (and not-so-shaded) seating. Nearby food stands serve fries, fresh fruit, barbecue, burgers, and ice cream.

Counter | American | Med. noise | Short waits | 11 am–closing

Fairfax Fare [G-3] — B $13, L $19, D $19 — DDP QS — 5 | 4 | 5

Part of the outdoor Sunset Ranch Market, this quick-service eatery offers a menu with chicken and ribs ($15.69), barbecued pork sandwich ($9.49), 1/2 slab of ribs ($12.99), and kids' meals of PB&J or mac & cheese ($5.99). Breakfast egg & cheese muffin ($5.99), yogurt ($1.99), and Danish ($2.69). Seating is outdoors at covered picnic benches. Other food stands are nearby.

Counter | American | Noisy | Med. waits | 11 am–closing

'50s Prime Time Cafe [E-5] — L $45, D $45 — DDP PT — 8 | 6 | 8

Clean your plate in an old kitchenette, while "Mom" serves gussied-up versions of home-cooked meals like meatloaf, pot roast, fried chicken, salmon, grilled pork tenderloin, pasta potpie, sandwiches, and salads ($13.49–$20.99), and scrumptious malts, milkshakes, and sundaes ($5.49–$6.49). Vintage TV clips of "I Love Lucy" and "The Honeymooners" play while you eat, and your "brother" and "sister" (your servers) boss you around when your "Mom" isn't watching. This is a unique dining experience if you're willing to play along—not recommended for the overly shy. Veggie burgers on request. The dining areas and adjoining bar/waiting area are a wonderland of '50s-vintage Formica, television sets, and knickknacks. Table and booth seating.

Table | American | Noisy | Reservations strongly recommended | Call 180 days | Long waits | 11 am–3:15 pm, 3:30 pm–closing

Eatery descriptions and ratings are explained on page 230.

Top Photo Slice: The "kitchen" at 50s Prime Time Cafe in Disney's Hollywood Studios (①8217) © Brigett Duncan

Disney's Hollywood Studios Eateries

(continued)

Jennifer | Dave | Readers

Hollywood & Vine [E-5] B $34, L $38, D $38 DDP T — 7 | 7 | 7

This 1940s-inspired "Cafeteria of the Stars" has star power with a character breakfast and lunch buffet ("Play 'n Dine") with Playhouse Disney friends, including Sofia the First, Doc McStuffins, Handy Manny, and Jake. It's a tasty and economical choice for a pre-Fantasmic! dinner. Stainless steel serving areas, comfy half-booths, retro tables, checkerboard tiles, and a mural of old Hollywood set the scene. The menu changes regularly—choices may include pot roast, salmon, baked chicken, and fish. The kids have their own buffet, and everyone can make sundaes. Breakfast is $26.62–$30.88 ($15.97–$17.03/kids), lunch is $30.88–$34.90 ($14.90–$18.10/kids), and dinner (no characters) is $30.88–$34.90 ($14.90–$18.10/kids). Available with the Fantasmic! dinner package at the same price (see below).

- **Buffet**
- American
- Noisy
- Reservations suggested
- Call 180 days
- 8:00–11:20 am, 11:40–2:25 pm, 4:00 pm–closing

The Hollywood Brown Derby [E-3] L $57, D $75 DDP 2 — 8 | 8 | 8

The famous Brown Derby, complete with "stars," serves enticing starters like sweet corn bisque ($11), crab cakes ($15), and the yummy and original Cobb Salad ($9/$16). Entrees include loin of lamb ($42), duck confit ($37), and pork tenderloin ($36). Dessert is your choice of three mini desserts for $9 (such as chocolate sphere, banana toffee cake, and grapefruit cake). Kids' entrees with drink are $6–$14. The Brown Derby is the Studios' most elegant establishment. Off-white walls covered with caricatures of the stars, dark wood trim, crisp, white table linens, and attentive, formal service set the tone. Hollywood "personalities" may jazz up the show. An outdoor lounge with walk-up only seating is also available. This restaurant offers some special meals—for information on the Fantasmic! Meal Package, see below; for the Dine with an Imagineer experience, see page 267.

- **Table**
- American
- Med. noise
- Reservations strongly recommended
- Call 180 days
- Long waits
- 12–3:25 pm, 3:30 pm–closing

Mama Melrose's Ristorante Italiano [A-4] L $48, D $48 DDP T — 6 | 5 | 7

Mama's is a brick wall and booth sort of place. A variety of individual wood-fired pizzas ($12.99-$13.99), light pasta specialties, and simple meats grace the menu at Mama's, which changes regularly. Starters include calamari ($11.99) and mozzarella with tomatoes ($8.99). Charred strip steak ($32.99), chicken parmigiana ($18.99), wood-grilled chicken ($18.99) or seafood arrabbiata ($23.99) may catch your eye. Sangria, a Bellini cocktail, and desserts like chocolate amarettini cheesecake ($5.49) may catch your attention. Ask about the Fantasmic! Dinner Package, which offers a three-course dinner plus seating at Fantasmic! (see pages 173 and below). Your little "bambini" can get pasta, pizza, grilled fish, or chicken parmigiana for $8.59.

- **Table**
- Italian
- Med. noise
- Reservations suggested
- Call 180 days
- Short waits
- 11:30–4:10 pm, 4:15 pm–closing

Fantasmic! Meal Package DDP 1 DDP 2

If you're thinking about a table service lunch or dinner at Disney's Hollywood Studios, consider the Fantasmic! Dinner Package. You get a meal at Hollywood Brown Derby, Mama Melrose, or Hollywood and Vine *plus* seats in the reserved section at the Fantasmic! nighttime show, at the price of the meal alone. To qualify, everyone in your party must order a meal (if you dine at Hollywood & Vine, you must get the fixed-price meal). Credit card deposit required, and there is a $10 cancellation fee if canceling less than 48 hours beforehand. Call 407-WDW-DINE to make reservations up to 180 days in advance, or ask about it at Lobby Concierge at your Disney hotel or at Guest Relations in the park (see map on page 172 for location). Availability is very limited. Note: Details may change and Fantasmic! is not held every night. Note that no rain checks are issued for your Fantasmic! seating if it is canceled for bad weather.

Top Photo Slice: Dining in "cars" at the Sci-Fi Dine-In Theater (14907) © Janet Simonsen

Planning | Getting There | Staying in Style | Touring | Feasting | Making Magic | Index | Notes & More

Disney's Hollywood Studios Eateries

(continued)

Jennifer | Dave | Readers

Rosie's All-American Cafe [G-3] L $18, D $18, S $7 DDPO — 4 | 4 | 6

Part of the outdoor Sunset Ranch Market mini food court on Sunset Blvd., Rosie's is really a hamburger stand offering 1/3 lb. cheddar cheeseburgers ($10.49), fried green tomato sandwich ($9.49), chicken nuggets ($9.29), soup ($3.29), and desserts ($4.29). Seating is outdoors at covered picnic benches. Other stands nearby offer pizza, barbecue, ice cream, and fresh fruit.

Counter | American | Med. noise | Med. waits | 11 am–closing

Sci-Fi Dine-In Theater Restaurant [C-4] L $47, D $47 DDPT — 7 | 7 | 6

Build a drive-in theater in a movie soundstage, seat folks in replica vintage cars, serve souped-up drive-in fare, and show old sci-fi movie trailers. Would anyone buy that script? You and the kids will at this fanciful eatery. The menu is fun and portions are huge. Definitely get a shake ($5.19)—you can get "adult" (alcoholic) shakes, too. The kids' menu is classic "drive-in," but the adult menu has upscale choices like New York strip steak with garlic herb butter ($31.99) and shrimp pasta ($23.99). At lunch, try the Angus chuck burger ($17.49) or smoked turkey sandwich ($13.99). The desserts are out of this world ($5.99–$7.99). Everyone faces the screen, so chatting is hard. Not all seats are "parked cars"—request one if you want it. Kids' menu is $8.99.

Table | American | Noisy | Reservations strongly recommended | Call 180 days | Med. waits | 11 am–4 pm, 4 pm–closing

Studio Catering Co. [B-3] L $18, D $18, S $7 DDPO — 7 | 6 | 6

This eatery offers a melting pot of flavors. Offerings include a beef brisket sandwich ($10.49), spicy ranch chicken ($9.69), turkey and cheese panini ($10.49), melon salad ($9.99), and strawberry parfait ($4.39). Kids can have the choice of chicken nuggets or a mini veggie wrap ($.49). Sangria is also offered ($6.95). Tables are outside but sheltered.

Counter | Mediterranean | Med. noise | Med. waits | 11 am–closing

Toy Story Pizza Planet [B-5] L $17, D $17, S $7 DDPO — 3 | 4 | 6

The name is familiar, but this pizzeria/arcade doesn't look all that much like the pizza palace in Toy Story. Choose from individual pizzas ($9.99), meatball sub ($9.49), or a antipasto salad ($8.49). There's also a cappuccino cupcake ($4.99) and cookies ($2.99). It's an OK place to eat and rest while your little "Andy" or "Jessie" hits the arcade. Seating upstairs and outside.

Counter | American | Very noisy | Long waits | 11 am–closing

Disney's Hollywood Studios Snack Shops and Carts

Name	Location	Specialties
Dinosaur Gertie's Ice Cream DDPS	Echo Lake	Soft-serve ice cream
Min & Bill's Dockside Diner DDPS	Echo Lake	Shakes & malts, sausage sub
Peevy's Frozen Concoctions DDPS	Echo Lake	Frozen slushes, bottled drinks
Herbie's Drive-In DDPS	Streets of America	Corn dogs, chili dogs
Anaheim Produce DDPS	Sunset Boulevard	Fresh fruit, drinks
Hollywood Scoops DDPS	Sunset Boulevard	Hand-dipped ice cream
Starring Rolls Cafe DDPS	Sunset Boulevard	Baked goods, coffee, sandwiches
Toluca Legs Turkey Co. DDPS	Sunset Boulevard	Turkey legs, beverages

Note: Some shops and carts may be seasonal.

Top Photo Slice: Dinosaur Gertie near Echo Lake at Disney's Hollywood Studios (11674) © Donald Willis

Disney's Animal Kingdom Eateries

(park map on page 186)

Jennifer Dave Readers

Flame Tree Barbecue [E-4] L $12, D $12, S $7 — 6 6 6

Although we're not sure how barbecue fits in with the Animal Kingdom motif, we can't knock it, because it's good stuff. Pork, chicken, turkey, and beef are smoked right on premises and is available sliced on sandwiches ($9.49) and arrayed on platters ($10.99–$16.19). You can even get a turkey leg meal ($13.49). The condiment stations offer traditional and mustard-based barbecue sauces. A watermelon salad ($8.99) is the light alternative. Chicken drumstick, chicken sandwich, hot dog, and PB&J for the kids ($5.49–$5.99). Shaded outdoor seating in a lovely Asian garden or on decks overlooking the lake and Expedition Everest.

© MediaMarx, Inc.

Outdoor seating at Flame Tree Barbecue

Counter | American/Barbecue | Quiet | No reservations | Med. waits | 11 am–5 pm

Harambe Market [B-4] L $14, D $14 — 6 ? 6

Inspired by African street food, this recently expanded eatery offers four walk-up stations with specialities like karubi ribs ($13.39), grilled chicken skewer ($8.99), beef and pork sausage ($8.99), and African milk tart ($4.49). Kids meals are $7.49 (grilled chicken skewer, snack pack, ribs or corn dogs).

Counter | African | 11:00 am–5:00 pm

Pizzafari [B-4] B $10, L $13, D $13 — 4 4 7

This popular pizzeria centrally located in Disney's Animal Kingdom serves individual cheese and pepperoni pizzas ($9.69–$10.69), chicken Caesar salad ($9.19), and a hot Italian sandwich ($9.49). You can also get a veggie pizza ($9.69). Kids meals are $5.99. Breakfast platters ($8.99), breakfast panini ($6.49), kids French toast ($4.99), and cinnamon rolls ($3.19) are offered in the morning. There's lots of indoor, air-conditioned seating in brightly decorated, uniquely themed dining areas. Look for quieter seating toward the back of the restaurant or outside on the patio. Kosher items available here. Closed for refurbishment at press time. Rumors are circulating that Pizzafari could be expanded to table service (either in full or part), or change into an entirely new restaurant—check passporter.com for details!

Counter | Italian | Very noisy | Long waits | 10:00 am–5:00 pm

Rainforest Cafe [B-7] B $18, L $48, D $48 — 5 6 7

Environmentally conscious dining in an artificial rainforest hidden behind a two-story waterfall? It even rains indoors! The Rainforest Cafe puts on quite a show and piles your plate with tasty, inventive foods representing many different cuisines. Hearty breakfasts ($8.99–$13.99), enormous sandwiches ($12.99–$16.99), pastas ($18.99–$21.99), steaks, chicken, and ribs ($18.99–$30.99), seafood ($22.99–$26.99), and mountainous salads ($15.99–$16.99) overflow the menu. Smoothies and specialty alcoholic drinks are popular. Located just outside the gates (no park admission required). This was the first table-service restaurant at Disney's Animal Kingdom. There's a special entrance for folks exiting and re-entering the park. For discounts, see page 229.

Table | American | Very noisy | Call 407-WDW-DINE for reservations | Long waits | 8:30 am–1.5 hours after closing

RESTAURANTOSAURUS

Disney's Animal Kingdom Eateries

(continued)

Jennifer Dave Readers

Restaurantosaurus [E-6] L $19, D $19, S $8 DDP DDPQ | 5 | 5 | 8

DinoLand's only sit-down meal offers choices like an Angus bacon cheeseburger ($10.69), mac and cheese hot dog ($9.99), chicken nuggets ($9.29), chicken BLT salad ($9.99), black bean burger ($10.19), and chocolate mousse or cheesecake in a glass ($4.59). Kids meals are $6.99–$7.49 for your choice of turkey wrap, PB&J, corn dog nuggets, or cheeseburger. The indoor, air-conditioned dining areas are fun—it's a weathered, dig site bunker with broken equipment, humorous signs, and educational displays. Note: The fries and nuggets here are no longer McDonald's versions but rather Disney's, and are pretty good.

Counter | American | Very noisy | No reservations | Long waits | 11:00 am–park closing

Tusker House Restaurant [B-2] B $37, L $41, D $44 DDP DDPT | 7 | 8 | 8

This buffet restaurant offers a character breakfast and lunch, plus imaginative food offerings for dinner. You can start your day with "Donald's Safari Breakfast Buffet" with friends like Mickey, Goofy, Daisy, and Donald (of course). Breakfast food includes biscuits and gravy, vegetable frittata, cheese blintzes, scrambled eggs, rotisserie honey-glazed ham, yam casserole, and warm cinnamon rolls for $29.99–$33.01 ($15.99–$18.01/kids). Lunch is $31.99–$35.14 ($17.03–$19.16/kids) and dinner is $31.99–$35.14 ($15.99–$18.10), and both include a wide variety of dishes, including salads, curried rice salad, vegetarian couscous, salmon filet, carved beef and pork, and curry chicken. A kids' station stocks corn dog nuggets, mac and cheese, chicken drumsticks, and corn (among other items). Desserts are fruit cobbler, warm banana-cinnamon bread pudding, and pastries. Seating is at tables and chairs in several large dining rooms.

© MediaMarx, Inc.

A couple of the inventive options at Tusker House

Buffet/Table | American | Noisy | Call 180 days | 8:00–10:55 am | 11:00 am–3:30 pm, 4:00–5:30 pm

Yak & Yeti (*Counter Service*) [E-3] L $14, D $14, S $7 DDP DDPQ | 6 | 5 | 7

This counter next door to the restaurant by the same name (see next page) offers familiar Asian favorites in cute little boxes, such as teriyaki beef bowl ($10.99), honey chicken ($9.99), Korean stir-fry barbecue chicken ($9.99), Asian chicken sandwich ($9.99), and ginger chicken salad ($9.99). Sides such as pork egg rolls ($3.29) and chicken fried rice ($3.99) are also available. Kids' meals are $5.49–$5.99 and include your choice of cheeseburger or chicken bites. Seating is at plentiful tables and chairs, though shade is something of a scarce commodity. You could also take your tray to the riverside seating area behind Drinkwallah (see photo to right).

© MediaMarx, Inc.

A Yak and Yeti meal

Counter | Asian | Noisy | No reservations | Long waits | 10:30 am–park closing

Eatery descriptions and ratings are explained on page 230.

Disney's Animal Kingdom Eateries

(continued)

Jennifer Dave Readers

Yak & Yeti (*Table Service*) [E-3] L $50, D $50 DDPT 8 8 8

The Asian-themed eatery offers interesting Asian-fusion cuisine. Menu offerings include appetizers such as lettuce cups ($13.99), Thai chili chicken wings ($9.99), and a dim sum basket for two ($13.99). Wonton soup ($4.99) and huge Mandarin chicken salad ($15.99) are also available. Entrees include seared miso salmon ($24.99), duck with Anandapur glaze ($23.99), Shaoxing steak and shrimp ($25.99), and maple tamarind chicken ($19.99). Lo mein noodles are also available ($17.99- $18.99). Desserts include mango pie ($6.99) and fried wontons ($7.99). Kids' entrees are $8.49 and include your choice of mini burger, veggie lo mein, chicken bites, or egg roll, and a drink. The dining rooms on both floors are imaginatively decorated and worth a tour after your meal. The theme is evocative of the Western Himalayan foothills in India and Nepal, the dining rooms full of Asian antiques. There's also a shop next door selling Asian-inspired items.

Table
Asian-American
Noisy
Call 180 days
10:00 am-3:30 pm
4:00 pm-closing

The upper floor of Yak & Yeti offers nice views of Asia ⓘ8088 © Cheryl Pendry

Enjoying lo mein noodles © MediaMarx, Inc.

Disney Animal Kingdom's Snack Shops and Carts

Name	Land	Specialties
Dawa Bar	Africa	Beer, cocktails
Harambe Fruit Market DDPS	Africa	Fresh fruit, juices, beverages
Kusafiri Coffee Shop & Bakery DDPS	Africa	Pastries, cappuccino & espresso
Tamu Tamu Refreshments DDPS	Africa	Burgers, shakes, and Dole Whip
Anandapur Ice Cream DDPS	Asia	Soft-serve ice cream, soda floats
Dino Bite Snacks DDPS	DinoLand U.S.A.	Ice cream, sundaes, churros
Dino Diner DDPS	DinoLand U.S.A.	Hot dogs, chips
Trilo-Bites DDPS	DinoLand U.S.A.	Smoked turkey legs, drinks

Note: Some shops and carts may be seasonal.

Tip: Expect some dining changes to come to this park when Rivers of Light opens sometime in 2016, as it will bring expanded hours and with it more dining opportunities.

Top Photo Slice: Windows above the entrance to Yak & Yeti (ⓘ14730) © Janet Simonsen

Disney Springs Marketplace Eateries

(map on page 206)

Jennifer Dave Readers

Earl of Sandwich — B $11, L $13, D $13, S — 6 6 7

The menu was updated and portions are a bit smaller, but it's still a good deal! This eatery is perfect for a lunch or a light supper in cozy British decor and the menu offers a dozen appetizing hot sandwiches on specialty bread (roast beef & cheddar, ham & brie, and a turkey, bacon, & swiss club—all $5.99-$6.99 each), Cobb and Chinese chicken salads ($6.99), and grab 'n go items—sandwiches ($4.95), tuna, fruit, or chicken salads ($5.99), and tomato soup ($3.99). Hot breakfast sandwiches ($3.99) in the morning, and a kids' menu ($2.99-$3.99). 10% discount for annual pass and DVC.

Counter | Eclectic | Noisy | Medium waits | 8:00 am–11:00 pm

Ghirardelli Soda Fountain & Chocolate Shop — S $12 — 6 6 8

Who can resist the pleasures of San Francisco's famed chocolatier? Sundaes, sundaes, and more sundaes ($8.95-$9.50) tempt dessert fans, or share an eight-scoop Earthquake ($34.95). If that's too much, cones, shakes, malts, and frozen mochas beckon ($6.25-$6.95). Their whipped cream-topped hot chocolate ($4.25) is perfect on cool winter evenings. Sugar- and fat-free ice cream, too.

Counter | American | Med. waits | 9:30 am–12:00 am

Rainforest Cafe — L $50, D $50 — 5 6 7

Another Rainforest Cafe? Yes, and it's very similar to the one at Disney's Animal Kingdom (see page 245 for menu items and descriptions). Differences include a smoking volcano atop the restaurant and lunch and dinner only (no breakfast). This is a very popular stop for families. Show up, sign up, and be prepared to wait. Occasional live animal demonstrations help pass the time. If the wait is too long, you can sit at the Juice Bar and order from the regular menu, or browse the Rainforest gift shop. Near the Disney Springs Marketplace bus stop. Open until midnight on Fridays and Saturdays. For discounts, see page 229.

Table | American | Very noisy | 407-WDW-DINE | Long waits | 11:30 am–11:00 pm

T-Rex — L $48, D $48 — 7 7 7

It's fair to call T-Rex a prehistoric-styled Rainforest Cafe (they're both owned by Landry's Restaurants). Roaring Audio-Animatronics dinos replace trumpeting elephants, and occasional meteor showers substitute for rainstorms. It's a greater, more elaborately-executed spectacle than the nearby Rainforest Café (look for mineral and fossil specimens). The food is good, with the same approach to flavor (big), serving size (huge) and theming (over the top) as its sister-restaurant—a wide choice of mostly American plus popular international items, with fanciful names. Appetizers ($9.99-$15.99) include bruschetta, nachos, quesadillas, reliably good flatbread pizzas, and a gargantuan and satisfying sampler ($18.99, or $24.99 with ribs). After that, if you have room for entrees, is a long list of oversized entrée salads ($15.99-$17.99), burgers and sandwiches ($12.99-$16.99), pastas ($17.49-$18.99), and meat and fish specialties ($17.99-$31.99). Desserts are $7.99-$14.99. Kids menu is a la carte, with entrees $6.99-$7.99, drinks $1.99, and desserts $2.99.

Table | American | Very noisy | Call 407-828-8739 for reservations | Very long waits | 11:30 am–11:00 pm

Wolfgang Puck Express — B $19, L $20, D $20, S — 6 6 7

Fast food for the trendy, upscale set. Puck's famous wood-fired pizzas ($11-$14), cavatappi chicken Alfredo ($15), half rotisserie chicken ($16), and oven roasted salmon ($18) are served hot. Salads ($7-$13), and appetizing sandwiches ($10-$13) are available in the refrigerator cabinet. Desserts are $2-$6, and children's items are $7. Drink homemade lemonade, frozen cafe mocha, wines by the bottle and glass, and beer on tap. Dine outside, or take out. See page 252 for Wolfgang Puck Grand Cafe over at the West Side.

Counter | American | Med. noise | Med. waits | 9:00 am–11:00 am, 11 am–10 pm

Top Photo Slice: Outdoor waterfront dining at Rainforest Cafe at Disney Springs © MediaMarx, Inc.

Disney Springs The Landing Eateries

(continued)

Jennifer / Dave / Readers

The BOATHOUSE — L $88, D $88 — – | – | –

This new upscale eatery features pricey waterfront dining with live music, "floating artwork" (classic wooden boats), and boat rides. Guided tours aboard a wooden, Venetian-style water taxi include champagne and chocolate-covered strawberries. Guided Amphicar cars (yes, cars!) launch from land, enter the water, and take guests on a 20-minute tour of the landmarks of Disney Springs. Managed by the folks behind Chicago's Gibsons Bar & Steakhouse, menu items include bone-in ribeyes, Chilean sea bass, fish tacos, and grouper. Opened in April 2015.

Table | Steak/seafood | Reservations accepted | 11 am–3:55 pm, 4 pm–11 pm

Cookes of Dublin — L $20, D $20, S — DDP QS — 6 | 6 | 7

This small "chippie" beside Raglan Road offers hand-battered fish & chips ($10.95), scallops ($12.95), chicken ($9.95), Dublin-style meat pies ($11.95) and fried (donut-battered) candy bars ($3.50). Seating is mostly outside and uncovered.

Counter | Irish | 3 pm–11 pm

The Edison (opening 2016) — L, D — – | – | –

In the mood for 1920s cabaret and contortionists? This new "industrial gothic" restaurant will serve you in one of several themed rooms, such as "The Tesla Lounge," "The Radio Room," or the "The Patent Office." Expect American food and craft beers. Read our review after it opens at PassPorter.com.

Table | American

Fulton's Crab House — L $59, D $77 — DDP 2 — 6 | 7 | 8

A boatload of seafood, served in a replica of a riverboat (sans paddlewheel) just outside The Landing. The fish is flown in fresh every day, and the prices suggest it flew First Class. Preparations are straightforward—grilled, steamed, fried, or raw, with appropriate sauces. Crab lovers can choose from nearly a dozen entrees featuring crab ($29–$65). Maine lobster ($49), and the finest seasonal fish, shrimp, oysters, and clams ($25–$35) also appear in many forms. Steaks make a strong showing, too ($48). Prices aren't too bad if you avoid crab and lobster. Try the créme brulée. Kids' entrees are $8–$10.

Table | Seafood | Very noisy | Reservations accepted | 11:30 am–3:55 pm, 4 pm–11 pm

Jock Lindsey's Hangar Bar — L D — – | – | –

Did you know that Indiana Jones' pilot was named Jock Lindsey? He was, and he now has his own restaurant with signature cocktails and small plates, such as "Air Pirates Everything Pretzels" and "Rolling Boulder Meatballs." Aviation decor filling the eatery, with, vintage travel posters covering the walls and correspondence between Jock, Indy and their fellow adventurers on display. You can even go outside to Jocks' old steamboat. Read more at PassPorter.com after it opens.

Table | American

Morimoto Asia (Fall 2015) — L, D — – | – | –

Morimoto Asia will be Iron Chef Masaharu Morimoto's first-ever pan-Asian restaurant featuring flavors from across the continent. This Disney Springs dining destination will include unique exhibition kitchens showcasing traditions like Peking duck carving, and dim sum. "I'm very excited to bring this new concept to Disney, something I've always dreamed of," said Chef Morimoto. "It's a wonderful chance to share some of my favorite foods from across the Asian continent." The two-story restaurant is scheduled to open in the fall 2015 at The Landing (formerly Pleasure Island) in Disney Springs. Morimoto Asia will feature waterside seating, terraces, a grand hall and a cocktail lounge.

Table | Asian

Top Photo Slice: Fulton's Crab House at Disney Springs (ⓘ27411) © Cheryl Pendry

Disney Springs The Landing and West Side Eateries

(map on page 206)

Jennifer Dave Readers

Paradiso 37: Taste of the Americas L $52, D $52 — 8 6 7

This waterfront eatery features street foods from the 37 countries of the Americas. Typical menu items include Barbacoa beef quesadilla ($14.99), South American crazy corn ($9.99), North American corn dogs ($11.99), shrimp ceviche ($12.99), steak ranch salad ($18.99), jalapeno burger ($16.99), steak burritos ($16.99), Baja fish tacos ($16.99), and Argentinian skirt steak ($25.99). Kids meals are $7.99 and include choices such as corn dogs, mac 'n' cheese, tacos, cheeseburgers, grilled fish, and chicken fingers. Desserts include the Mexican chocolate brownie ($7.99), churros ($7.99), guava cheesecake ($8.99), and pineapple upside down cake ($7.99). Also offered are signature frozen margaritas, an extensive tequila "tower" with more than 50 types, an international wine bar, and nightly entertainment. Seating is both outdoors and indoors at the colorful, two-level restaurant. We think both the food and atmosphere are unique, and this is a nice change of pace from other eateries at Disney Springs.

Table | American (North, South, & Central) | Noisy | Reservations recommended | Call 407-934-3700 for reservations | 11:30 am–11:00 pm (open until midnight on weekends)

Portobello L $40, D $50 — 5 6 8

Contemporary Italian specialties are served in a bustling setting. Meals are robust and flavorful, and sometimes memorable—we've been disappointed by mediocre meals and excess noise, but we enjoyed others and loved our first. Specialties include an extensive antipasto menu ($8–$16), grilled meats and fish, including a grilled mahi mahi ($28) and flat iron steak ($29). Pastas include ravioli gigante ($20) and linguine with shrimp ($25). There's a fine, if expensive, wine list. Desserts include sinful chocolates, fresh fruits, and sorbet ($5.95–$7.95). Lunch features pizzas and sandwiches ($9.95-$12.95).

Table | Italian | Very noisy | Reservations accepted | Call 180 days | Med. waits | 11:30 am–11 pm

Raglan Road L $52, D $56 — 6 7 7

This large and comfortable Irish pub has a great atmosphere, four bars, live entertainment after 9:00 pm, and an updated menu of old Irish comfort foods that make this a worthy stop. Starters of a "kiss before shrimp" ($13) and "mighty mussels" ($12) are satisfying choices, as are main courses like "bangers & booz" ($18), fish and chips ($19), a modernized Shepherd's Pie ($19), and a schnitzel ($21). Desserts ($8) include bread & butter pudding, fluffy lemon clouds, and black forest kiss. Kids' menu ($8–$10) includes burgers, fish & chips, and shepherd's pie.

Table | Irish | Call 180 days | Med. waits | 11 am–2:45 pm, 3–11 pm

STK Orlando (late 2015) L D — – – –

This modern, upscale steakhouse opens in late 2015 in the former spot of Comedy Warehouse (circa Pleasure Island). Notable features of this eatery—which already has locations in Los Angeles, Las Vegas, and NYC—include rooftop dining and a sleek lounge with a DJ. Menu items include a wide variety of steaks, from skirt steaks to porterhouses, as well as salads (romaine, apple and endive, chopped vegetable), burgers, sandwiches (grilled tuna club, pulled duck confit), and sides (creamy Yukon potatoes, sweet corn pudding, haricot vert, mac & cheese). There may also be a raw bar available for those interested in oysters and shrimp. Learn more after the restaurant opens at PassPorter.com.

Table | Steakhouse

Eatery descriptions and ratings are explained on page 230.

Disney Springs
The Landing and West Side Eateries

(map on page 206)

Jennifer | Dave | Readers

Bongos Cuban Cafe — L $53, D $53 — 4 | 6 | 7

The lively Latin sounds and flavors of Miami's South Beach make Gloria Estefan's Bongos a popular choice. Black bean hummus ($7), seafood platter ($45), creole shrimp ($26), skirt steak ($29), ropa vieja ($16), fried plantains ($6), and flan ($5.75) are some of the authentic Cuban choices. The lunch menu offers mainly sandwiches. The bar serves classic rum drinks, including the Mojito, a refreshing mix of white rum, mint, and sugar. An outdoor counter serves sandwiches and snacks from 9:30 am–midnight. Lunch served on Friday and Saturday only.

Table | Cuban | Noisy | No reservations | Long waits | 11 am–11 pm

Crossroads at House of Blues — L $48, D $48 — 8 | 7 | 8

The funky House of Blues' menu has changed away from its Cajun and creole offerings to a more varied menu. The cornbread ($7.99), pulled pork sliders ($9.99), and jambalaya ($18.49) are two beats ahead of any place similar in the "World," and you can get fine burgers, meatloaf, steaks, ribs, salads and sandwiches, too. The "HOB" looks like a weather-beaten wharfside dive. Inside is an equally aged interior with comfy booths. Live blues bands keep the joint cookin'. Headliners play at the concert hall next door. A Gospel Brunch is held every Sunday (see page 266 for details). Open to 2:00 am on Thu.-Sat.

Table | American | Very noisy | Reservations suggested | Long waits | 11:30 am–10:00 pm

FoodQuest (closing in 2016) — L $17, D $17, S — 4 | 6 | 6

FoodQuest serves chicken Caesar salad ($8.99), wraps ($9.29), chicken parmesan sandwich ($9.49), chicken nuggets ($9.29), and individual flatbread pizzas ($8.19–$9.99) to guests at DisneyQuest (you must have DisneyQuest admission to dine here). Desserts and snacks are $3.59-$4.19. Kids' meals are $4.99. Note: DisneyQuest is closing sometime in 2016.

Counter | American | Noisy | 12:00 pm–9:00 pm

Planet Hollywood — L $53, D $53 — 5 | 5 | 6

Everyone will be entertained and well-fed inside Planet Hollywood's big, blue globe full of movie and TV memorabilia. Every visitor gets the Hollywood treatment—you have to pass by the bouncers at the bottom of the stairs and walk under a long awning to reach the front door. There's seating on several levels, with views of projection video screens showing TV clips and movie trailers. You don't really come for the food, or do you? The menu can please almost anyone, with entree salads ($13.99–$19.99), sandwiches and burgers ($11.99–$14.99), pastas ($14.99–$19.99), fajitas ($19.99), and grilled and roasted meats ($19.99–$25.99). Kids' meals and desserts are $7.95. Portions are huge, quality is average, and service can be slow.

Table | American | Very noisy | Reservations at 407-WDW-DINE | Call 180 days | Med. waits | 11 am–1 am

Splitsville Luxury Lanes — L $50, D $50 — 6 | 7 | 7

Enjoy your eats while bowling, or just dine at a table and watch—either way this is a fun, if noisy, place to enjoy a meal. Typical American pub food such as loaded fries ($11) and pizza ($13–$16) join other offerings such as California roll ($11), barbecue chicken salad ($15) and mahi mahi with voodoo shrimp ($25). Kids meals are $7. If you want to bowl while you eat, it's $15–$20/person for 90 minutes (arrive before 5:00 pm for better deals)—but remember, you're on the clock if you eat while you bowl!

Table | American | Call 180 days | Med. waits | 10:00 am–2:00 am

Top Photo Slice: This old, rusty water tower serves as the sign for House Of Blues (3504) © Lynn Mirante

Planning | Getting There | Staying in Style | Touring | Feasting | Making Magic | Index | Notes & More

Disney Springs West Side Eateries

(continued)

Jennifer | Dave | Readers

The Smokehouse — L $14, D $14 — 7 | – | 7

The quick-service eatery opened up right next to (and as part of) the House of Blues in January 2014. Prices are good and the service is fast! Menu items include smoked turkey leg ($7.99), smokehouse nachos ($7.99), St. Louis ribs ($12.99), hot dog ($6.99), pulled chicken sandwich ($9.99), pulled pork sandwich ($9.99), smoked beef brisket ($11.99), baked beans ($1.99), cole slaw ($1.99), potato chips ($1.00), brownies ($1.25), soft drinks, beer, wine, and cocktails (full bar available). Meats are smoked on site in the House of Blues kitchen. Seating is outdoors on the "front porch" with local live music every night of the week.

Counter | Barbecue | Noisy | Medium waits | 11:30 am–5:00 pm, 10 pm–closing

Starbucks Coffee — B $13, S $8 — 6 | – | 8

A big, fancy Starbucks opened here in 2014 (there's a smaller one in the Marketplace) with innovative features such as a grass roof (fed by recycled coffee grounds), an interactive screen that links to the Starbucks in Anaheim (you can draw your own messages on it), and a special Starbucks Reserved counter with rare and exotic coffees (a wee bit higher priced, but not bad). Of course, your usual Starbucks favorites and bakery items are available for sale as well (see page 235). Indoor and outdoor seating (with outdoor fireplace and moss mural).

Counter | Coffeehouse | Noisy | Medium waits | 10:00 am–midnight

Wolfgang Puck Grand Cafe — L $54, D $54 — DDPT — 7 | 6 | 7

Puck is famous for nearly single-handedly popularizing California cuisine and for putting wood-fired, individual pizzas on the map. Menu favorites include crab cake ($16), bacon-wrapped meatloaf ($15), bruschetta ($12), pesto chicken ($23), those legendary pizzas including BBQ chicken ($17) and roasted salmon ($28), and his Chinois chicken salad ($16). Oh, and the sushi bar is to die for! Desserts include Florida key lime pie ($9), brownie sundae ($9), classic carrot cake ($10), and cheesecake ($9). Kids meals include spaghetti ($7), California roll ($9), and pepperoni pizza ($9). The decor is trendy, the tables for two are too small, service is spotty, and dinnertime seating requires long waits. If you're in a rush, dine at the bar or outdoors. Conditions are much nicer at lunch.

Table | American | Very noisy | Reservations at 407-WDW-DINE | Very long waits | 11:30 am–11:00 pm

Wolfgang Puck Dining Room — D $77 — DDP2 — 8 | 7 | 8

Climb the broad staircase inside Wolfgang Puck Grand Cafe and you'll reach the upscale Dining Room, offering refined respite from the crowds below, when not booked for parties. Starters include tuna tartare ($20), hibachi sashimi ($16), and sauteed sea scallops ($18). Entrees include roasted duck breast ($40), wild mushroom ravioli ($29), sashimi platter ($35), miso glazed salmon ($34), and crispy pork schnitzel ($33). Three- and Four-course "Chef Tours" are $50.95 and $54.95, respectively. Kids meals are $9-$10. Call 407-WDW-DINE for reservations and parties.

Table | American | Noisy | Reservations recommended | Call 180 days | Long waits | 6-10:00 pm

Wolfgang Puck Express — B $19, L $21, D $21 — DDPQ — 5 | 6 | 8

Fast food for the trendy, upscale set. Puck's famous wood-fired pizzas, rotisseried rosemary garlic chicken, real macaroni and cheese, soups, and pastas are served hot. Enjoy a wide choice of salads and appetizing sandwiches, soft drinks, and alcoholic beverages. Part of Wolfgang Puck Grand Cafe. Dine outside, or take out. See page 248 for Wolfgang Puck Express at Marketplace.

Counter | American | Med. noise | Med. waits | 11 am–11 pm

Top Photo Slice: Wolfgang Puck at Disney Springs West Side (①6281) © Cheryl Pendry

Resort Restaurants

Disney's Animal Kingdom Lodge Resort Restaurants

Ratings: Jennifer / Dave / Readers

☐ Boma–Flavors of Africa — B $26, D $48 — DDP T — 8 | 8 | 9

Savor the many flavors of Africa at a fabulous buffet. Breakfast is $20.23-$24.49 ($11.71-$13.84/kids) and dinner is $35.14-$39.40 ($17.03-$19.16/kids); tax included. At dinner, a dazzling array of unusual soups, stews, salads, veggies, and wood-grilled meats tempt both timid and adventuresome diners (including kids and vegetarians). The wood-burning grill and exhibit kitchen add extra flavor to the marketplace décor. And the dessert station is fabulous—be sure to try the Zebra Domes. Breakfast is equally wonderful but more down-to-earth. Diners are consistently amazed by the wide variety of pleasing new tastes, and even plain meat-and-potatoes lovers are delighted. Book ahead and arrive early, as even the line to check in can be long.

Buffet | African | Very noisy | Reservations strongly suggested | Call 180 days | Long waits | 7:30 am–11 am, 4:30–9:30 pm

☐ Jiko–The Cooking Place — D $85 — DDP 2 — 9 | 9 | 9

African flavorings meet Californian and Asian influences with grace and style at Jiko. Savory appetizers include grilled wild boar tenderloin, crispy duck bobotie roll, and flat breads from wood-burning ovens ($9–$16). Entrees include Senegal scallops ($40), maize-crusted tilefish ($40), vegetable and tofu sambusas ($30), Botswana beef short ribs ($46), and harissa chicken ($34). Jiko boasts a AAA Four Diamond rating, among other honors. Fish and vegetarian items take the limelight, and you'll also find a strong Afro-Mediterranean influence. For dessert, try the chocolate and tea safari ($10). Phenomenal South African wines. Kids have their own menu with appetizers ($3–$4) and entrees ($8–$12). Dress code is "business casual" (see page 228).

Table | African | Noisy | Reservations strongly suggested | Call 180 days | 5:30 pm–10:00 pm

☐ Sanaa — L $43, D $52 — DDP T — 7 | 9 | 8

Sanaa's menu is almost entirely Indian, including samosa appetizers ($8.99), lamb kefta sliders ($9.49), spiced chickpea cakes ($6.99), and a good line-up of Indian breads ($10.49 for a sampler that serves two or more) as well as a salad sampler ($7.49). Entrees include lamb shank ($26.99), traditional sosatie (braii lamb, $19.99), butter chicken ($20.99), tandoori chicken ($20.99), braaivleis sampler plate ($25.99), sustainable fish (market) and a New York Strip steak ($32.99). The dining room is very attractive, offering great views and a quieter, more intimate version of the rustic style seen at Boma. The wine service here is a big deal, but beer ($7.25 for imports) or a mango lassi smoothie ($4.99) would be more traditional. There's even Kenyan press pot coffee here ($6.79). Lunch offers a similar menu at somewhat lower prices. Kid's meals are $8.99 and include fish, grilled chicken with basmati rice, shrimp with quinoa, cheese pizza with naan crust, and cheeseburger. Desserts ($5.49-$6.99) are never a big deal at Indian eateries but here you get shahi turka bread pudding ($6.49), Tanzanian chocolate mousse ($5.99), stone fruit samosa ($5.49), and seasonal kulfi ($5.49. There are also a dozen specialty hot teas ($6.29).

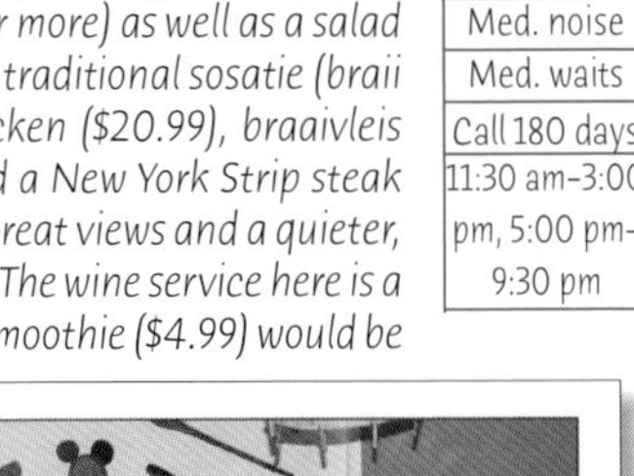

Table | African | Med. noise | Med. waits | Call 180 days | 11:30 am–3:00 pm, 5:00 pm–9:30 pm

(i)14543 © Cheryl Pendry

PassPorter friends together on opening night at Sanaa

Top Photo Slice: Pretty lights hanging over tables at Boma ((i)10899) © Gina Pesca

Resort Restaurants

Jennifer Dave Readers

BoardWalk Resort Restaurants

See page 261 for Beach Club eateries.

Big River Grille & Brewing Works L $47, D $47 DDP T — 3 | 4 | 4

No, you won't see Brewmaster Mickey, but this brewpub chain is a popular family dining spot at the BoardWalk (ESPN Club seems to siphon off the rowdier drinking crowd). Choices range from chicken quesadilla ($10.99) to a grilled chicken cashew salad ($12.99), barbecue pork sandwich ($9.99, lunch only), burgers ($10.99–$13.99), or meatloaf ($14.99). Steaks and ribs are also plentiful ($22.99–$25.99). The decor and seating are simple—we suggest you dine outdoors on the boardwalk in good weather. Our most recent visit was disappointing, with lackluster service, mediocre food, and a dirty floor. They do take reservations 24 hours in advance as well as reservations on the same day at 407-560-0253.

Table | American | Noisy | Reservations accepted within 24 hrs. | Med. waits | 11:30 am–11:00 pm

ESPN Club L $44, D $44 DDP T — 4 | 4 | 7

100 TVs pipe the big games into every nook and cranny of this very popular (and loud) sports bar. You can even go on camera for a live sports trivia quiz. The lineup is familiar—red wings ($11.49), nachos ($11.99), burgers and sandwiches ($10.49–$14.49), or try some rocky road cake ($5.99), plus beer and mixed drinks. Sit at booths or on stools. Open until 2:00 am on weekends. This eatery is very busy during any sport playoff as well as Sunday afternoons. No reservations.

Photo: ©945 © MediaMarx, Inc.

ESPN Club on the BoardWalk

Table | American | Very noisy | Med. waits | 11:30 am–1:00 am

Flying Fish Cafe D $82 DDP 2 — 8 | 8 | 8

This is a Disney dining hot spot and one of our favorites, serving uniquely prepared, fresh seafood in a trendy-but-fun atmosphere. The menu changes to suit the season and the catch. Appetizers are special. Dave was blown away by their plump steamed mussels ($18). The "Chef's Thunder" portion of the menu offers daily specialties, such as oak grilled Caribbean day-boat swordfish ($34), while the main menu may offer a red snapper in a crispy, sliced-potato wrapper ($36) or Maine diver scallops ($35). There's strip steak, pork, and pasta for the fish-shy ($28–$43) and not-to-be-missed desserts. The crowds here are loud—ask for a quieter table in the back. Inquire about the excellent prix fixe menu at the Chef's Counter! Open to 10:30 on Fri. and Sat. Dress code is "business casual" (see page 228).

Table | Seafood | Very noisy | Reservations strongly recommended | Call 180 days | Med. waits | 5:30 pm–10 pm

Trattoria al Forno B $18, L $49, D $49 DDP T — 7 | – | 7

This Italian restaurant (it replaced Kouzzina by Cat Cora) features classic Italian cuisine with housemade mozzarella, fresh cavatelli pasta, and wood-burning oven-fired pizzas. Breakfast is also served and includes frittata ($13.49), caramel apple crumb pancakes ($11.99), and cured Italian meats ($12.99). Dinner menu items include Caprese salad ($9.99), shaved Italian meats ($15.99), Margherita pizza ($16.99), baked lasagna ($18.99), chicken parmigiana ($21.99), cannoli pizzelle ($6.99), and "spaghetti" gelato and "meatballs" ($5.19).

Table | Italian | Reservations recommended | Call 180 days | Expect long waits

Eatery descriptions and ratings are explained on page 230.

Top Photo Slice: Neon fish above the Flying Fish Cafe sign © MediaMarx, Inc.

Resort Restaurants

Caribbean Beach Resort Restaurant

Jennifer | Dave | Readers

Shutters — D $55 — DDP T — 6 | 6 | 6

Serving American cuisine inspired by the flavors of the Caribbean, this 120-seat, casual family restaurant has a breezy, island atmosphere. Menu items include pan-seared crab cakes ($12.49), barbecue shrimp and grits ($11.49), banana-crusted mahi mahi ($22.99), Caribbean surf & turf ($32.99), and pork two ways ($23.99). For dessert, go with the flancocho ($5.99). Kids meals (pizza, steak, fish, pasta, chicken breast, or chicken nuggets) are $8.59.

Table | Caribbean/American | Reservations suggested | 5:30–10 pm

Contemporary Resort Restaurants

California Grill — D $101 — DDP 2 — 8 | 8 | 8

High atop the Contemporary, overlooking the Magic Kingdom, California Grill pours fine wines and serves seasonally-inspired California cuisine. This eatery reopened in September 2013 after a lengthy refurbishment with an updated menu and new decor. New offerings include an omakase service at 8:00 pm with 12–14 courses of sushi and more (chef's choice), pork two ways, baked local prawns, wild Columbia River salmon, and charcuterie on olive board. Guests sit at stand-alone tables, at the sushi bar, or at one of the two new solid teak tables that seat 10 guests each. The noise can be deafening, but the fireworks bursting over Cinderella Castle are spectacular. The menu changes weekly, but count on inventive dishes. When available, the peaceful Wine Room has the same menu, and you may see Epcot's IllumiNations. Dress code is "business casual" (see page 228). Note: Diners check in on the second floor of the Contemporary and are escorted up to the 15th floor when their table is ready. Only guests who have a reservation may watch the Magic Kingdom fireworks from the observation deck beside the restaurant (if you finish your meal before the fireworks, you may show your receipt at the podium to enter the observation deck).

Table | American | Very noisy | Reservations strongly recommended | Call 180 days | Long waits | 5:30 pm–10:00 pm

Chef Mickey's — B $43, D $54 — DDP T — 6 | 6 | 8

Chef Mickey's fills the Contemporary's cavernous lobby with all sorts of Goofy antics (not to mention Mickey, Minnie, and friends). Mickey's offers separate adult and kids dinner buffets ($41.53/$20.23 kids 3–9) and a sundae bar. Breakfast buffet ($37.99/$19.99) includes omelets and pancakes cooked to order. Brunch ($37.99/$19.99) was added in 2015 with selections from the breakfast and dinner buffets. Dinner items change, but we've seen roast beef, tasty pork loin, and cod with a curry crust, all of a quality and presentation befitting a deluxe resort. See pages 262–263 for character meal details.

Buffet | American | Very noisy | Reservations suggested | 7–11:30 am, 5:00–9:30 pm

Wave... of American Flavors — B $24, L $50, D $58 — DDP T — 7 | 8 | 7

In keeping with the Contemporary resort's theme, this eatery focuses on serving locally-grown foods that are organic and sustainable in a "wave of American flavors." Breakfast choices include sweet potato hash ($11.49) and a ham & cheese omelet ($12.49). The lunch menu offers items like Mediterranean tuna salad ($19.99), Reuben sandwich ($13.99) and vegetable stew ($17.49). Dinner brings a strawberry and blueberry salad ($8.99), lamb chops ($33.99), and chicken breast ($21.99). Dessert flights are $8.99 each and include three tasting portions of cakes, mousse, biscotti, etc. Kid's meals are $8.99–$10.99.

Table | American | Reservations suggested | Call 180 days | 7:30–11 am, Noon–2:00 pm, 5:30–10:00 pm

Top Photo Slice: A wave on the ceiling at The Wave in the Contemporary Resort (ⓘ12440) © Cheryl Pendry

Resort Restaurants

Coronado Springs Resort Restaurant

Jennifer Dave Readers

Maya Grill	D $56	5	6	5

Maya Grill has re-invented its menu yet again, returning to its Mexican roots. The restaurant is almost too elegant for a moderate resort, with grand, soaring architecture evoking a Mayan temple in warm yellows and accents of deep blue, shimmering gold, and rich woods. On the menu are green tortilla soup ($7), fried tomatillos ($11), shrimp tacos ($23), fajita skillet ($25), Mayan pork loin ($23), red snapper Vera Cruz ($27), Cornish hen ($20), and beef short ribs ($27). There are also some seasonal signature platters ($43-$58) with an array of tempting dishes. Kids' menu available with quesadilla, chicken taco, and chicken tenders, ranging in price from $6.95 to $9.50. Note: Breakfast and lunch are no longer served.

Table | American | Med. noise | Reservations suggested | Call 180 days | Short waits | 5:00 pm, 10:00 pm

Fort Wilderness Resort Restaurant

Trail's End Restaurant	B $22, L $40, D $30	7	6	6

One of the best dining deals on Disney property. While the vittles at Trail's End won't win awards for elegance, the food is plentiful, fresh, and tasty. Breakfast buffets ($19.16/$11.71 kids 3–9, tax. incl.) are hearty and heavy on home-style classics—eggs, French toast, Mickey waffles, hash, donuts, biscuits and gravy, cereals, yogurt, and fruit. Lunch is now a la carte, with chili, fried chicken and waffles, sauteed catfish, spicy grilled shrimp, burgers, and fried green tomatoes ($11.49-$15.99). The dinner buffet is gentle on the wallet at $26.62/$15.90, and you still get a tasty soup, salad bar, peel-and-eat shrimp, chicken, ribs, carved meat, fish, good veggies, pizza, and a daily regional specialty. Soup & Salad bar is $11.50.

Table/Buffet | American | Med. noise | Reservations accepted | Short waits | 7:30–11:30 am, 11:30–2:00 pm, 4:30–9:30 pm

Grand Floridian Resort Restaurants

Cítricos	D $86	9	8	9

A grand restaurant at the Grand Floridian, Cítricos blends the fresh flavors of Florida and the Mediterranean with simplicity and elegance. Warm colors, tall windows, and well-spaced tables make this a very comfortable place. The menu changes frequently. Sauteed shrimp ($14) and tapas plate ($14) are appealing appetizers. A wonderful braised veal shank is available as an entree ($46), along with pan-seared red snapper ($38), Berkshire pork two ways ($33) and seared tofu ($23). The wine pairings ($29.50) are a fine idea, and the desserts ($8-$10) are gorgeous! Now open seven days a week. Kids' menu entrees $6–$13. Dress code is "business casual" (see page 228).

Table | Floridian | Med. noise | Reservations suggested | Call 180 days | Short waits | 5:30–9:30 pm

Garden View Tea Room	$71	7	7	6

If you've ever yearned for afternoon tea, this is the place for it. The quiet, genteel Victorian setting is perfect for finger sandwiches, buttery scones, jam tarts, strawberries and creme, and pastries in all-inclusive tea "offerings," with or without champagne. Prices range from $30-$48 per person, or you can get "tea for two" for $150-$175. Mrs. Potts Tea, for the young ones, is $13. A good variety of teas is served. Site of "My Disney Girl's Tea Party" (see page 274).

Lounge | English | Call 180 days | 2–5 pm

Eatery descriptions and ratings are explained on page 230.

Top Photo Slice: Lemon cheesecake with raspberry sauce at Citricos (ⓘ10906) © Dawn Erickson

Grand Floridian Resort Restaurants *(continued)*

Jennifer | Dave | Readers

Grand Floridian Cafe — B $26, L $41, D $50 — 5 | 6 | 6

This "informal" cafe features an American menu with all the extra flourishes found in finer restaurants. Hearty breakfasts range from a frittata to lobster eggs Benedict ($9.99–$17.99). Lunch brings entree salads ($14.49–$18.49), shrimp and pasta ($16.99), and sandwiches include a Reuben and a burger with lobster, asparagus, and hollandaise ($10.99–$18.99). Dinner offers steaks, grilled fish, and pasta ($17.99–$28.99), and that over-the-top burger($18.99). Kids' complete meals are $6.09 at breakfast and $8.59 at lunch and dinner, with pizza, grilled chicken or salmon. Steak is a $2 up-charge.

Table | American | Very noisy | 7–11 am, 11:45 am–2 pm, 5–9 pm

Narcoossee's — D $99 — 8 | 8 | 8

Narcoossee's open kitchen serves an ever-changing menu of grilled seafoods with savory accompaniments. Perched on the edge of Seven Seas Lagoon, the restaurant has a sedate and casual dockside atmosphere, with lots of bare wood and windows affording views of the Magic Kingdom fireworks and the Electrical Water Pageant. Specials like tilefish with lobster fritters ($36), plus crispy whole snapper ($35) and steamed Maine lobster ($58) are tempting choices, and carnivores can have filet mignon ($45) or chicken breast ($29). Desserts ($8–$15) include a gelato sampler, key lime créme brulée, and a cheese plate. Kids' entrees are ($7–$12). Dress code is "business casual" (see page 228). A new waterfront brunch begins on Nov. 22, 2015—$69/adult, $41 kids.

Table | Seafood | Noisy | Reservations recommended | Call 180 days | Short waits | 6–10 pm (lounge open 5–10 pm)

1900 Park Fare — B $30, D $49 — 7 | 7 | 7

Daily character meals in a jolly Victorian setting, complete with an orchestrion ("player" organ). The upscale buffet breakfast is $22.36–$26.62 ($12.77–$14.90/kids) and features Mary Poppins, Alice in Wonderland, and the Mad Hatter. Waits can be long, but characters may be on hand to keep you occupied. Dinner is $38.33–$42.59 ($19.16–$21.29/kids) with Cinderella and friends hosting. This is one of Disney's finer buffets (keep your eyes open for the strawberry soup—it's scrumptious). The Wonderland Tea Party is held here for kids on Mondays–Fridays. See pages 262–263 and 274 for details.

Buffet | American | Very noisy | Reservations recommended | Call 180 days | 8:00–11:30 am | 4:30–8:30 pm

Victoria & Albert's — D $215 — 10 | 10 | 9

You have to dress up for Walt Disney World's five-star dining experience—jackets are required and a tux or gown isn't entirely out of place. The continental, five-course, prix fixe menu ($150, plus big up-charges for Kobe beef, caviar, and the like) is redesigned daily, a harpist fills the air with music, and ladies receive roses at meal's end. For an extra-special evening, reserve the "Chef's Table," an alcove in the kitchen where you observe and interact with the chef and staff, or the intimate Queen Victoria's Room—both serve a 10–12 course meal ($210/person, reserve six months in advance). Wine pairing ($60 in the main dining room, $95 for the Chef's Table and Queen Victoria's Room) perfectly match your meal. Is it all worth it? Without a doubt! Your dinner is elegantly prepared, and each course brings new delights. We held our wedding dinner here. Need we say more? State special dietary needs in advance. Must be at least 10 years old. Call 407-824-1089 to confirm 24 hours in advance.

Table | French | Quiet | Reservations required—call 407-824-1089 | Call 180 days | Short waits | 5:45 pm & 9:00 pm

Top Photo Slice: The orchestrion at 1900 Park Fare (ⓘ9659) © Cheryl Pendry

Old Key West Resort Restaurant

Jennifer | Dave | Readers

Olivia's Cafe — B $24, L $46, D $52 — DDPT — 6 | 6 | 5

Olivia's Cafe serves an enticing array of Key West- and Caribbean-tinged specialties in a homey, small-island atmosphere. Breakfast includes the classics and a lineup of healthy items ($9.99–$15.99). Lunch and dinner bring conch chowder ($7.99), salads ($5.50–$7.99), shrimp po boy ($14.49), Southernmost buttermilk chicken ($17.99), Mallory Square Cobb salad ($18.49), seven mile sea scallops ($24.99), and island barbecue pork ribs ($21.99). Don't pass up the key lime tart ($5.49). Kids meals are $8.59 and feature fish, grilled chicken cheeseburger, and Mickey pasta. Reservations are not always necessary here.

Table | Floridian | Med. noise | Short waits | Call 180 days | 7:30–10:30 am, 11:30 am–5 pm, 5–10 pm

Polynesian Village Resort Restaurants

See page 265 for the Spirit of Aloha Luau

Kona Cafe — B $23, L $43, D $56 — DDPT — 8 | 7 | 8

A stylish spot for coffee and full meals. Its Asian/eclectic menu brings welcome sophistication. Breakfast favorites include banana-stuffed "Tonga Toast" ($12.99) and tropical Liliko'i juice blend ($4.49). Lunch offers tempting appetizers ($6.99-$10.99), a huge teriyaki beef salad ($16.99), a satisfying Asian noodle bowl ($15.99), and a traditional Polynesian plate lunch ($15.99). Dinners offer steaks, chops, chicken, and seafood with an Asian flair ($16.99–$28.99), including teriyaki strip steak ($28.99). Sushi is available at lunch and dinner. Fabulous coffee bar (mornings only) and desserts ($5.49–$7.49), too!

Table | International | Noisy | Reservations recommended | Call 180 days | 7:30–11:30 am, Noon–3:00 pm, 5–10 pm

'Ohana — B $29, D $47 — DDPT — 8 | 7 | 7

Aloha, cousins! The Polynesian Village Resort welcomes you warmly to 'Ohana, a great, fun spot for families and groups. This is an all-you-care-to-eat feast for $36.20-$42.59 ($18.10-$20.23/kids). Appetizers (salad, fried dumplings, and wings) and veggies are served family-style, then the cast members circulate with long skewers of grilled steak, shrimp, chicken, and pork. Kids can do coconut races and hula hoop contests, and entertainers sing Hawaiian melodies. You may even see the Magic Kingdom fireworks! Soft drinks and bread pudding dessert included. The tropical drinks in unusual containers are extra. 'Ohana also hosts a character breakfast for $22.36–$26.62 ($12.77–$14.90/kids) with Lilo and Stitch: "'Ohana means family-style dining, which means no one gets leftovers!" See pages 262–263.

Table | Polynesian | Very noisy | Reservations strongly recommended | Call 180 days | Long waits | 7:30–11 am, 5–10 pm

Tip: Trader Sam's Grog Grotto is a great new lounge at the Polynesian Village. Be careful what you order—select drink orders can cause special effects! The terrace outside offers the same menu.

Port Orleans Riverside Resort Restaurant

Boatwright's Dining Hall — D $51 — DDPT — 7 | 5 | 7

Cajun cooking from down the bayou fits the bill perfectly. In keeping with the restaurant's theme, a wooden boat hangs overhead and boat-builders' tools hang on the rustic walls. This is a place for hearty, Southern-style dinners, with appetizers like crawfish bites ($10.49) and chicken andouille gumbo ($6.49). Main courses include jambalaya ($17.99), blackened fish filet ($21.99), voodoo chicken ($17.99), and pork chop with amber ale bbq sauce and cheesy grits ($21.99). Desserts ($5.49-$6.49) include bread pudding and pecan pie.

Table | American | Call 180 days | Short waits | 5:00–10:00 pm

Eatery descriptions and ratings are explained on page 230.

Top Photo Slice: Statues at 'Ohana (12482) © Cheryl Pendry

Resort Restaurants

Saratoga Springs Resort Restaurant

Jennifer | Dave | Readers

Turf Club Bar and Grill D $53 DDP T — 6 6 6

Table | American | Call 180 days | Short waits | 5:00-10:00 pm

This table-service eatery offers wholesome American fare. Menu items include calamari ($11.99), steamed mussels ($11.99), and onion rings ($6.99) for starters. Entrees include fettucine with shrimp ($20.99), prime rib ($31.49), New York strip ($34.49), lamb chops ($28.99), pasta with shrimp ($20.99), and grilled salmon ($21.99). Desserts are $4.49-$6.49. Kids' meals are $8.59 (cheeseburger, grilled chicken, or mac & cheese). Note this eatery now serves dinner only (no lunch).

8122 © Cheryl Pendry
Delicious calamari

Swan and Dolphin Resort Restaurants

bluezoo [Dolphin] D $93 — 6 7 7

Table | Seafood | Noisy | Call 180 days | 5 pm-11 pm

Star chef Todd English presents upscale, inventively prepared seafood at this visually striking establishment. The scallop appetizer with braised short rib ($14) was a savory adventure, the "Dancing Fish" (market) disappointing, king salmon ($33) a winner, and other choices ($25-$60) were satisfying. $79 chef's tasting menu. Separate, lighter menu at the crowded cafe/bar. Not kid-friendly.

Fresh Mediterranean Market [Dolphin] B $30, L $25 — 8 7 8

Buffet | Mediterranean | Med. noise | Call 180 days | 6 am-2 pm

This cheery and appealing eatery offers a wide variety of cooked-to-order items at a breakfast buffet ($17.95/$10.95). The very attentive chefs ply you with all sorts of temptations, both Mediterranean-style and American, all prepared with a light, "fresh" hand. Grilled and rotisseried meats, pastas, cold salads, veggies, and lots of desserts, too! Lunch is available seasonally and is a la carte off a menu.

Garden Grove [Swan] B $31, L $44, D $44 — 5 6 8

Table | American | Noisy | Call 180 days | 6:30-11:30 am, 11:30 am-2 pm, 5:30-10 pm

This out-of-the-way spot offers a weekday breakfast buffet ($22.99/$13.99 kids 3-9), a Japanese breakfast ($22), a la carte selections, and a character breakfast on weekends from 8:00 to 11:00 am ($24.99/$15.99). Lunch offers salads, sandwiches, and light entrees ($13-$16). In the evenings the eatery transforms into a character dining experience (see pages 262-263). Dinner offers a buffet ($29.99-$35.99/$13.99-$16.99 kids 3-9) with rotating seafood, Mediterranean, and bbq themes. Reserve at 407-934-1609 or online at MyDisneyExperience.

Kimonos [Swan] D $39, S — 6 7 6

Table | Japanese | Noisy | 5:30 pm-12 am

In search of excellent late-night sushi, drinks, and karaoke? Try the Swan! Now all a la carte. Feast on sushi (2-pc. orders, $5-$8), rolls ($5.50-$15.99) and hot items ($4.95-$17.95) while you get up the nerve to sing (if you dare). Very noisy. Reservations accepted for parties of 6+ (call 407-934-1609).

Top Photo Slice: Bubble baubles overhead at bluezoo (7991) © Cheryl Pendry

Resort Restaurants

Swan and Dolphin Resorts Restaurants *(continued)*

Ratings: Jennifer / Dave / Readers

Il Mulino New York Trattoria [Swan] D $63 — 8 8 7

This traditional Italian eatery offers an extensive (if pricey) menu which features dishes from the Abruzzi region of Italy, including arancini (rice balls) ($8), carpaccio ($14), pizzas ($16–$18), risotto con funghi ($26), gnocchi bolognese ($24), ribeye steak ($39), saltimbocca ($33), and seared red snapper ($31). Desserts are heavenly, especially the torta di cioccolati (flourless chocolate cake–$8). At meal's end, adults are served complimentary glasses of limoncello, a sweet digestif.

Il Mulino's Dining Room

© MediaMarx, Inc.

Table | Italian | Very noisy | Reservations suggested–407-WDW-DINE | 5 pm–11 pm

Shula's Steak House [Dolphin] D $114 — 8 8 9

This is the most upscale steakhouse on Disney property. Beautifully grilled, flavorful beef is the focus (if you finish the 48-oz. porterhouse, they'll engrave your name on a plaque!) but perfectly succulent fish ($33) gets the utmost respect. Grilled meats cost from $48 to $105. If you need to ask the "market price" of the 4-lb. lobster ($95), you can't afford it! With dark wood paneling, Sinatra on the speakers, gilt-framed football photos, and formal, attentive service, you may prefer to wear a jacket or dress. Veggies are $9–$15 (split an order, and get the potato gratin, too) but the "garnish" of peppers, watercress, and mushrooms on every plate may be enough. The wine list is expansive and expensive. And order the chocolate soufflé for two ($14)!

Table | Steakhouse | Med. noise | Reservations suggested; call 407-WDW-DINE | Call 180 days | Short waits | 5 pm–11 pm

Wilderness Lodge Resort Restaurants

Artist Point D $83 DDP2 — 10 9 8

This visually stunning restaurant serves flavorful contemporary fare from the Pacific Northwest and is among our favorites. The dining room is a soaring, log-beamed space graced by large murals of Western landscapes and furnished with comfortable, Mission-style tables and chairs. The menu changes seasonally. For starters, try Dungeness crab salad ($15), steamed mussels ($14), or smoky portobello soup ($10). The old-standby cedar plank Chinook salmon ($41) is always rewarding, or try the pork tenderloin ($33), buffalo strip loin ($49) or seafood and vegetarian entrees ($29–$36) like the vegan lo mein and the seared sea diver scallops. For dessert, the hot berry cobbler is a must ($11). The wine list is excellent–try a wine pairing. Dress code is "business casual" (see page 228).

Table | American | Med. noise | Reservations suggested | Call 180 days | Short waits | 5:30 pm–9:30 pm

Whispering Canyon Cafe B $25, L $45, D $57 DDPT — 8 6 8

If you hanker for house-made barbecue in a Wild West setting, sashay over to Whispering Canyon, long-famous for its family-style, all-you-can-eat meals ($34). At dinner, choose three of five for your platter: ribs, chicken, carved steak, fish, and sausage (a veggie entree can be requested). Sides and desserts are included, appetizers and drinks are extra. Breakfast and lunch is a la carte, with sandwiches and entrees ranging from $12.50-$17. There are activities for the kids, and the servers make sure all have fun. Just don't ask for ketchup. Trust us! Hours: 7:30–11:15 am, 11:45 am–2:30 pm, and 5:00–10:00 pm.

Table | Barbecue | Very noisy | Reservations a must | Call 180 days | Long waits | 7:30 am–10 pm

Eatery descriptions and ratings are explained on page 230.

Top Photo Slice: Windows above the entrance to Il Mulino (ⓘ6639) © Cheryl Pendry

Resort Restaurants

Yacht and Beach Club Resorts Restaurants

Jennifer Dave Readers

Beaches and Cream Soda Shop L $36, D $36, S — 8 6 8

This small, seaside-style ice cream parlor is always jammed. Sure, you can get classic luncheonette items like burgers ($15.99), Ruben sandwiches ($13.99), veggie falafel ($11.49), and hot dogs ($8.49), plus shakes and malts ($5.29), but you know everyone is here for the ice cream. Why not cut to the chase and go for an ice cream soda, float, ice cream, frozen yogurt, or sundae ($4.99-$8.49)? Or get the Kitchen Sink ($28.99), a huge sundae with every topping. Sit at tables, booths, or at the counter. The average meal costs above are for a "light" meal (no appetizers are available). Reservations now accepted. Take-out for ice cream is also available.

Table | American | Very noisy | Reservations suggested | Long waits | 11:00 am-11:00 pm

Cape May Cafe [Beach Club] B $34, D $52 — 7 7 8

Seafood lovers line up for this dinner buffet, which is within walking distance of Epcot. For $38.33-$42.59 ($18.10-$20.23/kids), you get an endless supply of chowder, steamed hard shell clams, mussels, baked fish, flank steak, ribs, corn on the cob, and all the trimmings, enough to make any seafood lover happy as a clam. There's plenty for the fish-shy, a kids' buffet (mac & cheese, mini hot dogs, fish nuggets, and chicken strips), a dessert bar, and they bring taffy with the check. The character breakfast buffet is $26.62-$30.88 ($13.84-$17.03/kids) and prized for its relaxed atmosphere (see pages 262-263). Chairs and booths.

Buffet | Seafood | Noisy | Reservations recommended | Call 180 days | 7:30-11 am, 5:30-9:00 pm

Captain's Grille [Yacht Club] B $21, L $42, D $56 — 4 5 8

Formerly the Yacht Club Galley, this casual hotel café offers pleasant surroundings at breakfast, lunch, and dinner. Traditional favorites and a healthy helping of meat and seafood dishes are the specialty here. Breakfast offers a buffet ($15.99/$8.99 kids 3-9) and a la carte selections ($4.49-$14.49). Lunch brings salads ($5.49-$17.49), burgers ($12.49-$14.99), and a lobster roll ($17.99). Dinner offers steaks, chops, and snow crab ($15.99-$29.99).

Table | American | Short waits | 7:00-11 am, 11:30 am-2 pm, 6:00-10:00 pm

Yachtsman Steakhouse [Yacht Club] D $94 — 8 7 9

Until Shula's opened, Yachtsman Steakhouse was the best steakhouse at Disney and it still comes close. Hardwood-grilled steaks are the main attraction at dinner, but vegetarians haven't been neglected. Appetizers include lobster bisque ($9), Maine diver scallops ($14), and salads ($9-$16). Plain and sauced meats ($34-$44) including a popular peppercorn-glazed strip steak ($42), porterhouse ($44), filet mignon ($40), rib-eye ($43), and rack of lamb ($34) fill the menu. Excellent wine and beer list. Kids entrees are $7-$12. Dress code is "business casual" (see page 228).

Table | Steakhouse | Med. noise | Reservations strongly suggested | Call 180 days | 5:30-9:45 pm

ESPN Wide World of Sports

ESPN Wide World of Sports Grill B $15, L $28, D $28 — 3 4 6

It's not all hot dogs at the Wide World of Sports complex. Menu offerings include cold sandwiches ($9.19-$9.49) like the roast beef and blue cheese, hot sandwiches ($8.49-$9.59) like the bbq pulled pork, soups ($2.99-$3.49) such as clam chowder, salads ($7.39-$8.99) including Cobb (not Ty), and desserts ($1.19-$3.79). Naturally, wings are available, both Buffalo and bbq ($9.79)!

Counter | American | Reservations not accepted | 8:00 am-7:30 pm

Top Photo Slice: The tops of colorful beach umbrellas at Cape May Cafe (7905) © Cheryl Pendry

Character Dining

Disney offers many opportunities to dine with characters, both those in full guise (like Mickey Mouse) and "face characters" in costume (like Cinderella). While they don't actually sit with you throughout your meal, they do roam around the restaurant and visit your table for interludes. Character meals are more expensive than comparable meals (ranging from $22 to $72 for adults and $13 to $43 for kids ages 3–9), but the chance to meet the characters in an unhurried atmosphere makes it worthwhile. Even if characters aren't at the top of your menu, character dinners are a good deal—the cost of these buffets and family-style meals is usually less than a la carte meals when you factor all costs. Character meals are *extremely* popular—make reservations as far in advance as possible at 407-WDW-DINE and have a credit card ready (required to book all character meals).

Be aware that there's a mad rush for reservations for meals at Chef Mickey's, Akershus, Crystal Palace, and Cinderella's Royal Table. Folks start phoning and logging in at 6:00 am Eastern time, exactly 180 days prior to their desired date, and tables are often gone in a matter of minutes. If you get a table at Cinderella's, expect to pay for the meal in full by credit card at the time of reservation—this payment is refunded if you cancel up to 48 hours in advance. If you miss out on these popular character meals, don't despair. Try again once you get to Disney. Cancellations are possible, so it never hurts to ask for a table, even as you're walking through Cinderella Castle. If you are set on dining with a princess, try the character dinner at 1900 Park Fare.

- ✔ Some character breakfasts start prior to park opening. All Disney resorts offer special Disney bus transportation to the early character breakfasts.
- ✔ For the best character experience, dine off-hours. While Mickey may only give you a quick hello during busy mealtimes, you might end up with a close, personal relationship when tables are empty.
- ✔ Don't be shy, grown-ups! Even if you aren't dining with kids, the characters visit your table. If you'd rather sit things out, they will simply give you a nod or handshake.
- ✔ The "head" characters don't speak, but that doesn't mean you have to keep quiet around them. Talk to them and they'll pantomime and play along!
- ✔ Most character meals take just one table-service credit on the Disney Dining Plan.

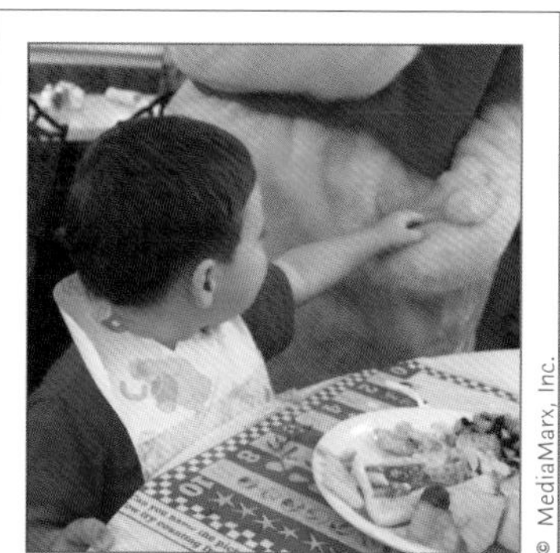
© MediaMarx, Inc.

Alexander holds hands with a furry friend at the Crystal Palace character meal. (His friend asked to remain anonymous because he's so bashful.)

Top Photo Slice: A happy little princess Belle watches the princesses at Akershus (ⓘ10002) © Nalagh

Character Dining Location Chart

The chart below shows all the character meals at the time of writing. The location of each meal is given in parentheses, along with the meal served (B=breakfast or brunch, L=lunch, D=dinner, All=all three meals), the type (buffet=buffet-style, family=family-style, plate=buffet items brought to you on a plate, menu=from the menu), and the prominent characters (note that a specific character's appearance is not guaranteed).

Restaurant	Meal	Type	Characters
Akershus Royal Banquet Hall DD P1	All	Family	Snow White, Belle, Jasmine
Dine in a castle with princesses Belle, Ariel, Jasmine, and Snow White. (Page 234)			
Cape May Cafe (Beach Club) DD P1	B	Buffet	Goofy, Donald, Pluto, Minnie
Casual, beach party atmosphere and good, standard breakfast foods. (Page 261)			
Chef Mickey's (Contemporary) DD P1	B/D	Buffet	Mickey, Minnie, Goofy, Pluto
Bustling, popular destination. Superior food. Try to dine at off-hours. (Page 255)			
Cinderella's Royal Table (MK) DD P2	All	Plate	Cinderella, Ariel, Aurora
Gorgeous setting, hottest reservation at WDW. Original "princess" meal. (Page 231)			
Crystal Palace (MK) DD P1	All	Buffet	Pooh, Tigger, Eeyore, Piglet
A favorite spot for satisfying meals in bright and airy surroundings. (Page 232)			
Donald's Safari (AK) DD P1	B/L	Buffet	Donald, Mickey, Goofy
Inventive cuisine and classic favorites in a market atmosphere. (Page 246)			
The Garden Grill (Epcot) DD P1	All	Plate	Mickey, Chip, Dale, Pluto
Tasty dining in an unusual setting. Good spur-of-the-moment choice. (Page 235)			
Garden Grove (Swan)	B/D[1]	Buffet/Menu	Timon or Goofy
A la carte menu makes this an expensive character dinner. (Page 259)			
Hollywood & Vine (Studios) DD P1	B/L	Buffet	Sofia, Doc, Manny, Jake
Play 'n Dine character meal appeals to the Playhouse Disney set. (Page 243)			
My Disney Girl's Tea Party (GF)	Tea[2]	Snack	Princess Aurora
A special tea and brunch, plus a My Disney Girl doll. (Page 274)			
1900 Park Fare (Grand Floridian) DD P1	B/D	Buffet	Mary Poppins (B) Cinderella (D)
First-rate food, comfy Victorian surroundings, and lots of character. (Page 257)			
'Ohana (Polynesian Village) DD P1	B	Family	Lilo, Stitch, Mickey, Pluto
Aloha, Cousins! A relaxed atmosphere (no more Minnie, alas!). (Page 258)			
Wonderland Tea Party (GF)	Tea[3]	Snack	Alice in Wonderland
"Tea," stories, and cupcakes with Alice at 1900 Park Fare. (Page 257)			

1 *Character breakfasts are weekends at 8:00–11:00 am; dinners are held 6:00–10:00 pm every night (Timon and Rafiki on Mon. and Fri., and Goofy and Pluto at all other times).*
2 *My Disney Girl's Princess Tea Party has limited availability—see page 274 for details.*
3 *Wonderland Tea Parties are held Monday through Friday, 1:30–2:30 pm.*

Note: The Liberty Tree Tavern character dinner ended in 2009.
PassPorter's Character Yearbook is a detailed guide to character meet-and-greets. See page 314.

Top Photo Slice: Looking down at Chef Mickey's at the Contemporary Resort (6628) © Cheryl Pendry

Hoop-Dee-Doo Musical Revue

DDP2

The Hoop-Dee-Doo Musical Revue is a **hilarious hoedown** in an Old West-style dance hall at the Fort Wilderness Resort. The song-and-dance vaudeville act relies heavily on slapstick humor, hokey gags, corny puns, and lots of audience participation. The Wild West performers interact with the audience, and guests celebrating birthdays and anniversaries may be singled out for special attention.

© MediaMarx, Inc.

We've been lucky to get this stage-side table at the Hoop-Dee-Doo twice!

The **all-you-care-to-eat meal** includes salad, barbecue ribs, fried chicken, corn, baked beans, and bread, with strawberry shortcake for dessert (kids can request mac and cheese and hot dogs instead). Complimentary beverages include soda, beer (Bud Light Draft), wine (house red, white, and rose), and sangria. Cocktails and bottled beer extra.

Prices vary by seat category—cheapest seats are in category 3 (left or right side of the balcony) at $58.99/adults and $32.99/kids 3–9 (includes tax and tip). Category 2 seats are $64.99/adults and $33.99/kids 3–9 and are located in the back of the main floor or in the center of the balcony. Category 1 premium seats are $67.99/adults and $36.99/kids 3–9, located front and/or center on the main floor. Guests who need wheelchair access may only be seated in category 1. Disney Dining Plan credits are accepted here—two credits per person) for category 1 (8:30 show only) and categories 2 and 3 (all shows). Shows are at 4:00 pm, 6:15 pm and 8:30 pm nightly (the 8:30 pm show is the easiest to get in). A photo is taken before the show, and the photo is saved to your My Disney Experience account (the print photo packages are no longer offered table-side).

This show is **very popular**—reserve up to 180 days in advance at 407-WDW-DINE. The earlier you reserve, the better your table (within your category, of course). Full payment is required with reservation, refundable up to 48 hours in advance. Hoop-Dee-Doo Musical Revue is located in Pioneer Hall at the Fort Wilderness Resort. See travel directions below.

Mickey's Backyard Barbecue DDP2

This old-fashioned, open-air barbecue features good ol' Disney characters (Minnie, Mickey, Goofy, Chip, and Dale), live country music, carnival games, and line dancing. Vittles include chicken, hot dogs, ribs, salads, corn, cole slaw, beans, vegetables, rolls, and (of course!) watermelon—all served buffet-style at picnic tables under a huge pavilion. Includes all-you-can-drink soft drinks and beer. Typically held on Thursdays and Saturdays at 6:30 (ends at 8:00 pm) from March through December. Cost: $56.99/adults and $32.99/kids 3–9 (prices include all taxes and gratuities). Call 407-WDW-DINE to inquire about availability and make reservations up to 180 days in advance. Full payment is required with your reservations, refundable up to 48 hours in advance, unless you're on a dining plan.

Getting to the Fort Wilderness Dinner Shows

To get to either Hoop-Dee-Doo or Backyard Barbecue, take the boat to Fort Wilderness from the Magic Kingdom, Contemporary, or Wilderness Lodge. Special buses run to and from some resorts, or take any Fort Wilderness-bound theme park bus. Driving (parking is free) is an option, too. The Hoop-Dee-Doo is in Pioneer Hall; Backyard Barbecue is next door to Pioneer Hall (around back). Allow 60 to 90 minutes for travel.

Top Photo Slice: Balcony seating at the Hoop-Dee-Doo Musical Revue (ⓘ120) © MediaMarx, Inc.

Spirit of Aloha Dinner (Luau)

DD P2

Aloha! The Spirit of Aloha Dinner is an **exotic, South Pacific-style celebration** of color, style, history, music, and dance. Everything you expect from a luau is here—women in "grass" skirts, men in face paint, fire dancers, traditional music, plus a little bit of Elvis—showcasing the cultures and traditions of Polynesia and connecting them all to the modern Hawaii seen in Lilo and Stitch. The show is held together by Auntie Wini, the heart of a group of young islanders who have learned to love traditional values including 'ohana (family). The show is held nightly in Luau Cove, an outdoor stage surrounded by a torch-lit garden. Upon arrival, guests are presented with a complimentary lei and entertained in the garden before dinner. While you wait for the show, you can buy drinks and souvenirs and have a family photo taken. Guests are seated at long, wooden tables that fan out from the stage, all under shelter in the event of rain.

The **all-you-care-to-eat meal**, served family-style for your party, includes tropical mixed greens with mango-poppyseed dressing, pineapple-coconut bread, sweet golden pineapple, barbecued pork ribs, roasted chicken, Polynesian rice, fresh seasonal vegetables, and Kilauea Volcano Delight for dessert. Included with your meal is your choice of unlimited soda, lemonade, coffee, iced tea, milk, beer (Bud and Bud Light Draft), and wine (house red, white, and rose). Specialty drinks are extra. The show begins after dinner with Hawaiian music and plenty of South Seas dancing by both men and women. Kids are quite welcome at the Luau—young ones will be invited on stage for a special dance number. A photo is taken before the show, and the photo is saved to your My Disney Experience account (the print photo packages are no longer offered table-side).

Prices vary by seat category—cheapest seats are in category 3 (extreme far left or right of the stage on the lower level, or on the upper level) at $60.99/adults and $33.99/kids 3–9 (prices include taxes and gratuities). Category 2 seats are $67.99/adults and $36.99/kids 3–9 and are located on the left or right side of the stage, or on the upper level tables in the center-rear. Category 1 premium seats are $72.99/adults and $39.99/kids 3–9, located front and/or center on the lower level. Disney Dining Plan credits are accepted here (two credits per person) for categories 2 and 3 only. The two-hour shows are held at 5:15 pm and 8:00 pm, Tuesdays through Saturdays. We prefer the later seating as the darkness adds to the mystique and romance of the show. Ask about discounts for the late show. In the cooler months, the late show may be canceled.

© MediaMarx, Inc.

The Spirit of "Alooooha!"

Make your reservations early (up to 180 days in advance)—they book up quick. Full payment is required with your reservation, refundable up to 48 hours prior to the show.

Getting to the Polynesian Dinner Show

To get to the Polynesian dinner show, either drive directly to the Polynesian Village Resort or take the monorail from the Magic Kingdom or Epcot. From other parks and resorts, bus to the Magic Kingdom and take the monorail (daytime) or bus to Disney Springs and transfer to a Polynesian Village bus. Once inside the resort, follow signs to Luau Cove. Allow plenty of time for travel, especially if coming from another resort.

Top Photo Slice: Fire dancer at the Spirit of Aloha Dinner (ⓘ3582) © Marnie Urmaza

Special Dinner Shows

Holidays

Holidays are always special at the Walt Disney World Resort. The parks and resorts overflow with special entertainment and decorations that vary from season to season and year to year (see pages 289 for details). The Christmas and New Year's season is especially magical, with all kinds of celebrations throughout the property. One big Christmas favorite is the Candlelight Processional at World Showcase in Epcot, which is available free to Epcot guests (show only) or as an Epcot lunch or dinner package offering special seating for the show (call 407-WDW-DINE).

House of Blues DD PT

House of Blues has a concert hall separate from its restaurant (page 250) that features performances by top musicians. On Sundays at 10:30 am and 1:00 pm, they serve an all-you-care-to-eat Gospel Brunch with soul food and glorious gospel music—price is $40–$53/adult, $32.25 child age 3–9. Reservations can be made up to a month in advance at the House of Blues box office (or call 407-934-2583). Tickets for evening performances are available through the box office or Ticketmaster, and range from $13 to $60. The House of Blues is located at Disney Springs West Side.

Restaurants With Entertainment

Several Disney restaurants offer performances or entertainment during meals. At the Magic Kingdom, a piano player may tickle the ivories at Casey's Corner. At Epcot, Biergarten has traditional German music and dancing, Restaurant Marrakesh features belly dancing and Moroccan musicians, and Rose & Crown plays host to pub performers. At Disney's Hollywood Studios, '50s Prime Time Cafe has TVs and cast members who act like "sisters" and "brothers," and the Sci-Fi Dine-In Theater Restaurant shows old movie trailers. Both 'Ohana (Polynesian Village) and Whispering Canyon Cafe (Wilderness Lodge Resort) offer fun activities for the kids (big and little). And Raglan Road at Disney Springs hosts Irish music, dancing, and storytelling.

①14198 © Janet Simonsen

Moroccan dancer and musicians at Restaurant Marrakesh

Top Photo Slice: Music and dancing at Biergarten in Epcot (①8018) © Cheryl Pendry

Special Dining Opportunities

On Mother's Day during Epcot's International Flower & Garden Festival (March 2–May 15, 2016), you can experience the **Food Among the Flowers Brunch**. This is an elaborate meal offering dozens of inventive and tantalizing choices—some may even include edible flower blossoms. Then, during Epcot's International Food & Wine Festival (anticipated dates are September 23–November 14, 2016), there are special **wine tasting dinners** and other special meals (see page 288 for more about the Festival). Finally, during the **Christmas season**, when all the familiar eateries are overflowing, there is often a **holiday buffet** at a special location. For all these meals, call 407-WDW-DINE for information and reservations, but walk-up diners are often welcome at the holiday buffet.

Holiday dinners at the resorts and selected theme park restaurants usually go unheralded, but you can be fairly certain that many resorts will have something happening on Easter Sunday, Mother's Day, Thanksgiving Day, Christmas week, and New Year's Eve. Start by phoning your Disney resort. If you strike out at your resort, call around to the various deluxe resorts (holiday meals aren't always listed with 407-WDW-DINE). Magic Kingdom and Epcot full-service restaurants are also good candidates. Call 407-WDW-DINE to ask about special meals at the theme parks.

Dine with a Disney Imagineer offers a close-up peek at the people who create Disney's entertainment, attractions, parks, and resorts. These special meals are available Mondays, Wednesdays, and Fridays at 11:30 am at Hollywood Brown Derby or 5:30 pm at the Flying Fish Cafe, and feature intimate conversations with an Imagineer. Guests are served a special four-course meal while they learn about "their" Imagineer's work. Each guest receives a souvenir that may be autographed. Available for groups of 2–10 guests, and groups may be combined. Lunch is $60.99 and dinner is $85.00 (guests must be age 14 or older to attend). Reserve up to 180 days in advance at 407-WDW-DINE—note that prepayment is required and you must cancel at least 48 hours in advance to get your money back.

Wishes Fireworks Dessert Party is a delicious way to view the Magic Kingdom's fireworks, from a reserved standing area. An elaborate buffet of dessert items (such as chocolate-dipped strawberries, chocolate mousse, character-themed cupcakes) and non-alcoholic beverages is served, starting about an hour before the fireworks, on select nights. $49/adults, $29/kids 3-9. Reserve 180 days ahead at 407-WDW-DINE. Prepayment is required.

Looking for the **Fantasmic! Meal Package**? See page 243.

Top Photo Slice: Food at Party of the Senses, a special dining event held during the Food & Wine Festival (ⓘ8000) © Cheryl Pendry

Electronic, interactive worksheet available—see page 316

Meal Worksheet

The first step in planning your meals is determining your needs. Start by checkmarking the meals you'll need in the worksheet below. Next, write down where you would like to eat your meals—be specific ("cereal in room" or "Brown Derby at Studios"). If you're using the Dining Plan (see pages 223-225), indicate the number of snacks S, quick-service Q, and table-service T credits to be used per meal. Circle the meals that require reservations, then use the worksheet on the next page to make the arrangements.

Meal	Location	S	Q	T	Meal	Location	S	Q	T
Day One—Date:		Dining Plan Credits			**Day Six—Date:**		Dining Plan Credits		
❑ Breakfast					❑ Breakfast				
❑ Lunch					❑ Lunch				
❑ Dinner					❑ Dinner				
❑ Other					❑ Other				
Day Two—Date:		Dining Plan Credits			**Day Seven—Date:**		Dining Plan Credits		
❑ Breakfast					❑ Breakfast				
❑ Lunch					❑ Lunch				
❑ Dinner					❑ Dinner				
❑ Other					❑ Other				
Day Three—Date:		Dining Plan Credits			**Day Eight—Date:**		Dining Plan Credits		
❑ Breakfast					❑ Breakfast				
❑ Lunch					❑ Lunch				
❑ Dinner					❑ Dinner				
❑ Other					❑ Other				
Day Four—Date:		Dining Plan Credits			**Day Nine—Date:**		Dining Plan Credits		
❑ Breakfast					❑ Breakfast				
❑ Lunch					❑ Lunch				
❑ Dinner					❑ Dinner				
❑ Other					❑ Other				
Day Five—Date:		Dining Plan Credits			**Day Ten—Date:**		Dining Plan Credits		
❑ Breakfast					❑ Breakfast				
❑ Lunch					❑ Lunch				
❑ Dinner					❑ Dinner				
❑ Other					❑ Other				

Top Photo Slice: A clock on Main Street, U.S.A. at the Magic Kingdom © MediaMarx, Inc.

Advance Reservations Worksheet

Electronic, interactive worksheet available–see page 316

Once you've determined what meals you plan to eat in table-service restaurants, note them in the chart below, along with your preferred dining time. Next, call 407-WDW-DINE or go online at DisneyWorld.com to make advance reservations (have a credit card handy for certain reservations). Note the actual meal time and confirmation number below. When dining arrangements are finalized, transfer the information to your PassPockets.

Our Resort:
Our Arrival Date:

Before calling, fill in everything to the left of this line.

Date	Restaurant Name	Preferred Time	Actual Time	Confirmation Number

A Recipe for Fun

Make the most of your dining experience at Walt Disney World with these tips and tricks from fellow vacationers like you:

"Advanced dining reservations for the most popular Walt Disney World restaurants can be very difficult to acquire, even when searching 180 days before your vacation, and especially during Free Dining dates. You can search for reservations months in advance, adjusting dates and times, and still not find any availability. Do not be discouraged! A credit card is required to reserve most reservations and will incur a fee if not cancelled at least one full day prior to the reservation. This cancellation window creates wonderful opportunities to acquire desirable reservations, which previously seemed impossible to get. Once you arrive at Disney, begin searching a day or two before you want a reservation. This trick has always worked for me on our annual vacations!"

– Contributed by Susan Fadel, a winner in our Reader Tip Contest

"Dining is a huge part of what makes our trips so much fun. On our last trip we had the Disney Dining Plan, which was awesome for us. I start planning (with my PassPorter in hand, of course!) which theme park we're going to do aim for. Notice I said 'aim for'—if things don't go to plan I don't sweat it. I then plan either a sit-down breakfast or a sit-down dinner on that day. The odd time we'll do two sit-down meals, but usually for us one is enough. Whatever else we end up doing that day, we really aim for the restaurant we've chosen so we make sure we put in lots of space for a nap beforehand or have some healthy snacks on hand for the morning if it's a late breakfast. I find this puts a nice anchor into our days even though I like to keep them laid back, and gives my husband and I something to look forward to each day. Since I'm the chief planner, he says to me, 'Where are we eating today?' and I tell him all about it. Sometimes the places we are eating are in the parks and that makes it a no-brainer as to which park we'll do that day. It works really well for us!"

– Contributed by Beth N., a winner in our Reader Tip Contest

Magical Memories

"On the morning of our vacation, I packed a little Disney surprise for the ride to the airport. I made non-alcoholic breakfast mock-tails I dubbed 'Disney Sunrise,' a bit of grenadine in the bottom of a clear disposable glass, followed by your favorite breakfast juice or juices. Check for sugar content and layer the highest sugar content on the bottom to least on the top. Do not mix. I added a skewer of fresh fruits, topped with a Mickey head cupcake pick. Mickey shaped rice crispie treats completed our breakfast."

...as told by Disney vacationer Teresa Weddelman

"On our last night of a seven-day vacation we ate at Columbia Harbour House in the Magic Kingdom. While I was waiting for my food I asked the cast member what an item in a small plastic bowl was. She told me it was a peach cobbler and handed me one to try. I was so excited and overwhelmed by her kindness. I thanked her profusely and told her 'You just made my day. We are leaving tomorrow and I am about to cry.' Then she stuck a swirly green Mickey Mouse straw in my drink cup and said 'Don't cry.'"

...as told by Disney vacationer Stacey Rahe

Top Photo: A birthday cupcake presented at Chef Mickey's (8064) © Cheryl Pendry

Making More Magic

You're bold. You're daring. You're a Disney vacationer. Now, here's your passport to an even more magical Walt Disney World Resort vacation!

Once you've tasted the Walt Disney World Resort, you'll hunger for more. Most visits can only *nibble* at the many wonders the "World" holds. There is much, much more that can be done to make your vacation magical. We've been to Disney more than most and yet there are *still* things we haven't done, and we add new discoveries to the wish list after every trip. It can all be a bit overwhelming, not to mention habit-forming.

To help you undertake your own magical explorations of the Walt Disney World Resort, we present a collection of useful information about some of its lesser-known aspects and attractions. This is our "everything else" chapter. To begin, we give you a backstage pass to the guided tours, special classes, and educational programs Disney offers—from peeks behind the scenes to dives under the seas. From there, we lead you on a treasure hunt for fun tucked away inside the parks—both real "treasure hunts" and hunts for items you'll treasure. We've even added a mini worksheet for those of you who love to shop! Next we share our special tricks for feeling and looking like a VIP on your trip—a little extra-special attention can go a long way! Then we give you the lowdown on childcare programs. Your kids may find these more fun than the theme parks themselves—no kidding! Special occasions and events aren't forgotten either, with ideas, tips, and details on celebrating birthdays, engagements, weddings, honeymoons, anniversaries, holidays, and more. Before we say goodbye, we'll leave you with information for explorations beyond Orlando at other Disney vacation spots—from exotic ports of call to home lands.

LEARN how to get special treatment at Disney!

So get out that pixie dust and don your sorcerer's hat—we're making magic, Disney-style!

Top Photo Slice: PassPorter reader dancing with a cast member on Main Street, U.S.A. (ⓘ13219) © Dawn Elliott

Backstage Passes

Disney does such a good job of hiding the figurative ropes and pulleys that you'll be disappointed if you hope to catch a glimpse of what makes Disney really work. To meet the growing demands of interminably curious guests, Disney offers tours and programs that satisfy the need to "peek."

Guided Tours

Unless otherwise noted, advance reservations may be (and should be) made up to 180 days in advance at 407-939-8687, or through your resort's Concierge desk. Some discounts are available to Annual Passholders, Disney Visa cardholders, or Disney Vacation Club members. Tours are only open to guests 16 and older unless otherwise noted. Many tours require substantial walking and most are wheelchair accessible. In general, no photos of backstage areas are allowed on the tours. Cancel 48 hours in advance to avoid penalties. Tours that require regular park admission are noted with the ticket ( ) icon. Important: Bring photo ID with you for tour check-in.

Backstage Magic [Magic Kingdom, Hollywood Studios, Epcot, and Animal Kingdom]

This seven-hour tour of all four major parks explores how Disney's magic is created and maintained. Go beneath the Magic Kingdom to explore the "utilidors," enjoy a special lunch at Whispering Canyon Cafe, visit Creative Costuming at the Studios, see backstage at The American Adventure at Epcot, and more! Tours depart Mon.–Fri. at 9:00 am. Price includes lunch. Park admission is not required.	**$249–$255** Ages 16 & up Backstage peek at four theme parks

Backstage Tales [Disney's Animal Kingdom]

A new, 3 1/2-hour tour gives you a behind-the-scenes peek at Disney's Animal Kingdom park to see how they care for our four-legged friends. No photography is allowed in backstage areas. Snack and souvenir included. Tour is mostly outdoors. Tours depart at 7:30 am daily. Park admission is required (not included in price).	**$90** Ages 12 & up Backstage peek

Disney's Family Magic Tour [Magic Kingdom]

This fun, 2 1/2-hour tour offers guests an interactive adventure through the Magic Kingdom in search of a Disney character (such as Peter Pan). The tour is open to all and is held daily at 10:00 am. This is a popular tour and reservations are strongly recommended. Park admission required.	**$34–$39** All ages On-stage only

Disney's Keys to the Kingdom [Magic Kingdom]

This 4 1/2-hour guided tour of Magic Kingdom gives an overview of the park's highlights, history, and backstage areas, plus lunch at Columbia Harbour House. The route varies, but usually visits up to three attractions and two backstage areas (even a peek in the "utilidors"). Offered daily at 8:30, 9:00, and 9:30 am. Guests without reservations can inquire at City Hall, but the tour is very popular and we recommend you book it well in advance. Park admission is required.	**$79** Ages 16 & up Backstage peek (including the utilidors)

Disney's Holiday D-Lights [Epcot, Hollywood Studios, Magic Kingdom]

Offered only during select nights in Nov. and Dec., this tour takes you to three parks to celebrate the season of lights. You'll see the Candelight Processional, the Osborne Lights, and the Castle Lighting Ceremony, then meet the cast members who do the decorating. Includes a holiday-themed meal and a trading pin.	**$259** Ages 16 & up Backstage peek

More at guided-tours backstage-magic keys-to-the-kingdom (tip: enter these keywords at

Top Photo Slice: Our tour guide studies Peter Pan's clues during the Family Magic Tour at Magic Kingdom © MediaMarx, Inc.

Looking for Epcot Seas Aqua Tour, Dolphins in Depth, or Divequest? See page 275.
Looking for the Sunset or Nighttime Safari Tours? See page 42.

☐ The Magic Behind Our Steam Trains [Magic Kingdom]

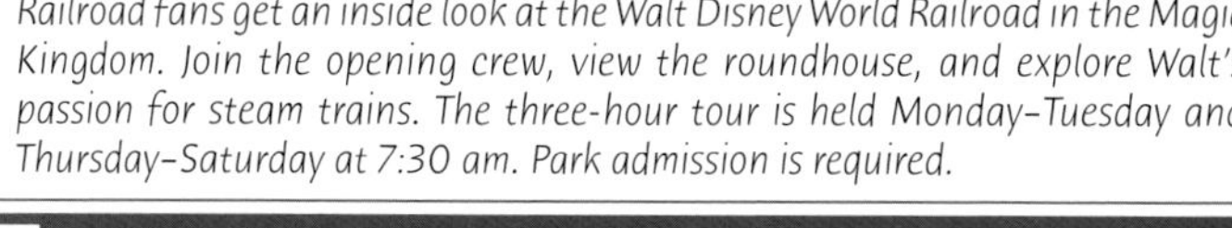

Railroad fans get an inside look at the Walt Disney World Railroad in the Magic Kingdom. Join the opening crew, view the roundhouse, and explore Walt's passion for steam trains. The three-hour tour is held Monday–Tuesday and Thursday–Saturday at 7:30 am. Park admission is required.

$54 | Ages 10 & up | Backstage peek

☐ UnDISCOVERed Future World [Epcot]

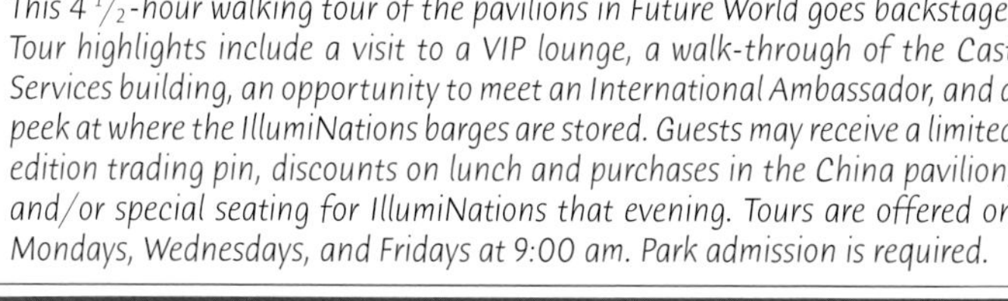

This 4 ½-hour walking tour of the pavilions in Future World goes backstage. Tour highlights include a visit to a VIP lounge, a walk-through of the Cast Services building, an opportunity to meet an International Ambassador, and a peek at where the IllumiNations barges are stored. Guests may receive a limited edition trading pin, discounts on lunch and purchases in the China pavilion, and/or special seating for IllumiNations that evening. Tours are offered on Mondays, Wednesdays, and Fridays at 9:00 am. Park admission is required.

$64–$69 | Ages 16 & up | Backstage peek (including Epcot marina)

☐ VIP Tours

Custom-designed six- to eight-hour tours may be booked by individuals or groups of up to ten people. Tours must include a meal. Cost is $360–$500+ per hour per tour guide (six-hour minimum) and does not include park admission. VIP Tours may be booked from 72 hours to three months in advance. Blackout dates apply; call 407-560-4033 for availability and reservations.

$299–$500 | All ages | On-stage only (no backstage)

☐ Walt Disney: Marceline to Magic Kingdom Tour [Magic Kingdom]

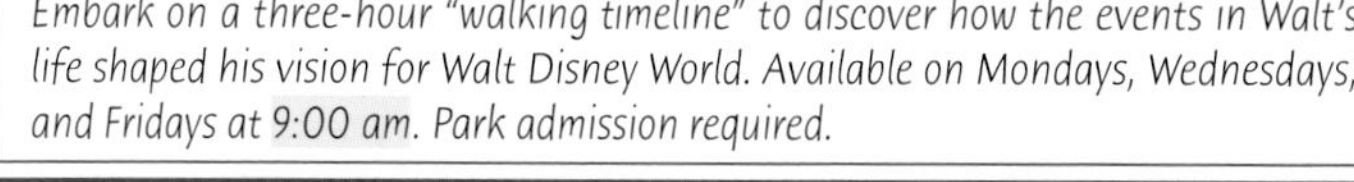

Embark on a three-hour "walking timeline" to discover how the events in Walt's life shaped his vision for Walt Disney World. Available on Mondays, Wednesdays, and Fridays at 9:00 am. Park admission required.

$30–$35 | Ages 12 & up | Backstage peek

☐ Wild Africa Trek [Disney's Animal Kingdom]

A special three-hour adventure at the Harambe Wildlife Reserve riding in open-air vehicles, walking over a rope bridge, and dining at a private safari camp. Must be between 45 and 300 lbs, at least 48 inches tall, and wear closed-toe shoes.

$139–$249 | Ages 8 & up | Backstage peeks

☐ Wilderness Back Trail Adventure Segway Tour [Fort Wilderness]

Take a ride on the Segway X2 off-road vehicles during this two-hour tour of Disney's Fort Wilderness Resort & Campground. The tour is offered on Tuesdays, Wednesdays, Thursdays, Fridays, and Saturdays at 8:30 am and 11:30 am. Minimum weight requirement of 100 lb./maximum weight of 250 lb.

$90 | Ages 16 & up | On-stage only

☐ World Showcase: DestiNations Discovered [Epcot]

This new five-hour walking tour takes you around all eleven countries of the World Showcase to learn about their history, culture, and food. Includes backstage peeks at several pavilions and lunch in Morocco! Most of the tour is spent outside. Tours leave at 7:30 am daily. Park admission required.

$109 | Ages 16 & up | Backstage peeks

☐ Yuletide Fantasy [Epcot, Magic Kingdom, Disney Resort]

Offered only on select nights in Nov. and Dec., this 3-hour tour takes you to Epcot to see how holidays are celebrated around the world, to the Magic Kingdom for the traditional trimmings on Main Street, and to a Disney resort to see its holiday decor. You'll also go behind-the-scenes to meet the Holiday services cast members.

$99 | Ages 16 & up | Backstage peek

Note: The Backstage Safari and Wild by Design tours have been discontinued.

More at ⓘ simply-segway | wild-by-design | wild-africa-trek | nature-inspired-design-segway-tour | wild-africa-trek

Children's Tours, Parties, and Activities

Fun stuff for kids! You can reserve fee-based activities by calling 407-WDW-DINE up to 90 days in advance; free activities take no reservations.

Albatross Treasure Cruise [Yacht Club Resort]

Follow the clues on this cruise around Crescent Lake, visit "exotic" ports of call, and listen to a reading of "The Legend of the Albatross." Cruise includes lunch (PB&J sandwich, cookie, and juice) and a split of the "buried treasure."

$37 | Ages 4–12 | 9:30–11:30 am

Disney's Pirate Adventure [Grand Floridian Resort]

Ahoy, mateys! Cast off from the Grand Floridian marina on a cruise around the Seven Seas Lagoon in search of treasure. Little buccaneers get a bandana to wrap around their heads, hear a reading of "The Legend of Gasparilla," learn pirate songs, and receive a bag of "loot" (treats). Lunch is included.

$37 | Ages 4–12 | 9:30–11:30 am M, W, Th, Sa

Wonderland Tea Party [Grand Floridian Resort]

Take tea with Alice in Wonderland! Kids make and eat cupcakes, participate in projects, and meet Alice, the Mad Hatter, and friends. Held in the 1900 Park Faire restaurant in the Grand Floridian Resort on Monday–Friday.

$43 | Ages 4–12 | 2:00–3:00 pm

My Disney Girl's Perfectly Princess Tea Party [Grand Floridian Resort]

Pure pampering for your little princess. This five-part party is held in the Grand Floridian's Garden View Lounge and may have a visit from Princess Aurora. Includes tea, brunch, dessert, a My DisneyGirl doll, and the participation of one adult. Siblings or friends can attend for $165 each and extra adults are $85 each. Many girls come dressed as their favorite princess, though this is not required, of course.

$281.25 | Ages 3–11 | 10:30–noon Su, M, W, Th, F

Bayou Pirate Adventure Cruise [Port Orleans Riverside]

Cruise along the Sassagoula River and hunt for Pirate Jean Lafitte's treasure. Includes a light snack and juice, and a share of the "treasure." Held on Sundays, Tuesdays, and Thursdays. Formerly the Sassagoula River Adventure.

$37 | Ages 4–12 | 9:30–11:30 am

Islands of the Caribbean Pirate Adventure [Caribbean Beach Resort]

Discover the story of Old Port Royale as you sail about Barefoot Bay in a boat resembling an old battle relic. Kids wear pirate bandanas, search for treasure, rustle up grub (snacks, juice), and divide the loot. Held on Tuesdays, Fridays, and Sundays.

$37 | Ages 4–12 | 9:30–11:30 am

Boma Kids' Activities [Disney's Animal Kingdom Lodge]

Daily activities for kids—such as cookie decorating—are available in the restaurant (Boma) and lobby of Disney's Animal Kingdom Lodge. Ask for the daily schedule of events at the hotel's front desk or at Boma.

Free | Ages 3–12 | Times vary

Making crayon rubbings of the African symbols on the floor of the Animal Kingdom Lodge lobby

Top Photo Slice: The Islands of the Caribbean Pirate Adventure takes place here on Barefoot Bay © MediaMarx, Inc.

Classes and Educational Programs

Behind the Seeds: A Special Guided Greenhouse Tour—This one-hour walking tour delves deeper into the innovative greenhouses seen in the Living With the Land exhibit at Epcot. Cost is $20/adult and $16/child age 3–9 (no minimum age), 13 people max. per tour. Park admission to Epcot is required. Sign up at the counter outside Soarin' (in The Land) or call 407-WDW-TOUR. Tours leave every 45 minutes between 10:30 am and 4:30 pm.

Dolphins in Depth—This unique three-hour program highlights the dolphin research at The Seas with Nemo & Friends in Epcot. Guests play an active part in the research as they learn about dolphin behavior. Guests must be 13 or older, and 13- to 17-year-olds must be with a participating adult. Offered on Tuesdays–Saturdays beginning at 9:45 am. Cost is $199/person and includes a photo, soda, and souvenir T-shirt. Dolphin interaction is not guaranteed. Park admission to Epcot is not required to participate in this program.

Epcot Divequest—Open Water SCUBA-certified divers ages 10 and older can dive the 6-million-gallon pool at The Seas with Nemo & Friends (guests 10–12 must be with a participating adult). The 3-hour program includes a presentation on marine research and conservation. Divers suit up and are guided in small groups for a 40-minute dive. The cost includes use of gear, refreshments, a certificate, a dive log stamp, and a shirt. Proof of certification must be shown and divers have to sign medical and legal waivers. Dives are Tuesdays–Saturdays at 4:30 and 5:30 pm. Cost is $175/person. Park admission to Epcot is not required. Advance reservations are required.

Epcot Seas Aqua Tour—A 2½-hour SNUBA-assisted snorkel that takes place in The Seas with Nemo & Friends. You do not need to be SCUBA certified; equipment and instructions are provided. Actual snorkel time is 30 minutes. Offered Tuesdays–Saturdays at 4:30 and 5:30 pm for guests ages 8 and up (8- to 12-year-olds must be with an adult). Cost is $175–$179 and includes use of gear, a backpack, and a group photo. Park admission not required.

Typhoon Lagoon Learn-to-Surf Program—The Learn-to-Surf program at Typhoon Lagoon water park teaches guests surfing basics. Learn on dry land for the first half-hour, then try your new skills on the big waves in the park's huge wave pool for the remaining two hours. The 2½-hour class is currently offered on Mondays, Tuesdays, Thursdays, and Fridays at 5:45 am, though starting time varies with park operating hours (class is held before the park opens). Class is open to resort guests ages 8 and up who are strong swimmers. Cost is $165/person, and park admission is not required. Call 407-WDW-PLAY for reservations. See pages 197–200 for details on Typhoon Lagoon. (You can book special "private surf parties" at Typhoon Lagoon—call 407-WDW-SURF for details.)

Recreation and Water Sports

A variety of options are available at moderate and deluxe resort hotels, water parks, and the Disney Springs marina. While not all activities are offered in all locations, you can expect to find biking (regular and surrey), fishing, canoeing, boating, sailing, parasailing, waterskiing, wakeboarding, tubing, surfing, horseback riding, and carriage rides somewhere in the World. Call 407-WDW-PLAY or your resort to get details. Sammy Duvall's Watersports Centre at the Contemporary offers personal watercraft excursions, waterskiing, parasailing, and wakeboarding (included in some packages)—call 407-939-0754 or visit http://www.sammyduvall.com. Also see page 216.

More at ⓘ dive-quest

Top Photo Slice: Ladybugs released on a head of lettuce during the Behind the Seeds tour at Epcot (ⓘ2398) © Denise Preskitt

Treasure Hunts

There is hidden treasure at the Walt Disney World Resort. While it may not consist of golden doubloons, it is every bit as priceless. There are countless sets of often-hidden and always-valuable Disneyesque items for you to find during your vacation. Sometimes these items are purposefully hidden; other times they are out in plain view for all to see but few to notice. Hunting for your favorite item can add a new dimension to your vacation! Here are our favorite things to collect:

Disney Characters and Autographs

Live Disney characters abound, and kids of all ages delight in spotting them. You can discover where some characters are "hiding" by checking with Guest Relations at each major park. If you want to "bag your catch," take photographs—and try to get yourself or your family in the picture! Keep in mind that characters are popular and crowds will form. If you know when your characters will appear, show up early to greet them. (Tip: Ask a Disney cast member about character appearances for the day.) You can also collect autographs from characters who are able to sign their name. Special autograph books are available at most shops, or you can bring your own. Or use the PassPorter's autograph space on pages 306–307. Try to bring a wide-barreled pen or marker so the character can hold it easily. You can also have the characters sign hats or shirts (which must be Disney or non-commercial), but shirts cannot be worn while they are being signed and you need something to slip under the fabric to provide a writing surface. We have an entire 266-page e-book called *PassPorter's Disney Character Yearbook*, which is all about finding, meeting, photographing, and getting character autographs, and includes a full page dedicated to each character you can meet at Walt Disney World—for details, see http://www.passporter.com/disney-character-yearbook.asp.

Pressed Pennies and Quarters

One of the least expensive souvenirs at the Walt Disney World Resort is pressed coins. Souvenir Pressed Coin machines, found throughout the "World," press different Disney designs onto pennies or quarters. Cost is 51 cents for a pressed penny and $1.25 for a pressed quarter, but there are two newer machines that are $1 per pressed coin (no penny needed) or $5–$10 for all 8–12 designs at the machine—you'll find the 8-die machine with Frozen designs at Once Upon a Toy in Disney Springs and the 12-die machine with Disney Heroine designs at the In Character shop at Disney's Hollywood Studios. Designs differ from machine to machine, making a complete collection a worthy achievement. Bring rolls of shiny pennies and quarters along with you—the hunt for a money-changing machine isn't as much fun. While there are good lists of pressed coin machine locations on the Internet (try http://www.presscoins.com), finding them is half the fun! **Tip**: Buy a keepsake book at Disney's gift shops to store your coins.

14685 © Lissette Brito

A pressed coin machine in Tomorrowland

Free Stuff

Disney may seem to be a mecca to capitalism, but there are still free things for the taking, and they make great souvenirs! Some may even become collector's items one day. You can collect guidemaps, brochures, napkins, paper cups and plates, containers, bags, menus, and more.

More at ⓣ unexpected-treasures

Top Photo Slice: An autograph from Mickey Mouse © MediaMarx, Inc.

Hidden Mickeys

Believe it or not, Disney intentionally hides "Mickeys" all over the place! The internationally recognized Mickey Mouse head (one big circle and two smaller circles for the ears) has been discovered hidden in murals, fences, shows—you name it, you can probably find a Mickey hidden somewhere in it! Disney fans maintain lists of these Hidden Mickeys—try http://www.hiddenmickeys.org and http://www.hiddenmickeysguide.com. You will also enjoy the "Hidden Mickeys" field guide by Steven M. Barrett, available in bookstores. We made a list of our favorite Hidden Mickeys for a rainy day activity—how many hiding places can you find? Write your answers below.

# Location	Hint	Hiding Place
1. General	Isn't it good to know Disney cares for the environment?	
2. General	Ka-ching! Look at what you get when the cash register rings!	
3. General	Bubble, bubble, toil, and trouble, look to laundry for three bubbles.	
4. Magic Kingdom	Clippity clop, clippity clop! I pull a trolley past the Main St. shops.	
5. Magic Kingdom	Look to your feet for the holes in the street.	
6. Magic Kingdom	A Mickey up a sleeve—no joke—check the Grim Reaper's cloak.	
7. Epcot	Test the Track, can you cope? Find the Mickey in the rope.	
8. Epcot	In the pretty koi pond in Japan, look down to the grate you can.	
9. Epcot	Now turn your glance to the gardens of France.	
10. Disney's Hollywood Studios	Look for a tower and we'll bet if you say "terror" you're all wet.	
11. Disney's Hollywood Studios	All around the park I run, my thin black bars protect the fun.	
12. Disney's Hollywood Studios	Writers Stop at the window display to check out the cookie jar, you say?	
13. Disney's Animal Kingdom	Amid the trees near Simba's fest hangs a house that holds a nest.	
14. Disney's Animal Kingdom	Near Pangani you'll pass some fruit. Don't squish Mickey under your boot!	
15. Disney's Animal Kingdom	There is a froggie near Pizzafari. Now that's the end of this safari!	

Hidden Mickey hiding places are found on page 291.

More at ⓘ hidden-mickeys

Top Photo Slice: A hidden Mickey in the hallway carpet at the BoardWalk Villas (ⓘ13340) © Melissa Potter

Taking Photos

Click! Whirrr! Zzzzzzzap! Clack! Whatever sound a still camera or camcorder makes, you can be sure you'll hear it at Walt Disney World. Disney characters wrap little ones in warm hugs, Nikon Picture Spots swim before beleaguered eyes, and everyone scrambles to **capture the legendary magic** on film and digital memory card. Many vacationers bring a camera or a camcorder to record their trip. Here are our tips for great vacation photos:

You've finally got your family lined up in front of Cinderella Castle for the biggest photo of your trip of a lifetime. "OK everyone, stand right there!" And you back up. And you zoom in. And back up some more. And zoom all the way in. But now that you can see everyone's faces, you can't see enough of the castle. So you back up until the entire castle is in view. Now you're 20 feet away from your family, and when you get your prints you need a microscope to see those happy faces. The trick is to **get closer to the people and the backdrop**, not farther away. Zoom the lens out to maximum wide angle, and walk in until the castle fills the viewfinder as desired. Now have everyone stand close to the camera, so they're all heads and shoulders (or at least waist up). That's right, get in their faces! When you frame things right your family will now loom as large as the World around them.

Here are some ideas for **fun photograph collections**: Disney puns and visual gags that often go unnoticed (try "holding up" Spaceship Earth in your photos); your favorite spot at different times of the day; all of the "Picture Spot" signs; and pictures through the eyes of your children (give them their own camera). How about a photo of each family member next to their favorite attraction? If you take these same photos on return trips, you can make a "growth chart" over time.

Another idea is to hold a family **photo scavenger hunt** for fun things and places around Walt Disney World.

You'll find many ideas for fun and magical photographs in our **photo supplement** at the back of this guidebook and in the large PassPorter Photo Archive online at http://www.passporter.com/photos.

Please Note: Selfie sticks are now banned at Walt Disney World theme parks.

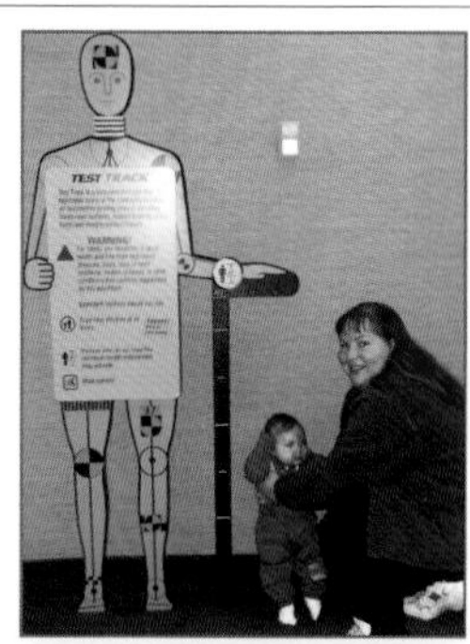

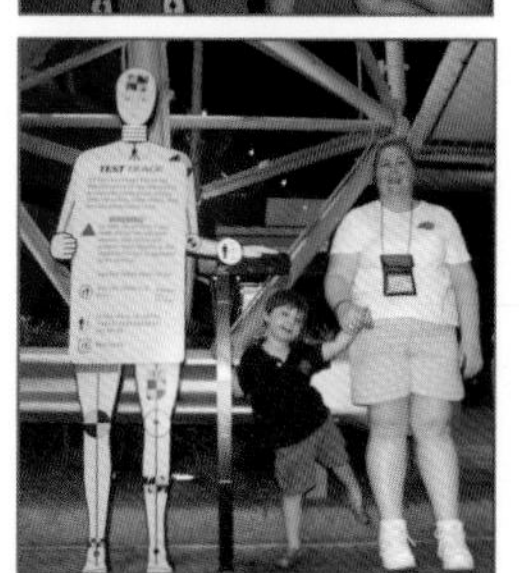

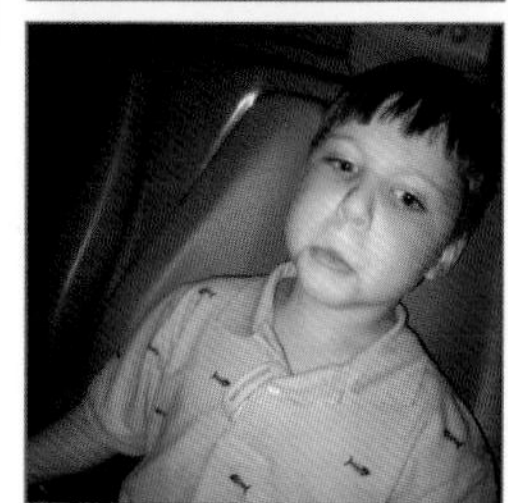

A photo "growth chart" at Epcot's Test Track (Alexander at 0, 1, & 2, and 4, riding for the first time!)

More at ⓘ great-photos | fireworks-photos | digital-camera-tips

Top Photo Slice: Laughing after goofing around in front of the camera at the Character Spot in Epcot (ⓘ14668) © Andrea Johnson

Disney's PhotoPass

Disney's parks have been awash in official photographers since Disney's PhotoPass hit the scene. PhotoPass has added new convenience to having professional photos taken in the parks, and its popularity has multiplied the ways you can enjoy (and purchase) those photos when you return home.

When you have your photo taken by an official Disney's PhotoPass photographer, you either show your MagicBand or are given a free PhotoPass card. There is **no cost** for the photographer to take your photo and code it to your MagicBand or PhotoPass card, and generally the photographers know the best spots, angles, and lighting for great pictures, so there's no reason not to give this a try. At the next photo op, show your MagicBand (or hand your PhotoPass card to the photographer and he/she will slide it through a card reader). Later, whether at a photo shop in the park or at the PhotoPass web site (http://www.disneyphotopass.com), all your photos will be together in one place. You can order prints with some or all of the shots from your vacation. If you use a card, you may continue using the same card on every visit, or combine the photos from several cards into a single online account. The best thing, as far as we're concerned, is that you don't have to wait in long lines at the park's photo shop to get your pictures. Just be sure to login and view new photos online within 30 days of when your first picture was taken—you'll then have 30 days from that login date to make modifications to your pictures (such as adding borders, cropping, etc.) and to order prints or gifts.

You'll find **PhotoPass photographers** nearly everywhere—at the most popular locations, at many character meet-and-greets, and just roaming the park. While park guests used to have (maybe) one "official" shot taken each day, some now seek out the PhotoPass photographers throughout the day. If you purchase the photo package offered at your character meal, those photos will be sent to PhotoPass, too. Even some official ride photos can be added to PhotoPass. Private PhotoPass Portrait Sessions can be arranged at some Disney resorts, and PhotoPass portraits are part of Bibbidi Bobbidi Boutique packages. You can also upload your own photos to the PhotoPass site. They can be combined with PhotoPass shots in your online albums for family and friends to view, professionally printed (4"x6" prints are $0.19 each), and added to PhotoPass merchandise. Not satisfied with your own shots and/or shots featuring your family? PhotoPass has a gallery of photos you can use in your online PhotoPass album and/or have printed on PhotoPass merchandise.

PhotoPass photos can be downloaded in JPG format for $14.95 each. For downloads of 10 or more images, consider purchasing **Memory Maker**, which gives you download access to all your photos for $199 (or $169 if purchased at least three days in advance). The Memory Maker web site lets you crop, and add Disney-themed borders and character autographs to the photos, too. You can even access your Family & Friends who share their photos with you! Plus, if you've purchased Memory Maker and are wearing a MagicBand, you'll get certain ride photos added automatically to your account thanks to the long-range RFID readers (currently that's Buzz Lightyear's Space Ranger Spin, Seven Dwarfs Mine Train, Space Mountain, Splash Mountain, Test Track, Twilight Zone Tower of Terror, Rock 'N' Roller Coaster, Expedition Everest, and DINOSAUR). Note that photos expire 45 days from the date the photo was taken. More details at https://disneyworld.disney.go.com/memory-maker.

You can also purchase photo gift products, such as **Disney's Photo Book**—this lets you customize an 11" x 8.75", hard cover souvenir book, starting at $79.95. Select up to four photos per page, choose background styles, layout, and add captioning/text, etc.

Tip: PhotoPass photographers will also usually take a photo with your own camera, as well as their own. Just ask!

More at ⓘ photopass

Top Photo Slice: A PhotoPass photographer taking photos in front of Cinderella Castle © MediaMarx, Inc.

Shopping for Souvenirs

If you enjoy taking home souvenirs but you're tired of the usual T-shirts or postcards, consider beginning a new collection. Chances are that if you can collect it, Disney has it somewhere on its property.

We list our favorite shops at each of the four major parks back in chapter 4 (look for the charts right after each fold-out map). What do we like to collect? Here are favorites: enamel trading pins (see page 283 for details), patches (you can sew them onto your packs), mugs, figurines, hats, clothing, stuffed animals, and Disney beanie babies. Love shopping? Use the worksheet below to help you organize the items you want to purchase for yourself and others at Walt Disney World! This is a great spot to make a note of those souvenirs you promised to bring back for friends and family, too!

ⓘ15313 © Lindsay Jones

Hats at the World of Disney store

The new "Shop Disney Parks" app allows guests to shop for exclusive Walt Disney World merchandise both in the parks and at home. Online maps allow guests to locate an item in the theme parks or scan an item, purchase it through the app, and have it shipped directly to their home! Look for the app in the App Store (iPhone) or Google Play (Android).

Who	What	Size/Color	$$	✓

More at ⓘ shopping-savings

Top Photo Slice: Plushy stuffed animals on display at The Seas With Nemo & Friends at Epcot (ⓘ6464) © Janet Simonsen

In Search Of...

Quite often we're on the lookout for specific items, whether they be souvenirs or necessities. To help hunt down your treasures, here is a partial list of places to find some of the more commonly sought items:

Alcohol—You can buy a mixed drink, wine, or beer at any of the resorts or parks—even the Magic Kingdom now serves beer and wine with meals at the Be Our Guest restaurant. You can also purchase bottled alcohol at most resort general stores and at Disney Springs.

Baby Needs—The baby care centers in the four major parks sell common baby items, such as diapers, wipes, and formula. Your resort's gift shop stocks these items as well.

Groceries—Snacks are available at most of the resort stores, and a small selection of groceries is available at resorts with in-room cooking facilities. For more serious marketing, visit the Winn-Dixie half a mile north of the Crossroads Shopping Center. You may also want to try GardenGrocer.com (http://www.gardengrocer.com) for deliveries!

Gum—Gum is not sold on Disney property nor at the airport to avoid messes.

Lost Items—Lost and Found centers are located everywhere you go—generally near the front of the park or complex. Jennifer dropped a favorite scarf at Disney Springs and within 15 minutes she had recovered it at Lost and Found (much to her relief). You can also call Lost and Found at 407-824-4245. Lost and found items are generally kept at each park only until closing. After that, they are usually transferred to Central Lost and Found at the Transportation and Ticket Center (inside the Kennel). Remember to label everything!

Medicine—Order prescription and over-the-counter drugs through Turner Drugs at 407-828-8125 from 8:00 am to 8:00 pm. Deliveries (for a fee) are available between 9:00 am and 9:00 pm. (Insurance paperwork is available so you may file claims upon your return.) Tip: Check with your insurance company to see which pharmacies will accept your insurance. Over-the-counter medicine and bandages are kept under the counter at many Disney shops—ask a cast member. Aspirin and bandages are also available at no charge at the first-aid stations staffed by licensed medical personnel in each park and resort front desks.

Missing or Lost Persons—Should you become separated, immediately alert a cast member or go to Guest Relations. Teach kids how to recognize cast members by their white or blue nametags. A message system is available at Guest Relations to help coordinate things, even if you aren't lost (yet). It's a good idea to choose a meeting place each day in the event you are separated from your family or friends. You may also find it helpful to give each member of your party a two-way radio or cell phone to stay in touch with one another. We also suggest you take a digital photo of kids each morning—this will help you if a child is lost.

Money—ATMs (cash machines) are located in all the parks and resorts. See our park maps or Disney's guidemaps for locations. The Walt Disney World Resort accepts American Express, MasterCard, Visa, Discover, JCB, Diner's Club, traveler's checks, cash, Disney Dollars and Gift Cards, and the Disney Dream Reward Dollars card (see page 10 for details on the Disney Rewards Visa card). Personal checks may be used to buy tickets or settle resort bills; checks can no longer be cashed unless it is a check from a Sun Trust bank. Travelers checks and some foreign currency may be cashed at the resort where you are staying up to $200 per day (no fee up to $100; fees apply for amounts over $100).

Rain Gear—If you didn't bring an umbrella or poncho along, Disney will sell you one at virtually any shop. You may need to ask, but chances are they'll have something. Tip: If your poncho rips, bring it back to any shop and they'll replace it. Disney sells clear ponchos to make it easier to spot your companions in the rain.

Top Photo Slice: Victoria searches Minnie's refrigerator in the now-gone Mickey's Toontown Fair (ⓘ1784) © Laura Dawson

More at ⓘ babies-at-disney | garden-grocer

Wake-Up Call

If you're staying at a Disney resort, start your day with a call from Mickey. Just use the phone system to arrange a wake-up call, and when the phone rings, Mickey, Stitch, or one of their friends welcomes you to the new day! When the phone rings with your wake-up call, press the speakerphone button so everyone in the room can hear it! Tip: Make your wake-up call for an off-time, such as 7:03, to help ensure you get Mickey.

Box Seats

Wishes Fireworks Dessert Party—The Tomorrowland Terrace hosts the new Wishes Fireworks Dessert Party on select nights. The party begins an hour before Wishes (check the schedule for times) and includes a self-service dessert buffet on the patio of the Tomorrowland Terrace. The dessert party is $49/adults and $29/kids ages 3-9. Call 407-WDW-DINE to inquire about availability (reservations are hard to obtain). Pre-payment is required.

ⓘ17320 © Monica Gauvin

Treats at the Dessert Party

Contemporary Resort—Enjoy a meal in the California Grill during the Magic Kingdom fireworks (the music that normally accompanies the fireworks is broadcast in the restaurant). While the California Grill observation deck is open only to diners, there's another viewing area on the north end of the Grand Concourse (4th floor).

Ferrytale Wishes: A Fireworks Dessert Cruise—This new cruise aboard the General Joe Potter ferryboat offers gorgeous views of the Magic Kingdom fireworks from the Seven Seas Lagoon along with a dessert buffet with sparkling wine, coffee, and punch. Cost is $99/adult and $69/kids ages 3–9.

Fireworks Cruises—Do you have something to celebrate? Rent a pontoon boat or the Grand 1 Yacht to view the fireworks at Epcot or the Magic Kingdom. Cruises are booked per boat rather than per passenger, and all include a pilot. Call 407-WDW-PLAY for rates and reservations. You can book up to 180 days in advance, and we recommend you call at 7:00 am Eastern Time exactly 180 days in advance, as these cruises are extremely popular. Note: These are sometimes called "specialty" cruises by Disney, as they can't promise that the fireworks won't be cancelled.

More at ⓘ fireworks-cruises

Top Photo Slice: Little PassPorter VIPs posing outside The Seas With Nemo & Friends Epcot (ⓘ14850) © Lisa Siverns-LeClair

Collectibles

Trading Pins

Colorful, enameled commemorative pins are a favorite Disney collectible, available at nearly every shop for $6.95 and up. Disney designs thousands of these colorful, cloisonné pins, which commemorate the theme parks, resorts, attractions, characters, and events. Over the years, Disney stepped up pin trading activity by introducing Pin Trading Stations at the parks and the Disney's Pin Traders shop at Disney Springs, where you can buy and swap pins. Bring (or buy) your own Disney pins, and trade pins with other guests and with cast members wearing special pin-trading lanyards around their neck or boards at their waist. Look for "Scoop Sanderson," a special Main Street, U.S.A. cast member who offers pin trading classes and tips. Note that cast members wearing green lanyards trade only with children. Buy a Disney pin lanyard, or display your pins in a scrapbook, or on a vest or hat. Tip: If pin collecting is your thing, keep an eye on Disney's Official Pin Trading page at http://www.disneypins.com, where news on pin releases and special events are announced.

Park Passports

The Epcot Passport is a great way to tour the World Showcase. Once you have a passport, you can get it "stamped" at each pavilion or land by a cast member. The passports—which kids love—can be purchased at shops and carts for about $12 and include an "I'm a World Showcase Traveler" pin and a set of stickers. A similar passport is available at Disney's Animal Kingdom.

Vinylmation Figures

These vinyl, designer toys—most are just 3" tall—are quite popular. They usually have a common shape (such as Mickey Mouse) but come in different designs—and typically you don't know what you get until you open the box! You can trade Vinylmation with others, or even trade one back in to Disney for one in a clear case or a mystery box. Prices start at $9.95 for a 3" tall figure. Learn more at http://www.disneystore.com/vinylmation.

Sorcerers of the Magic Kingdom Trading Cards

All park guests can get a free pack of trading cards for the fun Sorcerers of the Magic Kingdom game! Just stop by the firehouse on Main Street, U.S.A. and present your MagicBand or park admission. Spell Cards in the game are divided into nine different spell classes: Animal, Fairy, Hero, Machine, Monster, Mystic, Princess, Toy, and Warrior. A card's rarity is classified by the symbol in the bottom left corner, right above the number, so a Planet means that the card is common, a Crescent Moon means it's uncommon, a Star means it's rare and a Lightning Bolt means it's super rare. You can get a free 5-pack of cards every day you enter the Magic Kingdom by going to the firehouse. See page 134 for more details on the game itself.

More at ⓘ sorcerers

Top Photo Slice: A row of trading pins for sale at the Pin Trading Station in Epcot © MediaMarx, Inc.

Childcare Programs

"We're going to Walt Disney World. Why in the 'World' would we need childcare?" The Walt Disney World Resort is an adult playground, too! The "World" offers an exciting nightlife and leaves lots of room for romance. All you need is a sitter. Not surprisingly, Disney delivers with a variety of childcare options and a few programs that may seem like childcare to you (but don't tell the kids). The two main options are childcare programs at the resorts and private, in-room baby-sitting.

Many of Disney's deluxe resorts offer childcare programs. These childcare programs are a good bit like daycare, but unlike daycare, their "day" usually starts at 4:00 pm or 4:30 pm and runs until midnight. They offer a variety of structured activities and usually include a full meal. All programs accept children from 3 to 12 years of age (must be at least age 4 at Camp Dolphin), and all children must be potty-trained. Rates are $12/hour, and there is a two-hour minimum stay. Programs usually also have an overtime rate—the kids won't be evicted if your coach turns into a pumpkin on the way back from Cinderella Castle. Parents are given pagers, too. Some programs are available only to Disney resort guests, and some only for guests staying or dining in the particular resort. Make your status clear when you phone so there are no disappointments. No matter which program you contact, we recommend you call well in advance and ask plenty of questions. Reservations can be made with the club itself or at 407-WDW-DINE. Each resort offers different services and rules, and all are subject to change. Cancel at least 24 hours in advance to avoid a $20/kid fee. **Alex's KidTip:** "You can play video games and do crafts! I liked it better when I was younger (I'm 10 now), so maybe it's better for little kids." **Allie's KidTip:** "It's cool to stay at the kids' clubs so you can do what you like to do and grown-ups can do what they want to do."

Childcare Near Epcot and Disney's Hollywood Studios

☐ **Sandcastle Club** [Beach Club]	407-934-3750
Large club with plenty of Legos, games, computers, and video games (free) to play with. Meals are served at 6:00, 7:00, or 8:00 pm. This club is available only to Disney resort guests. **Allie's KidTip:** *"There are fun games to play."*	**$12/hour** 4:30 pm–Midnight

☐ **Camp Dolphin** [Swan and Dolphin]	407-934-4000 ext. 4241
Kids have fun with arts and crafts, video games, and movies. Price includes a meal at 7:00 pm—kids are usually taken to the Picabu eatery in the resort. Note that participation is not limited to Swan and Dolphin guests. Unlike the other childcare centers, kids must be at least 4 years old to participate here.	**$12/hour** 5:30 pm–Midnight

Top Photo Slice: Play things in Lilo's Clubhouse at the Polynesian Village Resort © MediaMarx, Inc.

Childcare Programs

Childcare Near Disney's Animal Kingdom

Simba's Cubhouse [Disney's Animal Kingdom Lodge]	407-938-4785
The club with a view of the savanna and animals. Plenty of movies and games. Price includes a meal (serving time varies). Allie's KidTip: *"This is my first choice! I liked the people and the decorations. And I loved watching the animals."*	$12/hour 4:30 pm–Midnight

Childcare Near the Magic Kingdom

Cub's Den [Wilderness Lodge]	407-824-1083
A smallish club with structured activities, movies, arts and crafts, and games. Price includes a meal (choice of hot dog, hamburger, cheeseburger, chicken strips, mac & cheese, or PB&J, plus ice cream) served between 6:30–8:00 pm.	$12/hour 4:30 pm–Midnight

Lilo's Playhouse [Polynesian Village]	407-824-2000
Formerly the Neverland Club. Price includes a meal (buffet of kid-friendly items) served 6:00–8:00 pm. The club has its own movie theatre and game arcade. The newly-redesigned club is themed to look like a fairytale brought to life, with touches from the classic Disney Little Golden Books, including "Alice In Wonderland," "Pinocchio" and "Lady and The Tramp." Ask about their open house daily from noon to 4:00 pm for Polynesian Village resort guests. Allie's KidTip: *"I like the people here, and the stairs are fun to sit on and watch movies. The TV here is big!"* Alex's KidTip: *"I pretended to be a pirate in Neverland!"*	$12/hour 4:00 pm–Midnight

Other Childcare Options

Kids Nite Out offers Disney-sanctioned, private in-room babysitting, 24 hours a day, seven days a week. Rates are $16/hour for one child, $18.50/hour for two children, $21/hour for three children, and $23.50/hour for four children. Note that a $10 fee for transportation is automatically applied for each session, and a $2/hour surcharge is applied to caregiving that begins after 9:00 pm. There is a four-hour minimum. Two other independent childcare agencies, **Fairy Godmothers** and **All About Kids**, offer similar services. The professional sitters will take kids to the theme parks if you make arrangements in advance (ask at time of reservation) and watch infants and children with some special needs. The sitters show up equipped to keep the kids occupied with games and activities. They are well-trained, bonded, and insured. Rates vary, depending on the age and number of kids under care. For reservations, contact Kids Nite Out at 800-696-8105 or 407-828-0920 or visit http://www.kidsniteout.com. Fairy Godmothers is at 407-275-7326. All About Kids is at 407-812-9300.

More at ⓘ toddlers-at-disney

Top Photo Slice: Having fun in "the club" © MediaMarx, Inc.

Special Occasions

It seems natural to celebrate a special occasion at Disney. It's designed for fun and comes predecorated! So whether you plan a trip around a special day or want to celebrate one that falls during your vacation, you can do it at Disney! Here are our tips and tricks for a magical celebration:

Birthdays—What better place to celebrate a birthday than at Disney? If you're at a Disney resort, press "0" on your room phone and ask for the special "birthday message." Be sure to request a free "Happy Birthday!" button at the Guest Relations desk at the theme parks or at your hotel's concierge. If you want to celebrate in style, all sorts of birthday parties and cruises can be arranged in advance—you can even "invite" Disney characters (though they're very expensive). For kids ages 4–12, you can arrange a birthday party at the BoardWalk or the Yacht & Beach Club—call 407-WDW-PLAY. For parties in other restaurants, call 407-WDW-DINE. Birthday cruises (407-WDW-PLAY) are also available. One year, Jennifer surprised her mom Carolyn with a special birthday event, planned in part by Gifts of a Lifetime (see sidebar on next page). Families that celebrate Quinceañera, a daughter's 15th birthday, are invited to contact Disney's event planning department to plan their party at 321-939-4555.

Engagements—Disney is a magical place to propose. For $300, you can propose at Cinderella's Royal Table—price includes a meal, glass slipper, photo, and special dessert!

Weddings—From intimate to traditional to themed, Disney's Fairy Tale Weddings have something for virtually every budget. Learn more at http://www.disneyweddings.com or call 407-828-3400. Vow renewals are also available. You can also get free "Just Married" buttons to wear—ask about them at Guest Relations in any of the four major parks and resort front desks. You may wish to purchase and wear the bridal Mickey ears (white veil and black top hat) for $20 each. Learn much more in our full-length guidebook, *PassPorter's Disney Weddings & Honeymoons* by Carrie Hayward—it's available immediately as an e-book or in a handy print edition. It includes hard-to-obtain information, prices, photos, and delightful details on planning a special wedding or honeymoon! Learn more at http://www.passporter.com/weddings.asp.

© Disney Event Group

The magical Dattalo wedding

More at ⓘ birthdays | intimate-weddings

Top Photo Slice: A birthday button from Walt Disney World © MediaMarx, Inc.

A diver at Coral Reef holds up a sign for a couple on their honeymoon

ⓘ7402 © Gina Winnette

Honeymoons—Walt Disney World is the #1 honeymoon destination in the world, believe it or not. Not only are romantic spots found around virtually every corner, but Disney goes out of its way to make newlyweds welcome. Lodging packages, romantic rooms, candlelit dinners, and adult-oriented entertainment abound. Even if you do nothing more than mention that it is your honeymoon to cast members, you may be in for a special treat. For details, call Disney at 407-934-7639.

Anniversaries—Like birthdays, anniversaries are always in style at the Walt Disney World Resort. You can get free "Happy Anniversary" buttons to wear—ask about them at Guest Relations or your resort front desk. You can plan a special night out at a romantic restaurant or shape an entire vacation around your special day. Be sure to mention your anniversary when making advance dining reservations (especially at Cinderella's Royal Table)—you may be pleasantly surprised.

Group Events—With all the conventions it hosts each year, Disney is a pro at group parties and functions. We've planned several ourselves and found plenty of options and many helpful cast members. You can have a private party virtually anywhere in the "World," for small or large groups. For parties in any of the resorts, call 407-828-3074. If you're interested in having a private party at one of the parks, call Group Sales at 407-828-3200. We can't say it'll be cheap, but you can plan one within a reasonable budget if you're careful. Of course, you can go all-out, too—companies rent entire theme parks. Planet Hollywood at Disney Springs hosts private functions, too.

In fact, PassPorter readers like to plan gatherings of like-minded individuals. If you'd like to learn about our next gathering, visit http://www.passporterboards.com/forums/backyard-gatherings-meets-group-trips.

Special Services for Special Occasions

It's a challenge to organize a special occasion long-distance. An innovative company, **Presentations: Gifts of a Lifetime**, helps you shop for that perfect gift, arrange a magical event, and even put on the whole show! To learn more, visit their web site at http://www.giftsofalifetime.com or call 407-909-0593.

You can also have **Disney Floral & Gifts** (http://www.disneyfloralandgifts.com, 407-827-3505) prepare a fruit or snack basket and deliver it to a guest room.

More at ⓘ romance-at-disney | vow-renewals | gatherings

Special Events at Disney

Disney really knows how to celebrate. Nearly every holiday seems to have at least one event, and Easter, Halloween, Christmas, and New Year's Eve spark extended festivities. Disney also is a master at battling periods of slow attendance with specially themed events throughout the year. Call Disney's main information line at 407-824-4321 or visit their web site at http://www.disneyworld.com for more information.

Sports

January brings the sell-out **Walt Disney World Marathon Weekend** (Jan. 6-10, 2016), which includes the Family Fun Run and the Kids' Festival (open to all ages), as well as Goofy's Race and a Half Challenge (Jan. 9-10)—call 407-939-7810 for information and sign-up. The **Princess Half-Marathon** is held February 18–21, 2016, with a focus on women's fitness. The new Star Wars Half Marathon in April 14-17, 2016. There's also the **Tinker Bell Half-Marathon** on May 5–8, 2016. The **Atlanta Braves** baseball spring training is in March and April. There's also another **Disney Spring Training** event in 2016, featuring team training for baseball, golf, lacrosse, softball, and track & field. Many more sport opportunities are available at ESPN Wide World of Sports Complex—for more details, visit http://www.disneyworldsports.com and http://www.rundisney.com.

Festivals and Fun

The **Epcot International Flower & Garden Festival** (March 2–May 15, 2016) fills the park with exhibits, seminars, tours, demonstrations, the Food Among the Flowers Brunch (see page 267), amazing character-shaped topiaries, and special entertainment at the America Gardens Theatre. On selected dates in May and June, Disney's Hollywood Studios has **Star Wars Weekends** with celebrity appearances and special events. The Friday and Saturday after Labor Day bring the popular **Nights of Joy** to Magic Kingdom to celebrate contemporary Christian music ($55/day/person in advance; see http://www.nightofjoy.com). The 21st Annual **Epcot International Food & Wine Festival**, which will be held September 23–November 14, 2016, turns the World Showcase into an even greater gourmet delight (see page 241). Note that the **ABC Super Soap Weekend** held its last event at Walt Disney World in 2009 and the last **Grad Night** was held in 2011.

Other Parties, Holidays, and Observances

May 31–June 6, 2016 are the **Unofficial Gay Days events** (visit http://www.gaydays.com). No word yet on whether **Destination D**, a D23 event, will return to Walt Disney World again, but it wouldn't surprise us if it did! There are smaller D23 events at Walt Disney World, however, such as the Sip & Stroll.

Check out *PassPorter's Festivals and Celebrations at Walt Disney World* for 78 pages of details on all the **wonderful and magical festivals**, celebrations, parties, and holidays at Walt Disney World. Details at http://www.passporter.com/wdw/festivals-celebrations.asp.

Tip: Fireworks for major holidays—Independence Day, New Years Eve, and often others—are normally given a "dress rehearsal" the night before. Go a day early and avoid the big crowds!

More at ⓘ food-and-wine-festival

Holidays at Disney

Easter *(March 27, 2016)*
Spring crowds reach a peak during Easter week. Easter egg hunts and candy scrambles may be held at some of the resorts for their guests. Check with your resort for details. Some restaurants offer Easter meals, such as Chef Mickey's (see page 255), 'Ohana (see page 258), Whispering Canyon Cafe (see page 260), and Mickey's Backyard BBQ (see page 264).

Independence Day *(July 4, 2016)*
The Magic Kingdom traditionally puts on a spectacular fireworks show, as does Disney's Hollywood Studios. Epcot's IllumiNations is enhanced with Fourth of July fun, too!

Halloween *(October 31, 2016)*
Mickey's Not So Scary Halloween Party brings kid-friendly spookiness to the Magic Kingdom for 24 nights (7:00 pm–midnight) in September and October (usually Tuesdays, Fridays, and Sundays, plus Halloween night). Enjoy Mickey's Boo to You Halloween Parade, a kids' costume parade, trick-or-treating around the park, Halloween-themed fireworks, storytellers, fortune tellers, and access to most rides. We recommend you make time for the Liberty Belle Riverboat, which offers Halloween cruises with storytellers and live entertainment—it was the highlight of our night! Advance tickets at press time were at $72.42–$84.14/adult, $67.10–$78.81/child (price includes tax). Call 407-934-7639 well in advance as tickets sell out, especially for Halloween night—expect tickets to go on sale on May 1, 2016.

Thanksgiving *(November 24, 2016)*
Crowds take a bump up for this All-American holiday. Disney's holiday decorations are already up, and a number of the full-service restaurants at the parks and almost all of the Disney resorts host special holiday dinners, with and without Disney characters.

Christmas *(December 25, 2016)*
Christmas is a very special time, with delightful decorations, holiday entertainment, and countless ways to enjoy the season. Decorations go up by mid-November, so there's more than a month of merriment. Try to come during the first two weeks of December when the crowds are a little thinner, rates are a little lower, the party is in full swing, and the "World" is decked with holiday cheer. **Mickey's Very Merry Christmas Party** is a big favorite. Packed full of special shows and special fun, the Magic Kingdom is open for five extra hours for about 20 nights in November and December. Snow falls on Main Street, fireworks and music fill the air, and the big rides are open. And let's not forget the castle lighting ceremony, holiday-themed entertainment, strolling carolers, and complimentary cookies and hot cocoa. Advance tickets at press time are $78.81–$87.33/adult, $73.49–$82.01/child, prices include tax—expect tickets to go on sale May 1, 2016. At Epcot, the **Candlelight Processional** runs two to three times nightly. A celebrity narrator, chorus, and orchestra present the Christmas tale. No extra admission required, but a special dinner package offers reserved seating (call 407-WDW-DINE). Be sure to **view the resort decorations** (try the Yuletide Tour—see page 273) and enjoy merriment at **Disney Springs**. The **Osborne Family Spectacle of Dancing Lights** sparkles throughout the Streets of America Set at Disney's Hollywood Studios in 2015, but closes in 2016—see page 179.

New Year's Eve *(December 31, 2016)*
The Magic Kingdom, Epcot, Disney's Hollywood Studios, and Atlantic Dance at the BoardWalk all host big New Year's celebrations. The theme parks overflow during the Christmas–New Year's week, and reservations at resorts are extremely hard to get. Disney does not charge anything more than regular admission to the parks on New Year's Eve.

More at ⓘ holidays-at-disney

Top Photo Slice: Iced turrets on Cinderella Castle at the Magic Kingdom (ⓘ10632) © JustLorri

Beyond Walt Disney World

We're pretty infatuated with Disney, but there is life beyond Walt Disney World. At least that's what we hear. We don't venture far beyond the gates, preferring to spend more time immersed in Disney's magic rather than battle traffic to get to another park. We do know that families hope to visit other theme parks during their visit to central Florida, so here is a list of Florida parks and attractions. For more information, check out *PassPorter's Orlando and Beyond: Everything but the Mouse* guidebook by Cheryl Pendry (coming soon).

Name	Number	Web Site
Busch Gardens	813-987-5082	http://www.buschgardens.com
Discovery Cove	407-370-1428	http://www.discoverycove.com
Gatorland	800-393-JAWS	http://www.gatorland.com
LEGOLAND Florida (see page 315)	877-350-5346	http://florida.legoland.com
Kennedy Space Center	321-452-2121	http://kennedyspacecenter.com
Medieval Times	407-396-1518	http://medievaltimes.com
Sea World	407-363-2613	http://seaworld.com
Universal Studios/Islands of Adv.	407-363-8000	http://www.universalorlando.com
Wet 'n' Wild	407-351-1800	http://www.wetnwild.com

Beyond Orlando

Like any other forward-thinking organization, The Walt Disney Company has expanded into other locales. Here are a few of them:

Disney Cruise Line—"Take the magic of Disney and just add water!" The Disney Cruise Line set sail in 1998 with the same enthusiasm and energy you find at the Walt Disney World Resort. See pages 106–107, and pick up a copy of our popular guidebook, *PassPorter's Disney Cruise Line and Its Ports of Call* (available in bookstores or order at http://www.passporter.com/dcl—more details about the guidebook on page 312).

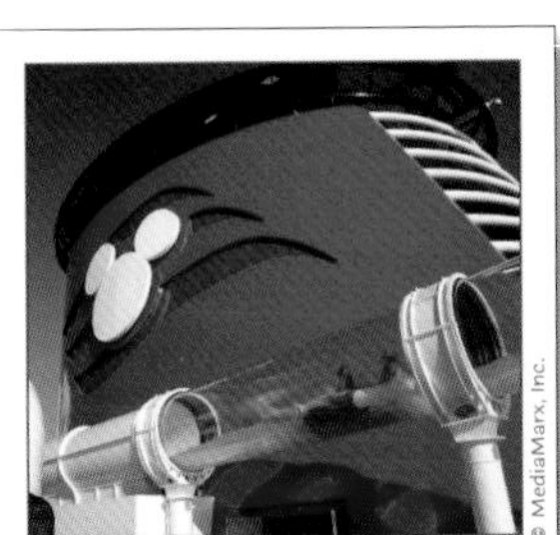
© MediaMarx, Inc.

The AquaDuck water coaster on the Disney Dream ship

Adventures by Disney—Adventures by Disney is making the world a Disney "park." These deluxe escorted tours feature separate activities for adults and kids as well as all together, and visit a growing list of fabulous destinations in the US and abroad. http://www.adventuresbydisney.com

Disney's Vero Beach Resort—Vero Beach, Florida, is Disney's first oceanside resort, a two-hour drive from Disney World. Call 561-234-2000 for more information, or visit http://verobeach.disney.go.com and click Resorts. Also learn about our in-depth e-book on the Disney Vacation Club at http://www.passporter.com/disney-vacation-club.asp.

Disney's Hilton Head Island Resort—For southern grace and charm, experience the South Carolina Low Country lifestyle at Disney's Hilton Head Island Resort. Hilton Head is a golfer's nirvana, boasting 12 nearby golf courses. The tennis and beaches are also big draws. It's an ideal spot for small group retreats. For more information, call 843-341-4100. Get more information at http://hiltonhead.disney.go.com.

More at ⓘ busch-gardens | kennedy-space-center | universal-orlando | disney-cruising | hilton-head

Top Photo Slice: Universal Studios globe with Islands of Adventure in the background (ⓘ1899) © Brad K.

Disney Parks Around the World

© MediaMarx, Inc.
Disneyland Resort

Disneyland Resort (California)—The original "Magic Kingdom," near Los Angeles. Disneyland was the model for the Magic Kingdom in Florida and still keeps a step or two ahead of its offspring, since Disney's Imagineers live close by. The official Disneyland hotels are right next door if you want to make a week out of it. Disneyland's "other" park, Disney California Adventure, recently completed a huge expansion and re-design, to rave reviews. We cover the entire Disneyland Resort and other area attractions, such as Universal Studios, Knott's Berry Farm, LEGOLAND, Hollywood, San Diego Zoo, and SeaWorld in our award-winning guidebook: *PassPorter's Disneyland Resort and Southern California Attractions*. For more details and to order a copy, visit http://www.passporter.com/dl (see page 313).

© MediaMarx, Inc.
Disneyland Paris

Disneyland Paris Resort (France)—The first (and only) Disney resort in Europe, the park has a similar layout to Disneyland, with the major change being a substitution of Discoveryland for Tomorrowland. A second park, the Walt Disney Studios, features several popular attractions from Disney's Hollywood Studios in Florida—and one of its original attractions (Lights, Motors, Action!) made its way to Florida, too. Visit http://www.disneylandparis.com. A third theme park, new eco-tourism resort hotel, and a housing development were reported to be built, but no recent updates! We visited and stayed at the Disneyland Hotel—immediately adjacent to the park—and adored it. Look for PassPorter's complete guidebook to Disneyland Paris (see page 315).

Tokyo Disney Resort (Japan)—Disney, Japan-style! Tokyo Disney Resort is located in Urayasu, just outside Tokyo. It is similar to Disneyland in California, incorporating the quintessential "American" things. When Jennifer visited, she found it squeaky clean and definitely Disney, with just a touch of Japanese peeking through. In 2001, the Tokyo DisneySea theme park opened immediately adjacent to Tokyo Disneyland. The aquatically themed park has seven lands and three resort hotels, including the new Tokyo Disneyland Hotel. Visit http://www.tokyodisneyresort.jp/en/.

Hong Kong Disneyland—Opened in September 2005, this theme park overlooks the water of Penny's Bay, Lantau. For details, visit http://www.hongkongdisneyland.com.

Hawaii—Aulani, a new Disney resort and spa, is located at the Ko Olina Resort and Marina west of Honolulu on the island of Oahu. The 21-acre facility offers a total of 800 hotel rooms and Disney Vacation Club villas, and opened on August 29, 2011. For more details, visit http://www.aulani.com.

Hidden Mickey Hiding Places (from list on page 277)

1) In the Disney Recycles logo on bags, napkins, etc.; 2) On cash register receipts; 3) The "Soap Stop" vending machines in the resort laundry rooms; 4) Main Street Vehicle horse harnesses; 5) In the center of manhole covers; 6) In the sleeve of a cloak on a Grim Reaper ghost in the Haunted Mansion; 7) In coiled ropes on Test Track (visible in the ride photo); 8) Drain grate in the goldfish pond in Japan; 9) Hedges trimmed into circles; 10) Earffel water tower; 11) The ironwork fence around Disney's Hollywood Studios; 12) The cookie jar in the Writer's Stop window; 13) Birdhouse near Festival of the Lion King; 14) On the sidewalk near the Harambe Fruit Market; and 15) On the frog statue outside of the women's restroom near Pizzafari.

Top Photo Slice: Celebrating Chinese New Year on Main Street at Disneyland Hong Kong (ⓘ5970) © Cheryl Pendry

Your Own Walt Disney World

Make Walt Disney World your personal playground with these tips:

"If you are traveling to Walt Disney World with a large family or many friends, purchase the Memory Maker and split the cost. Anyone linked to you on your My Disney Experience account can add pictures to the Memory Maker. Not only is it less money, but it gives you the chance to see some of the things everyone else in your party is doing. Only one person can edit prints, but it's not a big deal if all work together! We recently did this with our extended family of 19 and ended up with well over 1,000 pictures! It's a great value when the cost is split three ways!"

– Contributed by Jean Bussell, a winner in our Reader Tip Contest

"Buy glow necklaces at the dollar store. We generally buy two or three containers so we're able to hand out extras while we wait for fireworks. Saves money on the kids asking for glowing souvenirs they sell in the street before nighttime parades and fireworks and you get to spread the magic to other kids nearby!"

– Contributed by Kelly Van Eerden, a winner in our Reader Tip Contest

"Take home a memory of the magic by having silhouettes of you or your children made. We've done this every trip and have a unique souvenir of each one. It's a great way to remember your kids at that special age. It's not just for young kids either. On a recent trip, my daughter and her new husband had one made of the two of them together (his mother loved It!). You get three copies so they can make a great gift for the grandparents as well. Disney Springs is our favorite place to have them made. Special tip: Ask the artist to put the name of the person and the date on it."

– Contributed by Sherry Rohlfing, a winner in our Reader Tip Contest

Magical Memories

"*Our last trip to Walt Disney World in December was for my husband's 50th birthday. On our first day at Animal Kingdom we stopped at Guest Services to get a birthday celebration pin for my husband to wear. He was a little reluctant, but I encouraged him to wear it. He loved the birthday greetings he received from the Cast Members in all the parks as they called him by name and wished him a Happy Birthday. He was selected to join in the Magic Kingdom Parade (definitely got that on video), he received a free brownie at Casey's Corner, and a free pretzel at a street vending cart. It made for magical memories and the smile on my husband's face was great. He talked about our Walt Disney vacation for months after we got home.*"

...as told by Disney vacationer Pamela Feavel

"*I took a Father/Daughter trip with just my 9-year-old daughter, and had to write in about a Magical Moment we had. My daughter and I were waiting for Mary Poppins to come to the United Kingdom pavilion. We asked a Cast Member when Mary Poppins would arrive and she tells us that Mary Poppins doesn't meet there, but down the path next to the cottage. Just as we were about to go, the Cast Member says 'Oh, here comes Mary Poppins now,' and to my daughter's delight, she sees Mary Poppins walking towards her. Mary Poppins starts walking with my daughter down the path, alone, to the place where she needs to be for her meet and greet. When she gets to her destination and says 'Oh, I see there are people waiting to meet me, thank you for walking with me.' The smile on my daughter's face was priceless, this was a dream come true, not just for my daughter but me as well.*"

...as told by Disney vacationer Nathan Franco

Top Photo Slice: An anniversary cake and Magical Moment certificate (①13886) © Jodi Leeper

Index

We feel that a comprehensive index is very important to a successful travel guide. Too many times we've tried to look something up in other books only to find there was no entry at all, forcing us to flip through pages and waste valuable time. When you're on the phone with a reservation agent and looking for that little detail, time is of the essence.

You'll find the PassPorter index is complete and detailed. Whenever we reference more than one page for a given topic, the major topic is in **bold** and map references are in *italics* to help you home in on exactly what you need. For those times you want to find everything there is to be had, we include all the minor references. We have plenty of cross-references, too, just in case you don't look it up under the name we use.

P.S. This isn't the end of the book. More nifty features begin on page 306!

Symbols

A

D

N

O

P

Q

R

S

➢

V

W

Y

Web Site Index

Site Name	Page	Address (URL)
Maple Leaf Tickets	123	http://www.mapleleaftickets.com
MapQuest	15	http://www.mapquest.com
Marc Schwartz's Unofficial Disney Golf	214	http://www.wdwgolf.com
Medieval Times	290	http://medievaltimes.com
Military discounts	123	http://www.disneyworld.com/military
The Mouse For Less	7, 11	http://www.themouseforless.com
MouseMemories	286	http://www.mousememories.com
Mouse Pads Vacation Rentals	115	http://www.mousepadsorlando.com
MousePlanet Trip Reports	12	http://www.mouseplanet.com/wdwtr
MousePlanet Disney Vacation Club	109	http://www.mouseplanet.com/dtp/dvc
MousePlanet Trip Planner	viii	http://www.mouseplanet.com/dtp/wdwguide
MouseSavers.com	viii, 11	http://www.mousesavers.com
MouseStation podcast	7	http://www.mouseplanet.com
My Disney Experience	126	http://disneyworld.disney.go.com
Nature Conservancy	215	http://www.nature.org
Nickelodeon Family Suites	112	http://www.nickhotel.com
Orbitz	16	http://www.orbitz.com
Orlando International Airport	18	http://www.orlandoairports.net
Orlando Magicard	11	http://www.orlandoinfo.com/magicard
Orlando Sanford Airport	19	http://www.orlandosanfordairport.com
Orlando Stroller Rentals	121	http://www.orlandostrollerrentals.com
PassPorter Online	309	http://www.passporter.com *(see more on page 309)*
PassPorter Book Updates	6, 308	http://www.passporter.com/customs/bookupdates.htm
PassPorter Moms Podcast	308	http://www.passporter.com/podcast
PhotoPass	121, 279	http://www.disneyphotopass.com
Portofino Bay Hotel	113	http://www.portofinobay.com
Pressed Coin Collector Page	276	http://www.presscoins.com
Priceline	16	http://www.priceline.com
Planning Strategy Calculator	viii, 226	http://pscalculator.net
Quicksilver Tours & Transportation	22	http://www.quicksilver-tours.com
Radisson Resort Orlando-Celebration	112	http://www.radissonparkway.com
Rainforest Cafe	226	http://www.rainforestcafe.com
Regal Sun Resort	110	http://www.regalsunresort.com
Royal Pacific Resort	113	http://www.loewshotels.com/hotels/orlando_royal_pacific
Sea World	290	http://seaworld.com
Shades of Green	104	http://www.shadesofgreen.org
Sheraton Safari	112	http://www.sheratonsafari.com
Sheraton's Vistana Resort	114	http://www.sheraton.com
Southwest Airlines	16	http://www.southwest.com
Spencer Family's Disney Page	68	http://home.hiwaay.net/~jlspence
Steve Soares' Disney Entertainment	133	http://www.wdwent.com
Swan and Dolphin Resorts	105	http://www.swandolphin.com
Tagrel	7	http://www.tagrel.com
TicketMania	123	http://www.ticketmania.com
Transportation Security Administration	17	http://www.tsa.gov
Travelocity	16, 30	http://www.travelocity.com
Universal Studios Florida	290	http://www.usf.com
Unofficial Disney Information Station	viii, 7	http://www.disboards.com
Walker Mobility	36	http://www.walkermobility.com
Walt Disney Travel Co.	8	http://www.disneytravel.com
Walt Disney World Resort	7, 126	http://www.disneyworld.com
Walt Disney World Spas	215	http://www.relaxedyet.com
Walt Disney World Sports & Rec.	216	http://www.disneyworldsports.com
WDW Radio podcast	7	http://www.wdwradio.com
WDWToday podcast	7	http://www.wdwtoday.com

Autographs

Kids and kids-at-heart love to get autographs from Disney characters! These two pages beg to be filled with signatures, paw prints, and doodles from your favorite characters. We've even provided places to write the actual name of the character (they can be hard to read—they are autographs, after all), plus the location where you discovered the character and the date of your find. Even if you bring or purchase an autograph book, use these pages when you fill it up or just plain forget it. (Been there, done that!) Be sure to see page 276 for tips and tricks on how to get character autographs, too!

Character: *Location:* *Date:*

Character: *Location:* *Date:*

Character: *Location:* *Date:*

Autographs Anonymous

We know. We understand. Bouncing tigers and giant mice can be intimidating. After several months of research and development, we came up with the following system that can help both the interminably shy and the overstimulated. Just write your name in the blank below, take a deep breath, and hold out your book. Now, wasn't that easy?

Hi, my name is ____________. May I have your autograph?

(write your name here)

Character:
Location: *Date:*

Character:
Location: *Date:*

Character: *Location:* *Date:*

Character: *Location:* *Date:*

Register Your PassPorter

We are very interested to learn how your vacation went and what you think of the PassPorter, how it worked (or didn't work) for you, and your opinion on how we could improve it! We encourage you to register your copy of PassPorter with us—in return for your feedback, we'll send you **two valuable coupons** good for discounts on PassPorters and PassHolder pouches when purchased directly from us. You can register your copy of PassPorter at http://www.passporter.com/register.asp, or you can send us a postcard or letter to P.O. Box 3880, Ann Arbor, Michigan 48106.

Report a Correction or Change

Keeping up with the changes at Walt Disney World is virtually impossible without your help. When you notice something is different than what is printed in PassPorter, or you just come across something you'd like to see us cover, please let us know! You can report your news, updates, changes, and corrections at http://www.passporter.com/report.asp.

Contribute to the Next Edition of PassPorter

You can become an important part of the 2017 edition of *PassPorter's Walt Disney World*! The easiest way is to rate the resorts, rides, and/or restaurants. Your ratings and comments become part of our reader ratings throughout the book and help future readers make travel decisions. Want to get more involved? Send us a vacation tip, magical memory, or photograph—if we use it in a future edition of PassPorter, we'll credit you by name in the guidebook and send you a free copy of the edition! Do all this and more at http://www.passporter.com/customs.

Get Your Questions Answered

We love to hear from you! Alas, due to the thousands of e-mails and hundreds of phone calls we receive each week, we cannot offer personalized advice to all our readers. But there's a great way to get your questions answered: Ask your fellow readers! Visit our message boards at http://www.passporterboards.com/forums, join for free, and post your question. In most cases, fellow readers and Disney fans will offer their ideas and experiences! Our message boards also function as an ultimate list of frequently asked questions. Just browsing through to see the answers to other readers' questions will reap untold benefit! This is also a great way to make friends and have fun while planning your vacation. But be careful—our message boards can be addictive!

PassPorter Online

A wonderful way to get the most from your PassPorter is to visit our active web site at http://www.passporter.com. We serve up valuable PassPorter updates, plus useful Walt Disney World information and advice we couldn't jam into our book. You can swap tales (that's t-a-l-e-s, Mickey!) with fellow Disney fans, play contests and games, find links to other sites, get plenty of details, and ask us questions. You can also order PassPorters and shop for PassPorter accessories! The latest information on new PassPorters to other destinations is also available on our site. To get our page-by-page PassPorter updates, visit http://www.passporter.com/customs/bookupdates.htm.

PassPorter Web Links	Address (URL)
Main Page: PassPorter Online	http://www.passporter.com
Walt Disney World Forum	http://www.passporter.com/wdw
PassPorter Message Boards	http://www.passporterboards.com
PassPorter Photo Archive	http://www.passporter.com/photos
PassPorter Article Collection	http://www.passporter.com/articles
Book Updates	http://www.passporter.com/customs/bookupdates.htm
Contribute to PassPorter	http://www.passporter.com/contribute.asp
Register Your PassPorter	http://www.passporter.com/register.asp
PassPorter Deluxe Edition Information	http://www.passporter.com/wdw/deluxe.htm

Planning
Getting There
Staying in Style
Touring
Feasting
Making Magic
Index
Notes & More

PassPorter Articles and Photos

Still hungry for more information to make your Walt Disney World trip the best it can be? You'll **find all the things we couldn't fit** into our guidebook in our extensive photo and article collections, available online at the PassPorter.com web site. At press time, we offer more than 1200 articles (which amounts to about 6000+ pages of information) and nearlyh 70,000 images ... all neatly organized and searchable!

The **PassPorter Article Collection** (view at http://www.passporter.com/articles) contains full-length, feature articles on a variety of topics related to Disney and travel. Each article can be downloaded as a fully-formatted Adobe PDF, printed, and placed in your PassPorter for additional reference. You can search or browse the collection to find articles that interest you. Tip: Use the special keywords we've listed in the lower right margin of many pages in this guidebook and then type the keyword at http://www.passporter.com/i to zip right to a related article! Most of our articles come with photos, links to the related forum in our message boards, and reader comments! If you enjoy our articles, be sure you're subscribed to the free PassPorter News, in which most of our articles originally appear each week! Subscribe at http://www.passporter.com/news.

The huge **PassPorter Photo Archive** is a great way to get a closer look at Disney before you ever arrive. Photos are contributed by authors and readers, giving you a wide range of perspectives. Our archive offers several features, including searching and commenting. PassPorter's Club members (see page 316) can also zoom in on each photo up to 25 times in size to see all the delightful detail. We encourage all of our readers to contribute to the archive—your photo may be selected as a PhotoPick of the week or even chosen to appear in an upcoming PassPorter guidebook! Tip: Use the special numbers we've listed with most photos in this guidebook and then type the number at http://www.passporter.com/i to zip right to the photo for a better look! Tip: Play our Mystery Photo Contest to get contest

PassPorter Goodies

PassPorter was born out of the necessity for more planning, organization, and a way to preserve the memories of a great vacation! Along the way we've found other things that either help us use the PassPorter better, appreciate our vacation more, or just make our journey a little more comfortable. Others have asked us about them, so we thought we'd share them with you. Order online at http://www.passporterstore.com/store or use the order form below.

PassPorter® PassHolder is a small, lightweight nylon pouch that holds passes, ID cards, passports, money, and pens. Wear it around your neck for hands-free touring, and for easy access at the airport. The front features a clear compartment, a zippered pocket, and a velcro pocket; the back has a small pocket (perfect size for FASTPASS) and two pen slots. Adjustable cord. Royal blue. 4 7/8" x 6 1/2"

Quantity: ____ x $8.95

PassPorter® Badge personalized with your name! Go around the "World" in style with our lemon yellow oval pin. Price includes personalization with your name, shipping, and handling. Please indicate badge name(s) with your order.

Quantity: ___ x $4.00

Name(s): ________

Please ship my PassPorter Goodies to:

Name ....

Address ....

City, State, Zip ....

Daytime Phone ....

Payment: ☐ check (to "MediaMarx") ☐ charge card

☐ MasterCard ☐ Visa ☐ American Express ☐ Discover

Card number .... Exp. Date. ....

Signature ....

Sub-Total:

Tax*:

Shipping**:

Total:

* Please include sales tax if you live in Michigan.

**Shipping costs are:
$5 for totals up to $9
$6 for totals up to $19
$7 for totals up to $29
$8 for totals up to $39
Delivery takes 1-2 weeks.

Order online at http://www.passporterstore.com/store or send your order form to P.O. Box 3880, Ann Arbor, MI 48106.

More PassPorters

You've asked for more PassPorters—we've listened! We have eight PassPorter print books and fourteen e-books (and growing), all designed to make your Disney vacation the best it can be. And if you've wished for a PassPorter with all the flexibility and features of a daily planner, check out our Deluxe Editions (described below). To learn more about the new editions and release dates, visit us at http://www.passporter.com.

PassPorter's Walt Disney World Deluxe Edition

Design first-class vacations with this loose-leaf ring binder edition. The Deluxe Edition features the same great content as *PassPorter's Walt Disney World* spiral guide. Special features of the Deluxe Edition include ten interior storage slots in the binder to hold guidemaps, ID cards, and a pen (we even include a pen). The Deluxe PassPorter binder makes it really easy to add, remove, and rearrange pages ... you can even download, print, and add in updates, feature articles, and supplemental pages from our web site, and refills are available for purchase. Learn more at http://www.passporter.com/wdw/deluxe.htm. The Deluxe Edition is available through bookstores by special order—just give your favorite bookstore the ISBN is 978-1-58771-155-8 (2016 Deluxe Edition).

PassPorter's Disney Cruise Line and its Ports of Call

Updated annually! Get your cruise plans in shipshape with our updated, award-winning field guide ... includes details on all new ports and the new ships to come! Authors Dave Marx and Jennifer Marx cover the Disney Cruise Line in incredible detail, including deck plans, stateroom floor plans, color photos, menus, entertainment guides, port/shore excursion details, and plenty of worksheets to help you budget, plan, and record your information. We also include reader tips, photos, and magial memories! In its 13th edition in 2016, this is the original and most comprehensive guidebook devoted to the Disney Cruise Line, and is now in full color! Our 13th edition covers all four ships and over 70 ports of call that the Disney ships visit. Learn more and order your copy at http://www.passporter.com/dcl or get a copy at your favorite bookstore. ISBN for the 13th edition paperback, no PassPockets is 978-1-58771-147-3. Also available in a Deluxe Edition with organizer PassPockets (ISBN: 978-1-58771-148-0).

> ***Did you know?*** *If you purchase these guidebooks directly from PassPorter, you also get the online edition free! This offer is only available to those who order directly through PassPorter; we regret we're unable to offer it to those who purchase it from a bookstore.*

Even More PassPorters in Paperback

PassPorter's Disney 500

This popular book has more than 500 time-tested Walt Disney World tips—all categorized and coded! We chose the best of our reader-submitted tips over a six-year period for this book and each has been edited by author Jennifer Marx. For more details, visit http://www.passporter.com/wdw/disney500.asp. ISBN-13: 978-1-58771-090-2

PassPorter's Free-Book

It's hard to believe anything is free at Walt Disney World, but there are actually a number of things you can get or do for little to no cost. This book documents more than 150 free or cheap things to do before and during your vacation. Visit http://www.passporter.com/wdw/free-book.asp. ISBN-13: 978-1-58771-102-2

PassPorter's Disney Vacation Club Guide

A 170-page in-depth guide to all aspects of the Disney Vacation Club, from deciding whether to join to deciding where and when to use your points. Included are numerous photos and tips on maximizing your experience. If you've ever wondered what the club is all about or wanted to learn more, this is the perfect introduction. Get more details at http://www.passporter.com/disney-vacation-club.asp. ISBN-13: 978-1-58771-087-2

PassPorter's Disney Weddings & Honeymoons

This is both a guidebook and a bridal organizer tailored to the unique requirements of planning a wedding, vow renewal, or commitment ceremony at Walt Disney World or on the Disney Cruise Line. It takes you through the entire process, outline your options, offer valuable tips, organize your information, and help you plan down to the last detail! Details at http://www.passporter.com/weddings.asp. ISBN-13: 978-1-58771-088-9

PassPorter's Walt Disney World for British Holidaymakers

New in print! Brits, you can get super in-depth information for your Walt Disney World vacation from fellow Brit and PassPorter feature columnist Cheryl Pendry. More than 250 pages long and filled with amazing detail on Walt Disney World and Orlando-area attractions. Learn more at http://www.passporter.com/wdw/brits.asp. ISBN-13: 978-1-58771-094-0

PassPorter's Disney Speed Planner

Coming soon to print! Author Justine Fellows offers a fast, easy method for planning practically perfect vacations—great for busy people or those who don't have lots of time to plan. Follow this simple, ten-step plan to help you get your vacation planned in short order so you can get on with your life. For more details, visit http://www.passporter.com/wdw/speedplanner.asp. ISBN: 978-1-58771-089-6

PassPorter's Cruise Clues: First Class Tips for Disney Cruise Trips

Coming soon to print! Get the best tips for the Disney Cruise Line—all categorized and coded—as well as cruise line comparisons, a teen perspective, and ultimate packing lists! This popular e-book is packed with 250 cruiser-tested tips. For more details, visit http://www.passporter.com/dcl/cruiseclues.asp. ISBN-13: 978-1-58771-096-4

Planning | Getting There | Staying in Style | Touring | Feasting | Making Magic | Index | Notes & More

PassPorter E-Books

Looking for more in-depth coverage on specific topics? Look no further than PassPorter E-Books! Our e-books are inexpensive (from $5.95–$9.95) and available immediately as a download (Adobe PDF format). And unlike most e-books, ours are fully formatted just like a regular PassPorter print book. A PassPorter e-book will even fit into a Deluxe PassPorter Binder. We offer fourteen e-books at press time, and have plans for many, many more!

PassPorter's Disney 500: *Fast Tips for Walt Disney World Trips*
Our most popular e-book has more than 500 time-tested Walt Disney World tips—all categorized and coded! We chose the best of our reader-submitted tips over a six-year period for this e-book and each has been edited by author Jennifer Marx. For more details, a list of tips, and a sample page, visit http://www.passporter.com/wdw/disney500.asp.

PassPorter's Cruise Clues: *First-Class Tips for Disney Cruise Trips*
Get the best tips for the Disney Cruise Line—all categorized and coded—as well as cruise line comparisons, a teen perspective, and ultimate packing lists! This popular e-book is packed with 250 cruiser-tested tips—all edited by award-winning author Jennifer Marx. For more details, visit http://www.passporter.com/dcl/cruiseclues.asp.

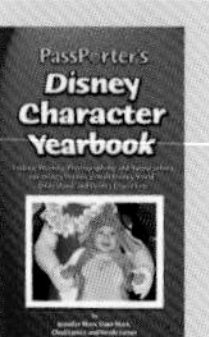

PassPorter's Disney Character Yearbook
A 268-page compendium of all the live Disney characters you can find at Walt Disney World, Disneyland, and on the Disney Cruise Line. Also includes tips on finding, meeting, photographing, and getting autographs, plus a customizable autograph book to print! For more details, visit http://www.passporter.com/disney-character-yearbook.asp.

PassPorter's Disney Speed Planner: *The Easy Ten-Step Program*
A fast, easy method for planning practically perfect vacations—great for busy people or those who don't have lots of time to plan. Follow this simple, ten-step plan to help you get your vacation planned in short order so you can get on with your life. For more details, visit http://www.passporter.com/wdw/speedplanner.asp.

PassPorter's Free-Book
A Guide to Free and Low-Cost Activities at Walt Disney World
It's hard to believe anything is free at Walt Disney World, but there are actually a number of things you can get or do for little to no cost. This e-book documents more than 150 free or cheap things to do before you go and after you arrive. Visit http://www.passporter.com/wdw/free-book.asp.

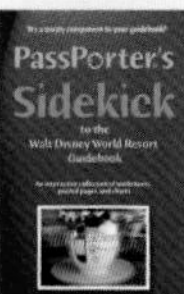

PassPorter's Sidekick for the Walt Disney World Guidebook
This is a customizable companion to our general Walt Disney World guidebook—you can personalize worksheets, journals, luggage tags, and charts, plus click links to all the URLs in the guidebook! Details at http://www.passporter.com/wdw/sidekick.asp.

PassPorter's Festivals and Celebrations *at Walt Disney World*

Get in on all the fun in this updated 78-page overview of all the wonderful and magical festivals, celebrations, parties, and holidays at Walt Disney World. Included are beautiful color photos and tips. Read more and see a sample page at http://www.passporter.com/wdw/festivals-celebrations.asp.

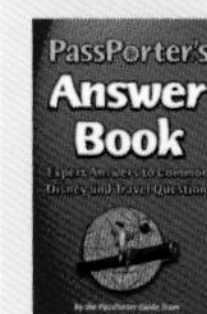

PassPorter's Answer Book

Get answers to the most popular topics asked about Walt Disney World, Disneyland, Disney Cruise Line, and general travel. You've asked it, we've answered it! The e-book's questions and answers are sorted geographically and topically. Details at http://www.passporter.com/answer-book.asp.

PassPorter's Disney Weddings & Honeymoons

This is both a guidebook and a bridal organizer tailored to the unique requirements of planning a wedding, vow renewal, or commitment ceremony at Disney World or on the Disney Cruise. It will take you through the entire process, outline your options, help you plan your event down to the last detail! Details at http://www.passporter.com/weddings.asp.

PassPorter's Disney Vacation Club Guide

A 170-page in-depth guide to all aspects of the Disney Vacation Club, from deciding whether to join to deciding where and when to use your points. Included are beautiful color photos and tips on maximizing your experience. If you've ever wondered what the club is all about or wanted to learn more, this is the perfect introduction. Get more details at http://www.passporter.com/disney-vacation-club.asp.

PassPorter's Walt Disney World for Brit Holidaymakers

Brits, you can get super in-depth information for your Walt Disney World vacation from fellow Brit and PassPorter feature columnist Cheryl Pendry. This e-book is more than 250 pages long and filled with amazing detail on both Walt Disney World as well as other Orlando-area attractions. Learn more at http://www.passporter.com/wdw/brits.asp.

PassPorter's Disneyland Paris

This comprehensive, 204-page book covers every aspect of visiting Disneyland Paris, including traveling to France from the United States and the United Kingdom. We provide all the information you need to get the most out of your stay! Read more and see a sample page at http://www.passporter.com/disneyland-paris.asp.

And coming soon ...

PassPorter's Orlando and Beyond: Everything But the Mouse!

This is the Disney fan's guide to Central Florida's numerous other theme parks, covering Universal Studios, Islands of Adventure, Wet 'n Wild, SeaWorld, Aquatica, Discovery Cove, LEGOLAND, Kennedy Space Center and Busch Gardens with the same helpful format and attention to detail found in *PassPorter's Walt Disney World*. Whether you're traveling to Orlando for the first time and want to see it all or returning for the umpteenth time and want to see something new, this book is for you!

Learn more and order at: http://www.passporterstore.com/store/ebooks.aspx

Do you want more help planning your Walt Disney World vacation? Join the PassPorter's Club and get all these benefits:

- ✔ "All-you-can-read" access to EVERY e-book we publish (see current list on the previous page). PassPorter's Club passholders also get early access to these e-books before the general public. New e-books are added on a regular basis, too.
- ✔ New! Anyone who commits to an annual pass in the PassPorter's Club also receives free access to all our Online Editions, including the one for this book!
- ✔ Interactive, customizable "e-worksheets" to help make your trip planning easier, faster, and smoother. These are the electronic, interactive worksheets we've been mentioning throughout this book. The worksheets are in PDF format and can be printed for a truly personalized approach! We have more than 50 worksheets, with more on the way. You can see a sample e-worksheet to the right.
- ✔ Access to super-sized "e-photos" in the PassPorter Photo Archives—photos can be zoomed in up to 25 times larger than standard web photos. You can use these e-photos to see detail as if you're actually standing there—or use them for desktop wallpaper, scrapbooking, whatever!
- ✔ Our best discount on print guidebooks ... 35% off!

PassPorter E-Worksheet — Daily Park and Reservations Coordinator

Daily Parks and Reservations

Use this worksheet to coordinate and plan your advance dining reservations around the places (i.e., parks) you intend to visit today. While you may only wish to stay in one park all day, space for alternate destinations are provided in the event you prefer to park hop or need to travel elsewhere for a meal because you could not get an advance dining reservation in the same park.

Today's Day and Date:

First Destination of the Day:
Hours:
Advance Dining Reservations:

Location	Time	Confirmation #

Transportation to Next Destination:

Next Destination of the Day:
Hours:
Advance Dining Reservations:

Location	Time	Confirmation #

Transportation to Next Destination:

Final Destination of the Day:
Hours:
Advance Dining Reservations:

Location	Time	Confirmation #

Transportation to Next Destination:

© MediaMarx, Inc. Do not distribute without explicit permission. For more information, visit http://www.passporter.com/club

There's more features, too! For a full list of features and current e-books, e-worksheets, and e-photos, visit http://www.passporter.com/club. You can also take a peek inside the Club's Gallery at http://www.passporterboards.com/forums/passporters-club-gallery. The Gallery is open to everyone—it contains two FREE interactive e-worksheets to try out!

Price: A PassPorter's Club pass is currently $5.95/month, or the cost of just one e-book!

How to Get Your Pass to the PassPorter's Club

Step 1. Get a free community account. Register simply and quickly at http://www.passporterboards.com/forums/register.php.

Step 2. Log in at http://www.passporterboards.com/forums/login.php using the Member Name and password you created in step 1.

Step 3. Get your pass. Select the type of pass you'd like and follow the directions to activate it immediately. We currently offer monthly and annual passes. (Annual passes save 25% and get extra perks!)

Questions? Assistance? We're here to help! Please send e-mail to club@passporter.com.

Electronic, interactive worksheet available—see page 316

My Important Numbers

Enter your important numbers in the boxes below. Once you obtain your park passes, write down the number on the back in the appropriate places below—you will need this number if your passes are ever lost. Consider using a personal code to conceal sensitive information.

Personal Information:

Personal Information
Driver's License number(s):
Passport number(s):
Frequent Flyer number(s):
Insurance number(s):
Park pass number(s):

Financial Information:

Financial Information
Voucher number(s):
Gift card number(s):
Traveler check number(s):
Other number(s):

Electronic, interactive worksheet available—see page 316

Vacation At-A-Glance

Create an overview of your itinerary in the chart below for easy reference. You can then make copies of it and give one to everyone in your traveling party, as well as to friends and family members who stay behind. Get a FREE electronic version of this worksheet at http://www.passporter.com/club.

Name(s):	
Departing on: Time: #:	
Arriving at:	
Staying at: Phone:	
Date:	Date:
Park/Activity:	Park/Activity:
Breakfast:	Breakfast:
Lunch:	Lunch:
Dinner:	Dinner:
Other:	Other:
Date:	Date:
Park/Activity:	Park/Activity:
Breakfast:	Breakfast:
Lunch:	Lunch:
Dinner:	Dinner:
Other:	Other:
Date:	Date:
Park/Activity:	Park/Activity:
Breakfast:	Breakfast:
Lunch:	Lunch:
Dinner:	Dinner:
Other:	Other:
Date:	Date:
Park/Activity:	Park/Activity:
Breakfast:	Breakfast:
Lunch:	Lunch:
Dinner:	Dinner:
Other:	Other:
Date:	Date:
Park/Activity:	Park/Activity:
Breakfast:	Breakfast:
Lunch:	Lunch:
Dinner:	Dinner:
Other:	Other:
Departing on: Time: #:	
Returning at:	

Reader Photo 48657: Bill Myers, 1951-2015

Disney Dreaming

Celebrating the magic of Disney through photographs by PassPorter authors and readers

A pictorial supplement

If you can dream it ...

Walt Disney World is for dreamers. Sometimes, it's a dream of a lifetime, born in front of a television in a childhood long ago, nurtured on VHS, DVD, and heartstring-tugging TV commercials—a dream that may not come to life until the dreamers have little dreamers of their own. Dreams of Tinker Bell, flitting through the night over a shimmering castle; a hug from Mickey, Minnie, Tigger, or the Goof; a childhood waiting to be revisited; a hope for magic at an age when "reality" overwhelms us daily.

For other dreamers, it's a return to a **golden childhood** that magically remains untarnished, with new marvels joining the old. Whole new worlds may have appeared, waiting to be explored. Old friends remain, waiting patiently for memories to be passed from parent to child.

Other dreamers just can't stay away, returning to their **laughing place** year after year, sharing the magic with family and friends. Their minds swirl with memories of castles, warm evening breezes, twinkling lights, kindness from strangers, familiar wonders shared with awestruck crowds, or perhaps a few moments when the crowds disappear into the mist and it's just two of you, dancing in front of an outdoor stage to a nameless rock band playing "Hotel California," finding a deeper love than you thought possible.

It's brides dreaming of horse-drawn coaches and liveried footmen, and a trio of siblings at the youngest's Golden anniversary, finding there are still new wonders to mingle with the memories. It's dreams of a **better, brighter world**, with less care, and more delight.

Reader Photo 11185: Diana Barthelemy

Reader Photo 22863: Rebecca Smith

PassPorter is a book about dreaming it and doing it—it's about charting a course, plotting a feast, maximizing the precious days and nights, and recording some of those moments for a cold night in Minnesota, or a bit of magic after a long, stressful day. It's learning where and how the magic and memories can find you (because the harder you chase the magic, the faster that pixie will fly from your grasp). It's about a place where tens of thousands of people labor daily to bring these dreams to life, and hundreds of millions have managed to explore fantasy, history, nature, humanity, childhood, the wide world, and the dreams of an extraordinary man, **Walt Disney**, and the people he continues to inspire.

Your authors have had a share in all these dreams and doings; shared with our closest family, and with strangers who are connected to us only by the pages of our books and an address on the Internet. What **began as a dream** of enhancing the magic for others and charting an independent course for ourselves was launched in print more than 15 years ago, on May 3, 1999. Over the years, PassPorter has become so much more—a community of readers sharing a common love, making new friends, nurturing each other's dreams and achievements, and exchanging knowledge, experience, and magic.

Join us as we **explore the magic** that is Walt Disney World, as seen through our eyes and the eyes of the PassPorter reader community. It is our dream that these images help you imagine yourself there.

... then you can do it!

Make believe

Finally there!

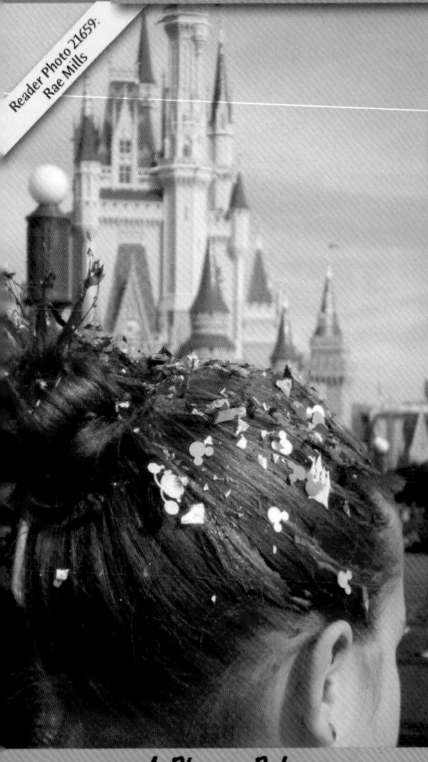

Reader Photo 21659:
Rae Mills

A Disney Do!

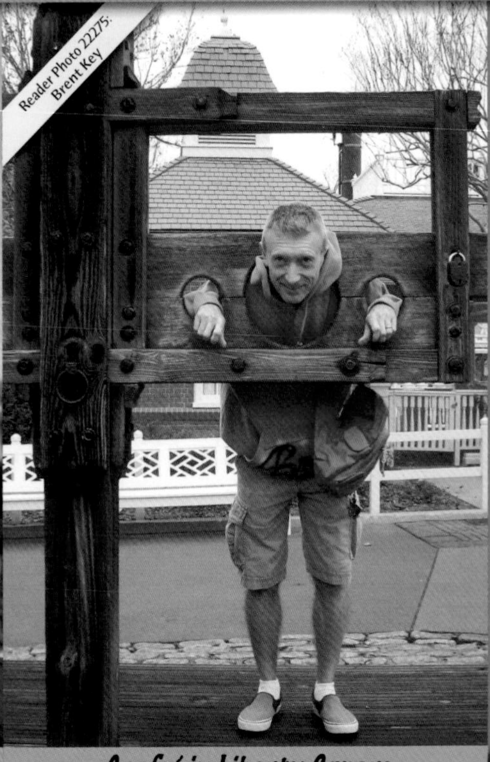

Reader Photo 22275:
Brent Key

Goofin' in Liberty Square

Reader Photo 21803: Charity Boughner

Reader Photo 38026: Vicki Lynn Collins

Highest score on Buzz Lightyear

Magic Kingdom

is a world of wonder for all ages. It is the place most of us think of when we picture Walt Disney World, and it is the embodiment of all things magical. Enter these gates and you look through the eyes of a child, where magic is real again and something extraordinary awaits you around every corner. Let your imagination soar!

Author Photo: Dave Marx

Play inside while you wait for your turn to fly with Dumbo

Find your inner child

Discover the world

Reader Photo 30641: Bill Myers

The enchantment of Mexico

Reader Photo 41358: Sam Fuller

Reader Photo 47766: Jill Koenigs

Making memories

Reader Photo 37749: Megan Caceres

Trying on the perfect hat in France

Epcot

is broad vistas, bold architectural statements, and a lagoon that unites a world. Go rocketing through space, glide peacefully over California, walk from Mexico to Norway, to China, and beyond.

Reader Photo 47495: Jana Ruf

Prepare for Rope Drop

Reader Photo 47980: Ben Gross

Reader Photo 21027: Debra Ortiz

Havin' a ball!

Wish upon a star

Getting in the Act!

Singin' in the rain

Disney's Hollywood Studios, where the star-struck and soundstage-struck gather to explore their dreams, the dream-maker's dreams, and the method behind the magic. The bold line up to be terrorized, star tourists rocket to Endor, stuntmen tumble, and wannabes hope to become Idols.

Larger Than Life

Reader Photo 37668: Melissa Lynn Page

Hugs and Kisses from Star Minnie

Reader Photo 21848: Sean Dunham

Jedi Training

Author Photo: MediaMarx, Inc.

Reader Photo 22571: Cam Matthews

Props!

Be more playful

Talk to animals

Tigger, is that you?

Jammin' in the jungle

Get up close and personal

Morning at the dig site

Disney's Animal Kingdom

allows you to explore the high Himalayas, dry African savannahs, and lush Asian rainforests. Encounter every creature from ant to elephant, dino to Yeti, and from Simba to Nemo. Fantasy may take a back seat to True Life Adventure, but whimsy and wonder are always close at hand.

Yellin' for the Yeti!

Spot little ones

Special delivery of fun

Be inspired by nature

Daydream

Sun-drenched Italy

Days of dazzling Florida sunshine, bright colors, broad vistas, glorious flowers and gardens at every turn, fanciful parades, enchanting faces, and unexpected encounters. Days at Walt Disney World can indeed be a living, waking dream. Sit on a bench, feel the warm breeze, and take a few minutes to let the quieter joys come to you.

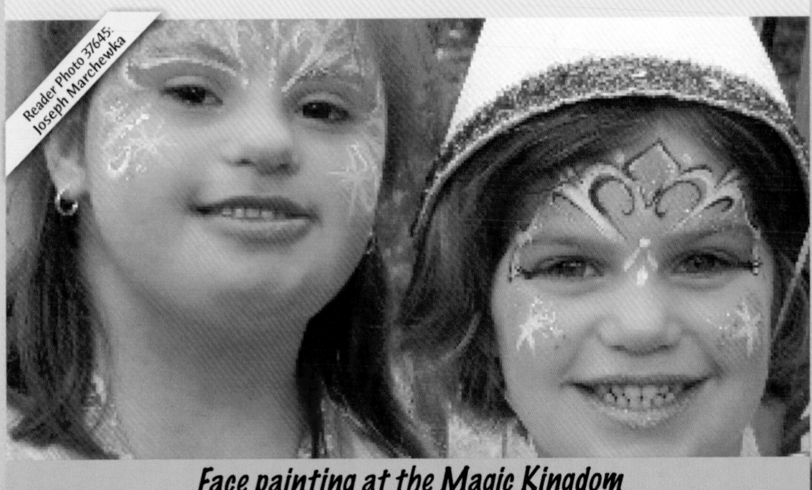

Face painting at the Magic Kingdom

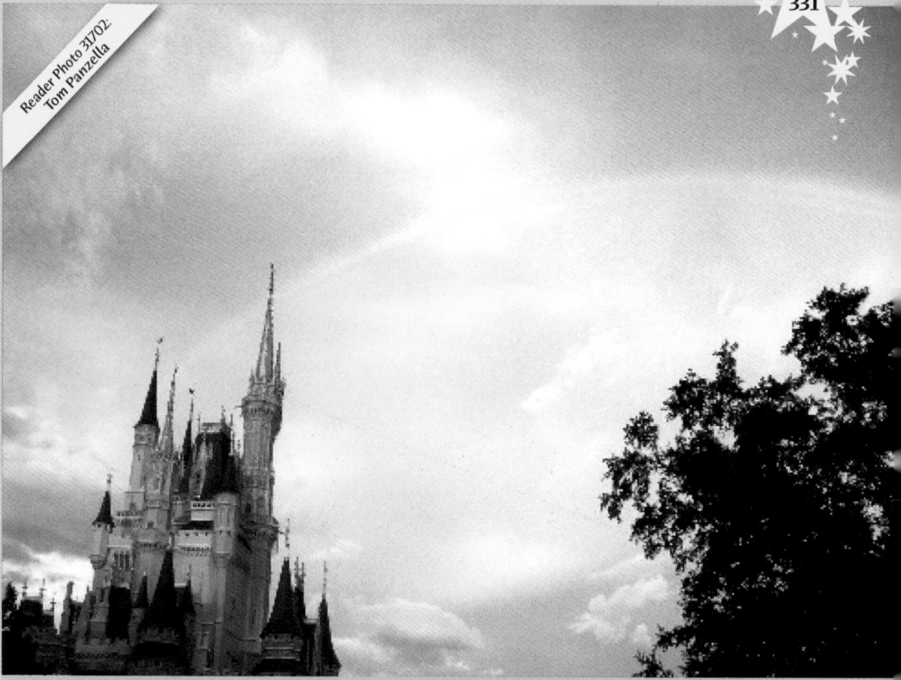

Reader Photo 31702:
Tom Panzella

Rainbow over the Magic Kingdom

Beast's Castle

Batters Up!

Sunshine comin' your way!

Enchanted evenings

Reader Photo 30624: Bill Myers

Imagine IllumiNations from a different perspective

Reader Photo 23084: Francis T. Tewey

Expedition Everest on an enchanted evening

Nights with fairy lights filling long, enchanted hours. Fear finds only those who seek it in haunted mansions and pirates' caves, while the rest of us revel in a midsummer night's dream. Everyone stays up way past bedtime for a bit of music, explosions, fireworks-filled awe, and the "extra magic," and we all wait for a "kiss goodnight."

Reader Photo 37713:
Jennifer Arnold
GOOD OLD
FRED

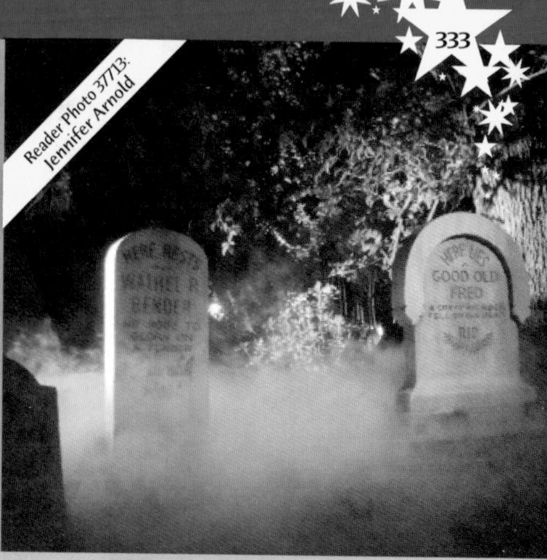

Haunted Mansion in Fog

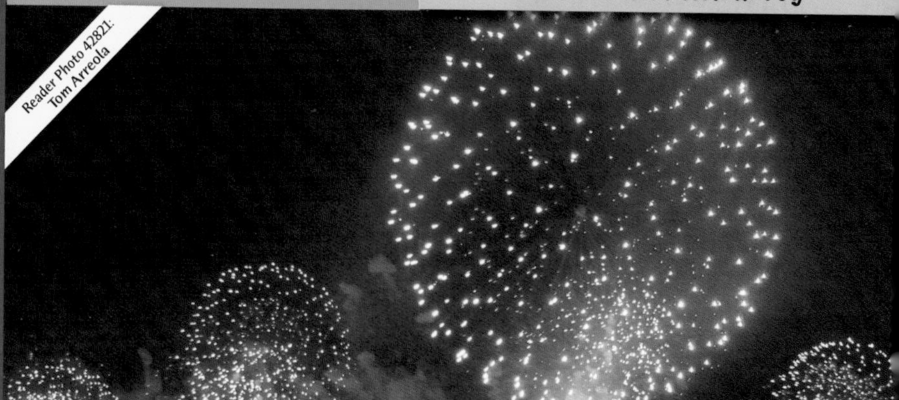
Reader Photo 42821:
Tom Arreola

A View of the Magnificent Fourth of July Fireworks

Dream with your eyes open

Feast on dreams

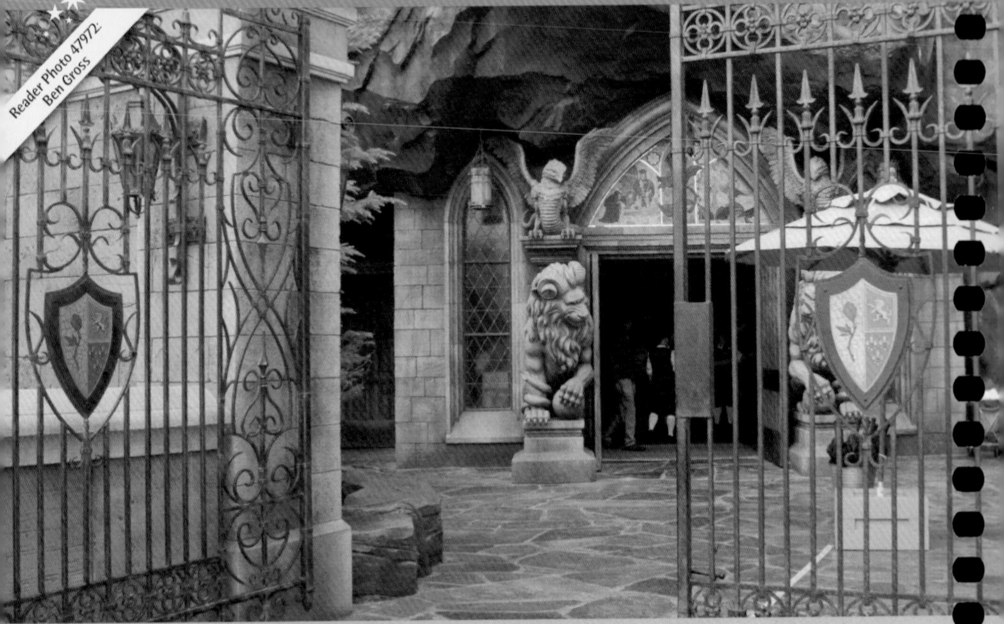
Reader Photo 47972:
Ben Gross

Dine in a Castle ... Beast's Castle!

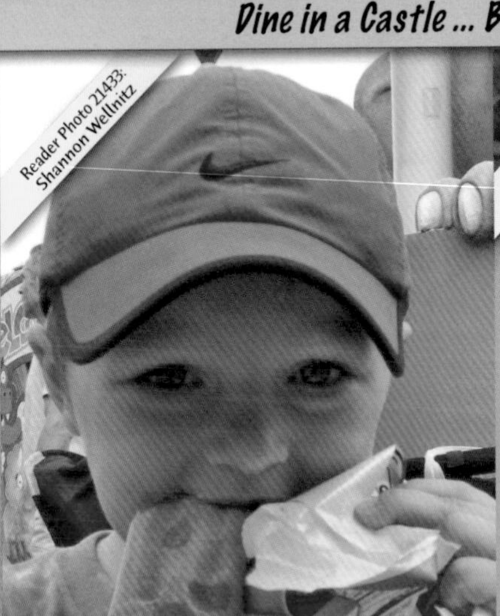
Reader Photo 21433:
Shannon Wellnitz

One child, two treats

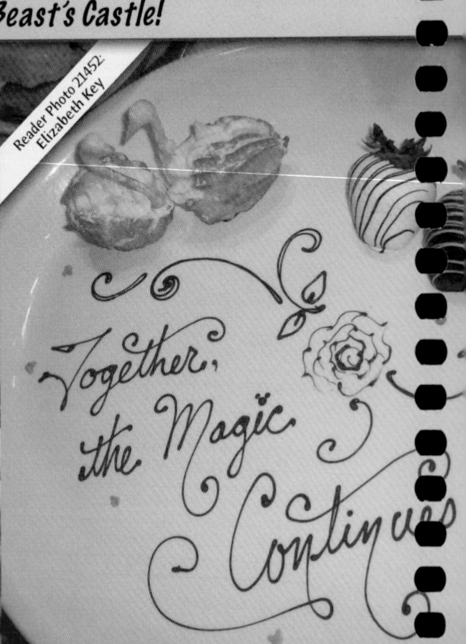
Reader Photo 21452:
Elizabeth Key
Together,
the Magic
Continues

Celebrating at 1900 Park Fare

Dining at the Walt Disney World Resort is truly fundamental, experimental, sentimental, and elemental. A world of flavors waits, from the simplest snack to five-star delights. Many find the feast as important as the fantasy, and reserve tables for dinners six months hence. A festival of food and wine packs the parks at the slowest time of year. Others savor simple chicken nuggets from a Mickey plate, a frozen treat that delights the taste buds on those hot Florida days, or a delectable dessert at tea time.

Narcoosees

Snacks on the Wild Africa Trek

Taking tea at the Garden View Lounge

Try something new

Sweet dreams

Reader Photo 22028: Heather DiFulvio

Sound asleep at Pop Century Resort

Reader Photo 13185: David Latoundji

Delight upon seeing the savanna

Reader Photo 36771: Penny J. Pettigrew

Port Orleans Royal Room

Breathtaking views at Coronado Springs Resort

Water fun at Bay Lake Tower

Lodging here is luxury, fantasy, nostalgia, and comfort. The savannah, South Seas, back woods, and seashore. New Orleans, New England, Southwest, and Northwest; keys, bayous, and boardwalks. Fantasies for the frugal. Elegant indulgence. A welcoming home for vacation club members, playful pools, and satisfying meals. Soft pillows, clean linens, and maybe even a towel sculpture greet you after a magical day in the parks.

Stay in style

Make some magic

Ready for the Luau

Going to see Nemo ... for the fifth time!

Picked as Grand Marshals for the Parade

Magic can be found anywhere in "The World," and there are countless ways that it can happen. Get a personal escort into your favorite park. See your movie friends come alive before your eyes. Dress up to the nines for a romantic dinner. Take in a pick-up game of duck duck goose. Make your own magic!

He proposed at Walt Disney World!

Notice the little things

Be together

Reader Photo 13191: Angie Lambert

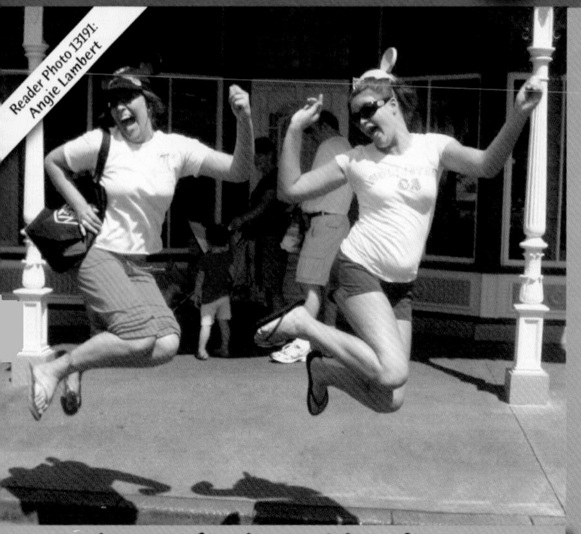

Jumpin' for Joy on Main Street

Families, including Walt Disney's own, inspired the theme park dream. Is there any doubt he succeeded? The joy he has given millions of families from around the world is incalculable. Loving moments, life-long memories, and uninhibited parent-and-child play await all those who take the time to be together here.

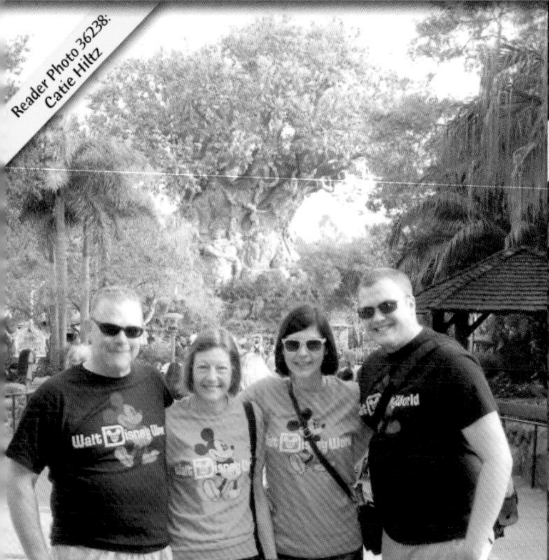

Reader Photo 36238: Catie Hiltz

We Go Together!

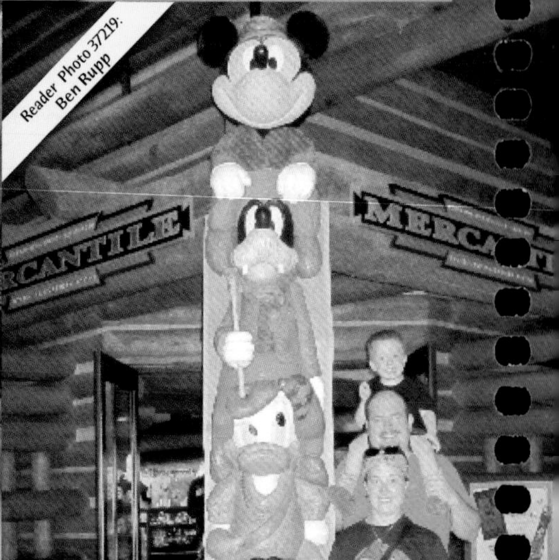

Reader Photo 37219: Ben Rupp

Family Totem Pole

Reader Photo 14954: Carrie Owens
my first ear hat

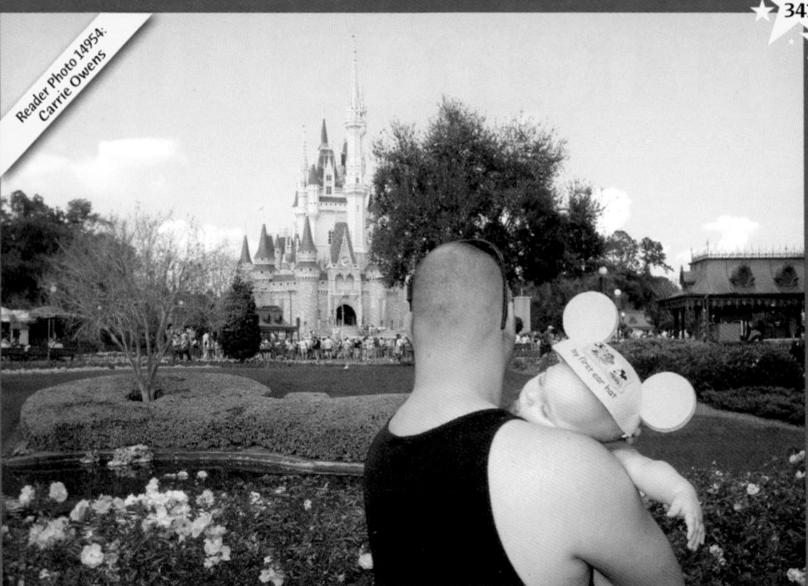

The best place to rest

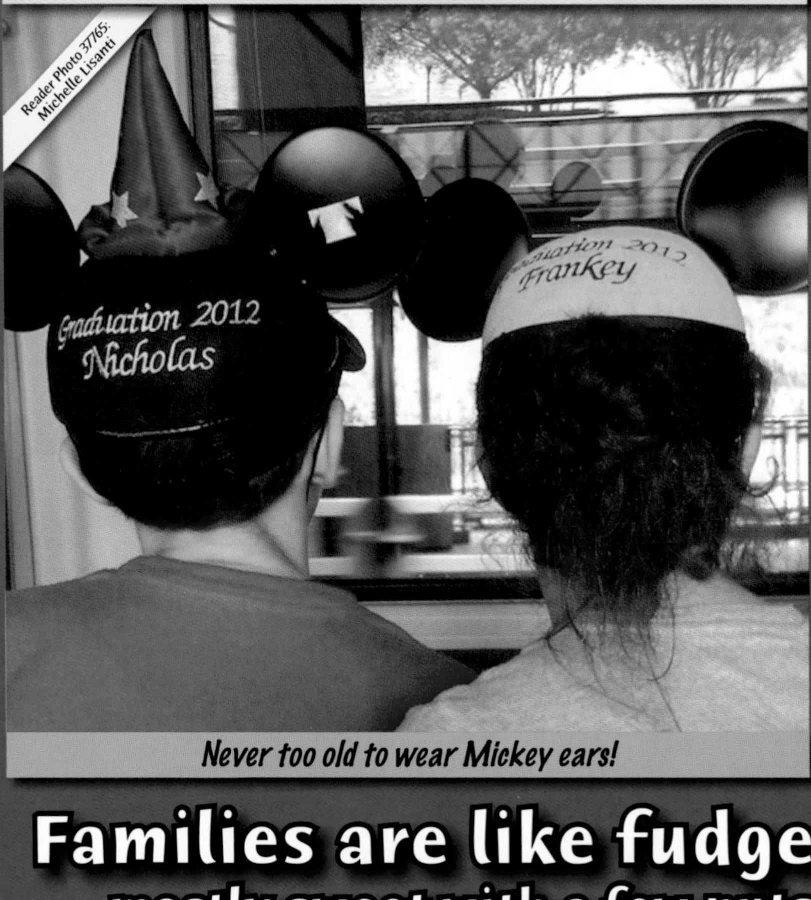
Reader Photo 37765: Michelle Lisanti
Graduation 2012
Nicholas
Frankey

Never too old to wear Mickey ears!

Families are like fudge
... mostly sweet with a few nuts

Friendships

We meet through PassPorter ... *... and even get engaged!*

Ohana Happy Fun Time PassPorter Reunion

Sharing a drink *Sharing a meal*

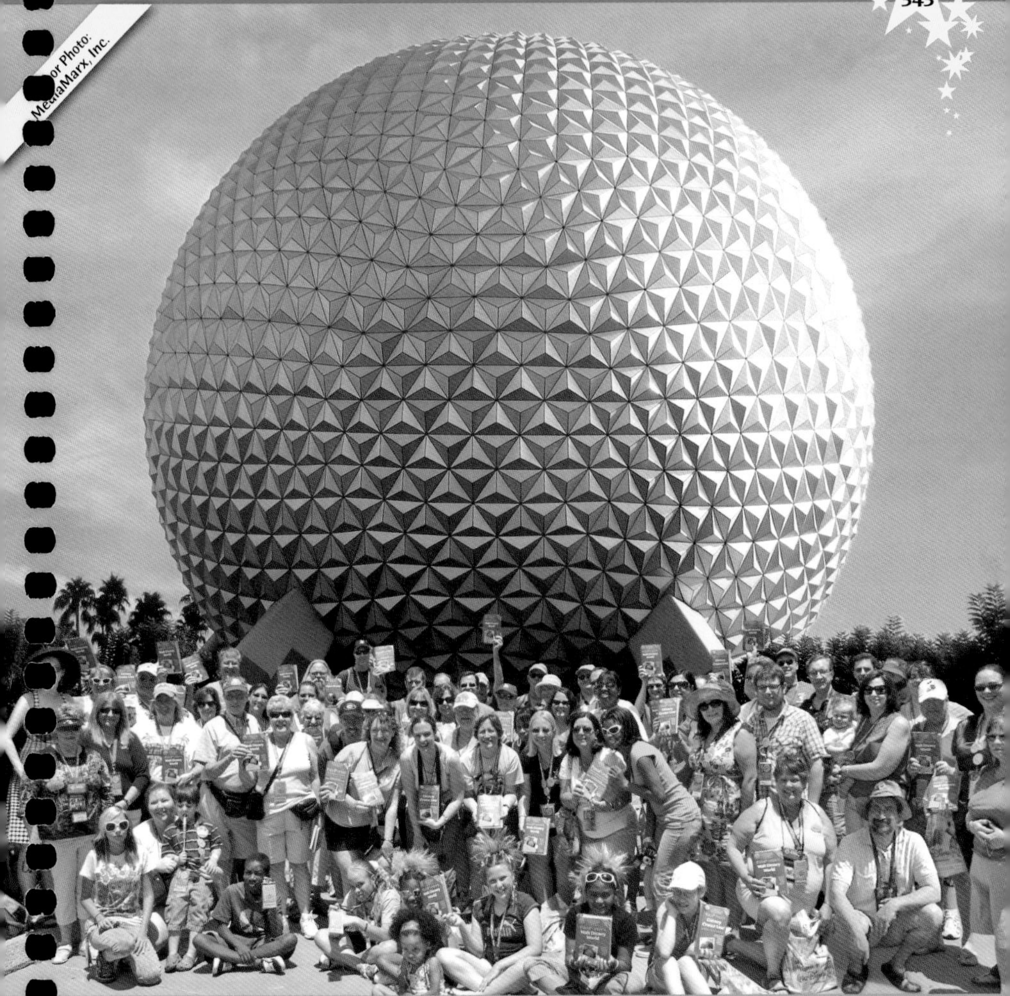
Author Photo:
MediaMarx, Inc.

Coming together for PassPorter's 10th birthday on May 3, 2009

Author Photo:
MediaMarx, Inc.

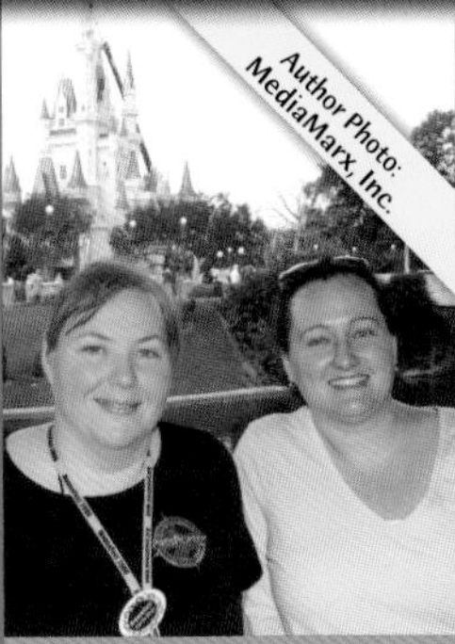

PassPorter Moms

Friends to share the good times. Reach beyond family to friends from back home, and even friends you meet online. Passion for all things Disney has spawned thousands of web sites, forums, podcasts, blogs, chats, and even marriages. Friendships are cemented here, as members of online communities "meet" to enjoy rides, share meals, do good works, and explore "The World."

It takes a village

Spread your wings

Invited to sit in the cockpit after landing in Orlando

Having fun and driving us crazy

"A Friendship" Can Take You Places

A Monorail Odyssey

Ride Home After a Long Day

Journeys of a thousand miles often end in Orlando. For some, it may be their first flight, or longest drive. Even after you've reached this sprawling place, it's an adventure to get from here to there. There's the astounding network of highways and byways, a fleet of boats shuttling between park and resort, buses headed everywhere, and the legendary monorail gliding quietly overhead.

Gold monorail pulls in to the station

Go on an adventure

Discoveries

Disneyland Paris

Bow of the Disney Magic

Pisa, Italy

Beyond this "World" lies much more to explore. There's nothing like a visit to "The World" to spark wanderlust, and Disney is happy to oblige. Cruise the seas and visit far-flung ports of call with Disney Cruise Line. Visit theme parks in California, Japan, France, and China, and the wondrous places nearby. Tour with Adventures by Disney, or maybe head east or west down the road to either of Florida's coasts—Gulf, or Space.

Tokyo and Big Thunder Mountain Railroad

Reader Photo 14169: Cheryl Pendry

Disneyland Railroad Station in California

Reader Photo 6093: Cheryl Pendry

Sleeping Beauty Castle at Hong Kong Disneyland

Explore your world

Decade of Dreams

PassPorter's 10th Birthday Party in The Seas VIP Salon at Epcot

We had a dream. We followed it and it led us to develop, write, and publish PassPorter more than ten years ago. Little did we know how it would grow and blossom! To celebrate this "decade of dreams," we invited our family, friends, and PassPorter readers to party with us onboard the Disney Magic, at Walt Disney World and Disneyland, and even on Broadway in New York City! Thank you to our core team and hundreds of thousands of readers who have supported PassPorter over the last ten years. Here's to another magical decade with you!

Storming the castle!

A surprise gift from our Guides

First Visit to American Idol

PassPorter Quest Winners

Celebrating onboard the Disney Magic

An evening on Broadway

All Gussied Up

I found treasure!

Bon Voyage Deck Party

Thanks for believing in me, Mom!

What's your dream?

Thank You ...

To our fabulous readers who contributed photos to the PassPorter Photo Archive and allowed us to reprint them for this supplement: *Jennifer Arnold, Tom Arreola, Diana Barthelemy, Charity Boughner, Megan Caceres, Vickie Lynn Collins, Tricia Davids, Heather DiFulvio, Sean Dunham, Debbie Ernest, LilyAnn Fisherman, Sam Fuller, Ben Gross, Susan Gross, Denise Hand, Catie Hiltz, Brent Key, Elizabeth Key, Jill Koenigs, Angie Lambert, David Latoundji, Michelle Lisanti, Joseph Marchewka, Cam Matthews, Bonnie McCarty, Lisa Miller, Rae Mills, Bill Myers, Amanda Nash, Lisa O'Meara, Debra Ortiz, Carrie Owens, Melissa Lynn Page, Tom Panzella, Cheryl Pendry, Penny J. Pettigrew, Andrea Popovits, Michelle Price, Jana Ruf, Ben Rupp, Hope Rupp, Danielle Sabato, Heather Shevland, Rebecca Smith, Keith Stanton, Francis T. Tewey, Regina Thomas, and Shannon Wellnitz*

And a special thank-you to the many readers who appear in the photographs—your smiling faces spread magic to us all!

You can view thousands of more photographs—both from your authors and fellow readers—online in the PassPorter Photo Archive at http://www.passporter.com/photos

Reader Photo 37694: Marc Lorenzo

Customize Your PassPorter

Use these labels to personalize your PassPockets for your trip. The color rectangles at the right can be folded over the edge of pages to create your own tabs or flags!

Our Cruise

Our Honeymoon

Our Wedding

Our Anniversary

Our Reunion

Our Gathering

My Birthday

Our Special Day

Our Journey

Our Eleventh Day

Our Twelvth Day

Our Thirteenth Day

Our Fourteenth Day

Our Return

PLANS PLANS

TRAVELS TRAVELS

ROOMS ROOMS

PLAY PLAY

FOOD FOOD

PLACES PLACES

MAGIC MAGIC

Create Your Own Labels & ← Tabs →

Keep everything you need for your journey together here in one place, such as maps, tickets, coupons, reservation numbers... even passports!

Our Journey

Departing at ______ Arriving at ______

Airline/Train/Bus Company ______

Flight/Route Number(s) ______

Flight Reservation Number(s) ______ Seat(s) ______

Cruise Reservation Number ______ Stateroom ______

Auto/Trip Insurance ______

Rental Car/Shuttle/Limo Company ______

Type ______ Reservation Number ______

Details ______

Returning at ______ Arriving home at ______

Flight/Route Number(s) ______ Seat(s) ______

Note(s) ______

Store small items in here like baggage claim tickets and receipts

Things to Do

- ☐ ______
- ☐ ______
- ☐ ______
- ☐ ______
- ☐ ______
- ☐ ______
- ☐ ______
- ☐ ______

Notes

Memories of Our Journey

The weather was... ______ ... when we left

and... ______ ... when we arrived

The best thing about our journey was... ______

The worst thing about our journey was... ______

The funniest thing about our journey was... ______

During our journey we tried... ______

and the result was... ______

The most magical moment during our journey was... ______

Photos and Snapshots

❑ Photos taken today (card/roll # ____)

Shot #	Description

Meals and Snacks

Breakfast: ______ $

Lunch: ______ $

Dinner: ______ $

Snacks: ______ $

Budget and Expenses

Target travel budget: $

Fares:	$
	$
Fuel:	$
Tips:	$
Meals:	$
	$
Other:	$
	$
Total:	$

Notes for Next Time

Use your notes here to remind yourself to inquire about special requests at check-in, such as room preferences, discounts, and amenities.

Our Room(s)

Hotel/Motel/Ship: ______________ Phone: ______________

Arriving: ______________ Departing: ______________

Room Type: ______________ Location: ______________

Special Requests: ______________

Reservation Number: ______________

Room Number: ______________ Floor/Building: ______________

Additional Stay: ______________ Phone: ______________

Arriving: ______________ Departing: ______________

Room Type: ______________ Location: ______________

Special Requests: ______________

Reservation Number: ______________

Room Number: ______________ Floor/Building: ______________

↓ *Store small items in here like card keys, receipts, and luggage tags* ↓

Things to Do

- ❑ ______________ ❑ ______________
- ❑ ______________ ❑ ______________
- ❑ ______________ ❑ ______________
- ❑ ______________ ❑ ______________

Notes

____

____

____

____

____

Memories of Our Rooms

The first impression of our room(s) was... ______

The best thing was... ______

______

The worst thing was... ______

______

The amenities were... ______

______

We tried... ______

and the result was... ______

______

The most magical moment was... ______

______

Photos and Snapshots

☐ Photos taken here (card/roll # ___)

Shot #	Description
______	______
______	______
______	______
______	______
______	______
______	______

Budget and Expenses

Target room budget: $ ______

Room(s): $ ______

$ ______

Options: $ ______

$ ______

Tips: $ ______

$ ______

Other: $ ______

$ ______

Total: $ ______

Rooms and Views

Our room was... ______

______

______

The view was... ______

______

______

Best feature: ______

Worst feature: ______

Notes for Next Time

______

Take it easy on your first day so you don't wear yourself out early in the trip. Your entire vacation is ahead of you—relax and enjoy it!

Our First Day

Confirmation Numbers

:	Wake up:
:	Early Morning:
:	Breakfast:
:	Morning:
:	
:	Lunch:
:	Afternoon:
:	
:	Dinner:
:	Evening:
:	
:	Before bed:

Special plans for today:

↓ *Store small items in here like ticket stubs and receipts for meals and purchases* ↓

Things to Do, Places to Go, Attractions to Visit

- ❑
- ❑
- ❑
- ❑
- ❑
- ❑
- ❑
- ❑

Notes

Day: **Date:**

Memories of Our First Day

The weather today was... ______

The best thing today was... ______

The worst thing today was... ______

The funniest thing today was... ______

Today we tried... ______

and the result was... ______

The most magical moment today was... ______

Photos and Snapshots

☐ Photos taken today (card/roll # ___)

Shot #	Description

Budget and Expenses

First day budget: $

Admission: $

Meals: $

$

$

Shopping: $

$

Other: $

$

Total: $

Meals and Snacks

Breakfast:

$

Lunch:

$

Dinner:

$

Snacks:

$

Notes for Next Time

*Remember to drink plenty of fluids,
eat substantial meals, use sunblock, wear a hat,
and take frequent breaks as necessary during your day.*

Our Second Day

Confirmation Numbers

: Wake up:

: Early Morning:

: Breakfast:

: Morning:

:

: Lunch:

: Afternoon:

:

: Dinner:

: Evening:

:

: Before bed:

Special plans for today:

↓ *Store small items in here like ticket stubs and receipts for meals and purchases* ↓

Things to Do, Places to Go, Attractions to Visit

- ❑
- ❑
- ❑
- ❑
- ❑
- ❑
- ❑
- ❑

Notes

Day: **Date:**

Memories of Our Second Day

The weather today was... ____________________

The best thing today was... ____________________

The worst thing today was... ____________________

The funniest thing today was... ____________________

Today we tried... ____________________

and the result was... ____________________

The most magical moment today was... ____________________

Photos and Snapshots

☐ Photos taken today (card/roll # ____)

Shot #	Description

Budget and Expenses

Second day budget: $

Admission: $

Meals: $

$

$

Shopping: $

$

Other: $

$

Total: $

Meals and Snacks

Breakfast: __________ $

Lunch: __________ $

Dinner: __________ $

Snacks: __________ $

Notes for Next Time

When you skip activities for lack of time or energy, flip ahead in your PassPorter and jot them down for another day so you don't forget to return!

Our Third Day

Confirmation Numbers

: Wake up:

: Early Morning:

: Breakfast:

: Morning:

:

: Lunch:

: Afternoon:

:

: Dinner:

: Evening:

:

: Before bed:

Special plans for today:

↓ *Store small items in here like ticket stubs and receipts for meals and purchases* ↓

Things to Do, Places to Go, Attractions to Visit

- [ ]
- [ ]
- [ ]
- [ ]
- [ ]
- [ ]
- [ ]
- [ ]

Notes

Day: **Date:**

Memories of Our Third Day

The weather today was... ______

The best thing today was... ______

______

The worst thing today was... ______

______

The funniest thing today was... ______

______

Today we tried... ______

and the result was... ______

______

The most magical moment today was... ______

______

Photos and Snapshots

☐ Photos taken today (card/roll # ____)

Shot #	Description

Meals and Snacks

Breakfast: ______ $

Lunch: ______ $

Dinner: ______ $

Snacks: ______ $

Budget and Expenses

Third day budget: $ ______

Admission: $ ______

Meals: $ ______

$ ______

$ ______

Shopping: $ ______

$ ______

Other: $ ______

$ ______

Total: $ ______

Notes for Next Time

______

When you find a souvenir you want, get it right away—there is no guarantee you'll be able to find that same treasure later in your trip.

Our Fourth Day

Confirmation Numbers

: Wake up:

: Early Morning:

: Breakfast:

: Morning:

:

: Lunch:

: Afternoon:

:

: Dinner:

: Evening:

:

: Before bed:

Special plans for today:

Store small items in here like ticket stubs and receipts for meals and purchases

Things to Do, Places to Go, Attractions to Visit

- ❑
- ❑
- ❑
- ❑
- ❑
- ❑
- ❑
- ❑

Notes

Day: **Date:**

Memories of Our Fourth Day

The weather today was... ______________________________

The best thing today was... ______________________________

____

The worst thing today was... ______________________________

____

The funniest thing today was... ______________________________

____

Today we tried... ______________________________

and the result was... ______________________________

____

The most magical moment today was... ______________________________

____

Photos and Snapshots

☐ Photos taken today (card/roll # ____)

Shot #	Description

Meals and Snacks

Breakfast: ______________________________ $

Lunch: ______________________________ $

Dinner: ______________________________ $

Snacks: ______________________________ $

Budget and Expenses

Fourth day budget: $ ________

Admission: $ ________

Meals: $ ________

$ ________

$ ________

Shopping: $ ________

$ ________

Other: $ ________

$ ________

Total: $ ________

Notes for Next Time

____

Take stock of what you wanted to do and what you've actually done while you still have time, then make the time to fulfill your dreams!

Our Fifth Day

Confirmation Numbers

: Wake up:

: Early Morning:

: Breakfast:

: Morning:

:

: Lunch:

: Afternoon:

:

: Dinner:

: Evening:

:

: Before bed:

Special plans for today:

↓ *Store small items in here like ticket stubs and receipts for meals and purchases* ↓

Things to Do, Places to Go, Attractions to Visit

- ❑
- ❑
- ❑
- ❑
- ❑
- ❑
- ❑
- ❑

Notes

Day: **Date:**

Memories of Our Fifth Day

The weather today was... ______

The best thing today was... ______

The worst thing today was... ______

The funniest thing today was... ______

Today we tried... ______

and the result was... ______

The most magical moment today was... ______

Photos and Snapshots

❑ Photos taken today (card/roll # ____)

Shot #	Description

Meals and Snacks

Breakfast: ______ $

Lunch: ______ $

Dinner: ______ $

Snacks: ______ $

Budget and Expenses

Fifth day budget: $

Admission: $

Meals: $

$

$

Shopping: $

$

Other: $

$

Total: $

Notes for Next Time

Break out of the typical tourist mold and customize your vacation with one of the tips in your PassPorter. Don't forget the sunglasses!

Our Sixth Day

Confirmation Numbers

: Wake up:

: Early Morning:

: Breakfast:

: Morning:

:

: Lunch:

: Afternoon:

:

: Dinner:

: Evening:

:

: Before bed:

Special plans for today:

↓ *Store small items in here like ticket stubs and receipts for meals and purchases* ↓

Things to Do, Places to Go, Attractions to Visit

- ❑
- ❑
- ❑
- ❑
- ❑
- ❑
- ❑
- ❑

Notes

Day: **Date:**

Memories of Our Sixth Day

The weather today was... __________

The best thing today was... __________

The worst thing today was... __________

The funniest thing today was... __________

Today we tried... __________

and the result was... __________

The most magical moment today was... __________

Photos and Snapshots

☐ Photos taken today (card/roll # ____)

Shot #	Description

Budget and Expenses

Sixth day budget: $

Admission: $

Meals: $

$

$

Shopping: $

$

Other: $

$

Total: $

Meals and Snacks

Breakfast:

$

Lunch:

$

Dinner:

$

Snacks:

$

Notes for Next Time

Address your postcards and store them in your PassPorter for safe keeping until you can mail them. This also helps you remember to send them!

Our Seventh Day

Confirmation Numbers

: Wake up: ____

: Early Morning: ____

: Breakfast: ____

: Morning: ____

: ____

: Lunch: ____

: Afternoon: ____

: ____

: Dinner: ____

: Evening: ____

: ____

: Before bed: ____

Special plans for today: ____

↓ *Store small items in here like ticket stubs and receipts for meals and purchases* ↓

Things to Do, Places to Go, Attractions to Visit

- ❑ ____
- ❑ ____
- ❑ ____
- ❑ ____
- ❑ ____
- ❑ ____
- ❑ ____
- ❑ ____

Notes

Day: **Date:**

Memories of Our Seventh Day

The weather today was... ______

The best thing today was... ______

______

The worst thing today was... ______

______

The funniest thing today was... ______

______

Today we tried... ______

and the result was... ______

______

The most magical moment today was... ______

______

Photos and Snapshots

☐ Photos taken today (card/roll # ____)

Shot #	Description

Budget and Expenses

Seventh day budget: $ ______

Admission:	$
Meals:	$
	$
	$
Shopping:	$
	$
Other:	$
	$

Total: $ ______

Meals and Snacks

Breakfast:	
	$
Lunch:	
	$
Dinner:	
	$
Snacks:	
	$

Notes for Next Time

______

Running out of steam? Try taking a day to relax away from the excitement. Take a dip in the pool, or just hang out in your room.

Our Eighth Day

Confirmation Numbers

: Wake up:

: Early Morning:

: Breakfast:

: Morning:

:

: Lunch:

: Afternoon:

:

: Dinner:

: Evening:

:

: Before bed:

Special plans for today:

↓ *Store small items in here like ticket stubs and receipts for meals and purchases* ↓

Things to Do, Places to Go, Attractions to Visit

- ❑
- ❑
- ❑
- ❑
- ❑
- ❑
- ❑
- ❑

Notes

Day: **Date:**

Memories of Our Eighth Day

The weather today was... ______

The best thing today was... ______

______

The worst thing today was... ______

______

The funniest thing today was... ______

______

Today we tried... ______

and the result was... ______

______

The most magical moment today was... ______

______

Photos and Snapshots

☐ Photos taken today (card/roll # ___)

Shot #	Description

Budget and Expenses

Eighth day budget: $ ______

Admission:	$
Meals:	$
	$
	$
Shopping:	$
	$
Other:	$
	$

Total: $ ______

Meals and Snacks

Breakfast: ______ $

Lunch: ______ $

Dinner: ______ $

Snacks: ______ $

Notes for Next Time

______

On the next to last day of your trip, confirm your return travel arrangements and pack whatever you can for a less stressful departure.

Our Ninth Day

Confirmation Numbers

: Wake up:

: Early Morning:

: Breakfast:

: Morning:

:

: Lunch:

: Afternoon:

:

: Dinner:

: Evening:

:

: Before bed:

Special plans for today:

Store small items in here like ticket stubs and receipts for meals and purchases

Things to Do, Places to Go, Attractions to Visit

- [ ]
- [ ]
- [ ]
- [ ]
- [ ]
- [ ]
- [ ]
- [ ]

Notes

Day: **Date:**

Memories of Our Ninth Day

The weather today was... ______

The best thing today was... ______

______

The worst thing today was... ______

______

The funniest thing today was... ______

______

Today we tried... ______

and the result was... ______

______

The most magical moment today was... ______

______

Photos and Snapshots

☐ Photos taken today (card/roll # ____)

Shot #	Description

Meals and Snacks

Breakfast: ______ $

Lunch: ______ $

Dinner: ______ $

Snacks: ______ $

Budget and Expenses

Ninth day budget: $

Admission: $

Meals: $

$

$

Shopping: $

$

Other: $

$

Total: $

Notes for Next Time

______

Your visit may be ending soon, but the memories you've made can last a lifetime. Record them in your PassPorter now before you forget.

Our Tenth Day

Confirmation Numbers

:	Wake up:
:	Early Morning:
:	Breakfast:
:	Morning:
:	
:	Lunch:
:	Afternoon:
:	
:	Dinner:
:	Evening:
:	
:	Before bed:

Special plans for today:

↓ *Store small items in here like ticket stubs and receipts for meals and purchases* ↓

Things to Do, Places to Go, Attractions to Visit

- ❑
- ❑
- ❑
- ❑
- ❑
- ❑
- ❑
- ❑

Notes

Day: **Date:**

Memories of Our Tenth Day

The weather today was... ______

The best thing today was... ______

The worst thing today was... ______

The funniest thing today was... ______

Today we tried... ______

and the result was... ______

The most magical moment today was... ______

Photos and Snapshots

☐ Photos taken today (card/roll # ___)

Shot #	Description

Meals and Snacks

Breakfast: ______ $

Lunch: ______ $

Dinner: ______ $

Snacks: ______ $

Budget and Expenses

Tenth day budget: $

Admission: $

Meals: $

$

$

Shopping: $

$

Other: $

$

Total: $

Notes for Next Time

Design your own PassPocket!
Use it for extra days, special events, projects, or remove it and bring it along on days you don't carry your book.

Confirmation Numbers

Write your day, event, or subject above.

↓ *Store small items in here like ticket stubs and receipts for meals and purchases* ↓

- [ ]
- [ ]
- [ ]
- [ ]
- [ ]
- [ ]
- [ ]
- [ ]

Notes

Day: **Date:**

Write your subject above.

Your memories will last longer if you record them while they are fresh in your mind. What made you laugh? Smile? Cry? Write it down here!

Our Magic Memories

Our most memorable day was... ______

because... ______

Our most memorable place was... ______

because... ______

Our most memorable attraction was... ______

because... ______

Our most memorable activity was... ______

because... ______

↓ *Store small items in here that you want to save as souvenirs and mementos* ↓

Our most memorable meal was... ______

because... ______

Our most magic moment of all was... ______

because... ______

Special memories of our vacation: ______

Our Trip Report

Use this page to write about your vacation for your family and friends, or even for the benefit of others at school, work, or on the Internet. A trip report is also a good activity for school-age children, especially if they missed school during their adventure. If you run out of room on this page, just continue it on paper and tuck the sheets in this PassPocket for safekeeping.

When did you go? ______________________

Who did you go with? What are their ages? ______________________

____

Was this your first trip? ______ If not, how many trips have you had? ______

Where did you sleep? ______________________

____

What attractions did you visit? ______________________

____

____

____

What special things did you do? ______________________

____

____

____

What would you do again? Why? ______________________

____

____

What would you never do again? Why not? ______________________

____

____

What tips do you have for your fellow vacationers? ______________________

____

____

____

____

____

____

____

Would you like to share your trip report with other PassPorter readers? Visit us on the web at http://www.passporter.com. You can also make a copy of this page and mail it to us—our address is P.O. Box 3880, Ann Arbor, MI, 48106. Please include your full name, address, and phone number so we may contact you if necessary.